Brief Contents

Contents

Parenting Today's Children
A DEVELOPMENTAL PERSPECTIVE

Lynn R. Marotz
University of Kansas

Sara Kupzyk
Munroe-Meyer Institute for Genetics
and Rehabilitation at the University
of Nebraska Medical Center

CENGAGE
Learning®

Australia • Brazil • Mexico • Singapore
• United Kingdom • United States

Parenting Today's Children: A Developmental Perspective
Lynn R. Marotz and Sara Kupzyk

Senior Product Director: Marta Lee-Perriard

Senior Product Manager: Cheri-Ann Nakamaru

Associate Content Developer: Jessica Alderman

Marketing Manager: Andrew Miller

Senior Content Project Manager: Samen Iqbal

Senior Designer: Helen Bruno

Senior Digital Content Specialist: Jaclyn Hermesmeyer

Manufacturing Planner: Doug Bertke

Production and Composition: MPS Limited

Photo Researcher: Uginevinnarasi Immanvel, Lumina Datamatics Ltd.

Text Researcher: Gracia Alan, Lumina Datamatics Ltd.

Cover and Text Designer: Lisa Delgado

Cover and Title Page Image: Rock and Wasp/Shutterstock.com

For product information and technology assistance, contact us at
Cengage Learning Customer & Sales Support, 1-800-354-9706.

For permission to use material from this text or product,
submit all requests online at **www.cengage.com/permissions.**
Further permissions questions can be e-mailed to
permissionrequest@cengage.com.

Library of Congress Control Number: 2016946785

Student Edition:
ISBN: 978-1-305-96430-3

Loose-leaf Edition:
ISBN: 978-1-305-96432-7

Cengage Learning
20 Channel Center Street
Boston, MA 02210
USA

Cengage Learning is a leading provider of customized learning solutions with employees residing in nearly 40 different countries and sales in more than 125 countries around the world. Find your local representative at **www.cengage.com**.

Cengage Learning products are represented in Canada by Nelson Education, Ltd.

To learn more about Cengage Learning Solutions, visit **www.cengage.com**.

Purchase any of our products at your local college store or at our preferred online store **www.cengagebrain.com.**

Printed in the United States of America
Print Number: 01   Print Year: 2016

Chapter 3 Understanding, Supporting, and Collaborating with Families 69

SECTION II Parenting: Nurturing and Supporting Children's Development

Chapter 4 Becoming a Parent 93

Monkey Business Images/Shutterstock.com

Chapter 5 Parenting Styles and Children's Socialization 127

Chapter 6 Parenting Infants   151

Chapter 7 Parenting Toddlers 189

Chapter 10 Parenting Early Adolescent Children 285

Pressmaster/Shutterstock.com

mangostock/Shutterstock.com

SECTION III Additional Considerations

Chapter 13 Family Violence and Child Maltreatment 357

Chapter 14 Parenting Children with Exceptionalities 383

Denis Kuvaev/Shutterstock.com

Preface

Children face a lifetime of learning, exploration, successes and failures—a path that parents, educators, and various professionals have themselves followed. The quality of their environments, early learning opportunities, and positive adult support and encouragement plays an influential role in mapping a route along which all future skill acquisition is acquired. Thus, an understanding of children's developmental needs, capabilities, and limitations enables parents and practitioners to create effective learning experiences and behavior guidance that will help children achieve a rich and fulfilling life.

Parenting advice typically has been handed down from one generation to the next. Generational knowledge transfer is less effective today because families are more mobile and diverse, and they encounter parenting issues that differ markedly from those in the past. Contemporary families are also faced with significant cultural and societal changes, stress, and challenges in their efforts to raise children. Such factors necessitate new approaches and interventions based upon a fundamental understanding of child development, changing family dynamics and environmental conditions, and the latest research findings. Consequently, contemporary parents often depend upon teachers, health clinicians, social workers, counselors, agency personnel, and many others for child-rearing information.

Today's parents and children are diverse in terms of their race/ethnicity, language, family structure, socioeconomic status, and religious beliefs. Teachers and practitioners must be knowledgeable about these differences so that they are able to support and collaborate with parents as children progress through their sequential developmental stages. *Parenting Today's Children* provides educators and professionals who work in numerous fields with the latest research-based information about common parenting challenges encountered in raising children, practices for positive behavioral guidance, strategies that support children's progress along a developmental continuum, and approaches to building positive relationships with diverse families.

Philosophical Approach and Organization

Many parenting textbooks are organized around a topical framework (i.e., children's cognitive or moral development is discussed as a single concept across a birth-to-adulthood continuum). This approach requires students to assimilate and form connections among isolated pieces of information in a way that may—but often does not—create meaning. Furthermore, a topical approach presumes that students are able to generalize understanding into effective parenting practices and applied behavioral interventions. Educators have shown that students have difficulty grasping and retaining the conceptual significance of stand-alone information and its relationship to responsive parenting. Thus, educational efforts may not always lead to successful learning and facilitation of effective parental practices.

A more pedagogically sound approach is to provide a developmentally-based organizational structure. *Parenting Today's Children* uses such a framework to support meaningful learning, improve retention, and foster critical thinking skills and innovation. This approach enables students to link, build, and integrate new knowledge along a progressive timeline. A developmental approach also promotes an understanding of ecological variables, their influence on child-rearing problems, and effective response strategies. For example, a developmental perspective helps students relate a toddler's overt displays of frustration to their limited language and social skills, and to then translate this understanding into positive learning and behavior guidance responses that encourage more desirable behaviors.

Students will find *Parenting Today's Children* to be especially helpful for understanding parenting roles, responsibilities, and challenges as well as timely—and sometimes controversial—parenting topics. The material is based upon the latest research findings, and addressed in a clear, concise, and thought-provoking manner. A developmental framework makes student learning easier because each chapter builds on material presented in the previous one. Students will also consider many contemporary topics (e.g., "helicopter" parents, sleep deprivation, eating disorders, teens and plastic surgery, overscheduled children, depression and suicide, social media) which are discussed throughout the book. Pedagogical features (e.g., *Key Terms*, *Learning Objectives*, *Responsive Parenting*, *Trending Now*, *Questions for Discussion and Self-Reflection*, and *Field Activities*) reinforce learning that is interesting, meaningful, applicable, and easy for students to retain. Students will also benefit from the *Suggestions for Parents* features that are provided throughout the book; these features translate chapter material into practical ideas that can be shared with parents. Students will also appreciate the chapter structure, visual summaries and presentations (e.g., photographs, illustrations, graphs), and the easy-to-read format.

The Intended Audience

Parenting Today's Children is designed to be a core text for collegiate-level majors and non-majors who are pursuing interests in early childhood, teacher education (primary and secondary), social welfare, nursing and ancillary health care, pre-med, psychology, counseling, and family studies. This book is also suitable for graduate-level courses in which the research and theoretical bases of parenting and family intervention are addressed. The format, writing style and subject matter also make it a valuable resource for students enrolled in parent educator certification programs offered through community colleges and universities, and for teen parenting and family and consumer science courses offered in secondary and vocational schools.

In addition, *Parenting Today's Children* can be an important asset for teachers, health care clinicians, school counselors, social workers, community educators, and other practicing professionals who work with, and mentor, children and their families. Often these busy individuals are looking for an easy-to-use reference book that contains the latest research results and answers to contemporary parenting challenges. Parents who are interested in learning additional ways to support their children's development and manage challenging behaviors will also find the book beneficial.

Organizational Overview

Parenting Today's Children addresses parenting from a contemporary perspective. It presents the latest information about the multiple challenges that today's parents face, and the skills they need to be successful in their parenting endeavors. The most current published research is used to support ideas, discussions, and conclusions.

- The textual material is organized within a developmental organizational framework that fosters improved student understanding, application, and learning retention. This approach enables students and practitioners who have worked with children—as well as those who are inexperienced—to link, build, and integrate new knowledge along a progressive timeline.
- Chapters provide information that helps students and practitioners to appreciate the supportive role, responsibilities, and challenges that contemporary parents encounter in their efforts to raise healthy, happy, and successful children. The developmental framework contributes to improved student understanding

about the ways that parents can promote children's development across all domains and at any given age. This approach also has pedagogical advantages for students who are trying to assimilate large amounts of new information.

- Each chapter includes extensive pedagogical material—*Key Terms, Learning Objectives,* end-of-chapter *Questions for Discussion and Self-Reflection,* and *Field Activities,* as well as *Responsive Parenting, Trending Now,* and *Suggestions for Parents* features—designed to foster student learning, information retention, and critical thinking. Each element strengthens students' ability to apply parenting concepts to everyday situations.

- The discussion of contemporary—and sometimes controversial—topics that reflect the concerns of today's parents is emphasized as preparatory material for class discussions and individual reflection.

- This text also comes with MindTap™ Education for *Parenting Today's Children.* MindTap™ is a fully customizable online learning platform with interactive content designed to help students learn effectively and prepare them for success in the classroom. Through activities based on real-life teaching situations, MindTap™ elevates students' thinking by providing everyday experiences in applying concepts, practicing skills, and evaluating decisions to guide them in becoming reflective educators.

Content Features

Each chapter includes pedagogical features designed to enhance reader comprehension, retention, critical thinking, and skill in applying the information to everyday experiences and settings:

- *Key Terms* are highlighted in the text, defined on the corresponding page, and included in a comprehensive glossary.

- *Learning Objectives* identify important concepts and skills that readers will achieve after working through each chapter.

- The *Trending Now* feature addresses the pros and cons of contemporary, and sometimes controversial, issues that today's parents may encounter. Discussion points are supported by the latest research findings, and include questions for readers to consider.

- The *Responsive Parenting* feature provides everyday case study scenarios that strengthen and reinforce students' ability to apply effective parenting concepts to address children's challenging behaviors in positive ways.

- *Suggestions for Parents* boxes translate chapter material into practical ideas that can be shared with parents.

- *Self-Reflection Questions* and *Field Activities* reinforce meaningful and applicable interactive learning based upon chapter content.

- *Current references* encourage further research and reading.

- *Visual aids* (e.g., photos, graphics, boxed and highlighted features) are designed to appeal to the media-based learner, and to expand upon and reinforce parenting concepts presented in the chapters.

Accompanying Teaching and Learning Resources

MindTap™: The Personal Learning Experience

MindTap™ Education for *Parenting Today's Children* represents a new approach to teaching and learning. A highly personalized, fully customizable learning platform with an integrated e-portfolio, MindTap™ helps students to elevate thinking by guiding them to:

- Know, remember, and understand concepts critical to becoming an effective practitioner;
- Apply concepts, create curriculum and tools, and demonstrate performance and competency in key course areas, including national and state education standards;
- Prepare portfolio artifacts in preparation for eventual state licensure and launching a successful professional career; and
- Develop the habits to become a reflective practitioner.

As students move through each chapter's Learning Path, they engage in a scaffolded learning experience, designed to move them up Bloom's Taxonomy, from lower- to higher-order thinking skills. The Learning Path enables preservice students to develop these skills and gain confidence by:

- Engaging them with chapter topics and activating their prior knowledge by watching and answering questions about authentic videos of parents and professionals collaborating to promote children's development.
- Checking their comprehension and understanding through Did You Get It? assessments, with varied question types that are autograded for instant feedback.
- Applying concepts through mini-case scenarios—students analyze typical teaching and learning situations, and then create a reasoned response to the issue(s) presented in the scenario.
- Reflecting about and justifying the choices they made within the teaching scenario problem.

MindTap Moves Students Up Bloom's Revised Taxonomy

Create
Evaluate
Analyze
Apply
Understand
Remember & Know

Anderson, L. W., & Krathwohl, D. (Eds.). (2001). *A taxonomy for learning, teaching, and assessing: A revision of Bloom's taxonomy of educational objectives.* New York: Longman.

MindTap™ helps instructors facilitate better outcomes by evaluating how future teachers plan and teach lessons in ways that make content clear and help diverse students learn, assessing the effectiveness of their teaching practice, and adjusting teaching as needed. MindTap™ enables instructors to facilitate improved outcomes by:

- Making grades visible in real time through the Student Progress App so that students and instructors always have access to current standings in the class.
- Using the Outcome Library to embed national education standards and align them to student learning activities, and also allowing instructors to add their state's standards or any other desired outcome.
- Allowing instructors to generate reports on students' performance against any standards or outcomes that are in their MindTap™ course with the click of a mouse.
- Giving instructors the ability to assess students on state standards or other local outcomes by editing existing MindTap™ activities or creating their own, and then aligning those activities to any state or other outcomes that the instructor has added to the MindTap™ Outcome Library.

MindTap™ Education for *Parenting Today's Children* helps instructors easily set their course; since it integrates into the existing Learning Management System, it saves instructors time by allowing them to fully customize any aspect of the learning path. Instructors can change the order of the student learning activities, hide activities they don't want for the course, and—most importantly—create custom assessments and add any standards, outcomes, or content they desire (e.g., YouTube videos, Google docs). Learn more at www.cengage.com/mindtap.

Online Instructor's Manual

The Instructor's Manual contains a variety of resources to aid instructors in preparing and presenting text material in a manner that meets their personal preferences and course needs. It presents chapter-by-chapter suggestions and resources to enhance and facilitate learning.

Online Test Bank

The Test Bank contains multiple choice, true/false, completion, and essay questions to challenge your students and assess their learning.

Cengage Learning Testing Powered by Cognero

The Test Bank also is available through Cognero, a flexible online system that allows you to author, edit, and manage test bank content, as well as to create multiple test versions in an instant. You can deliver tests from your school's learning management system, your classroom, or wherever you want.

Online PowerPoint Lecture Slides

These vibrant Microsoft PowerPoint lecture slides for each chapter assist you with lecture preparation by providing concept coverage using images, figures, and tables directly from the textbook!

Acknowledgments

A performance of any kind—a play, dance, exhibit, sporting event, or book—only comes to fruition with the efforts and support of many behind-the-scenes people who are not always recognized on the program. We would like to acknowledge and thank these individuals for their endless contributions to this project. There are others with whom we have worked closely to take hundreds of typed manuscript pages and transform them into a resource-rich book that is attractive and meaningful. We would like to say a special thank you to Jessica Alderman, our Content Developer, for her expertise in editing, keeping us on track, and guiding us through the writing process. We would also like to thank Samen Iqbal and Jill Traut for their indispensable production contributions. We cannot thank our families enough for their unending encouragement, support, and patience during the many months of writing, proofing, and finalizing this project. We would not have been able to do this without your help.

We are also grateful to our many reviewers who provided valuable insight, comments, and suggestions for improvement:

- Linda S. Behrendt, Ph.D., Indiana State University
- David Bowers, Ohio State University
- Jamie Brown, University of North Carolina at Charlotte
- J. Claire Cook, Middle Tennessee State University
- Jerry L. Cook, California State University, Sacramento
- Ming Cui, Florida State University
- April Dominguez, Ph.D., California State University, Bakersfield
- Donna L. Foster, Langston University
- Nerissa LeBlanc Gillum, Ph.D., Texas Woman's University
- Dr. Angel L. Gullon-Rivera, Western Michigan University

- Karleah Harris, Miami University
- Donna Hancock Hoskins, Bridgewater College
- Dr. Sharleen L. Kato, Seattle Pacific University
- April LaGue, Ph.D., California State University, Bakersfield
- Dr. Ravisha Mathur, San Jose State University
- Felicia McGowan, Ed.D., Alcorn State University
- Yolanda T. Mitchell, University of Nebraska - Lincoln
- Jennifer K. Moore-Kemp, Langston University
- Justin W. Peer, University of Michigan - Dearborn
- Janene Perez, MA, San Jose State University
- Dr. Kimberly Reynolds, LPC, Nicholls State University
- Rhonda A. Richardson, Kent State University
- Lori E. Staton, Mississippi State University
- Heather Von Bank, Minnesota State University, Mankato
- Tao Wang, The University of Tulsa
- Shadonna M. Watkins, Langston University
- Carrie G. Watson, Arizona State University
- Natalie A. Williams, Ph.D., University of Nebraska - Lincoln
- Dr. Cynthia B. Wilson, University of Montevallo
- Dr. Eileen Yantz, University of North Carolina at Charlotte
- Tammy Lowery Zacchilli, Saint Leo University

About the Authors

Lynn Marotz, R.N., Ph.D., professor emerita, was a member of the Department of Applied Behavioral Science faculty, University of Kansas, for over 35 years, and also served as the Associate Director of the Child Development Center. She taught large undergraduate and graduate courses in parenting, children's health, safety and nutrition, history and philosophy of early childhood education, and leadership and administration. She also worked closely with students in the Early Childhood teacher education program and the families of children enrolled in the Child Development Center.

Lynn has authored numerous invited book chapters in national and international publications about children's health and nutrition, legal issues, and environmental safety. She is also the author of *Health, Safety, and Nutrition for the Young Child, Developmental Profiles: Birth through Adolescence, Motivational Leadership*, and *By the Ages: Behavior & Development of Children Pre-birth Through Eight*. She has been interviewed for numerous articles about children's health and nutrition and parenting that have appeared in national trade magazines and has served as a consultant for children's museums and training film productions. In addition, she has presented extensively at international, national, and state conferences, and continues to hold appointments on national, state, and local committees and initiatives that advocate on behalf of children and their families.

Sara Kupzyk, Ph.D., is a licensed psychologist and an Assistant Professor of Psychology at the Munroe-Meyer Institute for Genetics and Rehabilitation at the University of Nebraska Medical Center. She provides outpatient integrated behavioral health services in a pediatric primary care clinic for children with various concerns including anxiety, depression, oppositional behavior, autism spectrum disorder, and attention and anger control problems. She also directs the Academic Evaluation and Intervention Clinic, which provides assessment and intervention development services to improve academic skills through parent tutoring. Sara teaches graduate-level courses for the Applied Behavior Analysis and School Psychology Programs at the University of Nebraska Omaha. She previously taught courses in the areas of education and issues in parenting.

Sara conducts research focused on issues of treatment integrity, academic problems, parent training, and early intervention for children with emotional and learning concerns. She has authored articles in several peer-reviewed journals, including the *Journal of Applied Behavior Analysis, Journal of Behavioral Education*, and *Psychology in the Schools*, as well as book chapters in *Behavioral Health Promotion and Intervention for People with Intellectual and Developmental Disabilities, APA Handbook of Applied Behavior Analysis*, and *The Practical Handbook of School Psychology: Effective Practices for the 21st Century*. She also presents at local and national conferences and reviews manuscripts for peer-reviewed journals.

Parenting in Historical, Cultural, and Theoretical Contexts

1

LEARNING OBJECTIVES

After reading the chapter, you will be able to:

1-1 Explain why families are important to any society and cultural group.

1-2 Compare and contrast the concept of parenting in America from colonial times to the present day.

1-3 Describe how child development is influenced by each of the levels or rings identified in Bronfenbrenner's ecological systems theory model.

naeyc Standards Linked to Chapter Content

1a and 1b: Promoting child development and learning

2a: Building family and community relationships

For centuries, political, religious, sociological, and ethnic background factors have had a collective influence on American approaches toward children, families, and parenting. Some represent milestones that have had a significant impact on the development of family

continued on following page

Figure 1-1 Projected Ethnic Changes in U.S. Population Diversity

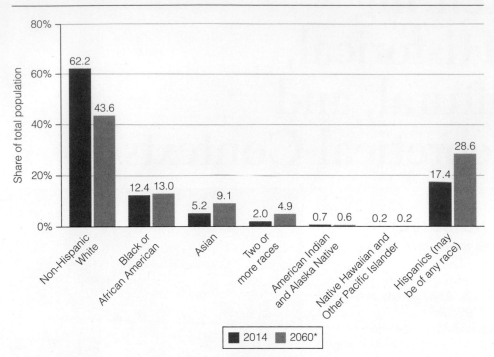

Source: U.S. Census Bureau (2014). National population projections.

arrangements, interactions, and parenting practices under challenging circumstances. Similarly, a steady and very large addition of people and families from other countries have, and continue to, substantially change the size, demographics, and complexity of the indigenous U.S. population (see Figure 1-1). An overview of only the most salient features and trends that have contributed to the rich diversity in this country and produced changes in the meaning of "family" and "parenting" follows. ■

1-1 The Meaning of Family

Is it necessary to describe the concept of family? Everyone has one, however defined, and interaction among families of various kinds is an everyday occurrence. Although the term is familiar and commonly used, we may not recognize that "family" often has very different meanings to many persons and cultural groups.

Although the family concept as a social construct has seemingly remained constant for centuries, its characteristics and functional relationships have undergone significant change in the past, and especially in recent decades. For example, family size has been steadily decreasing, single-person parenthood continues to increase, marriage and fertility rates are declining, and women are postponing childbearing longer—or remaining childless—as a result of career goals, personal choice, and economic challenges (Williamson & Lawson, 2015). Same-sex marriage, cohabitation, divorce, work-family balance, reproductive technologies, and adoption by single and same-sex parents have resulted in family configurations and roles that differ substantially from those in the past. Many contemporary families also find themselves caring for aging parents at the same time that they are raising their own young children. More grandparents are assuming primary care and custodial responsibility for their grandchildren, and adult children are moving back to their familial home because of economic or health issues.

These and many other factors have altered the nature of the traditional **nuclear family** and given rise to alternative family constructs. Some social scientists believe these developments are a positive sign of familial resilience that promote an ability to adapt to changing social conditions (Henry, Morris, & Harrist, 2015; Wall & Gouveia, 2014). Others have cited negative effects on children's development and on adults in nontraditional relationships (Brown, Manning, & Stykes, 2015; Harcourt & Adler-Baeder, 2015). Further research may resolve some of these contrasts, which may lead to a better understanding of how well alternative family structures function and their effect on children, parents, and society.

nuclear family a unit consisting of two parents and their biological offspring.

1-1a The Historical Importance of Family

Throughout history, the family, as a legal and kinship unit, has always been considered fundamental to a society's continuation. It has served in support of important functions, such as land ownership, inheritance, and social and economic development. Well into the twentieth century, families often included many children, partially to ensure that a percentage would survive at a time when diseases were rampant and medical care limited. Children born into familial relationships helped to ensure the passage of social values and cultural traditions from one generation to the next.

1-2 A Historical Perspective on Parenting: Roles and Responsibilities

Although children are essential for societal and cultural survival, attitudes toward and respect for children have not always been favorable. The concept of childhood as a distinct life stage was not generally recognized until the 17th century (Aries, 1965). Prior to this time, children were considered to be small adults who no longer required parental care, attention, and protection and were expected to work alongside their family members.

Parents' views toward children have since undergone radical transformation. Their ideas about children's role in a family system and how children should be reared have been reframed by historical and philosophical developments. Although some parenting practices may seem unusual to us today, it is likely that parents were doing their best based on the information available to them at the time. Their fundamental goals of caring for and nurturing children to ensure their health and safety, preparation for adulthood, and maintenance of cultural norms and values have remained important throughout history.

1-2a Parenting in Ancient and Modern Europe

Early Greek philosophers were among the first to formally acknowledge the importance of parenting for children's development and a society's future. Plato (428–348 BCE), for example, advocated that pregnant women take care of themselves (e.g., take walks, eat well) to help ensure that they would have a healthy baby. He also believed that the first 5 years of a child's life were the most important time for learning. Aristotle (384–322 BCE),

Photo 1-1 Parents' concepts of childhood and childrearing have changed throughout history. Library of Congress, Prints & Photographs Division, Reproduction number LC-USZC4-11327 (color film copy transparency post-conservation)

in turn, urged parents to identify each child's unique talents, especially those that were conducive to leadership, and to adjust their parenting style to address children's different personality types.

During the Roman era (200 BCE–400 CE), parents cared for, socialized, and taught their children to read, write, and to engage in play. They typically arranged their children's marriages when girls were in their early teens and boys were several years older. Fathers were considered to be the head of their family, and were expected to handle financial and decision-making responsibilities, while women principally oversaw household duties. It was a father's right to practice infanticide if an infant was not of a preferred gender, was born with a physical defect, or he was financially unable to provide for another child in the family (PBS, 2006).

Historians paint a picture of parenting and family life during the Middle Ages (400 CE–about 1300 CE) that was quite different from that of earlier times. Couples married and usually had three to five children. Mothers gave birth at home with the assistance of a midwife or neighbors. As a result, maternal and infant mortality rates were high, with an estimated one in twenty mothers dying during childbirth and one in three infants perishing before their first birthday (Singman, 1999).

Child-rearing practices during the Middle Ages have been described as being unusually cold, harsh, and uncaring (Hanawalt, 1993). Living conditions were difficult. Child abuse was fairly common, and reflected prevailing religious and philosophical beliefs which underscored the need to eliminate children's evil thoughts and behaviors. Parents met children's basic needs, but provided limited nurturing and showed little affection. From our 21st century perspective, it may be difficult to understand why parents would treat their children in this manner. However, their indifference afforded some emotional protection from the likelihood (25–35 percent) that children would die (Hill, 1990).

It is also true that parents did not understand children's developmental needs in the same way they are understood today and, thus, saw no reason for engaging in much interaction with an infant or young child. When children turned seven, they were treated as an adult and would be taught a craft or skill, or entered into an apprenticeship, so that they could contribute to the family's economic survival. Formal education was primarily reserved for male children from upper-class families. These ideas and practices remained relatively constant over the next several centuries, simply because societal and economic conditions in feudal times were similar from decade to decade.

Such parental attitudes toward children, child development, and parental roles began to change during the 17th and 18th centuries, a time period often referred to as the Enlightenment. Earlier beliefs that children were born wicked and immoral were gradually being set aside and replaced with ideals that encouraged parents to be more lenient, understanding, and nurturing (Kagan, 1978). Philosophers, including John Locke, Jean Jacques Rousseau, Johann Pestalozzi, and John Amos Comenius, touted the virtues and innocence of childhood and the importance of environmental influences on children's development. Parents were counseled to guide children's behavior with rewards rather than harsh punishments, to encourage play, and to use nature to promote curiosity and hands-on learning. They educated children at home and taught them to write and to read the Christian Bible in preparation for adulthood.

Many of these progressive ideas, however, were set aside during the later 18th and 19th centuries. The advent of the Industrial Revolution in Western Europe brought about social and political unrest that thrust many families into poverty and changed their way of living. Efforts to accelerate industrial productivity led to widespread urban crowding, poor living conditions, malnutrition, and rampant death and disease among the general population. Parents were forced to send children as young as nine and ten to work in factories to help support their family (Humphries, 2013). Fathers sought any employment in increasingly competitive labor markets, while mothers assumed

Photo 1-2 Children as young as nine were sent to work in factories. Library of Congress, Prints & Photographs Division, Reproduction number LC-DIG-nclc-01892 (color digital file from b&w original print)LC-USZ6-1226 (b&w film copy negative)LC-USZ62-15519 (b&w film copy negative)

full responsibility for all household tasks and children's education (Fitzgerald, 2000). However, difficult economic conditions forced many mothers to also seek work (usually service-related and at a lower wage than men), which represented a significant deviation from their traditional homemaker role.

Compulsory education became a priority, or was at least considered to be an important goal, in the latter half of the 19th century. Various groups throughout Europe argued that free public education should be available to all children (5 to 10 years); free also meant "not under the control of a religion-based organization" (Ramirez & Boli, 1987). Reading, writing, and arithmetic skills were considered necessary for people who were living in a rapidly industrializing world. This development also marked the movement of educational responsibility out of the home and into the public sector, which began to create a stronger sense of social and cultural identity—a way of defining what it meant to be "German" or "English," and, ultimately as the 20th century unfolded, Scandinavian, Italian, or Hispanic.

Families began leaving their farms and moving to the city in large numbers during the early 20th century. Rapid urbanization led to a higher standard of living for some families and an increase in poverty, substandard housing, and poor living conditions for others (Bairoch & Goertz, 1986). Poverty remained high among a large, unskilled working class (e.g., servants, laborers, farm workers) (Gazeley, 2003). Infant mortality declined and life expectancy increased as a result of improved wages, nutrition, sanitation, and living conditions. Fewer women were employed outside of the home, more regulations protected workers' safety, opportunities for advancement and free enterprise created a large middle class sector, and a new way of life existed for many families.

Twenty-first century parents continue their efforts to care for, nurture, and guide children to the best of their abilities. They worry about their children's well-being and the challenges they face as they grow up in a world that may be quite different from the one they knew as a child. At the same time, parents embrace new developments, celebrate their children's accomplishments, and hope that their children will enjoy a life that is equal to or better than their own.

1-2b Parenting in the United States

Many of the first immigrants to arrive in New England during the 1600s were intact Puritan families that worked closely together to survive in difficult conditions. They were passionately religious people who had fled Europe to live according to their fundamental religious beliefs and without fear of persecution. Fathers were in charge of family life, provided moral guidance, controlled all family property, and made all family decisions (Graham, 2000; Mintz & Kellogg, 1988). Because men were responsible for handling worldly affairs, they were often the only literate family member available to teach their children, mainly sons, to read and write. Girls were only taught to read (especially religious material) which explains why many colonial women often could read, but could not write or sign their names—with other than an "X" or initials (Monaghan, 1988).

The Christian Bible served as the family's main parenting manual. Verses provided guidance for proper behavior and encouraged parents to treat children with firmness and affection. "Firmness" is the key word in the parenting process, because early colonists considered children to be intrinsically "sinful" and, thus, in need of being taught to control their impulses (Chudacoff, 2007). Discipline was handled by fathers, who demanded children's strict obedience. Neighbors were also expected to help monitor and nurture the proper behavior of all children in the community.

Photo 1-3 Slaves were bought and sold as manual laborers to work on plantations. Library of Congress, Prints & Photographs Division, Reproduction number LC-DIG-ppmsca-11398 (digital file from original item, front)

Shortly after the Puritans had settled in Colonial America, other groups, such as the Quakers, followed. Their families were also close-knit and often included eight or more children, who helped to care for one another. The Quakers believed that children were born innocent and with goodness. They did not accept the notion of "breaking children's will," but taught children how to behave through example. Parents followed a parenting style that was less patriarchal or authoritarian than that used by the Puritans. They devoted much of their time to nurturing and teaching children in order to protect them against outside influences, although parental affection remained minimal so as not to "spoil" a child (Jensen, 1984).

Strong family unity was also characteristic of many early settler groups. The circumstances for some, however, were quite different. According to the 1860 census, African slaves, brought to America in large numbers, represented approximately 13 percent (4 of the 31 million) of the total population (U.S. Census Bureau, 2016). They often faced seemingly insurmountable challenges, especially those who worked on Southern plantations. Although some owners made an attempt to keep slave families intact, others sold or sent family members off to live and work on different farms. Work-related role differences and a failure to recognize African marriages caused mothers, fathers, and children to be separated from one another. Slaves were forced to give up their name, religion, customs, and any hope of an education—indignities that would have long-lasting effects (Independence Hall Association, 2014).

Parenting roles remained similar among colonial families until the Civil War (1861–1865). When husbands joined the military, women were forced to take over family finances and farm-related duties in addition to caring for their children. Many women also filled teaching positions in schools that had traditionally been held only by men. Their teaching style proved to be more nurturing than the customary stern male approach and forever changed the way that children's education would be conducted. When the war ended, women often remained in their new roles, which placed them in responsible positions that were equivalent to their male counterparts. The patriarchal family model, thus, began to slowly disappear and was replaced by relationships in which husband and wife were equal partners (Hacker, Hilde, & Jones, 2010).

A developing reverence for motherhood and a woman's role in children's development began to appear in the later 1800s. Families left their farms and moved to the city, fathers worked outside of the home, and mothers devoted their full attention to raising children. They nurtured, educated, and protected children from the perceived and real evils of city life, which, in turn, often meant that children became more dependent upon their parents. Some women also pursued interests other than homemaking, which paralleled a choice to have smaller families. Children could be considered a financial liability, given that they were no longer needed as a labor source for the family's endeavors.

These developments contributed to an increased interest in parent education, which led to publications, study clubs, research studies, and the eventual establishment of the National Congress of Mothers (later to become the PTA) (1897), the Children's Bureau (1912), and the National Association of Colored Parents and Teachers (1926). Parents took a greater interest in promoting children's health, nutrition, psychological well-being, and personality development. However, fathers' role became increasingly marginalized in the parenting process as psychologists promoted the importance of mothering and maternal bonding.

Despite these changes, the notion that women possessed a natural motherly instinct was abandoned (Watson, 1928). Mothers were advised to maintain strict feeding and sleeping schedules and not to immediately respond to children's requests, but rather to let them cry. "Never hug and kiss them, never let them sit on your lap. Shake hands with them in the morning." This was thought to prepare children for the world they would encounter as adults. There was also a general fear that giving too many hugs and kisses would turn boys into "sissies" (Grant, 2004).

Child-centered parenting practices continued to develop during the 1930s and 1940s. However, mothers were encouraged to follow a more relaxed and enjoyable approach to raising children. Parents had access to more informed approaches about how to support children's developmental progress and provide age-appropriate discipline based on the contributions of Arnold Gesell, Jean Piaget, and Dr. Benjamin Spock. Mothers were advised to follow their instincts and to try to understand children's seemingly troublesome behaviors from the child's perspective. Parents were made more aware of children's developmental delays and encouraged to seek professional guidance for maladjustment disorders, such as prolonged bed-wetting, temper tantrums, sleeping problems, and academic failure.

Such child-centered approaches endured even as family life itself changed significantly during the 1930s and 1940s. The Great Depression brought about high unemployment, poverty, and a decline in the birth rate. Marriage and birth rates surged at the onset of World War II as soldiers prepared to be sent overseas. Psychologists advised mothers to remain in the home, due to fears that their absence would cause changes in children's sense of well-being. However, the critical labor shortage that resulted while men served in the military meant that women were needed to work in factory, shipyard, military, and government jobs (Goldin, 1991). The Federal government responded by temporarily subsidizing a very limited national system of child care programs for working mothers (less than 1 percent of the approximately two million spaces that were needed) (Michel, 2011). Shortly after the war ended, the government ceased funding for child care centers despite the fact that demand remained high.

Prosperity and a renewed sense of optimism followed immediately after the war ended. Women married at an earlier age and had more children, which created a postwar "baby boom." The number of children living in two-parent households peaked during this period and remained the norm until the early 1960s. Many women returned to being full-time housewives; fathers resumed their role as the principal economic provider. Parents closely followed the advice of child development experts (e.g., Arnold Gesell, Erik Erikson, John Bowlby, Dr. Benjamin Spock) who encouraged them to be more nurturing and responsive to children's individual differences. Middle-class parents were determined to rear children who would ultimately be educated thinkers, tolerant of others, and successful in life.

Although life was good for many families during the 1950s and early 1960s, this was not true for everyone. Minority and immigrant families were often plagued by poverty, discrimination, unemployment, and high dropout rates among children (Elliott & Ionescu, 2003; Rumbaut, 1994). Families were encouraged to institutionalize children who were born with a disability. In some instances, mothers were blamed for causing their children's anxieties, mental health problems, and homosexuality (Rainer et al., 1960). Criticism was also leveled at parents for their leniency in raising a generation of children who failed to conform, questioned adult authority, and were seemingly uncontrollable.

By the late 1960s and early 1970s, military deployments and antiwar protests against United States involvement in the Vietnam War began to challenge family bonding and unity. The introduction of birth control measures and more readily available abortion procedures meant that having a child was now a "personal choice" and not a "responsibility." The birth rate hit its lowest point ever, and the average family size decreased from four children to two. Social and economic instability contributed to high rates of divorce, poverty, and births to teen and unwed mothers. Increasing numbers of children were living in single-parent families, and more mothers found it necessary to seek paid employment (Popenoe, 1993).

Child psychologists voiced concern about how these changes would affect children's development, which, in turn, prompted a renewed interest and financial investment in child-study research. Experts, like Jean Piaget, continued to encourage parents to devote more attention to promoting children's cognitive, emotional, and moral development. Parents responded by limiting children's free play and enrolling them in multiple structured opportunities (e.g., preschools, music lessons, sports, theater, and art activities) to advance their physical and academic skills. Soon parents would be criticized for overscheduling children's lives.

Humanitarian concerns reached an all-time high during the mid-1970s through the 1990s. New social service programs were established and existing programs, including Medicaid and Head Start, expanded to assist more families and children living in poverty.

Photo 1-4 Mothers were told to enjoy their children.
Library of Congress Prints and Photographs Division[LC-USF34-032902-D]

Wilma left her job as an elementary school teacher to **homeschool** her 6-year-old twin boys and 8-year-old daughter. The decision had been difficult, but she feared for her children's safety every day as they walked to and from school. Their once modest Detroit neighborhood was now lined with foreclosed homes, many of them abandoned and occupied by gang members. Wilma's daughter was a gifted learner and often told her mother that she already knew everything they were teaching her at school. There were also many days when she didn't want to go to school because she was afraid of several children in her classroom who had severe behavior problems. The loss of Wilma's salary would make it more difficult for their family to do some of the things they enjoyed, but she knew that homeschooling her children was far more important.

Wilma's decision reflects a fast-growing trend in America and throughout the world. According to the U.S. Department of Education (2015), approximately 2.2 million school-age children (or 3 percent) are currently being taught by a parent at home. Parents have cited a variety of reasons for assuming this responsibility. Some favor the practice because it appears to re-establish the strong connection between parent as educator and child as student, an approach similar to parent/child relationships that prevailed in the 18th and 19th centuries. Some express disappointment with public school education and want to have more control over what children are being taught. Some parents desire greater involvement in their children's education and development. Others feel strongly about providing their children with moral and religious instruction in addition to academics. Parents associated with various minority groups frequently cite concerns about safety, discrimination, and academic quality as their primary reasons for choosing to educate children at home (Mazamal & Lundy, 2015; Ray 2015). Homeschooling is also rapidly becoming a preferred educational option among parents of children who have a developmental disability.

The homeschooling trend embodies politics, religion, and parental choice, but it is not without controversy. Critics cite a lack of empirical evidence supporting some of the positive claims that have been made (Lubienski, Puckett, & Brewer, 2013). However, they have also acknowledged that research on such subject areas is often biased by the self-selected nature of parents (e.g., better educated, religious, financially stable) who choose to engage in homeschooling activities. Opponents also point to a lack of systematic oversight, inconsistent curriculum standards, and children's failure to achieve at grade level (Green-Hennessy, 2014). The National Education Association (NEA) and teachers' unions oppose homeschooling on the grounds that parents lack teacher credentialing and training in effective instruction. Furthermore, questions have been raised about the social isolation that children may experience when they are homeschooled and denied opportunities to participate in extracurricular school functions.

Advocates report that students who are homeschooled score above average on standardized achievement tests. Ray (2015) noted that homeschooled African American children averaged significantly higher scores on math, reading, and language tests than did African American children who were enrolled in public schools. Researchers have also determined that many homeschooled students are as well-prepared for college level math courses as their public schooled peers (Wilkens et al., 2015). Concerns that homeschooled children would lack social skill development have not been evident. Observers have noted that homeschooled children tend to exhibit fewer behavior problems and generally are quite mature, self-confident, and socially adept for their age. This may be attributed to the fact that they often have had opportunities to interact with peers as well as adult role models from diverse backgrounds during field trips, volunteer experiences, and participation in community activities. Vaughn et al. (2015) also found that homeschooled adolescents held unfavorable views of drugs and alcohol and were less likely than their public school peers to use these substances.

Parents have many decisions to make on behalf of their children, one of which is how to provide them with the best education possible. Their personal beliefs, values, goals, and expectations will serve to guide their ultimate choices. As a result, what works for one family may not necessarily be appropriate for another. Yet, many questions remain to be answered. Is homeschooling in a child's best interest? Does homeschooling isolate children from their peers and reality? Should parents be expected to meet certain requirements before they homeschool children?

---

homeschool parent-led, home-based education.

The passage of the Education for All Handicapped Children Act (1975) mandated free screening, special education services, and civil rights protection, and marked a turning point in public attitude and support for individuals with physical and mental disabilities.

Dual-income families became the norm during this period. Financial pressures made it difficult for fathers to remain as the sole breadwinner. More than fifty-percent of mothers with children younger than age 5 sought full- and part-time paid employment (Leibowitz & Klerman, 1995). As a result, many children spent their days in out-of-home child care programs. Families again began having fewer children and changed some of their child-rearing practices. Fathers assumed some responsibility for children's care and household duties out of necessity (Gershuny & Robinson,

1988). The media and others warned parents that day care was harmful to children's intellectual and psychological development (Belsky & Rovine, 1988; Barglow, Vaughn, & Molitor, 1987). This only added to the guilt that parents were already feeling, so they tried to compensate for their absence by spending concentrated periods of "quality" time together whenever possible. In fact, researchers discovered that working parents were actually spending more time engaged in activities with their children than parents had in previous decades (Sayer, Bianchi, & Robinson, 2004). Children's safety also became a predominant parental concern because of the amount of time they were away from home. As a result, parents dedicated considerable effort to teaching children about sexual abuse prevention, installing safety devices, and monitoring children's whereabouts.

Photo 1-5 The 1970s marked an era of humanitarian concern. Library of Congress Prints and Photographs Division[LC-DIG-ppmsca-03128]

Parents relied heavily on time-out, praise, and rewards to reinforce children's behavior. However, they were also reluctant to establish "too many" rules, criticize children's behavior, or use disciplinary measures that might be upsetting or reduce a child's self-esteem. Parents coached children to be independent and self-confident and tolerated their questioning of authority. As the 1990s drew to an end, it became evident that the American family and the way the current generation of children, commonly labeled "Generation Me," were being raised had changed.

Twenty-first century parents continue to experience new pressures and opportunities. Millions of jobs lost during the 2007–2009 recession led to extensive unemployment, poverty, and homelessness—trends that have been difficult to reverse. As a result, one in five U.S. children under the age of 18 lives in poverty, one of the highest rates among developed countries worldwide (U.S. Census Bureau, 2014). Parents struggle with increased drug use and abuse among their children as illicit substances became easier to obtain. They maintain busy lifestyles and try to balance work and family responsibilities. They have been blamed for escalating juvenile delinquency, gun violence, and early sexual activity rates, because of their seemingly lax parental control. They try to protect their children who are growing up in a digital age from overexposure to too much technology and social media, and struggle to keep their family connected.

Despite these challenges, 21st century parents have benefited from research advances and improved access to parenting information in books, articles, and on websites. As a result, they are often better informed about the importance of supporting children's health, nutrition, and early brain development. Today's parents are more aware of the need to seek professional consultation when a child's development may not be proceeding as expected. However, there are also times when parents may be overwhelmed by too much information or confused when contrasting viewpoints are presented. It is easy now to become a seeming "expert" in a variety of fields simply by self-promotion on social media.

Parents are also beginning to understand why it is important to participate in children's education. They purchase the latest electronic toys, learning videos, enroll children in private schools, and work with children at home in hopes of giving them an educational advantage. Some parents have taken this a step farther and chosen to homeschool their children. These trends are representative of the contemporary milieu that parents must decipher and act upon, and that may bode well for children and parents alike. Today's parents, like parents throughout history, continue to strive to create conditions and opportunities that may well make life better for their children than what they may have experienced.

1-2c A Nation of Immigrants

The historical overview of parenting in the United States outlined in the previous section highlighted the basic factors which have led to parental approaches that are considered fundamental to an American identity. The historical timeline also encompassed significant differences in parenting practices brought to the United States by immigrant families—and entire communities in some cases. A brief look at how their ideas have

Photo 1-6 The United States has historically been a refuge for immigrants.
Library of Congress Prints and Photographs Division[LC-DIG-highsm-15918]

influenced the concept of parenting provides an additional context for appreciating the diversity that exists in this country today.

Immigration to what is now the United States has been a continuous process since the 17th century. Indigenous Native Americans were joined by French, Spanish, English, and Dutch people who sought religious freedom and opportunity. Over the course of many decades, they would be joined by large numbers of immigrants from Ireland, Germany, Italy, and many other countries. Between the 17th and 19th centuries people from Africa were brought to this country by the hundreds of thousands to work as indentured slaves. Thousands of Asian immigrants arrived during the mid-1800s to work as laborers in mining and railroad construction. More recently, millions of Latino and Hispanic people have entered the United States, legally and illegally, from South America, Mexico, and the Caribbean to work primarily in agriculture, construction, and service industries.

As the immigration tides swept progressively through various parts of the country, conflicts also inevitably arose. Immigrants were rarely well-received, despite the fact that they often helped to mitigate critical labor shortages and were willing to accept lower wages and poorer living conditions. As a result, ethnic immigrant groups often formed or maintained close-knit neighborhoods and enclaves where they could preserve their language, customs, cultural, and family values.

Parenting and Socialization. Families' adaptation to new surroundings and expectations was highly influenced by the circumstances associated with their arrival in this country. Most early immigrant parents were poor, had limited English proficiency, and experienced significant stress caused by leaving their extended families, friends, and familiar way of life behind (Thomas, 1995). Economic and social stressors, such as these, have been blamed for the authoritarian style of parenting that was often practiced among many immigrant family groups.

Asian and Latino/Hispanic immigrant families came from cultures that upheld strong, collectivist and intra-family values which they continued to follow in this country. Traditional cultural views defined and shaped their ideas about parenting roles, responsibilities, and practices, although they were based on different religious philosophies (e.g., Confucian vs Catholicism). Children in both cultural groups were, and continue to be, highly valued and socialized to maintain close family ties. Mothers typically assumed principal familial responsibility for the home environment and child care; fathers filled the role of primary disciplinarian. The family's economic situation often required that mothers work and take their children along because they lacked an extended family network for support. As a result, children's strict obedience was expected and misbehavior was harshly punished.

Africans who were brought to this country as indentured slaves struggled to retain their cultural identity and beliefs despite the discrimination and oppression under which they lived for decades. These historical developments influenced, and continue to influence, African American parenting styles and practices which were intended to nurture, protect, and provide security for children who were growing up in unfavorable conditions. Strong, extended kinship ties and religious affiliations played, and continue to play, an important role in helping parents address prejudice and adversity. Children were expected to behave, and parents often used discipline that was perceived as being direct, restrictive, and accepting of corporal punishment (Yildirim & Roopnarine, 2015). However, it was also administered in a warm, caring, and non-authoritarian manner.

Education has historically served as a unifying theme among immigrant parents, and is considered a means to economic success and social integration into the larger American cultural landscape. The Latino and Hispanic family ethic has embraced education as an indication of personal accomplishment, but not necessarily as a priority.

African American parents support and value education as a pathway that will help their children to enjoy a better and personally-satisfying life. Likewise, Asian immigrant parents also place a high value on children's education and expect them to achieve well-paying jobs and high socioeconomic status.

The various historical events that melded cultures, parents, children, and parenting practices into the American landscape have created many opportunities to examine the interplay among and within familial structures (see Table 1-1). The outcome of these efforts worldwide has produced numerous theories and contributed to a rich and extensive literature about the parenting concept.

		Ancient Greeks	Romans	Middle Ages	1600–1700s	1700–1800s	1900s
Ancient and Modern Europe	**Childhood**	• Seen as repositories of knowledge	• Viewed as father's property-Infanticide • Perceived to be basically evil • Treated as small adults and most taught a trade		• Believed to be born innocent-tabula rasa • First years of life seen as formative • Increased access to education		
	Parenting	• Plato–pregnant women care for themselves • Aristotle–identify unique talents of children and adjust parenting style	• Arranged marriages • Parents cared for and educated children • Fathers head of families	• Parents married • Mothers gave birth at home • High infant mortality • Cold, harsh childrearing	• Families more involved in education/preparation for adulthood • More lenient and nurturing childrearing	• Increased poverty • Fathers worked in industry, mothers maintained household, but some forced to work for financial reasons	• Higher standard of living • Decreased mortality rate • Fewer women employed • Parents fostered development
		1600–1700s	**1700–1800s**	**1900–1940s**	**1950–1970s**	**1980–1990s**	**2000s**
North America	**Childhood**	• Puritans–believed children innately evil • Relied on children to help/contribute to family • "Putting out" to learn a trade	• Childhood viewed as a distinct life stage • Increase in children attending boarding schools and working in factories	• Child labor laws • Compulsory education	• Increase in child-related research • Laws and programs for children with disabilities and in poverty developed		• More relaxed scheduling of activities for children • Improved health care, education, and access to technology
	Parenting	• Puritans–fathers in charge of families, children treated firmly • Quakers–taught children to behave through example, more nurturing	• Expansion of women's role because of men's involvement in Civil War • Parenting responsibilities more equal • Children viewed as a financial liability • Strict feeding and sleeping routines	• Child-centered parenting • More relaxed and followed instincts • Increase in parents seeking professional help for childhood disabilities and disorders • Two parent households peaked • Baby boom following war	• Having a child becomes more of a choice because of birth control and availability of abortion • Decrease in family size • Increase single parent families	• Increase in services for children • Dual-income families become the norm • Use of time-out and praise common	• Increase in poverty • Emphasis on work family balance • Improved access to parenting information

Table 1-1 Childhood and Parenting Historical Timeline

1-3 Guiding Theories of Child Development and Parenting

Researchers have long debated whether development is a result of nature or nurture, but it is now widely acknowledged that both play an important and shared role in the process. The interaction that occurs between biology and environmental factors makes human behavior very complex. Researchers have proposed developmental theories to help us better understand this complexity, promote children's development, and support healthy family relationships. In this section, we highlight the primary theories that are applied in later chapters, including ecological systems theory, family systems theory, attachment theory, psychosocial theory, and learning theory.

1-3a Ecological Systems Theory

As a psychologist, Urie Bronfenbrenner noticed that all too often, researchers and service providers focused on an individual child with whom they were working, and did not consider how children function within their environment. This led him to develop the ecological systems theory (Bronfenbrenner, 1979, 1994; Bronfenbrenner & Ceci, 1993) (see Figure 1-2). This theory provides a framework for examining how individuals are influenced by direct interactions with their environment as well as indirectly by larger social and cultural variables across time. Bronfenbrenner

Figure 1-2 Bronfenbrenner's Ecological Model

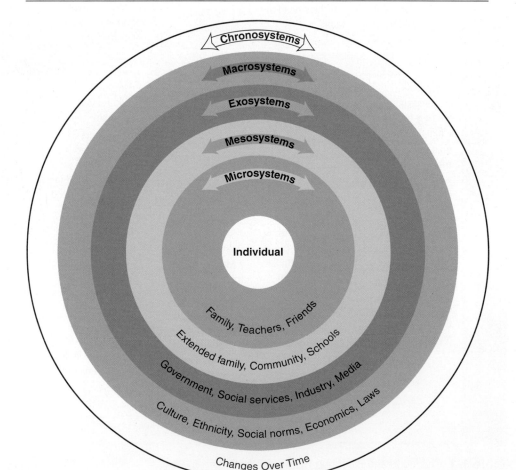

conceptualized the model as having several levels or rings of interacting environments, with the individual at the central core.

The first level of Bronfenbrenner's model, the **microsystem**, addresses the direct interactions that an individual has with others in his or her immediate environment. For example, a child's microsystem may consist of home (e.g., parents, siblings), school (e.g., teachers, principal), park (e.g., peers, neighbors), and offices (e.g., therapists, physician, social worker). Bronfenbrenner emphasized the bidirectional or reciprocal nature of interactions that occur within these settings. In other words, not only does the environment have an impact on an individual, but the individual also affects the environment or causes it to alter in some way. For example, a parent may try to use the same calming strategies that were successful with their first child only to find that the strategies (e.g., holding close and rocking) do not work with the second child and, thus, the parent needs to try alternative strategies (e.g., laying the child flat, singing). In this situation, the parent's behavior is affected by the infant's behavior and vice versa.

The system's second level or ring, the **mesosystem**, includes the reciprocal interactions and connections that form between various environmental entities in the individual's microsystem (e.g., child and peers, family and church, etc.). The relationship and spill over from one environment to another may be of a positive or negative nature. For example, children are more likely to benefit when their parents and teachers have a positive relationship, communicate effectively, and share common goals. In contrast, children may receive mixed or confusing messages and limited support in meeting learning goals if a poor or unsupportive relationship exists between their parent and teachers.

Bronfenbrenner referred to the next level as the **exosystem**. Here individuals are affected by institutional decisions or events, but they are not directly involved in the decision-making process. These large contextual environments may include, but are not limited to, entities such as parents' workplace, governmental policies, insurance criteria, and school board resolutions. For example, a family's inability to qualify for social service assistance may translate into less food or a lack of consistent medical care for their children. Similarly, a child may have an opportunity to participate in a gifted program because of a local school board's decision to provide additional funding. In each case, the child was not involved in making decisions but was directly affected.

The two outermost rings represent even more distant, but important contexts that influence human development and parenting. The **macrosystem** represents the societal culture and subcultures, including its associated beliefs, values, and customs, that influence (govern) the way in which individuals function and interact with one another. For example, Americans tend to consider education, individuality, hard work, and freedom fundamentally important, whereas effort, harmony, respect, and collaborative relationships are valued in the traditional Japanese culture. It is important for teachers and service providers to understand how the macrosystem shapes the beliefs and behaviors of children and their families, especially given that communities are becoming increasingly diverse. Familiarity with the societal culture in which children and their families live enables teachers to appreciate different perspectives and to provide learning environments that are meaningful and supportive.

Finally, the **chronosystem** focuses on factors of time, including external events (e.g., parent death or divorce, graduation, earthquake, sibling birth) and internal changes (e.g., physiological aging). For example, children growing up in the 1920s experienced a very different world than those growing up today. The chronosystem exerts an effect across all system levels and influences the way an individual experiences and responds to daily events.

Bronfenbrenner later revised his theory to include a greater acknowledgement of biological factors and the role they play in an individual's development. His bioecological theory has had a significant impact on a variety of fields, including education, psychology, health, and human resource management. It challenges professionals to consider individual and environmental factors, both immediate and more distal, that influence development.

microsystem the direct interactions that occur between the individual and immediate environments.

mesosystem the interactions and relationships that occur between the microsystems.

exosystem environments that have an indirect effect on the individual.

macrosystem the culture of society, including its beliefs, values, and customs.

chronosystem factors of time that influence development.

Photo 1-7 Everything children experience influences their development.

homeostasis maintaining equilibrium or balance; remaining the same.

implied rules expectations that guide behavior and are usually learned through a process of repetition and experience.

boundaries limits that are established within families and between the family and others.

1-3b Bowen's Family Systems Theory

Family systems theory was first proposed by M. Bowen, and is based on the work of general systems theory, which emphasizes that events, situations, or people can only be understood within the context of their environment (Bowen, 1976; von Bertalanffy, 1968). Systems theorists often use a cake as a metaphor to describe a family system. Although a cake is made up of individual ingredients, the final product (cake) is greater than each of its independent components. In other words, the whole is more than the sum of its parts. Families are described as complex emotional units in which changes in the relationship or roles of its members influence the functioning of the entire system. From an evolutionary perspective, maintaining a cohesive system was necessary to protect the individual members of a society. Similarly, the primary goal of a family system is to safeguard its members by maintaining the unit's stability or **homeostasis**.

Another way to understand family systems theory is to think about what happens when a person feels cold. Your body does several things: blood vessels contract to keep blood in the core, you shiver to create heat. You may also take several actions (e.g., put on a sweater, turn up the thermostat, drink a hot beverage) in order to feel warm again. A similar thing happens in families when a stressor or change presents itself. The family system must either take action or adapt in order to achieve a new stability or it is likely to experience conflicts. For example, when a new child becomes part of the family, the family members' roles, rules, and routines must be altered in order for the system to remain functional. If the family is unable to adapt or adjust to situations that produce a high stress level, there is an increased probability that it will become dysfunctional. The more **implied rules** and roles and closed outside **boundaries** a family has, the more likely it is to experience significant problems when changes are needed.

Families typically have a combination of explicit and implied rules and roles within their family systems. A parent may, for example, inform children that they are expected to pick up after themselves, complete certain chores on time, and treat each other with respect. They are also likely to have implied rules that gradually shape children's behavior over time, such as not sharing family problems with friends, turning homework in on time, or coming to the dinner table when called. Implied messages are inferred through the repetition of behaviors and experiences that family members encounter, but they are not openly stated. Similarly, family members' roles may be clearly outlined or they may be unspoken. For example, if grandparents move in with their son's family, the roles of all adults may need to be changed and clearly defined (e.g., who is responsible for disciplining the children, who will prepare food, who does the laundry). When both parents in a family work outside of the home, implied changes in the father's role may involve an increased assistance with child-rearing responsibilities.

Within families, boundaries between its members and people outside of the family may be either open or closed. Clear boundaries between subsystems, such as parents and children, are useful because they limit the impact that conflicts can have on other members. For example, parental disagreements about how to handle child misbehavior or financial concerns can be discussed and resolved within the parental subsystem without involving or affecting the relationship with the children. Additionally, the family system as a whole can be either closed or open to people outside of the unit. Closed family systems tend to have rigid rules for their members and input from others is rarely, if ever, accepted. For instance, a teacher may provide feedback that he believes could have a positive effect on the family, but the feedback is rejected because change within the family is not viewed as desirable. In contrast, open family systems are generally receptive to suggestions from others and more likely to use information to make positive changes within the family.

The **differentiation of the self** concept is basic to Bowen's family systems theory (Bowen, 1976). Individuals either become emotionally similar to other family members (fusion) or are able to maintain some degree of emotional separation which may include development of independent thoughts, beliefs, and opinions. In some ways, differentiation of the self is closely related to the idea of open and closed family systems. Although family members influence one another, some individuals have difficulty differentiating themselves from the family system. This is more likely to occur when systems are closed because differentiation is not promoted in order to maintain familial homeostasis. Poor differentiation may produce relational conformity and a desire for acceptance from others, which can lead to chronic anxiety and dysfunctional problems within the family (Kerr, 2000). People who are well-differentiated recognize their dependence on others, but they are able to think and make independent decisions based on information that they gather and assimilate. Kerr (2000) explained that the level of differentiation is influenced by the child's innate ways of responding to caregiver's moods, actions, and how they shape development. Children are likely to develop a level of differentiation that is similar to their parents. However, because there may be small differences in the degree of differentiation among siblings, familial relationships may look very different over the course of several generations.

1-3c Attachment Theory

John Bowlby received training in psychoanalysis, a field that often examines **attachment** retrospectively or in hindsight. For example, if an adult sought therapy for depression, substance abuse, or a troubled relationship, the therapist would examine the level of attachment and similar factors in an attempt to understand the individual's current problems. Bowlby, however, sought to understand attachment as it was happening in order to prevent or remediate mental health problems. He believed that attachment was best understood within a current relationship environment that exists between parents and children. He turned to **ethology** and his own observations of caregiver–child interactions to develop the attachment theory.

Bowlby's work was influenced by Lorenz (1935), as well as Harlow and Zimmermann (1958). Konrad Lorenz developed the concept of imprinting through his work with geese. He noted that geese did not have to be taught to follow their mother closely after hatching. In fact, this following behavior appeared to be innate or pre-programmed in geese; the goslings (baby geese) instinctively knew what they should do. Interestingly, he found that the goslings would follow other people (including him) or objects if they met certain criteria (size, sounds) and were encountered within a specific sensitive period.

Harlow and Zimmermann (1958) and Harlow and Harlow (1965) studied affectional systems in infant rhesus monkeys by observing their interactions with two surrogate monkeys, one made of cloth and the other of wire. They found that the infants spent more time with the cloth surrogate mother and would go to this seemingly more comforting mother when frightened. They hypothesized that the infants perceived the cloth mother to provide a more secure and safe base from which they could explore their environment. The infants also responded more favorably to the cloth mother even when the wire mother was constructed with milk-providing features. Thus, attachment was shown to be dependent upon more than simply satisfying an infant's physiological needs.

Bowlby (1969) concluded that human infants have several instinctual behaviors, including sucking, clinging, crying, smiling, and following, that help them to develop an emotional attachment to their caregivers. He argued that attachment development was

differentiation of the self the degree to which an individual distinguishes him- or herself from, and relies upon, family.

attachment an emotional bond that endures over time.

ethology objective study of animal behavior in the natural environment with a focus on behavior as a result of evolution.

Photo 1-8 Attachment is critical to an infant's development.

related more to the proximity of a responsive attachment figure than simply to one that provided nutrients. Viewed from an evolutionary perspective, keeping close proximity to a primary caregiver affords an infant protection and an improved chance for survival.

Over time, infants focus on, and become, more attached to caregivers who are responsive and provide a reliable secure base for exploration. Attachment quality is influenced by the caregiver's ability to respond sensitively to the child's signals and, conversely, by the child's response to the parents' efforts. Positive attachments emerge when both the caregiver and the infant experience pleasure and affirmation from their interactions. For example, a child cries, the parent picks up the child, the child clings to the parent and smiles, and the parent feels pleased and smiles in return. However, environmental conditions, such as the death of a caregiver, divorce, or mental illness, can influence the strength of the attachment formation and increase or decrease behaviors, such as confidence, stress, and anxiety.

Some caregivers and children do not have these positive interactions or may be separated (emotionally or physically) for a number of reasons. Bowlby wanted to understand the effect that such separations have on children's development. He and his colleague, James Robertson (Bowlby & Robertson, 1952), reviewed observations of children in orphanages and those who were separated from their caregivers for long periods of time (i.e., when hospitalized). They found that children older than 6 months of age responded to separations with protest, despair, and detachment (Bowlby, 1969). They also noted that these same behaviors were exhibited when the child's caregiver was continuously unavailable or when too many different caregivers were present. Bowlby (1951) wrote a report for the World Health Organization in which he articulated his belief that a nurturing and continuous relationship with a caregiver was essential to an individual's mental health. He also recommended practices that could be implemented to improve children's mental health in the event that they had to be separated from their primary caregiver.

Bowlby also proposed the idea of internal working models that children develop through interactions with caregivers. He believed that children, whose parents met their infant's needs for comfort and provided a secure base for exploration, developed a model of themselves as valued and reliable. In contrast, children who experienced rejection or little comfort were more likely to have a working model of themselves as unworthy or incompetent (Bretherton, 1992). Because these working models are developed through continuous interactions, attachment patterns are often transmitted across generations.

Mary Ainsworth (1978) expanded on Bowlby's works, and also made significant contributions to the attachment theory. She conducted naturalistic and more structured studies to observe attachment patterns in infants. She used the "strange" or unfamiliar situation to examine attachment patterns in low stress (with mother) and high stress (with a stranger or alone) situations. The results suggested that if children viewed their parent as available and responsive (i.e., a secure base), they are more likely to explore the environment. Children who had an insecure attachment became anxious or distressed when they were separated from their parent or left with a stranger.

Although attachment is always present, the quality of this relationship varies. In addition, attachment behaviors are heightened in threatening situations. For example, when a stranger enters a room, children may cling to their mothers and, thereby, explore less. Ainsworth, et al. (1978) identified three types of attachment based on their observations:

- Secure: the infant explores the room in her mother's presence, becomes mildly distressed when she leaves, avoids the stranger when left alone but is friendly when mother is present, and appears happy and approaches or acknowledges the mother when she returns.

- Ambivalent or Resistant: the infant is less likely to explore when the mother is present, becomes extremely distressed when she leaves, avoids the stranger, and starts to approach the mother when she returns, but then resists contact and attention from her.

- Avoidant: the infant avoids or ignores the mother and explores little when she is present, shows little emotion when she leaves, continues to play as before when alone with the stranger, shows little interest and emotion when the mother returns. In general, these infants did not seem to care who was in the room.

Main and Solomon (1990) described an additional form of attachment:

- Disorganized: infant shows disorganized or disoriented and unusual behaviors (e.g., freezing or becoming motionless, repetitive behaviors, slowed movements and expressions); they appear apprehensive of the parent.

These types of attachment behaviors may be seen as adaptive in some way. For example, if a parent is not reliable in responding to a child, the child is more likely to show anger and resistance when the parent returns, which may help the child hold the caregiver's attention (Duschinsky, 2015).

Overall, attachment theory proposes that children are pre-programmed to develop an attachment with a primary caregiver. If an attachment is not formed within a sensitive period, then the child is likely to experience problems in the future (e.g., mental health disorders, aggression). The quality of attachment between a child and caregiver also serves as a model for future relationships. In addition, the theory emphasizes how important it is for young children to form a stable and responsive relationship with caregivers.

Photo 1-9 Physical closeness and consistent, nurturing responses promote a strong parent–infant bond.

1-3d Psychosocial Theory

A basic premise of psychosocial theories suggests that conscious (e.g., thoughts) and unconscious processes (e.g., instincts, drives) are the primary motivators of human behavior. Sigmund Freud believed that certain inner thoughts (e.g., impulses, desires, sexual urges) emerge during different developmental stages (e.g., oral, anal, phallic, latency, and genital) which create conflict and anxieties that must be resolved before an individual can advance to the next stage (Freud, 1938). He suggested that individuals often use a series of defense mechanisms (e.g., repression, denial, projection, regression, displacement, sublimation) in an effort to overcome these desires and avoid guilt. Freud proposed his psychoanalytic theory based upon his beliefs that unresolved sexual and erogenous desires were the fundamental cause of adult psychological problems.

Erik Erikson extended the work of Freud in three significant ways: (1) he emphasized psychosocial development (as opposed to psychosexual) by describing the importance of family and society on individuals; (2) acknowledged that psychological development did not end in early adulthood, but continued throughout the lifespan; and (3) focused on the development of psychological health instead of on where problems originated or their remediation (Kivnick & Wells, 2014).

In the book, *Childhood and Society* (1963), Erikson proposed that individuals proceed through a series of eight stages, each of which is characterized by a social-emotional conflict that must be successfully resolved before the individual is able or motivated to move on to the next stage (see Figure 1-3). Each stage corresponds to a point of time in an individual's life that is associated with biological or maturational changes. For example, as children begin attending school, they encounter new learning challenges (e.g., reading, writing, cooperation) and, depending on their experiences, may or may not develop a sense of competence. Development proceeds in a positive manner when an individual's needs and abilities are consistent with environmental or societal expectations and rewards (Marcia, 2014). The resolution or outcome of conflicts helps to shape an individual's development, personality, and self-awareness in relationship to others (i.e., ego identity). The eight stages and corresponding conflicts are also associated with a positive outlook or virtue that fosters psychological health (Kivnick & Wells, 2014; Erikson, 1963).

Figure 1-3 Erikson's Stages of Psychosocial Development

Stage	Conflict	Positive Outlook
Infancy (0–12 months)	Trust vs. Mistrust: Learning to have a sense of trust with caregivers	Hope
Toddlerhood (1–3 years)	Autonomy vs. Shame and Doubt: Developing independence and gaining some control (toileting, self-feeding)	Will
Play Age (3–5 years)	Initiative vs. Guilt: Using social interactions to learn about roles and actively taking control to initiate and see tasks to completion	Purpose
School Age (6–12 years)	Industry vs Inferiority: Learning to work toward personal and social tasks. Developing pride and confidence in skills through successful accomplishments	Competence
Adolescence (13–20 years)	Identity vs. Confusion: Developing a sense of self and commitment to beliefs and a future	Fidelity
Young Adulthood (20–35 years)	Intimacy vs. Isolation: Forming intimate relationships	Love
Middle Adulthood (35–55 years)	Generativity vs. Stagnation or Self-absorption: Focusing on ways to contribute to family, work, and the larger society	Care
Older Adulthood (60s–death)	Integrity vs. Despair: Reflecting and developing a sense of wholeness, meaning, and satisfaction	Wisdom

Three principles underlie the stages of development: dynamic balance of opposites, vital involvement, and life in time (Kivnick & Wells, 2014). Dynamic balance refers to a favorable or appropriate ratio between two tendencies. For example, it is important for children to develop autonomy, but it is also necessary that they recognize when it is unsafe to do so (e.g., talking to a stranger on the street, putting hot food on a plate). This balance between being autonomous and being reliant on a caregiver changes over time to fit the situation. Vital involvement refers to the importance of meaningful involvement in society in relationship to good psychological health. The final principle, life in time, refers to the idea that although there are periods when certain conflicts are more central, people may encounter them at different times in their life and can anticipate conflicts through observation of older individuals, as well as reflect on their experiences when they were younger.

Although Erikson's theory does not specifically explain how a healthy balance can be achieved at each stage, or how the outcome affects later development, he points out important behaviors that can be encouraged through social interactions. In other words, the stages provide a useful framework for identifying, teaching, and reinforcing prosocial skills.

1-3e Learning Theory

Learning theories, behaviorism and social learning theory, represent attempts to explain how people learn from direct experiences with their environment. **Behaviorism** developed through the works of Ivan Pavlov, John B. Watson, and B. F. Skinner. Pavlov (1897) found that pairing a sound with the presentation of food (to a dog), ultimately led the canine to salivate when only the tone, and no food, was presented. He described the tone as a conditioned stimulus that evoked the conditioned response (salivation). This learning process of repeated pairings was later termed **respondent conditioning**. Watson and Rayner (1920) later used the same learning process to create a phobia in a young child. They first noted that a young child would startle and cry when he was frightened by a loud noise (hammering on a steel rod). The loud noise was then paired repeatedly with the sight of a live rat. Soon the child began to exhibit a startle or fear response whenever he was presented with the sight of a rat, even when no loud noise was present. Watson and Rayner concluded that many phobias (e.g., fear of spiders,

behaviorism a philosophy of human behavior based on observable changes that occur in a person's development as the result of environmental experiences.

respondent conditioning learning through repeated pairings of an unconditioned stimulus (e.g., food) and neutral stimulus (e.g., bell) until the neutral stimulus becomes conditioned to evoke the same response (e.g., salivation).

fear of going to school, fear of heights) develop in this manner. Thus to eliminate the fear, the connection between the original stimulus that evoked the reflex response (the loud noise) and the conditioned stimulus (the rat) had to be broken. Watson (1920) emphasized the importance of studying human behavior in objective ways and not by introspection or contemplation which was common at the time.

Skinner (1938) identified another type of learning through his work with animals, which he termed operant conditioning. In **operant conditioning**, learning takes place through contact with consequences (reinforcement and punishment) that follow behavior. For example, when a rat pushed a lever and a food pellet was delivered, the rat was more likely to press the lever again to receive more food (positive reinforcement). Skinner began applying such behavioral principles to human behavior in the 1950s.

Learning is said to occur as part of a three-term contingency that involves an antecedent, a behavior, and a consequence (see Figure 1-4). An antecedent is a stimulus (e.g., item, person, signal, or interaction) that comes before a behavior and, over time, may signal that a specific consequence is available. A behavior refers to what the individual does (e.g., an action, thought, or response). A consequence (reinforcement or punishment) describes what follows a behavior and influences whether or not a behavior will be repeated. Reinforcement increases the likelihood that the behavior will occur again in the future, whereas punishment decreases this probability. Consequences can be further divided into positive (adding something) and negative (taking something away). Note that what is reinforcing and punishing for a particular person will vary, and can only be identified by observing the effect of the consequence on behavior. For example, one child may be more likely to pick up toys (positive reinforcement) when the act is followed by enthusiastic praise from his mother; another child may be less likely to do so because she finds this type of praise overwhelming and, therefore, considers it aversive (positive punishment). Some behaviorists have added a fourth term, **establishing operations**, to describe factors which either increase (motivate) or decrease (abolish or extinguish) the value or effectiveness of a consequence.

For example, a child who is hungry (establishing operation) sees cookies (antecedent) and asks for one (behavior). When he asked his mother, she said "no" and sent him to his room (punishment), but when he asked his grandmother, she said "yes" (reinforcement). In this situation, the child is more likely to ask his grandmother, rather than his mother, for a cookie in the future because she reinforced his asking. In other words, his grandmother's presence gradually comes to signal that he can get a cookie when he asks. Figure 1-5 provides a description of these behavioral concepts in further detail.

Bijou further expanded behaviorism to child development in the 1960s. In his book, *Behavior Analysis of Child Development* (1993), he described how individuals develop through reciprocal interactions with their environment. He noted that children's early responses are largely reflexive and uncoordinated movements. Over time, these movements become more coordinated as they are reinforced through interactions with people, objects, or events. Thus, children continue to learn more complex skills through their repeated experiences in multiple environments.

operant conditioning
learning through consequences that either increase (reinforcement) or decrease (punishment) the likelihood of the behavior being repeated in the future.

establishing operations
distant antecedents that increase or decrease the value of a consequence.

Figure 1-4 Three-Term Contingency

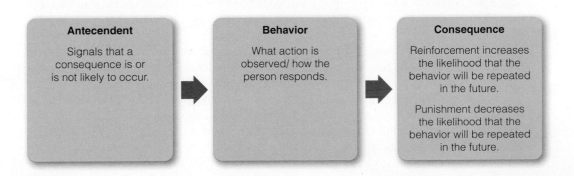

Antecendent	Behavior	Consequence
Signals that a consequence is or is not likely to occur.	What action is observed/ how the person responds.	Reinforcement increases the likelihood that the behavior will be repeated in the future. Punishment decreases the likelihood that the behavior will be repeated in the future.

Figure 1-5 Behavioral Concepts

Behavioral Concept	Effect on Behavior	Example of Behavior
Motivating operation	A state or situation that increases the motivation to engage in a certain behavior; something that increases the value of the consequence.	A child is more likely to eat lunch if he has not had a snack before dinner. He is motivated to eat by hunger.
Abolishing operation	A state or situation that decreases motivation to engage in a certain behavior, or decreases the value of the consequence.	A child is less likely to complete a chore in order to receive an allowance if her parents always purchase whatever she wants. Money is not an effective motivator because the child already receives everything she desires.
Positive reinforcement	An added incentive that increases the likelihood of a behavior occurring again in the future.	A parent acknowledges and gives a child positive attention for picking up his toys. As a result, the child is more likely to repeat this behavior (e.g., picking up toys) at another time because he enjoys his parent's positive attention.
Negative reinforcement	A response or incentive that is aversive, taken away, or terminated to increase the likelihood of a behavior happening again in the future.	A parent stays to soothe a child who cries when taken to school, and the child stops crying. The parent is more likely to soothe the child in the future because the aversive crying stopped when she did so.
Positive punishment	A response that is intended to decrease the likelihood of a behavior happening again in the future.	A child with an aversion to cleaning her room is given an extra cleaning chore to complete for breaking a curfew. She may then be less likely to arrive home late the next time because she does not want extra chores to complete.
Negative punishment	A reward or incentive that is taken away to decrease the likelihood of a behavior happening again in the future.	A child loses a privilege (e.g., watching TV, playing videogames) for hitting his brother. As a result, the child is less likely to repeat the behavior because he does not want to lose privileges again.

social learning theory
theory of learning in which individuals learn through their experiences and cognitive processes; learning through observation and modeling.

Social learning theory was developed through the work of Alfred Bandura and his colleagues. Bandura acknowledged that consequences (reinforcement and punishment) facilitated learning, but believed that other variables also led to learning, specifically, modeling and cognitive processes. Bandura and his colleagues (1961) published a key study that demonstrated how children learn (model) aggressive behaviors from observing other children exhibit such behaviors. In the study, children were assigned to different experimental groups. Some saw a person (male or female), who served as a model, act aggressively toward a blown-up doll ("Bobo," who resembled a clown); others saw no aggression exhibited by the model, and still others were placed in the room without a model. The children who saw an aggressive model were more likely to show similar aggressive behaviors at a later time; children who saw a nonaggressive male model were less likely to show aggression. Bandura and his colleagues concluded that role modeling is an important mechanism in learning behavior.

Additional studies have identified several features that increase the likelihood of learning from a model. The first relates to behaviorism: if a model is rewarded for a behavior, the child is more likely to act in a similar way (Bandura, 1965). In addition, children can learn from models in the media including television, video games, and songs, which has led to controversy about what and how much media children should be allowed to consume if they are to avoid harmful effects. Children also learn best if the model has similar characteristics to the child (e.g., gender, age) and the modeling happens close to the time that the behavior is needed.

Observational study outcomes clearly show that children are keen observers of their environment and are, thus, always learning from what they see. For example, a student quickly learns to raise her hand in the classroom after observing that a peer received the teachers' attention after doing so. A 3-year-old throws a ball at his sister after seeing his favorite television character do the same thing. A toddler hears an adult use an inappropriate word and she starts saying the word repeatedly.

Modeling can also be used in more purposeful interactions to teach new skills. For example, a child who attempts to stack blocks can learn more quickly and efficiently by observing a parent performing the same task. A child learns how to introduce himself to peers by watching video examples of children introducing themselves to others. Parents also learn how to parent from models such as their own parents, friends, family members, and parents depicted in the media.

Photo 1-10 Social learning theory suggests that children model behavior they have observed.

1-3f Cognitive Theory (Piaget)

Jean Piaget, a Swiss biologist, sought to determine how human behaviors evolve over time by studying individuals, especially his own children. He applied a **constructivist** approach to development in which individuals actively interact with the world to construct meaning. This approach shared a focus with behaviorism (learning through interactions with the environment), but differed because it emphasized active cognitive processes. Piaget believed that infants are born with reflexive behaviors that allow them to immediately begin constructing meaning about the world around them. He developed the concept of **schemas** to describe how children store and organize information to make sense of their experiences. The development and refinement of these mental patterns or groupings allow children to gradually develop more complex ways of thinking.

Piaget concluded that schemas are built upon, modified, and made new through the processes of assimilation and accommodation. For example, a child may develop a schema that a pet is something that walks on four legs and barks. Then one day the parent takes the child to a friend's house that has a pet bird. The child takes in this new information and tries to make it fit into her schema of "pet." The process of trying to make the information fit is called **assimilation**. Because a bird does not walk on four legs or bark, the child modifies the pet schema. Modifying or creating a new schema based on information is termed **accommodation**. For example, the child may revise the idea in such a way that a pet becomes an animal that lives with people. Thus, schemas are formed and modified, through assimilation and accommodation, to improve an understanding of the world.

As children develop, they undergo qualitative changes in the way information is interpreted and understood. In turn, they create new ways of thinking that were not possible when they were younger (Carey, 2015). Piaget (1952) described these changes and categorized them into four developmental stages: sensorimotor, preoperational, concrete operational, and formal operational (see Figure 1-6). Children's skills and their ability to understand the environment change with each developmental stage. Skills learned in earlier stages enable children to achieve increasingly complex skills as they continue to mature. Initially, he hypothesized that children learn primarily through their senses and accidental movements, and that thinking at its most advanced level involves the ability to think abstractly.

The progression of skills, as described by Piaget, has received additional support from researchers, although the proposed times when skills are said to develop have been contested. Baillargeon (1987) found that **object permanence** occurs earlier than Piaget suggested. In addition, children's cognitive skills and the mechanisms involved in their development are more complex than outlined in Piaget's stages (Barrouillet,

constructivist theory of development in which individuals actively interact with the world to construct meaning.

schemas mental patterns or categories that are used for organizing and storing information.

assimilation process of trying to make new information or experiences fit into existing schemas.

accommodation process of modifying or creating new schemas based upon additional information.

object permanence Piaget's sensorimotor stage whereby an infant is able to comprehend that an object exists even when out of sight.

Figure 1-6 Piaget's Stages of Cognitive Development

Stage	Age	Characteristics
Sensorimotor	Birth–2 years	Infants' first actions are reflexive (e.g., sucking, breathing). They respond to their environment through reflexes and senses. Children at this stage learn that objects exist even if they cannot be seen (object permanence), thinking becomes more complex by the end of this stage, and children learn that they are able to influence things around them. They begin to act more intentionally. For example, a toddler throws pea after pea from his highchair, releasing them at different points to see where they land.
Preoperational	2–7 years	Children learn to use language and symbols to represent things in their immediate environment. For example, a child may pick up a spatula and pretend it is a guitar. However, their thinking is not logical and they are egocentric, or unable to see things from another person's point of view. Magical thinking is common at this stage; children attempt to self-explain things they don't yet have an ability to understand.
Concrete operational	7–11 years	Children begin to think more logically about their immediate environment, but their thinking continues to be rigid and based on concrete information. They master skills such as classification by relying on several features (e.g., color, shape, size), and begin to understand numbers, mass, and weight conservation. Children are also able to consider other peoples' perspectives and to anticipate outcomes.
Formal operational	11 years and up	Thinking becomes more complex and abstract. Children are able to solve problems through visualization (without needing to see actual objects). They can think hypothetically about situations and solutions due to an ability to recall past events and think about the future. They understand the use of metaphors and analogies, and are able to explore values, beliefs, and philosophies.

zone of proximal development tasks that a child is unable to perform independently, but is able to achieve with guidance and support from a more experienced person.

Photo 1-11 Children learn best when they are personally involved.

2015). Nonetheless, the underlying idea that a child's way of thinking and understanding information changes over time has important implications for parenting and teaching. For example, asking a 3-year-old to consider how his sister feels after he pushed her down, and then asking why he didn't think that it is wrong to hurt another person is likely to have little impact on the boy's behavior. Because a 3-year-old has limited ability to understand and explain his actions, it would be more developmentally appropriate for the parent to respond with an actual consequence.

Similar to Piaget, Lev Vygotsky (1986) believed that children learn through active participation with their environment, and that cognitive development generally takes a particular course. However, he also placed more emphasis on the role of culture and socialization in learning than did Piaget. Vygotsky felt strongly that parents and teachers play an essential role in children's development by initially telling them what to do, how to behave, and providing an appropriate level of support with new tasks. He proposed that children have an actual developmental level (when children are able to do things on their own) and a potential level (when children can achieve a task with guidance from a more experienced person). To help children reach their potential level, children are given tasks within their **zone of proximal development**. For example, a child may not be able to hit a softball on her own, but if her father provides assistance (holding and swinging the bat with the child) she is able to hit the ball. Gradually, the father can decrease his support (hold the bat less tightly, give slightly less guidance to the movement) until the child is able to hit the ball on her own.

Responsive Parenting

Hayden's mother stopped to speak with his teacher one morning shortly after they had arrived at the preschool. She mentioned that Hayden's father had recently been deployed overseas. She also commented that 4-year-old Hayden seemed sad that he has not been able to kick a soccer ball as well as his friends, and that they have been taking the ball away from him. His mother said that she has tried to explain why his father isn't home, and that his friends probably weren't intentionally taking the ball away from him, but that Hayden did not seem to understand. What could you say to help Hayden's mother better understand his behavior based on the attachment, psychosocial and cognitive stages, and learning principles theories? What would you recommend that she talk about with Hayden to help him feel more successful?

Summary

- Families are critical to a society's survival. Their children preserve social and cultural values and traditions by learning and passing them on to future generations.

- Attitudes about children and how they should be treated have changed throughout history. Prior to the 17th century, children were treated as adults and expected to work once they turned seven. European philosophers gradually brought about a more enlightened understanding of children's unique developmental needs and abilities. Children living in America experienced a similar pattern of social views and treatment. Prior to the Civil War, they were raised in highly religious families and taught a trade. Following the war, formal schooling became compulsory, families moved to cities, and parents gained a better understanding of why it was important to nurture and guide children's development.

- Child-rearing philosophies and practices have undergone radical change during the course of American history. Early colonial families considered children evil and in need of firm correction. These ideas were abandoned following the Civil War when parenting began to assume a more nurturing, child-centered approach. This style continues to be followed despite newly-emerging social challenges and changes in family structure and roles.

- Theories that are important for understanding family relationships and parents' influence on children's development include: ecological systems theory, family systems theory, attachment theory, psychosocial theory, and learning theory.

Key Terms

accommodation (p. 21)
assimilation (p. 21)
attachment (p. 15)
behaviorism (p. 18)
boundaries (p. 14)
chronosystem (p. 13)
constructivist (p. 21)
differentiation of the self (p. 15)

establishing operations (p. 19)
ethology (p. 15)
exosystem (p. 13)
homeostasis (p. 14)
homeschool (p. 8)
implied rules (p. 14)
macrosystem (p. 13)
mesosystem (p. 13)

microsystem (p. 13)
nuclear family (p. 3)
object permanence (p. 21)
operant conditioning (p. 19)
respondent conditioning (p. 18)
schemas (p. 21)
social learning theory (p. 20)
zone of proximal development (p. 22)

Questions for Discussion and Self-Reflection

1. In what ways are contemporary families similar to, and different from, the historical concept of a nuclear family?

2. How did parenting roles change as a result of the Civil War?

3. In what ways did the parenting advice offered by J. Watson and Dr. Benjamin Spock differ?

4. How could theories of learning be applied to teaching new skills to children in a classroom?

Field Activities

1. Visit a local art museum (or search online museums, e.g., National Gallery of Art, Smithsonian, Library of Congress). Concentrate on paintings of children that were completed during two different centuries. For each period, write a paragraph describing what you think childhood was like during these periods based upon the paintings you observe.

2. Arrange an interview with two parents to discover how their experiences in raising children may be similar to, and different from, those of their own parents and grandparents. Prepare a written summary of what you learned.

3. Use Bronfenbrenner's ecological model to identify factors (e.g., relationships, groups, organizations) that have influenced your life during the past year.

REFERENCES

Ainsworth, M., Blehar, M., Waters, E., & Wall, S. (1978). *Patterns of attachment: A psychological study of the strange situation*. Hillsdale, NJ: Erlbaum.

Aries, P. (1962). *Centuries of childhood: A social history of family life*. New York: Vintage Books.

Baillargeon, R. (1987). Object permanence in 3 ½ and 4 ½ -month-old infants. *Developmental Psychology, 23*(5), 655–664.

Bairoch, P., & Goertz, G. (1986). Factors of urbanization in the nineteenth century developed countries: A descriptive and econometric analysis. *Urban Studies, 23*, 285–305.

Bandura, A. (1965). Influence of models' reinforcement contingencies on the acquisition of imitative responses. *Journal of Personality and Social Psychology, 1*(6), 589–595.

Bandura, A., Ross, D., & Ross, S. (1961). Transmission of aggression through imitation of aggressive models. *Journal of Abnormal and Social Psychology, 63*, 575–582.

Barglow, P., Vaughn, B., & Molitor, N. (1987). Effects of maternal absence due to employment on the quality of infant-mother attachment in a low risk sample. *Child Development, 58*(4), 945–954.

Barrouillet, P. (2015). Theories of cognitive development: From Piaget to today. *Developmental Review, 38*, 1–12.

Belsky, J., & Rovine, M. (1988). Nonmaternal care in the first year of life and the security of infant-parent attachment. *Child Development, 59*(1), 157–167.

Bijou, S. (1993). *Behavior analysis of child development*. Reno, NV: Context Press.

Bowen, M. (1976). Theory in practice of psychotherapy. In P. J. Guerin. (Ed.). *Family therapy*. New York: Gardner.

Bowlby, J. (1969). *Attachment and loss: Volume 1. Attachment*. New York: Basic Books.

Bowlby, J. (1951). *Maternal care and mental health*. Geneva: World Health Organization.

Bowlby, J., & Robertson, J. (1952). A two-year-old goes to hospital. *Proceedings of the Royal Society of Medicine, 46*, 425–427.

Bretherton, I. (1992). The origins of attachment theory: John Bowlby and Mary Ainsworth. *Developmental Psychology, 28*(5), 759–775.

Bronfenbrenner, U. (1979). *The ecology of human development: Experiments by nature and design*. Cambridge, MA: Harvard University Press.

Bronfenbrenner, U., & Ceci, S. (1993). Heredity, environment, and the question "how?": A new theoretical perspective for the 1990s. In R. Plomin and McClearn, G. (1993). *Nature, Nurture, & Psychology*. Washington, DC: APA Books.

Bronfenbrenner, U. (1994). Ecological models of human development. In, *International Encyclopedia of Education*, Vol. 3 (2nd Ed.). Oxford: Elsevier.

Brown, S., Manning, W., & Stykes, J. (2015). Family structure and child well-being: Integrating family complexity. *Journal of Marriage and Family, 77*(1), 177–190.

Carey, S., Zaitchik, D., Bascandziev, I. (2015). Theories of development: In dialog with Jean Piaget. *Developmental Review, 38*, 36–54.

Chudacoff, H. (2007). *Children at play*. New York: New York University Press.

Duschinsky, R. (2015). The emergence of the disorganized/disoriented (D) attachment classification 1979-1982. *History of Psychology, 18*(1), 32–46.

Elliott, J., & Ionescu, M. (2003). Postwar immigration to the deep South triad: What can a peripheral region tell us about immigrant settlement and employment? *Sociological Spectrum: Mid-South Sociological Association, 23*(2), 159–180.

Erikson, E. (1963). *Childhood and society* (2nd Ed.). New York: W. W. Norton.

Fitzgerald, R. (2000). The social impact of the industrial revolution. *Science and Its Times: Understanding the Social Significance of Scientific Discovery,* (4), 376–381. Ed. J. Lauer and N. Schlager. Detroit, MI: Gale. Retrieved on September 4, 2015 from http://find.galegroup .com/gic/infomark.do?&idigest=fb720fd31d9036c1ed2d1f3a0500fcc2&type=retrieve &tabID=T001&prodId=GIC&docId=CX3408502115&source=gale&userGroupName =itsbtrial&version=1.0.

Freud, S. (1938). In, *An outline of psycho-analysis*. James Strachey (translator). New York: W. W. Norton & Company.

Gazeley, I. (2003). *Poverty in Britain 1900-1965*. New York: Palgrave Macmillan.

Gershuny, J., & Robinson, J. (1988). Historical changes in the household division of labor. *Demography 25*(4), 537–552.

Goldin, C. (1991). The role of World War II in the rise of women's employment. *The American Economic Review, 81*(4), 741–756.

Graham, J. (2000). *Puritan family life: The diary of Samuel Seawall*. Boston, MA: Northeastern University Press.

Grant, J. (2004). A "real boy" and not a sissy: Gender, childhood, and masculinity, 1890-1940. *Journal of Social History, 37*(4), 829–851.

Green-Hennessy, S. (2014). Homeschooled adolescents in the United States: Developmental outcomes. *Journal of Adolescence, 37*(4), 441–449.

Hacker, J., Hilde, L., & Jones, J. (2010). The effect of the Civil War on southern marriage patterns. *Journal of Southern History, 76*(1), 39–70.

Harcourt, K., & Adler-Baeder, F. (2015). Family mapping: A cumulative measure of family structure and instability. *Journal of Divorce & Remarriage, 56*(3), 199–219.

Harlow, H., & Zimmermann, R. (1958). The development of affective responsiveness in infant monkeys. *Proceedings of the American Philosophical Society, 102*, 501–509.

Harlow, H., & Harlow, M. (1965). The affectional systems. In A. Schrier, H. Harlow, & F. Stollnitz (Eds.), *Behavior of Nonhuman Primates: Modern Research Trends*. New York: Academics Press.

Hanawalt, B. (1993). *Growing up in medieval London*. Oxford, UK: Oxford University Press.

Henry, C., Morris, A., & Harrist, A. (2015). Family resilience: Moving into the third wave. *Family Relations, 64*(1), 22–43.

Hill, K. (1990). The decline of childhood mortality. Johns Hopkins University, School of Hygiene and Public Health, Population Center. Retrieved on September 3, 2015 from https:// jscholarship.library.jhu.edu/bitstream/handle/1774.2/936/WP90-07_Childhood_Mortality .pdf?sequence=1.

Humphries, J. (2013). Childhood and child labour in the British industrial revolution. *The Economic History Review, 66*(2), 395–418.

Independence Hall Association. (2014). Slave life and slave codes. Retrieved March 30, 2016 from http://www.ushistory.org/us/27b.asp.

Jensen, J. (1984). Not only ours but others: The Quaker teaching daughters of the Mid-Atlantic, 1790-1850. *History of Education Quarterly, 24*(1), 3–19.

Kagan, J. (1978). The parental love trap. *Psychology Today, 12*(3), 54–61.

Kerr, M. (2000). One Family's Story: A Primer on Bowen Theory. The Bowen Center for the Study of the Family. Retrieved October 7, 2015 from http://www.thebowencenter.org.

Kivnick, H., & Wells, C. (2014). Untapped richness in Erik H. Erikson's rootstock. *The Gerontologist, 54*(1), 40–50.

Leibowitz, A., & Klerman, J. (1995). Explaining changes in married mothers' employment over time. *Demography, 32*(3), 365–378.

Lorenz, K. (1935). Der Kumpan in der Umwelt des Vogels. Der Artgenosse als auslösendes Moment sozialer Verhaltensweisen. *Journal für Ornithologie, 83*, 137–215, 289–413.

Lubienski, C., Puckett, T., & Brewer, T. (2013). Does homeschooling "work"? A critique of empirical claims and agenda of advocacy organizations. *Peabody Journal of Education, 88*(3), 378–392.

Main, M., & Solomon, J. (1990). Procedures for identifying infants as disorganised/disoriented during the Ainsworth Strange Situation. In M. Greenberg, D. Cicchetti, & E. Cummings (Eds.), *Attachment in the preschool years* (pp.121–160). Chicago, IL: University of Chicago Press.

Marcia, J. (2014). From industry to inferiority. *Identity: An International Journal of Theory and Research, 14*, 165–176.

Mason, M. (1994). Masters and servants: The American colonial model of child custody and control. *The International Journal of Children's Rights, 2*, 317–332.

Mays, S., & Eyers, J. (2011). Perinatal infant death at the Roman villa site at Hambleden, Buckinghamshire, England. *Journal of Archaeological Science, 38*(8), 1931–1938.

Mazamal, A., & Lundy, G. (2015). African American homeschooling and the quest for a quality education. *Education and Urban Society, 47*(2), 160–181.

Michel, S. (2011). The history of child care in the U.S. Retrieved March 23, 2016 from http://www.socialwelfarehistory.com/programs/child-care-the-american-history/.

Mintz, S., & Kellogg, S. (1988). *Domestic revolutions: A social history of American family life.* New York: Free Press.

Monaghan, E. J. (1988). Literacy instruction and gender in Colonial New England. *American Quarterly, 40*(1), 18–41.

Pavlov, I. P. (1897). *The work of the digestive glands.* London: Griffin.

Piaget, J. (1952). *The origins of intelligence in children.* New York: International University Press.

Popenoe, D. (1993). American family decline, 1960-1990: A review and appraisal. *Journal of Marriage and Family, 55*(3), 527–542.

Public Broadcasting Service (PBS). (2006). The Roman Empire in the first century. Retrieved on August 31, 2015 from http://www.pbs.org/empires/romans/empire/family.html.

Rainer, J., Mesnikoff, A., Kolb, L., & Carr, A. (1960). Homosexuality and heterosexuality in identical twins. *Psychosomatic Medicine, 22*(4), 251–258.

Ramirez, F., & Boli, J. (1987). The political construction of mass schooling: European origins and worldwide institutionalization. *Sociology of Education, 60*(1), 2–17.

Ray, B. (2015). African American homeschool parents' motivations for homeschooling and their Black children's academic achievement. *Journal of School Choice: International Research and Reform, 9*(1), 71–96.

Sayer, L., Bianchi, S., & Robinson, J. (2004). Are parents investing less in children? Trends in mothers' and fathers' time with children. *American Journal of Sociology, 110*(1), 1–43.

Singman, J. (1999). *Daily life in Medieval Europe.* Westport, CT: Greenwood Press.

Skinner, B. (1938). *The behavior of organisms: An experimental analysis.* New York: Appleton-Century.

Thomas, T. (1995). Acculturative stress in the adjustment of immigrant families. *Journal of Social Distress and the Homeless, 4*(2), 131–142.

U.S. Census Bureau. (2014). Poverty: 2014 highlights. Retrieved on September 22, 2015 from https://www.census.gov/hhes/www/poverty/about/overview.

U.S. Department of Education (2015). National Center for Education Statistics: Homeschooling. Retrieved October 10, 2015 from http://nces.ed.gov/fastfacts/display.asp?id=91.

Vaughn, M., Salas-Wright, C., Kremer, K., & Maynard, B. (2015). Are homeschooled adolescents less likely to use alcohol, tobacco, and other drugs? *Drug and Alcohol Dependence, 155*(1), 97–104.

von Bertalanffy, L. (1968). *General system theory: Essays on its foundation and development,* (Rev. Ed). New York: George Braziller.

Vygotsky, L. (1986). *Thought and language.* (2nd Ed.) Cambridge, MA: MIT Press.

Wall, K., & Gouveia, R. (2014). Changing meanings of family in personal relationships. *Current Sociology, 62*(3), 352–373.

Watson, J. (1928). *Psychological care of infant and child.* New York: Norton.

Watson, J., & Rayner, R. (1920). Conditioned emotional reactions. *Journal of Experimental Psychology, 3*, 1–14.

Wilkens, C., Wade, C., Sonnert, G., & Sadler, P. (2015). Are homeschoolers prepared for college calculus? *Journal of School Choice: International Research and Reform, 9*(1), 30–48.

Williamson, L., & Lawson, K. (2015). Young women's intentions to delay childbearing: A test of the theory of planned behavior. *Journal of Reproductive and Infant Psychology, 33*(2), 205–213.

Yildirim, E., & Roopnarine, J. (2015). The mediating role of maternal warmth in the associations between harsh parental practices and externalizing and internalizing behaviors in Hispanic American, African American, and European American families. *Cultural Diversity and Ethnic Minority Psychology, 21*(3), 430–439.

Contemporary Families

LEARNING OBJECTIVES

After reading the chapter, you will be able to:

2-1 Explain why families are important to a society.

2-2 Compare and contrast functional and dysfunctional families.

2-3 Discuss how children's development is influenced differently when they grow up in various family structural configurations: two-parent heterosexual; single-parent; stepparent; extended; adoptive; foster; or same-sex parent.

2-4 Describe children's role in two different cultural groups.

2-5 Discuss the positive and negative effects that are often associated with growing up in different family contexts: adolescent parent; grandparent; parent with a disability; military parent; and incarcerated parent.

2-6 Identify several ways that socioeconomic and religious diversity influence children's educational outcomes.

naeyc Standards Linked to Chapter Content

1b: Promoting child development and learning

2a: Building family and community relationships

Ask five of your best friends to define the term family and it is likely that you will end up with five different descriptions. Although most of us live in a family and know many others, our individual concept of what constitutes a family is often quite different and may not translate into

continued on following page

a common or shared understanding. A classic dictionary definition typically refers to family as a group of people who are related to one another. However, even officially-recognized entities differ in their efforts to establish a precise definition. For example, the U.S. Census Bureau (2015b) defines family as "a group of two people or more (one of whom is the householder) related by birth, marriage, or adoption and residing together; all such people (including related subfamily members) are considered as members of one family." According to the Canadian government, family refers to "a married couple (with or without children), a common-law couple (with or without children) or a lone parent of any marital status with at least one child" (Statistics Canada, 2011).

Families in the United States and many Western countries today reflect a wealth of diverse cultural, socioeconomic, ethnic, language, and religious differences. They also represent individuals who are facing unique challenges that require exceptions and adaptations to traditional notions about family. Furthermore, mass media, the Internet, and global travel have increased our exposure to families that have different ideas and customs, structural arrangements, and childrearing practices. For these reasons and more, it is important that teachers and other professionals gain an understanding of families that may be different from the stereotypical norm with which they are most familiar. To do so enables individuals (each one of us) to move outside of our comfort zone and to better relate, support, and appreciate what families are trying to achieve. ∎

2-1 What is a Family?

What makes the concept of family so perplexing to define? The difficulty may stem, in part, from the fact that family is a fluid social construct that can be described from multiple perspectives. For example, the term family may elicit romantic or idealistic notions (e.g., a mother, father, and their two children). It may also be defined in terms of structure (e.g., two-parent, single parent, adoptive parent), kinship (e.g., father/mother, grandparents, aunts/uncles, cousins), or individuals (e.g., guardians) who possess the legal authority to make certain decisions for children. Alternatively, the term family is sometimes used to describe members of a particular group who share a common characteristic (e.g., church congregation, ethnicity, "lefty's") or form a common bond (e.g., teammates, alumni, professionals, neighbors).

Social, political, and economic factors have historically exerted a strong influence on the concept of family, including the roles and responsibilities that it was expected to fulfill. For example, colonist families who settled in North America consisted of a husband and wife who were expected to have children and raise them to serve as laborers on their farms (Mintz & Kellogg, 1988). Such a family is in sharp contrast to present day notions about how contemporary families are structured and function. For example, the generation of "baby boomer" parents (born between 1946 and 1964) represents approximately 80 million adults who grew up after World War II. Although they were likely to have only a high school education, they had a strong work ethic and a desire to marry and raise children who would have more economic and educational opportunities than their parents. Mothers typically stayed home with children, who enjoyed considerable freedom, while fathers were employed in a full-time job (Plant, 2010).

Social and economic factors also played instrumental roles in shaping the next generation of approximately 51 million parents, commonly referred to as Generation X or GenX (born 1965–1977). This was the first and largest group of children to experience a dual-career family and out-of-home child care. Many also grew up in single-parent households as a result of the highest divorce rate in U.S. history. Gen X children, often referred to as "latchkey kids," were expected to care for themselves after school until their parent(s) returned home from work. Sixty-three percent of GenX'ers chose not to marry (Pew Research Center, 2014). Those who did focused on career-building and postponed childbearing until their mid-thirties. They tended to be less demanding of their children and often involved them in family-related decisions.

Millennial parents (born 1977–2005) are one of the most educated and ethnically-diverse generations (Yazykova & McLeigh, 2015; Downing, 2006). Many are immigrants or children of immigrants, with a reputation for tolerating diversity and engaging in civic responsibility. They have grown up in an era dominated by technology and social communication, but are even less likely to marry than Gen X adults. Pew Center researchers (2014) reported that only 23 percent of eligible adults between the ages of 18 and 30 were married. This trend has been attributed to an increased rate of **cohabitation** among this age group instead of marriage. Millennials who do marry are interested in having children and providing enriching opportunities that will improve their likelihood of economic and social success.

> **cohabitation** living together without legal or religious sanction (e.g., an unmarried couple).

2-2 Family: Roles, Responsibilities, and Functionality

Societies have historically relied on families to fulfill certain perceived roles and responsibilities, which may provide an alternative framework for defining family. Traditionally, families have been expected to:

- produce children—maintain or expand a society's population.
- socialize and educate children—ensure the survival of cultural values, beliefs, traditions, and social roles by transmitting them to children.
- provide resources and economic security—ensure that adequate housing, food, clothing, and medical care are available for all family members.
- provide companionship, affection, and emotional support—show love and respect for one another; have fun together and enjoy each other's company.
- maintain and preserve the family unit—practice effective leadership and decision-making skills, and establish rules for acceptable behavior that are beneficial for all family members.

In many respects, societies' ideas about family formation and the roles and responsibilities they are expected to fulfill parallel the ideas that Erik Erikson (1959) proposed in his psychosocial theory of human development. Erikson believed that self-assured young adults begin searching for a partner with whom they can form a long-term intimate relationship (stage 6, intimacy vs. isolation). If they are successful in achieving this goal, they will likely move on to the next stage, which centers on raising a family and developing a career (stage 7, generativity vs. stagnation).

Erikson's ideas, as well as those of many other developmental theorists, are based on biological changes (e.g., growth, hormonal fluctuations) that occur throughout an individual's lifetime. What these theories do not take into account

Photo 2-1 Members of functional families enjoy spending time together.
RonTech3000/Shutterstock.com

are environmental factors that may alter the expression of human development. For example, social and economic developments that began to occur during the late 1950s gradually eroded the traditional concept of family (e.g., wife, husband, and their children) and allowed individuals to consider alternative arrangements, including single parent households, cohabitation, and grandparents assuming parental responsibility for their grandchildren. In turn, these developments have altered the perceived roles and responsibilities that have long been attributed to families, including their efforts to socialize children. As a result, attempts to define family in terms of their traditional roles and responsibilities may no longer prove possible.

2-2a Attributes of Functional and Dysfunctional Families

Although contemporary families are diverse in terms of their composition, geographical location, ethnicity, goals, and values, they share certain qualities in common that cause them to be either successful or dysfunctional as a unit (see Figure 2–1). Researchers

---

Figure 2–1 Functional and Dysfunctional Family Characteristics

Characteristics of functional families:

- communication—listen respectfully to one another; share thoughts and opinions often and in an honest manner; remain receptive and open to alternative ideas
- flexibility—compromise and accept alternative views; adapt to change in rules, roles, and responsibilities (e.g., father may assume cooking and laundry tasks because mother works late); ability to cope with stress
- resilience—are able to cope with, and overcome, adversity
- commitment—form an emotional connection with one another; family members trust, cooperate, support, and take pride in each other's accomplishments while retaining their individuality
- defined roles—have parents who are in charge and make decisions in the family's best interest, but are also open to children's input
- standards (principles)—model behavior and establish rules consistent with family values
- social support—volunteer and participate in community activities and civil affairs; have friends and social resources to rely on in difficult times
- enjoyment—value and make time to have fun together as a family

Characteristics of dysfunctional families:

- distrustful—lack empathy and sensitivity; skeptical of other members' intentions
- poor communication—fail to listen; tell others what to do and discourage individuals from having any input; critical of others
- inconsistent—establish few boundaries; individuals act independently; minimal control exercised over children's behavior; family lacks cohesiveness
- unrealistic expectations—lack knowledge of children's development and appropriate behavioral guidance; role reversal
- low self-esteem—are negative and self-critical; feel shame or guilt; constantly seeking approval from others; apathetic; substance dependency
- lack of enjoyment—fail to experience fun together as a family; pessimistic; critical of one another

---

have studied family dynamics for decades in an effort to identify characteristics that enable family members to work effectively together, overcome adversity, and meet the needs of each individual. Families cannot be expected to function without stress all of the time. However, some families lack the ability to communicate, collaborate, and resolve conflicts in a healthy and positive manner.

Children who grow up in responsive families, within which they feel safe, secure, valued, and loved, are more likely to also have a positive relationship with their parents. When their families practice open communication, peaceful conflict resolution, flexible parenting expectations and guidance, and spend time together, children learn important social-emotional skills and develop positive self-esteem (Masten & Monn, 2015). Researchers have observed that children who enjoy warm, nurturing parent-child relationships are more resilient to negative experiences, such as bullying, chronic stress, and substance abuse (Kshipra, 2015; MacPhee, Lunkenheimer, & Riggs, 2015; Smokowski et al., 2015). These findings have important long-term implications for children's social-emotional well-being and ability to become productive adults.

Living in a dysfunctional family places children at increased risk for suffering adverse physical and behavioral consequences. Exposure to overly-controlling or lax parenting can lead to poor social-emotional skill development and contribute to low self-esteem, difficulty establishing and maintaining peer relationships, and peer victimization (Brock & Kochanska, 2015; Healy, Sanders, & Iyer, 2015). As a result, children are more likely to succumb to peer pressure and to engage in deviant behaviors (e.g., substance abuse, promiscuous sexual activity, violence, and crime). Researchers have also noted that children who live in chaotic and unpredictable home environments experience increased rates of acute and chronic illness, eating disorders, self-injurious behaviors, and maltreatment (Kerker et al., 2015; Tschan, Schmid, & In-Albon, 2015).

2-3 Family: Structural Characteristics

An alternative way to define family is in terms of its configuration or structure. For example, how many adults are in the family (e.g., two-parent, single-parent, several generations) and what is their relationship to one another (e.g., married, cohabitating, divorced with joint custody, relatives)? Is the family household comprised of teen parents, or grandparents who have assumed custodial responsibility for rearing their grandchildren? Does the family include children who are adopted, in foster care, or living in a same-sex family? Because families come in many shapes and sizes, it is important that teachers and service providers understand whom a child considers to be part of his or her family so they can work together more effectively.

2-3a Nuclear Families

For decades, the **nuclear family** remained the predominant family unit type in North America. A woman and man formed a lifelong **monogamous** union based upon self-selection, mutual love, common interests, and a desire for companionship. The nuclear family provided structure, stability, and enabled societies to advance socially, economically, and politically. Strict moral, cultural, and religious standards helped to maintain the sanctity of marriage and an intact family.

Until 1970, 85 percent of U.S. children under the age of 18 years lived in two-parent households. However, these numbers declined significantly as divorce rates escalated and more young adults decided to delay marriage or remain single. A study released by the Pew Research Center (2014) reported that the number of married households decreased from approximately 72 percent in 1960 to 50.5 percent in 2012, according to U.S. Census data. They also noted that marriage rates were highest among college graduates, and that young adults worldwide appeared to be waiting longer before entering into marriage. The average age of first marriages in the United States is 27 for women and 29 for men (U.S. Census Bureau, 2015a).

nuclear family a family consisting of a mother, a father, and their biological children.

monogamous being married to, or having a sexual relationship with, one partner at a time.

Although the number of nuclear families has been decreasing, it remains the preferred structural configuration in many societies. Researchers have noted that intact families, especially those that include children, experience a better quality of life in terms of economic benefits, safety, and secure feelings (Manning, Brown, & Stykes, 2015). Parents in nuclear families are more likely to provide a stable home, follow a consistent approach to children's socialization and behavior guidance, and be involved in children's educational activities. As a result, children raised in nuclear families tend to achieve higher academic outcomes and experience fewer behavior problems (Goldberg & Carlson, 2014; Myers & Myers, 2014).

Despite the benefits attributed to the nuclear family structure, scientists and scholars have also pointed out several disadvantages. For example, such families may have limited access to resources in time of need (e.g., financial, emotional support, child care, temporary housing) that might otherwise be available in an extended family arrangement. The nuclear family has also been cited for potentially creating isolation from extended family members. However, Mennen (1988) found that geographical distance, not family structure, was responsible for limiting interaction among nuclear families and relatives. Concerns have also been expressed about the homogeneous thinking and problem solving that may develop when family members function in a relatively closed unit. However, these challenges are not considered valid deterrents to the formation of nuclear families in light of the advantages it affords to parents and their children.

Cohabitation. Two adults, most commonly a female and her male partner, who choose to live together but not enter into a legal marriage, form a structural family unit that has become more popular, but is still considered unconventional in many societies. In the United States, for example, the number of cohabiting couples, including those who have a child, has increased by 40 percent in the last 10 years (see Figure 2–2). Premarital cohabitation among **heterosexual** couples is seen as a way to test compatibility and, thus, decrease the risk of a relationship ending in divorce. Others choose to cohabitate for reasons of convenience (e.g., saving on rent, companionship), shared political views, or lack of incentives for marrying. Although Americans view marriage as important, Europeans do not perceive the same level of significance and are more accepting of cohabitating relationships (Cherlin, 2014). For same-sex couples, cohabitation has long been the only option available to them in countries where marriage laws did not permit such unions.

> **heterosexual** romantic attraction to a person of the opposite sex.

Figure 2-2 Type of First Unions Among Women Aged 15–44: United States, 1995, 2002, and 2006–2010

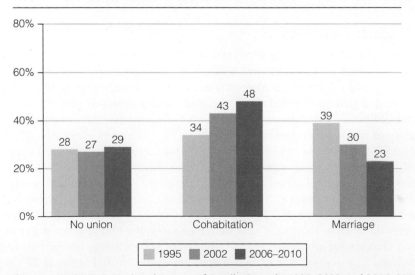

Source: CDC/NCHS, National Survey of Family Growth, 1995, 2002 and 2006–2010.

Socio-demographic data obtained from the 2014 American Community Survey revealed characteristic differences among heterosexual couples who marry and individuals in same-sex and heterosexual relationships who cohabitate (U.S. Census Bureau, 2014b). First-time married couples (opposite gender) who tend to delay matrimony until their late twenties and early thirties, are Caucasian, have a college education, employed, and maintain a stable and supportive relationship with their partner. In contrast, researchers have noted that cohabiting same-sex couples typically enter into this arrangement at an earlier age (early twenties), have less education and poorer employment status, and are unlikely to remain together longer than two or three years, especially if they have a child (Musick & Michelmore, 2015). According to data from the National Survey of Family Growth, 70 percent of women who cohabitated had less than a high school diploma (Copen, Daniels, & Mosher, 2013). Cohabitation in same-sex families is typically less stable and shorter-lived than in other family structures; male cohabiting couples experience the highest rate of relationship dissolution.

Because increasing numbers of children are living in cohabiting families, researchers are interested in learning how this structural arrangement may potentially affect children's development and well-being. Manning (2015) noted that cohabiting families typically have fewer economic and social resources available to them, which can result in poorer outcomes for children, especially when they are young. Krueger et al. (2015) also found that children living with cohabitating parents were at greater risk for adverse health and developmental outcomes. Researchers have observed that non-biological fathers in cohabiting relationships tend to spend less time with children than do biological fathers in two-parent families. These findings could help to explain why children in married, two-biological parent families tend to experience more favorable developmental outcomes compared to children living with cohabiting parents or married or cohabitating stepparents (Berger & McLanahan, 2015). However, other researchers have found no differences in children's health, cognitive development, or behavioral outcomes when cohabiting couples had a strong, stable relationship (Manning, 2015; Goldberg & Carlson, 2014).

2-3b Extended or Multigenerational Families

By definition, an extended or multigenerational family consists of at least three kinship generations, including parents, their children, and relatives (e.g., grandparents, aunts, uncles, cousins, nieces/nephews) who may live in close proximity or together in the same household. This configuration is particularly customary among families in the Middle East, Asia, South America, Eastern Europe, Pacific Islands, and parts of Africa (Mazzucato et al., 2015). According to a report prepared by the Child Trends and Social Trends Institute (2015), approximately 40 percent of children in these countries live in extended family households.

Extended family arrangements were fairly common in the United States during the 20th century. Although they are much less typical today, they are increasing in numbers. Many immigrant and first-generation families continue to maintain their multigenerational household customs. High unemployment and rising housing prices have forced many young adult children, as both single and married couples, to live with their parents until they are able to achieve financial independence (see Figure 2–3). In addition, the number of parents who are raising their own children in addition to grandchildren, or moving an aging parent into their home, represent another increasingly common trend in extended family formation.

In some cultures (e.g. Hopi Indians, Australian aborigines, Juchitecs in Mexico, and various African societies), the organization of extended family units is **matriarchal**. Women in these families are recognized as the head of household and they have legal authority to make all major decisions, including financial, that affect family members. In addition, they typically own the family's property, which is passed down to heirs on the mother's side of the family. The **patriarchal** model is common in many other cultures, especially industrialized societies, and follows a similar pattern with regard to legal and financial authority and property ownership.

matriarchal family unit in which authority and resources are controlled by the wife.

patriarchal family unit in which authority and resources are controlled by the husband.

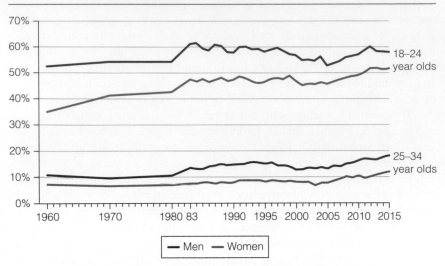

Figure 2-3 Adult Children Living in Their Parental Home: 1960 to Present

Source: U.S. Census Bureau, Decennial censuses, 1960 to 1980, and Current population survey, annual social and economics supplements, 1983 to 2015.

polygamy the practice of being married to more than one spouse simultaneously.

polygyny the practice of having more than one female spouse at the same time.

polyandry the practice of having more than one male spouse at the same time.

The practice of **polygamy** creates a variation of the extended family structure that persists in some cultures around the world. Polygamous families can take the form of either **polygyny** or the less common practice of **polyandry** (Ickowitz & Mohanty, 2015; Mkhize, & Nompumelelo, 2015). Although polygamy has been declared illegal in many countries, it continues to be practiced in some Middle Eastern and African nations. Smaller enclaves also exist in the United States, Canada, and Europe (Ault & Gilder, 2015). Governments in countries that have laws prohibiting polygamy face unique challenges when immigrants arrive from countries where the practice is permitted.

The extended family structure offers several advantages and limitations. In some instances, families pool their financial resources, assist with child-rearing, and share household responsibilities. Family members are also able to provide social and emotional support for one another, especially during times of stress or crisis, and preserve cultural values and customs by teaching them to younger generations. Children reared in extended families also have an opportunity to form a close day-to-day relationship with their relatives, an experience that eludes many of today's children because families are separated by considerable geographical distances. However, members of an extended family unit may not always interact harmoniously with one another.

2-3c Single-Parent Families

The number of single-parent households in the United States and many Western countries has increased dramatically in recent years. Currently, single-parent families account for more than half of all household units in the United States. They are formed for a variety of reasons including divorce, separation, personal preference, death, and abandonment. Single-parent families may also be created temporarily by military deployment or incarceration. Although mothers head the majority of single-parent households, an increasing number of fathers and grandparents are assuming this role. Approximately 35 percent of U.S. children younger than 18 years (or 24,689,000 children) are currently growing up in single-parent households—a number that has tripled since 1960 (Kids Count Data Center, 2015) (see Figure 2–4). African American and Hispanic or Latino children are at the highest probability of living in a single-parent family arrangement.

Figure 2-4 Living Arrangements of Children: 1960 to Present

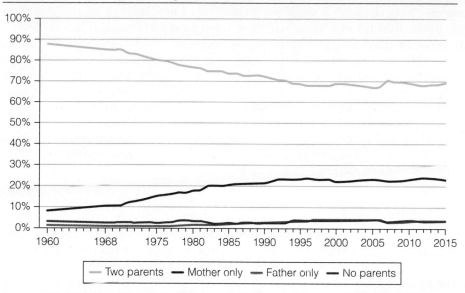

Source: U.S. Census Bureau, Decennial census, 1960, and Current population survey, annual social and economics supplements, 1968 to 2015.

Parenting is unquestionably one of the most challenging and difficult roles that adults assume. However, it can become even more intense when one person has to assume sole responsibility for performing all household and childrearing tasks. Poverty is also a significant concern for many single-parent families, especially among those headed by a mother. Approximately 83 percent of the 12 million single-parent families in the United States are headed by single mothers (U.S. Census Bureau, 2014b). More than half of all children who experience poverty live in single-mother households in contrast to only 21 percent who reside in a single-father household. Poverty among single-mother households is also common throughout the world (Colton, Janzen, & Laverty, 2015; Schmeer et al., 2015).

Single parents often deal with a range of personal emotional feelings (e.g., loss of a partner, social stigma, loss of self-esteem, depression) when they try to help children cope and adjust to change (Colton, Janzen, & Laverty, 2015). The combination of intense parenting pressures, inadequate resources, and limited parenting skills are known to increase the risk of child maltreatment and substance abuse in some single-parent families (Afifi et al., 2015). Stavrova and Fetchenhauer (2015) noted, however, that single parents were less likely to experience negative feelings and pressures in cultures where one-parent families are the norm.

Because a majority of children in the United States today will spend at least a portion of their time living in a single-parent family, social scientists have focused attention on how these changes may affect children's development. Ryan, Claessens, and Markowitz (2015) examined data from 3936 families who participated in the National Longitudinal Survey of Youth study and noted that change in family structure (from a two- to one-parent family) had a negative impact on children's development, particularly when children were younger than age 5. The most detrimental effects occurred in families with high to moderate incomes. Researchers concluded that reduced income created a greater financial strain and adjustment situations for these families than for low-income families who were already accustomed to limited economic resources. Colter et al. (2015) observed an increase in antisocial behavior among children of all ages after their fathers left the family unit. Food insecurity, poor mental and physical health, and high school dropout rates have also been closely linked to poverty in single-parent families (Slopen et al., 2016).

It is important, however, to understand that not all single-parent families are disadvantaged or dysfunctional. Divorce, for example, may eliminate a history of conflict, negative family interactions, and uncertainty. Many single parents are resilient and able to use their strengths to create a positive family experience even though their standard of living may have changed. A single parent may gain a new sense of control and they may begin to make decisions without worrying about joint agreement on family needs. They may make an effort to spend more quality time with children in order to compensate for the other parent's absence. Single parents may also increase children's involvement in household affairs so that a family has more time available to spend having fun together. However, even the most well-adjusted single parent is likely to encounter situations and days that are especially challenging. Single parents who reach out to friends and extended family members for support, participate in community activities and resource groups, and take advantage of job training opportunities are often able to increase their resilience to overcome seemingly insurmountable odds (Pollock, Kazman, & Deuster, 2015).

2-3d Stepfamilies

A stepfamily is a blended structural unit that is formed when a parent with children from a previous relationship marries a new same- or opposite-sex partner. One or both adults may have been divorced, widowed, single parents, or cohabiting partners who choose to marry. Men are three times more likely than women to remarry within 5–10 years following divorce or the death of a spouse (Poortman & Hewitt, 2015; Wu, Schimmele, & Ouellet, 2015). Current estimates suggest that approximately 40 percent of U.S. married couples with children from a previous relationship live in stepfamilies (U.S. Census Bureau, 2014b). Approximately 76 percent of children—especially older children—in stepfamilies live with their biological mother and a stepfather.

Stepfamilies are unique in that they form an instant family unit. As a result, parents face immediate challenges, which are unlike those experienced by intact families that gradually add children to their relationship. Newly married couples have many household responsibilities to work out, in addition to adjusting their parenting roles, helping children to cope with a different family arrangement, and strengthening their own relationship. These transitions can involve considerable conflict and stress which, in turn, contribute to high marriage failure rates and divorce among remarried couples (Manning, 2015b; Pace et al., 2015). Sears et al. (2016) observed that marital friction and negative parent-child interactions have a bidirectional effect on parental mood which may then exacerbate children's undesirable behavior and family turmoil. Experts caution stepfamilies that they can expect to encounter difficult periods during the assimilation phase, and that the process may take two to four or more years to achieve (APA, 2016). During this time, effective communication among parents and children is essential for reducing conflict, improving family resilience, and nurturing cohesiveness (Pace, 2015). Couples are also encouraged to focus on developing their own relationship in order to provide a positive model and strong foundation for family integration.

Assimilation into a new stepfamily can be a stressful process for children, particularly for adolescents (see Figure 2–5). Early studies tended to focus on the challenges and detrimental effects that children experienced when transitioning into a stepfamily. More recently, researchers have attempted to identify specific factors that can lead to successful integration. King, Amato, and Lindstrom (2015) noted that adolescents who enjoyed a positive relationship with their mother prior to stepfamily formation were able to establish an effective bond with stepfathers in a relatively short time period. Other researchers have also found that children who have a close, supportive relationship with their biological parent tend to experience less stress and are better able to make a successful adjustment (Jensen, Shafer, & Holmes, 2015; Urick & Limb, 2015). Children were more likely to describe the transition as a positive experience when their biological parent and stepparents maintained open communication and involved them early and throughout the family formation process (Suggestions for Parents 2–1) (Kellas et al., 2015).

Figure 2–5 Children's Development and Stepfamily Integration

Children's reactions to stepfamily integration vary depending on age, level of understanding, and experiences leading up to the event.

- *Infants and toddlers.* Very young children will not understand what is occurring, but they will notice changes in their location and daily routines. Stranger anxiety may cause older infants and toddlers to have difficulty warming up to and accepting a stepparent. Extra care should be taken to make children feel safe and secure. Parents can take comfort in knowing that this phase will gradually end.

- *Preschoolers (2 ½–5 years).* Children of this age have difficulty grasping the concept of time and the finality associated with divorce or death. They may believe that an absent parent will eventually return or blame themselves for having caused the event ("Daddy went away because I wasn't a good boy.") and, thus, need continued reassurance that this is not the case. However, preschoolers are generally adaptable, receptive to change, and able to form an attachment with a stepparent more quickly than older children.

- *School-age children (6–12 years).* School-age children understand the permanency of loss (e.g., divorce, death) and may experience remorse, guilt, and lack of control. These feelings have a negative spillover effect on academic performance and contribute to depression and oppositional behavior. Adjusting to a new stepfamily may revive old memories, and require that parents exercise patience, communicate, and provide opportunities for involving children in the integration process.

- *Early adolescents (13–14 years).* Children are beginning to form strong opinions about life, crave independence, and learn how to manage hormone-driven emotions. They may resent their parent's decision to remarry, and the need to share their time and attention with another individual. Consequently, children at this age have the most difficulty adjusting to a new stepfamily arrangement.

- *Middle and late adolescents (15–18 years).* Older adolescents are becoming more self-assured and independent. They are less interested in bonding with a stepparent and more likely to rely on peers for support. However, they still want to know that parents care about them. Adolescents are more comfortable with verbal compliments than physical affection (e.g., hugs, kisses); girls are often uncomfortable with physical affection shown by a stepfather.

Suggestions for Parents 2-1

Supporting Children's Integration into a Stepfamily

Guidelines for helping children assimilate into a stepfamily arrangement include:

- Proceed slowly. Take time to learn about children's interests, and don't insist that they participate in too many joint family activities early in the assimilation phase.

- Involve children in making decisions, especially those that affect their place in the family (e.g., bedroom assignments, daily routines, household responsibilities, rules).

- Build relationships slowly and in small steps. Children are more likely to form a bond with a non-biological parent when they are given mental space and if allowed to do so at their own pace. Allow biological children to have some "alone" time with their biological parent.

- Let children know often that they are loved, safe, and valued.

- Encourage open communication. Hold family meetings; listen to children's concerns and suggestions, but insist that they be offered in a respectful manner.

- Create new traditions, and find ways to have fun together as a family; let children help plan a picnic or a walk, go fishing, attend a movie, ride bicycles, or visit a local park or zoo.

- Set limits and agree on disciplinary approaches to prevent children from playing one parent against the other. Initially, it may be best for the biological parent to provide discipline until children gradually establish a bond with the stepparent.

- Seek professional help if continued integration efforts fail to achieve favorable results.

Brandon's mother called down the basement stairs and said that it was time for dinner. After he failed to come upstairs, Brandon's stepfather went down and told him that he needed to stop playing his video game and come to the table. Brandon was upset that his stepfather had interrupted his video game and shouted, "You are not my dad!" Brandon's mother and stepfather had only recently married and moved into the same household. How would you advise Brandon's stepfather to respond to this situation and to similar situations in the future?

2-3e Same-Sex Partnered Families

A majority of the more than 600,000 same-sex partnered households are located in California, New York, Oregon, and Florida (see Figure 2–6) (Lofquist, 2011). This figure represents approximately 1 percent of all current U.S. households, but may be an undercount of the actual number of same-sex couple households that exist. Forty percent of these households are comprised of racial and/or ethnic minorities (Gates, 2013). More than 200,000 children (e.g., biological, adopted, step) are being reared in same-sex partner families, including 22,000 who are adopted and another 3400 who are foster children (Gates, 2015).

In June 2015, the U.S. Supreme Court handed down a landmark decision *(Obergefell v. Hodges)* that guaranteed same-sex couples the constitutional right to marry. This decision has had important social, financial, and legal implications for same-sex families. Legal recognition has improved couples' access to a variety of financial benefits, including employer-based retirement plans and health insurance, which have important consequences for children's well-being. Researchers have long documented poorer outcomes,

Figure 2-6   Same-Sex Couple Households

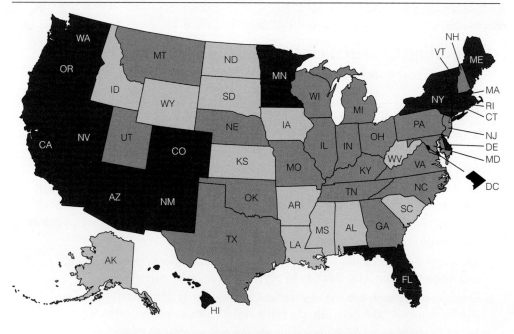

Percent of Same-Sex Couple Households

■ 1.76–4.01	■ 0.96–1.75	■ 0.67–0.95	☐ 0.29–0.66

United States = 0.95 percent

Source: U.S. Census Bureau, 2010 American community survey.

including family instability and poverty, for children who live with cohabitating parents verses those whose parents are married (Manning, 2015a). Dillender (2015) noted that improved access to health insurance has also led to changes in couples' work and caregiving arrangements. Same-sex female couples are more likely to switch from two employed parents to one employed parent; no change in work arrangements was observed among male same-sex couples.

Researchers have studied the relationship quality and health of partners in same-sex families that include children. Tornello, Kruczkowski, and Patterson (2015) examined the way in which male same-sex parents shared household and child care responsibilities and the effect this had on their relationship. Same-sex male couples report their relationship to be of high quality when these tasks are shared in an equal and democratic manner, but rate it low when there were discrepancies between what they expected and what was actually happening. The perceived approval or disapproval of a same-sex couple's relationship has also been reported to influence the strength of their resilience and bond. Power et al. (2015) found that lesbian, gay, and bisexual parents often described having a stronger connection to friends than to their own family of origin. Assumptions that social discrimination and stress increase same-sex partners' risk of developing health-related problems have not, for the most part, been substantiated. However, Cochran and Mays (2015) noted that female same-sex couples experience a higher rate of suicide than women in heterosexual relationships or male same-sex couples.

There are arguments that parenting capabilities are gender-exclusive and, therefore, children need both a mother and a father as parents. However, most research studies to date have not demonstrated any significant differences in children's developmental outcomes when they are reared by same-sex or heterosexual parents (Adams & Light, 2015; Sasnett, 2015). A meta-analysis of more than 30 studies involving over 5000 children concluded that children's sexual orientation and identity, psychological adjustment, and cognitive abilities are not determined by parents' sexual orientation or family type (Fedewa, Black, & Ahn, 2015). This position has also been endorsed by numerous professional organizations, including the American Academy of Pediatrics, American Psychological Association, and Child Welfare League of America. However, researchers have noted that children's well-being is affected significantly more by the quality of their parents' relationship, parenting skills, social support, and economic stability than by parents' sexual orientation (Perrin & Siegel, 2013).

Same-sex parents are more likely than parents in other family configurations to volunteer and to attend their children's school events (e.g., parent-teacher conferences, class performances) (Myers & Myers, 2014). They are also more likely to discuss concerns about their child's academic performance and experiences with teachers and to report problems their child may be having with other students or the parents of other children in the school. Researchers have also noted that same-sex couples spend more child-focused time with their children than typically occurs in heterosexual families (Prickett, Martin-Storey, & Crosnoe, 2015). Bos, van Gelderen, and Gartrell (2015) reported that adolescents in female same-gender families had higher self-esteem and fewer behavior problems than teens raised in heterosexual-parent families.

Although children of same-sex parents consider their families to be normal, they also report feeling different and being subjected to stigma and negative comments at school and in their communities (Crouch et al., 2015; Farr et al., 2015). Homophobic remarks are the most commonly reported form of harassment, even greater than those involving religion, race, ethnicity, or disability. Students are frustrated by peers' lack of understanding about their parental and family differences and often feel unsafe at school, which can increase their risk for mental health problems and substance abuse. However, having a positive family environment and supportive parents can help to neutralize the negative effects of peer harassment.

A significant percentage of children with same-sex parents are enrolled in private schools (both religious and non-religious), although the majority attend public institutions. Parents' reasons for selecting a particular school include the school's academic reputation, school population diversity, and how the school addresses problematic issues. They are also particularly interested in the school's counseling services and the availability of a supportive adult, factors that can make a difference for children's mental health and academic performance.

2-3f Foster Families

Parents who serve as foster families agree to provide a safe, nurturing environment for children who are in need of temporary care. Children may enter the foster care system through a process that is either voluntary or court-ordered. Although far less common, a biological family may decide to have their child placed in foster care because they are experiencing a personal crisis, such as homelessness or substance addiction, and are unable to provide adequate care. Children are most often removed from their biological family and placed in foster care by the courts because they are being abused or neglected (e.g., physically, emotionally, or medically) or have a single parent who dies or is incarcerated and no kinship care is available (English, Thompson, & White, 2015; Shaw, Bright, & Sharpe, 2015).

A reported 415,129 children were in foster care during 2014; 264,746 entered the system and 238, 230 exited during the year. Approximately 50,644 foster children were adopted in 2012 while 60,898 continued to wait for adoption. The average age of children in foster care was 8 years; slightly over half (52 percent) were male compared to 48 percent female (see Figure 2–7). Although the majority of children entering foster care were White, the number of children from minority backgrounds were approximately equivalent when all minority groups were combined (see Figure 2–8). These numbers have raised questions about the overrepresentation of children from minority backgrounds, compared to their non-minority counterparts, who have been placed in the child welfare system. Lanier et al. (2015) determined that poverty significantly increases the risk of maltreatment in minority families, particularly those headed by unmarried and teenage mothers, and contributes to the high removal rate of children from their homes. Horton and Watson (2015) noted that poverty and parents' level of educational attainment were also strongly associated with maltreatment and children's placement in foster care.

Recently, opportunities to become foster parents have opened to a broader array of families, including same-sex, bisexual, transgender, single-parent, extended, multiracial, and grandparent-led families (George, 2016; Manning, Fettro, & Lamidi, 2014). This trend followed changes in state laws, which acknowledged same-sex marriage, and research that provides evidence of positive outcomes when children are placed in diverse foster homes (George, 2016; Baiocco et al., 2015).

Figure 2-7 Ages of Children in Foster Care, 2014

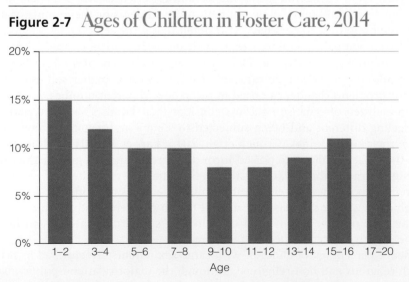

Source: U.S. Department of Health and Human Services (2015).

Figure 2-8 Race/Ethnicity of Children Entering Foster Care, 2014

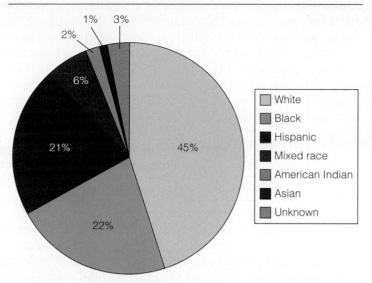

Legend:
- White
- Black
- Hispanic
- Mixed race
- American Indian
- Asian
- Unknown

Pie chart values: 45%, 22%, 21%, 6%, 2%, 1%, 3%

Source: U.S. Department of Health and Human Services (2014).

Adults who decide to become foster parents often do so because they have a sincere desire to help children in need, wish to include more children in their life, or they plan to use the experience as a step to adoption. However, it is imperative that all family members agree with this decision and understand how it will affect their lives. Application to become a licensed foster parent can be made through a private, county, state, or tribal agency. This process involves meeting State requirements and completing a background check, mental and physical evaluations, personal interview, family assessment, and home inspection. Once a family is approved, they are placed on a waiting list of potential placement homes.

Because many children who enter the foster care system have complex needs (e.g., developmental disabilities, medical conditions, a history of abuse, mental health disturbances) families must be adaptable and prepared to handle such challenges (Thakur, Creedon, & Zeanah, 2016; Szilagyi et al., 2015). Foster parents must be able to advocate for a child or children in their care and work effectively with case managers, therapists, teachers, medical personnel, and legal advisors. It is also likely that they will need to provide some financial support because the monthly stipend they receive seldom covers all of the child's expenses. Foster parents may be able to report unreimbursed expenses and qualify for a child tax credit on their tax form. Children in foster care may also be eligible to receive Medicaid benefits depending upon the eligibility rules in their state.

Child welfare systems in the United States and throughout the world face a continuous struggle to recruit and retain caring foster parents. Many families cite the chronic stress associated with children's troublesome behaviors, lack of resources, and inadequate training as reasons for discontinuing their involvement in foster care (Cooley, Farineau, & Mullis, 2015). Others express concern about the effect a troubled foster child may have had on their own children, or the emotional distress they experienced when a foster child leaves their home (Geiger, Hayes, & Lietz, 2014; Geiger, Hayes, & Lietz, 2013). However, many foster parents derive a great deal of satisfaction from their ability to have a positive impact on children's lives (Lo et al., 2015).

Removing children temporarily from chaotic and unsafe environments and placing them with a foster family can make a significant difference in the direction of the child's life. However, the harsh reality of abruptly separating children from their biological parents and moving them into a stranger's home can also be especially traumatizing. Young children may misinterpret these transactions as punishment for misbehavior or think that they are no longer wanted by their parents. Older children are better able to assess the situation, and often later acknowledge that the move was necessary and beneficial (Jones, 2015). Physiological evidence also supports this conclusion. For example, Bick et al. (2015) observed improved brain development in children who were removed from neglectful and abusive conditions and placed in settings with responsive caregivers.

Foster care also has its limitations. Failed placements and frequent moves from one foster home to another can jeopardize children's development. Insecure attachment formation and subsequent poor behavioral and social-emotional outcomes have been documented repeatedly in scientific studies (Zaccagnino et al., 2015; Zeanah & Gleason, 2015). Jacobsen et al. (2014), however, determined that very young children (2–3 years) were able to form secure attachments when they remained in a long-term foster home setting with consistent and caring providers. Foster children who experience frequent placements and accompanying school changes tend to develop poorer cognitive and social-emotional skills and drop out of school at a higher rate (Pears et al., 2015; Szilagyi, 2015). Berger et al. (2015) noted that foster children consistently scored lower on math and reading assessments. As a result, children who are aging out of the foster care system are often unprepared to assume an independent adult role. Communities around the country are developing programs that teach independent living skills to older foster children and will continue to provide support as they transition into adulthood.

No one would agree that foster care provides an ideal, long-term solution for children in need. State laws and agency efforts are aimed at preserving and strengthening family unity and returning foster children to their biological family. However, achieving this goal is not always possible. The passage of the Adoptions and Safe Families Act of 1997 was designed to prevent children from remaining in long-term foster care by requiring states to proceed with the termination of parental rights and provide financial incentives in order to increase adoptions.

2-3g Adoptive Families

According to the Child Welfare Information Gateway (2016), adoption "is the social, emotional, and legal process in which children who will not be raised by their birth parents become full and permanent legal members of another family while maintaining genetic and psychological connections to their birth family." Adoption provides a solution for families that desire children but are unable to conceive due to infertility, medical complications, or advanced age. Single adults and same-sex couples may pursue adoption because they wish to include a child(ren) in their life. Stepparents often adopt their partner's biological children—a practice that is common in the United States and throughout the world. Adults who themselves were adopted as children may adopt because they want to give other children in need a positive family experience. Some couples adopt for religious or ethical reasons (e.g., not wanting to increase the existing population). Additional information on the adoption process and challenges that children and families face is presented in Chapter 4.

According to U.S. Health and Human Services data, 29 percent (or 114, 529) of the children in foster care were adopted in 2014 (Kreider & Lofquist, 2014). The largest percentage of children were adopted by their foster parents (see Figure 2–9): 49 percent of children who were adopted were between the ages of birth and 4 years; 35 percent were 5–10 years of age; and 16 percent were 11–17 years of age. The majority of children had been in foster care less than 12 months before they were adopted. Approximately 45 percent of adopted children were White, 22 percent were Hispanic, 19 percent were Black or African American, and 1 percent were American Indian/Alaskan Native.

Although the primary goal of foster care is family preservation, this objective is not always achievable. For children who cannot be reunited with their family, adoption remains the next best option. Federal and state initiatives, support programs, and legal and financial assistance have been established to encourage more families to adopt children who are currently in foster care. Information about the resources and subsidies available in each state can be accessed on the North American Council on Adoptable

Figure 2-9 Adoptive Family Structure and Relationship to Child Prior to Adoption

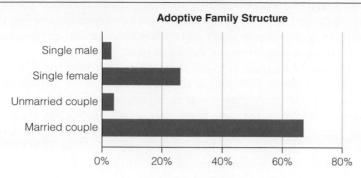

Adoptive Family Structure

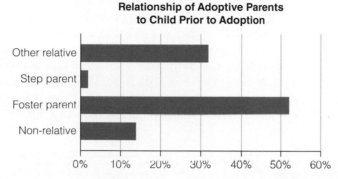

Relationship of Adoptive Parents to Child Prior to Adoption

Source: U.S. Department of Health and Human Services (2015).

Children's website. For example, approximately 91 percent of adoptive families received financial assistance subsidies in 2014 to help cover adoption expenses (Child Welfare Information Gateway, 2015).

It is difficult to determine how many adoptions are arranged annually through private or religious-affiliated agencies in the United States because there are no reporting requirements. However, the exact number of children adopted from foreign countries is well documented because they must apply for, and receive, an immigrant visa before entering the United States. Approximately three times as many children are adopted each year from China than from any other country; the remaining fraction of children come from Ethiopia, Haiti, Ukraine, and South Korea (U.S. State Department, 2015). The number of international adoptions has continued to decline to a low of approximately 6400 foreign-born children who entered the United States in 2014. This trend may be due, in part, to increased restrictions placed on international adoptions when the United States ratified the Hague Convention on Intercountry Adoption in 2008. The purpose of this international agreement is aimed at reducing human trafficking and increasing children's chances of adoption first in their own country. Concerns about undisclosed disabilities and the legality of parental rights terminations in some foreign countries have also caused more Americans to adopt U.S.-born children.

Adoptive parents experience challenges that are not always anticipated (Moyer & Goldberg, 2015). Their romantic image of parenthood may not always match the everyday reality of caring for a child who does not initially reciprocate the same loving feelings that are felt by their new parents. In some cases, this can lead to a condition known as post-adoption depression (Foli et al., 2014). Sleep deprivation, stress, and added responsibilities can cause some parents to feel sad and confused about their decision to adopt. Some adoptive parents worry that children will have difficulty forming an emotional attachment because of prior maltreatment or traumatic life experiences. However, most adoptive parents report having immediate positive feelings for a child that strengthen with time (Goldberg, Moyer, & Kinkler, 2013). Although parents understand that many children who are available for adoption, especially those from other countries, are more likely to have physical, mental health, or developmental disorders, they are willing to complete the adoption process (Diamond et al., 2015). However, they worry that years later they may experience disappointment when such a diagnosis is confirmed or behavior problems begin to emerge. Despite these special challenges, most adoptive parents don't regret their decision and experience great satisfaction in providing a loving home for a child in need.

An adoptive family may provide the first safe, stable household and caring parents that a child has known. However, a child's transition from a dysfunctional home environment or multiple foster placements to a permanent family may not always be a smooth process. Children often experience intense feelings of grief, sadness, and emotional loss associated with perceived abandonment and removal from their biological parents, even when living conditions have been harsh or unfavorable (Mariscal et al., 2015). Open adoption arrangements that allow children to maintain contact with their birth family have been shown to help resolve some of these concerns, except in situations where maltreatment has been involved (Boyle, 2015; Wang, Ponte, & Ollen, 2015).

Some internationally adopted children struggle with self-esteem and ethnic identity development issues, especially if they are of a different race or ethnicity than their adoptive parent (Boivan & Hassan, 2015). Parents of these children have expressed a need for improved education about how to answer children's questions and continue to support their cultural identities (Harf et al., 2015). Families who have adopted children with disabilities have also voiced a need for obtaining more professional assistance in meeting their child's unique physical and psychological needs (Hill & Moore, 2015).

2-4 Families: Cultural, Racial, and Ethnic Diversity

America has always been a multicultural society. Increased immigration activity here and in many countries throughout the world continue to add to population diversity. Approximately 48 percent (192 million) of U.S. children under age 18 are of a minority background and, as a group, are projected to become a majority (64.4 percent) of the U.S. population by the year 2044 (Colby & Ortman, 2015). All race and ethnic categories are expected to grow between 2014 and 2060, with the largest increases projected among the non-Hispanic–Two or More Races, non-Hispanic Asian, and Hispanic populations (see Figure 2–10).

Although cultures differ in many respects, they usually place a high value on children. Parents' ideas about child-rearing practices and children's role in families are influenced by traditional cultural values and beliefs. For example, Luo and Tamis-LeMonda (2016) observed that Mexican mothers with limited education typically communicate with their infants through gestures and guidance and are unlikely to engage in verbal interactions. Some African societies do not consider children younger than age two capable of communicating other than to indicate hunger or discomfort and, thus, consider it silly to converse with them (Lancy, 2014). These ideas may seem contrary to what is known about children's language development, but they reflect important cultural beliefs that are transmitted from one generation to the next.

Families immigrating to another country face challenges in learning different languages, customs, social behaviors, and how to balance a new manner of living with their customary ways. The **acculturation** process may take several years to complete. It can also become a source of considerable intra-family conflict, particularly when parents attempt to retain their native language and traditions while children begin to identify with their new culture (Goforth, Pham, & Oka, 2015; Lui, 2015). Stress associated with discrepancies that arise between parents' and children's acculturation is associated with a higher incidence of behavior problems and academic struggles. Children

acculturation the process of adopting the language and customs of another culture.

Figure 2-10 Projected Change in U.S. Population by Race and Ethnicity

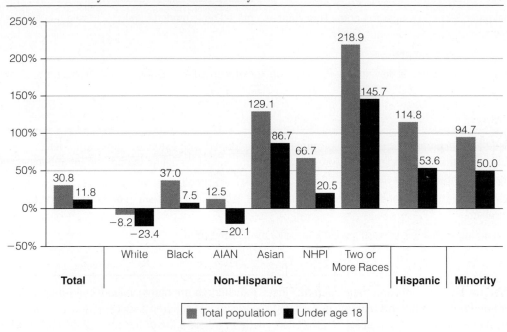

Note: AIAN = American Indian or Alaska Native; NHPI = Native Hawaiian or Other Pacific Islander.

Source: U.S. Census Bureau (2014c).

may also experience cultural discrimination and rejection, which can lead to variety of mental and physical health disorders (Inman et al., 2015; Sirin et al., 2015).

Learning about a family's cultural background is an important step in building respect and working effectively and collaboratively with parents. A family-focused approach is also beneficial for overcoming stereotypical misconceptions associated with a particular race or ethnicity. Although cultural orientation may provide a basic framework for understanding parents' behaviors, expectations, and child-rearing priorities, families within racial and ethnic subcultures can be quite different. For example, autonomy, individualism, and competition are qualities emphasized in many Western cultures, whereas collectivism and interdependence are more typical in Asian and Native American cultures. However, a Chinese couple that has completed their education in the United States or Canada, and holds dual citizenship, may prefer that their children adopt Western values as well as also maintain some Chinese traditions.

It is important for teachers and service providers to become familiar with some of the salient features associated with different cultures. However, it is equally important to remember that a family's cultural background is only one of many characteristics that make it unique. Efforts made to learn about a child's family, their heritage, language, traditions, strengths, challenges, and goals for children can begin to foster a trusting and effective working relationship. Figure 2–11 highlights general cultural characteristics that are considered representative of families in, and newly immigrated to, the United States. Because the statements are generalizations, they do not include many diverse differences that exist among individual families and subcultures within each group and, thus, must be viewed as an incomplete summary.

2-4a Multiracial and Interethnic Families

America has always been a mosaic of cultural, ethnic, and religious diversity. Immigration, legal and illegal, continues to add to the multiplicity of populations in the United States and other Western nations. Although public attitudes toward people of different races and ethnic backgrounds have improved, considerable prejudice still

Figure 2–11 Family and Parenting Concepts across Cultures

Mainstream American

- *Family*: Two married heterosexual parents are no longer the norm. Low emphasis placed on extended family. Increased gender-role sharing. More likely to follow an authoritative parenting style.
- *Children*: Taught to become independent and competitive.
- *Education*: Highly valued; high regard for personal achievements. Participation in extracurricular activities is considered an essential part of a child's education.

African American

- *Family*: High ratio and acceptance of single parents. Strong kinship connections are formed with extended family and friends. Elders are shown much respect. Some blurring of gender roles. More likely to use firm, direct discipline (authoritarian) and expect immediate response. Strong religious orientation and sense of pride.
- *Children*: May be expected to assist with household and caregiving responsibilities. Taught about racism in order to understand discrimination; taught to be self-reliant.
- *Education*: Highly valued as a way to improve one's upward mobility and give back to the community.

Asian

- *Family*: Typically, two married heterosexual parents and their children. Elders and children are highly valued; child-parent bond may be stronger than the bond between parents. Parents make sacrifices to support children's success. They closely supervise and guide children's development as a "sign of love." Efforts are made to follow a life of harmony and to preserve traditions.
- *Children*: Taught to be polite, respectful, obedient, and hard-working. Socialized to listen more than to speak. Emphasis is placed on collectivism versus individualism. Children are often more dependent upon parents for guidance than are mainstream American children.
- *Education*: Highly valued; teachers are held in high-esteem. Academic success is seen as a way to improve social status. Child's accomplishments are a source of parental pride or embarrassment.

Hispanic/Latino

- *Family*: Large family size and strong kinship ties are common. Elders and heritage held in high esteem. Male dominance (machismo) is common; in some families, males make decisions outside of the home while women run the household. Modest; may be reluctant to ask for help. Parents' role is to prepare children to become parents. Parenting style is more permissive with younger children, more authoritarian with older children.
- *Children*: Are important and considered a validation of marriage. Taught to respect elders. Young children enjoy relative freedom, and are not pressured to achieve developmental milestones in a timely manner. Older children are expected to obey and assist with household responsibilities.
- *Education*: Less pressure is placed on children to complete an education due to concerns that few jobs will be available and that education may erode traditional cultural heritage. Parent involvement in schools is often low. Dropout rate is high among students.

American Indians and Alaskan Natives

- *Family*: Two-parent families are declining in numbers. Children, elders, and extended family are respected and highly valued; elders are often very involved in child-rearing. Collectivism versus individualism is a predominant value. Experience the highest poverty rate of any cultural group.
- *Children*: Children are taught through example and elders' stories to live harmoniously with nature. Discipline and attitudes toward children's development are relaxed; children are not pushed to excel, but to become self-reliant. Children are taught to be quiet (listen, speak only when there is a purpose), patient, cautious, and cooperative.
- *Education*: Low incentive to complete education due to lack of jobs; experience the highest dropout rate of any cultural group. Education is focused on preservation of cultural traditions and rituals.

exists, especially toward mixed-race relationships and families (Leslie & Young, 2015; Rosenthal & Starks, 2015). For example, the last U.S. state to repeal laws prohibiting interracial marriage did so in 2000. Despite a sometimes difficult social and political environment, interracial and interethnic relationships and marriages continue to increase: approximately 15 percent of marriages in 2015 involved mixed-race couples, and about 320,000 interracial marriages took place in 2014 (Wang, 2015; Frey, 2014).

The 2000 census marked the first time that U.S. citizens were offered a choice to declare more than one race on a census questionnaire. This modification yielded data that was previously unavailable, and has led to an improved understanding about the ways in which American families are changing. For example, the percent of interracial married couples increased from 7 percent in 2000 to 10 percent in 2010, with the majority of these marriages occurring among the American Indian/Native Alaskan group (see Figure 2–12) (Wang, 2015; U.S. Census, 2000, 2010). States with the highest percentage of opposite-sex interracial married couples included California, Nevada, New Mexico, Oklahoma, Alaska, and Hawaii. Unmarried couples (opposite- and same-sex) accounted for the largest percentage of mixed-race partnerships.

Multiracial and interethnic families are also formed through the adoption of children who are of a race or ethnicity that is different from their adoptive parents. Twenty-four percent of children under age 18 and 15 percent of children 18 years and over were of a different race or ethnicity than their adoptive parents (Kreider & Lofquist, 2014). A majority of international adoptions involve children who also differ in race or ethnic heritage from their adoptive parents.

Although multiracial families are more common, they remain a small minority of all opposite-sex marriages in the United States. The low rate may be indicative of the difficulty interracial couples encounter in establishing and maintaining a long-term relationship. Bell & Hastings (2015) noted that parental disapproval of their children's interracial dating (e.g., Black and White) intensified the racial tension and stress that a couple was already experiencing. When at least one set of their parents approved of the relationship, tension and stress were somewhat diminished. However, when both

Figure 2-12 Multiracial Marriage for Specified Racial Groups, 1990–2010

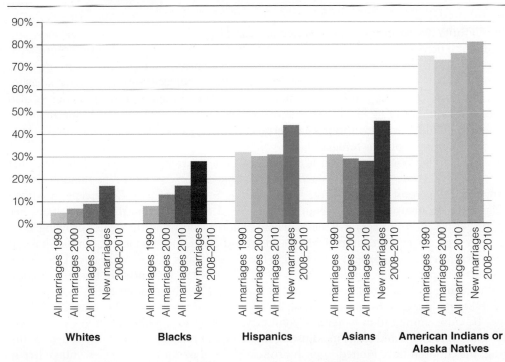

Source: 1990–2000 U.S censuses; American community survey, 2008–2010.

sets of parents approved, children felt emotionally stronger and more resistant to racial comments and social disapproval. Dual parental approval also enabled couples to feel psychologically safe when visiting either parents' home.

Researchers have observed that exposure to discriminatory and prejudicial comments can lead to chronic stress and an increase in poor relationship commitment, relationship dissolution, and intimate partner violence (Leslie & Young, 2015; Rosenthal & Stark, 2015). However, Canlas et al. (2015) did not find this to be true in the case of Asian and White interracial marriage relationships, and noted that personal fulfillment, relationship stability, and social approval were equivalent to that experienced by same-race White couples.

Parents play an important role in shaping multiracial children's concept of racial-ethnic identity so that they develop a sense of belonging, behave according to expected norms, and are more resistant to prejudice, discrimination, and peer pressure (Derlan & Umaña-Taylor, 2015; Seshadri & Knudson-Martin, 2013). However, not all parents are prepared or comfortable discussing ethnicity and racism with their children. Racial-ethnic socialization is important for biological children as well as for international children who are adopted. The importance and role that parents play in this process is drawing considerable attention as the number of children with mixed racial heritage continues to increase faster than any single race group.

Researchers have historically focused their studies on the challenges and disadvantages (e.g., poverty, less education, higher incidence of mental health disorders) that biracial or multiracial children often experience. Although these problems continue to exist, more studies are currently focusing on the positive developmental outcomes associated with racial socialization. Csizmadia, Rollins, and Kaneakua (2014) observed that when parents of biracial children identified their child as White, they engaged in minimal ethnic-racial socialization efforts. In contrast, parents who identified their biracial children as either Black or biracial were more likely to talk frequently with children about their heritage. However, identifying with a single racial category overlooks the diversity that often exists within a group and can limit an individual's self-identity perspective. Gaither (2015) reported that persons of mixed backgrounds often develop multiple racial identities which enable them to move between racial groups. This flexibility affords them protection against the negative effects of discrimination and preserves the richness of experiencing multiple cultural heritages.

2-4b Immigrant Families

Immigrants arrive in the United States in four categories: legal, refugees, asylees, and undocumented. The Immigration and Naturalization Service grants permission to legal immigrants to enter the United States either permanently or temporarily. A refugee is a person who is forced to flee their country because of persecution or war and is either granted refugee status prior to, or upon entering the United States. An asylee is also someone who is fleeing his or her country because of persecution or war, but an asylee enters the United States without legal permission. Once an asylee is in the United States, he or she must apply for refugee status.

The foreign-born population in the United States currently exceeds 41 million. First or second-generation immigrants account for about 62 percent of the population of Los Angeles; 54 percent in New York; 43 percent in San Diego; and 72 percent in Miami (Zigler and Camarota, 2015). About one-quarter of the children in the United States live in first-generation immigrant families. These children constitute the fastest-growing population segment in the country. Children in second-generation immigrant families have at least one foreign-born parent; were born in the United States (79 percent); have U.S. citizen parents (64 percent); live in their family-owned homes (55 percent); are fluent in English (74 percent); and most (60 percent) have at least one English-fluent parent. About one-half of children older than five speak English "very well" (Migration Policy Institute, 2015).

Because immigration is never a voluntary decision for a child, it often causes them considerable stress and effort in adjusting to a new environment. About one-fourth of immigrant children have limited English proficiency, and about the same percentage live in linguistically isolated households in which no one over age 13 speaks English exclusively, or very well. Children who have limited English proficiency are less likely to have academic success in school and to assimilate into their peer group (Baker, 2016). Garcia-Reid, Peterson, and Reid (2015) noted that Latino children with limited English language experienced a higher rate of behavior problems and were more likely to drop out of school early unless they had additional teacher support. In contrast, Gong, Marchant, and Cheng (2015) observed that Asian students tended to achieve greater academic success than Hispanic students, and attributed this difference to higher family income and parents' educational expectations for their children.

Immigrant children, and especially adolescents, are strongly influenced by family, peer, community, and environmental factors as they attempt to adjust to a new culture. Discriminatory remarks, prejudice, and rejection from peers in school and social settings can increase children's internalizing behaviors and also have a negative effect on their academic engagement (Kawabata & Crick, 2015). In some cases, children exhibit better social functioning than do their parents, which may be an indication of greater flexibility and resiliency against difficult circumstances. Parental adaptation can take longer, particularly if economic and health circumstances are unfavorable for lengthy periods. However, parental dissatisfaction with work conditions and/or perceived workplace discrimination can cause an increase in children's externalizing behaviors and delay their adjustment (Wheeler, Updegraff, & Crouter, 2015).

Children and their families need time, patience, and compassionate understanding to help them succeed in transitioning from a familiar to an unfamiliar culture. Their reasons for immigrating to a new country are often so diverse and complex that an individualized approach must be taken to gaining trust and addressing their essential needs. Efforts to support family strengths and cohesion are important for maintaining children's feelings of safety and security (Ibáñez et al., 2015). Steps can also be taken to help them locate information and connect with state and community programs and service agencies.

Photo 2-2 Families from many cultures are represented in this country.
Juriah Mosin/Shutterstock.com

Trending Now The Immigration Dilemma

Immigrants have always been a characteristic feature of the American landscape. The United States has remained a popular destination for waves of European, Asian, Mexican, and Latin American families that have left their countries to escape religious persecution, war, and poverty in hopes of finding a better life. However, their arrival and residency have not always been welcomed. Many groups and individuals have endured significant discrimination, racism, and marginalization as a result of their "foreigner" status in this country.

Between 1970 and 2013, there was a fourfold increase in the number of immigrants entering the United States; 60 percent of these individuals entered before 2000 (Migration Policy Institute, 2015). At present, there are approximately 41.3 million individuals (or 13 percent of the total population) currently residing in the United States who identify themselves as immigrants (i.e., no U.S. citizenship at birth); Hispanics and Latinos account for nearly half of this number. When children who are born in the United States to immigrant parents are included, this number increases to approximately 80 million (Migration Policy Institute, 2015).

Slightly less than half of all immigrants are naturalized U.S. citizens. The remainder include unauthorized immigrants, legalized permanent residents, and individuals (e.g., students, temporary workers) on provisional visas. Nearly half of the 11.3 million unauthorized immigrants in 2014 were Mexicans, although this number has continued to decrease each year (Krogstad & Passe, 2015). More than 80 percent of unauthorized immigrants were in the United States working or looking for work. The majority of those who had jobs were working in Nevada, California, Texas, and New Jersey.

The United States, like many countries, continues to struggle to find ways to strike a balance between the needs of its citizens and those of its immigrant populations. The dilemma clearly presents a number of moral, economic, logistical, and legal issues. For example, some individuals fear that immigrants will alter a community's composition and political direction. Others argue that immigrants, especially those who are in the country illegally, take jobs away from native workers and cause wages to be lower (Guan et al., 2015; Ross & Rouse, 2015). Those who are against immigration have raised concerns about the

Continued

potential security risk that immigrants from some countries might pose; those who have a criminal background; individuals who take up limited spaces in higher education classrooms; and immigrant families that require social assistance resources which may be diverted from permanent U.S. citizens. Educators have emphasized the burden that K-12 immigrant children, who frequently either do not speak English or have poor academic skills, place on often limited financial and personnel resources. Researchers have also drawn attention to the negative effect that immigrant children's presence can have on the academic performance of other children in the classroom (Potochnick & Mooney, 2015; Diette & Oyelere, 2014).

Immigration proponents note that U.S. population growth stagnation is creating a labor shortage that immigrants are able to partially fill, which can have a positive effect on the economy, particularly in agriculture and technical fields. Hong and McLaren (2015) observed that immigration influx increased demand for local community services (e.g., banks,

restaurants, groceries) which, in turn, led to an increase in native workers' wages. They calculated that 1.2 local jobs were added for every new immigrant who moved into a community. Chassamboulli and Peri (2015) reported similar findings. They determined that legalizing some immigration policies reduced unemployment among low-skilled natives and increased their wages because employers had more available revenue to create additional jobs and raise salaries. They noted that immigrants who are in the United States legally or illegally contributed to the economy through goods purchased locally and because they pay income taxes. Researchers also have noted that few immigrants rely on, or are eligible for, government assistance programs.

The immigration debate began decades ago in the United States and other countries, and is likely to continue for a long time. Should the number of immigrants entering the country be limited? What measures need to be taken to protect permanent citizens? What services should immigrants be eligible to receive?

2-5 Families: Contextual Factors

Family functionality and quality of life are influenced by a number of contextual variables. Each circumstance can alter the roles, responsibilities, and interactions of family members and ultimately affect their ability to address children's needs and development.

2-5a Adolescent Parent Families

Teen pregnancy and births in the United States among girls aged 15–19 have continued to decline over the last 20+ years and have recently reached historic lows (see Figures 2–13 and 2–14). Pregnancy rates have decreased by 51 percent and teen birth

Figure 2-13 Birth Rates Per 1000 Females Ages 15–19, by Race/Ethnicity, 1990–2013

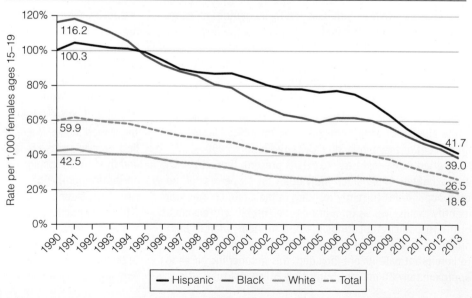

Source: CDC/NCHS. National Vital Statistics Report (2015). Births: Final data for 2013.

Figure 2-14 U.S. Birth Rates (2013)

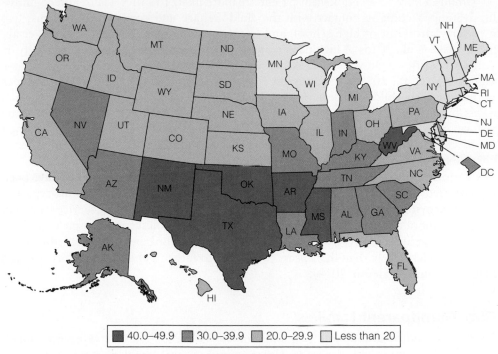

Legend: ■ 40.0–49.9 ■ 30.0–39.9 ■ 20.0–29.9 □ Less than 20

Note: U.S. teen birth rate was 26.5 in 2013

Source: Martin, Hamilton, & Ventura, (2015).

rates are down by 57 percent, although birth rates for girls aged 10–14 were unchanged over the same period. Downward trends occurred in all 50 states and across all racial and ethnic groups (CDC, 2015). Contraceptive use and increased awareness of sexually transmitted diseases have contributed to the large decline in pregnancy rates among sexually active teens (MMWR, 2015).

Despite the overall decrease, teen pregnancy and birth rates for young people aged 15–19 in the United States remain among the highest for developed countries. More than 400,000 infants are born annually to adolescent females aged 15–19. Nearly 89 percent of these births will occur outside of marriage (CDC, 2015). About 25 percent of girls will be pregnant at least once before age 20; about 25 percent of teen mothers will have a second child before they turn 20. According to a 2010 analysis by the National Campaign to Prevent Teen and Unplanned Pregnancy, the annual public cost of teen childbearing—due to the cost of public health care, foster care, incarceration, and lost tax revenue—is estimated to be about $9.4 billion (The National Campaign, 2016).

Adolescents who live in poverty and/or experienced abuse or neglect are at high risk for becoming pregnant (Garwood et al., 2015). Teens whose mothers gave birth as a teenager and/or only had a high school education are more likely to have a baby before age 20 than are teens whose mothers were older at the time of their birth, or who attended at least some college. Salas-Wright et al. (2015) also noted a strong relationship between prior substance use and adolescent pregnancy, and that many pregnant teens continue to use these substances (which may be harmful to the developing fetus) throughout their pregnancy.

Adolescent pregnancy and parenthood are closely associated with a host of social and economic issues that affect teen parents, their children, and society (Desai & Drake, 2015). Thirty percent of teenage girls cite pregnancy or parenthood as their primary reason for leaving high school. The dropout rate is highest among Hispanic (36 percent) and African American teens (38 percent). Approximately 50 percent of all teenage mothers are able to complete their high school degree (or GED) by age 22, and less than 2 percent complete a college degree by age 30. Teenage mothers who do not complete high school are more likely to live in poverty, depend upon public assistance, and be in poorer health than women who become pregnant in their early twenties.

Children born to an adolescent parent are more likely to suffer health and cognitive disadvantages, come in contact with the child welfare and correctional systems, live in poverty, drop out of high school, and become teen parents themselves (Jeha et al., 2015; Vaske et al., 2015). A high percentage of these infants will be born prematurely or with a low birth weight which increases their risk of developmental disorders and delays (Ganchimeg et al., 2014). They are less likely to perform as well as children of older mothers on early childhood development indicators and school readiness measures, such as communication, cognition, and social skills. They also tend to have lower academic performance, score lower on standardized tests, and are twice as likely to be retained (Madzwamuse et al., 2015). Less than two-thirds of children born to teen mothers earn a high school diploma, compared to 81 percent of children born to older mothers.

National initiatives, along with school- and community-based programs, have been implemented to address the challenge of teenage pregnancy. These programs typically focus on providing sex education, contraception, youth development, service learning, and after-school activities. Researchers have found that adolescents who participate in after-school activities, have positive attitudes toward school, perform well education- ally, and are less likely than their peers to have or to father a child (Secor-Turner et al., 2015; Tsui-Sui & Salerno, 2014).

2-5b Grandparent Families

Families headed by grandparents (grandfamilies) as householders have become much more common over the last decade. Unforeseen economic problems that cause adult children and their children to return home, an unwed mother and child, parental child abandonment, the necessity of caring for a child with health problems or a disability that the parents fail to attend to, substance abuse by one or both parents, and/or di- vorce are factors that frequently contribute to this trend. About 2.7 million grandpar- ents are "grandparent caregivers," defined as those who have primary responsibility for grandchildren under the age of 18 who are living with them (Ellis & Simmon, 2014). Sixty-seven percent of grandparents who report responsibility for grandchildren are under age 60. More than one-third of grandparents who have grandchildren living with them have not completed high school.

U.S. Census Bureau (2014b) statistical details provide some reasons for increased attention on grandparent families. About 10 percent of all U.S. children under age 18 (or 7.3 million children) currently live in a household with a grandparent present. Almost one-third (29 percent) of grandchildren live in their grandparent's household without their mother or father present. Children living with a grandparent are more likely to be Black, Hispanic, and younger than age 6 (see Figure 2–15).

Grandparents and other relatives in grandparent households provide care, stability and continuity to millions of potentially vulnerable children. This responsibility can have a significant negative effect on the lives, financial well-being, and the physical and mental health of individual family members, as well as the family structure. Financial concerns are often paramount given that a majority of grandparents are living on fixed incomes or near the end of their working career (Doley et al., 2015). Nearly 75 percent of grandchil- dren who live with their grandparents without a parent present receive public assistance (Ellis & Simmon, 2014). Many grandparent caregivers use tobacco products and suffer from health or mobility disorders (e.g., heart disease, arthritis) that make child care more challenging. Depression, chronic stress, and other mental health disorders primarily re- sulting from the added responsibilities associated with rearing children and lack of social interaction are also more common among these grandparents (Hayslip, Blumenthal, & Garner, 2015). However, many grandparents say they are motivated by an unconditional love for their grandchildren and would not hesitate to take a child in again if necessary.

Despite continued growth in the number of grandparents who are caring for grandchildren, relatively little is known about children's experiences in these situations.

Figure 2-15 Percentage of Children Under 18 Living with Grandparents by Race and Hispanic Origin, 1992–2012

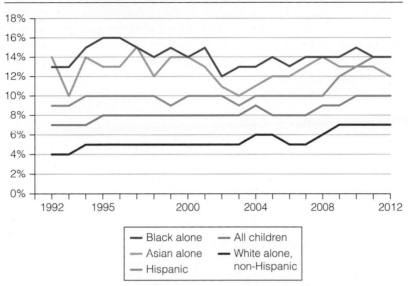

Source: U.S. Census Bureau (2015b).

The data show that the risks for children (e.g., poverty, access to medical and mental care housing stability) vary by the composition of the household, which is directly related to different levels of social support and access to resources (Coleman & Wu, 2016). Grandparent-and-grandchildren household composition is also highly variable (i.e., two grandparents present; just a grandmother or grandfather present; two parents, one parent, or no parent also present in the household) and each variation appears to be associated with a specific set of issues. For example, grandmother-headed households experience a higher prevalence of poverty compared with households where two grandparents are present or there is only a grandfather (Meyer & Abdul-Malak, 2015).

Grandparents' mental health status and parenting skills are known to have a significant effect on children's development (Smith, Cichy, & Montoro-Rodriguez, 2015). Children who were raised in households where grandparents experienced elevated levels of psychological distress, depression, poor coping skills, and had few or ineffective parenting skills showed an increase in problem behaviors. The reciprocal nature of the grandparent-grandchild relationship has also been reported by other researchers.

Goodman (2012) studied adults who had been raised by grandparents or great-grandparents to determine the nature of their relationship and if it had changed over time. Participants expressed having an intense emotional bond with their grandparent caregivers that they equated to a parent-child relationship. They were grateful for these relationships and respected their grandparents' efforts in raising them. Participants also reported how emotional support from their grandparent caregivers had provided them with a sense of stability and unconditional love, which they believed was crucial during their school years.

Grandparents are more likely to engage in discussions with their grandchildren about personal matters that are either neglected or viewed differently by children's parents. For example, Cornelius and Xiong (2015) found that grandparents are often more open to discussing sexual matters and information with grandchildren in their care. In contrast, parents are more likely to minimize discussions about such subjects, or they may suggest that their children practice behavioral patterns without explaining or justifying their point of view.

Access to information about effective child-rearing practices, support services, resources, programs, benefits, laws, and policies can help grandparents successfully fulfill their caregiving role (Coleman & Wu, 2016). Teachers and service providers should also be familiar with these resources so they can support and assist grandparents with their efforts. The American Association of Retired Persons (AARP), the Brookdale Foundation Group, Casey Family Programs, Child Welfare League of America, Children's Defense Fund, Generations United, and the National Committee of Grandparents for Children's Rights are examples of just some of the organizations that are taking an active role in partnering with grandparents who are caring for grandchildren. A national partnership among the latter has led to the creation of *GrandFacts: State Fact Sheets for Grandparents and Other Relatives Raising Children*, the development of local and national conferences on grandfamilies, and the efforts of individuals to form the Grandfamilies of America organization.

2-5c Military Families

About 2.3 million U.S. servicemen and -women typically serve in the four major and related military organizations each year. More than a third of the total were deployed more than once, and some as many as five times (Department of Defense, 2014). Thirty percent of enlisted personnel were married with children, almost 5 percent were single parents, and the majority were White (see Figure 2–16). Wars, combat missions, and overseas assignments have claimed the lives of almost 7000 service personnel; approximately 50,000 have suffered physical injuries.

Active-duty service assignments can lead to extended parental absences that result in missing important family events: birthdays, the middle school championship soccer game, high school graduation, and anniversaries. Children and adolescents often experience elevated anxiety and depression as a result of long parental absences. Older children (3–10 years) tend to develop emotional symptoms related to parental deployment that are more significant than do younger children (birth–5 years) (Alfano et al., 2016; Mustillo, Wadsworth, & Lester, 2015). Extended parental absence can also have a negative effect on children's academic performance (Moeller et al., 2015). However, children who are able to maintain relatively frequent contact (e.g., via Skype, telephone) with their absent parent are less likely to experience significant emotional problems.

The length of time a parent is away from home appears to have a crucial effect on the mental health of family members (Rodriguez & Margolin, 2015). Military

Figure 2-16 Race of Active Duty Enlisted U.S. Service Members

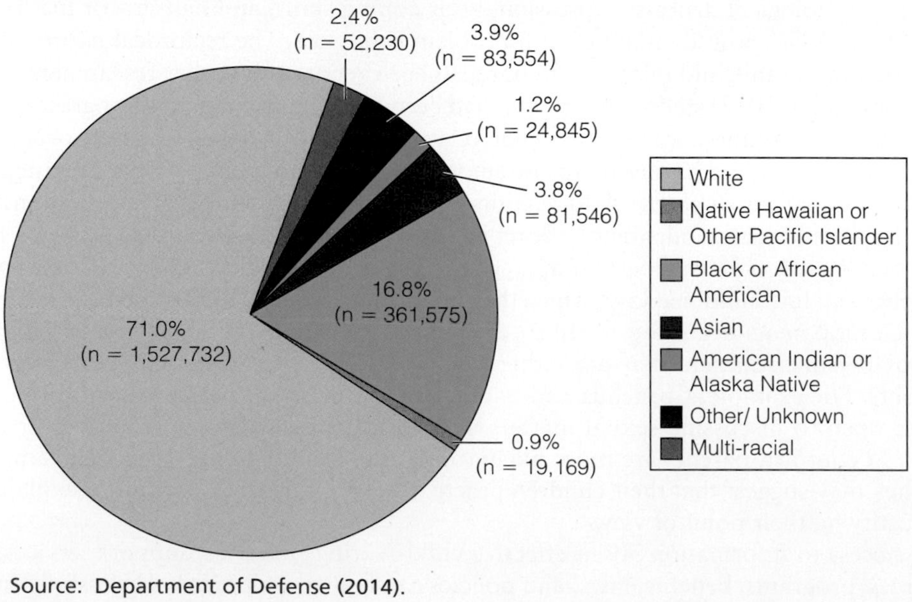

Source: Department of Defense (2014).

assignments that require absences longer than 1 year are associated with higher rates of depressive disorders, sleep disorders, anxiety disorders, acute stress reaction, and adjustment disorders among family members (Alfano et al., 2016; Lester et al., 2016).

Gender differences have also been observed in the way that children react to parental absence. Boys watch substantially more television and play more violent video games than do girls, which may expose them to greater violence-related media coverage. This may translate into an increased acceptance of aggressive behaviors toward friends or fellow students and participation in higher risk behaviors that could further add to the difficulty of coping with parental absence (Reed, Bell, & Edwards, 2011). Boys and girls may also differ in their role responsibilities at home, in their relationship with the absent parent, or in their response to mental health difficulties experienced by absent parents upon their return. For example, boys may face more challenges reconnecting emotionally with an absent parent (usually the father), or may struggle with renegotiating family roles when the parent returns home (Creech, Hadley, & Borsari, 2014).

Photo 2-3 It is difficult for children to cope with a parent's extended absence.
wavebreakmedia/Shutterstock.com

An increase in child maltreatment is known to occur following parental deployment, and has been attributed to the emotional stress and additional responsibilities placed on the resident parent. Taylor et al. (2016) noted that the rate of maltreatment increases significantly during repeat deployments and during the first 6 months following a deployed parent's return. Numerous organizations, including Head Start, Zero to Three, Child Welfare Information Gateway, and The National Child Traumatic Stress Network have developed extensive resources and programs to help military families and their children cope with the absence and return of parents in the military.

Many men and women who return from active military duty experience post-traumatic stress disorder (PTSD)—a mental health condition triggered by a terrifying event that was either experienced or witnessed. A parent who has PTSD may have flashbacks, nightmares, and severe anxiety, as well as uncontrollable thoughts about the event. They often experience changes in thinking and mood (e.g., hopelessness, negative feelings about self and others, lack of interest in activities once enjoyed, memory problems, difficulty maintaining close relationships) (U.S. Department of Veterans' Affairs, 2015). Emotional reactions (e.g., irritability, angry outbursts or aggressive behavior, always concerned about danger, overwhelming guilt or shame, insomnia) and self-destructive behaviors (e.g., drinking too much, driving recklessly) are also common. Some symptoms, effects, and behaviors may last for years. PTSD education for veterans is provided through various channels, including the U.S. Department of Defense *Strength of a Warrior* program.

The U.S. Defense Department's Office of Family Policy supports Families Overcoming Under Stress (FOCUS), which provides Family Resilience Training specifically designed to help active duty service members, veterans, and their families stay strong and supportive of each other during stressful times. FOCUS provides services for military children and families at several U.S. Navy, Marine Corps, Army, and Air Force installations. Stress demands placed on civilian spouses may equal or surpass their active duty partners because they frequently lack clear information about the risk status of their partner and are unable to act personally on their behalf. FOCUS programs improve family functioning and adjustment, which in turn significantly reduces child distress. Both parents and children participating in FOCUS demonstrate significant improvement in their emotional and behavioral adjustment (Lester et al., 2016).

2-5d Parents with a Disability and Their Families

Medical advances have enabled an increasing number of adults who have disabilities to enjoy the pleasures of parenthood. Approximately 6.2 percent of all parents (4.1 million) have a physical, mental, or intellectual disability and have children under the age of 18 living in their household (Stevens, 2012). However, disability rates are significantly different across ethnicities. For example, approximately 13.9 percent of American Indian/Alaska Native parents have a disability, whereas only 5.5 percent of Latino/Hispanic parents and 3.3 percent of Asian/Pacific Islander parents have a reported disability (National Council on Disability, 2012).

The right to bear children and to parent is considered a fundamental human right protected by the U.S. Constitution. However, this right is also balanced by state laws that have been established to protect children's welfare and safety. Despite these protections, parents who have disabilities face discrimination and significant barriers to health care access and employment opportunities (Iezzoni et al., 2015; Oberoi et al., 2015). Concerns persist about whether such parents, particularly those who have an intellectual disability, are capable of raising children. As a result, these parents are at increased risk of having children removed from their home and placed in foster care. Lightfoot and DeZelar (2015) reported that approximately 25 percent of children in foster care had been removed due to a parent's disability; some sources suggest this number may be as high as 40 to 80 percent.

Few studies have examined the effects that a parent's intellectual impairment may have on children's developmental outcomes. A literature review conducted by Collins and Llewellyn (2012) found no conclusive evidence that children's behavioral or developmental outcomes were positively or negatively affected by a parent's intellectual disability. Hindmarsh, Llewellyn, and Emerson (2015) also observed no difference in the developmental progress of 9-month-old infants whose mothers had an intellectual impairment. Researchers have noted that parents who have an intellectual disability typically experience higher stress levels associated with children's problematic behaviors than do other parents, and that having access to appropriate social support helped to mitigate this stress (Meppelder et al., 2015). Many parents, particularly those who have an intellectual disability, are able to provide appropriate and sufficient care for children with the aid of support services and parent training (Weiber et al., 2015; Llewellyn, 2013).

2-5e Families with Incarcerated Parents

About 2.6 million children, or roughly one in twenty-eight minors, had an incarcerated parent in 2013. Estimates are that 5 million U.S. children have had at least one parent imprisoned, which equates to approximately one in every fourteen children under age 18 (Murphey & Cooper, 2015). More than half of all state and federal prisoners were the parents of at least one minor child; approximately 65 percent (138,900) of incarcerated females were mothers. Fewer than 44 percent of fathers and 64 percent of mothers lived with their children prior to incarceration. Black children are twice as likely as White children to have a parent who has been incarcerated (Murphey & Cooper, 2015).

Researchers have studied the lives of inmates to determine if there are common personality and environmental factors that increase the likelihood of imprisonment. Nearly all studies have noted an accumulation of adverse life experiences and antisocial behaviors prior to an offender's arrest, including non-completion of a high school education. Roxburgh and MacArthur (2014) found that African American men and women were more likely to have experienced long-term negative emotional effects resulting from physical and sexual abuse. Many prison inmates, particularly Hispanic women and White men and women, also reported being victims of abuse and having resided in foster care as a child.

Higher rates of mental health problems and a history of involvement with juvenile justice and child welfare systems were also commonly observed among incarcerated mothers and fathers (Borja, Nurius, & Eddy, 2015). Many inmates report growing up in poverty and dysfunctional homes where they were exposed to multiple adversities, such as parents arguing and abusing substances, having a parent deployed or sent off to prison, experiencing homelessness, or being close to someone who had died as the result of suicide or a serious illness. Mitchell et al. (2015) noted that adolescents are especially vulnerable to these types of stressful situations and, thus, are more prone to impulsivity and antisocial behaviors resulting from diminished cognitive abilities and unpredictable emotional regulation. Adolescents in these situations are also at increased risk of suffering from mental health disorders and repeating the generational cycle of antisocial behavior displayed by their parents (Will, Whalen, & Loper, 2014).

Children experience significant stress and negative repercussions as a result of parental incarceration. Researchers have established a strong relationship between parental incarceration and children's mental health problems (e.g., anxiety, depression, delinquency), substance abuse, and poor educational performance. Dallaire, Zeman, and Thrash (2015) observed that children of incarcerated mothers exhibited an increase in internalizing (e.g., sadness, anxiety, depression, withdrawal) and externalizing (e.g., defiance, bullying, aggression) behaviors. They also noted that African American children developed fewer of these behaviors compared to other nonwhite children in the study. Researchers have also found that children of incarcerated parents suffer more acute illnesses (e.g., respiratory infections, asthma attacks), serious injuries, and obesity (Miller & Barnes, 2015). Many children also experience academic failure, grade retention, disciplinary problems, and leave school early. However, some researchers have also questioned whether a teacher's possibly negative perceptions may contribute to some of the problems (Turney & Haskins, 2014).

Parental imprisonment also has a significant effect on family dynamics. Distances between children and an imprisoned parent are often problematical: 63 percent of state prison facilities are located more than 100 miles from inmates' families (Rabuy & Kopf, 2015). As a result, slightly less than 50 percent of incarcerated parents are visited by their minor-aged children when prison distances are less than 50 miles; this figure drops to 40 percent when prisons are located more than 100 miles away. Visitation policies (e.g., frequency of allowed visits, intimidating environment, lack of privacy, cost of background checks) can further impede contact between parents and their children.

Incarceration also affects parents' relationship with one another. Mothers, but not fathers, reported a decrease in their relationship quality following paternal incarceration (Turney, 2015). These feelings lead to an increased probability of relationship dissolution, divorce, and cohabitation with another partner (Turney & Wildeman 2013). Legal debt, social disapproval, and extended family separation often have long-term detrimental effects on family relationships.

2-6 Family: Religious and Socioeconomic Diversity

A family's religious beliefs and socioeconomic status exert a direct influence on their value systems, parenting practices, and home environment. In turn, these factors affect the nature of complex bidirectional interactions that take place among family members and ultimately shape children's physical, mental, and intellectual development.

2-6a Religious Diversity

Religious affiliation or preference may provide an alternative method for defining families. Although Christianity (e.g., Protestant, Catholic, Orthodox Christian, Mormon, Jehovah's Witness) remains the predominant religion in the United States, the percentage of Americans who identify themselves as Christians has dropped from 78.4 to 70.6 percent since 2007 (Pew Research Center, 2015). In part, this decline can be attributed to increased ethnic population diversity and decreasing religious affiliation among young adults. Participation in non-Christian religions (e.g., Muslim, Judaism, Hindism, Buddhism) increased by 1.2 percent between 2007 and 2014; individuals who identified themselves as nonreligious increased by approximately 6.7 percent during the same time period.

Most religions provide documents and promote practices that are intended to guide personal conduct, choices, and morals (e.g., Christianity, Ten Commandments; Judaism, Torah; Confucianism, Five Classics and Four Books; Hinduism, Manusmriti,

Photo 2-4 A family's religious affiliation influences their belief system. DiversityStudio/Shutterstock.com

or Laws of Manu; Shintoism, One Hundred Poems of the World; Islam, The Five Pillars). For many parents, their religious beliefs and training serve as a guide for their childrearing practices and parenting style.

Kelly et al. (2015) conducted a meta-analysis of published studies that examined the relationship between adolescents' religious involvement and the likelihood of their participation in substance abuse and delinquent behavior. They consistently found that teens who attended church regularly and held religious beliefs were less likely to engage in delinquent acts or alcohol and drug use, and more likely to be focused on educational attainment. Jorgensen et al. (2015) observed that parents who held strong religious beliefs and participated in religious activities were also highly involved with their children and spent more time together as a family. Researchers have made similar observations and noted that the strength of parents' religious convictions is often associated with a positive parent-child relationship (Fredericks & Greeff, 2015).

Teachers and practitioners may find it helpful to learn the importance that religion plays in a family's life, especially its relationship to food restrictions, children's participation in some activities (i.e., birthday celebrations), and holiday observances. Such information should always be verified by a child's family in order to insure that modifications are consistent with their religious beliefs and preferences.

2-6b Socioeconomic Diversity

A family's socioeconomic status (SES) is a reflection of multiple factors, including parents' educational achievement, occupation, and household income. Economic pressures have forced increased numbers of single and married women to enter the labor force and to divide their time between childrearing responsibilities and paid employment. At present, approximately 40 percent of mothers in the United States serve as the primary source of household income. Seventy percent of women with children under the age of 18 years were employed in the labor force in 2014 (see Figure 2–17) (U.S. Bureau of Labor Statistics, 2015).

Socioeconomic differences have been shown to influence parenting style and practices, children's development, and access to resources. Park and Lau (2016) examined the child socialization priorities of parents in 90 countries and observed a strong correlation between parents' socioeconomic status and their socialization goals. Parents with

Figure 2-17 Mothers' Labor Force Participation Rates

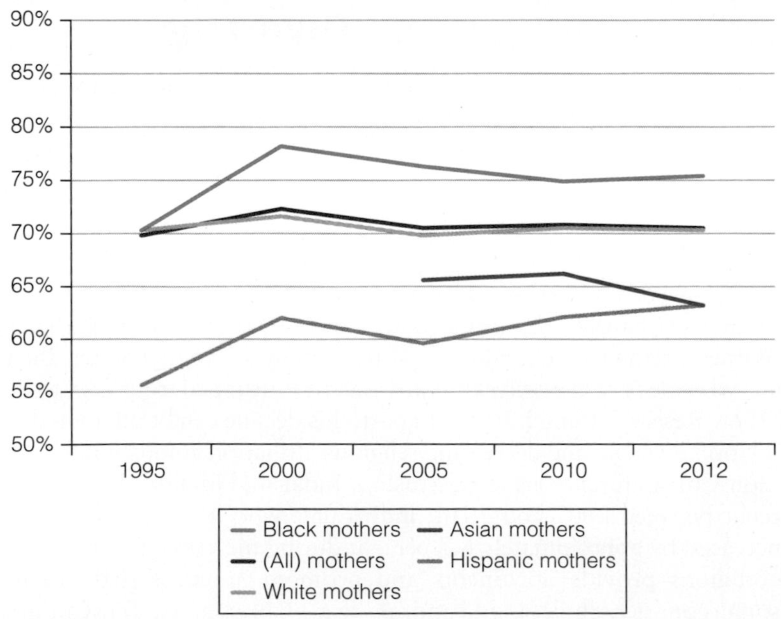

Legend:
- Black mothers
- Asian mothers
- (All) mothers
- Hispanic mothers
- White mothers

Source: U.S. Bureau of Labor Statistics (2015).

higher SES value children's independence over obedience, whereas parents with low SES are more likely to stress obedience over independence. Similarly, parents with higher SES are more likely to use an authoritative parenting style when interacting with children, whereas an authoritarian style is more commonly used in lower-SES families (Granero, Louwaars, & Ezpeleta, 2015). Disadvantaged parents who are dealing with daily stress and limited resources consider a direct approach toward their children more efficient and more likely to achieve the intended response. However, researchers have long established a link between high power assertion and low parental responsiveness that is associated with an increase in children's problematic behaviors (Kim & Kochanska, 2015).

Socioeconomic status also has important implications for children's educational outcomes. Children from low-SES households experience higher rates of delayed cognitive, language, and self-regulation skills that place them at a distinct disadvantage when they enter school (Norbury et al., 2016; Schmitt et al., 2015). High teacher turnover rates and disparities in teacher qualifications compromise the quality of many schools located in disadvantaged neighborhoods and further diminish children's academic development (Goldhaber, Lavery, & Theobald, 2015). Low parental involvement rates and chronic stress related to unsafe environments, food insecurity, and untreated health problems place many disadvantaged children at even greater risk for educational failure. Children from low-SES families also have fewer opportunities to participate in extracurricular activities, despite positive outcomes that have been demonstrated on school engagement, academic performance, physical and mental well-being, and a reduction in conduct disorders (Crosnoe, Smith, & Leventhal, 2015; Forneris, Camiré, & Williamson, 2015).

Summary

- The concept of family is a reflection of prevailing social, political, religious, and economic factors. As a result, families change in terms of their roles, responsibilities, goals, and objectives.

- Functional families enjoy being together, supporting one another, and working toward common goals. Children reared in these families are more likely to reach their developmental potentials. Children growing up in dysfunctional families experience a greater risk of developmental and behavioral problems.

- Families come in an array of structural arrangements, from two-parent heterosexual families to single-parent, foster, adoptive, same-sex, and stepfamilies. Each has associated benefits and challenges for parents and their children.

- Cultural, racial, ethnic, religious, and socioeconomic variants add to a family's diversity and uniqueness.

- The context in which a family functions (e.g., adolescent parents, grandparenting, parent with an intellectual disability, military service, incarceration) exerts a direct effect on children's health and development.

Key Terms

acculturation (p. 44)

cohabitation (p. 29)

heterosexual (p. 32)

matriarchal (p. 33)

monogamous (p. 31)

nuclear family (p. 31)

patriarchal (p. 33)

polyandry (p. 34)

polygamy (p. 34)

polygyny (p. 34)

Questions for Discussion and Self-Reflection

1. In what ways are "baby boomer" parents similar to, and different from, colonial parents?

2. What qualities increase a family's risk of becoming dysfunctional?

3. How might a child's life differ growing up in a two-parent heterosexual family versus a single adolescent parent family?

4. What are some of the reasons that individuals cite for wanting to become foster parents?

5. In what ways might Hispanic cultural values contribute to a child's inclination to drop out of school early?

Field Activities

1. Interview ten people and ask them to define the term *family*. Identify and record similar characteristics in one column and dissimilar characteristics in a second column. Form a definition of *family* from the characteristics that interviewees shared in common.

2. Compile a list of television shows in which families of different configurations are portrayed (e.g., nuclear, one-parent, divorced, blended, cohabiting, adoption, foster, same-sex). How realistic are the families in these programs compared to the descriptions in this chapter?

3. Imagine for a moment that you are a 5-year-old child and someone knocks on the door of your parent's home and announces that you have ten minutes to pack up some clothing and a few of your favorite toys before they whisk you away. Shortly thereafter they drop you off at a stranger's home. Make a list of five or ten things that you would put in your suitcase. Write a brief story describing your reactions to being removed from your family and placed with a foster family. How might you have reacted initially, and how did you feel when the social worker left you with a new family? Read your stories aloud in class or post them on a discussion board. What did you learn from this activity—about yourself and about others?

REFERENCES

Adams, J., & Light, R. (2015). Scientific consensus, the law, and same sex parenting outcomes. *Social Science Research, 53*, 300–310.

Afifi, T., Taillieu, T., Cheung, K., Katz, L., Tonmy, L., & Sareen, J. (2015). Substantiated reports of child maltreatment from the Canadian Incidence Study of Reported Child Abuse and Neglect 2008: Examining child and household characteristics and child functional impairment. *Canadian Journal of Psychiatry, 60*(7), 315–323.

Alfano, C., Lau, S., Balderas, J., Bunnell, B., & Beidel, D. (2016). The impact of military deployment on children: Placing developmental risk in context. *Clinical Psychology Review, 43*, 17–29.

American Psychological Association (APA). (2016). Planning for remarriage. Retrieved January 31, 2016 from http://www.apa.org/helpcenter/stepfamily.aspx.

Ault, M., & Gilder, B. (2015). Polygamy in the United States: How marginalized religious communities cope with stigmatizing discourses surrounding plural marriage. *Journal of Intercultural Communication Research, 44*(4), 307–328.

Baiocco, R., Santamaria, F., Ioverno, S., Fontanesi, L., Baumgartner, E., Laghi, F., & Lingiardi, V. (2015). Lesbian mother families and gay father families in Italy: Family functioning, dyadic satisfaction, and child well-being. *Sexuality Research and Social Policy, 12*(3), 202–212.

Baker, C. (2016). Fathers' and mothers' language acculturation and parenting practices: Links to Mexican American children's academic readiness. *Journal of Early Childhood Research*. Published online before print January 13, 2016. doi:10.1177/1476718X15614044.

Bell, G., & Hastings, S. (2015). Exploring parental approval and disapproval for Black and White interracial couples. *Journal of Social Issues, 71*(4), 755–771.

Berger, L., Cancian, M., Han, E., Noyes, J., & Rios-Salas, V. (2015). Children's academic achievement and foster care. *Pediatrics, 135*(1), e109–116.

Berger, L., & McLanahan, S. (2015). Income, relationship quality, and parenting: Associations with child development in two-parent families. *Journal of Marriage and Family, 77*(4), 996–1015.

Bick, J., Zhu, T., Stamoulis, C., Fox, N., Zeanah, C., & Nelson, C. (2015). Effect of early institutionalization and foster care on long-term white matter development. A randomized clinical trial. *JAMA, 169*(3), 211–219.

Boivin, M., & Hassan, G. (2015). Ethnic identity and psychological adjustment in transracial adoptees: A review of the literature. *Ethnic and Racial Studies, 38*(7), 1084–1103.

Borja, S., Nurius, P., & Eddy, J. (2015). Adversity across the life course of incarcerated parents: Gender differences. *Journal of Forensic Social Work, 5*(1-3), 167–185.

Bos, H., van Gelderen, L., & Gartrell, N. (2015). Lesbian and heterosexual two-parent families: Adolescent-parent relationship quality and adolescent well-being. *Journal of Child and Family Studies, 24*(4), 1031–1046.

Boyle, C. (2015). What is the impact of birth family contact on children in adoption and long-term foster care? A systematic review. *Child & Family Social Work.* doi:10.1111/cfs.12236.

Brock, R., & Kochanska, G. (2015). Decline in the quality of family relationships predicts escalation in children's internalizing symptoms from middle to late childhood. *Journal of Abnormal Child Psychology, 43*(7), 1295–1308.

Canlas, J., Miller, R., Busby, D., & Carroll, J. (2015). Same-race and interracial Asian-White couples: Relational and social contexts and relationship outcomes. *Journal of Comparative Family Studies, 46*(3), 307–328.

Centers for Disease Control and Prevention (CDC). (2015). National marriage and divorce rate trends. National Center for Health Statistics. Retrieved December 6, 2015 from http://www.cdc.gov/nchs/nvss/marriage_divorce_tables.htm.

Chassamboulli, A., & Peri, G. (2015). The labor market effects of reducing the number of illegal immigrants. *Review of Economic Dynamics, 18*(4), 792–821.

Cherlin, A. (2014). First union patterns around the world: Introduction to the special issue. *Population Research and Policy Review, 33*(2), 153–159.

Child Trends and Social Trends Institute. (2015). *Mapping family change and child well-being outcomes.* World Family Map 2015. Retrieved on December 3, 2015 from http://worldfamilymap.ifstudies.org/2015/.

Child Welfare Information Gateway. (2016). Adoption. Retrieved on January 22, 2016 from http://www.childwelfare.gov/topics/adoption/.

Cochran, S., & Mays, V. (2015). Mortality risks among persons reporting same-sex sexual partners: Evidence from the 2008 General Social Survey—National Death Index Data Set. *American Journal of Public Health, 105*(2), 358–364.

Colby, S., & Ortman, J. (2015). Projections of the size and composition of the U.S. population: 2014-2060. Retrieved January 31, 2016 from http://www.census.gov/content/dam/Census/library/publications/2015/demo/p25-1143.pdf.

Coleman, K., & Wu, Q. (2016). Kinship care and service utilization: A review of predisposing, enabling, and need factors. *Children and Youth Series Review, 61*, 201–210.

Collins, S., & Llewellyn, G. (2012). Children of parents with intellectual disability: Facing poor outcomes or faring okay? *Journal of Intellectual and Developmental Disability, 37*(1), 65–82.

Colter, M., McLanahan, S., Notterman, D., Hobcraft, J., Brooks-Gunn, J., & Garfinkel, I. (2015). Family structure instability, genetic sensitivity, and child well-being. *American Journal of Sociology, 120*(4), 1195–1225.

Colton, T., Janzen, B., & Laverty, W. (2015). Family structure, social capital, and mental health disparities among Canadian mothers. *Public Health, 129*(6), 639–647.

Cooley, M., Farineau, H., & Mullis, A. (2015). Child behaviors as a moderator: Examining the relationship between foster parent supports, satisfaction, and intent to continue fostering. *Child Abuse & Neglect, 45*, 46–56.

Copen, C., Daniels, K., & Mosher, D. (2013). First premarital cohabitation in the United States: 2006-2010. *National Health Statistics Report, 64.* Retrieved on December 2, 2015 from http://www.cdc.gov/nchs/data/nhsr/nhsr064.pdf.

Cornelius, J., & Xiong, P. (2015). Generational differences in the sexual communication process of African American grandparent and parent caregivers of adolescents. *Journal of Specialists in Pediatric Nursing, 20*(3), 203–209.

Creech, S., Hadley, W., & Borsari, B. (2014). The impact of military deployment and reintegration on children and parenting: A systematic review. *Professional Psychology: Research & Practice, 45*(6), 452–464.

Crosnoe, R., Smith, C., & Leventhal, T. (2015). Family background, school-age trajectories of activity participation, and academic achievement at the start of high school. *Applied Developmental Science, 19*(3), 139–152.

Crouch, S., Waters, E., McNair, R., & Power, J. (2015). The health perspectives of Australian adolescents from same-sex parent families: A mixed methods study. *Child: Care, Health, and Development, 41*(3), 356–364.

Csizmadia, A., Rollins, A., & Kaneakua, J. (2014). Ethnic-racial socialization and its correlates in families of Black-White biracial children. *Family Relations*, *63*(2), 259–270.

Dallaire, D., Zeman, J., & Thrash, T. (2015). Children's experiences of maternal incarceration-specific risks: Predictions to psychological maladaptation. *Journal of Clinical Child & Adolescent Psychology*, *44*(1), 109–122.

Department of Defense. (2014). Demographics: Profile of the Military. Retrieved February 10, 2016 from http://download.militaryonesource.mil/12038/MOS/Reports/2014-Demographics-Report.pdf.

Derlan, L., & Umaña-Taylor, A. (2015). Brief report: Contextual predictors of African American adolescents' ethnic-racial identity affirmation-belonging and resistance to peer pressure. *Journal of Adolescence*, *41*, 1–6.

Desai, M., & Drake, P. (2015). Sexual activity and contraception use and attitudes among teen mothers. *Journal of Adolescent Health*, *56*(2), S40–S41.

Diamond, G., Senecky, Y., Reichman, H., Inbar, D., & Chodick, G. (2015). Parental perception of developmental vulnerability after inter-country adoption: A 10-year follow-up study: Longitudinal study after inter-country adoption. *International Journal on Disability and Human Development*, *14*(1), 75–80.

Diette, T., & Oyelere, R. (2014). Gender and race heterogeneity: The impact of students with limited English on native student's performance. *The American Economic Review*, *104*(5), 412–417.

Dillender, M. (2015). Health insurance and labor force participation: What legal recognition does for same-sex couples. *Contemporary Economic Policy*, *33*(2), 381–394.

Doley, R., Bell, R., Watt, B., & Simpson, H. (2015). Grandparents raising grandchildren: Investigating factors associated with distress among custodial grandparent. *Journal of Family Studies*, *21*(2), 101–119.

Downing, K. (2006). Next generation: What leaders need to know about millennials. *Leadership in Action*, *26*(3), 3–6.

Ellis, R., & Simmon, T. (2014). Population characteristics. Coresident grandparents and their grandchildren: 2012. U.S. Census Bureau. Retrieved January 30, 2016 from http://www.census.gov/content/dam/Census/library/publications/2014/demo/p20-576.pdf.

English, D., Thompson, R., & White, C. (2015). Predicting risk of entry into foster care from early childhood experiences: A survival analysis using LONGSCAN data. *Child Abuse & Neglect*, *45*, 57–67.

Erikson, E. (1959). *Identity and the life cycle*. New York: International Universities Press.

Farr, R., Crain, E., Oakley, M., Cashen, K., & Garber, K. (2015). Microaggressions, feelings of difference, and resilience among adopted children with sexual minority parents. *Journal of Youth and Adolescence*, *45*(1), 85–104.

Fedewa, A., Black, W., & Ahn, S. (2015). Children and adolescents with same-gender parents: A meta-analytic approach in assessing outcomes. *Journal of GLBT Family Studies*, *11*(1), 1–34.

Foli, K., Lim, E., South, S., & Sands, L. (2014). "Great expectations" of adoptive parents: Theory extension through structural equation modeling. *Nursing Research*, *63*(1), 14–25.

Forneris, T., Camiré, M., & Williamson, R. (2015). Extracurricular activity participation and the acquisition of developmental assets: Differences between involved and noninvolved Canadian high school students. *Applied Developmental Science*, *19*(1), 47–55.

Fredericks, F., & Greeff, A. (2015). Own and perceived parental religiosity and the quality of the parent-child relationship. *Journal of Beliefs & Values: Studies in Religion & Education*, *36*(2), 252–258.

Frey, W. (2014). *Multiracial marriage on the rise*. Diversity Explosion Series, No. 2. Washington, DC: Brookings Institute.

Gaither, S. (2015). "Mixed" results. Multiracial research and identity explorations. *Current Directions in Psychological Science*, *24*(2), 114–119.

Ganchimeg, T., Ota, E., Morisaki, N., Laopaiboon, M., Lumbiganon, P., Zhang, J., . . . & Mori, R. (2014). Pregnancy and childbirth outcomes among adolescent mothers: A World Health Organization multicountry study. *BJOG: An International Journal of Obstetrics & Gynaecology*, *121*(S1), 40–48.

Garcia-Reid, P., Peterson, C., & Reid, R. (2015). Parent and teacher support among Latino immigrant youth. Effects on school engagement and school trouble avoidance. *Education and Urban Society*, *47*(3), 328–343.

Garwood, S., Gerassi, L., Jonson-Reid, M., Plax, K., & Drake, B. (2015). More than poverty: The effect of child abuse and neglect on teen pregnancy risk. *Journal of Adolescent Health*, *57*(2), 164–168.

Gates, G. (2015). Marriage and family: LGBT individuals and same-sex couples. *The Future of Children, 25*(2), 67–87.

Gates, G. (2013). LGBT parenting in the United States. Retrieved on February 5, 2016 from http://williamsinstitute.law.ucla.edu/wp-content/uploads/LGBT-Parenting.pdf.

Geiger, J., Hayes, M., & Lietz, C. (2014). Providing foster care for adolescents: Barriers and opportunities. *Child and Youth Services Review, 35*(3), 237–254.

Geiger, J., Hayes, M., & Lietz, C. (2013). Should I stay or should I go? A mixed methods study examining the factors influencing foster parents' decisions to continue or discontinue providing foster care. *Child and Youth Services Review, 35*(9), 1356–1365.

George, M. (2016). Agency nullification: Defying bans on gay and lesbian foster and adoptive parents. *Harvard Civil Rights-Civil Liberties Law Review* (CR-CL), *51*(2), 1–56. Columbia Public Law Research Paper No. 14–487.

Goforth, A., Pham, A., & Oka, E. (2015). Parent-child conflict, acculturation gap, acculturation stress, and behavior problems in Arab American adolescents. *Journal of Cross-Cultural Psychology, 46*(6), 821–836.

Goldberg, J., & Carlson, M. (2014). Parents' relationship quality and children's behavior in stable married and cohabiting families. *Journal of Marriage and Family, 76*(4), 762–777.

Goldberg, A., Moyer, A., & Kinkler, L. (2013). Lesbian, gay, and heterosexual adoptive parents' perceptions of parental bonding during early parenthood. *Couple and Family Psychology: Research and Practice, 2*(2), 146–162.

Goldhaber, D., Lavery, L., & Theobald, R. (2015). Uneven playing field? Assessing the teacher quality gap between advantaged and disadvantaged students. *Educational Researcher, 44*(5), 293–307.

Gong, X., Marchant, G., & Cheng, Y. (2015). Family factors and immigrant students' academic achievement: An Asian and Hispanic comparison study. *Asian Education and Development Studies, 4*(4), 448–459.

Goodman, C. (2012). Caregiving grandmothers and their grandchildren: Well-being nine years later. *Children and Youth Services Review, 34*(4), 648–654.

Granero, R., Louwaars, L., & Ezpeleta, L. (2015). Socioeconomic status and oppositional defiant disorder in preschoolers: Parenting practices and executive functioning as mediating variables. *Frontiers in Psychology, 6*, 1412. http://doi.org/10.3389/fpsyg.2015.01412.

Guan, Z., Wu, F., Roka, F., & Whidden, A. (2015). Agriculture labor and immigration reform. *CHOICES, 30*(4). Retrieved February 15, 2016 from http://www.choicesmagazine.org/UserFiles/file/cmsarticle_476.pdf.

Harf, A., Skandrani, S., Sibeoni, J., Pontvert, C., Revah-Levy, A., & Moro, M. (2015). Cultural identity and internationally adopted children: Qualitative approach to parental representations. *PLoS ONE 10*(3): e0119635. doi: 10.1371/journal.pone.0119635.

Hayslip, B., Blumenthal, H., & Garner, A. (2015). Social support and grandparent caregiver health: One-year longitudinal findings for grandparents raising their grandchildren. *The Journals of Gerontology, Series B, 70*(5), 804–812.

Healy, K., Sanders, M., & Iyer, A. (2015). Facilitative parenting and children's social, emotional and behavioral adjustment. *Journal of Child and Family Studies, 24*(6), 1762–1779.

Hill, K., & Moore, F. (2015). The postadoption needs of adoptive parents of children with disabilities. *Journal of Family Social Work, 18*(3), 164–182.

Hindmarsh, G., Llewellyn, G., & Emerson, E. (2015). Mothers with intellectual impairment and their 9-month-old infants. *Journal of Intellectual Disability Research, 59*(6), 541–550.

Hong, G., & McLaren, J. (2015). Are immigrants a shot in the arm for the local economy? The National Bureau of Economic Research. NBER Working Paper No. 21123.

Horton, A., & Watson, J. (2015). African American disproportionate overrepresentation in the Illinois child welfare systems. *Race, Gender & Class, 22*(1/2), 65–76.

Ibañez, G., Dillon, F., Sanchez, M., de la Rosa, M., Tan, L., & Villar, M. (2015). Changes in family cohesion and acculturative stress among recent Latino immigrants. *Journal of Ethnic and Cultural Diversity in Social Work, 24*(3), 219–234.

Ickowitz, A., & Mohanty, L. (2015). Why would she? Polygyny and women's welfare in Ghana. *Feminist Economics, 21*(2), 77–104.

Iezzoni, L., Wint, A., Smeltzer, S., & Ecker, J. (2015). Physical accessibility of routine prenatal care for women with mobility disability. *Journal of Women's Health, 24*(12), 1006–1012.

Inman, A., Tummala-Narra, P., Kaduvettoor-Davidson, A., Alvarez, A., & Yeh, C. (2015). Perceptions of race-based discrimination among first-generation Asian Indians in the United States. *The Counseling Psychologist, 43*(2), 217–247.

Jacobsen, H., Ivarsson, T., Wentzel-Larsen, T., Smith, L., & Moe, V. (2014). Attachment security in young foster children: Continuity from 2 to 3 years of age. *Attachment & Human Development, 16*(1), 42–57.

Jeha, D., Usta, I., Ghulmiyyah, L., & Nassar, A. (2015). A review of the risks and consequences of adolescent pregnancy. *Journal of Neonatal-Perinatal Medicine*, *8*(1), 1–8.

Jensen, T., Shafer, K., & Holmes, E. (2015). Transitioning to stepfamily life: The influence of closeness with biological parents and stepparents on children's stress. *Child and Family Social Work*. Online before print. doi: 10.1111/cfs.12237.

Jones, L. (2015). "Was taking me out of the home necessary?" Perspectives of foster youth on the necessity for removal. *Families in Society: The Journal of Contemporary Social Service*, *96*(2), 108–115.

Jorgensen, B., Mancini, J., Yorgason, J., & Day, R. (2015). Religious beliefs, practices, and family strengths: A comparison of husbands and wives. *Psychology of Religion and Spirituality*, *8*(2), 164–174.

Kawabata, Y., & Crick, N. (2015). Direct and interactive links between cross-ethnic friendships and peer rejection, internalizing symptoms, and academic engagement among ethnically diverse children. *Cultural Diversity and Ethnic Minority Psychology, 21*(2), 191–200.

Kellas, J., Baxter, L., LeClair-Underberg, C., Thatcher, M., Routsong, T., Normand, E., & Braithwaite, D. (2015). Telling the story of stepfamily beginnings: The relationship between young-adult stepchildren's stepfamily origin stories and their satisfaction with the stepfamily. *Journal of Family Communication, 14*(2), 149–166.

Kelly, P., Polanin, J., Jang, S., & Johnson, B. (2015). Religion, delinquency, and drug use: A meta-analysis. *Criminal Justice Review, 40*(4), 505–523.

Kerker, B., Zhang, J., Nadeem, E., Stein, R., Hurlburt, M., Heneghan, A., ... & Horwitz, S. (2015). Adverse childhood experiences and mental health, chronic medical conditions, and development in young children. *Academic Pediatrics, 15*(5), 510–517.

Kids Count Data Center. (2015). Children in single-parent families. Retrieved December 7, 2015 from http://datacenter.kidscount.org/data#USA/1/23/2488,24,2592,26,2721.

Kim, S., & Kochanska, G. (2015). Mothers' power assertion; children's negative, adversarial orientation; and future behavior problems in low-income families: Early maternal responsiveness as a moderator of the developmental cascade. *Journal of Family Psychology, 29*(1), 1–9.

King, V., Amato, P., Lindstrom, R. (2015). Stepfather-adolescent relationship quality during the first year of transitioning to a stepfamily. *Journal of Marriage and Family, 77*(5), 1179–1189.

Kreider, R., & Lofquist, D. (2014). Adopted children and stepchildren: 2010. U.S. Department of Health and Human Services. (2015). *The AFCARS Report*. Administration for Children and Families, Administration on Children, Youth and Families, Children's Bureau. Retrieved January 22, 2016 from http://www.acf.hhs.gov/programs/cb.

Krogstad, J., & Passe, J. (2015). 5 facts about illegal immigration in the U.S. Pew Research Center. Retrieved February 15, 2016 from http://www.pewresearch.org/fact-tank/2015/11/19/5-facts-about-illegal-immigration-in-the-u-s/.

Krueger, P., Jutte, D., Franzini, L., Elo, I., & Hayward, M. (2015). Family structure and multiple domains of child well-being in the United States: A cross-sectional study. *Population Health Metrics, 13*(6). doi: 10.1186/s12963-015-0038-0.

Kshipra, V. (2015). Perceived parenting: A correlate of mental health and social maturity among adolescents. *Journal of Psychosocial Research, 10*(1), 55–64.

Lancy, D. F. (2014). "Babies aren't persons": A survey of delayed personhood. In H. Keller & O. Hiltrud (Eds.). *Different faces of attachment: Cultural variations of a universal human need,* (pp. 66–109). Cambridge, England: Cambridge University Press.

Lanier, P., Maguire-Jack, K., Walsh, T., Drake, B., & Hubel, G. (2015). Race and ethnic differences in early childhood maltreatment in the United States. *Journal of Developmental & Behavioral Pediatrics, 35*(7), 419–426.

Leslie, L., & Young, J. (2015). Interracial couples in therapy: Common themes and issues. *Journal of Social Issues, 71*(4), 788–803.

Lester, P., Liang, L., Milburn, N., Mogil, C., Woodward, K., Nash, W., ... & Saltzman, W. (2016). Evaluation of a family-centered preventive intervention for military families: Parent and child longitudinal outcomes. *Journal of the American Academy of Child & Adolescent Psychiatry, 55*(1), 14–24.

Llewellyn, G. (2013). Parents with intellectual disability and their children: Advances in policy and practice. *Journal of Policy and Practice in Intellectual Disabilities, 10*(2), 82–85.

Lightfoot, E., & DeZelar, S. (2015). The experiences and outcomes of children in foster care who were removed because of a parental disability. *Children and Youth Services Review, 62*, 22–28.

Lo, A., Roben, C., Maier, C., Fabian, K., Shauffer, C., & Dozier, M. (2015). "I want to be there when he graduates:" Foster parents show higher levels of commitment than group care providers. *Children and Youth Services Review, 51*, 95–100.

Lofquist, D. (2011). Same-sex couple households. American Community Survey briefs. Retrieved on February 5, 2016 from http://www.census.gov/prod/2011pubs/acsbr10-03.pdf.

Lui, P. (2015). Intergenerational cultural conflict, mental health, and educational outcomes among Asian and Latino/a Americans: Qualitative and meta-analytic review. *Psychological Bulletin, 141*(2), 404–446.

Luo, R., & Tamis-LeMonda, C. (2016). Mothers' verbal and nonverbal strategies in relation to infants' object-directed actions in real time and across the first three years in ethnically diverse families. *Infancy, 21*(1), 65–89.

MacPhee, D., Lunkenheimer, E., & Riggs, N. (2015). Resilience as regulation of developmental and family processes. *Family Relations, 64*(1), 153–175.

Madzwamuse, S., Baumann, N., Jaekel, J., Bartmann, P., & Wolke, D. (2015). Neuro-cognitive performance of very preterm or very low birth weight adults at 26 years. *Journal of Child Psychology and Psychiatry, 56*(8), 857–864.

Manning, W. (2015a). Cohabitation and child wellbeing. *The Future of Children, 25*(2), 51–66.

Manning, W. (2015b). Remarriage in the United States: If at first they don't succeed, do most Americans "Try, try again?" A briefing paper prepared for the Council on Contemporary Families. Retrieved January 30, 2016 from http://contemporaryfamilies.org/remarriage-brief-report/.

Manning, W., Brown, S., & Stykes, J. (2015). Family complexity among children in the United States. *The ANNALS of the American Academy of Political and Social Science, 654*(1), 48–65.

Manning, W., Fettro, M., & Lamidi, E. (2014). Child well-being in same-sex parent families: Review of research prepared for American Sociological Association Amicus Brief. *Population Research & Policy Review, 33*(4), 485–502.

Mariscal, E., Akin, B., Lieberman, A., & Washington, D. (2015). Exploring the path from foster care to stable and lasting adoption: Perceptions of foster care alumni. *Child and Youth Services Review, 55*, 111–120.

Masten, A., & Monn, A. (2015). Child and family resilience: A call for integrated science, practice, and professional training. *Family Relations, 64*(1), 5–21.

Mazzucato, V., Schans, D., Caarls, K., & Beauchemin, C. (2015). Transnational families between Africa and Europe. *International Migration Review, 49*(1), 142–172.

Mennen, F. (1988). The relationship of race, socioeconomic status, and marital status to kin networks. *The Journal of Sociology and Social Welfare, 15*(4), Article 6. Available at http://scholarworks.wmich.edu/jssw/vol15/iss4/6.

Meppelder, M., Hodes, M., Kef, S., & Schuengel, C. (2015). Parenting stress and child behaviour problems among parents with intellectual disabilities: The buffering role of resources. *Journal of Intellectual Disability Research, 59*(7), 664–677.

Meyer, M., & Abdul-Malak, Y. (2015). Single-headed family economic vulnerability and reliance on social programs. *Public Policy & Aging Report, 25*(3), 102–106.

Migration Policy Institute. (2015). Frequently requested statistics on immigrants and immigration in the United States. Retrieved February 15, 2016 from http://www.migrationpolicy.org/article/frequently-requested-statistics-immigrants-and-immigration-united-states.

Miller, H., & Barnes, J. (2015). The association between parental incarceration and health, education, and economic outcomes in young adulthood. *American Journal of Criminal Justice, 40*, 765–784.

Mintz, S., & Kellogg, S. (1988). *Domestic revolutions: A social history of American family life.* New York: Free Press.

Mitchell, K., Tynes, B., Umaña-Taylor, A., & Williams, D. (2015). Cumulative experiences with life adversity: Identifying critical levels for targeting prevention efforts. *Journal of Adolescence, 43*, 63–71.

Mkhize, Z., & Nompumelelo, Z. (2015). Enlightened women and polygamy: Voices and perspectives from within. *Indilinga African Journal of Indigenous Knowledge Systems, 14*(1), 118–129.

Moeller, J., Culler, E., Hamilton, M., Aronson, K., & Perkins, D. (2015). The effects of military-connected parental absence on the behavioural and academic functioning of children: A literature review. *Journal of Children's Services, 10*(3), 291–306.

Morbidity and Mortality Weekly Report (MMWR). (2015). Vital Signs: Trends in use of long-acting reversible contraception among teens aged 15–19 Years seeking contraceptive services—United States, 2005–2013. *MMWR, 64*(13), 363–369.

Moyer, A., & Goldberg, A. (2015). 'We were not planning on this, but …': Adoptive parents' reactions and adaptations to unmet expectations. *Child & Family Social Work*. Online before print. doi: 10.1111/cfs.12219.

Murphey, D., & Cooper, P. (2015). Parents behind bars. Retrieved January 31, 2016 from http://www.childtrends.org/wp-content/uploads/2015/10/2015-42ParentsBehindBars.pdf.

Musick, K., & Michelmore, K. (2015). Change in the stability of marital and cohabitating unions following the birth of a child. *Demography, 52*(5), 1463–1485.

Mustillo, S., Wadsworth, S., & Lester, P. (2015). Parental deployment and well-being in children. *Journal of Emotional and Behavioral Disorders*. doi: 10.1177/1063426615598766.

Myers, S., & Myers, C. (2014). Family structure and school-based parental involvement: A family resource perspective. *Journal of Family and Economic Issues, 36*(1), 114–131.

National Council on Disability. (2012). Rocking the cradle: Ensuring the rights of parents with disabilities and their children. Retrieved January 31, 2016 from http://www.ncd.gov/publications /2012/Sep272012.

Norbury, C., Gooch, D., Baird, G., Charman, T., Simonoff, E., & Pickles, A. (2016). Younger children experience lower levels of language competence and academic progress in the first year of school: Evidence from a population study. *Journal of Child Psychology and Psychiatry, 57*(1), 65–73.

Oberoi, A., Balcazar, F., Suarez-Balacazar, Y., Fredrik, F., Langi, G., & Lukyanova, V. (2015). Employment outcomes among African American and White women with disabilities: Examining the inequalities. *Women, Gender, and Families of Color, 3*(2), 144–164.

Pace, G., Shafer, K., Jensen, T., & Larson, J., (2015). Stepparenting issues and relationship quality: The role of clear communication. *Journal of Social Work, 15*(1), 24–44.

Park, H., & Lau, A. (2016). Socioeconomic status and parenting priorities: Child independence and obedience around the world. *Journal of Marriage and Family, 78*(1), 43–59.

Pears, K., Kim, H., Buchanan, R., & Fisher, P. (2015). Adverse consequences of school mobility for maltreated children in foster care: A prospective longitudinal study. *Child Development, 86*(4), 1210–1226.

Perrin, E., & Siegel, B. (2013). *Promoting the well-being of children whose parents are gay or lesbian*. American Academy of Pediatrics. Tufts University, Boston Medical Center, Committee on Psychosocial Aspects of Child and Family Health. Technical Report. *Pediatrics, 131*(4): e1374–e1383.

Pew Research Center. (2015). America's changing religious landscape. Retrieved January 31, 2016 from http://www.pewforum.org/2015/05/12/americas-changing-religious-landscape/.

Pew Research Center. (2014). Millennials in adulthood. Retrieved November 17, 2015 from http://www.pewsocialtrends.org/2014/03/07/millennials-in-adulthood/.

Plant, R. (2010). *Mom: The transformation of motherhood in modern America*. Chicago, IL: University of Chicago Press.

Pollock, E., Kazman, J., & Deuster, P. (2015). Family functioning and stress in African American families. *Journal of Black Psychology, 41*(2), 144–169.

Poortman, A., & Hewitt, B. (2015). Gender differences in relationship preferences after union dissolution. *Advances in Life Course Research, 26*, 11–21.

Potochnick, S., & Mooney, M. (2015). The decade of immigrant dispersion and growth: A cohort analysis of children of immigrants' educational experiences 1990-2002. *International Migration Review, 49*(4), 1001–1041.

Power, J., Schofield, M., Farchione, D., Perlesz, A., McNair, R., Brown, R., … & Bickerdike, A. (2015). Psychological wellbeing among same-sex attracted and heterosexual parents: Role of connectedness to family and friendship networks. *Australian and New Zealand Journal of Family Therapy, 36*(3), 380–394.

Prickett, K., Martin-Storey, A., & Crosnoe, R. (2015). A research note on time with children in different- and same-sex two-parent families. *Demography, 59*(3), 905–918.

Rabuy, B., & Kopf, D. (2015). Separation by bars and miles: Visitation in state prisons. Retrieved January 30, 2016 from http://www.prisonpolicy.org/reports/prisonvisits.html.

Reed, S., Bell, J., & Edwards, T. (2011). Adolescent well-being in Washington State military families. *American Journal of Public Health, 101*(9), 1676–1682.

Rodriguez, A., & Margolin, G. (2015). Military service absences and family members' mental health: A timeline followback assessment. *Journal of Family Psychology, 29*(4), 642–648.

Rosenthal, L., & Stark, T. (2015). Relationship stigma and relationship outcomes in interracial and same-sex relationships: Examination of sources and buffers. *Journal of Family Psychology, 29*(6), 818–830.

Ross, A., & Rouse, S. (2015). Economic uncertainty, job threat, and the resiliency of the Millennial generation's attitudes toward immigration. *Social Science Quarterly, 96*(5), 1363–1379.

Roxburgh, S., & MacArthur, K. (2014). Childhood adversity and adult depression among the incarcerated: Differential exposure and vulnerability by race/ethnicity and gender. *Child Abuse & Neglect, 38*(8), 1409–1420.

Ryan, R., Claessens, A., & Markowitz, A. (2015). Associations between family structure and change and child behavior. *Child Development, 86*(1), 112–127.

Salas-Wright, C., Vaughn, M., Ugalde, J., & Todic, J. (2015). Substance use and teen pregnancy in the United States: Evidence from the NSDUH 2002–2012. *Addictive Behaviors, 45,* 218–225.

Sasnett, S. (2015). Are the kids all right? A qualitative study of adults with gay and lesbian parents. *Journal of Contemporary Ethnography, 44,* 196–222.

Schmeer, K., Piperata, B., Rodriguez, A., Torres, V., & Cardenas, F. (2015). Maternal resources and household food security: Evidence from Nicaragua. *Public Health Nutrition, 18*(16), 2915–2924.

Schmitt, S., McClelland, M., Tominey, S., & Acock, A. (2015). Strengthening school readiness for Head Start children: Evaluation of a self-regulation intervention. *Early Childhood Research Quarterly, 30*(Part A), 20–31.

Sears, M., Repetti, R., Reynolds, B., Robles, T., & Krull, J. (2016). Spillover in the home: The effects of family conflict on parents' behavior. *Journal of Marriage and Family, 78*(1), 127–141.

Secor-Turner, M., Griese, E., Baete, D., Kenyon, D., & Randall, B. (2015). Sexual risk behavior among frontier adolescents: Profiles of pregnancy risk and protection. *Health Behavior and Policy Review, 2*(2), 144–153(10).

Seshadri, G., & Knudson-Martin, C. (2013). How couples manage interracial and intercultural differences: Implications for clinical practice. *Journal of Marital and Family Therapy, 39*(1), 2013.

Shaw, T., Bright, C., & Sharpe, T. (2015). Child welfare outcomes for youth in care as a result of parental death or parental incarceration. *Child Abuse & Neglect, 42,* 112–120.

Sirin, S., Rogers-Sirin, L., Cressen, J., Gupta, T., Ahmed, S., & Novoa, A. (2015). Discrimination-related stress effects on the development of internalizing symptoms among Latino adolescents. *Child Development, 86,* 709–725.

Slopen, N., Shonkoff, J., Albert, M., Yoshikawa, H., Jacobs, A., Stoltz, R., & Williams, D. (2016). Racial disparities in child adversity in the U.S.: Interactions with family immigration history and income. *American Journal of Preventive Medicine, 50*(1), 47–56.

Smith, G., Cichy, K., & Montoro-Rodriguez, J. (2015). Impact of coping resources on the well-being of custodial grandmothers and grandchildren. *Family Relations, 64*(3), 378–392.

Smokowski, P., Bacallao, M., Cotter, K., & Evans, C. (2015). The effects of positive and negative parenting practices on adolescent mental health outcomes in a multicultural sample of rural youth. *Child Psychiatry & Human Development, 46*(3), 333–345.

Statistics Canada. (2011). Census family. Retrieved November 16, 2015 from http://www12 .statcan.gc.ca/census-recensement/2011/ref/dict/fam004-eng.cfm.

Stavrova, O., & Fetchenhauer, D. (2015). Single parents, unhappy parents? Parenthood, partnership, and the cultural normative context. *Journal of Cross-Cultural Psychology, 46*(1), 1134–1149.

Stevens, K. (2012). *Current demographics of parents with disabilities in the U.S.* Berkeley, CA: Through the Looking Glass.

Szilagyi, M., Rosen, D., Rubin, D., & Zlotnik, S. (2015). Health care issues for children and adolescents in foster care and kinship care. *Pediatrics, 136*(4), e1142–e1166.

Taylor, C., Ross, M., Wood, J., Griffis, H., Harb, G., Mi, L., … & Rubin, D. (2016). Differential child maltreatment risk across deployment periods of US Army soldiers. *American Journal of Public Health,106*(1), 153–158.

Thakur, A., Creedon, J., & Zeanah, C. (2016). Trauma- and stressor-related disorders among children and adolescents. *Psychiatric Treatment of Children and Adolescents, 14*(1), 34–45.

The National Campaign to Prevent Teen and Unplanned Pregnancy. (2016). Counting it up: The public costs of teen childbearing. Retrieved January 28, 2016 from http:// thenationalcampaign.org/why-it-matters/public-cost.

Tornello, S., Kruczkowski, S., & Patterson, C. (2015). Division of labor and relationship quality among male same-sex couples who became fathers via surrogacy. *Journal of GLBT Family Studies, 11*(4), 375–394.

Tschan, T., Schmid, M., & In-Albon, T. (2015). Parenting behavior in families of female adolescents with nonsuicidal self-injury in comparison to a clinical and a nonclinical control group. *Child and Adolescent Psychiatry and Mental Health, 9*(17). doi.org/10.1186/ s13034-015-0051-x.

Tsui-Sui, A., & Salerno, J. (2014). Keeping adolescents busy with extracurricular activities. *Journal of School Nursing, 30*(1), 57–67.

Turney, K. (2015). Hopelessly devoted? Relationship quality during and after incarceration. *Journal of Marriage and Family, 77*(2), 480–495.

Turney, K., & Haskins, A. (2014). Falling behind? Children's early grade retention after paternal incarceration. *Sociology of Education, 87*(4), 241–258.

Turney, K., & Wildeman, C. (2013). Explaining the countervailing consequences of paternal incarceration for parenting. *American Sociological Review, 78*(6), 949–979.

Urick, M., & Limb, G. (2015). The quality of residential parent-child relationships and its impact on stepfamily experiences. *Journal of Sociology and Social Work, 3*(1), 27–33.

U.S. Bureau of Labor Statistics. (2015). Women in the labor force: A databook. Retrieved February 6, 2016 from http://www.bls.gov/opub/reports/cps/women-in-the-labor-force-a-databook-2015.pdf.

U.S. Census Bureau. (2014a). 2014 American community survey. Retrieved December 3, 2015 from http://www.census.gov/hhes/socdemo/marriage/data/acs/ElliottetalPAA2012figs.pdf.

U.S. Census Bureau. (2014b). Family and living arrangements 2014. Retrieved January 15, 2016 from http://www.census.gov/hhes/families/data/cps2014FG.html.

U.S. Census Bureau. (2014c). 2014 National population projections. Retrieved April 14, 2016 from http://www.census.gov/population/projections/data/national/2014.html.

U.S. Census Bureau. (2015a). America's families and living arrangements: 2015: Family households (F table series). Retrieved December 10, 2015 from http://www.census.gov/hhes/families/data/cps2015F.html.

U.S. Census Bureau. (2015b). Current population survey. Retrieved April 14, 2016 from https://www.census.gov/programs-surveys/cps/technical-documentation/subject-definitions.html#family.

U.S. Department of Health and Human Services, Administration for Children and Families, Youth and Families, Children's Bureau. (2015). AFCARS report 2014. Retrieved from http://www.acf.hhs.gov/sites/default/files/cb/afcarsreport22.pdf.

U.S. Department of Veterans Affairs. (2015). Symptoms of PTSD. Retrieved January 30, 2016 from http://www.ptsd.va.gov/public/PTSD-overview/basics/symptoms_of_ptsd.asp.

U.S. State Department. (2015). FY 2014 Annual report on intercountry adoption. Retrieved January 22, 2016 from http://travel.state.gov/content/dam/aa/pdfs/fy2014_annual_report.pdf.

U.S. Supreme Court. (2015). Obergefell et al. v. Hodges, Director, Ohio Department of Health, et al. Retrieved on April 14, 2016 from http://www.supremecourt.gov/opinions/14pdf/14-556_3204.pdf.

Vaske, J., Newsome, J., Boisvert, D., Piquero, A., Paradis, A., & Buka, S. (2015). The impact of low birth weight and maternal age on adulthood offending. *Journal of Criminal Justice, 43*(1), 49–56.

Wang, W. (2015). Interracial marriage: Who is "Marrying out". Washington, DC: Pew Research Center. Retrieved April 15, 2016 from http://www.pewresearch.org/fact-tank/2015/06/12/interracialmarriage-who-is-marrying-out.

Wang, L., Ponte, I., & Ollen, E. (2015). Letting her go: Western adoptive families' search and reunion with Chinese birth parents. *Adoption Quarterly, 18*(1), 45–66.

Weiber, I., Tengland, P., Berglund, J., & Eklund, M. (2014). Social and healthcare professionals' experiences giving support to families where the mother has an intellectual disability: Focus on children. *Journal of Policy and Practice in Intellectual Disabilities, 11*(4), 293–301.

Wheeler, L., Updegraff, K., & Crouter, A. (2015). Mexican-origin parents' work conditions and adolescents' adjustment. *Journal of Family Psychology, 29*(3), 447–457.

Will, J., Whalen, M., & Loper, A. (2014). From one generation to the next: Childhood experiences of antisocial behavior and parental incarceration among adult inmates. *Journal of Offender Rehabilitation, 53*(3), 190–210.

Wu, Z., Schimmele, C., & Ouellet, N. (2015). Repartnering after widowhood. *The Journals of Gerontology, 70*(3), 496–507.

Yazykova, E., & McLeigh, J. (2015). Millennial children of immigrant parents: Transnationalism, disparities, policy, and potential. *American Journal of Orthopsychiatry, 85*(5), S38–S44.

Zaccagnino, M., Cussino, M., Preziosa, A., Veglia, F., & Carassa, A. (2015). Attachment representation in institutionalized children: A preliminary study using the child attachment interview. *Clinical Psychology & Psychotherapy, 22*(2), 165–175.

Zeanah, C., & Gleason, M. (2015). Annual research review: Attachment disorders in early childhood–clinical presentation, causes, correlates, and treatment. *Journal of Child Psychology and Psychiatry, 56*(3), 207–222.

Zigler, K., & Camarota, S. (2015). U.S. immigrant population hits record 42.4 million in 2014. Center for Immigration Studies. Retrieved on January 31, 2016 from http://cis.org/us-immigrant-pop-hit-record-42-million-2014.

Understanding, Supporting, and Collaborating with Families

3

LEARNING OBJECTIVES

After reading the chapter, you will be able to:

3-1 Define family-school partnerships, describe two benefits of partnering with families, and list three variables that influence the level of partnerships with families.

3-2 Identify the components necessary for establishing positive, collaborative relationships between professionals and parents.

3-3 Describe three strategies that foster open and effective communication with families.

naeyc Standards Linked to Chapter Content

2a, 2b, and 2c: Building family and community relationships

3d: Observing, documenting, and assessing to support young children and families

4a and 4d: Using developmentally effective approaches to connect with children and families

Parents serve many roles—provider, caregiver, motivator, and most importantly, children's first and most valuable teachers. They also have unique knowledge about their children's likes, dislikes, strengths, limitations, and needs. Although families are expected to assume primary

continued on following page

responsibility for raising their children, other individuals will also influence and help to shape the person a child ultimately becomes. The adage *"It takes a village to raise a child"* conveys a powerful message of philosophical and practical importance. The phrase reflects the responsibility that professionals (e.g., teachers, health care providers, counselors, social workers) have to engage, support, and join with families to enhance child outcomes. ■

3-1 Partnering with Families

When children transition to child care, formal schooling, or begin new services, parents may find it difficult to accept and make the adjustment. They may feel a loss of control by entrusting their child's care and education to other adults (Welchons & McIntyre, 2015). Although professionals and parents have traditionally maintained separate responsibilities in children's upbringing, many contemporary professionals have undertaken an expanded role. For example, although teachers' focus remains on academics, it also now includes the promotion of children's health and development and provision of support for families. When professionals work collaboratively with families, they can help to alleviate some parental concerns and improve the consistency of goals, practices, and expectations between settings.

Most parents want some degree of involvement in their child's education, therapy, child care, and other intervention services. However, challenges such as impoverishment, language differences, or parents' uncertainty about the role they should play may limit their participation. For this reason, professionals should take the initiative to reach out, invite, and empower all families, especially those of diverse backgrounds, to become active partners in their children's education and treatment. Organizations serving children can establish a collaborative framework by creating a welcoming atmosphere and providing opportunities that encourage all families to be involved. Although the language used in this chapter often refers to family-school partnerships, the concepts and principles involved can be extended to other professionals such as early interventionists, therapists, social workers, child advocates, and staff working in community organizations.

3-1a What are Family-School Partnerships?

Historically, parents have always played an important role in educating their children (see Figure 3-1). However, schools have not always welcomed parents' participation in children's educational activities. When they did solicit parents' help, it typically involved volunteering in the classroom, assisting with fundraising activities, bringing treats for class parties, attending parent conferences, or accompanying children on field trips. Although these are beneficial activities, they tend to minimize parent input and provide negligible educational support for individual children. They also prevent parents who work or have other daytime constraints from participating because the activities often take place during school hours. As a result, teachers could easily conclude that families who do not participate in school activities do not value their child's education which, in turn, could have a negative effect on parent-teacher relationships.

More recently, researchers and professional organizations have challenged educators to move beyond simply involving parents in limited or sporadic activities and to instead create authentic family-school partnerships. This step requires educators to establish a relational process with family members who share information, values,

Figure 3-1 Family-School Partnerships: Historical Developments in North America

Parents have always played an important role in educating children, but the nature of their involvement in public school education programs has been varied.

- 1600s–1800s—families were instructed by their church to serve as children's primary educators.

- 1852—Massachusetts passes the first compulsory school attendance law. Children 8–14 years of age were required to attend school a minimum of 3 months per year; 6 of the 12 weeks had to be consecutive.

- 1890s—parents participated in organizations that focused on school improvement (e.g., better sanitation, serving school meals, creating playgrounds).

- 1897—National Congress of Mothers is established; it was later renamed Parent Teacher Association (PTA).

- 1926—National Congress of Colored Parents and Teachers (NCCPT) is formed; it would merge with the PTA in 1970.

- 1930s—school-community relationships became more important; schools were used for neighborhood gatherings, recreational activities, and parent meetings with teachers.

- 1945–1950s—parent involvement declined as schools assumed full responsibility for children's education.

- 1960s—families demanded that schools become more aware and responsive to issues of cultural diversity.

- 1965–1970s—legislation mandates parent involvement in Head Start, Follow Through, and special education programs. Federal funding expanded for parent training programs. Parents are increasingly being used as volunteers and paraprofessionals in classrooms.

- 1980s—federal legislation (Elementary and Secondary Education Act) (ESEA) mandates that parents be included on Title 1 advisory boards and councils that make curriculum decisions. Increased attention is drawn to the influence of children's home environment on academic success and the need for parent training.

- 1994—the Goals 2000: Educate America Act is passed and requires schools to partner with families and communities. Researchers study and develop new parent involvement models.

- 2002—the No Child Left Behind Act is signed into law. It requires schools to expand families' involvement and engagement in children's education.

- 2015—the Every Student Succeeds Act (ESSA) was signed into law, and expands the nation's commitment to assuring equal educational opportunity for all students, and preparing them to succeed in college and careers.

---

expertise, and goals with one another and assume mutual responsibility for supporting student learning and success (Haines et al., 2015; Watson & Bogotch, 2015). All parties within a partnership are viewed as equal contributors to the development and implementation of plans that will help students succeed. The establishment of strong family-school partnerships is considered a mark of a quality educational program and a commitment to meeting the needs of all students (Haines et al., 2015; DEC, 2014).

Successful partnerships are built on a platform of effective communication, trust, and a mutual understanding of the positive outcomes that result from family-school collaboration. They take time to develop, and require effort and cooperation on the part of all stakeholders involved. The process of forming a partnership must be individualized and take into account the family's unique strengths and needs. Studies have also shown that family-school partnerships are more likely to be established and persist when parents become involved during children's early school years.

Figure 3-2 Positive Outcomes of Parent Involvement

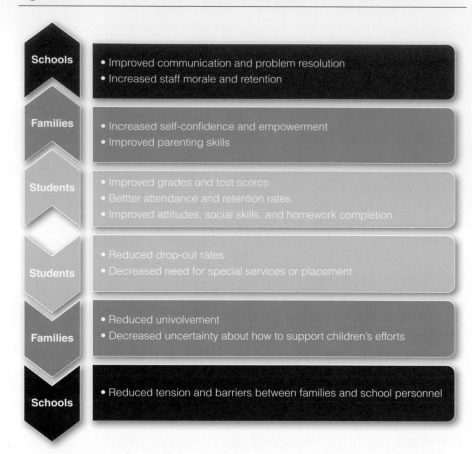

Schools
- Improved communication and problem resolution
- Increased staff morale and retention

Families
- Increased self-confidence and empowerment
- Improved parenting skills

Students
- Improved grades and test scores
- Bettter attendance and retention rates
- Improved attitudes, social skills, and homework completion

Students
- Reduced drop-out rates
- Decreased need for special services or placement

Families
- Reduced univolvement
- Decreased uncertainty about how to support children's efforts

Schools
- Reduced tension and barriers between families and school personnel

3-1b What are the Benefits of Family-School Partnerships?

Extensive empirical data support the conclusions that family-school partnerships produce positive outcomes for children, families, and teachers (see Figure 3-2). So impressive are the long-term results that policy makers have included parent engagement guidelines in No Child Left Behind, Individuals with Disabilities Education Act (IDEA), and Head Start legislation. Professional organizations, including the National Association for the Education of Young Children (NAEYC) and National Parent Teacher Association (PTA), have also established parent involvement recommendations.

Children. Family-school partnerships are especially beneficial for children, particularly those who are struggling, and are associated with improved academic achievement, engagement with schooling, and prosocial behaviors (Castro et al., 2015; Kim & Hill, 2015). For example, Steiner (2014) noted that participation by culturally diverse parents in a family literacy program, which included a family-school partnership component, contributed to the use of more effective reading strategies at home. As a result, their children demonstrated higher scores on basic reading assessments when compared to students whose families were not included in the program. Furthermore, children have demonstrated better cognitive and academic achievement skills and attained higher levels of education when parents provide rich language and learning opportunities at home,

Photo 3-1 Children demonstrate higher achievement and engagement when parents are involved.

promote positive attitudes and beliefs about school, have high academic aspirations for their children, and encourage participation in school activities (Chang, Choi, & Kim, 2015; Harding, Morris, & Hughes, 2015).

When parent involvement is combined with other factors, such as academic **self-efficacy**, positive effects on students' academic achievement are especially significant during the middle and high school years (Choi et al., 2015; Núñez et al., 2015). In addition, involvement tends to foster better parent-child communication about school activities, higher expectations for children's academic performance, and the use of an authoritative parenting style (Shute et al., 2011). Although fewer parents continue to monitor and assist children with homework in the advanced grades, their interest and involvement remains influential on student's self-control and regulation of study behaviors (Núñez et al., 2015).

Students whose parents show concern and involvement are also more likely to attend school consistently, be engaged in their studies, and participate in school-related activities. Brown and Lee (2014) observed that children who participated in early childhood intervention programs that emphasized parent involvement not only scored higher on tests but also had better attendance, were retained less often, and required fewer disciplinary referrals. Older students whose parents were involved in their school activities showed an increase in motivation and interest in education, reduced absenteeism, and decreased incidence of school-related and high risk behavior problems (Reynolds et al., 2015; Schlauch et al., 2013). Studies have repeatedly demonstrated that children experience long-term positive outcomes when parent involvement is initiated in early childhood settings (Pears et al., 2015; Brown & Lee, 2014).

Students also exhibit improved social behaviors and self-esteem when parents are informed and involved in their children's education. Baer and Bullock (2015) found that when the parents of students who had emotional and behavioral disorders participated in a collaborative program that targeted parenting skills, children showed improved prosocial behaviors, enhanced relationships with adults and peers, a reduced risk for substance abuse, and fewer serious mental health problems. Fite and Cooly (2013) noted that parent involvement, homework assistance, and collaborative relationships formed with teachers may help to buffer the negative effects of peer bullying or victimization on student's academic performance. Similarly, Erwin and colleagues (2015) demonstrated improvement in the self-determination skills of young children with disabilities when their parents participated in a family-school intervention program. In this study, parents and practitioners worked collaboratively to assess a child's needs, select and implement appropriate intervention strategies, and evaluate their effect on the child's skill development.

Families. Family-school partnerships are also beneficial for families. Parents tend to develop a better understanding of the school's efforts and goals and gain confidence in their ability to help their child become a better student (Grant & Ray, 2015; O'Donnell & Kirkner, 2014). In addition, parents are able to access teachers and other professionals for information related to children's development, appropriate expectations, ways to promote learning, behavior management strategies, and how to help children succeed in school.

Frequent communication with teachers is especially beneficial for families. These contacts are important for keeping parents informed about children's progress as well as new developments. They also build parent's confidence in their skills, support children's efforts in school, and develop feelings of control and competence (Murray, McFarland-Piazza, & Harrison, 2015). When parents are engaged in children's academic endeavors they gain knowledge of the education system and trust in schools and school personnel. This step is critical for bridging a potential gap that can exist between home and school environments (McDonald, Miller, & Sandler, 2015).

Home-school interventions can also be designed to address specific parenting skills that will improve family functioning and children's school outcomes based upon this information. For example, Pears and her colleagues (2015) developed an intervention program for children with developmental disabilities and behavioral difficulties who were transitioning to kindergarten. They included sessions for parents to help them learn

> **self-efficacy** an individual's confidence in their ability to succeed.

Photo 3-2 Partnering with families improves mutual understanding and increases parents' confidence in their ability to help children at home.

more effective ways to manage children's behavior and to prepare them for this change. Parents who participated in these sessions showed a reduction in the use of ineffective parenting practices and increased involvement in their child's school activities. Involved parents may also experience improvement in family functioning and a decrease in stress and conflict (Benson, 2015).

Teachers. Effective family-school partnerships are an important characteristic of a quality school. Such parent-teacher relationships lead to more positive attitudes toward families and an improved ability to respond to their unique needs (Family and Provider/Teacher Relationship Quality [FPTRQ] Project, 2014). Teachers who form effective partnerships with families are also more likely to receive higher evaluation ratings and report greater personal satisfaction with their position and efforts (Grolnick & Raferty-Helmer, 2015). This result is important because teacher satisfaction is directly related to retention and turnover rates. When teachers feel appreciated, they tend to remain in the profession longer and change schools less often which results in more consistent staffing and better outcomes for children (FPTRQ, 2014).

3-1c What Variables Influence Family-School Partnerships?

Many variables can affect the establishment, maintenance, and quality of effective family-school partnerships (see Figure 3-3). Some factors have a positive impact on partnership-building, whereas others may present significant barriers that hinder relationship formation. Unless teachers take specific steps to include all parents, there may be some families, especially those from culturally- and linguistically-diverse backgrounds, who remain uninvolved even though they are interested in their child's education.

Child. The nature of parents' participation may be influenced by one or more child-related variables, such as the child's age, disability status, and behavior. Parents of younger children, for example, are typically involved in partnerships at a higher rate,

Figure 3-3 Variables that Influence Family-School Partnerships

Child	Age and developmental level
	Disability status
	Behavioral problems
Families	Beliefs about their role in a child's education
	Beliefs about being competent to help
	Perceptions related to invitations from teachers and parents
	Skills and knowledge about collaboration and helping
	Resources including time, energy, financial, and social support
	Language proficiency
Organization and Educator	Extent of administrative, training, and financial support for family-school partnerships
	Practices for evaluating family-school partnership programming
	Attitudes toward diverse families
Laws and Regulations	Guidance on how to follow recommendations for collaboration with families
	Methods for collecting information over time to determine progress and success with parent involvement practices

in part, because elementary school teachers may provide clearer reasons and higher expectations for their participation. In addition, parents of younger children tend to have more free time and show a stronger interest in volunteering to assist with school-related activities. This is especially true if the child is their first-born and, thus, has no siblings who require care or are involved in organized school activities, such as sports. As children move into middle school years, parent involvement rates tend to decrease as students begin to seek greater autonomy and the opportunities for parent involvement become fewer (Kim & Hill, 2014). It is important that schools continue to encourage parents' participation in activities by finding ways that are innovative and sensitive to adolescents' changing needs, because their involvement is especially important during this developmental stage.

Studies have shown that a high percentage of parents who have children with special physical and developmental needs participate in their child's educational process (Welchons & McIntyre, 2015). These parents are also more likely to persist in providing long-term assistance with children's homework, attending school meetings, and participating in parent-teacher conferences than the families of typically-developing students. However, it is important that teachers reach out to parents who are new to, or unfamiliar with, the special education process and provide them with the information and support needed to establish an effective partnership. Parents, who are well-versed in special education language and rights and have similar approaches to problem solving as their child's teachers, are more likely to advocate and achieve positive outcomes developed through family-school partnerships (Anderson, Howland, & McCoach, 2015).

Fewer parents of children who have emotional and/or behavioral disorders form partnerships with teachers or become involved in their child's school. This disparity may, in part, be due to the increased difficulty that parents face in managing children's behavior and supporting learning at home. For example, a parent may find it easier to avoid situations, such as helping with homework, when a child refuses to follow directions or becomes overly aggressive. Children who have behavioral problems are also less likely to participate in the types of school-related extracurricular activities, such as sporting events or musical performances that encourage parent involvement and attendance (Samek et al., 2015).

Families. Most parents express a desire to support their child's educational endeavors. Although parents may indicate an interest in supporting their child in school, they may not know how to become involved or are hesitant for a variety of reasons. They may worry that a child's behavior problems are reflective of their parenting skills or they may have had personal negative experiences with the education system. Some parents also have concerns about cultural or linguistic differences which may contribute to discrimination and biased teacher expectations.

Teachers should remain non-judgmental if parents are initially unresponsive when they have been invited to take an active role in their child's education. For example, African-American parents are more likely to assist children with their educational activities at home than they are to participate in activities held in schools (Hoglund et al., 2015). Teachers may not be aware that a child's family is providing educational support at home and may incorrectly conclude that they have no interest in their child's success or in collaborating with teachers.

Motivational beliefs also exert a strong influence on the importance that parents attach to their role in a child's education and how competent (self-efficacy) they feel about assisting with homework and other school-related activities. Parents' motivation is often shaped by personal experiences they have had with an education system, as well as their own social and cultural expectations (Miller, 2015). For example, parents who have had negative experiences when they were students are more likely to feel incompetent and disempowered when interacting with school professionals. As a result, they may adhere to traditional beliefs that hold schools responsible for educating children. Thus, the challenge for teachers is to help parents understand the value of their involvement, explain their expectations for collaboration, invite parents to participate, and create a welcoming school climate.

Photo 3-3 It is important that fathers be included in interactions with schools and service providers.

Parents who lack experience with formal educational systems may not value involvement in children's education or understand its purpose. For example, immigrant families from countries where formal educational systems are limited, or differ substantially from those in the United States, face significant challenges. Not only do they have language and cultural barriers to overcome but they must also attempt to navigate an unfamiliar educational system and determine their role within it (Tyler & Fazel, 2014).

Family-school partnerships are also affected by a parent's social role expectations. Fathers, for example, have traditionally had less involvement in children's educational endeavors due to work commitments, adherence to traditional gender and parenting roles, and a lack of policies and activities that encouraged their participation. It may also be true that researchers have not always captured the unique ways that fathers' involvement may differ from that of mothers, even though they both have the same positive effect on children's outcomes (Kim & Hill, 2015).

Parents' confidence in their ability to help children with learning also affects their level of involvement. Researchers have observed that the more education a mother has, the greater is her involvement in children's school-related activities (Harding, Morris, & Hughes, 2015). Low-income parents who have high self-efficacy for helping with homework are more likely to do so than those who lack confidence in their abilities (O'Sullivan, Chen, & Fish, 2014). Thus, teachers must make an effort to learn about each parent's strengths and limitations and identify involvement opportunities that are matched to their abilities. For example, teachers can provide structure for homework assignments, request assistance with classroom projects, encourage participation on field trips, and work with parents on newsletter preparation. Training and various support services can also be provided to help parents gain additional skills and confidence and increase their participation.

Personal invitations typically increase parent involvement (Fisherman & Nickerson, 2014). Meaningful invitations are written clearly, sensitive to gender, cultural, language, and economic differences, and focused on ways that parents can participate. However, invitations alone may not be enough to motivate parents who lack confidence in their skills, perceive racism by school staff, do not have access to transportation or child care, or experience depression or other mental health problems (Murray et al., 2014). In addition, invitations that parents may perceive to be coercive can lead to lower participation and an increase in negative attitudes regarding future requests (Grolnick, 2015). When teachers are sensitive to these potential issues, they can take steps to identify alternative ways to invite and engage families in school-related activities.

Personal life contexts, including financial resources, family size and structure, and employment status, also determine the extent and nature of parents' involvement (Hoglund et al., 2015). For example, families in affluent communities are more likely to participate in children's school activities because parents tend to have more education, disposable income, and experience with professional interactions. Single parents and those of lower socioeconomic status are less likely to be involved due to limited finances, transportation availability, and family support (Choi et al., 2015; Myers & Myers, 2014). Participation rates are also known to decline as family size increases. Language barriers and limited knowledge of school systems and how to work with teachers restrict migrant parents' participation (Free, Kriz, & Konecnik, 2014). Demanding and inflexible work schedules can also impede parent involvement across all socioeconomic groups.

It is important to recognize and accept that not every parent will be interested in becoming involved in their child's formal education. However, teachers can take small steps to increase family-school collaboration by identifying unique barriers that affect individual families, establishing and maintaining frequent and open communication, and striving to meet the student's and family's needs through individualized planning.

Organizational and Educator Effects. An organizational lack of support, such as an absence of policies, limited funding, and poor evaluation practices, can present significant barriers for the successful establishment of family-school partnerships. For example, inadequate funding can limit the hiring of interpreters and translators who may be needed to communicate effectively with non-English speaking families (Goldberg & Smith, 2014). The failure to gather parent feedback and use the information to inform practice can also create barriers to effective partnership building. For example, one study found that even when educators believed they were communicating well with parents, many of the parents perceived the type and amount of communication to be insufficient and desired more (Tejero Hughes & Martinez Valle-Riestra, 2014). Gathering meaningful information regularly from teachers and parents allows practices to be changed so they better fit the families they serve.

Teachers' knowledge, skills, and attitudes in working with parents can also affect their ability to engage families. Teachers who receive pre-service and ongoing additional training, and have an administrator who values family involvement, are more

Trending Now "Overinvolved Parents"

Many teachers make a valiant effort to help parents overcome obstacles that might otherwise limit their participation in children's education. However, they may also find "helicopter" or "hummingbird" parents—those who make it a practice to be overly engaged—equally as challenging.*

Helicopter parents tend to be highly concerned and involved in their child's activities (e.g., completing their homework assignments, coaching from the sidelines, selecting their friends). They are also more likely to be quite controlling (e.g., not allowing children developmentally appropriate autonomy) and to solve their child's problems (e.g., contacting a teacher to request a grade change, demanding that their child make the team). For example, there are parents who are continuously telling their toddler what and how to play, or interfering during play activities to ensure that their child does not get hurt. Parents of elementary-age students may complete a portion of the child's homework, demand certain teachers or programs for their child, or force their child to participate in specific extracurricular activities even though the child may not show any interest. Although such interactions occur at all developmental levels, the rate of helicopter parenting seems to peak during students' high school and college years. Helicopter parents may contact professors to request grade changes, complete admission applications, or contact administrators on behalf of their child to resolve a conflict.

Motivational reasons for this level of involvement include anxiety about the child's future success, desire to maintain the connection they once had with children when they were young, or to fulfill their own emotional needs (Marano, 2014). Although parents' actions may be well-intentioned, research indicates that over-parenting lowers the quality of parent-child communication, decreases family satisfaction, and increases youths' sense of entitlement (Segrin et al., 2012). In addition,

children are more likely to experience increased stress and anxiety because they have fewer opportunities to develop autonomy and mature coping skills.

However, helicopter parenting may not always lead to negative outcomes. Children can achieve greater academic success, enjoyment of school, and self-confidence when parents work closely to support autonomous learning (Froiland, 2015). Nelson, Padilla-Walker, and Nielson (2015) found that children experienced fewer maladjustment outcomes in adulthood when overinvolved parents also conveyed feelings of warmth and caring during their interactions.

Some teachers, particularly those who are dissatisfied with their career choice or current position, may also experience difficulties as a result of their interactions with some helicopter parents. New teachers remain in the profession for an average of 4.5 years, and many report issues with parents as the primary reason for changing careers (Struyven & Vanthournout, 2014; Clark, 2013). Therefore, learning how to effectively work with overly involved parents is important.

Teachers may consider, at a minimum, several questions that can help construct a framework for addressing potentially difficult situations. When does involvement become problematic and interfere with a child's development? How can a teacher collaborate effectively with parents who hover? How can a teacher facilitate developmentally appropriate parenting practices? What are some limits that teachers may set for parental involvement? Some guidance is provided by McNerney, Goodman, & Scott (2011) who recommend three steps for working with helicopter parents: (1) decrease parental anxiety by listening and validating concerns, focusing on strengths, and inviting them to be involved in productive and appropriate ways; (2) communicate parental and student responsibilities clearly; and (3) reinforce healthy parental boundaries and practices.

*Dr. Haim Ginott (1969) first introduced the term "helicopter parenting" in his book, *Parents and Teenagers*. Its use became so common that in 2011 the term was included in the English dictionary (Bayless, 2013).

Build gross motor skills in art. Cassidy shakes a box with paint and balls inside to create a picture.

Photo 3-4 IDEA requires schools to communicate children's progress with parents on a regular basis.

likely to work effectively with parents. Teachers' perceptions of parenting behaviors can influence their interactions with families. Pepe and Addimando (2014) found that teachers frequently reported counterproductive behaviors, such as a lack of cooperation and limited or no involvement in school educational activities among parents from low socioeconomic backgrounds, whereas parents from upper socioeconomic groups were more likely to be excessively worried about children's academic achievements. Teachers' preconceived notions about these families hindered the development of a positive working relationship.

Laws and Regulations. Several laws and regulations require family involvement in children's education, and have set expectations that schools must meet to receive funding. Teachers should be familiar with two major laws, the Individuals with Developmental Disabilities Education Act (IDEA) and Title I of the Elementary and Secondary Education Act (ESEA), as well as legislation and recommendations in their state that are related to family involvement.

Parental involvement was first incorporated into laws that focused on students with disabilities during the 1970s. The Education for All Handicapped Children Act (Public Law 94-142; 1975) guaranteed children, ages 3 to 21, the right to a free and appropriate education. This law, amended in 1990 and renamed IDEA (Public Law 101-476), outlined responsibilities for the identification, assessment, and educational programming for struggling students. It also emphasized parents' inclusion in the process—from obtaining their consent to have a child evaluated for special education services to the development and monitoring of individualized instructional goals. Part C of IDEA (Public Law 99-457; 1986) outlines the special education process for children birth through age 3 and requires that an Individualized Family Service Plan (IFSP) be developed to support both the child and family. IDEA also requires schools to communicate children's progress information with parents on a regular basis.

Another law that specifically requires schools to involve parents is Section 1118 of Title I of the ESEA (2005). This law provides government funding to schools that include a high percentage of students from low income families to ensure that all children meet academic standards. In order to receive Title I funds, schools must:

- develop and implement strategies for parent involvement
- establish policies and provide parents with written information that describes how they will be involved in the development and review of educational plans
- provide effective supports for implementing parent involvement plans
- build school and parent capacity for involvement
- involve parents in the evaluation of programs

Legislators consider the positive outcomes associated with parent involvement so significant that they have recently reintroduced a bill amending ESEA. The Family Engagement in Education Act 2015 would authorize states to use a small amount of their Title 1 funding to increase school-based family involvement, establish Local Educational Agencies (LEA), and create a central State Educational Agency (SEA) to assist schools in developing a coordinated statewide plan for strengthening family engagement.

Many states have also instituted laws and policies that support parent engagement, but there is considerable variation in their focus and intent. For example, some states limit their attention to one or two specific goals, such as improving communication, establishing parent leadership in decision making, developing plans to meet families' needs, or providing incentives or sanctions to encourage family participation; others adopt a broader and more comprehensive approach (National PTA, 2015). Additionally, not all states have designated policy-makers who value or are even responsible for establishing parent partnership guidelines. Furthermore, budget cuts, frequent leadership turnover, and policy-making responsibilities that are spread across multiple state offices can make it difficult for states to develop effective and consistent guidelines for schools to follow.

The U.S. Department of Education recognizes that individual states face numerous challenges in their efforts to facilitate effective parent and family engagement and, thus, has posted resources and recommendations on their website. A framework consisting of four basic components is presented in the document, *Partners in education; A dual capacity-building framework for family-school partnerships* to help guide schools in developing and evaluating their partnership programs; however, the components described can be applied to other organizations as well (Mapp & Kuttner, 2013) (see Figure 3-4). The first component focuses on identifying obstacles and building a shared understanding among teachers, families, and community members through workshops, seminars, and training sessions. The second component addresses the processes and organizational conditions necessary for creating productive relationships. The Department of Education recommends that family-school initiatives be linked to student learning and development, focused on collaborative relationships, and systematically integrated with other programs. The third component, policy and program goals, includes four targeted components: capabilities (skills and knowledge); connections (trust and respect between home, school and the community); confidence (sense of comfort engaging in partnerships); and cognition (beliefs and assumptions regarding partnerships). The fourth and final component focuses on the establishment of a school culture that acknowledges families' strengths, creates a welcoming environment for diverse families, and encourages family involvement in student learning.

Figure 3-4 Family School Capacity-Building Framework

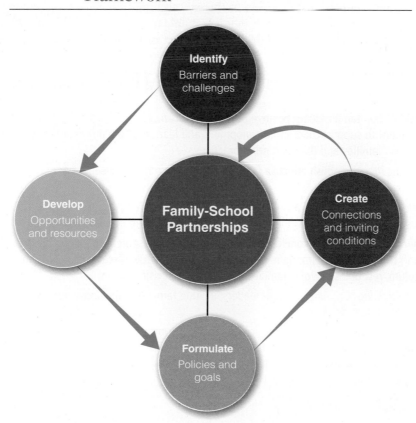

3-2 Establishing Successful Collaboration

Despite federal legislation, state laws, and organizational policies that highlight the need for family-school partnerships, professionals continue to struggle with *how* to effectively collaborate with families. Epstein (2011) proposed six principal strategies for promoting successful family-school partnerships that focus on achieving what is best for the child and go beyond traditional forms of parent involvement (see Figure 3-5). The framework also reinforces the need to treat families with respect, value their opinions, and take their desires and interests into consideration. Expansion of the conceptualization of active parent involvement provides an invitation to families who might otherwise not have considered the possibility. Epstein also recognizes that teachers are in an ideal position to encourage and answer parents' questions about children's development, nutrition and health matters, behavior management problems, and strategies for supporting appropriate learning activities in the home.

Photo 3-5 Inviting parents into the classroom provides opportunities for teachers to learn about the families' strengths and needs.

An understanding of the benefits and variables that influence family-school partnerships is essential in order to plan strategies and goals for family engagement and empowerment. Christenson and Sheridan (2001) identified four components of family-school collaboration that are essential for maximizing student outcomes: approach, attitudes, atmosphere, and actions (see Figure 3-6). These components are applicable to other professional settings for establishing effective partnerships with families. Across all components, there is a focus on appreciating family diversity, identifying common barriers that impede involvement, and developing trust and respect—all important elements for establishing strong relationships with families.

3-2a Approach

The first component, approach, refers to the overarching framework for understanding and interacting with families. Although it is possible to work with children without ever talking to a parent or becoming familiar with their community, such an approach can

---

Figure 3-5 Epstein's Six Keys to Successful Family Involvement

1. *Parenting*: Help families learn positive parenting skills and how to arrange the home environment to support children's development and learning; help professionals to better understand families and their parenting practices.

2. *Communicating*: Establish effective two-way communication between school programs and student progress.

3. *Volunteering*: Offer parents a variety of volunteer opportunities (e.g., different locations, various times, different tasks) that will support the school and its students.

4. *Learning at home*: Provide families with information and resources to extend classroom learning to the home environment (e.g., homework, activities, discussions related to the curriculum, resources); involve families in curriculum decisions.

5. *Decision making*: Encourage parent leaders; include families in making school-wide and individual student decisions.

6. *Collaborating with the community*: Coordinate with community resources and services to best meet the needs of the school, families, and students.

Source: Adapted from Epstein (2011).

⩒ Professional Resource Download

lead to incorrect assumptions about a student's performance and progress in achieving specific goals. A positive approach requires an appreciation of family diversity and the environmental variables that influence a child's development. Bronfenbrenner's ecological systems theory (1979, 1993, 1994) (see Chapter 1) provides a useful model for understanding how multiple interrelated systems continuously shape a child's and family's ideas and behavior. The model also recognizes the unique contributions that families and others make, and illustrates how multiple entities share in, and contribute to, student outcomes.

Establishing a productive approach necessitates that careful consideration is given to the unique characteristics, strengths, and needs of all involved parties (e.g., child, family, teacher, service providers) as well as to the larger environmental systems that influence individuals. Although teachers do not have control over many of these elements, it is important to understand how they may affect the approach to creating a meaningful relationship between home and school.

Figure 3-6 Four A's of Family-School Collaboration

3-2b Attitudes

The second framework component encompasses the attitudes held by teachers and family members which affect children's success and beliefs about school. It is especially important that teachers examine their personal beliefs and biases about families and family-school partnerships and consider how these may potentially influence their own behaviors. For example, would you respond differently to a parent who repeatedly arrives late to pick up their child than to parents who are always on time? Are you less responsive toward parents who never volunteer or attend conferences than to those who are always present? Do you blame parents who seem uncaring or uninvolved for their child's problematic classroom behaviors?

Teachers who have negative attitudes toward collaboration or adhere to stereotypes based on certain individual characteristics (e.g., ethnicity, language, socioeconomic status, behavior) are unlikely to form effective partnerships with children's parents. Conversely, teachers who make an effort to learn more about a child's family may discover that inflexible work schedules, lack of transportation, poor communication from the school, cultural variables, or medical problems may be preventing them from participating. This information may lead to positive changes in a teacher's attitude about a family and thoughts about ways to overcome barriers that are limiting collaboration. Teachers are professionals who have a moral and ethical responsibility to support and work collaboratively with all children, families, and colleagues regardless of their diverse backgrounds (AAE, 2015; NAEYC, 2011).

Parental attitudes, including feelings of inadequacy, disrespect from school personnel, or sensing blame for a child's disruptive behavior or poor academic progress, may also create barriers to successful collaborative relationships. However, these obstacles can be overcome when teachers commit to an attitude that acknowledges, respects, and builds upon the diversity and assets of individual children and their families.

Photo 3-6 Signs can help to create a welcoming environment that values parents.

3-2c Atmosphere

The third component of the family-school framework addresses the school's atmosphere. When families enter the building or stop to converse with a school staff member, the physical and emotional setting should make them feel welcomed, trusted, and valued. Elements of the physical school environment that create a respectful and collaborative atmosphere include:

- Welcome signs, preferably prepared by children
- Pictures and murals that promote the importance of involvement and reflect the diversity of families
- Establishment of an open and welcoming administrative office that is accessible to parents
- Easily accessible, user-friendly maps placed near an entrance door to help parents and staff locate room destinations
- A comfortable seating/greeting area where parents can mingle and meet with school personnel
- Available policies and documents that support family-school partnerships

Efforts should also be made to create an emotional atmosphere conducive to family-school collaboration. Christenson and Sheridan (2001) cite trust and respect as two invisible but critical elements which foster positive interactions and a sense of importance. To achieve them, they recommend that educators:

- Take time to learn from families about their cultural norms (values, practices, and preferences), community, strengths, needs, and desires for their child
- Establish effective two-way communications that emphasize the family's contributions
- Focus on solutions rather than problems
- Follow through with agreed-upon plans
- Provide multiple ways for families to be involved at different times of the day or week (e.g., extend invitations at the beginning of the school year as opposed to waiting until a crisis occurs)
- Show parents how their efforts contribute to student progress and success so they realize the value of their input, feel empowered to continue participating, and see themselves as an equal and respected part of their child's education
- Coordinate resources and activities with the communities in which families live
- Designate a family liaison or coordinator who can connect parents with resources and staff

3-2d Actions

When the first three components (i.e., approach, attitudes, and atmosphere) have been achieved, schools are ready to plan and implement strategies to actively engage families in children's education. Christenson and Sheridan (2001) identify several measures that schools can take to facilitate a shared family-school responsibility:

- Have strong administrative and leadership support and policies in place.
- Invite parents and staff to serve as system advocates and who can make changes focused on long-term outcomes (e.g., family-school evaluation plan, policy formation and revision).
- Provide training to increase teachers' communication skills and ability to manage relationships and conflicts with families.
- Establish family-school teams or parent advisory boards to increase involvement in decision- making at the school and district levels.
- Employ a structured problem-solving process that is focused on participant strengths and a shared responsibility for times when intervention is needed.
- Support families' efforts to encourage learning at home through workshops, contracts, and personal assistance.

Figure 3-7 NAEYC Effective Family Engagement Principles

Principle	What it means
Principle 1: Programs invite families to participate in decision making and goal setting for their child	Programs invite families to actively take part in decision-making opportunities concerning their children's education. Programs and families collaborate in establishing goals for children's education and learning both at home and at school.
Principle 2: Teachers and programs engage families in two-way communication	Communication takes multiple forms and is responsive to families' linguistic preferences. Communication is both school- and family-initiated and timely and continuous, inviting conversations about the child's educational experience as well as the larger program.
Principle 3: Programs and teachers engage families in ways that are truly reciprocal	Teachers seek information about children's lives, families, and communities and integrate this information into their curriculum and instructional practices. Programs help families share their unique knowledge and skills and encourage active participation in the life of the school.
Principle 4: Programs provide learning activities for the home and in the community	Programs plan activities to enhance each child's early learning and encourage and support families' efforts to support their child's learning beyond the program.
Principle 5: Programs invite families to participate in program-level decisions and wider advocacy efforts	Programs invite families to take an active part in decision-making opportunities regarding the program. Families are encouraged to advocate for early childhood education and supportive services for children and families in the community.
Principle 6: Programs implement a comprehensive program-level system for family engagement	Programs institutionalize family engagement policies and practices and ensure that leadership and teachers receive the support they need to fully engage families.

Source: National Association for the Education of Young Children (NAEYC). Effective family engagement principles. Retrieved October 24, 2015 from http://www.naeyc.org/familyengagement.

⋙ Professional Resource Download

Organizations that work primarily with children and parents have also placed a high value on establishing partnerships with families. The National Association for the Education of Young Children (NAEYC), for example, has historically supported family-school collaboration. They have identified six principles for forming effective engagement with diverse families (2011) (see Figure 3-7). NAEYC considers family collaboration so important that one of its seven core standards for teacher preparation programs is devoted exclusively to this responsibility. Although teachers play an essential role in forming reciprocal relationships with families, their success depends on administrative commitment, support, and policies that value parent involvement.

Responsive Parenting

Jill is a 3-year old child with a developmental delay. She currently receives special education services through a local early childhood program. Her grandmother (legal guardian) regularly attends Jill's Individual Family Service Plan (IFSP) meetings. She listens to the information presented, but does not contribute to the discussion or ask any questions. However, she is frustrated that Jill has not been making as much progress as she expected. How would you advise the teachers to work differently with Jill's grandmother in order to build a more effective partnership? In what ways could Jill's grandmother be encouraged to take a more active role in supporting Jill's developmental progress?

Schools are increasingly being held to higher accountability standards. Although researchers agree that schools benefit from adopting and implementing programs that encourage family-school partnerships, administrators are expected to provide evidence that such efforts are worthwhile. Student academic performance data gathered through state competency assessment testing (No Child Left Behind) and participation in Race to the Top grants, typically serve this purpose. Schools can also develop their own surveys or access a variety of evaluation instruments electronically in order to measure the effects of family-school partnerships. One such instrument, the *National standards for family-school partnerships assessment*, is available from the National PTA and is frequently used for this purpose.

The Office of Administration for Children and Families (ACH) also has an instrument, *A measure of family and provider/teacher relationship quality* (FPTRQ), that is accessible on their website. This tool has been developed specifically for evaluating the quality of parent partnerships in early childhood programs that serve children birth to 5 years. Separate teacher and parent surveys assess: (1) family-specific knowledge; (2) practices, including collaboration, responsiveness, communication, and family-focused concern; and (3) attitudes, including commitment, understanding context, respect, and openness to change (FPTRQ Project, 2014). The results can be combined with other data (e.g., achievement scores, attendance rates, common behavioral problems) to inform programming and refinement of practices for improved family engagement.

3-3 Fostering Open Communication and Action

Effective family-professional collaboration is dependent upon meaningful communication and mutual understanding. When information is shared with families, professionals must consider:

- when and how often the information needs to be communicated
- what information should be included in the message
- any special cultural and linguistic needs that may exist
- the efficiency and effectiveness of the communication method

Parents may not always ask questions or have time to contact professionals for information during the day. Therefore, it is important that teachers and other professionals take the initiative to share children's progress, achievements, and activities with their parents.

3-3a Timing, Content, and Delivery of Information

An ideal time to initiate positive interactions with parents is early in the school year or when services are beginning. Face-to-face events, such as open houses, school tours, and parent meetings, provide teachers with valuable opportunities for learning about children and their family and parents' preferred communication and involvement styles. Parents may also feel more comfortable initiating questions in these informal group environments.

Careful attention should be given to the content of any communication. When professionals articulate a clear desire to work with parents, they create an atmosphere that is likely to influence the nature of future interactions. Information stated clearly and in a manner respectful of individual differences (e.g., gender, cultural, linguistic, socioeconomic, and geographic) is generally well-received. Conversation content should remain focused on student performance, positive outcomes, and input from family members. Often, parents are contacted only when a problem arises. If this becomes a pattern, it can lead to negative family-professional interactions, misunderstandings, and a lack of collaboration. Parents report feeling a stronger commitment to their child's education and a greater satisfaction with teachers when they share positive as well as negative information (Goldberg &

Smith, 2014). Involving parents in identifying solutions to problems also conveys an expressed desire to support the child and family (Christenson & Sheridan, 2001).

The way in which information is delivered can also influence its effectiveness. Organizations tend to rely on one-way communication methods (e.g., newsletters, memos, fliers, materials posted on school websites) for transmitting information to families. However, these approaches limit parent input and also lend themselves to greater misunderstanding. Written communications are especially prone to misunderstanding because of the author's word choice or information that may be missing. Content delivered in person makes it easier for participants to check for understanding and provide clarification. The use of two-way communication methods (e.g., face-to-face meeting, Skype) helps to reduce potential misunderstandings and encourage an open sharing that is more conducive to successful family-professional partnerships.

Two-way communication methods involve active observation, listening, and speaking skills. Participants are able to check for mutual understanding by observing each other's body language (e.g., posture, eye contact, facial expressions, fidgeting, and head nods) for signs of tension, uncertainty, or agreement. Active listening communicates interest, respect, understanding, and encourages the speaker to continue sharing information. Listeners can also use their verbal skills to:

Photo 3-7 Regular and open communication is essential to building trust with families.

- encourage the speaker to continue talking (e.g., "Oh," "Mm-hm," "I see")
- paraphrase, summarize, or ask for confirmation ("Is that correct?" "Did I address all of your concerns?")
- reflect information to check for understanding of the information that was shared (e.g., "I noticed . . .," "It sounds like . . .," "I hear you saying. . . .").

These strategies are especially effective to use when professionals observe a discrepancy between what parents may be saying and actually feeling. Misunderstandings can be avoided by restating the message or following up with a parent after they have had time to reflect on the conversation.

Questions are also an important part of the conversational process, and can either encourage or discourage information sharing. Open-ended questions are effective for initiating a conversation and are typically used to engage parents in the discussion. For example, a teacher might begin by asking, "What would you like to talk about today?" or "What do you think would be most helpful for your child?" Close-ended questions are useful when more factual information is needed. For example, a teacher might ask, "Which activity do you think your child would most likely enjoy?" or "How long have you been living in town?" Questions stated in a manner that require more than a "yes" or "no" response are more likely to elicit useful information and encourage further discussion. The use of too many close-ended questions can create a conversation that feels more like an interrogation, and may limit the quality and quantity of information the parent is willing to share.

Ongoing developments in technology provide additional opportunities for professionals to connect with families. For example, teachers can communicate via email, website updates, deliver information through confidential school portals (e.g., view schedules, grades, assignments, send messages), and they can provide access to online learning activities. Use of school portals can help parents of older students feel more informed. However, parents report that such systems should not replace other, more personal forms of communication (Starkie, 2013). Teachers who use technological means should make efforts to invite parent responses and engagement, so that communication is a two-way process.

Furthermore, if electronic information transfer is used, professionals must be aware of families' accessibility to devices that are required for viewing the information and whether they have the skills to effectively use the technology. When new platforms are introduced, trainings and information on ways to access and utilize the information should be provided. Schools may also consider the use of technological platforms, such as televisions and DVD players that are often readily accessible for establishing connections between home and school. For example, Walsh, Cromer, and Weigel (2014) used classroom DVD newsletters to extend learning concepts discussed at school to encourage more meaningful conversations at home. Parents responded favorably and reported that the resource was helpful for making connections with classroom learning activities.

3-3b Communicating in a Culturally-Sensitive Manner

Schools and other organizations are serving increasingly diverse populations today. Some teachers feel unprepared to work with children's culturally and linguistically diverse families due to the lack of a common language, differences in communication styles and value systems, differences in ideas about children's development, and difficulty in locating and working with interpreters (Banerjee & Luckner 2014).

One of the first steps in establishing meaningful communication and partnerships with culturally and linguistically diverse families involves self-reflection. This requires teachers to closely examine their own cultural values and to understand how stereotypical assumptions may affect their interactions and relationships with families. Although most professionals are well-meaning, they may unintentionally communicate insults or snubs that convey negative messages about a particular group. These subtle forms of bias have been termed **microaggressions** and can make families feel that they do not belong or are not valued (Sue et al., 2016). For instance, a teacher who is meeting with an African American father of a student who recently transferred to the school remarked that his son looks like he's a great basketball player. Although the teacher's intention was to compliment the student (who does not play sports), the father was upset by the statement because he felt that the teacher's reference to the athletic stereotype of African American males undermined his son's academic accomplishments. In another example, a teacher told a parent from a low socioeconomic status background that the school has winter coats available for students. The parent was offended because her daughter has been wearing her favorite purple winter coat to school, one that was given to her by her sister, even though it is too big.

Although it is common in the dominant U.S. culture to shake hands, make eye contact, be assertive or ask clarifying questions, and use nonverbal gestures as signs of friendliness and interest when meeting with another individual, these behaviors may be interpreted differently in some ethnic groups. For example, making eye contact is viewed as disrespectful in many Native American and Middle Eastern cultures. Touch, especially between individuals of opposite genders, can be seen as inappropriate in Muslim cultures. Although patting a child's head in a friendly manner is acceptable in the American culture, it is viewed as inappropriate in Asian cultures because the head is believed to be a sacred part of the body (Vermont Department of Health, 2015). For these reasons, it is essential that teachers take time to learn about cross-cultural differences before meeting with families. It is also important that they avoid making generalized assumptions about individuals belonging to any particular cultural group because they may not always adhere to the same beliefs and practices.

A second step consists of getting to know a family by inviting them (including any extended family members who may be involved) into the classroom or session, making home visits, or arranging flexible meeting times when family members are able to attend. Care should be taken during these interactions not to rush through information as parents may need more time to decipher and respond to what is being said. Looking directly at parents when speaking, enunciating words carefully,

---

microaggressions
everyday, subtle, unintentional forms of bias that convey negative messages about a particular group.

and avoiding the use of slang or jargon also contribute to improved understanding. Teachers can also use these opportunities to learn more about an individual family's culture and preferences.

A third step for forming effective partnerships with diverse families is to identify ways to maintain communication once it has been established. Initial efforts may require the assistance of interpreters, family liaisons, or cultural brokers and must always accommodate the family's preferences. For example, some parents may prefer in-person meetings with an interpreter present, whereas others may be more comfortable with phone contacts through an interpreter, translated notes, or email communications. When professionals send out invitations, memos, or forms to be completed, the information should be provided at an appropriate reading level and translated into the family's native language if possible. Alternatively, an interpreter may contact a family to translate and explain the information.

Photo 3-8 When working with diverse families, information should be communicated in the family's native language.

Working with Interpreters. Professionals must not depend upon children to interpret information for their family members. Trained interpreters and translators should be used to communicate information directly to linguistically-diverse families, especially if the professional does not speak the family's native language. Learning to work effectively with interpreters requires patience, commitment, and a cooperative effort toward building trusting partnerships with families. Celliti (2010) outlined strategies for working effectively with interpreters, a summary of which follows.

Professionals should meet with the family's interpreter before scheduling a meeting with the family members. Several issues, such as the interpreter's skills, mode of interpretation, the use of technical words that are specific to the context, the meeting's purpose, cultural considerations for delivering information, and confidentiality, should be discussed and agreed upon ahead of time. It is also important to ensure that an interpreter has the necessary language and cultural skills required to interpret effectively. For example, although an individual may speak Spanish, their interpretations may not always be accurate if they are from a different region or have a dialect that differs from the family's.

Interpreters may also use different interpretive methods. For example, consecutive interpretation requires the speaker to pause periodically while the interpreter translates and delivers the information. In simultaneous interpretation, the interpreter translates and relays the message as the speaker talks. Reviewing technical words or specific phrases beforehand, such as those used to describe special education disability categories or medical information, helps to ensure that the intent of the words spoken is properly communicated. Materials that will be distributed to the family should first be given to the interpreter to review and translate. Interpreters should also be apprised of a meeting's purpose so they know what to expect. If the interpreter is familiar with the family's cultural community, information about appropriate greetings or social features of communication can be discussed. It is also important to review confidentiality with the interpreter to protect the student and family's privacy. Lastly, communication signals for transitioning between speakers and any anticipated difficulties (e.g., side-conversations between family and interpreter) and potential resolutions should be discussed.

During the meeting, the physical setting should be arranged so that the interpreter is seated to the side and slightly behind the person who is providing the majority of information, rather than between the professional and family members. This arrangement allows family members to face the professional and interpreter at the same time so that everyone present can hear and note nonverbal behavior (body language). It is also important that the professional look at, and speak directly to the family members and not the interpreter. Individuals present at the meeting may need to be reminded to pause from time to time so that the information can be properly translated and not simply summarized. In addition, the professional should follow the meeting plan, monitor the family members' nonverbal responses, and ask questions periodically to be sure that parents understand the information being discussed. When the meeting has ended, it is recommended that the professional and interpreter meet to discuss the meeting outcomes, process, and any problems have arisen including communication or cultural considerations. The professional and interpreter can share their observations in order to gain a better understanding of the family and culture. Written feedback or a planned follow-up meeting should also be arranged with the interpreter.

Responsive Parenting

Daniel and his family recently came to the United States as refugees from Somalia. The teacher tried to contact Daniel's parents by phone to discuss his academic progress and to refer him for a special education evaluation, but she has not heard back from the family. When the teacher sees Daniel's father in the hallway, she tells him that he needs to sign a form so that the school can move forward with testing. The father takes the form, but is unsure of what to do with it and how to work with the teacher. What factors appear to be challenging efforts to establish an effective home-school partnership? What advice would you give to Daniel's father and the teacher?

Summary

- Successful family collaboration requires that professionals acknowledge and respect family diversity (e.g., structure, roles, economics, stressors, culture, religious, linguistic differences).

- Partnerships with families are characterized by an active, relational process in which educators and family members share information, values, expertise, goals, and responsibility for student learning and success. All parties are viewed as equal contributors in the development and implementation of plans to help students succeed.

- Numerous variables at the level of the child, family, professional, and government affect the quality of relationships between home and school.

- A positive relationship between home and school leads to long-term positive outcomes for children, families, and educators.

- Four components—approach, attitudes, atmosphere, and actions—are necessary to establish successful collaboration that responds to the needs of children, families, and teachers.

- Open communication can be fostered by making early, positive, and regular two-way contacts with parents, using effective personal communication skills such as active listening, using technology to provide information access, and being sensitive to family differences.

Key Terms

microaggressions (p. 86)   **self-efficacy** (p. 73)

Questions for Discussion and Self-Reflection

1. Describe the concept of family-professional partnerships, and explain why they are important.

2. What does the research tell us about why some families seem indifferent or reluctant to become involved in their children's education?

3. What steps can professionals take to gain family support and increase family participation?

4. What steps can be taken to improve communication with culturally and linguistically diverse families?

Field Activities

1. Complete an online search to locate the Family and Provider/Teacher Relationship Quality Measures tool. Ask a teacher and parent to each complete the evaluation. Conduct a follow-up interview to learn about their collaboration experiences, and discuss ways to improve family-school partnerships.

2. Research information about your state's laws or recommendations related to family engagement in schools through the U.S. Department of Education's Family and Community Engagement resources, and request copies of policies or handbooks from local schools. After reviewing the information, make a list of recommendations to improve the policies and practices for building family-school partnerships based on your reading.

3. Research the educational system and cultural norms of a foreign country. Imagine yourself as a parent taking your child to school on the first day. Consider how you would feel in this situation (e.g., Is the school safe? Do you agree with the content of the material taught? Do the student groupings make sense, and are teachers prepared? Will the length of the school day fit your schedule?). How could teachers or other staff help with the transition and improve your understanding of the educational system?

REFERENCES

Anderson, J., Howland, A., & McCoach, D. (2015). Parental characteristics and resiliency in identification rates for special education. *Preventing School Failure: Alternative Education for Children and Youth*, 59(2), 63–72.

Association of American Educators (AAE). (2015). *Code of ethics for educators*. Retrieved October 24, 2015 from http://www.aaeteachers.org/index.php/about-us/aae-code-of-ethics.

Baek, J., & Bullock, L. (2015). Evidence-based parental involvement programs in the United States of America and Korea. *Journal of Child and Family Studies*, 24(6), 1544–1550.

Bayless, K. (2013). What is helicopter parenting? *Parents*. Meredith Corporation. Retrieved August 12, 2015 from http://www.parents.com/parenting/better-parenting/what-is-helicopter-parenting/.

Benson, P. (2015). Longitudinal effects of educational involvement on parent and family functioning among mothers of children with ASD. *Research in Autism Spectrum Disorders*, 11, 42–55.

Bronfenbrenner, U. (1979). *The ecology of human development: Experiments by nature and design*. Cambridge, MA: Harvard University Press.

Bronfenbrenner, U., & Ceci, S. (1993). Heredity, environment, and the question "how?": A new theoretical perspective for the 1990s. In R. Plomin and McClearn, G. (1993). *Nature, Nurture, & Psychology*. Washington, DC: APA Books.

Bronfenbrenner, U. (1994). Ecological models of human development. In *International Encyclopedia of Education*, Vol 3, 2nd Ed. Oxford: Elsevier.

Brown, A., & Lee, J. (2014). School performance in elementary, middle, and high school: A comparison of children based on HIPPY participation during the preschool years. *The School Community Journal*, 24(2), 83–106.

Castro, M., Exposito-Casas, E., Lopez-Martin, E., Lizasoain, L., Navarro-Asencio, E., & Gaviria, J. (2015). Parental involvement on student academic achievement: A meta-analysis. *Educational Research Review*, 14, 33–46.

Cellitti, A. (2010). Working effectively with interpreters. *Dimensions of Early Childhood*, 38(1), 31–37.

Chang, M., Choi, N., & Kim, S. (2015). School involvement of parents of linguistic and racial minorities and their children's mathematics performance. *Educational Research and Evaluation*, 21(3), 209–231.

Choi, N., Chang, M., Kim, S., & Reio, T. (2015). A structural model of parent involvement with demographic and academic variables. *Psychology in the Schools, 52*(2), 154–167.

Christenson, S., & Sheridan, S. (2001). *School and families: Creating essential connections for learning.* New York: The Guilford Press.

Clark, R. (2013). What teachers really want to tell parents. Special to CNN. Retrieved August 12, 2015 from http://www.cnn.com/2011/09/06/living/teachers-want-to-tell-parents/index.html.

Division for Early Childhood (DEC). (2014). *DEC recommended practices in early intervention/early childhood special education 2014.* Retrieved July 11, 2015 from http://www.dec-sped.org/recommendedpractices.

Erwin, E., Maude, S., Palmer, S., Summers, J., Brothersons, M., Haines, S., . . . Peck, N. (2015). Fostering the foundations of self-determination in early childhood: A process for enhancing child outcomes across home and school. *Early Childhood Education Journal,* 1–9. doi: 10.1007/s10643-015-0710-9.

Family and Provider/Teacher Relationship Quality (FPTRQ) Project. (2015). Development of a measure of family and provider/teacher relationship quality (FPTRQ), 2010–2015. Office of Planning, Research and Evaluation, Administration for Children and Families, U.S. Department of Health and Human Services. Retrieved July 25, 2015 from http://www.acf.hhs.gov/programs/opre/research/project/development-of-a-measure-of-family-and-provider-teacher-relationship-quality-fptrq.

Family and Provider/Teacher Relationship Quality (FPTRQ) Project. (2014). Quality connections in early care and education: Measuring relationships between families and providers or teachers. Office of Planning, Research and Evaluation, Administration for Children and Families, U.S. Department of Health and Human Services. Retrieved July 25, 2015 from http://www.acf.hhs.gov/programs/opre/resource/for-practitioners-quality-connections-in-early-care-and-education-measuring-relationships-between-families-and-providers-or.

Fisherman, C., & Nickerson, A. (2015). Motivations for involvement: A preliminary investigation of parents of students with disabilities. *Journal of Child and Family Studies, 24*(2), 523–535.

Fite, P., & Cooley, J. (2013). Parental school involvement as a moderator of the association between peer victimization and academic performance. *Children and Youth Services Review, 44,* 25–32.

Free, J., Kriz, K., & Konecnik, J. (2014). Harvesting hardships: Educators' views on the challenges of migrant students and their consequences on education. *Children and Youth Services Review, 4*(part 3), 187–197.

Goldberg, A., & Smith, J. (2014). Predictors of school engagement among same-sex and heterosexual adoptive parents of kindergarteners. *Journal of School Psychology, 52,* 463–478.

Froiland, J. (2015). Parents' weekly descriptions of autonomy supportive communication: Promoting children's motivation to learn and positive emotions. *Journal of Child and Family Studies, 24*(1), 117–126.

Grant, K., & Ray, J. (2015). *Home, school, and community collaboration: Culturally responsive family engagement.* Thousand Oaks, CA: Sage Publications.

Grolnick, W. (2015). Mothers' motivation for involvement in their children's schooling: Mechanisms and outcomes. *Motivation and Emotion, 39*(1), 63–73.

Grolnick, W., & Raftery-Helmer, J. (2015). Core components of family-school connections: Toward a model of need satisfying partnerships. *Foundation of Family-School Partnership Research, 1,* 15–34.

Haines, S., Gross, J., Blue-Banning, M., Francis, G., & Turnbull, A. (2015). Fostering family-school and community-school partnerships in inclusive schools. *Research and Practice for Persons with Severe Disabilities, 40*(3), 227–239.

Harding, J., Morris, P., Hughes, D. (2015). The relationship between maternal education and children's academic outcomes: A theoretical framework. *Journal of Marriage and Family, 77*(1), 60–76.

Hoglund, W., Jones, S., Brown, J., & Aber, J. (2015). The evocative influence of child academic and social-emotional adjustment on parent involvement in inner-city schools. *Journal of Educational Psychology, 107*(2), 517–532.

Hoover-Dempsey, K., Walker, J., Sandler, H., Whetsel, D., Green, C., Wilkins, A., & Closson, K. (2005). Why do parents become involved? Research findings and implications. *The Elementary School Journal, 106*(2), 105–130.

Kim, S., & Hill, N. (2015). Including fathers in the picture: A meta-analysis of parental involvement and students' academic achievement. *Journal of Educational Psychology, 107*(4), 919–934.

Mapp, K., & Kuttner, P. (2013). Partners in education. A dual capacity-building framework for family-school partnerships. Retrieved October 22, 2015 from http://www2.ed.gov /documents/family-community/partners-education.pdf.

Marano, H. (2014). Helicopter parenting—it's worse than you think. Post published on Jan 31, 2014 in *Nation of Wimps*. Retrieved August 12, 2015 from https://www.psychologytoday .com/blog/nation-wimps/201401/helicopter-parenting-its-worse-you-think.

McDonald, L., Miller, H., & Sandler, J. (2015). A social ecological, relationship-based strategy for parent involvement: Families and schools together (FAST). *Journal of Children's Services*, *10*(3), 218–230.

McNerney, N., Goodman, E., & Scott, J. (2011). Three steps for dealing with helicopter parents. Retrieved August 12, 2015 from https://www.schoolcounselor.org/magazine/blogs/january -february-2011/three-steps-for-dealing-with-helicopter-parents.

Miller, K. (2015). From past to present: How memories of school shape parental views of children's schooling. *International Journal of Early Years Education*, *23*(2), 153–171.

Murray, E., McFarland-Piazza, L., & Harrison, L. (2015). Changing patterns of parent-teacher communication and parent involvement from preschool to school. *Early Child Development and Care*, *185*(7), 1031–1052.

Murray, K., Finigan-Carr, N., Jones, V., Copeland-Linder, N., Haynie, D., & Cheng, T. (2014). Barriers and facilitators to school-based parent involvement for parents of urban public middle school students. *SAGE Open*, October-December 2014: 1–12.

Myers, S., & Myers, C. (2014). Family structure and school-based parental involvement: A family resource perspective. *Journal of Family and Economic Issues*, *36*(1), 114–131.

National Association for the Education of Young Children (NAEYC). (2009). Engaging diverse families. Effective family engagement principles. Retrieved October 23, 2015 from http:// www.naeyc.org/familyengagement.

NAEYC. (2011). *NAEYC Code of ethical conduct and statement of commitment*. Retrieved October 24, 2015 from https://www.naeyc.org/files/naeyc/image/public_policy/Ethics%20 Position%20Statement2011_09202013update.pdf.

National Education Goals Panel. (1999). The National Education Goals report: Building a nation of learners, 1999. Washington, DC: U.S. Government Printing Office. Retrieved July 20, 2015 from http://govinfo.library.unt.edu/negp/reports/99rpt.pdf.

National Parent Teachers Association (PTA). (2015). State laws on family engagement in education. *National PTA Reference Guide*. Retrieved October 21, 2015 from https://s3.amazonaws.com /rdcms-pta/files/production/public/State_Laws_Report.pdf.

Núñez, J., Suárez, N., Rosário, P., Vallejo, G., Valle, A., & Epstein, J. (2015). Relationships between perceived parental involvement in homework, student homework behaviors, and academic achievement: Differences among elementary, junior high, and high school students. *Metacognition and Learning*, 1–32. doi: 10.1007/s11409-015-9135-5.

Nelson, L., Padilla-Walker, L., & Nielson, M. (2015). Is hovering smothering or loving? An examination of parental warmth as a moderator of relations between helicopter parenting and emerging adults' indices of adjustment. *Emerging Adulthood*, *3*(4), 282–285.

O'Donnell, J., & Kirkner, S. (2014). The impact of a collaborative family involvement program on Latino families and children's educational performance. *The School Community Journal* *24*(1), 211–234.

O'Sullivan, R., Chen, Y., & Fish, M. (2014). Parental mathematics homework involvement of low-income families with middle school students. *The School Community Journal*, *24*(2), 165–187.

Pears, K., Hyoun, K., Healy, C., Yoeger, K., & Fisher, P. (2015). Improving child self-regulation and parenting in families of pre-kindergarten children with developmental disabilities and behavioral difficulties. *Prevention Science*, *16*(2), 222–232.

Pepe, A., & Addimando, L. (2014). Teacher-parent relationships: Influence of gender and education on organizational parents' counterproductive behaviors. *European Journal of Psychology in Education*, *29*(3), 503–519.

Reynolds, A., Crea, T., Medina, J., Degnan, E., & McRoy, R. (2015). Mixed-methods case study of parent involvement in an urban high school serving minority students. *Urban Education*, *50*(6), 750–775.

Samek, D., Elkins, I., Keyes, M., Iacono, W., & McGue, M. (2015). High school sports involvement diminishes the association between childhood conduct disorder and adult antisocial behavior. *Journal of Adolescent Health*, *57*(1), 107–112.

Schlaugh, R., Levitt, A., Connell, C., & Kaufman, J. (2013). The moderating effect of family involvement on substance use risk factors in adolescents with severe emotional and behavioral challenges. *Addictive Behaviors*, *38*(7), 2333–2342.

Segrin, C., Woszidlo, A., Givertz, M., Bauer, A., & Murphy, M. (2012). The association between overparenting, parent-child communication, and entitlement and adaptive traits in adult children. *Family Relations, 61*(2), 237–252.

Shute, C., Hansen, E., Underwood, J., & Razzouk, R. (2011). A review of the relationship between parental involvement and secondary school students' academic achievement. *Education Research International, 11*, 1–10.

Starkie, B. (2013). Data sharing through parent portals: An exploration of parental motivation, data use, and the promise of prolonged parent involvement. *Family Involvement Network of Educators (FINE) Newsletter, 5*(2), Retrieved July 20, 2015 from http://www.hfrp.org/publications-resources/publications-series/family-involvement-research-digests/data-sharing-through-parent-portals-an-exploration-of-parental-motivation-data-use-and-the-promise-of-prolonged-parent-involvement.

Steiner, L. (2014). A family literacy intervention to support parents in children's early literacy learning. *Reading Psychology, 35*(8), 703–735.

Struyven, K., & Vanthournout, G. (2014). Teachers' exit decisions: An investigation into the reasons why newly qualified teachers fail to enter the teacher profession or why those who do enter do not continue teaching. *Teaching and Teacher Education, 43*, 37–45.

Sue, D., Jackson, K., Rasheed, M., & Rasheed, J. (2016). Multicultural social work practice: A competency-based approach to diversity. Hoboken, NJ: John Wiley & Sons.

Tejero Hughes, M., & Martinez Valle-Riestra, D. (2014). Examining the perceptions of families, teachers, and administrators of preschool programs meeting the needs of young children with disabilities. *Journal of Education and Human Development, 3*(4), 21–32.

Tyrer, R., & Fazel, M. (2014). School and community-based interventions for refugee and asylum seeking children: A systematic review. *PLos ONE 9*(2), e89359.

U. S. Department of Education. (2015). Family and community engagement. Retrieved August 12, 2015 from http://www.ed.gov/parent-and-family-engagement.

Vermont Department of Health. (2015). Cultural differences in non-verbal communication. Retrieved August 17, 2015 from http://healthvermont.gov/family/toolkit/tools%5CF-6%20Cultural%20Differences%20in%20Nonverbal%20Communic.pdf.

Walker, J., Wilkins, A., Dallaire, J., Sandler, H., & Hoover-Dempsey, K. (2005). Parental involvement: Model revision through scale development. *The Elementary School Journal, 106*, 85–104.

Walsh, B., Cromer, H., & Weigel, D. (2014). Classroom-to-home connections: Young children's experiences with a technology-based parent involvement tool. *Early Education and Development, 25*(8), 1142–1161.

Watson, T., & Bogotch, I. (2015). Reframing parent involvement: What should urban school leaders do differently? *Leadership and Policy in Schools, 14*(3), 257–278.

Welchons, L., & McIntyre, L. (2015). The transition to kindergarten for children with and without disabilities: An investigation of parent and teacher concerns and involvement. *Topics in Early Childhood Special Education, 35*(1), 52–62.

Becoming a Parent

4

LEARNING OBJECTIVES

After reading the chapter, you will be able to:

4-1 Discuss different pathways to becoming a parent and the stressors associated with each.

4-2 List the stages of pregnancy, and describe the associated changes that occur in fetal development.

4-3 Describe lifestyle changes that may occur after becoming a parent.

naeyc Standards Linked to Chapter Content

1b: Promoting child development and learning

2a: Building family and community relationships

Monkey Business Images/Shutterstock.com

The transition to parenthood often brings a combination of new experiences, unanticipated demands, and unexpected joys. Parents may experience a range of conflicting feelings such as apprehension, excitement, disbelief, and worry. Some parents relish and adapt

continued on following page

quickly to their new role and responsibilities while others adjust more slowly or not at all. However, the way that parents adapt to their new role may be influenced by the level of social support they receive from others and their own self-confidence. New mothers often depend upon and receive considerable emotional support from their parents and relatives, although fathers are less likely to do so (Chong, Gordon, & Don, 2016). Mulherin and Johnstone (2015) observed that social support was also an important factor in helping adolescent and young mothers adjust to becoming a parent while stigmas had a negative effect on their transition. Lawler, Begley, and Loalor (2015) found that women who had disabilities felt pathologized and were under greater surveillance from clinicians (e.g., concerned they would be unable to care for the child), which disrupted their belief that they would be competent mothers and led to additional stress. However, it was also noted that these women were able to provide adequate care without close monitoring by clinicians and, thus, were able to achieve a positive sense of themselves as mothers. ∎

4-1 Pathways to Becoming a Parent

assisted reproduction
use of technology (e.g. fertility medications, *in vitro* fertilization, intracytoplasmic sperm insertion, egg and gamete donation, and surrogacy) to conceive a child.

There are many pathways available to individuals who desire to become a parent, including natural conception (planned or unplanned), **assisted reproduction**, adoption, foster parenting, or legal guardianship. Although all parents respond differently as they transition to becoming a parent, the stressors they face also differ depending on the unique avenue they have chosen to achieving parenthood.

Individuals contemplate many factors in determining if and when to attempt pregnancy. For example, some women may consider their desire to become pregnant and end contraceptive use, whether or not they feel that they have reached an ideal moment in their life, and whether or not their partner consents (McQuillan et al., 2015; Barrett & Wellings, 2002). However, many women are delaying pregnancy in order to obtain higher levels of education or to establish a career. Some women are choosing to postpone parenthood because of more effective contraception methods, changes in personal values, increased emphasis on gender equality, changes in partnership types, and lack of social family support policies (Mills et al., 2011). Factors that influence a father's decision to have a planned pregnancy include relationship stability, financial security, job stability, social pressure from partner and family, age, desire to have children and family, and readiness for a new life stage (deMontigny, Gauthier, & deMontigny, 2013).

Parents report several reasons or motivations for wanting children, although they may differ somewhat by culture (see Figure 4-1) (Astone & Peters, 2014). For example, Dyer (2007) found that individuals in Western countries and those in African nations both desired children for reasons related to happiness, well-being, and parenthood. However, African parents placed a greater emphasis on having children to better their culture and society, to solidify gender identity (e.g., having children as a prerequisite for womanhood), and continuity of the family lineage.

Figure 4-1 Reasons Commonly Cited for Becoming a Parent

- To feel pleasure interacting and spending time with children
- For intrinsic reasons (e.g., happiness, well-being, share love)
- To leave a legacy
- To improve or cement a relationship
- To succeed at doing something difficult and challenging
- To maximize "genetic fitness" or the number of children to carry on family genes
- To contribute to society
- To meet family and friends' expectations

Source: Astone & Peters (2014).

4-1a Planned versus Unplanned Pregnancy

According to the National Survey for Growth (Mosher, Jones, & Abma, 2012), older women and those who have achieved higher education are more likely to report that their pregnancy was intended. A majority of married couples report that their pregnancy was planned compared to those who are cohabitating or not married (see Figure 4-2). However, over one third (37 percent) of all births are either unwanted (14 percent) or mistimed (i.e., pregnancy happened sooner than planned; 23 percent). These data indicate that many people do not purposefully decide to enter into parenthood.

Unintended births are more common among less educated and low-income women (Borreo et al., 2015; Finer & Zolna, 2014). Although the number of teen pregnancies have declined over the past two decades, 77 percent of teen mothers have unplanned pregnancies (Office of Adolescent Health, 2016; Mosher et al., 2012). Researchers have identified a number of reasons for this pattern, including a lack of contraception because women underestimate the risk of pregnancy or poor adherence to contraceptive use, which decreases the effectiveness of these medications (Mosher et. al., 2012). In addition, a lack of insurance, dissatisfaction with contraceptive methods, and holding religious beliefs that are inconsistent with

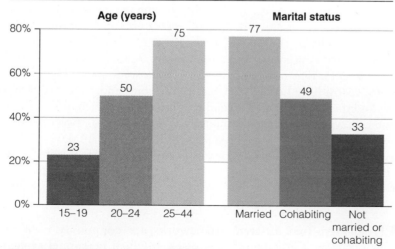

Figure 4-2 Percentage of Intended Births Based on Age and Marital Status

Source: Mosher, Jones, & Abma (2012).

Photo 4-1 An unplanned pregnancy may be a welcomed event or cause of significant distress. CandyBox Images/Shutterstock.com

contraceptive use are also associated with an increased likelihood of unplanned pregnancy (Kornides et al., 2015).

Unfortunately, women who have unplanned pregnancies are less likely to receive prenatal care during the first trimester and more likely to smoke, experience postpartum depression, and give birth to a low-weight infant (Coller et al., 2014; Mosher et al., 2012). Although women who intend to get pregnant report a high level of happiness upon finding out about the pregnancy, those with untimed or unwanted pregnancies are less likely to do so (Mosher, Jones, & Abma, 2012). Unplanned pregnancies can also cause couples to question whether or not to continue the pregnancy and what the pregnancy will mean to their relationship. Furthermore, some men experience negative effects from unplanned pregnancy, such as decreased life and relationship satisfaction (Sipsma et al, 2012). However, unplanned pregnancy can also have positive effects on individuals. For example, some men report feeling happy about the transition to fatherhood when unplanned pregnancies are continued to term because they view it as an indicator of status and an increased purpose in life (Astone, 2014). Some adolescent mothers feel that taking on the social role of mother made their life better, and encouraged them to reassess their values and aspirations and to move in a more positive direction (Anwar & Stanistreet, 2015).

Efforts to reduce the incidence of unplanned pregnancy among adolescents has led to initiatives, such as the National Campaign to Prevent Teen and Unplanned Pregnancy, that provide education and information resources to women and conduct research that will lead to improved practices. Data collected on the implementation of an online birth control support network developed through this initiative showed that women who participated were less likely to have a pregnancy scare, unintended pregnancy, or unprotected sex (Antonishak, Kay, & Swiader, 2015). These findings also showed that nurturant-responsive parenting, having a future goal orientation, and involvement in academic pursuits can decrease the risk of externalizing problems, including risky sexual behavior, among teens (Kogan et al., 2013).

4-1b Conception and Pregnancy

Female infants are born with millions of eggs (ovum) that gradually reach maturity during puberty; boys do not begin producing sperm until they enter puberty. A mature egg is released each month following the onset of a woman's menstrual cycle. An egg only lives for approximately 12–24 hours, during which time it can be fertilized by any available sperm (which live 1–2 days). If fertilization does not occur, the lining that has formed in the uterus (in preparation for pregnancy) is shed during the menstrual cycle.

chromosomes thread-like structures (DNA) present in every cell that determine all human characteristics (e.g., eye color, height, vision).

Reproductive cells (e.g., ovum, sperm) each contain 23 single **chromosomes**, whereas all other cells in the human body have 23 chromosome pairs (46 single chromosomes). When conception occurs, the sperm and ovum unite to create a small mass, called a zygote, that now contains 23 chromosome pairs. Ovum only carry X chromosomes; sperm have both X and Y chromosomes and, thus, are responsible for determining an infant's gender (XX, female child or XY, male child).

The two-cell zygote continues to multiply and divide (e.g., two cells become four, four become eight, and eight become sixteen) during the next 14 days until it reaches a total of 16 cells. At this point, the zygote attempts to attach itself to the uterine wall so that it can obtain nutrients and continue to grow. This process is called implantation. Once the zygote has successfully attached itself, it is referred to as an embryo. Approximately two thirds of zygotes survive this stage.

Stages of Pregnancy. Two different frameworks are commonly used to describe changes that occur as a pregnancy progresses. Medical personnel typically divide pregnancy into trimesters. Each trimester is associated with different symptoms for the mother (see Figure 4-3).

Figure 4-3 Pregnancy and Maternal Changes by Trimester

Trimester	Weeks	Signs and Symptoms
First	0–12	• hormonal changes can cause mood swings, "morning sickness" (e.g., nausea, vomiting), headaches • menstruation stops • fatigue • breasts become tender and swollen • cravings or distaste for certain foods • heartburn may develop • urination becomes more frequent • constipation • weight gain or loss
Second	13–28	• nausea and vomiting decrease • body aches, such as back, abdomen, groin, or thigh pain may develop due to increased pressure from the growing fetus • skin changes (e.g., stretch marks, patches of skin darkening, itching) may develop • ankles, fingers, and face may swell • begin to feel fetal movement around 16th week
Third	29–40	• discomfort (e.g., aches, swelling, heartburn) may become more frequent • shortness of breath • hemorrhoids • breasts become tender; may leak colostrum (pre-milk) • sleeping may become difficult • fetus "drops" into the lower abdomen in preparation for birth • contractions become more regular and frequent • gains ½ pound per week during the 8th month and 1 pound per week during the 9th month

- First trimester—0–3 months (weeks 0–12)
- Second trimester—4–6 months (weeks 13–24)
- Third trimester—7–9 months (weeks 25–40)

An alternative framework divides fetal development into stages and focuses on physiological changes that take place as the fetus matures (see Figure 4–4):

- Germinal stage—weeks 0–2
- Embryonic stage—weeks 3–8
- Fetal stage—weeks 9–40

The germinal stage begins when fertilization occurs and ends when the zygote is successfully implanted. Until the cell cluster is firmly attached, it is relatively protected from exposure to potentially harmful substances. However, once implanted, the embryo begins to share everything in common with its mother.

The embryonic stage marks an especially tenuous or critical point in any pregnancy because of the many developments that must occur. Hormonal changes prepare the mother's body for pregnancy, including the growth of specialized cells that will form

Figure 4-4 Characteristics of Fetal Development

PERIOD OF THE OVUM	PERIOD OF THE EMBRYO						PERIOD OF THE FETUS			
Weeks 1–2	Week 3	Week 4	Week 5	Week 6	Week 7	Week 8	Week 12	Week 16	Weeks 20–36	Week 38
Period of early embryo development and implantation.	CNS heart	eye heart	eye	ear	palate	ear		brain		
			limbs		teeth	external genitals				
	Central Nervous System (CNS)–Brain and Spinal Cord									
	Heart									
		Arms/Legs								
		Eyes								
				Teeth						
				Palate						
					External Genitals					
Pregnancy loss	Ears									

■ Period of development when major defects in bodily structure can occur.

■ Period of development when major functional defects and minor structural defects can occur.

Source: CDC (2016).

the structures (e.g., placenta, umbilical cords, chorionic fluid) necessary to support the developing embryo. Miscarriage is likely to ensue if any of these critical structures fail to develop properly.

The embryo increases in size and complexity as a result of continued cell division. All major fetal organ systems (e.g., heart, lungs, skeleton, brain, blood) that are essential for survival develop during the embryonic stage. Congenital deformities are also more likely to occur as critical organ systems are forming. Approximately 20 percent of embryos are aborted during this stage. Those that remain are now referred to as a fetus.

The fetal stage encompasses the remaining weeks of a pregnancy and concludes with the onset of labor and delivery. All fetal systems are now in place and functioning. However, they will continue to mature and grow in size until the fetus is able to live independently of its mother. Almost all of the infant's weight (7–8 pounds) is gained during this final stage. The majority of 7-month-old fetuses are able to survive birth although they are considered high-risk infants because their organ systems (especially respiratory) are not yet fully developed.

Some fathers feel an emotional connection from the moment they find out about the pregnancy, but others may experience a sense of disbelief. Feeling the fetus move and seeing the fetus through ultrasounds can increase a father's sense of connection (Pho, Koh, & He, 2014). In a review of interview data, Kowlessar and colleagues (2015) identified five themes related to fathers' experiences during pregnancy:

1. Reacting to early pregnancy: worries and conflicting emotions that range from joy to disappointment.

Photo 4-2 Some fathers form an immediate emotional connection with their unborn child. glenda/Shutterstock.com

2. On the outside looking in: feeling distant or disconnected from the pregnancy experience during the first trimester; feeling left out during prenatal appointments and classes.

3. The pregnant male: experiencing physical and emotional changes during the second trimester.

4. A journey of acceptance: increased acceptance of the pregnancy reality related to feeling and seeing the fetus; feeling more involved and attached to the baby in the second trimester.

5. Redefining self as a father: begin to make lifestyle adjustments during the third trimester, re-evaluating what is important, and reflecting on their own fathering and the roles they want to fulfill.

Throughout the pregnancy, it is important for service providers to consider the psychological needs of both parents as well as attending to the mother's medical care.

Labor and Delivery. Childbirth is a natural process that occurs every day, but the way it is perceived and experienced varies significantly by culture. For example, fathers in Arabic, Indonesian, Chinese, Korean, and Mexican cultures seldom witness or participate in their child's birth (Callister, 2014). More often the mother's female relatives are summoned to assist with the delivery. Women in some African, South American, and Asian cultures typically maintain a squatting or kneeling position during labor and delivery, whereas women in North America and Europe are more likely to assume a reclining or sitting position (Lavender & Mlay, 2006). Cultural differences have also been noted in the way that mothers interpret and respond to pain during labor and delivery (Van der Gucht & Lewis, 2015). For example, women in cultures that hold strong religious beliefs may accept pain as having spiritual meaning and, thus, are likely to endure it without medication.

Although the experience of giving birth may be unique for individual mothers, the fundamental labor and delivery process is quite similar. Approximately 2 weeks before active labor begins, a pregnant woman may notice that she is carrying the baby lower in her abdomen. This phenomenon is referred to as lightening, and occurs as the fetus descends into the birth canal, usually headfirst, in preparation for delivery. At the same time, the mild contractions that a mother has experienced throughout pregnancy become stronger and more regular. When active labor begins, she may notice a small bloody discharge as the mucus plug that has protected the birth canal opening is released. Some of the amniotic fluid that surrounds the fetus may also begin to leak at this time.

The birthing process is divided into 3 stages. The first stage is the longest, averaging 10–17 hours for first-time mothers and 6–8 hours in subsequent births. During this stage, the birth canal dilates in preparation for delivery. The second stage lasts approximately 1–2 hours during which time the infant continues to move through the birth canal until it is delivered. Contractions usually become more intense, frequent, and painful during this stage. The third and final stage lasts only a few minutes, and begins once the infant has been delivered and ends after the placenta is expelled. Throughout the birthing process, the infant is monitored for signs of respiratory distress and reevaluated immediately upon delivery and again 5 minutes later.

Although most births proceed with few complications, there are occasional situations that require medical intervention. The induction of labor is one of the most common of these procedures, and is used in approximately one out of every four U.S. births (Osterman & Martin, 2014). Labor may be induced when a woman is past her due date, is younger than 18 or older than 35 years, labor doesn't begin after a woman's water has broken, a multiple birth is involved, or there is a maternal or infant health risk (Hamou et al., 2016; Walker et al., 2016).

Caesarean section (C-section) deliveries are also relatively common, and occurred in approximately 32.2 percent of all deliveries in the United States in 2014 (CDC, 2016). A surgical delivery may be deemed medically necessary in certain high-risk situations,

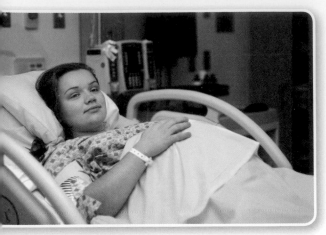

Photo 4-3 A caesarean delivery may be necessary when medical complications develop. Mikhail Tchkheidze/Shutterstock.com

breech birth when a fetus is positioned in the birth canal feet or bottom first versus headfirst.

such as complications associated with pregnancy (e.g., infections, multiple birth, problems with the placenta, high blood pressure, diabetes) or when problems develop during labor and delivery (e.g., **breech birth**, infant is too large, labor stops, infant is in distress, certain birth defects). However, the increased number of elective C-section procedures performed in recent years for reasons of convenience, pain avoidance, or low-risk conditions has raised significant public health concerns (Jou et al., 2015; Stoll, Edmonds, & Hall, 2015). Caesarean sections place mothers at increased risk for infection, blood loss, an extended hospital stay, and a longer recovery period. Infants delivered via C-section are more likely to experience breathing and respiratory problems and a higher mortality risk than infants delivered vaginally (Xie et al., 2015).

4-1c Infertility

Six percent of married women between the ages of 15 and 44 in the United States are infertile, and 11 percent have an impaired ability to get pregnant or carry a fetus to full term (Chandra, Copen, & Stephen, 2013). In addition, 12 percent of men between the ages of 25 and 44 have some form of infertility (Chandra et al., 2013). Approximately one third of infertility cases are related to male factors, one third to female factors, and the remaining one third to either a combination of male and female or unexplained factors (see Figure 4-5) (American Society for Reproductive Medicine [ASRM], 2015a).

Infertility can cause significant distress and negative emotions (e.g., anger, guilt, fear, anxiety) for couples who desire a child. Women are more likely than men to experience emotional maladjustment problems, such as depression and low self-esteem, when infertility problems arise (Ying, Wu, & Loke, 2015). Those who seek medical treatments for infertility often endure a series of emotional ups and downs (hopes and disappointments) throughout the demanding and challenging process of trying to conceive. However, individuals who have strong social support and a more positive outlook tend to experience better mental health outcomes (Ramírez-Uclés, Del Castillo-Aparicio, & Moreno-Rosset, 2015).

Cultural variables also influence a couple's responses to infertility. For example, in a review of the literature related to infertility in African countries, Dyer (2007) noted that infertility is sometimes associated with limited status, abuse, divorce, stigma, and social isolation. Although such social repercussions occur less often in more industrialized

---

Figure 4-5 Common Causes of Infertility

- Men
  - Azoospermia (no sperm cells are produced)
  - Oligospermia (few sperm cells are produced)
  - Malformed sperm cells or cells that die before reaching the egg
  - Genetic diseases such as cystic fibrosis or a chromosomal abnormality
  - Smoking
- Women
  - Ovulation disorder
  - Blocked fallopian tubes
  - Birth defects involving structural deformities of the uterus
  - Uterine fibroids (noncancerous growths) are associated with repeated miscarriages
  - Being under- or overweight
  - Smoking

---

countries, they do continue to exist among immigrant groups. Batool & de Visser (2016), for example, noted that childless Pakistani women were subjected to significant social consequences associated with infertility, including divorce and social exclusion, even when they were living in another country (England).

Support for individuals who experience infertility has changed over the last several decades from a focus on treating psychological conflicts in women (believed to be a main cause of infertility) in the 1930s, to helping individuals grieve in the 1970s when medical treatments were often unsuccessful, and finally to a more integrative approach that currently provides individualized psychological support before, during, and after medical treatment (Boivin & Gameiro, 2015). Empirical evidence continues to validate the importance of providing psychological counseling to help individuals cope with infertility and the emotional stress associated with its treatment (Gamerio et al., 2015; Yu et al., 2014).

4-1d Assisted Reproduction

Advances in alternative reproductive technology provide individuals who are unable to conceive naturally a different approach to having children. It also gives same-gender couples an opportunity to build their family with one parent being biologically related to the child. Lesbian couples, however, report unique challenges in their efforts to become parents. For example, non-biological co-mothers cite (a) stress related to their partner achieving a pregnancy and worries about legal protections (i.e., inability to adopt the child until after birth), (b) difficulty creating a distinctive role, (c) lack of support from the lesbian community for attempting to emulate heterosexual families, and (d) feeling ignored by medical professionals (Wojnar & Katsenmeyer, 2014).

Although the use of alternative reproduction technologies has become increasingly common in recent years, fewer than 2 percent of infants born in the United States are conceived in this manner (see Figure 4-6) (Centers for Disease Control and

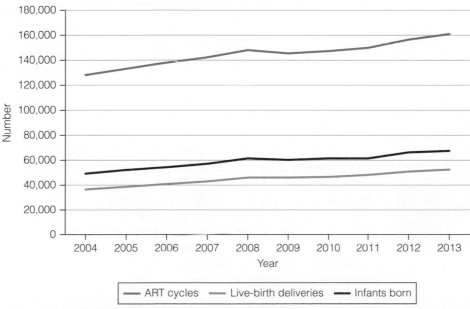

Figure 4-6 Number of Alternative Reproductive Technology (ART) Cycles Performed, Live Birth Deliveries and Infants Born Using ART

Source: Centers for Disease Control and Prevention, American Society for Reproductive Medicine, Society for Assisted Reproductive Technology (2015a).

Prevention [CDC], 2015a). Perinatal outcomes for children born via assisted reproduction technology have improved over time, with fewer infant deaths, pre-term births, and low birth weight infants (Henningsen et al., 2015).

Medications. Eighty-five to 90 percent of infertility cases are treated successfully with medication and/or surgery (ASRM, 2015b). Some medications are used to treat infertility while others prepare the body for procedures, such as *in vitro* fertilization (IVF), by increasing the likelihood of implantation, decreasing the risk of bacteria and infection, and increasing the quality of the uterine lining. Women who do not ovulate regularly or have no, infrequent, or long menstrual cycles often have success with medications that help to induce or stimulate ovulation and increase egg production (American Pregnancy Association, 2015).

***In Vitro* Fertilization (IVF).** IVF involves removing eggs from the female and placing them together with sperm in a laboratory petri dish. If fertilization occurs, the embryo is allowed to begin growing and then transferred back into the woman's uterus. The procedure is typically indicated for women who have blocked fallopian tubes or if the male has a low sperm count. The first recorded birth resulting from *in vitro* fertilization occurred in 1978 (Ombeliti & Van Robays, 2015). Although IVF is perhaps the most widely known infertility treatment, it accounts for only 5 percent of the methods used in the United States (ASRM, 2015b).

Intracytoplasmic Sperm Insertion (ICSI). ICSI differs from IVF in the way that eggs are fertilized. Specifically, a single sperm is injected directly into each egg. If fertilization is successful, the embryo is allowed to develop in a petri dish for several days and then implanted directly into the woman's uterine lining. More than one embryo is often implanted to increase the likelihood of pregnancy; thus, ICSI often results in a multiple birth.

Egg and Gamete Donation. Infertility is sometimes treated through the use of eggs, sperm, or embryos that have been donated by an individual who is known or unknown to the intended parents. Egg donation is used when a woman is unable to produce eggs, her eggs are of poor quality, or a couple wants to avoid transmitting a genetic disorder. A donor, typically between 21 and 30 years of age, undergoes medical testing and then is given hormones to increase the number of eggs produced each month. The eggs are then harvested from the donor's ovaries, fertilized with sperm from the intended father or a donor (**gamete donation**), and then implanted into the recipient woman. In some cases, women who are being treated with IVF will donate extra eggs for use by other infertile couples. Gamete donation may be indicated when the male is unable to produce usable sperm. In these situations, the recipient(s) are listed as the birth parents even though they are not genetically-related to the infant (ASRM, 2014a).

> **gamete donation** sperm donated by a known or anonymous person.

Surrogacy. In some cases, a woman is unable to become pregnant or to carry a child to full-term due to postmenopausal changes, medical conditions, or structural defects of reproductive organs. In these situations, the family may investigate the possibility of contracting with a surrogate who agrees to become pregnant and have a child for the family. However, there are significant legal, financial, medical, and psychological issues that must be considered carefully when contemplating gestational surrogacy (Dar et al., 2015). Once the decision has been made, a formal contract outlining the fees to be paid for services (e.g., medical procedures, attending appointments, transportation, maternity wardrobe, travel, food, etc.) and an agreement regarding parental rights is drawn up. Costs associated with surrogacy typically include agency and attorney fees, surrogate screenings, medical expenses, and insurance costs.

Photo 4-4 A variety of assisted reproductive techniques are available to help couples who have difficulty conceiving.

The practice of egg donation has risen dramatically in the last decade and, consequently, has posed several practical, legal, and ethical questions for the participating individuals, physicians, and the legal system. One of the most common dilemmas centers around donor selection and compensation. Some couples use eggs that are donated anonymously to clinics, while others recruit a donor through organizations or websites, or select a known donor such as a family member or friend.

Another dilemma concerns whether or not the genetic parents (donors) have parental rights. Laws governing parental rights in the case of IVF or egg donations vary from state to state and are often interpreted on a case-by-case basis. In order to avoid such questions, many clinics will only fertilize eggs with sperm from the intended father or a donor known to the family when they are ready to attempt a pregnancy. However, some clinics also create embryos from selected donors that can be purchased for implantation.

Some infertility clinics have been accused of creating 'designer babies' by only recruiting donors who possess certain specific and highly desirable characteristics (e.g., thin, attractive, athletic, intelligent, preferred skin color). Similarly, a California company has received a U.S. patent for a technique (23andMe) that identifies and selects specific DNA for use in creating children with chosen characteristics (Naik, 2013). Some authorities say these practices verge on eugenics (the practice of encouraging the reproduction of individuals with desirable traits and discouraging the reproduction of others) and express concern about their regulation.

Questions have also arisen about how much donors should be paid. The American Society for Reproductive Medicine Ethics Committee (2007) recommends paying donors approximately $4000 to cover the time, inconvenience, and physical and emotional demands associated with the donation process. However, compensation rates vary widely from region to region. Donors who are recruited for specific desirable characteristics have been offered as much as $50,000 and more in some cases. Researchers have found that women who donate eggs primarily for the financial incentives or those who have some ambivalence about their decision to donate are more likely to regret their decision and experience emotional harm (Boutelle, 2014; Skoog, et al., 2013) Furthermore, because the medical procedure is relatively complex and the long-term effects (on donors) are unknown, donors may not fully understand the procedure or the associated risks.

What to do with leftover embryos following a successful pregnancy and what to tell a child who is conceived with donor eggs also present significant ethical dilemmas. Couples have many options with regard to remaining embryos, including destroying them, donating them to research, donating them to another family, or having them frozen for future use. This decision can be very difficult for couples to make because their initial attention is usually focused on conceiving and not on what to do with any remaining embryos.

Couples must also consider what to tell their child about his or her conception. Prior to the 1980s, many families were advised not to inform the child. However, experts now recommend more openness and encourage parents to share this information with children. Recent findings show that 40 percent of parents now disclose information about the use of a donor with their child and another 31 percent intend to tell their child at some future time (Readings et al., 2011). The American Society for Reproductive Medicine (2014b) strongly recommends that parents disclose this information to children because it builds trust and honesty, eliminates the threat of betrayal, enables parents to provide accurate information about medical history, and allows parents to have control so that the child does not find out from someone else.

Egg donation offers families who are unable to conceive an option for experiencing pregnancy and having children. However, many moral, ethical, and legal dilemmas remain to be answered as technologies improve and infertility procedures become more commonplace. Is it morally fair to only allow couples who have the financial resources to attempt pregnancy through egg donation? Is it ethical to jeopardize a donor's health (e.g., medication, surgery) to provide eggs for an older, infertile woman? Who legally owns embryos that have been conceived through egg donation?

Depending upon the couples' needs, the surrogate may be required to go through the process of embryo implantation, artificial insemination, or *in vitro* fertilization. In most cases, the surrogate relinquishes parental rights upon delivery, and the contracting family is granted legal custody of the infant.

4-1e Foster Parenting

Foster parenting provides families a unique opportunity to parent. Foster parents typically contract with an agency that places children who have been abandoned or removed from their parent's custody. Foster parents are expected to provide a safe and nurturing environment for children until they can be returned to their parental home or placed

Figure 4-7 Roles and Responsibilities of Biological Parents, the State, Foster Parents, and Adoptive Parents

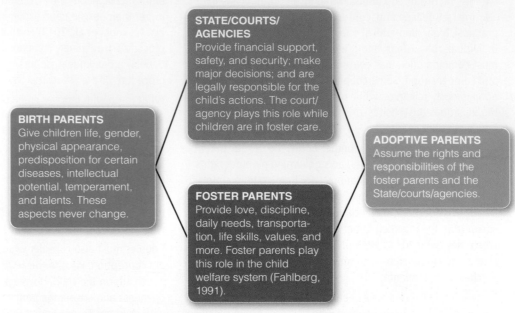

STATE/COURTS/ AGENCIES
Provide financial support, safety, and security; make major decisions; and are legally responsible for the child's actions. The court/ agency plays this role while children are in foster care.

BIRTH PARENTS
Give children life, gender, physical appearance, predisposition for certain diseases, intellectual potential, temperament, and talents. These aspects never change.

ADOPTIVE PARENTS
Assume the rights and responsibilities of the foster parents and the State/courts/agencies.

FOSTER PARENTS
Provide love, discipline, daily needs, transporta- tion, life skills, values, and more. Foster parents play this role in the child welfare system (Fahlberg, 1991).

Source: Child Welfare Information Gateway (2012).

with a permanent family (Child Welfare Information Gateway, 2014). Until this time, the state assumes legal and financial responsibility for the child's care (see Figure 4-7).

Several steps are involved in the approval process to become foster parents. Once an application has been received, an on-site visit is arranged to determine if the foster home is clean, safe, and has adequate space. An agency worker (often a social worker) conducts interviews with family members and contacts their references to determine if the potential foster parent is physically and mentally fit for the role. Often, potential foster parents must meet general requirements in addition to criteria specific to the state in which they reside (see Figure 4-8).

Most individuals desire to be foster parents for child-centered reasons such as providing a child with love and a good home. Others may pursue foster par- enting because they are unable to have children of their own, their own children are grown or have died, or they believe that being a foster parent is beneficial to society (De Maeyer et al., 2014). Regrettably, children placed in foster care, especially those who are older and have physical disabilities or mental health concerns, find themselves being moved frequently from one foster home to an- other. As a result, many of these children present increasingly difficult behaviors which foster parents must handle. However, researchers have determined that such children are less likely to experience multiple moves when they are placed with extended family members or foster parents who are committed to providing long-term placement stability (Koh et al., 2014).

4-1f Adoption

Adoption involves a legal agreement between a child's biological parents and an agency or another individual who consents to become the child's lawful parent. Reasons for adoption include an altruistic desire to provide a permanent home for a child in need, expand their own family, and an inability to have biological children. Adoption types differ by a family's motivations (see Figure 4-9).

Photo 4-5 Adoption can be a gratifying option for becoming a parent.

Figure 4-8 Foster Parent Requirements

Individual Requirements	Training Requirements	Home Study Requirements

• Any work profession or background
 	
• Able to provide a safe and nurturing environment
 	
• Willingness to work with social service agency and birth families
 	
• All family members in the home must pass a background check
 	
• No significant mental or physical health problems that would interfere with caring for children
 	
• 36 states require individuals to be 21 years old (age 18 in 5 states, age 19 in 2)
 	
• Single or married (5 states require couples to be legally married)
 	
• 4 states require applicant to be able to read and write
 	
• 9 states require individuals to be U.S. citizens
	• 44 states require prospective foster parents to complete orientation and training
	
	• Topics addressed in training may include:
	  • Agency policies and procedures
	  • Roles and responsibilities of foster parents
	  • Child development
	  • Behavior management
	  • Cultural sensitivity
	  • Attachment, separation, and loss
	  • Home and child safety
	  • Impact on own families
		• Safe, clean environment (smoke and carbon monoxide detectors, working appliances, hot and cold water)
		
		• Sufficient space to accommodate foster children, including areas for living, eating, studying, playing, and sleeping
		
		• Hazardous materials must be placed out of children's reach
		
		• 38 states require firearms to be locked in a cabinet or gun safe
		
		• Some agencies require inspection by the state health department or a fire and safety inspector in addition to a home study

Modified from: Child Welfare Information Gateway (2014).

⌄ Professional Resource Download

Figure 4-9 Percentage of Adopted Children by Parents' Reasons for Choosing to Adopt, by Adoption Type

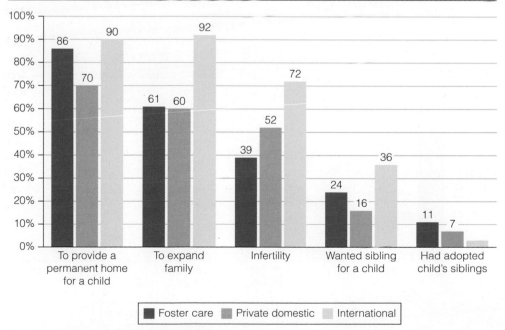

Source: Vandivere, Malm, & Radel (2009).

Adoptive parents face some stressors that other parents do not encounter. These challenges may include an undefined waiting period (2 weeks to 5 years) which leads to an unpredictable transition to parenthood, undergoing extensive agency assessments to determine if they are fit to parent, and receiving a child who has special needs or may have had a difficult past (Goldberg et al., 2014).

Adoptions can take several forms, depending upon the child's country of origin and the nature of contact that will be maintained with the biological parent following adoption. International adoptions have become increasingly popular, but are also often the most expensive adoption form (see Figure 4-10). Costs usually surpass $10,000 and can reach $50,000 depending on agency application fees, home study, background checks, donation to the foreign country, travel and medical expenses, and legal adoption finalization (Heron, 2013). Most agencies use a sliding scale based on family income, but the costs can still be prohibitive for some families. In addition, it can often take years to complete the adoption process.

Private domestic adoption is slightly more affordable (especially when a family member is adopting the child) and typically takes less time to complete. Costs include agency fees, background check, home visit, medical expenses, and termination of parental rights (Heron, 2013). Adoption can also take place through the foster care system and is typically the least costly to complete. Although children adopted from foster care may require more services than those adopted through other avenues, three fourths of these adoptions are subsidized by the state so that the adoptive parents have additional funds to address the child's specific needs (e.g., mental health, medical) (Vandivere, Malm, & Radel, 2009). Families who adopt children through the foster care system may also qualify for a federal adoption tax credit or for employer-funded financial assistance.

Adoptions can be either closed or open. In a closed adoption, the adoptive and biological parents receive non-identifying information about each other. Once the adoption is finalized, the case is sealed and no further contact is made between the families.

Figure 4-10 Percentage Distribution of Adopted Children According to the Cost of the Adoption, by Adoption Type

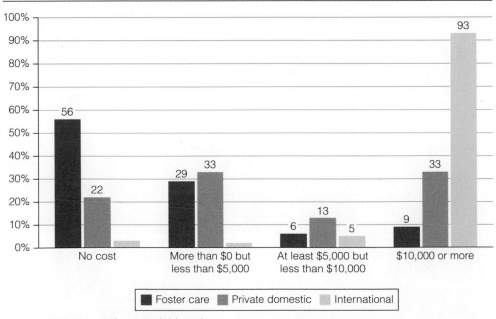

Source: Vandivere, Malm, & Radel (2009).

However, in almost all states, adoptive children have the right to obtain nonidentifying information about their birth parents when they turn 18, and can seek identifying information if the birth parent has provided consent for release or if there is a compelling reason that information is needed (Child Welfare Information Gateway, 2015a). Open adoptions enable the adopted child and birth parent to have some form of continued contact. The nature of this contact can vary from letters to phone conversations and in-person visits. Approximately one third of children adopted by nonrelatives maintain contact with their biological family. Post-adoption contact with the birth family is more common for children who are adopted privately (68 percent) than for those adopted from foster care (39 percent), and very rare for children adopted internationally (6 percent) (Vandivere et al., 2009). Regardless of whether or not the adoption is closed or open, 97 percent of all adopted children know that they are adopted (Vandivere et al., 2009). The Child Welfare Information Gateway (2012) provides suggestions for talking with children about their origins (Suggestions for Parents 4-1).

4-1g Legal Guardianship

Legal guardianship allows another person to make important decisions for a child, but does not require the termination of the biological parents' rights. This type of arrangement is often used when a family member agrees to provide a permanent home for a child in need. The Guardianship Assistance Program was developed by Congress to provide financial assistance to legal guardians, and has been approved in 31 states as of July 2013 (Children's Bureau, 2015). The program's goals are designed to help children stay connected to their family, increase the stability of children's placement, prevent children from continuing in the foster care system, decrease frequency of agency supervision, and support relatives who provide a permanent home for these children's (Allen et al., 2012). Twenty-eight states also permit parents to appoint a standby guardian for children in the event that a parent experiences a serious illness or disabling condition. This arrangement ensures that a plan is in place if a parent's condition worsens and they are temporarily unable to provide care for a child during the parent's lifetime (Child Welfare Information Gateway, 2015b).

Five-year-old Misaki was still upset when her mother picked her up after school. "The kids were making fun of me today and said that I wasn't really born, that I was adopted because I don't look like you or daddy." Misaki's parents had been waiting for the right time to talk with her about being adopted, and now realize that they should have had this conversation sooner. How would you advise Misaki's mother to respond to her daughter's immediate concerns? What suggestions would you offer to Misaki's parents for talking with her about being adopted?

4-2 **Preparing for a Healthy Infant**

Long before a pregnancy is attempted, both parents can take steps to improve their chances of giving birth to a healthy infant. For example, this is an ideal time to address any pre-existing medical conditions and practice good physical and mental health habits. It is also equally important that parents avoid excessive use of alcohol, tobacco, and drugs (unless prescribed by a physician), and follow a nutritious diet for at least several months prior to conceiving.

However, some environmental and social factors, such as poverty, disparities in access to health care, hazardous living conditions, and food and water supply safety may present significant obstacles that are difficult for an individual or family to overcome. Public health efforts continue to work toward improving environmental conditions and ensuring that pregnant women have access to essential food and health services beneficial for children, their families, and society as a whole.

4-2a **Healthy Lifestyle Practices**

teratogens harmful substances that may cause birth defects.

Couples can take important steps to increase their probability of giving birth to a healthy infant. However, waiting until a pregnancy is confirmed may not be as effective because critical fetal development is taking place during the early weeks following conception. For this reason, couples are encouraged to follow a healthy lifestyle throughout their reproductive years to improve their chances of conceiving and minimizing the risk of fetal birth defects. Years of empirical evidence support a number of practices that are known to have positive outcomes for mothers and their unborn child, including:

- timing of pregnancies
- obtaining early prenatal care
- consuming a nutritious diet
- maintaining a healthy weight
- getting adequate sleep
- avoiding **teratogens**

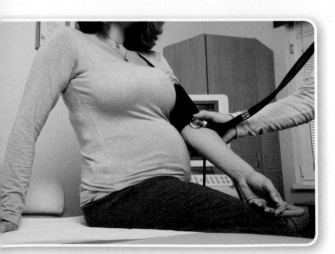

Photo 4-6 Early medical care is important for a healthy pregnancy and infant.
Nejron Photo/Shutterstock.com

Timing of Pregnancies. Couples have many factors to consider when they are deciding whether or not to have a child. Parental age may be among one of the most important. Research evidence suggests that the years between the mid-twenties and late thirties is an ideal time, from a physiological perspective, for conceiving, experiencing a healthy pregnancy, and giving birth to a healthy infant. Adolescent pregnancies are considered high-risk for several reasons. Teenage girls' physical development is still quite immature and there is a high probability that they live in poverty, consume an unhealthy diet, and/or engage in substance abuse (Barrett et al., 2015; Wright et al., 2015). Consequently, infants born to adolescent mothers experience a high rate of prematurity, developmental disabilities, inadequate growth, infection, chemical dependency, and early death (Callegari, Schiff, & Debiec, 2015). In contrast, women who become pregnant in their late thirties and beyond are at higher risk for miscarrying, developing medical complications (e.g., gestational diabetes, high blood pressure) during their pregnancy, having an infant with a birth defect, and requiring a caesarean delivery (Schimmel et al., 2015). Advanced paternal age (40–50 years) at the time of conception has been associated with difficulty conceiving, pregnancy loss, and an increase in birth defects, autism, and other developmental disabilities (Lee & McGrath, 2015; Ramasamy et al., 2015).

Another aspect of timing that is important for parents to consider is the spacing between pregnancies. Adverse outcomes, including premature birth, low birth weight, birth defects, and infant mortality, are more likely to occur when the interval between pregnancies is less than 12 months or greater than 60 months. Durkin, DuBois, and Maenner (2015) also noted a twofold increase in the rate of autism among infants conceived less than 12 months apart. Allowing an interval of at least 18–24 months between pregnancies improves the chances of giving birth to a healthy infant.

Early and Regular Prenatal Care. As soon as a woman suspects that she may be pregnant, she should arrange to visit with her health care provider. Early and continued prenatal visits are important for reviewing family history, identifying and treating existing medical conditions, updating immunizations, receiving advice about vitamin and mineral supplementation, and asking questions (see Figure 4-11). The mother's weight and blood pressure are monitored closely during each visit to assure that fetal development is progressing according to schedule and if any complications, such as **gestational diabetes** or **preeclampsia**, may be developing.

At present, only 73.7 percent of U.S. pregnant women receive prenatal care during their first trimester and 6 percent wait until the third trimester before seeking medical care (U.S. Department of Health and Human Services, 2013) (see Figure 4-12). Adolescent mothers account for almost half of these percentages. Mothers who wait until late in their pregnancy or fail to obtain any prenatal care experience significantly higher rates of **premature births, low birth weight** infants, and infant deaths. Barriers commonly associated with poor utilization of prenatal care include age (19 years and younger), race/ethnicity (non-Hispanic white, non-Hispanic black, Hispanic), limited

gestational diabetes
a form of diabetes that only occurs during pregnancy and is often associated with excessive weight gain, certain ethnicities (e.g., Latina, Native American, African American, Asian, Pacific Islander), or a family history of diabetes.

preeclampsia
a pregnancy complication that can develop after the 20th week; signs include high blood pressure that can damage the kidneys and be fatal to mother and infant unless promptly treated.

premature birth delivery prior to the 37th week following conception.

low birth weight an infant who weighs less than 5.5 pounds (2.5 kg) at birth.

Figure 4-11 Prevalence of Chronic Diseases Among Women of Reproductive Age

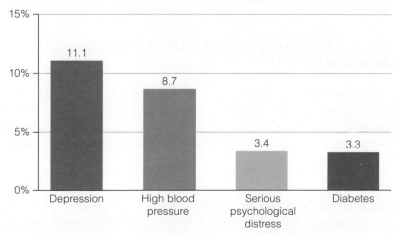

Source: Centers for Disease Control and Prevention (CDC). (2015).

Figure 4-12 Timing of Prenatal Care Initiation

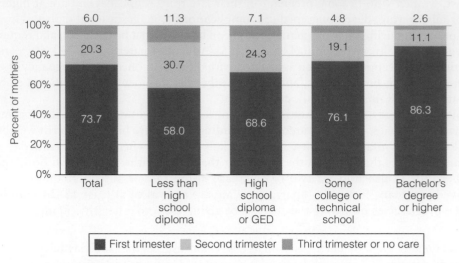

Timing of Prenatal Care Initiation, by Maternal Education, 2011

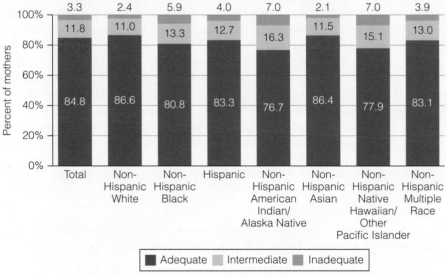

Adequacy of Prenatal Care Utilization Upon Initiation, by Maternal Race/Ethnicity, 2011

Source: Centers for Disease Control and Prevention. National Center for Health Statistics. 2011 Natality Public Use File Analysis conducted by the Maternal and Child Health Bureau.

spina bifida
a malformation
of the infant's spinal
column.

anencephaly
a malformation of the
skull and brain; some areas
may be missing.

cleft lip, cleft palate a
deformity caused by an
incomplete closure of the
lip, palate (roof of the
mouth), or both.

financial resources, difficulty accessing prenatal care (e.g., distance to a medical facility, no health insurance, unreliable transportation), and limited education.

Consuming a Nutritious Diet. Maternal diet plays a critical role in the ability to conceive and throughout pregnancy. A well-balanced diet that includes adequate calories, fluids, protein, vitamins (A, folate, B_6, B_{12}, C, D), and the minerals iron and calcium is essential for healthy fetal tissue and organ system development. Folate (folic acid) intake (a minimum of 400 micrograms daily) is especially important in the months prior to conceiving and during the first trimester when critical fetal systems are forming (Suggestions for Parents 4-2). Researchers have confirmed a direct correlation between folic acid consumption and a significant reduction in birth defects affecting the infant's brain and spine (e.g., **spina bifida, anencephaly**), heart, and oral cavity (e.g., **cleft lip, cleft palate**) (Cordero et al., 2015; Figueiredo et al., 2015). Low folic acid intake has also been linked to behavior

Foods Rich in Folates

Food sources of folate include:

- orange juice
- green vegetables (spinach, edamame, asparagus, broccoli, avocado, peas)
- lentils, dried peas, beans
- whole grain products, fortified (breads, crackers, cereals, pasta, rice)

and autism spectrum disorders in children and the development of certain chronic diseases as they reach adulthood (Langley-Evans, 2015; Ornoy, Weinstein-Fudim, & Ergaz, 2015). The results of numerous studies were so convincing that the U.S. and Canadian governments passed laws in 1998 requiring food manufacturers to enrich all grain products (e.g., flour, cereals, breads, pastas) with folic acid. As a result, there has been a substantial reduction in folate-related birth defects.

Maternal food choices during pregnancy should consist primarily of items rich in essential nutrients (e.g., protein, vitamins, and minerals). Although seafood provides high-quality protein and is low in calories, the Environmental Protection Agency (EPA) advises pregnant women to avoid certain varieties because they contain high mercury and pesticide levels (EPA, 2015). Foods high in calories and with few other nutrients (e.g., cake, cookies, doughnuts, candy, and soda) should be limited to avoid excessive weight gain.

Women are encouraged to take prenatal vitamins during their pregnancy. However, they should not be taken in place of a healthy diet because supplements lack the calories, proteins, fiber, and other essential nutrients that are required for optimum fetal development. Nutrients in food also improve the body's ability to absorb and utilize the vitamins and minerals in supplements. Herbal preparations are not recommended because they lack safety testing and consistent manufacturing standards. Some herbal medicines have been associated with harmful effects for the fetus and mother (Frawley et al., 2015).

Weight. Women are encouraged to gain between 25 and 35 pounds (10–14 kg) during their pregnancy unless they were under- or overweight before becoming pregnant. Excessive or inadequate weight gains are associated with poor outcomes for both the mother and her infant (Headen et al., 2015; Starling et al., 2015). Insufficient weight gain may result in a low birth weight infant (less than 5 pounds, 5 ounces or 2.5 kg), while too much weight gain can lead to premature birth, miscarriage, a large infant, or gestational diabetes. Following a diet that includes a variety of fruits and vegetables, lean protein (meats and plant-derived proteins), whole grains, and low-fat dairy products is ideal for promoting fetal growth and maintaining maternal health. Engaging in daily physical activity (with physician approval) also aids in moderating weight gain and improves the mother's muscle tone, circulation, and elimination.

Sleep. Pregnancy places an additional physical and emotional strain on the mother's body. Hormonal changes, weight gain, and stress often cause fatigue and an increased need for nighttime sleep and daytime rest periods. However, frequent urination, nausea, heartburn, leg cramps, and generalized physical discomforts can result in disturbed sleep. Inadequate sleep increases a mother's chances of developing depression, anxiety, excessive weight gain or loss, and eating disorders

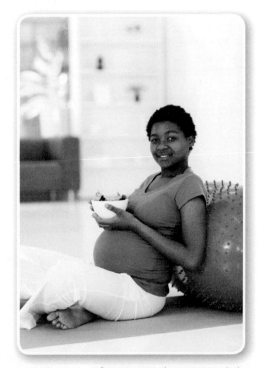

Photo 4-7 Engaging in daily activity has important physical and mental health benefits.
michaeljung/Shutterstock.com

(Bei, Coo, & Trinder, 2015). Sleep quality can be improved by maintaining a consistent bedtime routine, reducing fluid intake in the evening, participating in daily physical activity, avoiding spicy or fatty foods, and practicing relaxation techniques.

Acute and prolonged stress experienced during pregnancy can also disrupt sleep and have undesirable physical and psychological effects on maternal and infant well-being. Stone et al. (2015) observed that pregnant women who reported having high stress levels were more likely to develop **postpartum** depression. A number of studies have established a strong association between prenatal maternal stress and long-term effects on fetal brain development, learning potential, and emotional regulation (Betts et al., 2015; Bock et al., 2015). Thus, it is important that health care providers assess, monitor, and address a woman's stress levels and sleep quality throughout her pregnancy.

postpartum the months following childbirth.

4-2b Avoiding Teratogens

Researchers have identified a number of environmental substances that may cause birth defects if a mother is exposed to them during her pregnancy (see Figure 4-13). Some substances are especially harmful during critical early periods, often referred to as "sensitive windows," when certain fetal organ systems are developing. Exposure to these substances may result in fetal malformations and death. For example, facial deformities (e.g., cleft lip and cleft palate) are more likely to occur between the fifth and eighth weeks following conception; heart abnormalities are more likely between weeks three and five. Consequently, it is important that women take steps to avoid teratogen exposure during their childbearing years.

The relationship between exposure to teratogens and fetal abnormalities is complex and does not always involve a direct cause-and-effect process. Several factors, including the timing of exposure (fetal age), dose (amount of exposure), and genetic makeup (of the mother and fetus) will determine if or how the fetus will be harmed. Although some substances are more likely to harm the fetus in the early weeks when organ systems are forming, others are never safe to consume during pregnancy. For this reason, women who are contemplating pregnancy or believe they may be pregnant should take steps to avoid any use of, or exposure to, all known teratogens.

Alcohol. Maternal alcohol consumption prior to and during pregnancy is associated with increased health risks for both mother and infant. For this reason, the CDC advises women to avoid all alcoholic products during the time they are attempting to get pregnant and throughout the pregnancy (CDC, 2016). All alcoholic products now include labels warning women about the health hazards associated with drinking alcohol during pregnancy. Because a mother and her developing fetus share a common circulatory system (through the placenta and umbilical cord), they both experience the effects

---

Figure 4-13 Teratogens Harmful to Fetal Development

Efforts should be made to avoid these substances before and during pregnancy:

- alcohol
- nicotine
- illicit drugs (e.g., amphetamines, cocaine, heroin, marijuana)
- chemicals (e.g., mercury, lead, carbon monoxide, pesticides, insecticides)
- certain medications (e.g., antidepressants, antihistamines, hormones, anticonvulsants [to treat seizures], diet pills, antivirals, thyroid drugs, anticoagulants [to thin blood], large doses of vitamin A)
- infectious illnesses (e.g., chicken pox, herpes, German measles, cytomegalovirus [CMV], Fifth disease, syphilis, hepatitis C, HIV)

of any alcohol or other teratogens that are consumed. However, alcohol remains in the fetal circulatory system twice as long as in the mother's because the liver is not yet fully developed. Maternal alcohol consumption prior to and during pregnancy is known to cause fetal brain damage, birth defects (e.g., behavior and learning disabilities, oral and facial deformities), and fetal alcohol spectrum disorders (FASD) (Khoury, Milligan, & Girard, 2015). Researchers have also linked it to an increased risk of respiratory infections and cancers, including leukemia, in children (Libster et al., 2015; Yan et al., 2015). All of these conditions are preventable if women abstain from alcohol consumption during pregnancy.

Nicotine. Many pregnant women continue to smoke during pregnancy despite numerous health warnings printed on all tobacco products. Smoking and exposure to second-hand smoke can interfere with fertility, increase the risk of premature birth, miscarriage, and birth defects (e.g., cleft lip, cleft palate), and cause infants to have a low birth weight. Tobacco smoke produces chemicals (e.g., nicotine, tar, ammonia) and carbon monoxide gases that cross the placenta and reduce the amount of oxygen available to the fetus. Children whose mothers smoked during pregnancy are more likely to develop Sudden Infant Death Syndrome (SIDS), asthma, ear and respiratory tract infections, and/or learning and behavior problems. Han et al. (2015) also noted that the rate of attention deficit hyperactivity disorder (ADHD) was 2.6 times greater among children whose mothers smoked.

Photo 4-8 Smoking during pregnancy is harmful to the developing fetus. VGstockstudio/Shutterstock.com

Medications. Women who believe they may be pregnant should always check with a health care provider before taking any medication (including over-the-counter medications) and to use medications cautiously. In some instances, a physician may be able to prescribe an alternative medication in place of one known to have a higher risk for causing fetal abnormalities. However, a woman should never stop medication or treatments that have been prescribed for chronic conditions without first consulting with her health care provider.

Infectious Illnesses. Some infectious agents are also potentially harmful to a pregnant mother and her fetus because they increase the risk for miscarriage, premature birth, and congenital birth defects (Arnesen et al., 2015; Silasi et al., 2015). Although the placenta filters out many of these organisms, it is not able to eliminate them all. Whether or not they will cause harm to the fetus depends on the timing (stage of fetal development; see Figure 4–4) and the mother's general state of health. For example, infants born to mothers who were exposed to cytomegalovirus during their first trimester are more likely to have hearing loss, intellectual disabilities, seizures, or cerebral palsy. A mother who becomes infected with rubella (German measles) during her first trimester is at increased risk of giving birth to an infant who has hearing loss, blindness, heart defects, or all three abnormalities.

4-2c Pregnancy Loss

One fourth of all pregnancies end in either miscarriage, stillbirth, or neonatal death, with older women and African American mothers being at highest risk (Hutti, Armstrong, Myers, & Hall, 2015). In addition, 6 out of every 1000 infants born in the United States die during their first year, with the most common causes being birth defects, preterm birth, Sudden Infant Death Syndrome (SIDS), pregnancy complications, and injuries (CDC, 2015b).

The death of an infant, whether it occurs during pregnancy or following birth, is usually a devastating experience for parents and is often followed by symptoms similar to post-traumatic stress disorder (PTSD), including high rates of depression, anxiety, distress, suicidal thoughts, and negative well-being. Although these feelings tend to peak during the early months following a loss, they can last for several years (Campbell-Jackson & Horsch, 2014). Women who experience the death of an infant show higher levels of depression and anxiety during subsequent pregnancies (Blackmore et al., 2011). In addition, they tend to access health care more frequently during future pregnancies because of worries related to fetal health and development (Hutti, Armstrong, & Myers, 2011). Extreme and prolonged grief can interfere with the quality of a partner relationship or lead to its dissolution, especially if couples have different expectations about how to respond, behave, and the amount of time needed for grieving (Hutti et al., 2015). In a cross-cultural study conducted by Youngblut et al. (2015), it was observed that grandparents experience similar psychological problems in addition to an increase in health conditions (e.g., high blood pressure, heart conditions, cancer) following a grandchild's death.

Social support from a partner, service providers, and organizations seems to be effective for helping parents cope with the unexpected loss of a child (Kenner, Press, & Ryan, 2015; Randolph, Hruby, & Sharif, 2015). Several national organizations also provide families with grief support, including Share Pregnancy and Infant Loss Support, First Candle, March of Dimes, MISS Foundation, and Compassionate Friends. Several new Internet-based interventions have been developed and proven to be effective in treating post-traumatic stress associated with pregnancy loss (Kersting et al., 2013).

4-3 New Challenges and Adjustment

4-3a Lifestyle Changes

Becoming a new parent often brings a sense of pride, joy, and meaning to one's life. However, it also requires considerable patience and sacrifice. An individual's ability to make a successful adjustment is influenced by a combination of personal characteristics (e.g., mental health, personality, temperament, self-efficacy), a child's characteristics (e.g., temperament, physical health), and contextual factors (e.g., support from others, family communication and cohesiveness, financial stability) (Belsky, 1984). Some parents relish and adapt quickly to their new role and responsibilities while others adjust more slowly or not at all. Although children provide many rewarding interactions and have positive effects on their parents, they also present numerous challenges related to time, finances, and relationships. Hansen (2012) identified four aspects of well-being that are affected when parents have children, including:

- Psychological—worries, fatigue, sleep deprivation, loss of freedom
- Marital relationship—marital discord, dissatisfaction, decreased time spent together, decreased affection
- Financial obligations—food, shelter, medical care, and child care/schooling expenses
- Opportunities—career, income, education.

Psychological. Some parents worry that they will not know how to respond appropriately to their infant. However, Parsons et al. (2013) conducted a literature review and determined that the majority of parents respond intuitively to their infant's cues. In other words, most adults seem to know instinctively what to do when infants cry or show certain behaviors (e.g., reaching, clinging, facial expressions) without being specifically taught. In addition, they found that infant cues activate areas within the adult's brain that integrate sensory and affective information and motivate the parent to respond. Proximity and responsiveness to infants' behavioral cues also helped parents to establish an attachment or emotional bond with their infant, which they described as being pleasurable and inherently rewarding.

Nelson and colleagues (2013) summarized the literature on parenthood and well-being and found that parents are more or less likely to be happy depending on their experiences during pregnancy and in the months immediately following delivery. They noted that parents who experience greater meaning in life (i.e., children serve as a goal and source of affection), have their basic needs satisfied, and enjoy more positive emotions and enhanced social roles tend to have a greater sense of well-being and happiness. In contrast, adults who have more negative emotions, significant financial problems, marital conflicts, and sleep disturbances tend to experience a lower level of personal satisfaction and well-being when they become parents.

Hansen (2012) reported that in general, people who have children report lower levels of happiness compared to those who are childless. He concluded that adults may mistake happiness for meaning or a sense of purpose and direction in life, or for contributing to something larger than oneself. Thus, even though happiness may decline for some parents, meaning may increase, perhaps in part due to the challenges and sacrifices that are made during parenthood.

Single parents may experience lower life satisfaction and poorer emotional well-being because of increased financial responsibility, career limitations, limited social support, and custody issues with an ex-partner. However, Stavrova and Fetchenhauer (2014) found that these effects are only present for single parents in countries and cultures that have a strong two-parent family norm. In cultures where single parenting is more acceptable, parents often have more flexibility in childrearing practices and may not feel compelled to provide a traditional family structure (Stravrova & Fetchenhauer, 2014).

Parents' mental health can also affect the pleasure they derive from interactions with their infant. Approximately 15 percent of women experience varying degrees of postpartum depression following childbirth (NIMH, 2015). Depression, including postpartum depression, may affect women and men prior to, during, and/or following the birth of a child (see Figure 4-14). For these reasons, it is important to be aware of parents' psychological state because conditions such as anxiety and depression can affect their ability to provide quality care and engage in positive interactions with children. Early diagnosis and treatment can prevent prolonged mental health disorders and their negative effect on children's development.

Photo 4-9 Single parents face added responsibility and stress in raising children on their own.

Figure 4-14 Depression Symptoms

The symptoms of depression include:

- A sad or anxious mood.
- Loss of interest in fun activities.
- Changes in eating, sleeping, and energy levels.
- Problems in thinking, concentrating, and making decisions.
- Feelings of worthlessness, shame, or guilt.
- Thoughts that life is not worth living.

Postpartum depression symptoms are similar to these, but they can also include:

- Difficulty sleeping at times when your infant is asleep (more than the lack of sleep that new mothers usually experience).
- Feeling numb or disconnected from your infant.
- Having frightening or negative thoughts about the infant (e.g., thinking that someone may abduct or harm your infant).
- Worrying that you will hurt the infant.
- Feeling guilty about not being a good mother, or ashamed that you cannot care for your infant.

Source: Centers for Disease Control and Prevention (2015c).

The physical and psychological changes that accompany the transition to parenthood along with increased caregiving demands place women at higher risk of childbirth-related health problems and decreased self-care (Fahey & Shenassa, 2013). Female depression rates, for example, tend to be highest during pregnancy and in the early years immediately following birth with approximately 9–18 percent of women experiencing postpartum depression symptoms (CDC, 2015c; Barker, 2013). Women are at highest risk for depression if they have had difficulty getting pregnant, a baby as a teenager, premature labor, an infant who has a birth defect or disability, complications with pregnancy or delivery, a previous perinatal loss, or an infant that requires hospitalization (CDC, 2015c). Mothers who have children with poor health or a difficult temperament and receive limited help or emotional support during their postpartum period are more likely to experience depressive symptoms for as long as 2 years. These findings highlight the need for monitoring postpartum mothers closely for signs of depression (McMahon et al., 2015).

Children of chronically depressed mothers are more likely to experience contextual risks and interpersonal stress (e.g., food insecurity, poverty, poor relationships, low social support, and marital conflict) (Garg et al., 2015; Barker, 2013). These children also display poorer self-regulation during their development which can contribute to more significant mental health concerns, such as conduct disorder and depression as they are growing up (Slykerman et al., 2015).

Men can also develop pregnancy-related depression. Approximately 10 percent of men experience depression between the first trimester and up to 1 year following a child's birth. This rate is significantly higher than occurs in the general population (4.8 percent) (Singley & Edwards, 2015). Paternal depression may express itself differently in men than it does in women, and include anger, withdrawal, fatigue, sleep disturbance, and substance abuse. Risk factors for paternal depression include a history of psychiatric illness, poor spousal support, low relationship satisfaction, low parenting self-efficacy, previous perinatal loss, difficult child temperament, and changes in hormone levels (Singley & Edwards, 2015; deMontigny et al., 2013).

Symptoms of male depression may differ depending on whether or not a father lives with his children. Resident fathers, for example, have a decrease in depressive symptoms just prior to becoming fathers, an increase when their children are ages 0–5, and a decrease as children become older. Fathers who do not live with their children show increased symptoms prior to becoming a father and decreased levels during early and later fatherhood (Garfield, 2014). Culture can also influence fathers' health in these situations. For example, fathers in Middle Eastern cultures tend to have poorer health outcomes if the child born is a girl because boys are the preferred gender (deMontigny Gauthier & deMontigny, 2013).

Adoptive parents may also experience depression. For example, if adoptive parents have expectations for their child, their own parenting abilities, and presumed family supports that do not match reality, they are more likely to experience postadoption depression (Foli, 2014). An adopted child's early trauma or challenging behaviors can also interfere with parent-child bonding and increase parental aggravation. Furthermore, parents who adopt older children report added stress and tension related to behavioral and attachment problems and if children show a preference for one parent over the other (Goldberg et al., 2014). Individual, couple, and family therapy can be beneficial to these families.

Rather than focusing solely on women's physical health at postpartum medical visits, Fahey and Shenassa (2013) proposed a model of health promotion that focuses on enhancing four life skills which can be targeted through educational activities and messages: mobilization of social support, positive coping skills, self-efficacy, and realistic expectations. Intervention during the postpartum period can decrease depression and increase self-efficacy in at-risk mothers (Surkan et al., 2012). At-risk parents who receive intensive, goal-focused support prior to and following delivery experienced improved general health and were better able to cope with the transition to parenthood, understand their infant, and care for themselves and the child (Kemp et al., 2015).

4-3b Marital Relationship

The addition of a child to a family unit can change the relationship that exists between parents. Studies generally show a decline in relationship satisfaction during the transition to parenthood because of new challenges (e.g., increased household chores, child care, participation in children's activities) and the need to redefine roles within the family system. Traditionally, fathers invested their time and energy in earning a living, whereas mothers focused their attention on household and child-related activities. However, researchers have observed that this division of labor between partners has changed in recent years. Men (especially married men) are spending more time with their children and participating more in their care (Astone & Peters, 2014). Despite these changes, parents typically report having less time to spend with one another, friends, or even alone. Lesbian and gay couples who have adopted or conceived a child through IVF also report stress within their relationship after becoming a parent, in part, because the partners were no longer able to provide each other with the same level of undivided attention as before (Goldberg & Garcia, 2015; Tornello, Druczkowski, & Patterson, 2015).

One of the most significant sources of marital conflict and tension associated with the transition to parenthood involves the division of childcare responsibilities (Fillo et al., 2015). Reasons that new parents commonly mention include:

- Childcare tasks are new for parents, especially for men who are less likely to have experienced them prior to becoming a parent.
- Determining how to divide child care and household tasks within the relationship.
- Childcare tasks are demanding and cannot be postponed.
- Childcare tasks are unpredictable, which causes parents to feel a loss of control.

A child's arrival necessitates that parents make significant adjustments in their roles in order to maintain positive functioning within the family system. However, the impact that a child can have on a relationship may differ by culture and an adult's personality. For example, Taiwanese parents report an increase in intimacy which may be related to the cultural view that physical and emotional closeness is strengthened by spousal contributions to the child's care, whereas intimacy in Western cultures is based more on self-disclosure (Wu & Hung, 2015). In the Mexican-American culture, family harmony is related to fathers' value of *familism* (i.e., sense of attachment and shared obligation, loyalty, and respect that is greater for family than for self) and positive *machismo* (i.e., a strong feeling of male honor, pride, protection, and sense of responsibility to family) (Roubinoz et al., 2015).

Parents who report high parenting self-efficacy also experience greater and more consistent relationship satisfaction, perhaps because they are better able to balance the demands associated with parenting (Fillo et al., 2015). Father involvement is also positively related to life satisfaction in couples who live together. Specifically, when fathers are more involved, both the mother and father experience a steep increase in life satisfaction upon the birth of a child, which returns to pre-child levels by the time the child turns three (Agache et al., 2014). Researchers have also observed that adoptive parents seem to have less difficulty adjusting to parenting than do biological parents. They attribute this difference to the early processes that adoptive parents must go through (e.g., screening, finances, health, support) which causes them to deal with stress and potential conflicts before the child's arrival (Ceballo, 2004). However, differences in individual personalities and cultural values and expectations also influence this transition (Pace et al., 2015).

If fathers are less involved, their satisfaction decreases following the birth of the child (Agache et al., 2014). Furthermore, when mothers have sole responsibility for child care, they report lower relationship satisfaction compared to couples with more distributed responsibility (Trillingsgaard et al., 2014). Parents who have an avoidant attachment

Photo 4-10 Couples tend to enjoy greater satisfaction when both parents are actively involved with their children. Rob Marmion/Shutterstock.com

are less likely to seek support from their spouse. As a result, they tend to experience more work-family conflict and a decline in relationship satisfaction (Trillingsgaard et al., 2014; Fillo et al., 2015). In addition, cohabitating mothers are more likely to experience poor relationship satisfaction during the transition to becoming a parent, possibly related to a lower perceived commitment to the relationship (Mortensen et al., 2012).

4-3c Financial Obligations

When couples are deciding whether or not to have children, they may give careful consideration to the direct and indirect costs associated with increasing their family size. In 2013, the U.S. Department of Agriculture (2014) estimated the cost of raising a child from birth to age 18 to be approximately $245,340. This estimate includes housing (the largest expense), child care and education, food, clothing, medical care, and other related expenses (see Figure 4-15). However, this figure does not include costs associated with pregnancy or higher education expenses after a child turns 18 years (estimated to be between $18,390 and $40,920 per year). The cost of childrearing also varies by income level and geographical location. Families with higher incomes and those who live in urban Northeast areas typically have higher expenses than lower income families living in urban Southern and rural locations. Financial obligations are also affected by family size. For example, a family with three or more children typically spends 22 percent less per child because children are more likely to share rooms, toys, clothes, and receive discounts for schooling.

Children's special medical and mental health needs also add to the lifetime cost of raising a child. For example, families of children who are diagnosed with cancer incur many additional costs associated with diagnosis, treatment, and follow-up care including travel, loss of income, and out-of-pocket treatment not covered by insurance (Miedema et al., 2015). Parents of children who have autism experience similar financial burdens. Parish (2015) and her colleagues estimated that parents spend an average of $9.70 per $1000 of annual income on children's health care costs. As a result, these families often face long-term financial obligations and insecurity that, in turn, can affect the well-being of all family members.

Indirect costs of having a child may also include loss of income if a parent decides to leave employment and stay home to care for the child. However, this choice may also lead to some savings from child care fees, transportation, clothing purchases, and miscellaneous work-related expenses.

Figure 4-15 Costs of Raising a Child to Age 18

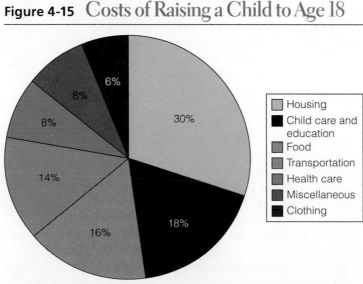

Data Source: U.S. Department of Health and Human Services (HHS). Health Resources and Services Administration, Maternal and Child Health Bureau (2013).

4-3d Opportunities

Young and unmarried fathers typically increase their work effort after becoming a parent, while older fathers may decrease their work commitment in order to spend more time with their children (Astone & Peters, 2014). Unfortunately, social expectations continue to focus on fathers as primary breadwinners. As a result, fathers who leave the traditional workforce employment to become full-time parents may experience social conflict and stigma (Gatrell & Cooper, 2016). Fathers who are not living with their children may view their financial responsibilities as a barrier to any interaction. In other words, the predominant view that men must provide monetary support for their families may cause them to avoid having contact with children if they are unable to provide for them (Astone & Peters, 2014).

In contrast, mothers in the workplace tend to earn lower wages and be viewed as less dedicated employees than women who do not have children (Glynn, 2014). This may be due, in part, to the fact that women are more likely to reduce employment hours in order to care for young children because they are already being paid less than men. Mothers are more likely than fathers to report that being a parent has made it more difficult to advance their career plans, even though they are just as dedicated and focused as are fathers (Patten, 2015).

Almost 60 percent of working parents report that it is difficult to balance their work and family responsibilities; mothers and college graduates express the most frustration (Pew Research Center, 2015). Despite public awareness regarding the importance of a child's first months of development, only 12 percent of parents have access to paid family leave and 40 percent risk losing vacation or pay if their child becomes ill (Glynn, 2014). Clearly, changes in public and workplace policies are needed to help decrease the work-family conflict that many parents experience.

Summary

- Individuals may take many different pathways to becoming a parent including natural conception, conception through assisted reproductive technology, foster parenting, adoption, and legal guardianship. Each approach is accompanied by unique challenges.

- Pregnancy can be described in terms of trimesters or developmental stages that focus on physiological changes which take place as the fetus matures.

- Healthy lifestyle practices before and during pregnancy can improve the chances of becoming pregnant and giving birth to a healthy infant. Practices that should be considered include the timing of pregnancies, obtaining prenatal care, consuming a nutritious diet, maintaining a healthy weight, getting an adequate amount of sleep, and avoiding teratogens.

- The transition to parenthood is associated with several challenges which individuals must navigate to adjust to new roles and responsibilities, including psychological issues, relationships, financial obligations, and opportunities/employment.

Key Terms

anencephaly (p. 110)

assisted reproduction (p. 94)

breech birth (p. 100)

chromosomes (p. 96)

cleft lip, cleft palate (p. 110)

gamete donation (p. 102)

gestational diabetes (p. 109)

low birth weight (p. 109)

postpartum (p. 112)

preeclampsia (p. 109)

premature birth (p. 109)

spina bifida (p. 110)

teratogens (p. 108)

Questions for Discussion and Self-Reflection

1. How do foster parenting, adoption, and legal guardianship differ?

2. In what ways might the experiences of becoming a parent be similar and different for a pregnant heterosexual couple and a same sex couple?

3. What are some common causes of infertility? What reproductive technologies are currently available for treating infertility?

4. What lifestyle practices would you recommend that individuals follow when trying to become pregnant to increase their chances of giving birth to a healthy infant?

5. In what ways does the birth of a child affect parents' lifestyle and marital relationship?

Field Activities

1. Conduct an Internet search for the USDA Cost of Raising a Child Calculator. Calculate the cost for a single- and two-parent household with varying numbers of children and income levels for your geographic location. Compare the charts produced. How might families of different family configurations and income be affected by the costs of raising children?

2. Interview five family members or friends to learn about the challenges and adjustments they faced when they became parents, and how having children changed their lives.

3. Visit and gather information from several local support programs for parents who may be experiencing postpartum depression or the loss of a child. Compile a resource for families.

REFERENCES

Agache, A., Leyendecker, B., Schafermeier, E., & Scholmerich, A. (2014). Paternal involvement elevates trajectories of life satisfaction during transition to parenthood. *European Journal of Developmental Psychology*, *11*(2), 259–277.

Allen, M., Sprow, S., Jordan, E., & Fletcher, M. (2012). Making it work: Using the Guardianship Assistance Program (GAP) to close the permanency gap for children in foster care. Children's Defense Fund and Child Trends. Retrieved November 24, 2015 from http://www.americanbar.org/content/dam/aba/administrative/child_law/Gapreport.authcheckdam.pdf.

American Pregnancy Association. (2015). Infertility medications. Retrieved on November 24, 2015 from http://americanpregnancy.org/infertility/infertility-medications/.

American Society for Reproductive Medicine. (2014a). Gamete (egg and sperm) and embryo donation. Retrieved on November 24, 2015 from http://www.reproductivefacts.org/uploadedFiles/ASRM_Content/Resources/Patient_Resources/Fact_Sheets_and_Info_Booklets/Gamete_embryo_donation_2014.pdf.

American Society for Reproductive Medicine. (2014b). Gamete and embryo donation: Deciding whether to tell. Retrieved on December 3, 2015 from http://www.reproductivefacts.org/uploadedFiles/ASRM_Content/Resources/Patient_Resources/Fact_Sheets_and_Info_Booklets/GameteDonation.pdf.

American Society for Reproductive Medicine. (2015a). Frequently asked questions about infertility. Retrieved on November 16, 2015 from http://www.reproductivefacts.org/awards/index.aspx?id=3012.

American Society for Reproductive Medicine. (2015b). Quick facts about infertility. Retrieved on November 16, 2015 from http://www.reproductivefacts.org/detail.aspx?id=2322.

American Society for Reproductive Medicine Ethics Committee. (2007). Financial compensation of oocyte donors. *Fertility and Sterility*, *88*(2), 305–309.

Antonishak, J., Kay, K., & Swiader, L. (2015). Impact of an online birth control support network on unintended pregnancy. *Social Marketing Quarterly*, *21*(1), 23–36.

Anwar, E., & Stanistreet, D. (2015). 'It has not ruined my life; it has made my life better': A qualitative investigation of the experiences and future aspirations of young mothers from North West of England. *Journal of Public Health*, *37*(2), 269–276.

Arnesen, L., Martínez, G., Mainero, L., Serruya, S., & Durán, P. (2015). Gestational syphilis and stillbirth in Latin America and the Caribbean. *Journal of Gynecology & Obstetrics*, *128*(3), 241–245.

Astone, N., & Peters, E. (2014). Longitudinal influences on men's lives: Research from the transition to fatherhood project and beyond. *Fathering*, *12*(2), 161–173.

Barker, E. (2013). The duration and timing of maternal depression as a moderator of the relationship between dependent interpersonal stress, contextual risk and early child dysregulation. *Psychological Medicine*, *43*, 1587–1596.

Barrett, D., Katsiyannis, A., Zhang, D., & Kingree, J. (2015). Predictors of teen childbearing among delinquent and non-delinquent females. *Journal of Child and Family Studies*, *24*(4), 970–978.

Barrett, G., & Wellings, K. (2002). What is a 'planned' pregnancy? Empirical data from a British study. *Social Science & Medicine*, *55*, 545–557.

Batool, S., & de Visser, R. (2016). Experiences in infertility in British and Pakistani women: A cross-cultural qualitative analysis. *Health Care for Women International*, *37*(2), 180–196.

Bei, B., Coo, S., & Trinder, J. (2015). Sleep and mood during pregnancy and the postpartum period. *Sleep Medicine Clinics*, *10*(1), 25–33.

Belsky, J. (1984). The determinants of parenting: A process model. *Child Development*, *55*(1), 83–96.

Betts, K., Williams, G., Najman, J., & Alati, R. (2015). The relationship between maternal depressive, anxious, and stress symptoms during pregnancy and adult offspring behavioral and emotional problems. *Depression and Anxiety*, *32*(2), 82–90.

Blackmore, E., Cote-Arsenault, D., Tang, W., Glover, C., Evans, E., Golding, J., et al. (2011). Previous perinatal loss as a predictor of perinatal depression and anxiety. *The British Journal of Psychiatry*, *198*(5), 373–378.

Bock, J., Wainstock, T., Braun, K., & Segal, M. (2015). In utero: Prenatal programming of brain plasticity and cognition. *Biological Psychiatry*, *78*(1), 315–326.

Boivin, J., & Ganeiro, S. (2015). Evolution of psychology and counseling in infertility. *Fertility and Sterility*, *104*(2), 251–259.

Borreo, S., Nikolajski, C., Steinberg, J., Freedman, L., Akers, A., Ibrahim, S., & Schwartz, E. (2015). "It just happens": A qualitative study exploring low-income women's perspectives on pregnancy intention and planning. *Contraception*, *91*(2), 150–156.

Boutelle, A. (2014). Donor motivations, associated risks, and ethical considerations of oocyte donation. *Nursing for Women's Health*, *18*(2), 112–121.

Callegari, L., Schiff, M., & Debiec, K. (2015). Labor and delivery outcomes among young adolescents. *American Journal of Obstetrics and Gynecology*, *213*(1), 95.e1–95.e8.

Callister, L. (2014). Integrating cultural beliefs and practices when caring for childbearing women and families. In, K. Simpson & P. Creehan (Eds.), *AWHONN's perinatal nursing (pp.41–64). Alphen aan den Rijn*, Netherlands: Wolters Kluwer.

Campbell-Jackson, L., & Horsch, A. (2014). The psychological impact of stillbirth on women: A systematic review. *Illness, Crisis, and Loss*, *22*(3), 237–256.

Chandra, A., Copen, C., & Stephen, E. (2013). Infertility and impaired fecundity in the United States, 1982–2010: Data from the National Survey of Family Growth. *National health statistics reports*, no. 67. Hyattsville, MD: National Center for Health Statistics. Retrieved November 9, 2015 from http://www.cdc.gov/nchs/fastats/infertility.htm.

Ceballo, R., Lansford, J., Abbey, A., & Stewart, A. (2004). Gaining a child: Comparing the experiences of parents, adoptive parents, and stepparents. *Family Relations*, *53*(1), 38–48.

Centers for Disease Control and Prevention (CDC). (2016). Alcohol and pregnancy. Retrieved on March 9, 2016 from http://www.cdc.gov/media/dpk/2016/dpk-vs-alcohol-pregnancy.html.

Centers for Disease Control and Prevention, American Society for Reproductive Medicine, Society for Assisted Reproductive Technology. (2015a). *2013 Assisted Reproductive Technology National Summary Report*. Atlanta (GA): U.S. DHHS.

Centers for Disease Control and Prevention (CDC). (2015b). Infant mortality. Retrieved December 11, 2015 from http://www.cdc.gov/reproductivehealth/maternalinfanthealth/infantmortality.htm.

Centers for Disease Control and Prevention (CDC). (2015c). Depression among women of reproductive age. Retrieved December 11, 2015 from http://www.cdc.gov/reproductivehealth/depression/.

Child Welfare Information Gateway. (2015a). Access to adoption records. Retrieved March 12, 2016 from https://www.childwelfare.gov/pubPDFs/infoaccessap.pdf.

Child Welfare Information Gateway. (2015b). Standby Guardianship. Retrieved on November 24, 2015 from https://www.childwelfare.gov/pubPDFs/guardianship.pdf.

Child Welfare Information Gateway. (2014). Home study requirements for prospective foster parents. Retrieved on November 20, 2015 from https://www.childwelfare.gov/systemwide/laws_policies/statutes/homestudyreqs.cfm.

Child Welfare Information Gateway. (2012). Helping your adopted foster child transition to your adopted child. Retrieved December 3, 2015 from https://www.childwelfare.gov/pubPDFs/f_transition.pdf.

Children's Bureau. (2015). Title IV-E Guardianship Assistance. Retrieved November 24, 2015 from http://www.acf.hhs.gov/programs/cb/resource/title-iv-e-guardianship-assistance.

Chong, A., Gordon, A., & Don, B. (2016). Emotional support from parents and in-laws: The roles of gender and contact. *Sex Roles*, 1–11. doi: 10.1007/s11199-016-0587-0.

Cordero, A., Crider, K., Rogers, L., Cannon, M., & Berry, R. (2015). Optimal serum and red blood cell folate concentrations in women of reproductive age for prevention of neural tube defects: World Health Organization guidelines. *Morbidity and Mortality WeeklyReport (MMWR)*, 64(15), 421–423.

De Maeyer, S., Vanderfaeillie, J., Vanschoonlandt, F., Robberechts, M., & Van Holen, F. (2014). Motivation for foster care. *Children and Youth Services Review*, 36, 143–149.

deMontigny Gauthier, P., & deMontigny, F. (2013). Conceiving a first child: Fathers' perceptions of contributing elements to their decision. *Journal of Infant Psychology*, 31(3), 274–284.

deMontigny, F., Girard, M., Lacharite, C., Dubeau, D., & Devault, A. (2013). Psychological factors associated with paternal postnatal depression. *Journal of Affective Disorders*, 150(1), 44–49.

Durbin, M., DuBois, L., & Maenner, M. (2015). Inter-pregnancy intervals and the risk of autism spectrum disorder: Results of a population-based study. *Journal of Autism and Developmental Disorders*, 45(7), 2056–2066.

Dyer, S. (2007). The value of children in African countries - insights from studies on infertility. *Journal of Psychosomatic Obstetrics and Gynecology*, 28(2): 69–77.

Environmental Protection Agency (EPA). (2015). Advisories and technical resources for fish and shellfish consumption. Retrieved November 13, 2015 from http://www2.epa.gov/fish-tech.

Fahey, J., & Shenassa, E. (2013). Understanding and meeting the needs of women in the postpartum period: The perinatal maternal health promotion model. *Journal of Midwifery & Women's Health*, 58(6), 613–621.

Figueiredo, R., Figueiredo, N., Feguir, A., Bieski, I., Mello, R., Espinosa, M., & Damazo, A. (2015). The role of the folic acid to the prevention of orofacial cleft: An epidemiological study. *Oral Diseases*, 21(2), 240–247.

Fillo, J., Simpson, J., Rholes, W., & Kohn, J. (2015). Dads doing diapers: Individual and relational outcomes associated with the division of childcare across the transition to parenthood. *Journal of Personality and Social Psychology*, 108(2), 298–316.

Finer, L., & Zolna, M. (2014). Shifts in intended and unintended pregnancies in the United States, 2001–2008. *American Journal of Public Health*, 104(S1), S43–S48.

Foli, K., Lim, E., South, S., & Sands, L. (2014). "Great Expectations" of adoptive parents: Theory extension through structural equation modeling. *Nursing Research*, 63(1), 14–25.

Frawley, J., Adams, J., Steel, A., Broom, Al, Gallois, C., & Sibbritt, D. (2015). Women's use and self-prescription of herbal medicine during pregnancy: An examination of 1835 pregnant women. *Women's Health Issues*, 25(4), 396–402.

Gameiro, S., Boivin, J., Dancet, E., de Klerk, C., Emery, M., Lewis-Jones, C., . . . & Vermeulen, N. (2015). ESHRE guideline: Routine psychosocial care in infertility and medically assisted reproduction—a guideline for fertility staff. *Human Reproduction*, 30(11), 2476–2485.

Garfield, C., Duncan, G., Rutsohn, J., et al. (2015). A longitudinal study of paternal mental health during transition to fatherhood as young adults. *Pediatrics*, 133(5), 836–843.

Garg, A., Toy, S., Tripodis, Y., Cook, J., & Cordella, N. (2015). Influence of maternal depression on household food insecurity for low-income families. *Academic Pediatrics*, 15(3), 305–310.

Gatrell, C., & Cooper, C. (2016). A sense of entitlement? Fathers, mothers and organizational support for family and career. *Community, Work & Family*, 19(2), 134–147.

Geiger, J., Hayes, M., & Lietz, C. (2013). Should I stay or should I go? A mixed methods study examining the factors influencing foster parents' decisions to continue or discontinue providing foster care. *Children and Youth Services Review*, 35(9), 1356–1365.

Glynn, S. (2014). Explaining the gender wage gap. Center for American Progress. Retrieved November 24, 2015 from https://www.americanprogress.org/issues/economy/report/2014/05/19/90039/explaining-the-gender-wage-gap/.

Goldberg, A., & Garcia, R. (2015). Predictors of relationship dissolution in lesbian, gay, and heterosexual adoptive parents. *Journal of Family Psychology*, 29(3), 394–404.

Hamou, B., Wainstock, T., Mastrolia, S., Beer-Weisel, R., Staretz-Chacham, O., Dukler, D., ... & Erez, O. (2016). Induction of labor in twin gestation: Lessons from a population based study. *The Journal of Maternal-Fetal & Neonatal Medicine*. eAhead of print. doi:10.3109/14767058 .2016.1152252.

Han, J., Kwon, H., Ha, M., Paik, K., Lim, M., Lee, S., Yoo, S., & Kim, E. (2015). The effects of prenatal exposure to alcohol and environmental tobacco smoke on risk for ADHD: A large population-based study. *Psychiatry Research*, 225(1-2), 164–168.

Hansen, T. (2012). Parenthood and happiness: A review of folk theories versus empirical evidence. *Social Indicators Research*, 108(1), 29–64.

Headen, I., Mujahid, M., Cohen, A., Rehkopf, D., & Abrams, B. (2015). Racial/ethnic disparities in inadequate gestational weight gain differ by pre-pregnancy weight. *Maternal and Child Health Journal*, 19(9), 1672–1686.

Henningsen, A., Gissler, M., Skjaerven, R., Bergh, C., Tiitinen, A., Romundstad, L., Wennerholm, U., ... & Pinborg, A. (2015). Trends in perinatal health after assisted reproduction: A Nordic study from the CoNARTaS group. *Human Reproduction*, 30(3), 710–716.

Heron, J. (2013). Adoption vs. surrogacy financial costs. ABC World News. Retrieved November 16, 2015 from http://abcnews.go.com/Business/cost-comparisons-international -domestic-adoption-surrogacy-foster-adoption/story?id=19962169#3.

Hutti, M., Armstrong, D., Myers, J., Hall, L. (2015). Grief intensity, psychological well-being, and the intimate partner relationship in the subsequent pregnancy after a perinatal loss. *Journal of Obstetric, Gynocologic, & Neonatal Nursing*, 44(1), 42–50.

Hutti, M., Armstrong, D., & Myers, J. (2011). Healthcare utilization in the pregnancy following a perinatal loss. MCN. *The American Journal of Maternal Child Nursing*, 36(2), 104–111.

Jou, J., Koxhimannil, K., Johnson, P., & Sakala, C. (2015). Patient-perceived pressure from clinicians for labor induction and cesarean delivery: A population-based survey of U.S. women. *Health Services Research*, 50(4), 961–981.

Kemp, L., Harris, E., McMahon, Kemp L., Harris E., McMahon C., Matthey S., Vimpani G., Anderson T., ... & Aslam H. (2013). Benefits of psychosocial intervention and continuity of care by child and family health nurses in the pre- and postnatal period: Process evaluation. *Journal of Advanced Nursing*, 69(8), 1850–1861.

Kenner, C., Press, J., & Ryan, D. (2015). Recommendations for palliative and bereavement care in the NICU: A family-centered integrative approach. *Journal of Perinatology*, 35, S19–S23.

Kersting, A., Dolemeyer, R., Steinig, J., Walter, F., Kroker, L., Baust, K., & Wagner, B. (2013). Brief internet-based intervention reduces posttraumatic stress and prolonged grief in parents after the loss of a child during pregnancy: A randomized controlled trial. *Psychotherapy and Psychosomatics*, 82(6), 372–381.

Khoury, J., Milligan, K., & Girard, T. (2015). Executive functioning in children and adolescents prenatally exposed to alcohol: A meta-analytic review. *Neuropsychology Review*, 25(2), 149–170.

Kogan, S., Cho, J., Allen, K., Lei, M., Beach, S., Gibbons, F., ... & Brody, G. (2013). Avoiding adolescent pregnancy: A longitudinal analysis of African-American youth. *Journal of Adolescent Health*, 53(1), 14–20.

Koh, E., Rolock, N., Cross, T., & Eblen-Manning, J. (2014). What explains instability in foster care? Comparison of a matched sample of children with stable and unstable placements. *Children and Youth Services Review*, 37, 36–45.

Kornides, M., Kitsantas, P., Lindley, L., & Wu, H. (2015). Factors associated with young adults' pregnancy likelihood. *Journal of Midwifery & Women's Health*, 60(2), 158–168.

Kowlessar, O., Fox, J., & Wittowski, A. (2015). The pregnant male: A metasynthesis of first-time fathers' experiences of pregnancy. *Journal of Reproductive and Infant Psychology*, 33(2), 106–127.

Langley-Evans, S. (2015). Nutrition in early life and the programming of adult disease: A review. *Journal of Human Nutrition and Dietetics*, 28(s1), 1–14.

Lavender, T., & Mlay, R. (2006). Position in the second stage of labor for women without epidural anaesthesia: RHL commentary. Geneva, Switzerland: The WHO Reproductive Health Library, World Health Organization.

Lawler, D., Begley, C., & Lalor, J. (2015). (Re)constructing myself: The process of transition to motherhood for women with a disability. *Journal of Advanced Nursing*, 71(7), 1672–1683.

Lee, B., & McGrath, J. (2015). Advancing paternal age and autism: Multifactorial pathways. *Trends in Molecular Medicine*, 21(2), 118–125.

Libster, R., Ferolla, F., Hijano, D., Acosta, P., Erviti, A., & Polack, F. (2015). Alcohol during pregnancy worsens acute respiratory infections in children. *Acta Paediatrica*, *104*(11), e494–e499.

McEachern, A., Dishion, T., Wilson, M., Fosco, G., Shaw, D., & Gardner, F. (2013). Collateral benefits of the family check-up in early childhood: Primary caregivers' social support and relationship. *Journal of Family Psychology*, *27*(2), doi: 10.1037/a0031485.

McMahon, K., Boivin, J., Gibson, F., Hammarberg, K., Wynter, K., & Fisher, J. (2015). Older maternal age and major depressive episodes in the first years after birth: Findings from the Paternal Age and Transition to Parenthood Australia (PATPA) study. *Journal of Affective Disorders*, *175*, 454–462.

McQuillan, J., Greil, A., Shreffler, K., & Bedrous, A. (2015). The importance of motherhood and fertility intentions among U.S. women. *Sociological Perspectives*, *58*(1), 20–35.

Miedema, B., Easley, J., Fortin, P., Hamilton, R., & Mathews, M. (2008). The economic impact on families when a child is diagnosed with cancer. *Current Oncology*, *15*(4), 173–178.

Mills, M., Rindfuss, R., McDonald, P., & teVelde, E. (2011). Why do people postpone parenthood: Reasons and social policy incentives. *Human Reproductive Update*, *17*(6), 848–860.

Mortensen, O., Torsheim, T., Melkevik, O., & Thuen, F. (2012). Adding a baby to the equation: Married and cohabiting women's relationship satisfaction in the transition to parenthood. *Family Process*, *51*(1), 112–139.

Mosher, W., Jones, J., & Abma J. (2012). Intended and unintended births in the United States: 1982–2010. *National health statistics reports, no 55*. Hyattsville, MD: National Center for Health Statistics.

Mulherin, K., & Johnstone, M. (2015). Qualitative accounts of teenage and emerging adult women adjusting to motherhood. *Journal of Reproductive and Infant Psychology*, *33*(4), 388–401.

Naik, G. (2013). Designer babies: Patented process could lead to selection of genes for specific traits. *Wall Street Journal*. October 3, 2013. Retrieved December 21, 2015 from http://www.wsj.com/articles/SB10001424052702303492504579113293429460678.

National Institutes of Mental Health (NIMH). (2015). Postpartum depression facts. Retrieved December 28, 2015 from https://www.nimh.nih.gov/health/publications/postpartum-depression-facts/index.shtml.

Nelson, S., Kushlev, K., & Lyubomirsky, S. (2013). The pains and pleasures of parenting: When, why, and how is parenthood associated with more or less well-being? *Psychological Bulletin*, *140*(3), 846–895.

Office of Adolescent Health. (2016). Trends in teen pregnancy and childbearing. Retrieved March 12, 2016 from http://www.hhs.gov/ash/oah/adolescent-health-topics/reproductive-health/teen-pregnancy/trends.html#

Ombeliti, W., & Van Robays, J. (2015). Artificial insemination history: hurdles and milestones. *Facts, Views, & Visions in Obgyn*, *7*(2), 137–143

Ornoy, A., Weinstein-Fudim, L., & Ergaz, Z. (2015). Prenatal factors associated with autism spectrum disorder (ASD). *Reproductive Toxicology*, *56*, 155–169.

Osterman, M., & Martin, J. (2014). Recent declines in induction of labor by gestational age. Retrieved on March, 9, 2016 from http://www.cdc.gov/nchs/data/databriefs/db155.htm.

Pace, C., Santona, A., Zavattini, G., & Folco, S. (2015). Attachment states of mind and couple relationships in couples seeking to adopt. *Journal of Child and Family Studies*, *24*(11), 3318–3330.

Parish, S., Thomas, K., Williams, C., & Crossman, M. (2015). Autism and families' financial burden: The association with health insurance coverage. *American Journal on Intellectual and Developmental Disabilities*, *120*(2), 166–175.

Parsons, C., Stark, E., Young, K., Stein, A., & Kringelbach, M. (2013). Understanding the human parental brain: A critical role of the orbitofrontal cortex. *Social Neuroscience*, *8*(6), 525–543.

Patten, E. (2015). How American parents balance work and family life when both work. Pew Research Center. Retrieved December 7, 2015 from http://www.pewresearch.org/fact-tank/2015/11/04/how-american-parents-balance-work-and-family-life-when-both-work/.

Pew Research Center. (2015). Raising a household: How working parents share the load. Retrieved December 7, 2015 from http://www.pewsocialtrends.org/files/2015/11/2015-11-04_working-parents_FINAL.pdf.

Poh, H., Kph, S., & He, H. (2014). An integrative review of fathers' experiences during pregnancy and childbirth. *International Nursing Review*, *61*, 543–554.

Ramasamy, R., Chiba, K., Butler, P., & Lamb, D. (2015). Male biological clock: A critical analysis of advanced paternal age. *Fertility and Sterility*, *103*(6), 1402–1406.

Ramírez-Uclés, I., Del Castillo-Aparicio, M., & Moreno-Rosset, C. (2015). Psychological predictor variables of emotional maladjustment in infertility: Analysis of the moderating role of gender. *Clinica y Salud*, *26*, 57–63.

Randolph, A., Hruby, B., & Sharif, S. (2015). Counseling women who have experienced pregnancy loss: A review of the literature. *Adultspan Journal*, *14*(1), 2–10.

Readings, J., Blake, L., Casey, P., Jadva, V., & Golombok, S. (2011). Secrecy, disclosure and everything in-between: Decisions of parents of children conceived by donor insemination, egg donation and surrogacy. *Reproductive Biomedicine Online*, *22*(5), 485–495.

Roubiov, L., Lueken, L., Gonzales, N., Crnic, K. (2015). Father involvement in (Mexican-origin families) Preliminary development of a culturally informed measure. *Cultural Diversity and Ethnic Minority Psychology*, Advance online publication. http://dx.doi.org/10.1037/cdp0000063.

Silasi, M., Cardenas, I., Kwon, J., Raciocot, K., Aldo, P., & Mor, G. (2015). Viral infections during pregnancy. *American Journal of Reproductive Immunology*, *73*(3), 199–213.

Sipsma, H., Divney, A., Niccolai, L., Gordon, D., Magriples, U., & Kershaw, T. (2012). Pregnancy desire among a sample of young couples who are expecting a baby. *Perspectives on Sexual & Reproductive Health*, *44*(4), 244–251.

Singley, D., & Edwards, L. (2015, June 22). Men's perinatal mental health in the transition to fatherhood. *Professional Psychology: Research and Practice*. Advance online publication. http://dx.doi.org/10.1037/pro0000032.

Skoog Svanberg, A., Lampic, C., Gejerwall, A., Gudmundsson, J., Karlstrom, P., Solensten, N., Sydsjö, G. (2013). Gamete donors' satisfaction; Gender differences and similarities among oocyte and sperm donors in a national sample. *Acta Obstetricia et Gynecologica Scandinavica*, *92*(9), 1049–1056.

Slykerman, R., Thompson, J., Waldie, K., Murphy, R., Wall, C., & Mitchell, E. (2015). Maternal stress during pregnancy is associated with moderate to severe depression in 11-year-old children. *Acta Paediatrica*, *104*(1), 68–74.

Starling, A., Brinton, J., Glueck, D., Shapiro, A., Harrod, C., Lynch, A., Siega-Riz, A., & Dabelea, D. (2015). Associations of maternal BMI and gestational weight gain with neonatal adiposity in the Healthy Start study. *American Journal of Clinical Nutrition*, *101*(2), 302–309.

Stoll, K., Edmonds, J., & Hall, W. (2015). Fear of childbirth and preference for cesarean delivery among young American women before childbirth: A survey study. *Birth*, *42*(3), 270–276.

Stravrova, O., & Fetchenhauer, D. (2014). Single parents, unhappy parents? Parenthood, partnership and the cultural normative context. *Journal of Cross-Cultural Psychology*, *46*(1), 134–149.

Stone, S., Diop, H., Declercq, E., Cabral, H., Fox, M., & Wise, L. (2015). Stressful events during pregnancy and postpartum depressive symptoms. *Journal of Women's Health*, *24*(5), 384–393.

Surkan, P., Gottlieb, B., McCormick, M., Hunt, A., & Peterson, K. (2012). Impact of a health promotion intervention on maternal depressive symptoms at 15 months postpartum. *Maternal and Child Health Journal*, *61*(1), 139–148.

Tornello, S., Kruczkowski, S., & Patterson, C. (2015). Division of labor and relationship quality among male same-sex couples who became fathers via surrogacy. *Journal of GLBT Family Studies*, *11*(4), 375–394.

Trillingsgaard, T., Baucom, K., & Heyman, R. (2014). Predictors of change in relationship satisfaction during the transition to parenthood. *Family Relations*, *63*(5), 667–679.

Trillingsgaard, T., Sommer, D., Lasgaard, M., & Elklit, A. (2014). Adult attachment and the perceived cost of housework and child care. *Journal of Reproductive and Infant Psychology*, *32*(5), 508–519.

Vandivere, S., Malm, K., & Radel, L. (2009). Adoption USA. A chartbook based on the 2007 National Survey of Adoptive Parents. Washington, D.C.: The U.S. Department of Health and Human Services, Office of the Assistant Secretary for Planning and Evaluation. Retrieved December 3, 2015 from http://aspe.hhs.gov/report/adoption-usa-chartbook-based-2007-national-survey-adoptive-parents.

U.S. Department of Health and Human Services (HHS). Health Resources and Services Administration, Maternal and Child Health Bureau. (2013). *Child Health USA 2013*. Retrieved November 11, 2015 from http://mchb.hrsa.gov/chusa13/health-services-utilization/p/prenatal-care-utilization.html.

Van der Gucht, N., & Lewis, K. (2015). Women's experiences of coping with pain during childbirth: A critical review of qualitative research. *Midwifery*, *31*(3), 349–358.

Wainstock, T., Mastrolia, S., Beer-Weisel, R., Staretz-Chacham, O., Dukler, D., ... & Erez, O. (2016). Induction of labor in twin gestation: Lessons from a population based study. *The Journal of Maternal-Fetal & Neonatal Medicine*. eAhead of print. doi:10.3109/14767058 .2016.1152252.

Walker, K., Bugg, G., Macpherson, M., McCormick, C., Grace, N., Wildsmith, C., ... & Thornton, J. (2016). Randomized trial of labor induction in women 35 years of age and older. *New England Journal of Medicine*, 374, 813–822.

Wright, A., Duffy, J., Kershner, S., Flynn, S., & Lamont, A. (2015). New opportunities in teen pregnancy prevention: Identifying individual and environmental differences between youth who abstain, use contraception, and use no contraception. *Journal of Community Psychology*, 43(8), 931–953.

Wu, W., & Hung, C. (2015). First-time mothers' psychiatric health status during the transition to motherhood. *Community Mental Health Journal*, 1–7. Http://dx.doi.org/10.1007/s10597 -015-9892-2.

Xie, R., Gaudet, L., Krewski, D., Graham, I., Walker, M., & Wen, S. (2015). Higher cesarean delivery rates are associated with higher infant mortality rates in industrialized countries. *Birth*, 42(1), 62–69.

Yan, K., Xu, X., Liu, X., Wang, X., Hua, S., Wand, C., & Xin, L. (2015). The associations between maternal factors during pregnancy and the risk of childhood acute lymphoblastic leukemia: A meta-analysis. *Pediatric Blood & Cancer*, 62(7), 1162–1170.

Ying, L., Wu, L., & Lo, A. (2015). Gender differences in experiences with and adjustments to infertility: A literature review. *International Journal of Nursing Studies*, 52(10),1640–1652.

Youngblut, J., Brooten, D., Blais, K., Kilgore, C., & Yoo, C. (2015). Health and functioning in grandparents after a young grandchild's death. *Journal of Community Health*, 40(5), 956–966.

Yu, Y., Peng, L., Chen, L., Long, L., Wei, H., Li, M., & Wang, T. (2014). Resilience and social support promote posttraumatic growth of women with infertility: The mediating role of positive coping. *Psychiatry Research*, 215(2), 401–405.

Parenting Styles and Children's Socialization

5

LEARNING OBJECTIVES

After reading the chapter, you will be able to:

5-1 Discuss the transactional nature of parenting.

5-2 Define the term communication and describe the elements that make it effective.

5-3 Compare and contrast the four parenting styles described in Baumrind's classification model.

5-4 Describe four factors that influence an adult's parenting style.

5-5 Identify five features of an effective family education program.

naeyc Standards Linked to Chapter Content

1a, 1b, and 1c: Promoting child development and learning

2a, 2b, and 2c: Building family and community relationships

4a: Using developmentally effective approaches to connect with children and families

Many first-time parents are overly optimistic and unprepared to meet the challenges and responsibilities that accompany child-rearing. This is particularly true if either parent is an only child or the child is the parents' first born. Once children arrive, parents often engage

continued on following page

in a "learn as you go" process. They rely on a mixture of trial-and-error, intuition, personal experience, advice from family and friends, and information gleaned from articles and/or online sources. Some parents also benefit from taking parent education classes. Unfortunately, these classes are not available in all communities despite evidence that they lead to improved outcomes for children, including a reduction in maltreatment. ■

5-1 Parent-Child Relationships

Parents play an irreplaceable role in children's lives. Although infants are born with primitive reflexes that are designed to ensure their survival, they are dependent upon parents to provide the food, shelter, warmth, protection, and guidance required for continued growth and development. Children also rely on their parents for unconditional love, respect, and a trusting parent-child relationship—emotional needs that are easily satisfied when adults respond to children in a warm, loving, and consistent manner.

5-1a What Do Children Need From Parents?

The early nature of parent-child interactions is known to have significant, long-term effects on children's behavior. Landmark studies conducted by Harlow (1958), Bowlby (1969), and Lorenz (1935) demonstrated an intense human need for emotional attachment (see Chapter 1). They all concluded that it was vital for survival, brain development, and social competence. Scientists have since determined that children are less likely to experience long-term emotional and behavioral problems, including substance abuse, when they are reared by parents who are attentive, supportive, and nurturing (Ordway et al., 2015; Goldberg & Carlson, 2014). Lee et al. (2015) noted that children who experience a secure emotional attachment with their parents are also more socially competent, adaptable, and likely to succeed in forming stable peer and adult relationships. Additionally, they tend to establish a similar nurturing and supportive style with their own children if and when they become parents.

In contrast, early exposure to a pattern of maltreatment or negative parent-child interactions is known to have detrimental effects on a child's social-emotional development (Hajal et al., 2015). Neuroscientists are discovering that a child's cognition, emotional regulation, and decision-making abilities may also be impaired when an emotional attachment with a parent is unstable, punitive, or absent (Oshri et al., 2015; Sampaio & Lifter, 2014). In a recent longitudinal study, Moutsiana et al. (2015) documented physical changes in specific areas of children's brains that are directly related to insecure infant attachment and poor early caregiving interactions. They have discovered that stress related to disorganized attachment, neglectful caregiving, and abuse causes an enlargement of the neural areas responsible for emotional processing and regulation. As a result of this alteration, children exhibit an increase in negative behaviors, including anxiety, ambivalence, anger, disorganization, withdrawal, and depression.

Children also depend upon their parents to teach them the skills they will need to assume a productive role in society. However, a parent's ability to recognize and successfully satisfy a child's needs is influenced by multiple factors, including, educational background, available resources (e.g., personal, family, community), family structure, cultural and religious norms, geographical differences, and social value systems. For example, a single parent who has limited time, education, and financial resources may not recognize or consider a child's medical condition or developmental delay problematic or a may not have sufficient time, support, or resources needed to address the concerns. As a result, children reared in families with limited means are often at increased risk for academic failure, health complications, and behavior problems (Abenavoli, Greenberg, & Bierman, 2014). Cultural beliefs and social stigmas can also present significant barriers that prevent parents from seeking treatment for children's behavioral and mental health problems. Rusch, Frazier, and Atkins (2015) found that Hispanic parents are less likely than African American and Caucasian parents to acknowledge children's mental health problems and to utilize treatment services. Other studies have reported similar findings (Burkett et al., 2015; Dempster et al., 2015; Lawton et al., 2014). Differences in cultural beliefs also influence Asian parents' emphasis on children's academic performance versus friendships and play (Zhao & Gao, 2014). Thus, judgments about the ways in which parents are or are not meeting their children's needs must be withheld until an effort is made to understand the family's actions within the context of their goals, circumstances, and social value systems.

5-1b Parenting: A Transactional Relationship

Child-rearing is often viewed as a one-way process whereby parents continuously socialize children to conduct themselves in certain ways until they are ready to leave home. However, such an approach overlooks the dynamics involved in a parent-child relationship, and the transactional, or bidirectional, effect that children's behavior has on parenting practices. Contemporary research efforts have contributed to a more informed understanding of the complexity of parent-child interactions, and the mutual influence they exert on each other's behavior (Crouter & Booth, 2003; Paschall et al., 2015; Pratt, 2015). In a sense, parents and children enter into a dance with one another in which the behavior of each person affects the way the other moves and responds.

In the days and weeks preceding and immediately following a child's birth, parents begin to form strong emotional connections with their children based upon early expectations of their new role. In most instances, these include feelings of joy, adoration, and affection. An infant coos and smiles, his parent(s) respond by smiling back, he returns the smile, and the parent feels a sense of pride. These positive or negative feelings continue to develop as parents and children interact with one another. For example, a toddler cries because she does not want to go to bed, her parent soothes and comforts her, she stops crying and falls asleep, and the parent experiences a sense of relief and satisfaction. However, a child's behavior may also have the opposite effect. For example, an adolescent's rebellious behaviors may cause his parents to feel angry and frustrated. As a result, they may deny the teen's requests for special privileges which, in turn, may cause him to act out even more. In each case, parents' actions influenced children's behavior, and children's behavior affected the nature of the parental response.

For some parents, a child's arrival stirs a range of negative emotions which may include displeasure and rejection, especially if an unwanted pregnancy, illness, or other personal hardship is involved. Changes in a family's circumstances (e.g., structure, stability, or instability) and the interaction of child and adult temperaments continue to influence the way in which a parent perceives the child (Merwin, Smith, & Dougherty, 2015; Barbot et al., 2014). In turn, these positive or negative feelings have a direct effect on the transactional nature of the parenting relationship.

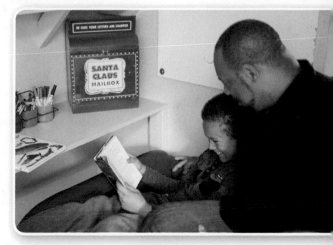

Photo 5-1 Parents and children influence the nature of their interactions with one another.

Wayne, age 4, watched his father place the TV remote control on the sofa and then leave the room to get a snack. He picked up the control and became fascinated with the way the channels changed when he pushed the buttons. When Wayne's father returned, he shouted at Wayne to put the remote down and told him that "he should know better." Wayne tried to hide the remote behind his back, but then threw it across the room as his father approached. How did Wayne's behavior affect his father's response? How did his father's reactions influence Wayne's behavior? How would you advise Wayne's father to respond differently the next time to achieve a more positive outcome?

Photo 5-2 Parents often adjust their parenting style to meet children's personality and unique needs.

Stress also affects the transactional nature of parenting. Poverty, raising a child who has a physical or intellectual disability, marital discord, job loss, and many other factors can increase a parent's stress level and affect the quality of the parent-child relationship. Until recently, researchers limited their studies to a single dimension: either examining the effect that raising a child with a disability or living in poverty has on parental stress, or the way that parental stress contributes to children's behavior. A longitudinal study by Woodman, Mawdsley, and Hauser-Cram (2015) is one of the first to investigate the transactional processes which occur in families that include a child who has a developmental disability. They concluded that these parents do not consider young children's (3 to 5 years) "troublesome" behaviors particularly stressful. This suggests that parents may view such behaviors as typical and, thus, find them acceptable. However, parents found challenging behaviors especially stressful when they were exhibited by older children (5 to 15 years). The authors also noted that parental stress can actually foster challenging behaviors in middle- and late adolescent children. Thus, this study clearly draws attention to the complexity of the parent-child relationship, and the developmental variations that occur in bidirectional interactions.

5-2 Communication and the Use of Authority

The term parenting style describes the relatively predictable manner in which parents communicate with children and use their authority to address perceived misbehavior. Each parent develops a unique pattern of communication, behavioral expectations for children, and disciplinary methods, often modeling them after those they experienced during their own childhood. These interaction patterns are known to have different effects on children's behavior (Mackler, et al., 2015; Ramsey & Gentzler, 2015). In some families, parents may make an intentional effort to modify or to abandon familiar styles, especially if they considered these methods to be punitive or dysfunctional. Some parents may intentionally choose an alternative approach in order to accommodate differences in family structure, resources, personal values, conflicting parenting styles, or newer trends. Adapting or experimenting with different parenting styles may also be necessary to cope with a child's developmental disability, temperament, or specific personality traits.

5-2a What Is Communication?

Sixteen-year-old Laura receives a phone call from her father, who asks if she will pick up her brother after drama practice and meet him at 5:30 p.m. for dinner at the café. She replies "yes," finishes her homework, and drives to pick up her brother from school only to find that he is not outside waiting for her. Laura sends her brother a text, but he does not respond. Although she is growing irritated, Laura continues to wait. She sees one of her friends leaving the school and stops to talk. Laura's father calls at 5:40 P.M. because he was expecting her at the café, and becomes upset when he hears people laughing in the background. At about the same time, she receives a text message from her brother informing her that he is waiting at the theater where his drama practice took place, not at the school.

This scenario is a classic example of failed **communication**. Although Laura intended to meet her father on time for dinner, she assumed that her brother's drama practice was being held at the school. At the same time, Laura's father assumed that she was being irresponsible for not following through with the plan. Clearly, the incomplete messages led to frustration for all parties involved. Effective communication requires that both the sender and receiver have a shared understanding of the intended message (see Figure 5-1). If either participant lacks or misinterprets any of the information, communication will not achieve the expected results.

The communication process is comprised of verbal and nonverbal messages. Verbal communication refers specifically to the words that are used to convey information. Nonverbal communication includes a person's tone of voice, body language, emotional expressions, and active listening skills. Both forms transmit important information about what the sender and receiver is thinking and feeling. In the case of one-way communication (e.g., text messaging, email, newsletter, memo) participants do not have an opportunity to use nonverbal clues for feedback or to check for mutual understanding. As a result, the chances for miscommunication are significantly greater.

Effective communication is a distinguishing feature of functional or successful families, and includes the way in which members speak and listen to each other. Parents who maintain a positive and open communication style with their partner are likely to interact with children in a similar manner. What parents say and how they talk with their children affects a child's feelings, self-confidence, and self-esteem. Furthermore, children tend to be more cooperative and experience fewer behavior problems when parents include them in frequent and respectful dialogue (Grebelsky-Lichtman, 2014; Waller et al., 2014). In addition, parents are modeling a communication style that becomes familiar to children and that they are also likely to imitate.

Several factors influence the nature of parent-child communication: the child's age, the child's behavior, the parent's objective or concern, and the context or situation in which communication occurs. For example:

This is the third time that Amita has asked her 5-year-old son, Deepak, to stop playing with his toy cars, wash his hands, and come to the dinner table. He acknowledges her request each time but continues to play. Finally, Amita raises the tone of her voice and threatens to take away Deepak's toy cars or to send him to his room without dinner if he doesn't come at once.

communication an exchange of information that is mutually understood by both the sender and receiver.

Figure 5-1 Effective or Successful Communication is a Two-Way Process

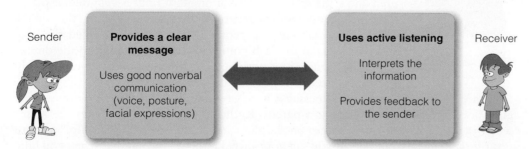

Consider for a moment how variations in one or more of these factors could potentially alter the communication style and eventual outcome. For example, how might Amita have changed the nature of her request if her son were 2 or 12 years old instead of 5? Would she have spoken in a different tone of voice or not threatened to banish Deepak to his room if they were dining at a friend's house? If Amita thought that Deepak was deliberately ignoring her requests, how might this perception have influenced her reaction? What could Amita have done to make the communication more effective?

A majority of the verbal exchanges that occur in families, especially when children are young, are triggered by behavior that parents perceive to be in conflict with their own expectations or standards (Bergmeier, Skouteris, & Hetherington, 2015). As a result, a high percentage of these interactions have negative overtones. Often these events are accompanied by considerable frustration and anger which also alter the parent's communication style. Stress, family disagreements, and cultural conflict can further escalate the frequency, intensity, and harshness of these interactions (Robinson & Neece, 2015; Woodman, Mawdsley, & Hauser-Cram, 2015).

Several effective strategies can be used to create positive parent-child communications. **Active listening** involves not only hearing what a child is saying but also noting body language, tone of voice, and emotional expressions. It also requires that an adult keep an open mind and restrain themselves from making a preconceived judgment until all of the information has been obtained. For example, a child might come running to his mother and shout, "Joel hates me." This statement could have several different implied meanings. If the boy's mother responds, "I'm sure Joel doesn't hate you," the conversation is likely to end abruptly. In addition, her response sends a clear message that she either is not interested in hearing how her son has come to his conclusion or does not really care. Instead, if the boy's mother says, "Why do you think Joel doesn't like you?" or "What happened to make you think that Joel doesn't like you?," she indicates empathy and an interest in understanding her son's reasons for arriving at this conclusion. By taking this approach, she also shows respect for her son's feelings and invites further conversation.

Another communication technique that fosters positive parent-child interactions involves the use of **I-messages**. This method is especially effective for parents to use when they are angry or upset and likely to say something that they would later regret. I-messages consist of three statement components: how the parent feels; the behavior in question; and why the parent finds this behavior particularly upsetting. For example, a father might be tempted to confront his daughter who did not come straight home from school by saying, "You are late again! There will be no television for you tonight." However, addressing his daughter in this negative manner does not allow her an opportunity to explain why she was late, and is likely to arouse hostile feelings toward her father. The girl's father would have created a more positive situation if he had said: "I worry about your safety when you are late coming home from school." By eliminating a reference to "you" in this statement, the father is removing blame and helping his daughter to understand why he is upset about her tardiness.

The I-message is also an effective strategy for reflecting and reinforcing children's positive behaviors. These statements let children know the specific behavior an adult finds acceptable or pleasing, and encourages its repetition by acknowledging the child's efforts. For example, a parent might say, "I really liked the way you remembered to wash your hands before coming to the dinner table." By focusing on positive behaviors, children are more likely to be motivated to repeat the desired behavior.

Care must be taken to use I-messages in a way that does not cause children to feel guilty or responsible for pleasing a parent. Rather than saying, "It makes me angry when you throw your dirty clothes on the floor and I have to pick them up," a more positive statement would be "If you put your dirty clothes in the hamper when you take

Photo 5-3 Positive behaviors can be effectively reinforced through the use of I-messages.

them off, we will have more time to read a story before you go to bed." Restating the message by removing accusations reduces angry feelings and is more likely to gain the child's cooperation. The positive quality of parent-child interactions also helps to promote children's language development, self-esteem, self-regulation, and the likelihood that they will continue to engage in open communication (Chang et al., 2015; Boyce, Riley, & Patterson, 2015).

5-2b Parental Use of Authority

In most societies, parents are responsible for socializing their children according to the prevailing beliefs and values. They are expected to guide children's development so that it ultimately complies with social standards and enables them to live and function harmoniously within a particular group. Parents are also expected to use their authority to make decisions that will protect a child's well-being. This responsibility includes addressing children's basic needs for housing, health care, nourishing food, education, safety, and nurturing. Because a child's survival depends on having these needs satisfied, state laws have been established to assure that minimally acceptable care is provided and penalties are enforced whenever parental care is deficient.

Parents also use their authority for disciplinary purposes, especially to establish and enforce rules that address children's misbehavior. Beliefs about how children are expected to behave are shaped by a combination of personal and societal values. Often these ideas are handed down from one generation to the next and learned through personal experiences during childhood. Although these child-rearing practices may not always be the most appropriate or effective, they are often the ones that parents use simply because they are the most familiar.

Cultural beliefs also exert a strong influence on parents' expectations about children's behavior and how parental authority should be used. Each culture has written and implied rules that govern how its members should conduct themselves. Some cultures expect children's strict obedience and emotional regulation, whereas others place a strong emphasis on children's autonomy and academic performance (Moilanen, Rasmussen, & Padilla-Walker, 2015; Koury & Votruba-Drzal, 2014). For example, Chinese parents, particularly mothers, are often viewed as being highly controlling with regard to their children's social and academic development (Ng, Pomerantz, & Deng, 2014). Their intentions may appear to be overly harsh or punitive to someone who is not familiar with the Confucian philosophy that adheres to respect, self-control, and the importance of education. Children of Mexican heritage, where initiative and family commitment are highly valued qualities, may perform household duties without being asked but show reserve in the classroom or among their peers (Telzer et al., 2015; Coppens, Alcalá, Mejía-Arauz, & Rogoff, 2014). Many Filipino American families place a high value on closeness, affection, and mutual support. Although cultural groups may value certain behaviors, not all of its members may uphold the same beliefs. Therefore, caution must always be exercised to avoid forming preconceived ideas about children or their families strictly on their basis of their cultural heritage.

Photo 5-4 There is often less tension experienced between children and parents when they share similar temperaments.

Temperament, or personality, also plays a critical role in the way that parents perceive, respond to, and use their authority to guide children's behavior. For example, a calm, low-key parent may actually encourage her toddler to continue pulling pots and pans out of the cabinet because she knows that he is learning, whereas an intense, controlling parent may consider the child's actions disruptive and scold him for the same behavior. Positive relationships are more likely to occur when parents and children share similar temperaments. When their temperaments differ or clash, the level of parent-child conflict and stress typically increases (Merwin, Smith, & Dougherty, 2015).

5-3 Parenting Styles

Seldom do parents deliberately think about or determine their parenting style in advance. More often a communication and response pattern begins to emerge during the early months following an infant's birth and gradually evolves as the child is growing up.

5-3a Baumrind's Classification Model

Developmental psychologists and family scientists have had a long-standing interest in parenting and its effects on children's behavior. Baumrind (1967) was interested in studying this relationship, and focused her research efforts on determining how parents' responsiveness influenced children's socialization. She proposed three fundamental parenting styles based on extensive parent interviews and parent-child observations: authoritative, authoritarian, and permissive. Baumrind believed that parents should establish rules and enforce them in a responsive, nurturing, and accepting manner. However, Maccoby and Martin (1983) suggested that parental demandingness also played a critical role in this equation. As a result, they added a fourth category to Baumrind's original classification model which they identified as rejecting or neglectful parenting (see Figure 5-2). Baumrind later acknowledged that parenting styles were defined by both demandingness and responsiveness qualities, and accepted the addition.

5-3b Authoritative Parenting

authoritative parenting style provides a balance between demandingness and responsiveness and is sometimes referred to as a democratic style; associated with the most positive child outcomes.

The **authoritative parenting style** is often referred to as democratic parenting, and is recognized for achieving the most positive developmental outcomes for children (Jungert et al., 2015; Jabagchourian et al., 2014). Parents who practice this style maintain an ideal balance of demandingness and responsiveness. They respect children's individuality and set high, developmentally appropriate expectations for their behavior. They value two-way communication, provide rationales for rules and limits, use discipline for teaching purposes, and willingly listen to children's perspective when they disagree. Authoritative parents also understand the importance of helping children develop autonomy, self-control, and self-confidence. Consequently, they involve children in decision-making and gradually relinquish parental control as a child ages and matures. They grant children limited freedom as long as the child's actions don't interfere with, or cause harm to, others. They are also successful in creating a warm, supportive parent-child relationship while maintaining respect, limits, and high standards.

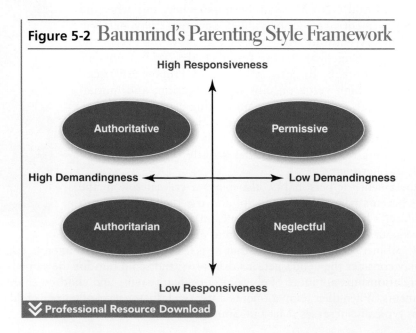

Figure 5-2 Baumrind's Parenting Style Framework

Research has shown that children develop many positive qualities, including self-esteem, problem-solving skills, empathy, trust, and self-control when they are reared by parents who follow an authoritative style. These children also have better social-emotional skills and achieve a higher level of academic success than do their peers who grow up in households where authoritarian, permissive, or neglectful parenting is practiced (Watkins & Howard, 2015; Watabe & Hibbard, 2014). Children whose parents use an authoritative child-rearing style also present fewer behavior problems, and are less likely to engage in delinquent, high-risk, or bullying behaviors (Pezzella, Thornberry, & Smith, 2015; Rajendran, Kruszewski, & Halperin, 2015).

Photo 5-5 Children have difficulty learning impulse control when their parents use an authoritarian parenting style.

5-3c Authoritarian Parenting

Parents who practice an **authoritarian parenting style** tend to be extremely rigid, directive, and demanding. They have a significant need for control and are disinterested in children's involvement. Authoritarian parents set high behavioral standards for their children and expect unquestioning obedience. Nonnegotiable rules are established to maintain order, no explanations are offered for why they are needed, and strict compliance is demanded. An authoritarian parent is likely to rebuke a child's questions ("Why do I have to be home by 6:00 P.M.?"; "Why can't I buy that toy?") by responding, "Because I told you so!" In other words, parents are in charge and provide children with limited support, input, and constructive guidance. Verbal interactions with children are more likely to be negative (e.g., yelling, screaming, abusive) and critical (e.g., name-calling, threatening, belittling) in nature. Harsh discipline, including the use of corporal punishment, is also considered more acceptable by parents who practice an authoritarian style.

Children who are exposed to authoritarian parenting have difficulty learning impulse control and self-regulation. Because parents are in charge of establishing and enforcing rules and provide little or no explanation, children become dependent upon others for behavioral control. As a result, these children are highly susceptible to rebellion and a range of risky behaviors, including drugs, alcohol, and promiscuity (Hartman et al., 2015; Hoskins & Simons, 2014). Researchers have also noted a direct link between the authoritarian parenting style and an increased incidence of childhood obesity and eating disorders (Kakinami et al., 2015; Zubatsky, Berge, & Neumark-Sztainer, 2015).

Children of authoritarian parents tend to be average students in school, although they often lack social skills, creativity, and self-confidence. As a result, they also experience a high rate of anxiety, fear, and depression when faced with a new or especially challenging task (Asselman et al., 2015). This form of parenting is used more commonly among certain ethnic and cultural groups, including Asian, Hispanic, Latino, African American, and low SES Caucasians (Kelch-Oliver & Smith, 2015; Lansford et. al., 2014). However, it is important to note that child outcomes may vary across family situations because an authoritarian style of parenting may be adaptive, protective, or consistent with different cultural norms (Sangawi, Adams, & Reissland, 2015).

> **authoritarian parenting style** high in demandingness and rigidity and low in warmth; children raised by authoritarian parents often develop poor impulse control and self-regulation.

> **permissive parenting style** high in nurturing and warmth, but low in demandingness; is associated with poor decision making and long-term reliance on parents for guidance.

5-3d Permissive Parenting

In many respects, the **permissive parenting style** is a direct opposite of the authoritarian approach. Permissive parents are nurturing, caring, and exceedingly tolerant. However, their relationship with children resembles one of equals or friends, and not one in which they are a respected authority figure. Permissive parents make few demands on children, including assigning any responsibilities, and exert minimal control. They are generous with gifts and privileges in order to gain a child's favor and compliance. They accept children's impulsive behavior as a sign of immaturity and, therefore, establish few rules or limits because they believe this will hinder the child's development.

Permissive parents may even consult with their children when family policies and limits are being determined. If rules do exist, their enforcement is often lax or inconsistent. Basically, children are relatively free to do as they please and are left to self-regulate their own behavior. Permissive parents believe that children will learn from their mistakes and, therefore, do not require adult interference.

Children who grow up in a permissive environment typically do not fare well. They do not learn how to control their behavior or conform to social expectations. Because they have enjoyed unrestrained freedom during their childhood, they tend to act impulsively, make poor decisions that may place them at risk, and make demands without regard to others' feelings (Hartman et al., 2015; Paschall et al., 2015). They lack a sense of purpose, connectedness, and self-worth due to years of parental overindulgence and lack of involvement. These deficits also contribute to children's long-term dependency on their families for care and guidance.

Responsive Parenting

Amelia's parents received a telephone call from the school principal informing them that she would be serving detention after school for the next 5 days. Amelia had been caught stealing a cell phone from another girl's locker. Her parents don't understand why she would do such a thing since they have always given her whatever she wanted and made few demands on her behavior. What parenting style do Amelia's parents appear to be following? Why would Amelia be more likely than other children to engage in this type of behavior? How would you advise Amelia's parents to handle this and similar situations?

5-3e Neglectful Parenting

neglectful parenting style low in demandingness and warmth; associated with poor academic achievement and an increase in risky behaviors.

The **neglectful parenting style** is sometimes referred to as uninvolved child-rearing. These parents make few if any demands on children and show minimal interest in their welfare other than meeting the basic needs for food and shelter. Their lack of concern and emotional connection with children results in a parent-child attachment relationship that is of poor quality. Neglectful parents are often depressed, under considerable duress, or simply lack the time or energy to care. As a result, children are basically left to provide for themselves and to make their own decisions. In its extreme form, this approach to parenting represents maltreatment or neglect.

Parents who are indifferent to their children's social and emotional needs place them at significant risk for failure. These children are typically not interested in academics and tend to perform poorly in school (Arora, 2014). Although they get along relatively well with their peers, children whose parents are indifferent are more likely to experiment with dangerous behaviors, including alcohol, drugs, risky driving, and sex due to a lack of impulse control (Seibert & Kerns, 2015; Hoskins & Simons, 2014). Researchers have noted these outcomes consistently across different ethnicities, cultures, socioeconomic groups, and geographical areas (Khaleque, 2015).

Photo 5-6 Variations in parenting practices must be considered within the family's context.

5-3f Baumrind's Model and Controversy

Baumrind's research has drawn attention to the potential long-term effects that parenting style can have on children's behavior and development. Her findings are especially relevant in light of brain research findings that have demonstrated how behavior changes the brain's physical structure and neural connections (Guyer et al., 2015; Lianos, 2015). However, although Baumrind's parenting style model continues to prove useful, it is not without controversy. Some researchers have expressed concern about the subjective nature of value-laden terms (e.g., warmth, nurturing, respectful) that she used to

Trending Now "Free-Range Parenting"

An international movement, commonly referred to as "**free-range parenting**," began shortly after journalist Lenore Skenazy and her husband made a controversial decision to let their 9-year-old son ride the New York subway home alone on a Sunday afternoon. He had been begging his parents to do this for some time, so they prepared him with a map, extra money, and a MetroCard. Several days later, his mother wrote about her son's experience in a newspaper column, and was immediately labeled "America's Worst Mom" by the media.

In December 2014 a Silver Spring, Maryland couple permitted their 6-year-old daughter and 10-year-old son to walk unaccompanied to a park located approximately one mile away. The children were later picked up by the police and turned over to Child Protective Services while their parents were being investigated for child neglect.

Both sets of parents have explained their decision to allow children these unsupervised experiences as a way to foster competence, self-esteem, and autonomy. They expressed concern that many of today's parents over-regulate their children's lives and over-protect them from risk-taking or failure. They fear that, as a result, children are not developing the social, emotional, problem solving, and coping skills they will need later in life. Critics of "free-range parenting" cite irresponsible parenting and child endangerment. They believe this approach exposes children to increased risk of danger, abduction, bullying, stress, and serious bodily injury.

These and similar incidences have raised questions about which parenting style is better or achieves the best outcomes for children. Has the media caused parents to be overly concerned about children's safety? How can parents balance a need to protect children's welfare with their responsibility to guide and support optimum learning and development? Piaget, Vygotsky, Dewey, Montessori, and other prominent philosophers and educators advocated a constructivist approach to children's learning. They suggested that children learn best and form culturally and socially relevant knowledge and understanding as a result of experience. Rogateg-Sariz and Sakic (2014) found that adolescents had higher self-esteem and life satisfaction when parents practiced a permissive versus authoritarian parenting style. However, some children whose parents practiced a permissive style reported feeling overly stressed and anxious when faced with unfamiliar situations (Park & Walton-Moss, 2012).

The debate about whether "free-range parenting" or a more authoritarian style, such as "**helicopter parenting**," is better for children is unlikely to be resolved anytime soon. What is right and works for one family may not be acceptable or functional for another. The fundamental question is how can parents achieve the right balance between too much and too little control?

---

categorize parental behaviors. Others have questioned the lack of cultural relevance and suggested that certain parenting styles may work better in some cultures. For example, Gao, Zhang, and Fung (2015) explain that although the Asian parenting style is often categorized as authoritarian, these children tend to experience outcomes that are more positive than they are for Caucasian children. To explain the difference, researchers have proposed an additional dimension, **guan**, which they suggest should be considered with regard to the parenting style practiced in Asian cultures. Still other researchers have criticized Baumrind's failure to take temperament and environmental differences into account.

Social scientists have also challenged the strength of the cause-effect correlations that Baumrind has suggested occur between parenting style and children's behavioral outcomes. Few people today would acknowledge parenting as the sole cause of children's behavior. Bronfenbrenner (1979, 1993) was among the first to describe behavior as a product of the numerous interactions that occur between an individual's genetic makeup and environment (e.g., family, friends, culture, religion, employment, geographical location, social activities) in his ecological model of human development. His holistic views continue to influence the way we think about the complexity of human behavior today.

5-4 Factors that Influence Parenting Style

Several variables known to influence a parent's unique child-rearing style include:

- personal philosophy and experiences
- goals and objectives for a child's behavior

free-range parenting giving children freedom to engage in experiences without close parental monitoring; parents believe this builds self-confidence and an independent spirit.

helicopter parenting overly involved, overly protective parenting that interferes with children's autonomy, lowers self-esteem, and increases anxiety.

guan a dimension of Asian parenting styles characterized by caring, monitoring, and teaching appropriate behaviors such as self-discipline and hard work.

- child's age, gender, and temperament
- family size
- parent's education, ethnicity and culture, and social class
- stress

5-4a Familiarity

Familiarity and personal choice are two of the most common reasons why parents may adopt a particular parenting style. Parents may not even be aware that they are raising children in a manner similar to what they experienced while growing up in their own family. However, there are also parents who make a deliberate choice to alter or to adopt a different style based on information obtained from friends, mass media, parent education classes, and/or health professionals.

Some parents make an intentional decision to use a particular parenting style or a combination of styles to help their children achieve three universal goals: survival, health, and happiness; financial independence and self-sufficiency; and adherence to cultural values and traditions. How parents help their children to attain these goals is determined by a combination of family beliefs, traditions, and available resources. For this reason, child-rearing practices must always be considered within the context of a family's environment and culture. For example, researchers have noted that families who live in particularly dangerous or high risk neighborhoods frequently use an authoritarian style to protect children's safety (Cuellar, Jones, & Sterre, 2015). Chinese parents may be perceived as being exceedingly authoritarian due to their strict, demanding, and even coercive expectations when it comes to children's effort and academic achievements. However, these same parents also enjoy a close, nurturing relationship with their children and justify their actions as a sign of concern and love for the child.

Photo 5-7 Family beliefs, resources, and cultural norms influence one's parenting style.

5-4b Children's Age

A child's age also plays a significant role in the type of child-rearing style a parent is likely to use. Ellen Galinsky's (1981) six developmental stages of parenting illustrate how changes in children's developmental needs and abilities necessitate that parents adjust their expectations and interaction style as children mature (see Figure 5-3). For example, although parents may use a style that is more directive (authoritarian) when

Figure 5-3 Galinsky's Six Stages of Parenting

Image-making stage	Envisioning what it is like to become a parent.
Nurturing stage	Forming an emotional attachment to a new infant.
Authority stage	Using parental authority to establish and implement rules and limits to guide children's social-emotional development (toddler, preschool-age).
Interpretive stage	Instilling family values, answering children's questions, and teaching decision-making skills (school-age, pre-adolescent).
Interdependent stage	Establishing interactions and demands that are protective while supporting the adolescent's desire for independence.
Departing stage	Relinquishing parental control and authority; respecting a child as an adult.

Adapted from Galinsky (1981).

children are very young and safety is an issue, they often shift to a style that supports greater independence (authoritative) as children mature and develop self-regulatory behaviors (Ansari & Crosnoe, 2015). By reducing the amount of demandingness associated with the authoritarian style, parents help children achieve greater autonomy while also increasing their cooperation and compliance (e.g., picking up their room, completing homework, adhering to curfews). When parents fail to adjust their child-rearing style to meet children's changing developmental needs and abilities, family conflict and stress tend to increase.

5-4c Gender

Contemporary studies have been unable to confirm the effect of children's gender on parenting style that researchers have described in the past. Global efforts to raise gender equality may, in part, help to explain this change. However, strict adherence to gender role stereotypes is still practiced in many cultures today despite these efforts, and continues to perpetuate differential expectations and treatment for boys and girls. Van der Pol et al. (2015) noted that mothers often used a more authoritarian and demanding approach with boys than with girls, while fathers tended to be more lax about boys' noncompliant behaviors. Varmer and Mandara (2014) also noted that later-born boys were given more autonomy than their older female siblings, and that parents held girls to higher behavioral and academic standards than they did boys.

5-4d Temperament

A child's temperament is also known to influence the quality of a parent's interaction style. Temperament is thought to be biologically based and relatively stable over a person's lifetime. It influences the way children interpret and react to their environment, and the way that others often respond to a child's behavior. For example, a parent is likely to interact differently with a child who is exuberant, curious, and impulsive than they would if the child is reserved or irritable. In fact, siblings within the same family may demonstrate different temperaments, leading parents to modify how they interact with each child.

It is also important to factor a parent's own temperament into this equation. When children and parents share similar or compatible temperaments, their relationship tends to result in fewer conflicts and more positive outcomes for both individuals (Baer et al., 2015). When their personalities clash, the resulting friction and conflict can have a negative effect on children's social-emotional development, as well as on their mothers' health (Danzig et al., 2015). Although fundamental personalities cannot be changed, parents can take steps to create an environment that respects and accommodates differences in parent-child temperaments, including:

- being a positive role model
- anticipating children's needs and likely reactions
- exercising patience and flexibility
- acknowledging and being sensitive to the child's personality traits
- understanding how responses may affect a child's behavior

5-4e Family Size

Family size also affects the way that children are parented. Jabagchourian et al. (2014) found that fathers shifted from an authoritative to authoritarian parenting style when family size increased, whereas mothers' pattern did not change. Families with fewer children are able to devote more quality attention to each child, respond more quickly to their individual needs, and provide greater economic and emotional resources (Theunissen, Vogels, & Reijneveld, 2015; Sputa & Paulson, 1995). As a result, the rate of positive parent-child interactions is often significantly greater in small versus large families. In large families, parents are more likely to use an authoritarian style because

Photo 5-8 Family tension and conflict can cause children considerable stress.

it offers an efficient way to address children's misbehavior and achieve immediate compliance. Because children in large families must compete for parents' attention, they frequently rely on their siblings for advice and guidance.

Education, Culture, and Social Class. Numerous studies have also been conducted to determine if variables such as parents' education, culture, ethnicity, and socioeconomic status (SES) influence parenting style. Azad, Blacher, and Marcoulides (2014) found that mothers who have more education and accessible income tend to engage in more positive interactions with their children. Parents who have a higher SES status and educational attainment are also more inclined to practice an authoritative parenting style. They involve children in family decision-making processes and are supportive of their educational endeavors. Families in many cultures (e.g., Asian, Hispanic, Latino, African American) where a strict authoritarian approach has often been the norm, are beginning to transition to a more authoritative child-rearing style as they better understand the positive effects that a democratic style can have on children's development (Trifan, Stattin, & Tilton-Weaver, 2014).

5-4f Stress

Stress also affects the type of parenting style that a parent is likely to use. Poverty and its accompanying anxiety (e.g., job uncertainty, housing instability) can detract from the time, energy, and emotional resources that a parent has available to focus on nurturing children's development. As a result, parents may view an authoritarian approach as a more direct and effective method for addressing children's behavior. Van Gundy et al. (2015) and other researchers have found that the strength of a family's interpersonal relationship and external support system can negate some of the negative effects that poverty and stress have on children's health and development (Pollock, Kazman, & Deuster, 2015). However, marital discord and parenting a child who has a developmental disability significantly increase family stress and the likelihood that an authoritarian parenting style will be used (Robinson & Neece, 2015).

5-4g When Parents Don't Agree

Until recently, researchers described the type of interactions that mothers and fathers have with their children as being distinctly different. Mothers spent more time nurturing and caring for children's needs and were considered to be more sensitive and patient than fathers. They engaged in more conversation with children than did fathers, and they provided considerable instruction during play activities. In contrast, fathers have traditionally been viewed as being either overly permissive or strict disciplinarians. They were less likely than mothers to initiate play with children and, when they did participate, they gravitated toward activities that involved risk-taking, physical rough-housing, or a sport or other recreational activity (John, Halliburton, & Humphrey, 2013). As a result, children had to learn how to adjust to quite different parenting styles and expectations, but they also acquired a broader array of lifelong skills.

Fortunately, these stereotypical roles have undergone notable change in recent years. Modern-day fathers are assuming more daily caregiving responsibilities and becoming more involved in their children's lives. Additionally, mothers in two-parent families are often balancing child care tasks with outside employment. As a result, they are more likely to encourage and support fathers' participation in child-rearing activities. This movement has allowed both parents to make unique gender-related contributions to children's development, and increased the likelihood that children will model similar parenting styles in the future.

Despite these trends, it is not unusual for parents in the same family to adhere to distinctly different child-rearing methods. Although they may agree on common behavioral goals and objectives, their communication style, interpretation of children's behavior, and disciplinary measures may be quite dissimilar. When these differences are relatively minor, children learn unique skills from both parents, including how to negotiate, cooperate, and compromise, that will be beneficial in future relationships.

However, numerous studies have also drawn attention to the negative consequences, including various psychopathologies (e.g., anxiety and conduct disorders, antisocial behaviors, obesity) that can occur when parents do not agree or they practice conflicting or inconsistent parenting styles. For example, Braza et al. (2015) reported that the combination of an authoritarian maternal style and permissive paternal style was strongly associated with an increase in children's aggressive behavior. Boys experienced a higher rate of maladjustment problems when they had one authoritative parent and one parent who followed a different parenting style (Panetta et al., 2014). Rinaldi and Howe (2012) observed a similar pattern of externalizing behaviors when mothers were permissive and fathers practiced an authoritarian parenting style. Adolescents are particularly vulnerable to conflicting or inconsistent parenting styles. Hartman et al. (2015) noted the importance of studying mother-child and father-child relationships separately in order to eliminate any potential moderating effect that either parent's style might have on children's behavior. What they learned was that adolescent drinking-related behaviors increased when mothers used an authoritarian parenting style, whereas alcohol use and impaired drinking control were less likely to occur when fathers practiced an authoritative style. They also noted that children's gender made no difference in the outcome.

Photo 5-9 Parenting can be an extremely challenging and rewarding role.

The authoritative parenting style is used by a majority of mothers and fathers, at least a portion of the time, and has been shown to achieve the most favorable outcomes for children (Pinquart, 2015; Panetta et al., 2014; Rinaldi & Howe, 2012). However, most parents will use a combination of parenting styles over the course of a child's lifetime. The ability to adapt and modify one's style to address different situations is highly desirable and a characteristic of effective parenting. It also models important coping skills for children, including situational flexibility, tolerance, empathy, and resilience. In contrast, a parent's rigid adherence to a single parenting style can create a negative family atmosphere and have adverse effects on children's development. When parents have conflicting goals, expectations, and child-rearing styles, children may experience considerable stress and confusion. For this reason, it is essential that parents make a concerted effort to work out their differences so they present a unified approach to parenting (see Figure 5-4).

Figure 5-4 How to Manage Differences When Parenting Styles Conflict

Parents are unlikely to agree on all decisions that involve children's behavior, whether they relate to sleep routines, mealtimes, discipline, or special privileges. However, parents can take constructive steps to reach a compromise that is in children's best interest. To accomplish this, both parents should:

- Identify their individual parenting style and the specific child-rearing practices they consider important.
- Set aside time when there are no distractions to discuss your parenting goals with one another. Note areas where there are similarities and differences.
- Discuss what the child needs to be successful.
- Negotiate opinions that differ and work to reach a compromise that is acceptable to both parents. The outcome is not about one parent winning or losing, but what is ultimately best for the child.
- Avoid arguing in front of children, or blaming each other for the child's behavior. Disagreements should be addressed in private.
- Enroll in a parenting class to learn new or alternative strategies for addressing children's problematic behaviors.
- Seek professional counseling if a compromise cannot be reached and significant differences remain.

5-5 Family Education Programs

Parenting may be one of the most challenging and important roles that adults will ever undertake. Yet, few parents receive any formal preparation or training for the task that lies ahead. They may assume that parenting skills will come naturally once children arrive or that others will be there to assist with child care responsibilities if needed. However, the support that extended families and friends often provided to new parents in the past has diminished as societies have become increasingly busy and mobile. As a result, young parents often experience considerable stress as they attempt to raise their children. Many also face additional challenges, such as financial hardships, living in dangerous neighborhoods, changes in family size and structure, military deployment, or caring for a child who has a developmental disability, which can detract from their ability to parent (Crandall, Deater-Deckard, & Riley, 2015; Foody, James & Leader, 2015).

Although most parents are able to meet children's physical needs, they are often less well-informed about how to promote learning, problem solving, and social-emotional development. Many parents also struggle with children's challenging behaviors because they lack information about effective management strategies. Over the years, there have been sporadic efforts to develop educational programs that would help parents with these and similar child-rearing issues. Some proved to be successful, while others were short-lived due to a lack of interest or failure to achieve positive results.

A renewed interest in studying children's behavior and well-being occurred during the 1960s and 1970s and led to the beginning of a concerted parent education movement. Several programs, including the Parent Effectiveness Training (PET) and Systematic Training for Effective Parenting (STEP), were developed during this time period and remain in use today. Both programs have a long-standing success record for improving family communication and effectiveness, reducing problematic behaviors and child maltreatment, and increasing positive developmental outcomes for children (Baek & Bullock, 2015; Pears et al., 2015).

Continued efforts to strengthen parent education have resulted in a wide range of community-based programs being offered through churches, county extension offices, child development agencies, hospitals, universities, and school districts. For example, because children are typically seen in primary care for well-child and sick visits, there has been a recent emphasis on the development of patient-centered medical homes to meet the unique needs of individual families (Ader et al., 2015). The goal of a medical home is to increase coordination and accessibility of services such as parent education. For example, the medical care office may integrate behavioral health providers into their practice, provide parent education programs, or provide access to social workers to help families navigate community services. Several new parent education programs have recently been developed and are being offered and tested online. Because these programs vary in terms of their quality and purpose, it is important that parents take time to investigate each one carefully before they enroll (see Figure 5-5). In some cases, a family may not have this option because a specific court-ordered program is mandated as a result of custody arrangements or child maltreatment charges.

A number of well-known family education programs have undergone rigorous scientific evaluation to validate their effectiveness. This process requires that a program's content and objectives be based on scientific evidence, and that the outcomes can be replicated on multiple occasions. STEP is one example of an evidence-based program. Training is delivered in a small-group setting, and focused on positive behavior guidance and the management of children's

Photo 5-10 Many evidence-based family education programs are available to help parents address children's behavior in positive ways.

Figure 5-5 Characteristics of an Effective Family Education Program

- Identifies goals and targets specific areas of children's development
- Focuses on particular parenting skills and builds on family strengths
- Tailors information to meet the diversity (e.g., culture, language, economic, education level, traditions) and needs of parents in the group
- Offers classes at a time and location that is accessible for parents
- Is taught by qualified professionals
- Delivers information over a period of several weeks so that parents have an opportunity to make adjustments and ask questions
- Evaluates and measures changes in parent competence; provides parents with feedback
- Follows-up and maintains contact with families after the sessions have ended

misbehavior. During the 7-week course, parents receive help in understanding conditions that may be contributing to children's behavior problems. They also learn cognitive-behavioral strategies that can be used to create a more positive parent-child environment. Studies have shown that family dynamics improve significantly as a result of this program.

The Incredible Years® is also an evidence-based program that is designed to boost parent confidence and competency. Several variations are available, including cultural adaptations and new components that address autism spectrum and language delay disorders (Baumann et al., 2015). The Incredible Years® program consists of 12 to 20 weekly sessions. Parents are grouped according to their child's age (e.g., infants, toddlers, preschool, school-age) so that developmentally appropriate content can be delivered. Parents are taught how to improve interpersonal communications, manage disciplinary problems, and promote children's social and emotional competence. The Incredible Years® program also places a strong emphasis on parents' involvement in their children's schools and educational endeavors.

The Triple P (Positive Parenting Program) is another well-known, evidence-based family support program that aids parents in addressing and preventing children's emotional and behavioral problems. Sessions are organized into a five-level system, and cover a range of topics from general parenting skills to strategies for managing severe behavior problems and maltreatment prevention. The Triple P program offers several different instructional components, including:

- Triple P, for parents of children birth to age 12
- Teen Triple P, for parents of teens between the ages of 12 and 16 years
- Stepping Stones, for parents of children who have a disability
- Family Transitions, for parents who are going through separation or divorce
- Lifestyle, for parents of overweight children
- Indigenous, for indigenous families

These programs are backed by more than 30 years of research, and endorsed by the World Health Organization (WHO), the United Nations, and the U.S. Centers for Disease Control and Prevention (CDC). They have proven successful with audiences of diverse cultures, family structures, and socioeconomic backgrounds.

The Nurturing Parenting™ is an evidence-based intervention program designed for at-risk families who are receiving social services. This federally recognized program teaches basic parenting and communication skills. Instructors help parents of children birth to 18 years to better understand developmentally appropriate expectations and learn positive behavior management skills. The goal is to reduce teen pregnancy, alcohol abuse, juvenile delinquency, the use of corporal punishment, and the

Figure 5-6 A Sampling of Family Education Programs

- Common Sense Parenting
- 1 2 3 Magic: Effective Discipline for Children 2–12
- Strengthening Families Program
- Parent Management Training: The Oregon Model (PMTO)®
- Parent-Child Interaction Therapy (PCIT)
- Parent Effectiveness Training (P.E.T.)
- Parenting Wisely
- Circle of Security™—Home Visiting
- The Adolescent Transitions Program
- Helping the Noncompliant Child

intergenerational cycle of child abuse. The Nurturing Parenting program has been modified to serve a variety of audiences, including different cultural groups, teen parents, military families, adoptive and foster families, parents of children who have medical challenges or developmental disabilities, and families in treatment and recovery programs (Vesely, Ewaida, & Anderson, 2014).

Parents As Teachers® (PAT) is a nationally-recognized intervention program that is familiar to many families and professionals. Parents, especially first-time and those at-risk (e.g., teens, low-income, single), are eligible to receive services throughout their pregnancy and until their children enter kindergarten. Sessions are delivered during in-home visits on a weekly, biweekly, or monthly basis and are focused on teaching basic parenting and family wellness skills, as well as maltreatment prevention (Carroll, Smith, & Thomson, 2015; PAT, 2015).

There are many well-respected family education programs available, only a few of which have been described here (see Figure 5-6). Additional program reviews can be located through the National Registry of Evidence-Based Programs and Practices (NREPP). Researchers continue to document the positive, long-term effects these programs have on strengthening family dynamics and competence, improving outcomes for children, and reducing risky and maltreatment behaviors. The proven success of these programs has led family educators to explore and experiment with alternative delivery methods such as online video sessions, websites, podcasts, and electronic newsletters in order to reach parents who otherwise may not have an opportunity to access classes any other way.

Summary

- Children rely upon parents for the satisfaction of their basic needs. The nature of the parent-child relationship is interactive, and influenced by a variety of factors, including the child's behavior, temperaments, stress, and environmental conditions.

- Communication is achieved through a combination of verbal (words that are spoken, tone of voice) and nonverbal (body language, behavior) information. The ultimate goal of communication is mutual understanding. This is achieved when both the sender and receiver agree on the intended message.

- Diane Baumrind described three basic parenting styles based on her extensive observations of parent-child interactions: authoritative, authoritarian, and permissive. These categories reflected the level of responsiveness and demandingness that parents exhibited. Maccoby and Martin added a fourth category which they labeled neglectful or rejecting. Each parent style was noted to have a different shaping effect on children's development and behavior.

- Numerous factors, ranging from personal experience to family size, stress, temperament, and cultural beliefs, can collectively influence one's parenting style.
- Evidence-based family education programs have proven effective in preparing adults for their role as parents, supporting and strengthening parenting skills, and promoting positive family relationships and outcomes for children.

Key Terms

active listening (p. 132)

authoritarian parenting style (p. 135)

authoritative parenting style (p. 134)

communication (p. 131)

free-range parenting (p. 137)

guan (p. 137)

helicopter parenting (p. 137)

I-messages (p. 132)

neglectful parenting style (p. 136)

permissive parenting style (p. 135)

Questions for Discussion and Self-Reflection

1. What effects does repeated exposure to negative parent-child interactions have on children's development?

2. How do verbal and nonverbal forms of communication differ? Describe the features of effective communication.

3. Why do children who are reared by permissive parents and given ample freedom experience a higher rate of social and emotional problems as adults?

4. What factors may influence a person's parenting style?

5. What is the difference between a community-based parent education program and one that is evidence-based?

Field Activities

1. Interview a local social worker or family court judge. Learn the reason(s) that a parent might be referred to a family education program. What types of parent-child problems do they encounter most often? How often do these problems involve inappropriate discipline or other behavior management conflict?

2. Conduct a literature search for parent education programs. Compare and contrast the programs based on the intended audience, teaching methods, length of the program, content, cultural considerations, and research support.

3. Locate and attend at least two sessions of a community-based parent education program. Describe the experience and how effective you found the sessions to be. Consider whether the program was appropriate for parents from different cultural, religious, and socioeconomic groups. Are the resources in your community sufficient to meet the parent education needs?

REFERENCES

Abenavoli, R., Greenberg, M., & Bierman, K. (2015). Parent support for learning at school entry: Benefits for aggressive children in high-risk urban contexts. *Early Childhood Research Quarterly, 31*(2nd Quarter), 9–18.

Ader, J., Stille, C., Keller, D., Miller, B., Barr, M., & Perrin, J. (2015). The medical home and integrated behavioral health: Advancing the policy agenda. *Pediatrics, 135*(5), 1–9.

Ansari, A., & Crosnoe, R. (2015). Children's elicitation of changes in parenting during the early childhood years. *Early Childhood Research Quarterly, 32*, 139–149.

Arora, M. (2014). The impact of authoritative and neglectful parenting style on educational performance of learners at high school level. *International Journal for Research in Education, 3*(6), 44–57.

Asselmann, E., Wittchen, H., Lieb, R., & Beesdo-Baum, K. (2015). The role of the mother-child relationship for anxiety disorders and depression: Results from a prospective-longitudinal study in adolescents and their mothers. *European Child & Adolescent Psychiatry, 24*(4), 451–461.

Azad, G., Blacher, J., & Marcoulides, G. (2014). Longitudinal models of socio-economic status: Impact on positive parenting behaviors. *International Journal of Behavioral Development, 38*(6), 509–517.

Baek, J., & Bullock, L. (2015). Evidence-based parental involvement programs in the United States of America and Korea. *Journal of Child and Family Studies, 24*(6), 1544–1550.

Baer, J., Schreck, M., Althoff, R., Rettew, D., Harder, V., Ayer, L., Albaugh, M., Crehan, E., Kuny-Slock, A., & Hudziak, J. (2015). Child temperament, maternal parenting behavior, and child social functioning. *Journal of Child and Family Studies, 24*(4), 1152–1162.

Barbot, B., Crossman, E., Hunter, S., Grigorenko, E., Luthar, S. (2014). Reciprocal influences between maternal parenting and child adjustment in a high-risk population: A 5-year cross-lagged analysis of bidirectional effects. *American Journal of Orthopsychiatry, 84*(5), 567–580.

Baumann, A., Powell, B., Kohl, P., Tabak, R., Penalba, V., Proctor, E., Domenech-Rodriguez, M., & Cabassa, L. (2015). Cultural adaptation and implementation of evidence-based parent-training: A systematic review and critique of guiding evidence. *Children and Youth Services Review, 53*, 113–120.

Baumrind, D. (1967). Child-care practices anteceding three patterns of preschool behavior. *Genetic Psychology Monographs, 75*, 43–88.

Bergmeier, H., Skouteris, H., & Hetherington, M. (2015). Systematic research review of observational approaches used to evaluate mother-child mealtime interactions during preschool years. *American Journal of Clinical Nutrition, 101*(1), 7–15.

Bowlby, J. (1969). *Attachment. Attachment and Loss: Vol. 1. Loss.* New York: Basic Books.

Boyce, J., Riley, J., & Patterson, L. (2015). Adult-child communication: A goldmine of learning experience. *Childhood Education, 91*(3), 169–173.

Braza, P., Carreras, R., Muñoz, J., Braza, F., Azurmendi, A., Pascual-Sagastizabal, E., Cardas, J., & Sanchez-Martin, J. (2015). Negative maternal and paternal parenting styles as predictors of children's behavioral problems: Moderating effects of child's sex. *Journal of Child and Family Studies, 24*(4), 847–856.

Bronfenbrenner, U. (1979). *The ecology of human development: Experiments by nature and design.* Cambridge, MA: Harvard University Press.

Bronfenbrenner, U., & Ceci, S. (1993). Heredity, environment, and the question "how?": A new theoretical perspective for the 1990s. In Plomin, R. and McClearn, G. (Eds). (1993). *Nature, Nurture, & Psychology.* Washington, DC.: APA Books.

Burkett, K., Morris, E., Manning-Courtney, P., Anthony, J., & Shambley-Ebron, D. (2015). African American families on autism diagnosis and treatment: The influence of culture. *Journal of Autism and Developmental Disorders, 45*(10), 3244–3254.

Carroll, L., Smith, S., & Thomson, N. (2015). Parents as Teachers health literacy demonstration project. Integrating an empowerment model of health literacy promotion into home-based parent education. *Health Promotion Practice, 16*(2), 282–290.

Chang, H., Shaw, D., Dishion, T., Gardner, F., & Wilson, M. (2015). Proactive parenting and children's effortful control: Mediating role of language and indirect intervention effects. *Social Development, 24*(1), 206–223.

Chen, X., & Schmidt, L. (2015). Temperament and personality. *Handbook of Child Psychology and Developmental Science. 3*(5), 1–49.

Coppens, A., Alcalá, L., Mejía-Arauz, R., & Rogoff, B. (2014). Children's initiative in family household work in Mexico. *Human Development, 57*(2-3), 116–130.

Crandall, A., Deater-Deckard, K., & Riley, A. (2015). Maternal emotion and cognitive control capacities and parenting: A conceptual framework. *Developmental Review, 36*, 105–126.

Crouter, A., & Booth, A. (2003). *Children's influence on family dynamics: The neglected side of family relationships.* New Jersey: Lawrence Erlbaum.

Cuellar, J., Jones, D., & Sterre, E. (2015). Examining parenting in the neighborhood context: A review. *Journal of Child and Family Studies, 24*(1), 195–219.

Danzig, A., Dyson, M., Olino, T., Laptook, R., & Klein, D. (2015). Positive parenting interacts with child temperament and negative parenting to predict children's socially appropriate behavior. *Journal of Social and Clinical Psychology, 34*(5), 411–435.

Dempster, R., Davis, D., Jones, V. F., Keating, A., & Wildman, B. (2015). The role of stigma in parental help-seeking for perceived child behavior problems in urban, low-income African American parents. *Journal of Clinical Psychology in Medical Settings, 22*(4), 265–278.

Dyer, N., Owen, M., & Caughy, M. (2014). Ethnic differences in profiles of mother-child interactions and relations to emerging school readiness in African American and Latin American children. *Parenting: Science and Practice, 14*(3-4), 175–194.

Foody, C., James, J., & Leader, G. (2015). Parenting stress, salivary biomarkers, and ambulatory blood pressure: A comparison between mothers and fathers of children with autism spectrum disorders. *Journal of Autism and Developmental Disorders, 45*(4), 1084–1095.

Galinsky, E. (1981). *Between generations: The six stages of parenthood.* New York: Times Books.

Gao, Y., Zhang, W., & Fung, A. (2015). The associations between parenting styles and proactive and reactive aggression in Hong Kong children and adolescents. *International Journal of Psychology, 50*(6), 463–471.

Goldberg, J., & Carlson, M. (2014). Parents' relationship quality and children's behavior in stable married and cohabiting families. *Journal of Marriage and Family, 76*(4), 762–777.

Grebelsky-Lichtman, T. (2014). Parental patterns of cooperation in parent-child interactions: The relationship between nonverbal and verbal communication. *Human Communication Research, 40*(1), 1–29.

Guyer, A., Jarcho, J., Pérez-Edgar, K., Degnan, K., Pine, D., Fox, N., & Nelson, E. (2015). Temperament and parenting styles in early childhood differentially influence neural response to peer evaluation in adolescence. *Journal of Abnormal Child Psychology, 43*(5), 863–874.

Hallers-Haalboom, E., Groeneveld, M., van Berkel, S., Endendijk, J., van der Pol, L., Bakermans-Kranenburg, M., & Mesman, J. (2016). Wait until your mother gets home! Mothers' and fathers' discipline strategies. *Social Development, 25*(1), 82–98.

Hajal, N., Neiderhiser, J., Moore, G., Leve, L., Shaw, D., Harold, G., Scaramella, L., Ganiban, J., & Reiss, D. (2015). Angry responses to infant challenges: Parent, marital, and child genetic factors associated with harsh parenting. *Child Development, 86*(1), 80–93.

Harlow, H., & Zimmermann, R. (1958). The development of affective responsiveness in infant monkeys. *Proceedings of the American Philosophical Society, 102*, 501–509.

Hartman, J., Patock-Peckham, J., Corbin, W., Gates, J., Leeman, R., Luk, J., & King, K. (2015). Direct and indirect links between parenting styles, self-concealment (secrets), impaired control over drinking and alcohol-related outcomes. *Addictive Behaviors, 40*, 102–108.

Hoskins, D., & Simons, L. (2014). Predicting the risk of pregnancy among African American youth: Testing a social contextual model. *Journal of Child and Family Studies, 24*(4), 1163–1174.

Huang, G., & Grove, M. (2015). Asian parenting styles and academic achievement: Views from eastern and western perspectives. *Education, 135*(3), 389–390.

Jabagchourian, J., Sorkhabi, N., Quach, W., & Strage, A. (2014). Parenting styles and practices of Latino parents and Latino fifth graders' academic, cognitive, social, and behavioral outcomes. *Hispanic Journal of Behavioral Sciences, 36*(2), 175–194.

John, A., Halliburton, A., & Humphrey, J. (2013). Child-mother and child-father play interaction patterns with preschoolers. *Early Child Development and Care, 183*(3-4), 483–497.

Jungert, T., Landry, R., Joussemet, M., Mageau, G., Gingras, I., & Koestner, R. (2015). Autonomous and controlled motivation for parenting: Associations with parent and child outcomes. *Journal of Child and Family Studies, 24*(7), 1932–1942.

Kakinami, L., Barnett, T., Séguin, L., & Paradis, G. (2015). Parenting style and obesity risk in children. *Preventive Medicine, 75*, 18–22.

Kelch-Oliver, K., & Smith, C. (2015). Using an evidence-based parenting intervention with African American parents. *The Family Journal, 23*(1), 26–32.

Khaleque, A. (2015). Perceived parental neglect, and children's psychological maladjustment, and negative personality dispositions: A meta-analysis of multi-cultural studies. *Journal of Child and Family Studies, 24*(5), 1419–1428.

Koury, A., & Votruba-Drzal, E. (2014). School readiness of children from immigrant families: Contributions of region of origin, home, and childcare. *Journal of Educational Psychology, 106*(1), 268–288.

Lansford, J., Sharma., C., Malone, P., Woodlief, D., Dodge, K., Oburu, P., . . . & Di Giunta, L. (2014). Corporal punishment, maternal warmth, and child adjustment: A longitudinal study in eight countries. *Journal of Clinical Child & Adolescent Psychology, 43*(4), 670–685.

Lawton, K., Gerdes, A., Haack, L., & Schneider, B. (2014). Acculturation, cultural values, and Latino parental beliefs about the etiology of ADHD. *Administration and Policy in Mental Health and Mental Health Services Research, 41*(2), 189–204.

Lee, R., Lawler, J., Shlafer, R., Hesemeyer, P., Collins, W., & Sroufe, A. (2015). The interpersonal antecedents of supportive parenting: A prospective, longitudinal study from infancy to adulthood. *Developmental Psychology, 51*(1), 115–123.

Lianos, P. (2015). Parenting and social competence in school: The role of preadolescents' personality traits. *Journal of Adolescence, 41,* 109–120.

Lorenz, K. (1935). "Der Kumpan in der Umwelt des Vogels: Der Artgenosse als auslösendes Moment sozialer Verhaltensweisen. *Journal für Ornithologie, 83,* 137–215, 289–413.

Maccoby, E., & Martin, J. (1983). Socialization in the context of the family: Parent–child interaction. In P. H. Mussen (Ed.), *Handbook of child psychology* (Vol. 4). *Socialization, personality, and social development* (4th Ed., pp.1–101). New York: Wiley.

Mackler, J., Kelleher, R., Shanahan, L., Calkins, S., Keane, S., & O'Brien, M. (2015). Parenting stress, parental reactions, and externalizing behavior from ages 4 to 10. *Journal of Marriage and Family, 77*(2), 388–406.

Merwin, S., Smith, V., & Dougherty, L. (2015). "It takes two": The interaction between parenting and child temperament on parents' stress physiology. *Developmental Psychobiology, 57*(3), 336–348.

Moilanen, K., Rasmussen, K., & Padilla-Walker, L. (2015). Bidirectional associations between self-regulation and parenting styles in early adolescence. *Journal of Research on Adolescence, 25*(2), 246–262.

Moutsiana, C., Johnstone, T., Murray, L., Fearon, P., Cooper, P., Pliatsikas, C., Goodyer, I., & Halligan, S. (2015). Insecure attachment during infancy predicts greater amygdala volumes in early adulthood. *Journal of Child Psychology and Psychiatry, 56*(5), 540–548.

Ng, F., Pomerantz, E., & Deng, C. (2014). Why are Chinese mothers more controlling than American mothers? "My child is my report card." *Child Development, 85*(1), 355–369.

Ordway, M., Webb, D., Sadler, L., & Slade, A. (2015). Parental reflective functioning: An approach to enhancing parent-child relationships in pediatric primary care. *Journal of Pediatric Health Care, 29*(4), 325–334.

Oshri, A., Sutton, T., Clay-Warner, J., & Miller, J. (2015). Child maltreatment types and risk behaviors: Associations with attachment style and emotion regulation dimensions. *Personality and Individual Differences, 73,* 127–133.

Panetta, S., Somers, C., Ceresnie, A., Hillman, S., & Partridge, R. (2014). Maternal and paternal parenting style patterns and adolescent emotional and behavioral outcomes. *Marriage & Family Review 50*(4), 342–359.

Parents as Teachers® (PAT). (2015). Parents as Teachers. Retrieved on July 5, 2015 from http://www.parentsasteachers.org.

Park, H., & Walton-Moss, B. (2012). Parenting style, parenting stress, and children's health-related behaviors. *Journal of Developmental Behavioral Pediatrics, 33*(6), 495–503.

Paschall, K., Gonzalez, H., Mortensen, J., Barnett, M., & Mastergeorge, A. (2015). Children's negative emotionality moderates influence of parenting styles on preschool classroom adjustment. *Journal of Applied Developmental Psychology, 39,* 1–13.

Pears, K., Kim, H., Healey, C., Yoerger, K., & Fisher, P. (2015). Improving child self-regulation and parenting in families of pre-kindergarten children with developmental disabilities and behavioral difficulties. *Prevention Science, 16*(2), 222–232.

Pezzella, F., Thornberry, T., & Smith, C. (2015). Race socialization and parenting styles links to delinquency for African American and White adolescents. *Youth Violence and Juvenile Justice.* doi: 10.1177/1541204015581390.

Pinquart, M. (2015). Associations of parenting styles and dimensions with academic achievement in children and adolescents: A meta-analysis. *Educational Psychology Review 24*(1), 1–19.

Pollock, E., Kazman, J., & Deuster, P. (2015). Family functioning and stress in African American Families. *Journal of Black Psychology 41*(2), 144–169.

Pratt, M., Singer, M., Kanat-Maymon, Y., & Feldman, R. (2015). Infant negative reactivity defines the effects of parent–child synchrony on physiological and behavioral regulation of social stress. *Development and Psychopathology, 27*(4), 1191–1204.

Rajendran, K., Kruszewski, E., & Halperin, J. (2015). Parenting style influences bullying: A longitudinal study comparing children with and without behavioral problems. *Journal of Child Psychology and Psychiatry, 57*(2), 188–195.

Ramsey, M., & Gentzler, A. (2015). An upward spiral: Bidirectional associations between positive affect and positive aspects of close relationships across the life span. *Developmental Review, 36,* 58–104.

Rinaldi, C., & Howe, N. (2012). Mothers' and fathers' parenting styles and associations with toddlers' externalizing, internalizing, and adaptive behaviors. *Early Childhood Research Quarterly, 27*(2), 266–273.

Robinson, M., & Neece, C. (2015). Marital satisfaction, parental stress, and child behavior problems among young children with developmental delays. *Journal of Mental Health Research in Intellectual Disabilities*, 8(1), 23–46.

Rogateg-Sariz, Z., & Sakic, M. (2014). Relations of parenting styles and friendship quality to self-esteem, life satisfaction and happiness in adolescents. *Applied Research in Quality of Life*, 9(3), 749–765.

Rusch, D., Frazier, S., & Atkins, M. (2014). Building capacity within community-based organizations: New directions for mental health promotion for Latino immigrant families in urban poverty. *Administration and Policy in Mental Health and Mental Health Services Research*, 42(1), 1–5.

Sampaio, A., & Lifter, K. (2014). Neurosciences of infant mental health development: Recent findings and implications for counseling psychology. *Journal of Counseling Psychology*, 61(4), 513–520.

Sangawi, H., Adams, J., & Reissland, N. (2015). The effects of parenting styles on behavioral problems in primary school children: A cross-cultural review. *Asian Social Science*, 11(22), 171–186.

Seibert, A., & Kerns, K. (2015). Early mother-child attachment. Longitudinal prediction to the quality of peer relationships in middle childhood. *International Journal of Behavioral Development*, 39(2), 130–138.

Telzer, E., Tsai, K., Gonzales, N., & Fuligni, A. (2015). Mexican American adolescents' family obligation values and behaviors: Links to internalizing symptoms across time and context. *Developmental Psychology*, 51(1), 75–86.

Theunissen, M., Vogels, A., & Reijneveld, S. (2015). Punishment and reward in parental discipline for children aged 5 to 6 years: Prevalence and groups at risk. *Academic Pediatrics*, 15(1), 96–102.

Trifan, T., Stattin, H., & Tilton-Weaver, L. (2014). Have authoritarian parenting practices and roles changed in the last 50 years? *Journal of Marriage and Family*, 76(4), 744–761.

van der Pol, L., Mesman, J., Groeneveld, M., Endendijk, J., van Berkel, S., Hallers-Haalboom, E., & Bakermans-Kranenburg, M. (2015). Sibling gender configuration and family processes. *Journal of Family Issues*. doi: 10.1177/0192513X15572369.

Van Gundy, K., Mills, M., Tucker, C., Rebellon, C., Sharp, E., & Stracuzzi, N. (2015). Socioeconomic strain, family ties, and adolescent health in a rural northeastern county. *Rural Sociology*, 80, 60–80.

Varmer, F., & Mandara, J. (2014). Differential parenting of African American adolescents as an explanation for gender disparities in achievement. *Journal of Research on Adolescence*, 24(4), 667–680.

Vesely, C., Ewaida, M., & Anderson, E. (2014). Cultural competence of parenting education programs used by Latino families: A review. *Hispanic Journal of Behavioral Sciences*, 236(1), 27–47.

Waller, R., Gardner, F., Viding, E., Shaw, D., Dishion, T., Wilson, M., & Hyde, L. (2014). Bidirectional associations between parental warmth, callous unemotional behavior, and behavior problems in high-risk preschoolers. *Journal of Abnormal Child Psychology*, 42(8), 1275–1285.

Warren, E., & Font, S. (2015). Housing insecurity, maternal stress, and child maltreatment: An application of the family stress model. *Social Service Review*, 89(1), 9–39.

Watabe, A., & Hibbard, D. (2014). The influence of authoritarian and authoritative parenting on children's academic achievement motivation: A comparison between the United States and Japan. *North American Journal of Psychology*, 16(2), 359–382.

Watkins, C., & Howard, M. (2015). Educational success among elementary school children from low socioeconomic status families: A systematic review of research assessing parenting factors. *Journal of Children and Poverty*, 21(1), 17–46.

Woodman, A., Mawdsley, H., Hauser-Cram, P. (2015). Parenting stress and child behavior problems within families of children with developmental disabilities: Transactional relations across 15 years. *Research in Developmental Disabilities*, 36(1), 264–276.

Zhao, X., & Gao, M. (2014). "No Time for Friendship." Shanghai mothers' views of adult and adolescent friendships. *Journal of Adolescent Research*, 29(5), 587–615.

Zubatsky, M., Berge, J., & Neumark-Sztainer, D. (2015). Longitudinal associations between parenting style and adolescent disordered eating behaviors. *Eating and Weight Disorders*, 20(2), 187–194.

Parenting Infants

6

BIRTH TO 12 MONTHS

LEARNING OBJECTIVES

After reading the chapter, you will be able to:

6-1 Describe how the infant growth patterns differ between birth to 6 months and 6 to 12 months.

6-2 Explain how parents can support infants' development in the cognitive, motor, language, and social-emotional awareness domains, and understand how temperament, nutrition, health care, sleep behavior, and environmental safety contribute to an infant's well-being.

6-3 Identify ways in which parents can mitigate the stress of parenting infants and take care of their own well-being.

6-4 Describe three strategies to soothe an infant, and three positive behavior guidance techniques.

naeyc Standards Linked to Chapter Content

1a, 1b, and 1c: Promoting child development and learning

2a, 2b, and 2c: Building family and community relationships

4a and 4b: Using developmentally effective approaches to connect with children and families

The transformation from newborn to 12-month-old is a truly remarkable journey in every respect. Rapid growth during this period significantly alters the infant's appearance and contributes to dramatic developmental changes in motor, cognitive, language, and social-emotional

continued on following page

abilities. From the moment of birth, infants are continuously assessing and learning about the world around them, even though they may seem to spend a majority of their time sleeping. They are able to capture and hold their parents' and caregivers' attention through cries, smiles, movements, and ability to imitate expressions. They learn quickly as new cognitive, language, motor, and social-emotional skills emerge almost daily. ■

6-1 Typical Growth and Development Overview

Infants depend upon their parents and caregivers for survival. When their basic physical (e.g., food, warmth, sleep, touch) and psychological (e.g., love, nurturing, trust) needs are met in a responsive and consistent manner, infants thrive and begin to form trust and an emotional attachment with their parents. Once established, these qualities facilitate continued brain development and create a sense of confidence that permits infants to reach out, explore, and interact with their environment.

6-1a Growth

fontanels soft spots in the bony skull that are covered by a tissue membrane.

mongolian spots bluish-grey patches of normal pigment (melanin) that may be present on the lower back of dark-skinned children.

Most infants are approximately 18–21 inches (45.7–53.3 cm) in length and weigh 7–9 pounds (3.2–4.1 kg) at birth; boys usually weigh more than girls. However, the infant's size varies depending on ethnicity and race, gender, birth order, parents' size, and maternal health during pregnancy. Growth standards developed by the World Health Organization (WHO) more accurately reflect the ethnic and racial diversity of today's children (CDC, 2010).

The infant's head appears large in proportion to their body (approximately one fourth of the body's length). "Soft spots" (called **fontanels**) are present in the skull bones to allow for continued bone growth during the first year. The skin tends to be light in color, regardless of race or ethnicity, and gradually darkens over time. Infants who are of Asian, African American, Native American, and Hispanic heritage may have **Mongolian spots** present on their back. These bluish-grey patches vary in size and location, and look like bruises but typically do not disappear until children reach the age of 6 or 7.

Infants grow at a rapid rate during the first 6 months, add approximately 1 inch (2.54 cm) in length per month, and gain weight at approximately ¼ to ½ pound (0.11–0.22 kg) per week (which results in a near doubling of their birth weight by 6 months of age). Their eyes are sensitive to light. They begin to cry with tears (1 to 4 months); color vision, depth perception, and true eye color are established (5 to 8 months). During the first 2 months, infants are unable to focus or control their eye movements (eyes may appear crossed or to wander) and only see objects at a distance of about 10 inches (25 cm). Gradually, their eye movements become more coordinated and distant vision improves. Hearing is acute and fully functional at birth. Hair becomes thicker, and teeth begin to erupt between 4 and 8 months of age.

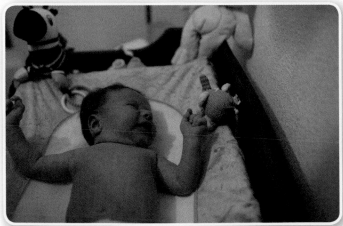

Photo 6-1 Reflexes help to ensure that an infant survives and thrives.

The infant's growth rate slows significantly between 6 and 12 months. Body length increases by about ½ inch (1.3 cm) per month; total length reaches approximately 1½ times the birth length by 12 months. A weight gain of approximately 1 pound (0.5 kg) per month is typical; the infant's birth weight is tripled by 12 months. The fontanels close, the head and chest become approximately equal in size, and their legs may remain bowed. By 12 months, most infants will have four upper and four lower teeth.

6-1b Developmental Tasks

Infants are born with primitive reflexes (e.g., sucking, swallowing, gagging, stepping, grasping, startling) that are designed to help assure their early survival. However, many of these involuntary movements disappear by the child's first birthday and are replaced with intentional and persistent skills. (Note: The failure of involuntary reflexes to fade according to schedule may be an early indication of neurological problems that require evaluation.) As a result, infants devote considerable time and effort to developing basic communication, motor, and social-emotional skills during their first year (see Figure 6-1).

So dramatic are the developmental advancements that occur during infancy, that children will never again experience changes that are as significant. The newborn, for example, progresses from a lack of mobility to learning to roll over, sit up, crawl, stand up, and perhaps even walk within a 12-month period. This rapid progression is only made possible through continued brain development and neurological maturation. Although infants begin learning from the moment they are born, the process is more likely to be positive and accelerated when infants form a trusting relationship with parents and caregivers (Erikson's stage of trust versus mistrust) and they have access to a variety of stimulating opportunities.

Every learning experience (positive and negative) forms and strengthens critical connections among brain cells which, in turn, increase the size of different brain regions (Kok et al., 2015). For example, Noble et al. (2015) observed that children who are brought up in impoverished environments in which play opportunities and positive verbal interactions were limited have a smaller brain size than do children who are reared in higher socioeconomic circumstances. Linton, Choi, and Mendoza (2016) noted that children who grow up in immigrant families that experience socioeconomic disadvantage, cultural challenges, and linguistic limitations show lower levels of cognitive development. However, the authors also note that many immigrant children, especially those from Asian and African groups, show higher levels of high school completion and standardized test scores compared to those from the same cultural groups whose parents were born in the United States.

Figure 6-1 Major Developmental Tasks of Infancy

Infants begin to make sense of their world through the acquisition of skills in several critical developmental areas:

- Understanding—learning through sensory and motor exploration; developing *object permanence.*

- Locomotion and hand-eye coordination—learning to roll over, sit up, crawl, and stand; pick up, shake, rotate and throw objects; assist with feeding self; imitate actions.

- Communication—reproducing sounds, acquiring a few words, understanding words, and how language works.

- Social-emotional awareness—learning trust and emotional expression through responsive care; discovering relationships and forming emotional attachments; understanding self as distinct from others.

Photo 6-2 Early identification of physical and developmental disorders improves the success of intervention measures.

Parents can promote infants' skill acquisition in each of the developmental task areas (e.g., cognitive, motor, and language) by providing simple toys and activities and engaging in frequent verbal and nonverbal interactions. Toys and play materials need not be commercial or expensive, but they *must* be safe (e.g., no sharp edges, no small parts, no harmful chemicals, developmentally appropriate) (Suggestions for Parents 6-1). Piaget (1952) suggested that infants learn primarily through a process of sensory exploration (Piaget's sensorimotor stage of cognitive development). In other words, they develop understanding by feeling, tasting, hearing, and observing, which explains why most objects usually end up in the infant's mouth. Offering play items that appeal to these senses support the infant's preferred mode of learning.

Tomasello (2016) noted that cultural preferences often influence the nature of parent-child interactions and the type of learning experiences that are presented to infants to help ensure cultural consistency and conformity. Luo & Tamis-LeMonda (2016) observed that Mexican mothers were more likely to use nonverbal methods (e.g., gestures, guidance) to attract an infant's attention or to encourage verbalization than did African America and/or Dominican

Suggestions for Parents 6-1

Developmentally Appropriate Toys and Play Activities for Infants

Safe, developmentally appropriate play materials and activities are effective for supporting infant learning.

- Birth to 6 months:
  - Crib mobiles, geometric pictures hung near the crib, unbreakable mirrors
  - Soft, stuffed animals or dolls, large textured balls, teething rings, rattles, toys that squeak
  - Plastic blocks and stacking cups
  - Cloth or board books (especially poems and those with rhyming lines)
  - Talk with your infant and read aloud often; infants won't understand but will begin to learn about sounds, rhythm, and voice inflection
  - Play quiet music, gently dance and sing while holding your infant.
- 6 to 12 months:
  - Push and pull toys, large rubber balls
  - Pots/pans or mixing bowl and wooden spoon, plastic bowls or containers, wet sponges, and plastic water toys
  - Shape sorters, plastic stacking cups, and large blocks
  - Puppets and stuffed toys
  - Continue reading aloud often (even the newspaper or a magazine); point to and name objects; talk to your infant during baths, meals, and throughout the day.
  - Look at photo albums together.
  - Play simple games together ("peek-a-boo," "patty-cake," "where is baby's nose"); singing to your infant, dancing gently to quiet music while holding your infant.

Adapted from: *Good toys for young children*. National Association for the Education of Young Children. http://www.naeyc.org/ecp/resources/goodtoys.

≫ Professional Resource Download

mothers. Keller et al. (2010) reported that Indian mothers tend to be more directive in their play interactions with children, whereas German mothers follow children's lead and encourage their independence. The culturally-relevant nature of parent-child interactions that occur during play is currently being studied for its potential to identify early autism spectrum disorders in infants and very young children (Elsabbagh et al., 2015).

6-1c Early Identification and Intervention

On rare occasions an infant may be born with an identifiable impairment or disability. Infants who are born prematurely, with low birth weight, or to mothers who experienced high risk pregnancies related to poverty, poor nutrition, or teratogen exposure have a greater chance of having developmental disabilities or delays. Each year, approximately 3 percent of infants (or 120,000) in the United States are born with a birth defect (CDC, 2015). Some conditions are not immediately apparent, and may not be detected until the infant is older and fails to achieve typical developmental milestones. However the delayed acquisition of a single skill is usually not considered significant or cause for undue concern unless the infant's progress continues to be inconsistent or lacking in one or more developmental domains (Marotz & Allen, 2016).

The early identification of impairments, developmental disabilities, and/or delays is essential to helping infants continue to achieve their skill potential (Suggestions for Parents 6-2). Many hospitals administer screening tests, such as the Apgar, Brazelton

---

Suggestions for Parents 6-2

Early Warning Signs

Parents play a critical role in the early identification of children's developmental delays and disabilities. Concerns about any of the following behaviors should be discussed with a health care provider.

- By 1 month of age, if your infant does not:
  - startle or respond to loud noises or make eye contact when held close
  - grasp your finger with equal strength in both hands
  - turn head when placed on stomach
  - accept milk readily or continue to grow
- By 4 to 6 months of age, if your infant does not:
  - focus on and follow a moving object
  - turn to locate a sound
  - bring hands together over mid-chest; reach for objects
  - coo or make babbling sounds
  - roll over
- By 8 to 12 months of age, if your infant does not:
  - search for hidden objects
  - reach for, grasp, and pick up objects; show interest in feeding self
  - respond to simple requests ("no," "stop," "come"); look when name is called
  - sit without support; crawl; pull up to standing position
  - imitate simple sounds ("ma-ma," "ba-ba")

Adapted from Marotz & Allen (2016).

≫ Professional Resource Download

Neonatal Behavioral Assessment Scale, and universal hearing screening, soon after an infant is born in order to detect gross neurological problems, breathing difficulties, and deafness (Brosco, Grosse, & Ross, 2015). Although these tests are not definitive, they are useful for identifying infants who may be at-risk and in need of further evaluation. Many states have also mandated newborn blood testing (tandem mass spectrometry or MS/MS) for metabolic disorders, including phenylketonuria (PKU) and approximately 20 other inherited conditions (Brown & Lichter-Konecki, 2016; Ombrone et al., 2016; Therrell et al., 2015). Treatment for disorders that are identified can be initiated immediately and, thus, limit or prevent potentially harmful effects on the child's development.

Continuous monitoring and assessment are essential for ensuring that an infant's development is progressing as expected. These efforts should include an awareness of physical and behavioral indicators that may suggest abusive and neglectful treatment (see Chapter 13). Developmental screening programs are offered in many communities through local schools, public health departments, clinics, universities, and health care providers (Williams et al., 2015). Additional information on laws and intervention services is provided in Chapter 14.

Understandably, parents may be emotionally devastated if they are told that their newborn has a congenital deformity or a disability that affects intellectual capacity, such as Down syndrome. In some cases, parents may have had prior knowledge of the condition through prenatal testing. However, when the reality is confirmed upon an infant's birth it may still be difficult news for parents to receive. It is important to understand and accept that these parents will experience a range of emotional feelings and responses, including anger, grief, guilt, depression, rejection, and fear and will need continued support (Fernández-Alcántara et al., 2015; Havermans et al., 2015).

Researchers have noted that parents of infants who have disabilities experience increased rates of stress and health-related problems (Miodrag et al., 2015). Mothers tend to worry about the burden of caregiving responsibilities and the effect a child's disability will have on family well-being; fathers are more likely to report concerns about the child's self-esteem, learning challenges, and potential for bullying. However, cultural context, values, and traditions tend to influence a family's perception of disability and the way they are likely to manage caregiving stress. For example, Cohen et al. (2015) noted that Latina mothers of children who had a disability experienced higher self-efficacy than White mothers when their partner or spouse provided emotional support. Ekas et al. (2016) also observed that partner and family support reduced the incidence of depression and increased optimism among Hispanic and non-Hispanic White mothers of children with autism spectrum disorder. Similar findings have been reported among other cultural groups (e.g., Korean, Asian, Native American, Caribbean, African American) in which extended families play a shared role in child rearing responsibilities (Linton, Choi, & Mendoza, 2016; Park & Chung, 2015; Zhang et al., 2015a).

6-2 Supporting Infant Development

At no other time in a person's life will growth or learning occur as rapidly as it does during infancy. However, premature birth, low birth weight, and unhealthy or adverse family situations can place infants at significant risk, compromise their development, and reduce lifelong productivity (Brumberg & Shah, 2015; Currie & Rossin-Slater, 2015). Good nutrition, quality sleep, a safe environment, and opportunities for learning are essential for protecting infants' well-being during this particularly vulnerable period and helping them to reach their biological potentials (Jensen & Bouhou, 2015; Robinson, 2015).

6-2a Promoting Cognitive Development

From the moment infants are born, they begin to take in sensory information from the environment. They are able to recognize their mother's voice and facial expressions, and seek out, and respond to, touch. Infants are born with an excess of disorganized neurons that are gradually arranged into functional pathways as a result of learning experiences; any unused neurons are discarded. This process can cause the brain to nearly double in size during the first year (Urban Child Institute, 2015). The cerebellum, the largest part of the brain that is involved in higher order processing (e.g., memory and learning), triples in size as the result of improved motor skill development (Urban Child Institute, 2015). However, prenatal exposure to teratogens can have a long-term negative impact on the way the brain functions. For example, prenatal exposure to alcohol is associated with decreased gray matter, which affects how information is processed, and differences in the hypothalamus (which is involved in consolidation of memory and social organization) (Donald et al., 2015).

Sensitive periods provide "windows of opportunity" for the maximization of potential brain development, but they also make it more vulnerable to stressors, such as emotional trauma or the lack of a nurturing environment (Gee & Casey, 2015). It is important for service providers to share information with parents about sensitive developmental periods as this knowledge may help to encourage them to engage in quality interactions with their infants. Researchers have noted that children who grow up in orphanages where they receive limited personalized attention show lower brain volume, larger amygdala volume, decreased cortical activity, altered frontal and limbic activity, and irregular hormone levels (Perego, Caputi, & Oglari, 2015). These outcomes may be the result of decreased interaction, limited stimulation and nurturing, and the lack of a consistent caregiver. In general, infants who are not exposed to sensitive and enriching environments show differences in areas of the brain associated with cognitive functioning, memory, emotion regulation, and processing reward signals and, thus, are more likely to have problems with impulsivity, attention, and social interactions (Perego et al., 2015).

Exposure to moderate stressors, such as ongoing parental conflict and trauma, also have implications for children's brain development. Graham and colleagues (2015) found that infants whose parents reported higher levels of conflict had differences in brain connections associated with negative emotionality (e.g., irritability, soothability, anxiety, sadness, anger), and experienced an increased vulnerability to mental health problems later on. Maternal depression and postnatal PTSD (post-traumatic stress disorder) can interfere with mother-infant attachment and her ability to respond quickly to the infant's cues which, in turn, has a negative effect on children's cognitive and emotion regulation development (Parfitt, Pike, & Ayers, 2014). Living in poverty may also expose the infant to increased environmental stress and negative parental interactions which can inhibit cognitive development.

Parental sensitivity (responsiveness to an infant's signals) and guidance provided during activities also play a critical role in infant's cognitive development. Paternal sensitivity appears to have a more significant effect than maternal sensitivity on cognitive outcomes, when socioeconomic status is taken into account (Malmberg et al., 2015). However, having at least one responsive parent may buffer any negative effects of the less sensitive parent (Malmberg et al., 2015). Strong neural connections are fostered when parents are responsive and provide a range of varied learning opportunities for infants, such as:

- placing objects, such as geometric shapes, mobiles, and mirrors where infants can view
- talking to the infant about daily routines, and describing what you see
- imitating infants' verbalizations, and following their lead in play

Photo 6-3 Brain development is a product of continuous learning experiences.

sensitive periods window of time for optimal development of specific abilities or skills. Although it may be more challenging, development can also happen outside of this window.

- encouraging play with toys and household items that have different textures and sounds (e.g., plastic cups, pans, boxes) (*Note*: all toys given to infants should be no smaller than the infant's fist [approximately 1.5 inches or 3.8 cm in diameter])
- allowing infants to safely explore the environment
- singing calming and action songs (e.g., This Little Piggy, Wheels on the Bus, The Itsy Bitsy Spider), and reading stories aloud
- playing games that emphasize social interaction, such as peek-a-boo and rolling a ball back and forth
- helping older infants begin to learn to follow simple directions by showing and providing gentle guidance

6-2b Promoting Motor Development and Physical Activity

The infant's motor skills improve dramatically during the first year (see Figure 6-2). According to Piaget, infants respond to, and learn about, the environment through their reflexes and sensory system. At birth, infants show several involuntary reflexive behaviors, such as:

- Swallowing, gagging, sucking, coughing, yawning, blinking, tears, and elimination
- Rooting—infants turn their heads when their check is gently touched (disappears between 1 and 4 months)

Figure 6-2 Examples of Infant Motor Skill Development

Age	Motor Skill Development
0–1 month	• Reflexes are present • Maintains the fetal position; holds hands in a fist • Turns head from side to side when lying down • Tries to follow objects with eyes • Has no hand-eye coordination
1–4 months	• Begins to hold hand in more open position • Makes large, jerky movements that later become smoother • Begins rolling from stomach to back near the end of this period • Raises head when pulled up to a sitting position • Begins to gain more head control when in a supported sitting position and while lying on stomach
4–8 months	• Reaches for objects; places items in mouth • Sits independently • Begins rolling from back to stomach • Gets into a crawling position and rocks; and may begin to crawl • Scoots around when placed on the floor • Begins using a pincer grasp (thumb and finger grasp)
8–12 months	• Manipulates and moves objects from one hand to the other • Reaches for objects offered; hands objects to others • Begins stacking, dropping, and throwing objects • Pulls self to a standing position, side-steps while holding on to furniture • Walks with support or may begin to walk independently

Adapted from: Marotz & Allen (2016).

- Moro—infants startle when there is a loud noise, touch, or quick movement (disappears between 4 and 8 months)
- Grasping—infants' fingers tightly wrap around objects placed in their hands (disappears between 1 and 4 months)
- Stepping—infants move their feet in a walking motion when held upright with their feet touching a surface (disappears between 1and 4 months)
- Plantar—infants' toes curl when the ball of the foot is touched (disappears between 8 and 12 months)
- Landau—infant extends legs, straightens back, and lowers head when held in a horizontal position (disappears between 12 and 18 months)

These reflexes serve as a basis for early survival and future learning. Their presence and fading according to schedule are important indicators of normal brain and neuro-muscular development (Marotz & Allen, 2016). Jerky motor movements become increasingly smooth, precise, and controlled with experience and neurological maturation. For example, an infant may accidently hit a toy hanging from a mobile as he moves his arms in large quick movements. Gradually he learns—with encouragement from caregivers—how to focus on the object and move his hands in an intentional way to hit or grab the toy. As new skills are acquired, infants are better able to explore, discover their environment, and advance skills in other developmental areas. For example, when an infant learns to sit up or to walk, she is able to experience and interact with her environment in ways that are different from earlier efforts (Leonard & Hill, 2014).

Scientists now understand that a child's development results from the continuous interactions of genetic and environmental factors, including cultural practices. Consequently, children may acquire skills at different rates due to the conditions in which they are growing up. For example, infants in rural areas of northern China are often placed in a sandbag during the day during the first 12 to 24 months to keep them safe and clean. Infants in central Asia are often swaddled, placed on a cradle, and carried around while their mother works (Adolph & Robinson, 2015). Although infants reared in these ways typically sit and walk later than the milestones noted in Figure 6-2, their developmental progress is considered typical or normal within their culture. Similarly, beliefs related to infant exercise also differ by culture. For example, parents in parts of Africa, the Caribbean, and India often perform vigorous stretching, massage, and shaking of the infant's limbs, and expect infants to support their own body weight, hold up their head, sit, and stand from the time of birth (Adolph & Robinson, 2015).

Motor activity during the first year has been associated positively with early attention skills, and with academic achievement and social development in older children (Libertus & Landa, 2014). Chiang et al. (2015) found that motor development was more advanced when parents interacted frequently with their infants and felt competent in providing their daily care. Furthermore, an association has been found to exist between a fathers' relationship quality with their infants and more advanced motor development. This difference may be related to the fact that fathers often engage in play that is typically more vigorous and physically stimulating than play initiated by mothers (Parfitt, Pike, & Ayers, 2014).

Motor skill development can be encouraged by providing learning opportunities that are within, and build upon, the infant's existing abilities (*zone of proximal development*) (Vygotsky, 1978). For example, Libertus and Landa (2014) found that when parents provided specific activities each day that were focused on reaching and grasping skills (e.g., toy placement, encouraging reaching, placement of toy in infant's hand, sticky mittens), 3-month-old infants' motor skills improved. In contrast, although infant walkers are thought to encourage early walking, they may actually delay motor skill development. The American Academy of Pediatrics (AAP) (2016b)

Photo 6-4 Cultural variations influence parenting practices and the expectations parents have for their children.

Marcus, a single father, picks up his 8-month-old son from his grandmother's house each day on his way home from work. Andre is unable to sit for long without support and shows little interest in crawling or reaching for toys that are offered to him. Is Andre's development typical? What advice would you offer to Marcus?

discourages their use because they are associated with numerous deaths and injuries (e.g., falls, reaching harmful items that would have otherwise been out of reach). Leaving infants in car seats, swings, or stationary walkers for prolonged periods of time also restricts movement and can slow motor development.

6-2c Promoting Communication and Language Development

From the moment they are born, infants communicate with their caregivers through crying. Cries gradually become more distinct and signal different needs and wants. For example, a high-pitched shrill cry may indicate pain, a wail may suggest sleepiness, and a whimper may express a desire to be picked up. Parents and caregivers can begin to distinguish an infant's unique cries by associating them with specific needs. Infants' cries also elicit an autonomic arousal (e.g., heart rate, blood pressure) in caregivers, which may help them to respond more quickly to the infant. However, this response may be minimal in parents who are diagnosed with depression (Parsons et al., 2013).

Healthy newborns are prepared to process sounds in a predictable manner (Háden et al., 2015). They react to loud sounds (startle) and show a preference (quiet, relax) for soothing sounds and human voices (especially mother's) (see Figure 6-3). Within weeks, they begin to engage in vocal interactions with caregivers, and are able to use learned information to discriminate between their native language and other languages (Molnar, Gervin, & Carreiras, 2013). Some infants, in particular those at-risk for autism spectrum disorder, may process voices differently which, in turn, interferes with their language and social development (Blasi et al., 2015). In other words, these infants appear to have a reduced ability to integrate visual and auditory cues to achieve understanding.

Parents and caregivers typically speak to infants differently than they do to other adults. Their interactions are characterized by a higher and more variable pitch, exaggerated sounds, slower rate of speech, limited vocabulary, shorter phrases, and increased melodic features. This form of talking has been termed "**motherese**" or infant-directed speech, and its role in infants' language development has received much attention. Golinkoff and colleagues (2015), for example, outlined three ways that infant-directed speech serves as a language-learning tool. It:

"motherese" a pattern of speech (simple words, rhythmic, exaggerated sounds, variable pitch) that adults often use when speaking to infants.

- increases the infant's attention to language,
- fosters social interaction between the infant and caregiver, and
- informs infants about the unique features of their native language by emphasizing certain aspects (e.g., vowels, consonants, chunking or segmenting sounds, questioning).

Photo 6-5 Verbal and nonverbal interactions promote infants' language development.

Infant's language development is highly influenced by the quality of their social interactions. For example, mothers who show frequent and intense positive attention through speech, gestures, and expressions help to maintain children's interest and motivation

Figure 6-3 Examples of Infant Language Development

Age	Language Development
Birth–1 month	• Communicates by crying and fussing • Shows preference for mother's voice and soothing sounds • Blinks and startles to loud noises
1–4 months	• Babbles and coos • Looks to locate sounds • Makes and imitates sounds • Laughs out loud
4–8 months	• Recognizes and responds to name and simple requests • Produces a series of sounds (ba, ba, ba; mm, mm, mm) • Talks to toys and stuffed animals • Expresses different emotions—squeals when excited, cries when displeased
8–12 months	• Imitates sounds and gestures • Shakes head to indicate "no" • Says simple words: ma ma, da da, oh oh • Understands the meaning of words ("Give the ball to me," "Point to your nose") • Uses sounds (e.g., shouts or squeals and then listens) to gain attention • Begins to associate gestures with words (e.g., waving and saying "Hi" or "Bye-bye")

Adapted from: Marotz & Allen (2016).

during reciprocal interactions and, thereby, increase their language skills (Grau et al., 2015). Furthermore, Hirsh-Pasek et al. (2015) noted that the quality of parent-child interactions—the fluency and connectedness of verbal and nonverbal interactions—was more important than the quantity of language to which an infant was exposed. Quality interactions were predictive of better language abilities as children grew older. Positive mother-infant relationship quality has also been linked to optimal language development, whereas prenatal depression is often associated with poorer infant language skills (Parfitt, Pike, & Ayers, 2014). Northrup and Iverson (2015) found that individual infant behaviors did not always predict a language delay, but that poor communication coordination with others was predictive. In other words, infants who developed a language delay were more likely to have latent response times and to talk at the same time as their mothers.

In a literature review on the effects of parent-infant interactions on language development, Topping and colleagues (2013) identified four strategies that are associated with increased infant language development. In order of evidence strength, they are:

• Contingency or extent to which the recipient of a communication is fully oriented, receiving, and processing information: making eye contact, facing the child when talking or playing, responding to infant cues,

• Pre-literacy activities: facilitating learning through shared book reading, telling and discussing stories, visiting libraries and museums,

• Parental elaboration: engaging in conversations, varying intonation to emphasize interesting or important points, explaining and narrating activities, talking about prior activities or events, and

• Gestures: responding to an infant's gaze, facial expressions, motions, and sounds.

Infants learn language and other communication skills better through live interactions than from video-based presentations. This is because live presentations may engage parts of the brain that are involved in integrating language and visual input (Jones et al., 2015). The American Academy of Pediatrics (AAP, 2015a) recommends that television and other entertainment media be avoided for children under the age of 2 years because they learn best through play and social interaction with people.

6-2d Promoting Social and Emotional Attachment

Infants enter into a social world showing an immediate preference for faces; in fact, this predilection continues to increase during the course of the first year (Frank, Amso, & Johnson, 2014). For example, when infants are shown social versus non-social stimuli their frontal lobe is activated (Jones et al., 2015). This preference helps infants to establish an early social connection with their parents and caregivers, and activates regions in the brain that play an active role in processing and regulating social and emotional behaviors.

Infants are also quickly learning whether or not they can trust their primary caregivers. Erikson described this stage of psychosocial development as a conflict between trust and mistrust. The nature of interactions that occur between infant behavior (e.g., temperament), parent behavior (e.g., level of responsiveness), and the environment (e.g., stressors and trauma) determine if this conflict will be successfully resolved and, thus, allow the infant to form a secure emotional attachment to caregivers.

Healthy social-emotional development occurs when children experience positive, supportive, and trusting relationships with parents and caregivers (see Figure 6-4).

Figure 6-4 Examples of Infant Social-Emotional Development

Age	Social-Emotional Development
Birth–1 month	• Gazes at parents
	• Shows preference for mother's voice
	• Enjoys being held
	• Begins to develop an attachment and sense of trust with caregivers
1–4 months	• Begins to show social smiles
	• Coos and babbles; participates in back and forth "conversations" with others
	• Recognizes familiar people
	• Enjoys routines and gentle physical play (e.g., tickling, bouncing)
	• Begins to imitate expressions
4–8 months	• Exhibits increased self-awareness
	• Distinguishes and responds differently to parents, teachers, and strangers
	• Seeks attention from others through movements and vocalizations
	• Imitates facial expressions; laughs out loud
	• Enjoys watching people and activities in their surroundings
8–12 months	• Shows stranger anxiety
	• Enjoys new experiences and exploring new toys
	• Responds when name is called
	• Follows simple directions; points to familiar people and objects when prompted
	• Begins to understand that others exist even when they cannot be seen (object permanence)

Adapted from: Marotz & Allen (2016)

Grossman (2015) proposed a framework outlining six key principles involved in the development of the infant's social brain:

1. Self-relevance: shows sensitivity (e.g., eye contact, facial expressions, infant-directed speech) to signs or changes in other people's behavior; deficits in this ability have been linked to neurodevelopmental disorders, such as autism.

2. Joint engagement: exhibits a shared understanding about an object or event with another individual (e.g., looks at a toy, turns to locate a voice, follows an eye gaze).

3. Predictability: shows sensitivity to a caregiver's actions; recognizes behaviors that help the infant to anticipate what will happen next or the purpose of an action.

4. Categorization: shows sensitivity to other people's features; this ability allows infants to use cues (e.g., species, race, gender) to attain a sense of identity.

5. Discrimination: shows sensitivity to changeable features (e.g., facial expressions, tone of voice, movements) that enable the infant to identify another person's emotions.

6. Integration: shows ability to integrate information from multiple senses (e.g., hearing a voice, seeing a parent, feeling a parent's touch) and uses the information for enhanced understanding.

The quality of early experiences that infants have with caregivers can have long-term effects on their mental health as well as social development. For example, low rates of parental vocal interactions, responsiveness, and involvement in play with 1-year-old infants are associated with disruptive behaviors and emotional disorders at age 7 (Allely et al., 2013). Some infants show early signs of mental health problems related to unresponsive caregiving, including excessive crying, sleep disturbances, and eating disorders. Such problems can have a negative effect on an infant's development and the quality of parent-infant relationship unless they are identified and treated early (Bolten, 2013). These studies reaffirm the important role that nurturing and supportive caregiving play in the promotion of children's social and emotional development.

Sensitive Period of Attachment. Attachment is critical to later learning, emotional health, physical growth, trust, and self confidence. Although a positive attachment can happen later in life, the period from birth to 9 or 10 months appears to be most important (Feldman, 2015). Researchers have observed that when infants are moved from institutionalized care (e.g., orphanages) to quality foster homes prior to the age of 24 months, they are more likely to develop a strong sense of attachment to caregivers and a normal stress response system (McLaughlin et al., 2015). As a result, these children tend to experience fewer developmental and attachment problems than if they had remained in an impersonal institutional setting where neglect and frequent caregiver changes are more common (Zeanah & Gleason, 2014).

The classic work of John Bowlby and Mary Ainsworth provides a basis for understanding the attachment relationship that occurs between parents and their infants (see Chapter 1). Attachments to caregivers form through close proximity (e.g., touch, sound) and physical and emotional nurturance. Many parents begin to have feelings of an attachment during pregnancy as evidenced by the sadness and grief that may be witnessed after a miscarriage or stillbirth. Following birth, infants engage in instinctual behaviors (e.g., crying, sucking, and clinging) that signal important needs. When caregivers respond and attend to these behaviors in a consistent manner, infants develop a sense of trust that their needs will be met. When both parties experience pleasure in these interactions, a positive attachment is more likely to form. Schaffer and Emerson (1964) proposed four stages of the attachment process based upon their observations of 60 infants from birth

attachment an emotional bond that endures over time.

Photo 6-6 A trusting relationship forms when parents are sensitive and responsive to an infant's needs.

Figure 6-5 Schaffer and Emerson's Stages of Infant Attachment

Preattachment/Asocial (Birth to 6 weeks)	• Infants respond to social and non-social stimuli with favorable reactions • Infants do not show attachment to a specific caregiver and are therefore okay with being held by unfamiliar people • Infants' instinctive behaviors attract the caregiver • Infants' response to the caregiver's behaviors encourage close proximity • Infants recognize their mother's smell, voice, and face
Indiscriminate Attachment (6 weeks to 7 months)	• Infants begin to smile and show enjoyment during interactions; they also become upset when the interactions stop • Infants are more easily comforted by familiar caregivers • Infants learn that their actions influence those of others • Infants begin to develop a sense of trust when caregivers respond to their signals
Discriminate (7 to 11 months)	• Infants show attachment or preference for familiar caregivers • Infants look to familiar caregivers for security, comfort, and protection • Infants show signs of separation anxiety with unfamiliar people
Multiple Attachments (9 months and beyond)	• Infants begin to form attachments with other caregivers including grandparents, siblings, and neighbors • Children develop stronger attachments when caregivers respond appropriately to their signals

Adapted from: McLeod (2009).

to 18 months (see Figure 6-5). As the infants aged, the types of attachment that were formed—secure, avoidant, ambivalent or resistant, and disorganized—became more apparent (Chapter 1; Ainsworth et al, 1978; Main & Solomon, 1990). Children who form secure attachments demonstrate healthy development, and continue to use parents as a base for exploration and learning.

The development of a secure attachment is facilitated by close interactions following birth and the establishment of **bio-behavioral synchrony**. Early touch-based interventions such as skin-to-skin contact and massage have been shown to promote bonding and enhance social-emotional development (Case-Smith, 2013). Feldman, Rosenthal, and Eidelman (2015) utilized an intervention in which mothers engaged in skin-to-skin contact (commonly referred to as "kangaroo care") with their pre-term infants for one hour per day for at least the first fourteen days following birth. They followed these children for ten years and found that those in the intervention group showed improved mother-child reciprocity as well as more organized sleep, better cognitive control, and increased resilience to stress.

Feldman (2015) described a phenomenon, called bio-behavioral synchrony, that develops between parent and infant during sensitive periods, and has long-term implications for social growth, stress management, emotion regulation, and mental health. This connection forms through physical touch, proximity to caregivers, eye gaze, facial expression, and vocal tonality. Synchrony between mother and child tends to be focused on visual and affective cues (rhythmic-calm synchrony) and is closely related to later self-regulation, moral understanding, and decreased likelihood of internalizing and externalizing problems. Father-infant synchrony typically involves more physical

bio-behavioral synchrony when biological markers such as heart rate and behaviors such as eye gaze and facial expressions of an infant and caregiver synchronize or occur at the same time.

Strategies to Promote Attachment

- Care for your own physical and mental health needs
- Spend quality time with your infant; devote your full attention and minimize distractions
- Provide newborns with nurturing, affectionate touch (e.g., skin-to-skin contact, holding, kissing, massage)
- Make eye contact, smile, exchange facial expressions, use voice tone appropriate to the situation (remaining calm when child is in distress)
- Respond to an infant's needs in a predictable way; this helps the infant to anticipate what will happen and begin to trust that the caregiver will meet her needs
- Show enthusiasm during play and when the infant learns a new skill
- Soothe and provide comfort when an infant is upset

contact, has brief peaks of positive arousal, and is focused on orienting the infant to the environment (physical synchrony). This type of synchrony is predictive of lower aggression and greater ability to handle peer conflict. Over time, caregiver-infant interactions become more reciprocal rather than occurring at the same time. Additional strategies to increase the likelihood of a secure attachment are provided in the Suggestions for Parents 6-3.

Several factors can pose obstacles to the development of a strong attachment. Prior to birth, parents who experience an unwanted pregnancy or relationship problems may be less likely to have feelings of happiness or to form a healthy attachment with their infant (Mosher, Jones, & Abma, 2012). Medical problems may necessitate that an infant remain in a neonatal intensive care unit or be hooked up to specialize equipment. These arrangements can limit the amount of time parents are able to spend holding and interacting with their infant during a critical bonding period (Pennestri et al., 2015). Parents' depressive symptoms or PTSD can cause decreased sensitivity and responsiveness and, thus, have a negative effect on their relationship with the infant (Parfitt, Pike, & Ayers, 2014; Puura et al., 2013). In addition, a mismatch in temperament between parents and infants can affect the amount of fulfillment obtained from interactions and, thereby, decrease synchrony if parents do not adjust their parenting strategies to better fit the infant's temperament (see Understanding Temperament, Section 6-2e). It is important for service providers to acknowledge these obstacles and to remain nonjudgmental in making recommendations to parents. They can help parents to recognize their child's unique personality and skills and implement strategies to improve the attachment quality (Suggestions for Parents 6-3).

Photo 6-7 Placing infants in non-parental child care does not interfere with the quality of their attachment to parents.

Child Care. Some parents worry that placing their infant in child care will have a detrimental effect on parent-infant attachment. At present, approximately 61 percent of children under the age of 5 spend at least a portion of their day in child care arrangements; a majority of this care is provided by a grandparent, father, or other relative (Laughlin, 2013). Infants whose mothers are employed outside of the home spend more time in care (36 hours) than those with mothers who do not work. Although the research has presented mixed findings, placement in high quality care arrangements does not have a negative effect on attachment, especially if parents also spend quality time with their infant and are responsive to the infant's needs (Bornstein, Putnik, & Suwalsky, 2016). It is important for parents to understand that infants can develop secure attachments with more than one person and that this development does not detract from the quality of parental attachment.

There are many important factors that parents should consider when selecting an early childhood care setting (Suggestions for Parents 6-4). However, research shows that parents often seek out arrangements that are close in proximity to their home or work, least expensive, and have availability (Liu, 2015). Child care costs account for approximately 7 percent of a family's income; however, families living in poverty may spend up to 30 percent of their income on child care (Laughlin, 2013).

Parents have several child care options to choose from. Care may be provided by a relative, friend, or nanny in the family's own home. Children may also be cared for in a licensed or unlicensed child care home (not all states require small group care to be licensed). Licensed programs are typically inspected and must meet specific health, safety, educational, and nutritional standards. The primary advantages to these two arrangements are that group size is typically small, caregivers are consistent, scheduling may be more flexible, and they are generally less expensive (Forry, Davis, & Welti, 2013). However, they also have potential disadvantages, including uncertainty if the caregiver becomes ill or goes on vacation, caregivers who lack training in child development, and the availability of only one caregiver to meet all of the children's needs.

A third child care option involves larger, center-based programs. The primary advantages to this arrangement are that these programs are usually required to be licensed, include greater diversity among children and staff, and have multiple, trained or credentialed caregivers present. Disadvantages associated with center-based programs can include the presence of more children, higher costs, and less flexibility in scheduling. Children in large group care settings are often exposed to more gastrointestinal and respiratory infections, including acute otitis media and, thus, may be an important consideration when parents are searching for infant care (Hoog et al., 2014).

Suggestions for Parents 6-4

Selecting a Quality Child Care Setting

Questions that parents should consider when evaluating the quality of a child care setting include:

- What are the teacher/staff credentials? Do teachers/staff have an early education background and do they receive ongoing supervision and training?
- Is there an appropriate ratio of adults to children?
- Are the group sizes small?
- Is the environment clean, safe, and large enough for the number of children present?
- Are nutritious meals provided?
- Are there varied opportunities for learning? What types of activities are organized and presented? Are the toys and equipment developmentally appropriate? Are there enough toys so that children do not always have to share?
- Are teachers sensitive to diversity?
- How do teachers/staff communicate with one another and with the children?
- How do teachers/staff partner with parents? Are parents welcome to visit? How is information communicated between home and school?

When evaluating child care options, parents should closely attend to the quality of care provided. One of the most important indicators of quality child care is the relationship or bond that teachers develop with the children in their care, as this bond helps to facilitate development (Brebner et al., 2015). Parents must not only talk with the teachers but also observe their interactions with children at different times. Teachers should be responsive to the infants' cues, provide a variety of opportunities for learning (not leaving the infant in one area for long periods), talk directly to infants (not only to other caregivers who are present), remain calm during trying times, and maintain open lines of communication with parents.

6-2e Understanding Temperament

Temperament is the relatively stable way that an individual reacts to the world. Infants are generally described as being easy, difficult, or slow-to-warm-up. There are nine traits commonly associated with temperament (Center for Early Childhood Mental Health Consultation, 2015):

- Activity level—degree of physical activity (e.g., high, low)
- Regularity—predictability of biological functions (e. g., toileting, eating, sleeping)
- Adaptability—initial response and ease in adjusting to changes
- Distractibility—ability to focus
- Sensitivity—degree of sensitivity to sensations (e.g., sight, texture, sounds)
- Persistence—duration spent on challenging tasks
- Intensity—level of emotional response (relaxed to intense)
- Approachability—response to novel situations
- Mood—positive or negative reactions

Although there is a biological basis for temperament, culture and environmental experiences also shape its expression. Sung et al. (2014) found that U.S. infants received higher ratings on negative affectivity, activity level, and vocal reactivity, whereas Dutch infants received higher ratings on low-intensity pleasure and soothability. These findings may reflect a combination of genetic differences and variations in the way that parents in different cultures interact and interpret infant behavior. For example, American parents place an emphasis on cognitive stimulation; in contrast, Dutch parents emphasize rest, regular schedules, and play and are less likely to interpret mild fussing as negative affect (Sung et al., 2014). Infants who are perceived by parents to have a difficult temperament and sleep disturbances are less likely to experience optimal development across all domains (Parfitt, Pike, & Ayers, 2014).

Parents and infants are likely to vary in at least some of their temperament traits. A mismatch between parent and infant temperament can impede development of a secure attachment. For example, if a parent who is laid back, calm, and appreciates routines has an infant who shows high levels of activity and intense emotional responses, he or she may have difficulty being sensitive and responsive to the child's ever changing moods and needs. Similarly, a parent who is active and distractible may have greater difficulty noticing subtle cues from a relaxed, low-keyed infant and, thus, not respond contingently. Infants' level of trust is likely to decline if their signals do not produce predictable caregiver responses. However, parents can intentionally change the way they interact to meet the infant's needs and, thus, create a "**goodness of fit**." The Center for Early Childhood Mental Health Consultation (2015) developed the *Infant Toddler Temperament Tool* (or IT³), which provides suggestions to help parents and caregivers identify and meet their child's preferred response style in order to improve the relationship. For example, if a parent is more spontaneous, but the infant prefers predictability, the parent may need to learn ways to develop and follow daily routines and to prepare older infants in advance when routines change.

Self-Awareness. Rochat (2003) described five levels of self-awareness, the first two of which apply to infants. The first level is differentiation. Infants are born with some level

"goodness of fit" compatibility between caregiver and child temperaments; caregiver adjusts methods to fit the child's individual temperament style.

Photo 6-8 Infants are able to distinguish themselves from others.

of self-awareness as they are able to differentiate themselves from others. For example, infants can distinguish the difference between self- and non–self-touch, and respond differently to each. At the second level, situated, 2-month-old infants begin to show an understanding of themselves in relation to others. For example, infants may imitate facial expressions, engage in turn-taking, or coordinate their movements to reach for a toy.

Additional research findings support the idea that from the time of birth, infants are affectively tuned to others' emotional states and are able to empathize (Jensen, Vaish, & Schmidt, 2014). These early forms of awareness are influenced by culture and related to a later development of self-concept (Kristen-Antonow et al., 2015). Specifically, infants reared in societies that emphasize distal parenting with a lot of face-to-face contact as opposed to cultures that emphasize body contact, identify themselves earlier on measures of self-recognition.

Separation Distress. Separation distress or stranger anxiety typically appears between 7 to 12 months of age and is related to two primary developments. First, infants at this age have established a discriminate attachment with their primary caregivers and, therefore, show preference for them over unfamiliar people. In addition, they are becoming more aware of their surroundings, but have not fully mastered object permanence. When parents understand that separation anxieties are universal and typical, they can take positive steps to help infants transition through this stressful phase (Suggestions for Parents 6-5).

6-2f Supporting Development and Wellness Through Nutrition

Good nutrition is especially critical during the child's first year of a life. Rapid growth and brain development are dependent upon an adequate intake of essential fats, protein, carbohydrates, vitamins, and minerals as well as calories to meet the infant's high energy needs. Inadequate nutrition during infancy can result in stunted growth and a reduction in brain size, neural connections, and **neural plasticity** (Georgieff, Brunette, & Tran, 2015; Prado & Dewey, 2014).

neural plasticity the ability of the brain to reorganize and form new connections between cells.

Suggestions for Parents 6-5

Helping Infants Adjust to Separations

- Keep in mind infants' level of development; specifically, that they are not always able to understand that people and objects exist when they are out of sight.
- Remain calm and patient.
- Allow infants to have a comfort object (e.g., blanket, soft toy) to increase secure feelings.
- Practice brief, safe separations.
- Create a consistent routine when leaving (don't rush away or sneak out, and also do not prolong leaving).
- Allow the caregiver to comfort the infant upon leaving (resist the urge to return to comfort the infant yourself).
- Use distractions such as toys, talking, or feeding.
- Convey a sense of confidence; smile, give the infant a hug, and reassure her that you will return.

During the first 6 months, infants require approximately 50 calories per pound of body weight; older infants need only 45 calories per pound of body weight because their growth rate is beginning to slow (Marotz, 2015). An infant's nutrient needs are easily met with breastmilk or infant formula. Although manufacturers are able to produce formulas that closely mimic most nutrients found in human breastmilk, they are not able to replicate the protective **antibodies** that mothers produce. These antibodies are known to safeguard infants against Sudden Infant Death Syndrome (SIDS), ear infections, diarrhea, pneumonia and other infectious illnesses, and leukemia and, thus, are important for infant health (Leung, Chisti, & Pavia, 2016; Moon & Hauck, 2016). This antibody protection is even more critical for premature and low birth-weight infants and infants who are growing up in poverty and developing countries. For these reasons, the American Academy of Pediatrics (AAP), Canadian Paediatric Society (CPS), and the World Health Organization (WHO) recommend that mothers breastfeed their infants exclusively for at least 6 months and longer if possible (WHO, 2015; CPS, 2014; AAP, 2012).

> **antibodies** substances (proteins) produced by the immune system that protect an individual against specific infectious disease.

Human breastmilk offers several advantages in addition to satisfying all of an infant's essential nutrient requirements. It contains proteins, fats, and carbohydrates in forms that are easy for infants to digest. It also is lower in sodium than most formulas, supplies beneficial intestinal bacteria, is sterile (which reduces the risk of contamination), and less likely to cause food allergies. Breastmilk is convenient, always the correct temperature, available when needed, and less expensive than the cost of formula. Infants who are breastfed are also less likely to develop chronic health conditions, such as obesity and type 2 diabetes (Horta, de Mola, & Victora, 2015).

Research has shown that mothers who have breastfed an infant tend to experience lower rates of breast and ovarian cancer, hypertension (high blood pressure), and diabetes (Islami et al., 2015; Zhang et al., 2015b). There are, however, some perceived drawbacks associated with breastfeeding. Mothers must be accessible unless they pump and store breastmilk and they must increase their nutrient (protein, vitamins A and C, folacin, calcium), fluid, and caloric intakes.

Some mothers choose not to breastfeed their infant or are not able to do so for medical reasons (e.g., poor health, taking medications that could be harmful to the infant, substance abuse, transmittable infectious diseases such as HIV, Ebola, hepatitis). However, it is always important that mothers discuss these concerns with a health care provider. Cultural differences are also known to influence mothers' breastfeeding decisions. Masho, Cha, and Morris (2015) noted that prepregnancy obesity reduced the initiation of breastfeeding among non-Hispanic white and non-Hispanic black women. In fact, breastfeeding rates in the United States are lowest among women of minority ethnic/racial backgrounds (Jones et al., 2015). Cultural traditions and beliefs that a "heavy baby is a healthy baby" also influence early breastfeeding cessation and the introduction of solid foods (Cartagena et al., 2015; Lee & Brann, 2015). However, cultural values and practices can also be effective in supporting exclusive breastfeeding (Wambach et al., 2016).

The benefits of human breastmilk for infant health and development have led to the establishment of nonprofit and for-profit breastmilk banks throughout the United States and Canada. Nursing mothers can donate or sell their surplus milk to these programs, where it is tested and pasteurized. Breastmilk banks make it possible for mothers who are unable to nurse or whose milk is inadequate to obtain breastmilk for their infant. However, families should exercise caution and carefully investigate these organizations, especially if breastmilk is sold online, to be sure that donors are screened and milk is handled safely and pasteurized to protect infants from illness (St-Onge, Chaudhry, & Koren, 2015).

Photo 6-9 Breastmilk provides many healthful advantages.

Photo 6-10 Sensitivity to the infant's behavioral cues prevents overfeeding.

As previously mentioned, infant formulas are currently manufactured with ingredients similar to those found in breastmilk and, thus, they provide a satisfactory substitute when circumstances prevent breastfeeding. Care must be taken to carefully follow the manufacturer's mixing guidelines so as not to create a solution that is either too weak (and lacking in nutrients) or overly rich. Infants should always be fed in an upright position (to reduce the risk for ear infections) and burped often. Feedings should be relaxed and a time when mother and infant can enjoy being together. The infant's gums should be wiped with a damp cloth after feedings to help reduce the incidence of tooth decay. Prolonged feedings (longer than 20 minutes or so) should be avoided to prevent the sugars in breastmilk and formula from remaining in contact with the infant's teeth for an extended period.

Infants do not require any food in addition to breastmilk or formula during the first 6 months. They eat often, especially in the early months, because their stomach can only hold small amounts of food at a time. Crying does not always indicate hunger. It may be a sign of discomfort (e.g., wet diaper, gas), too much stimulation, or simply a desire to be picked up (Suggestions for Parents 6-6). Supplemental water should only be offered to prevent dehydration (e.g., vomiting, diarrhea, fever, warm climate).

Five- to six-month-old infants are developmentally ready to begin accepting solid foods such as iron-fortified cereals (to prevent anemia) in addition to breastmilk or formula. They are now able to move food from the front of their mouth to the back and swallow, chew, sit upright in a highchair, show an interest participating, and communicate hunger and refusal (see Figure 6-6). Foods, such as pureed vegetables, fruits, and proteins, should only be added to the infant's diet when advised by a health care provider. Some foods, such as meat proteins, cannot be digested until the infant's digestive system is more mature. However, there are also "sensitive periods" when infants are more receptive to accepting solid foods. Delaying their introduction too long can lead to food refusal and prolonged feeding disorders (Romano et al., 2015). It is also recommended that new food items be introduced one at a time (and for several days) in order to observe for any potential allergic reaction. Mealtimes should be a pleasant, shared experience during which parents and caregivers can interact and reinforce an infant's learning, language, social interaction, and motor skills.

Suggestions for Parents 6-6

Behavioral Indicators of Hunger and Fullness

Changes in an infant's behavior provide useful clues for assessing hunger and satiety (no longer hungry).

Hunger	Satiety
thrusts tongue out	turns head away
makes sucking sounds	falls asleep
puts fingers or fist in mouth	releases latch on nipple
searches for breast or bottle	pushes away from bottle or breast
begins crying (a late sign)	clamps mouth/lips closed
becomes restless, fidgets	

Figure 6-6 Infant Eating and Feeding Behaviors

Infants' interest in eating and learning how to feed themselves is highly variable, and is influenced by their developmental skills, special needs, and diverse environments in which they are growing up.

1 to 3 months	sucks on fingers or fist when hungry
	licks lips in anticipation of food; turns to breast or nipple
	sucks vigorously when hungry; often chokes
4 to 6 months	reaches for, picks up, and brings small food pieces to mouth
	leans forward and opens mouth as spoon approaches
	sucking becomes voluntary
	places hand on breast or around bottle
6 to 9 months	chews with up-and-down motion
	closes lips around spoon; moves food around in mouth
	drinks from a cup
	picks up food between thumb and fingers
9 to 12 months	begins to grasp small plastic spoon; not always successful at delivering food into mouth
	enjoys tossing food over edge of tray and onto the floor; delights in having adult retrieve the items
	holds and drinks from own cup; frequently spills liquid in cup
	picks up, releases, and transfers food pieces from one hand to the other
	bites cracker or biscuits with teeth; chews with rotary motion

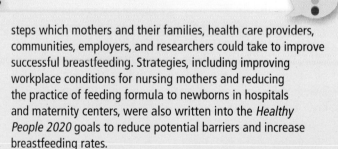

Trending Now Breastfeeding in Public Places

Dietitians, health care providers, and lactation specialists have long encouraged mothers to breastfeed their infants. Researchers have consistently demonstrated breastmilk's beneficial attributes and its positive effects on infant and maternal health. Scientists have used advanced technologies to identify stem cells in human milk and detect their transfer to infants during breastfeeding (Hassiotou et al., 2015; Sani et al., 2015). Additionally, they have discovered that these cells may play an important role in infant development and that variations may be associate with premature birth and low maternal milk production (Twigger et al., 2015).

Efforts to increase breastfeeding support have led to a number of national initiatives and legislative acts. The U.S. Surgeon General announced plans in 2000 for a major national awareness plan that was designed to increase exclusive infant breastfeeding rates (no supplemental formula or other food). However, the percentage and duration of breastfeeding in this country remained low. The *Affordable Care Act* (2010) requires employers to provide a private room (other than a bathroom) and a reasonable amount of time for nursing mothers to pump or express breastmilk for up to 1 year after giving birth. A new *Call to Action to Support Breastfeeding* campaign was launched by the U.S. Surgeon General in 2011 that outlined 20 action

steps which mothers and their families, health care providers, communities, employers, and researchers could take to improve successful breastfeeding. Strategies, including improving workplace conditions for nursing mothers and reducing the practice of feeding formula to newborns in hospitals and maternity centers, were also written into the *Healthy People 2020* goals to reduce potential barriers and increase breastfeeding rates.

Although breastfeeding offers compelling benefits for infants and their mothers, the decision is ultimately a personal choice. However, progress toward achieving the *Health People 2020* breastfeeding targeted goals has remained slow. According to the Breastfeeding Report Card 2014, the rate of U.S. mothers who have breastfed their infant for at least 1 month has risen slightly to 79 percent; the Healthy People 2020 objective/target was set at 81.9 percent (CDC, 2014). However, the duration that infants are being breastfed has continued to decrease; only 49 percent of infants were nursed exclusively for at least 6 months (*Health People 2020* target 60.6) and 27 percent (target 34.1) were breastfed for 12 months (see Figure 6-7). Rates among women of racial/ethnic minority and those living in poverty were significantly lower.

(Continued)

Figure 6-7 Exclusive Breastfeeding Rates by Age Among U.S. Children Born in 2012

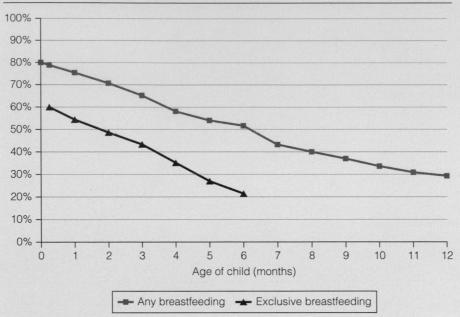

Source: National Immunization Surveys, Centers for Disease Control and Prevention, Department of Health and Human Services.

So, why don't more mothers breastfeed their infants? When asked, they often cite reasons for not initiating breastfeeding or curtailing it early that include unsupportive workplace environments, concerns that milk supply is inadequate, depression and pain, inconvenience, and lack of partner support (Brown, Rance, & Bennett, 2016; Henshaw et al., 2015; Rozga, Kerver, & Olson, 2015). Others express significant concern about reactions to breastfeeding in public, including harassment and negative attitudes (Patenaude, Knol, & Turner, 2015; Roche, Owen, & Fung, 2015; Mulready-Ward & Hackett, 2014).

Although almost every state has passed laws permitting breastfeeding in public places, few have included any enforcement provisions (NCSL, 2016). They also vary in terms of the protections afforded. For example, some states excuse breastfeeding mothers from jury duty or require the provision of a private area, other than a bathroom, for breastfeeding. Only 29 states protect breastfeeding mothers from public indecency laws. The lack of enforcement provisions in state laws has allowed employers (with the exception of government agencies) and private businesses to dismiss nursing mothers from their jobs, ask them to leave restaurants and shopping malls, and call in security or law enforcement without experiencing any significant repercussions.

Mothers understand the importance of doing what is best for their infant but they continue to receive mixed messages. It is unlikely that rates of exclusive and prolonged breastfeeding will increase until some of these inconsistencies are resolved.

6-2g Well-Child Care and Immunizations

Routine visits with a health care provider are important for ensuring that an infant is growing and developing normally, and for treating occasional health problems that may arise. These visits also enable health care personnel to appraise the family's emotional well-being and to answer parents' questions. The American Academy of Pediatrics recommends that infants be seen within several days of being discharged from the hospital, then every 2 months until age 6 months, and every 3 months until the age of 2 years (AAP, 2016a). Parents can access age-relevant questionnaires, called *Bright Futures*, from the AAP website (www .healthychild.org) to print and complete prior to each well-child visit. These forms may be useful for framing and prompting questions that parents may want to ask.

During well-child visits, the health care provider will examine the infant, measure height and weight, evaluate developmental progress, and provide anticipatory guidance regarding nutrition, safety, and behavior. Scheduled immunizations against preventable

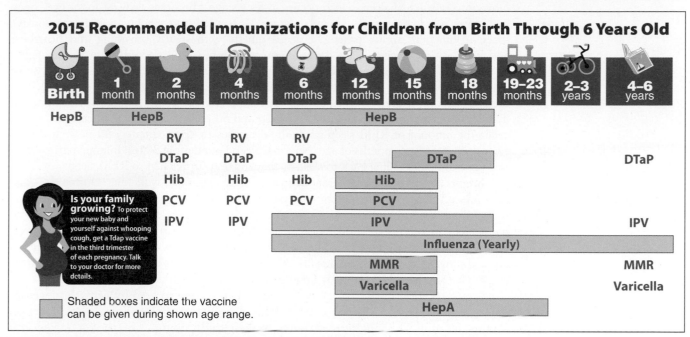

2015 Recommended Immunizations for Children from Birth Through 6 Years Old

Birth	1 month	2 months	4 months	6 months	12 months	15 months	18 months	19–23 months	2–3 years	4–6 years
HepB	HepB				HepB					
		RV	RV	RV						
		DTaP	DTaP	DTaP	DTaP					DTaP
		Hib	Hib	Hib	Hib					
		PCV	PCV	PCV	PCV					
		IPV	IPV	IPV						IPV
				Influenza (Yearly)						
				MMR						MMR
				Varicella						Varicella
				HepA						

Is your family growing? To protect your new baby and yourself against whooping cough, get a Tdap vaccine in the third trimester of each pregnancy. Talk to your doctor for more details.

Shaded boxes indicate the vaccine can be given during shown age range.

Source: Centers for Disease Control and Prevention (CDC). http://www.cdc.gov/vaccines/parents/downloads/parent-ver-sch-0-6yrs.pdf.

communicable diseases will usually be administered at this time (see Figure 6-8). Some parents are hesitant to have their children immunized due to concerns about vaccine safety, the number of required immunizations, and belief that many diseases no longer pose a threat. Others may refuse immunizations on the basis of religious beliefs or because of a child's medical condition. Although rare side effects have been linked to some vaccines, experts consistently report their efficacy and safety (AHRQ, 2014). Information about vaccine schedules, safety, and the diseases they prevent is available on the CDC website.

6-2h Sleep Behavior and Sleep-Wake Patterns

There is a perception that infants spend a majority of their time sleeping. Proud parents are often heard boasting that their newborn is "already sleeping through the night," only to learn that this phase is likely to soon end. This is, in part, due to the fact that newborns are not yet able to distinguish day from night. They typically sleep 8 or 9 hours during the daytime and 8 or more hours at night. They also awaken every 2 or 3 hours to be fed, changed, or held.

Sleep patterns begin to change at around 3 or 4 months of age. Infants start sleeping 6 to 8 hours at a stretch during the nighttime because they are now able to consume more at a feeding. However, some infants may not reach this point for several more months. Daytime sleep is gradually replaced with morning and afternoon naps and an increase in uninterrupted nighttime sleeping. The National Sleep Foundation (2015) recommends that infants 4 to 11 months get between 12 and 15 total hours of sleep each day.

Infants experience stages and intensities of sleep that are similar to those of an adult. During the final months of pregnancy, a fetus develops a sleep-wake cycle patterned after its mother's. Following birth, infants begin to establish their own circadian pattern based on exposure to light and maternal activity (Thomas, Burr, & Spieker, 2015). Two forms of sleep develop—REM (rapid eye movement)

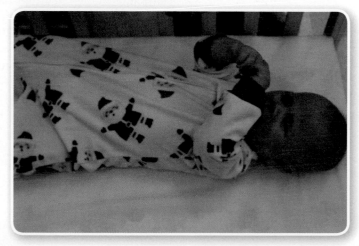

Photo 6-11 Infants may spend hours sleeping.

and non-REM (NREM). During REM sleep, infants are in a stage of light or active sleep. They may smile, their eyes may move about, and their extremities may twitch. They soon move into non-REM sleep, which occurs in four stages: becomes drowsy, fussy, eyes open and close, breathing may be irregular (stage 1); has few movements, but still responsive to environmental stimuli (stage 2); sleeps quietly with steady breathing and heartbeat and no body movement (stage 3); and, enters a deep, sound sleep, has no muscle activity and is difficult to arouse (stage 4). Sleep progresses systematically through each stage (e.g., REM, stage 1, 2, 3, 4) and then reverses the pattern (e.g., stage 4, 3, 2, 1, REM). This cycle repeats itself several times during each sleep period. Young infants spend approximately 50 percent of their time in REM sleep and 50 percent in NREM sleep during each cycle; the amount of REM sleep gradually decreases to approximately 30 percent during each sleep cycle by 6 months of age (National Sleep Foundation, 2016). Infants may awaken and have difficulty falling back to sleep as they move from NREM to REM sleep.

Infants also experience different degrees of alertness upon awakening. During the quiet alert phase, infants may lie quietly and stare or look around the crib. The active alert phase soon follows and the infant may begin to make sounds, wiggle around, and/or play with hands, feet, or the sleeve of their sleeper. The infant becomes aware of sounds and movements in the room; older infants may turn to locate the source. Finally, the infant begins to cry and move about in the crib. Ideally, it is best to pick infants up and feed or change their diapers before they become overly upset and are then difficult to feed or console.

Scientists have linked the quality of an infant's sleep to healthy growth, development, and behavior. Seehagen et al. (2015) demonstrated sleep's positive effects on infants' learning and long-term memory. In their study, infants who took a nap several hours before learning a new task had better recall after 24 hours than did infants who had not napped. Gómez and Edgin (2015) noted that sleep promoted neural development and improved infants' ability to generalize learning to novel situations. Poor sleep quality during infancy interferes with attention regulation and has been linked to the development of problematic behaviors in toddlers (Sadeh et al., 2015). Sleep deficit in infancy has also been shown to increase children's risk of becoming overweight or obese (Halal et al., 2016).

Parents and caregivers can promote quality infant sleep by implementing a reasonably predictable bedtime routine and creating a safe sleep environment. For example, a warm bath followed by a story and gentle rocking may signal bedtime and help the infant to relax and drift into sleep. A consistent, unhurried bedtime routine also fosters the infant's ability to establish a sleep-wake pattern, experience a better sleep quality, and gradually sleep longer through the night. Placing infants in their crib when they first show signs of sleepiness (e.g., closing eyes, rubbing face, restless) helps them to develop an ability to soothe themselves to sleep (Allen et al., 2016). This skill is especially important given that infants awaken frequently during REM and NREM sleep cycles, and is also beneficial for older infants when they begin to experience separation anxiety. However, consistent bedtimes are not practiced in all world cultures.

Parents have many different ideas about infant sleep and sleeping arrangements that are influenced by personal preferences, culture, and media. However, an infant's safety must always be a prime consideration when creating infant sleeping environments. The American Academy of Pediatrics (AAP), CDC, World Health Organization (WHO), and numerous other professional organizations have issued guidelines and launched public campaigns designed to prevent Sudden Infant Death Syndrome (SIDS), a major cause of infant death (particularly between 1 and 4 months of age) (see Figure 6-9) (Suggestions for Parents 6-7). These recommendations have resulted in a 50 percent reduction in the number of SIDS deaths since they were first issued (NICHD, 2015).

Yet, some parents and caregivers continue to ignore the guidelines, particularly as they apply to sleeping arrangements. Kendall-Tackett, Cong, and Hale (2016) noted that African American and American Indian mothers, as well as single and lower income mothers, were more likely to practice bed-sharing. Gaydos et al. (2015) reported that African American mothers in their study were aware of safe sleep recommendations but chose not to abandon bed-sharing practices for reasons related to inconvenience,

Figure 6-9 Sudden Unexpected Infant Death by Race/Ethnicity, 2010–2013

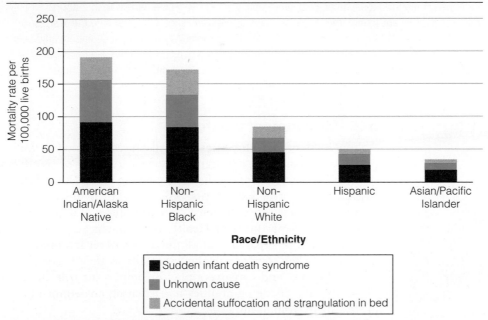

Source: CDC/NCHS, National Vital Statistics System, Period linked birth/infant death data.

sleep quality, and conflicting advice from family members. Some mothers who had not originally planned on bed-sharing cite the ease of breastfeeding, emotional closeness, and reduction in infant fussiness and nighttime crying as reasons for changing their mind (McKenna & Gettler, 2016; Tully, Holditch-Davis, & Brandon, 2015). However, researchers have also determined that bed-sharing not only raises safety concerns, but also has a negative effect on infant and maternal sleep quality. Infants who slept with their mother experienced more night awakenings than did infants who slept in their own beds, and mothers who slept with their infants had more fragmented sleep than did mothers who did not co-sleep with their infant (Volkovich et al., 2015). Consequently, experts continue to recommend room-sharing (placing the infant's crib next to the parent's bed or in the same room) as a safe substitute for bed-sharing.

Suggestions for Parents 6-7

Creating Safe Sleep Environments for Infants

Important steps can be taken to reduce the risk of SIDS by creating a safe sleeping environment for infants.

- Always put infants on their back for sleep (e.g., nighttime, naps)
- Place infants in their own safety-approved crib (one that has a firm mattress that is covered with a fitted sheet). Cribs can be placed next to a parent's bed or in the same room.
- Remove all soft and loose items from the crib (e.g., blankets, bumper pads, toys, pillows)
- Make sure nothing is covering the infant's head
- Dress infants in a light, one-piece sleeper to prevent overheating
- Locate infant cribs away from windows, window coverings, and other furniture
- Do not let anyone smoke near the infant

Ramona's 6-month-old daughter, Enid, woke up crying after sleeping for less than 2 hours. Ramona didn't want to miss the rest of her favorite television show, *Dancing with the Stars*, so she picked the infant up and brought her into the living room. When the episode ended, Enid was wide awake and not at all interested in going back to sleep. Why do you think Enid was no longer sleepy? How would you advise Ramona to manage this situation differently the next time?

Photo 6-12 Infants must never be left unattended when they are awake.

6-2i Environmental Safety

Although infant mortality rates from all causes continue to decline, deaths due to unintentional injuries remain a matter of significant concern. The majority of deaths among young infants are related to suffocation, whereas falls, burns, poisonings, drownings, and motor vehicle accidents are the most common causes of death in older infants (U.S. Department of Health and Human Services, 2013). Infants should be supervised at all times, and never left unattended in a car or when they are awake, especially as they become more mobile. Parents and caregivers play an important role in recognizing infants' changing abilities and creating environments that protect them from harm.

Infants of all ages must *always* be securely fastened in a size- and age-appropriate seat restraint whenever they are transported in a motor vehicle. In a recent study, researchers observed that 50 percent of young children (birth to age 9 years) who died in a motor vehicle accident were not in a car seat or wearing any type of child restraint, and 20 percent were riding in the front seat (Lee, Farrell, & Mannix, 2015). The proper use of car seats has been shown to reduce infant deaths by as much as 71 percent (Durbin, 2011). Selection guidelines and product recalls are available on the Consumer Product Safety Commission (CPSC) and National Highway Traffic Safety Administration (NHTSA) websites. Infant car seats should be installed in the back seat and rear-facing to protect children in the event that passenger airbags deploy. Infants should continue to use these seats until they turn 1 year of age or weigh at least 20 pounds (9.1 kg).

Parents should pay special attention to safety features when selecting infant furniture (e.g., cribs, highchairs, changing tables, carriers, strollers), toys, window coverings, clothing, pacifiers, and supplies. Comprehensive safety guidelines can be accessed on the CPSC website and used when making purchases. Caution should be exercised when buying items on the Internet or at garage sales to be sure they meet current safety standards. For example, the use of lead-based paints was banned after 1978, new safety standards for cribs were implemented in 2011, and efforts are currently in place to eliminate corded window coverings by 2018.

Care must be taken to prevent burns and choking during infant feedings. Bottles should never be heated in a microwave; liquids heat unevenly and can cause burns even though the outside of the bottle may feel cool. Feeding infants in a semi-upright position reduces the potential for choking and ear infections. Parents and caregivers should also prepare themselves to handle choking emergencies by completing a CPR course. Hot adult beverages (e.g., coffee, tea, soup) and foods should not be carried around or set in places where infant care is being provided. Water temperature should always be tested before bathing an infant; the infant's thin skin can burn quickly in temperatures that may feel comfortable to a parent (Shields et al., 2015). Setting the temperature of hot water heaters at 120°F (49° C) or lower can also help to reduce this risk.

Precautions should also be taken during outings to protect infants (especially those younger than 6 months) from the sun. Their skin burns easily, even in winter and on cloudy days, because it is quite thin and contains minimal amounts of protective melanin.

Outdoor trips should be scheduled before 10 A.M. or after 2 P.M. to minimize harmful sun exposure. A hat and lightweight clothing can protect exposed areas of the infant's body. Small amounts of sunscreen (with at least 15 SPF) can be applied to areas (e.g., face, hands) that cannot be covered with clothing (AAP, 2015b). Plastic sunglasses with 97 to 100 percent UVA and UVB protection, held in place with a soft elastic strap, safeguard the infant's sensitive eyes.

6-3 Parental Stress and Well-Being

Parenting infants can be stressful and, at times, an overwhelming responsibility. Infants who are born prematurely or who have medical or disability conditions may present needs that are even more challenging for parents to meet (Miodrag et al., 2015). Consequently, it is easy for parents to neglect their own needs in the process of caring for young children, but doing so can have negative health consequences. Stress can cause a parent to feel exhausted, irritable, angry, and resentful. Chronic stress increases the risk of infectious illness, sleep disturbances, depression, tension in relationships, and abusive treatment of children (Anding et al., 2016; Whitesell et al., 2015).

Some parents experience additional pressure in their efforts to conform or live up to cultural childrearing expectations (Mesman et al., 2015). For example, a sample of African American women believed that mothers who breastfed were "good mothers," whereas mothers who fed their infants formula were "lazy and selfish" (Carter & Anthony, 2015). Japanese mothers are expected to practice *hansei* (reflection) and continuously evaluate their parenting behaviors to determine how they might do things better; no response is considered perfect and always has room for improvement. Asian parents believe that infants and young children are a divine gift and, thus, are expected to dedicate themselves to meeting children's needs before their own.

It is important that parents find a healthy balance between childrearing responsibilities and meeting their own personal needs without feeling guilty about doing so (Suggestions for Parents 6-8). Making time to walk or engage in other physical activity, eat a nutritious diet, obtain adequate sleep, practice relaxation techniques, and maintain social connections with family and friends are important measures for reducing stress, increasing resilience, and improving the quality of parental care and interactions (Hannan et al., 2015; White et al, 2015).

Suggestions for Parents 6-8

Caring for Your Own Physical and Mental Health Needs

Meeting your own physical and emotional needs improves energy, attitude, and self-esteem.

- Spend time outdoors (e.g., go for a walk, sit outside and read a book or magazine for 10 minutes, work in the garden)
- Connect with friends (e.g., call, email, meet at the mall or grocery store and shop together, join a group at your church or local school)
- Set aside quiet time together with your partner (e.g., watch a movie or television program, visit a favorite restaurant or coffee bar, make plans for the weekend)
- Take a warm bath or shower, breathe deeply, and think about something pleasant (e.g., travel, family, hobby)
- Take a class through your local parks and recreation department, YMCA, or county extension office (e.g., craft, cooking, aerobics, yoga, dancing, gardening, woodworking)

(Continued)

- Play your favorite music while you go about your daily activities; dance or run up and down stairs for a few minutes in between tasks
- Learn to let things go (e.g., do the laundry tomorrow instead of today, prepare a meal that takes less time but is just as nutritious, let your partner or an older child walk the dog)
- Ask for help and accept that they may not do things in the same manner that you would
- Plan fun things to do together as a family (e.g., have a picnic dinner in the park or on a blanket in the living room, swim at a municipal pool, visit the library, invite friends over for a potluck dinner)
- Join a parent group, or attend activities for mothers and infants at a local library or museum
- Talk to your medical provider about mental health symptoms; seek therapeutic support to learn ways to better manage stress, sadness, or anxiety

⩔ Professional Resource Download

6-4 Developmentally Appropriate Behavior Guidance

Infants need unconditional love from caregivers, and thrive when there is consistency and predictability. Parents must avoid blaming or punishing infants for their behavior. Instead, parents should respond in positive ways to encourage the development of appropriate behavior (Suggestions for Parents 6-9).

One of the most difficult times for parents is when they have met all of an infant's needs (feeding, changing diaper, cuddling), but the baby continues to cry. These times can be very challenging because parents often feel like they are doing something

Suggestions for Parents 6-9

Positive Behavior Guidance

Infant behavior is rewarding and challenging. Arranging the environment to encourage safe exploration and responding patiently can help to improve the parent-infant relationship and prevent future behavior problems.

- Provide unconditional love and attention.
- Childproof the environment to keep the infant safe.
- Attend closely to the infant's cues that indicate when he is ready to eat, sleep, cuddle, or change placement (e.g., move from playing on the floor to sitting in a highchair to see you better).
- Be responsive to infant cues, and attend to all infant cries during the first 4 months.
- Hold and have frequent "conversations" with the infant.
- Establish predictable routines and simple rules to set the occasion for sleep so infants know that their needs will be met.
- Provide praise and encouragement.
- Use distraction and modeling to redirect infants to appropriate activities as they become more mobile.
- Allow infants to learn to soothe themselves.

Figure 6-10 Period of PURPLE Crying

P   **Peak of crying:**
2 weeks through 3–4 months, with crying peaking in the second month.

U   **Unexpected:**
Crying comes and goes with no apparent reason.

R   **Resists soothing:**
Infant does not respond to typical strategies to end crying.

P   **Pain-like face:**
Looks like the infant is in pain even though there is nothing physically wrong.

L   **Long lasting:**
Infants may cry for up to 5 hours per day, with approximately 10 percent of the crying being inconsolable.

E   **Evening:**
Crying is most likely to happen in the late afternoon and evening.

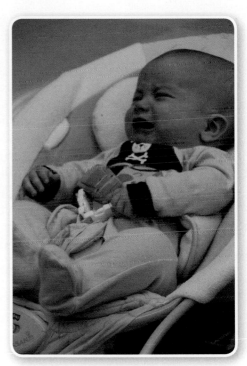

Photo 6-13 Infants need unconditional love.

wrong. It is important for parents to remember that infants do not purposefully cry to make them angry or frustrated. The National Center on Shaken Baby Syndrome (Barr, 2016a) has developed the Period of PURPLE Crying Campaign to educate caregivers about what is normal and how to handle inconsolable crying (see Figure 6-10).

All infants go through this phase, with some crying more than others. However, it is important for parents to understand that the crying will usually end, and that the amount of crying will gradually decrease. Although parents should be aware of different strategies that can be used to soothe their infant (Suggestions for Parents 6-10), they must also understand that the same approach may not always work, and sometimes nothing will work. When crying becomes overly frustrating, it is recommended that parents place the baby in a safe place, such as a crib, and walk away to calm down. Taking a break can help parents regain their composure before returning to comfort the infant. In addition, this brief respite reduces the potential for harming or violently shaking the baby—both of which can result in serious brain damage and death.

Suggestions for Parents 6-10

Strategies for Soothing an Infant
Strategies for soothing an infant:

- Check to make sure all of the infant's needs have been met—hunger, need for sleep, diaper changed
- Change the infant's position—if the child has been lying in her crib, try picking her up or propping her in a sitting position; a warm bath or novel activity may also settle the infant

(Continued)

- Use repetitive and rhythmic sounds and movements—singing a song, making quiet sounds, rocking, bouncing gently, going for a walk or a ride in the car
- Create white noise—turn on the vacuum cleaner or a fan
- Hold the infant close—skin-to-skin contact, placing the infant in a sling or carrier
- Engage the infant's senses—use affectionate touch, calming sounds, stimulating visuals

Adapted from: Barr (2016b).

Summary

- The growth and developmental changes that an infant undergoes during the first year are more dramatic and significant than they will ever again experience. Consequently, the early identification of developmental delays or disabilities is especially important to minimize any effect they may have on other developmental areas.
- Infants begin to learn from birth. Parents and caregivers can take important steps to support the infant's cognitive, motor, language, and social-emotional development by providing nurturing, responsive care, and varied opportunities for discovery and learning.
  - A secure attachment to parents and/or caregivers affects the quality of an infant's development across all domains.
  - Temperament is shaped by a combination of biological, environmental, and cultural factors, and influences the nature of infant-parent interactions.
  - Older infants begin to experience separation anxiety. Parents and caregivers can take steps to help make separations easier for infants.
- Optimal infant development is dependent on good nutrition, sufficient sleep, medical supervision, and a safe environment. Breastmilk offers advantages to infants; formula provides similar nutrients with certain exceptions.
- Parents must not overlook their own needs in the process of caring for young children.
- Positive behavior guidance is based on unconditional love, a safe environment, and responsive parenting.

Key Terms

antibodies (p. 169)

attachment (p. 163)

bio-behavioral synchrony (p. 164)

fontanels (p. 152)

"goodness of fit" (p. 167)

mongolian spots (p. 152)

"motherese" (p. 160)

neural plasticity (p. 168)

sensitive periods (p. 157)

Questions for Discussion and Self-Reflection

1. In what ways does nutrition influence an infant's growth and development (e.g., cognition, motor, language, social-emotional)?

2. What are some of the ways that caregivers can engage in positive social interactions with an infant?

3. What can parents do to promote an infant's motor development?

4. Why is it important for parents to nurture their own physical and emotional well-being in the process of caring for young children?

5. In what ways can parents and caregivers support infants' language development? What effect might poverty have on an infant's language acquisition?

Field Activities

1. Conduct an Internet search for the Infant Toddler Temperament Tool developed by the Center for Early Childhood Mental Health Consultation. Assess your own temperament and then enter the following infant characteristics: highly active, easily distracted, intense personality, spontaneous, highly sensitive, less approachable, less adaptable, less persistent, serious mood. Examine the strategies for working with infants who display styles that are different from your own. How might an infant's temperament influence the nature of interactions with his or her parent?

2. Survey your community, and prepare a list of resources that parents can contact if they have concerns about their infant's developmental progress. Visit your local early intervention program or contact the director via telephone. Find out what types of conditions or delays are identified most often, and what services are provided.

3. Visit a local store that sells infant toys. Describe the types of toys that are available. Select five toys and explain why you believe they are or are not safe and developmentally appropriate. Compare and discuss your findings with those of your classmates.

REFERENCES

Adolph, K., & Robinson, S. (2015). Motor development. In R. M. Lerner (Series Eds.) & L. Liben & U. Müller (Vol. Eds), *Handbook of child psychology and developmental science: Vol. 2: Cognitive processes* (7th Ed.) New York: Wiley, pp. 114–157. Retrieved on January 15, 2016 from http://www.psych.nyu.edu/adolph/publications/AdolphRobinson-inpress -MussenMotorDev.pdf.

Agency for Healthcare Research and Quality (AHRQ). (2104). Safety of vaccines used for routine immunizations in the United States. Retrieved on March 3, 2016 from http://effectivehealthcare .ahrq.gov/ehc/products/468/1929/vaccine-safety-executive-140701.pdf.

Ainsworth, M., Blehar, M., Waters, E., & Wall, S. (1978). *Patterns of attachment: A psychological study of the strange situation.* Hillsdale, NJ: Erlbaum.

Allely, C., Purves, D., McConnachie, A., Marwick, H., Johnson, P., Doolin, O., et al. (2013). Parent-infant vocalisations at 12 months predict psychopathology at 7 years. *Research in Developmental Disabilities, 34*(3), 985–993.

Allen, S., Howlett, M., Coulombe, J., & Corkum, P. (2016). ABCs of SLEEPNG: A review of the evidence behind pediatric sleep practice recommendations. *Sleep Medicine Reviews, 29*, 1–14.

American Academy of Pediatrics (AAP). (2016a). AAP schedule of well-child care visits. Retrieved January 7, 2016 from http://www.healthychildren.org/English/family-life/health -management/Pages/Well-Child-Care-A-Check-Up-for-Success.aspx.

American Academy of Pediatrics (AAP). (2016b). Baby walkers: A dangerous choice. Retrieved January 16, 2016 from https://www.healthychildren.org/English/safety-prevention/at-home /Pages/Baby-Walkers-A-Dangerous-Choice.aspx.

American Academy of Pediatrics (AAP). (2015a). Media and children. Retrieved January 16, 2016 from https://www.aap.org/en-us/advocacy-and-policy/aap-health-initiatives/pages /media-and-children.aspx.

American Academy of Pediatrics (AAP). (2015b). Sun and water safety tips. Retrieved January 8, 2016 from http://www.aap.org/en-us/about-the-aap/aap-press-room/news-features-and-safety -tips/pages/sun-and-water-safety-tips.aspx.

American Academy of Pediatrics (AAP). (2012). Policy statement: Breastfeeding and the use of human milk. Retrieved January 7, 2016 from http://pediatrics.aappublications.org/content /129/3/e827.full#content-block.

Barr, R. (2016a). What is the period of PURPLE crying? National Center on Shaken Baby Syndrome. Retrieved January 15, 2016 from http://purplecrying.info/what-is-the-period -of-purple-crying.php.

Barr, R. (2016b). Common features and principles of soothing. National Center on Shaken Baby Syndrome. Retrieved January 15, 2016 from http://purplecrying.info/sub-pages /soothing/common-features-and-principles-of-soothing.php.

Blasi, A., Lloyd-Fox, S., Sethna, V., Brammer, M., Mercure, E., Murray, L., et al. (2015). Atypical processing of voice sounds in infants at risk for autism spectrum disorder. *Cortex, 71*, 122–133.

Bolten, M. (2013). Infant psychiatric disorders. *European Child Adolescent Psychiatry, 22*(Suppl 1), S69–S74.

Bornstein, M., Putnik, D., & Suwalsky, J. (2016). Infant-mother and infant-caregiver emotional relationships: Process analyses of interactions in three contemporary childcare arrangements. *Infancy, 21*(1), 8–36.

Brebner, C., Hammond, L., Schaumloffel, N., & Lind, C. (2015). Using relationships as a tool: Early childhood educators' perspectives of the child–caregiver relationship in a childcare setting. *Early Child Development and Care, 185*(5), 709–726.

Brosco, J., Grosse, S., & Ross, L. (2015). Universal state newborn screening programs can reduce health disparities. *JAMA Pediatrics, 169*(1), 7–8.

Brown, C., & Lichter-Konecki, U. (2016). Phenylketonuria (PKU): A problem solved? *Molecular Genetics and Metabolism Reports, 6*(1), 8–12.

Brown, A., Rance, J., & Bennett, P. (2016). Understanding the relationship between breastfeeding and postnatal depression: The role of pain and physical difficulties. *Journal of Advanced Nursing, 72*(2), 273–282.

Brumberg, H., & Shah, S. (2015). Born early and born poor: An eco-bio-developmental model for poverty and preterm birth. *Journal of Neonatal-Perinatal Medicine, 8*(3), 179–187.

Canadian Paediatric Society (CPS). (2014). Nutrition for health term infants six to 24 months: An overview. Retrieved January 7, 2016 from http://www.cps.ca/en/documents/position /nutrition-healthy-term-infants-6-to-24-months.

Cartagena, D., Ameringer, S., McGrath, J., Masho, S., Jallo, N., & Myers, B. (2015). Factors contributing to infant overfeeding in low-income immigrant Latina mothers. *Applied Nursing Research, 28*(4), 316–321.

Case-Smith, J. (2013). Systematic review of interventions to promote social-emotional development in young children with or at risk for disability. *American Journal of Occupational Therapy, 67*(4), 395–404.

Centers for Disease Control and Prevention (CDC). (2015). Birth defects: Data and statistics. Retrieved January 6, 2015 from http://www.cdc.gov/ncbddd/birthdefects/data.html.

Centers for Disease Control and Prevention (CDC). (2014). Breastfeeding report card: U.S. 2014. National Center for Chronic Disease Prevention and Health Promotion. Retrieved January 9, 2016 from http://www.cdc.gov/breastfeeding/pdf/2014breastfeeding reportcard.pdf.

Centers for Disease Control and Prevention (CDC). (2010). WHO Growth Standards are recommended for use in the U.S. for infants and children 0 to 2 years of age. Retrieved January 4, 2016 from http://www.cdc.gov/growthcharts/who_charts.htm#The%20WHO %20Growth%20Charts.

Center for Early Childhood Mental Health Consultation. (2015). Infant Toddler Temperament Tool. Retrieved January 16, 2016 from http://eclkc.ohs.acf.hhs.gov/hslc/tta-system/health /mental-health/ec-mental-health-consultation/materials-for-families.html.

Chiang, Y., Lin, D., Lee, C., & Lee, M. (2015). Effects of parenting role and parent–child interaction on infant motor development in Taiwan Birth Cohort Study. *Early Human Development, 91*(4), 259–264.

Currie, J., & Rossin-Slater, M. (2015). Early-life origins of life-cycle well-being: Research and policy implications. *Journal of Policy Analysis and Management, 34*(1), 208–242.

Donald, K., Fouche, J., Roos, A., Koen, N., Howells, F., Riley, E., et al. (2015). Alcohol exposure in utero is associated with decreased gray matter volume in neonates. *Metabolic Brain Disease*. Advance online publication, doi: 10.1007/s11011-015-9771-0.

Durbin, D. (2011). Technical report: Child passenger safety. *Pediatrics, 109*(3), 550.

Ekas, N., Ghilain, C., Pruitt, M., Celimli, S., Gutierrez, A., & Alesandri, M. (2016). The role of family cohesion in the psychological adjustment of non-Hispanic White and Hispanic mothers of children with autism spectrum disorder. *Research in Autism Spectrum Disorders, 21*(1), 10–24.

Elsabbagh, M., Bruno, R., Wan, M., Charman, T., Johnson, M., & Green, J. (2015). Infant neural sensitivity to dynamic eye gaze relates to quality of parent-infant interaction at

7-months in infants at risk for autism. *Journal of Autism and Developmental Disorders*, *45*(2), 283–291.

Feldman, R. (2015). Sensitive periods in human social development: New insights from research on oxytocin, synchrony, and high-risk parenting. *Developmental and Psychopathology*, *27*(2), 369–395.

Feldman, R., Rosenthal, Z., Eidelman, A. (2014). Maternal-preterm skin-to-skin contact enhances child physiologic organization and cognitive control across the first 10 years of life. *Biological Psychiatry, 75*(1), 56–64.

Fernández-Alcántara, M., García-Caro, M., Laynez-Rubio, C., Pérez-Marfil, M., Martí-García, C., Benítez-Feliponi, A., Berrocal-Castellano, M., & Cruz-Quintana, F. (2015). Feelings of loss in parents of children with infantile cerebral palsy. *Disability and Health Journal, 8*(1), 93–101.

Forry, N., Davis, E., & Welti, K. (2013). Ready or not: Associations between participation in subsidized child care arrangements, pre kindergarten, and Head Start and children's school readiness. *Early Childhood Research Quarterly, 28*(3), 634–644.

Frank, M., Amso, D., & Johnson, S. (2014). Visual search and attention to faces during early infancy. *Journal of Experimental Child Psychology, 118*, 13–26.

Gee, D., & Casey, B. (2015). The impact of developmental timing for stress and recovery. *Neurobiology of Stress, 1*, 184–194.

Georgieff, M., Brunette, K., & Tran, P. (2015). *Development and Psychopathology*, *27*(2), 411–423.

Golonkoff, R., Can, D., Soderstrom, M., & Hirsh-Pasek, K. (2015). (Baby) talk to me: The social context of infant-directed speech and its effects on early language acquisition. *Current Directions in Psychological Science*, *24*(5), 339–344.

Gómez, R., & Edgin, J. (2015). Sleep as a window into early neural development: Shifts in sleep-dependent learning effects across early childhood. *Child Development Perspectives*, *9*(3), 183–189.

Graham, A., Pfeifer, J., Fisher, P., Carpenter, S., & Fair, D. (2015). Early life stress is associated with default system integrity and emotionality during infancy. *Journal of Child Psychology and Psychiatry, 56*(11), 1212–1222.

Grau, J., Duran, P., Castellanos, P., Smith, E., Silberman, S., & Wood, L. (2015). Developmental outcomes of toddlers of young Latina mothers: Cultural, family, and parenting factors. *Infant Behavior & Development, 41*, 113–126.

Grossman, T. (2015). The development of social brain functions in infancy. *Psychological Bulletin, 141*(6), 1266–1287.

Háden, G., Németh, R., Török, M., & Winkler, I. (2015). Predictive processing of pitch trends in newborn infants. *Brain Research, 1626*, 14–20.

Halal, C., Matijasevich, A., Howe, L., Santos, I., Barros, F., & Nunes, M. (2016). Short sleep duration in the first year of life and obesity/overweight at age 4 years: A birth cohort study. *The Journal of Pediatrics, 168*, 99–103.e3.

Hassiotou, F., Mobley, A., Geddes, D., Hartmann, P., & Wilkie, T. (2015). Breastmilk imparts the mother's stem cells to the infant. *The FASEB Journal, 29*(1), S876.8.

Havermans, T., Tack, J., Vertommen, A., Proesmans, M., & Boeck, K. (2015). Breaking bad news, the diagnosis of cystic fibrosis in childhood. *Journal of Cystic Fibrosis, 14*(4), 540–546.

Henshaw, E., Fried, R., Siskind, E., Newhouse, L., & Cooper, M. (2015). Breastfeeding self-efficacy, mood, breastfeeding outcomes among primiparous women. *Journal of Human Lactation, 31*(3), 511–518.

Hirsh-Pasek, K., Adamson, L., Bakeman, R., Owen, M., Golinkoff, R., Pace, A., . . . Suma, K. (2015). The contribution of early communication quality to low-income children's language success. *Psychological Science, 26*, 1071–1083.

Hoog, M., Venekamp, R., van der Ent, C., Schilder, A., Sanders, E., Damoisequx, R., et al. (2014). Impact of early daycare on healthcare resource use related to upper respiratory tract infections during childhood: Prospective WHISTLER cohort study. *BMC Medicine, 12*, 107. Published online. doi: 10.1186/1741-7015-12-107.

Horta, B., de Mola, C., & Victora, C. (2015). Long-term consequences of breastfeeding on cholesterol, obesity, systolic blood pressure and type 2 diabetes: A systematic review and meta-analysis. *Acta Paediatrica, 104*(S467), 30–37.

Islami, F., Liu, Y., Jemal, A., Zhou, J., Weiderpass, E., Colditz, G., . . . & Weiss, M. (2015). Breastfeeding and breast cancer risk by receptor status—a systematic review and meta-analysis. *Annals of Oncology, 26*(12) 2398–2407.

Jensen, K., Vaish, A., & Schmidt, M. (2014). The emergence of human prosociality: Aligning with others through feelings, concerns, and norms. *Frontiers in Psychology, 5*, 822. Published online. doi.org/10.3389/fpsyg.2014.00822.

Jensen, S., & Bouhou, R. (2015). Enhancing the child survival agenda to promote, protect, and support early child development. *Seminars in Perinatology, 39*(5), 373–386.

Jiang, Y., Ekono, M., & Skinner, C. (2015). *Basic Facts about Low-Income Children: Children under 3 Years, 2013*. New York: National Center for Children in Poverty, Mailman School of Public Health, Columbia University.

Jones, E., Venema, K., Lowy, R., Earl, R., & Webb, S. (2015). Developmental change in infant brain activity during naturalistic social experiences. *Developmental Psychobiology, 57*(7), 842–853.

Jones, K., Power, M., Queenan, J., & Schulkin, J. (2015). Racial and ethnic disparities in breastfeeding. *Breastfeeding Medicine, 10*(4), 186–196.

Keller, H., Borke, J., Chaudhary, N., Lamm, B., & Kleis, A. (2010). Continuity in parenting strategies: A cross-cultural comparison. *Journal of Cross-Cultural Psychology, 41*(3), 391–409.

Kendall-Tackett, K., Cong, Z., & Hale, T. (2016). Factors that influence where babies sleep in the United States: The impact of feeding method, mother's race/ethnicity, partner status, employment, education, and income. *Clinical Lactation, 7*(1), 18–29.

Kok, R., Thijssen, S., Bakersman-Kranenburg, M., Jaddoe, V., Verhulst, F., White, T., van IJzendoorn, M., & Tiemeier, H. (2015). Normal variation in early parental sensitivity predicts child structural brain development. *Journal of the American Academy of Child and Adolescent Psychiatry, 54*(10), 824–831.e1.

Kristen-Antonow, S., Sodian, B., Perst, H., & Licata, M. (2015). A longitudinal study of the emerging self from 9 months to the age of 4 years. *Frontiers in Psychology, 6*, 789. Published online. doi: 10.3389/fpsyg.2015.00789.

Laughlin, L. (2013). *Who's Minding the Kids? Child Care Arrangements: Spring 2011*. Current Population Reports, P70–135. U.S. Census Bureau, Washington, DC.

Lee, A., & Brann, L. (2015). Influence of cultural beliefs on infant feeding, postpartum and childcare practices among Chinese-American mothers in New York City. *Journal of Community Health, 40*(3), 476–483.

Lee, L., Farrell, C., & Mannix, R. (2015). Restraint use in motor vehicle crash fatalities in children 0 to 9 years old. *Journal of Trauma and Acute Care Surgery, 79*(3), S55–S60.

Leonard, H., & Hill, E. (2014). Review: The impact of motor development on typical and atypical social cognition and language: A systematic review. *Child Adolescent Mental Health, 19*(3), 163–173.

Leung, D., Chisti, M., & Pavia, A. (2016). Prevention and control of childhood pneumonia and diarrhea. *Pediatric Clinics of North America, 63*(1), 67–79.

Libertus, K., & Landa, R. (2014). Scaffolded reaching experiences encourage grasping activity in infants at high risk for autism. *Frontiers in Psychology, 5*(Article 1071), 1–8.

Linton, J., Choi, R., & Mendoza, F. (2016). Caring for children in immigrant families. Vulnerabilities, resilience, and opportunities. *Pediatric Clinics of North America, 63*(1),115–130.

Liu, M. (2015). An ecological review of literature on factors influencing working mothers' child care arrangements. *Journal of Child and Family Studies, 24*(1), 161–171.

Luo, R., & Tamis-LeMonda, C. (2016). Mothers' verbal and nonverbal strategies in relation to infants' object-directed actions in real time and across the first three years in ethnically diverse families. *Infancy, 21*(1), 65–89.

Main, M., & Solomon, J. (1990). Procedures for identifying infants as disorganised/disoriented during the Ainsworth Strange Situation. In M. Greenberg, D. Cicchetti, & E. Cummings (Eds.), *Attachment in the preschool years* (pp.121–160). Chicago, IL: University of Chicago Press.

Malmberg, L., Lewis, S., West, A., Murray, E., Sylva, K., & Stein, A. (2015). The influence of mothers' and fathers' sensitivity in the first year of life on children's cognitive outcomes at 18 and 36 months. *Child: Care, Health and Development*. Advance online publication. doi: 10.1111/cch.12294.

Marotz, L. (2015). *Health, safety, and nutrition for the young child*. (9th Ed.). Stamford, CT: Cengage Learning.

Marotz, L., & Allen, K. (2016). *Developmental profiles: Pre-birth through adolescence*. Boston, MA: Cengage Learning.

Masho, S., Cha, S., & Morris, M. (2015). Prepregnancy obesity and breastfeeding noninitiation in the United States: An examination of racial and ethnic differences. *Breastfeeding Medicine*, 10(5), 253–262.

McCormick, D., Jennings, K., Ede, L., Alvarez-Fernandez, P., Patel, J., & Chonmaitree, T. (2016). Use of symptoms and risk factors to predict acute otitis media in infants. *International Journal of Pediatric Otorhinolaryngology*, 81, 55–59.

McKenna, J., & Gettler, L. (2016). There is no such thing as infant sleep, there is no such thing as breastfeeding, there is only breastsleeping. *Acta Paediatrica*, 105(1), 17–21.

McLaughlin, K., Sheridan, M., Tibu, F., Fox, N., Seanah, C., & Nelson, C. (2015). Causal effects of the early caregiving environment on development of stress response systems in children. *Proceedings of the National Academy of Sciences of the United States of America*, 112(18), 5637–5642.

McLeod, S. (2009). Attachment theory. Retrieved May 6, 2016 from http://www.simplypsychology.org/attachment.html.

Molnar, M., Gervin, J., & Carreiras, M. (2013). Within-rhythm class native language discrimination abilities of Basque-Spanish monolingual and bilingual infants at 3.5 months of age. *Infancy*, 19(3), 326–337.

Moon, R., & Hauck, F. (2016). SIDS risk: It's more than just the sleep environment. *Pediatrics*. Retrieved January 7, 2016 from http://hw-f5-pediatrics.highwire.org/content/137/1/e20153665.

Mosher, W., Jones, J., & Abma, J. (2012). Intended and unintended births in the United States: 1982–2010. National health statistics reports, no 55. Hyattsville, MD: National Center for Health Statistics.

Mulready-Ward, C., & Hackett, M. (2014). Breastfeeding in public in New York City. *Journal of Human Lactation*, 30(2), 195–200.

National Conference of State Legislatures (NCSL). (2016). Breastfeeding state laws. Retrieved January 10. 2015 from http://www.ncsl.org/research/health/breastfeeding-state-laws.aspx.

National Institute of Child Health and Human Development (NICHD). (2015). Safe to Sleep. Retrieved January 10, 2016 from http://www.nichd.nih.gov/sts/about/SIDS/Pages/progress.aspx.

National Sleep Foundation. (2016). Children and sleep. Retrieved January 10, 2016 from http://sleepfoundation.org/sleep-topics/children-and-sleep.

National Sleep Foundation. (2015). National Sleep Foundation recommends new sleep times. Retrieved January 10, 2015 from http://sleepfoundation.org/media-center/press-release/national-sleep-foundation-recommends-new-sleep-times.

Noble, K., Engelhardt, L., Brito, N., Mack, L., Nail, E., Angal, J., . . . & Elliott, A. (2015). Socioeconomic disparities in neurocognitive development in the first two years of life. *Developmental Psychobiology*, 57(5), 535–551.

Northrup, J., & Iverson, J. (2015). Vocal coordination during early parent–infant interactions predicts language outcome in infant siblings of children with Autism Spectrum Disorder. *Infancy*, 20(5), 523–547.

Ombrone, D., Giocaliere, E., Forni, G., Malvagia, S., & la Marca, G. (2016). Expanded newborn screening by mass spectrometry: New tests, future perspectives. *Mass Spectrometry Reviews*, 35(1), 71–84.

Parfitt, Y., Pike, A., & Ayers, S. (2014). Infant developmental outcomes: A family systems perspective. *Infant and Child Development*, 23(4), 353–373.

Park, H., & Chung, G. (2015). A multifaceted model of changes and adaptation among Korean mothers of children with disabilities. *Journal of Child and Family Studies*, 24(4), 915–929.

Parsons, C., Stark, E., Young, K., Stein, A., & Kringelbach, M. (2013). Understanding the human parental brain: A critical role of the orbitofrontal cortex. *Social Neuroscience*, 8(6), 525–543.

Patenaude, E., Knol, L., & Turner, L. (2015). Social cognitive theory constructs associated with mothers' breastfeeding in public comfort levels: Results from a national study. *Journal of the Academy of Nutrition and Dietetics*, 115(9), A82.

Pennestri, M., Gaudreau, H., Bouvette-Turcot, A., Moss, E., Lecompte, V., Atkinson, L., . . . & Meaney, M. (2015). Attachment disorganization among children in Neonatal Intensive Care Unit: Preliminary results. *Early Human Development*, 91(10), 601–606.

Perego, G., Caputi, M., & Ogliari, A. (2015). Neurobiological correlates of psychosocial deprivation in children: A systematic review of neuroscientific contributions. *Child Youth Care Forum*. Advance online publication. doi: 10.1007/s10566-015-9340-z.

Piaget, J. (1952). *The origins of intelligence in children*. New York: International University Press.

Prado, E., & Dewey, K. (2014). Nutrition and brain development in early life. *Nutrition Reviews, 72*(4), 267–284.

Puura, K., Mäntymaa, M., Leppänen, J., Peltola, M., Salmelin, R., Luoma, I., et al. (2013). Associations between maternal interaction behavior, maternal perception of infant temperament, and infant social withdrawal. *Infant Mental Health Journal, 34*(6), 586–593.

Robinson, S. (2015). Infant nutrition and lifelong health: Current perspectives and future challenges. *Journal of Developmental Origins of Health and Disease, 6*(5), 384–389.

Rochat, P. (2003). Five levels of self-awareness as they unfold early in life. *Consciousness and Cognition, 12*(4), 717–731.

Roche, A., Owen, K., & Fung, T. (2015). Opinions toward breastfeeding in public and appropriate duration. *ICAN: Infant, Child, & Adolescent Nutrition, 7*(1), 44–53.

Rozga, M., Kerver, J., & Olson, B. (2015). Self-reported reasons for breastfeeding cessation among low-income women enrolled in a peer counseling breastfeeding support program. *Journal of Human Lactation, 31*(1), 129–137.

Romano, C., Hartman, C., Privitera, C., Cardile, S., & Shamir, R. (2015). Current topics in the diagnosis and management of the pediatric non organic feeding disorders (NOFEDs). *Clinical Nutrition, 34*(2), 195–200.

Sadeh, A., De Marcas, G., Guri, Y., Berger, A., Tikotzky, L., & Bar-Haim, Y. (2015). Infant sleep predicts attention regulation and behavior problems at 3–4 years of age. *Developmental Neuropsychology, 40*(3), 122–137.

Sani, M., Hosseini, S., Salmannejad, M., Aleahmad, F., Ebrahimi, S., Jahanshahi, S., & Talaei-Khozani, T. (2015). Origins of the breast milk-derived cells: An endeavor to find the cell sources. *Cell Biology International, 39*(5), 611–618.

Schaffer, H., & Emerson, P. (1964). The development of social attachments in infancy. *Monographs of the Society for Research in Child Development, 29*(3), 1–77.

Seehagen, S., Konrad, C., Herbert, J., & Schneider, S. (2015). Timely sleep facilitates declarative memory consolidation in infants. *Proceedings of the National Academy of Sciences in the United States of America, 112*(5), 1625–1629.

Shields, W., McDonald, E., Pfisterer, K., & Gielen, A. (2015). Scald burns in children under 3 years: An analysis of NEISS narratives to inform a scald burn prevention program. *Injury Prevention, 21*(5), 296–300.

St-Onge, M., Chaudhry, S., & Koren, G. (2015). Donated breast milk stored in banks versus breast milk purchased online. *Canadian Family Physician, 61*(2), 143–146.

Sung, J., Beijers, R., Gartstein, M., de Weerth, C., & Putnam, S. (2014). Exploring temperamental differences in infants from the USA and the Netherlands. *European Journal of Developmental Psychology, 12*(1), 15–28.

Therrell, B., Padilla, C., Loeber, J., Kneisser, I., Saadallah, A., Borrajo, G., & Adams, J. (2015). Current status of newborn screening worldwide: 2015. *Seminars in Perinatology, 39*(3), 171–187.

Thomas, K., Burr, R., & Spieker, S. (2015). Maternal and infant activity: Analytic approaches for the study of circadian rhythm. *Infant Behavior and Development, 41*, 80–87.

Tomasello, M. (2016). The ontogeny of cultural learning. *Current Opinion in Psychology, 8*(1), 1–4.

Topping, K., Dekhinet, R., & Zeedyk, S. (2013). Parent–infant interaction and children's language development. *Educational Psychology, 33*(4), 391–426.

Trevarthen, C. (2015). Infant semiosis: The psychobiology of action and shared experience from birth. *Cognitive Development, 36*, 130–141.

Tully, K., Holditch-Davis, D., & Brandon, D. (2015). The relationship between planned and reported home infant sleep locations among mothers of late preterm and term infants. *Maternal and Child Health Journal, 19*(7), 1616–1623.

Urban Child Institute. (2015). Baby's brain begins now: Conception to age 3.

U.S. Department of Health and Human Services, Health Resources and Services Administration, Maternal and Child Health Bureau. (2013). *Child Health USA 2013*. Rockville, Maryland: U.S. Department of Health and Human Services. Retrieved January 8, 2016 from http://mchb.hrsa.gov/chusa13/perinatal-health-status-indicators/p/infant-mortality.html.

Volkovich, E., Ben-Zion, H., Karny, D., Meiri, G., & Tikotzky, L. (2015). Sleep patterns of co-sleeping and solitary sleeping infants and mothers: A longitudinal study. *Sleep Medicine, 16*(11), 1305–1312.

Vygotsky, L. (1978). *Mind in society: The development of higher psychological processes.* Cambridge, MA: Harvard University Press.

Wambach, K., Domian, E., Page-Goertz, S., Wurtz, H., & Hoffman, K. (2016). Exclusive breastfeeding experiences among Mexican American women. *Journal of Human Lactation, 32*(1), 103–111.

Williams, A., Cormack, C., Chike-Harris, K., Durham, C., Fowler, T., & Jensen, E. (2015). Pediatric developmental screenings: A primary care approach. *Nurse Practitioner, 40*(4), 34–39.

World Health Organization (WHO). (2015). Infant and young child feeding. Retrieved January 7, 2016 from http://www.who.int/mediacentre/factsheets/fs342/en/.

Zeanah, C., & Gleason, M. (2014). Annual Research Review: Attachment disorders in early childhood – clinical presentation, causes, correlates, and treatment. *Journal of Child Psychology and Psychiatry, 56*(3), 207–222.

Zhang, Y., Wei, M., Shen, N., & Zhang, Y. (2015a). Identifying factors related to family management during the coping process of families with childhood chronic conditions: A multi-site study. *Journal of Pediatric Nursing, 301*(1), 160–173.

Zhang, B., Zhang, H., Liu, H., Li, H., & Wang, J. (2015b). Breastfeeding and maternal hypertension and diabetes: A population-based cross-sectional study. *Breastfeeding Medicine, 10*(3), 163–167.

Parenting Toddlers

7

12 TO 30 MONTHS

LEARNING OBJECTIVES

After reading the chapter, you will be able to:

7-1 Briefly describe several growth and developmental milestones that are characteristic of 1- and 2-year-olds.

7-2 Provide an example of how parents can support toddlers' development in each domain: cognitive, motor, language, social-emotional, and daily living.

7-3 Describe three developmentally appropriate behavior guidance techniques.

naeyc Standards Linked to Chapter Content

1a, 1b, and 1c: Promoting child development and learning

2a, 2b, and 2c: Building family and community relationships

4a and 4b: Using developmentally effective approaches to connect with children and families

Toddlers are an endearing work in progress. They are inquisitive and fascinated by the world around them. They have abundant enthusiasm, curiosity, and energy that seldom dwindles until they are fast asleep. They are in the earliest stages of learning right from wrong, how they are expected to behave, and how to get along with others. At the same time, they are driven by an

continued on following page

intense desire to do things for themselves, even though their limited language and motor skills, reasoning, and efforts may easily lead to frustration and defiance. Shouting "no" and running away, throwing objects, biting, or having a tantrum are some of the only ways seemingly available to express their frustration and other intense emotions, regardless of their effects on other people. Toddlers also have difficulty following directions, have no patience, don't understand sharing, and believe the world centers around them. Is it any wonder then that frequent conflicts arise, or that parents often find toddlers' behavior exasperating? ■

7-1 Typical Growth and Development Overview

It becomes easier to cope with a toddler's conduct if parents understand that these behaviors are typical of the growth and developmental changes that occur during this stage. Toddlers obviously have much to learn, and they depend upon parents to provide constructive guidance, and to do so with patience, respect, sincerity, and compassion. They also rely on parents for the nutritious foods, physical activities, health care, emotional interactions, and safe environments that foster wellness. Only when children are healthy and safe will they be ready and able to learn.

7-1a Growth

The toddler's growth rate begins to slow significantly during this life stage. One-year-olds will typically gain 4–6 pounds (1.81–2.7 kg) during the year, and weigh an average of 21–27 pounds (9.6–12.3 kg). Their height increases by 2–3 inches (5–7.5 cm) over the next 12 months. Most toddlers will be an average of 32–35 inches (80–87.5 cm) tall by their second birthday, and have reached approximately one-half of their adult height potential.

Teeth continue to erupt in pairs until most 1-year-olds will have a total of 16 primary or "baby" teeth. Their body begins to appear more streamlined, although 1-year-olds still have a relatively large upper body, small buttocks, bowed legs, and protruding abdomen (Marotz & Allen, 2016). The toddler's head increases in size as the brain continues to grow, and appears large in proportion to the rest of the body.

Two-year-olds' growth proceeds at a rate that is even slower than that which occurred during the previous year. A weight gain of about 2–3 pounds (0.90–1.36 kg) per year is typical, so that most 2-year-olds will weigh 26–32 pounds (11.2–14.6 kg), or approximately four times their birth weight. They will also add 3–5 inches (7.5–12.5 cm) in height per year, and reach an average height of 34–38 inches (85–95 cm) by their third birthday. Two-year-olds begin to appear more adult-like as they grow taller and muscle gradually replaces "baby fat." Four remaining teeth erupt during this year, resulting in a total of 20 primary teeth. The 2-year-old's brain continues to increase in size as neural networks form in response to learning experiences. As toddlers approach their third birthday, their brains will have reached approximately 80 percent of their adult size.

7-1b Developmental Tasks

Toddlers begin this stage with limited skills and understanding. However, they will undergo significant developmental changes in their abilities to think, learn, communicate, navigate, manipulate, and socialize during the next 2 years. Although development proceeds in a relatively predictable manner, the rate at which individual children achieve skills in each domain is highly variable. Genetic and environmental differences, including the ethnic, cultural, socio-economic, and environmental contexts in which a child is being raised, shape when and how skills are learned (Cuellar, Jones, & Sterrett, 2015; Stephens, Markus, & Phillips, 2014).

The values that families transmit to children, the behaviors they consider acceptable and unacceptable, the encouragement and learning opportunities they provide, and the discipline strategies they use exert a strong, shaping effect on children's overall development. For example, children in many Latino families are taught to maintain a strong sense of respect and loyalty, or *familismo*, to preserve family cohesion and cultural norms (Calzada et al., 2014). As a result, some children may be slower to warm up to a new teacher or child in the classroom. Parenting practices in many middle class Western families encourage children to think and act independently, whereas traditional Asian families teach caring and respect toward one's parents, or *filial piety*, and unquestioning obedience to maintain peace and harmony (Ho, 2015; Li et al., 2014). Although such assumptions are generalizations and certainly not applicable to all Latino, Asian, or Western families, they highlight the diversity that exists among parenting styles, values, beliefs, and expectations. These differences must be acknowledged and respected, and families supported in their efforts to raise children.

Continued growth, brain development, and neuromuscular system maturation make it possible for toddlers to attempt, practice, and achieve increasingly complex skills. Much of their early efforts will be concentrated on learning new words and speech patterns, how to walk, run and jump, how to interact appropriately with other children and adults, how things work, and how to do some things for themselves. They begin to insist on feeding, dressing, and washing themselves, and may protest any adult assistance. They are eager for adult attention and enjoy participating in simple games, songs, and movement activities. Toddlers consider nothing in their environment off-limits, and use their rudimentary reasoning abilities, including understanding simple cause and effect, recall, and object functionality, to explore everything within reach (Walker & Gopnik, 2014). Despite their increasing awareness, curiosity, and desire for **autonomy**, toddlers want and need continued reassurance that a caring adult is nearby.

autonomy a sense of self and/or being independent.

7-1c Early Identification and Intervention

Parents, early childhood teachers, and health care providers are in ideal positions to observe and monitor toddlers' developmental progress, and to note when it may not be progressing as expected. Identifying young children who may be experiencing or are at risk for developmental delays or disabilities is of utmost importance. However, a cautious approach must always be taken when there are questions about a child's development. Individual differences in genetic makeup and environmental conditions (e.g., geographical, psychological, economic, cultural) influence the rate and nature of a child's skill acquisition. As a result, a child's developmental pattern or progress may not always be consistent with typical expectations. Professional evaluation should always be sought when there is a concern about a child's development, especially if delays are evident in more than one domain. The earlier a child's delay or disability is identified and intervention services are initiated, the less adverse the effect may be on future learning and social interactions. Additional information on the identification process and intervention programs is presented in Chapter 14.

7-2 Supporting the Toddler's Development

Between the ages of 1 and 3 years, toddlers devote a majority of their time, attention, and effort to achieving skills in four major developmental areas: cognitive, motor, language and communication, and social-emotional (see Figure 7-1). For the most part, skills in each of these domains are mastered in a sequential manner that is

Figure 7-1 Toddlers' Developmental Tasks

Toddlers focus their time, attention, and energy on several major developmental tasks:

solitary play playing alone.

onlooker play watching other children play.

parallel play playing alongside other children and imitating their actions, but not interacting with them in any way.

- Cognition—understanding, experimenting with cause-effect, discovery, and problem solving
- Locomotion and motor skills—learning to navigate, perform purposeful movements, and manage daily living activities
- Language skills and communication—acquiring words, understanding how language works, and learning how to express thoughts and requests
- Social-emotional skills—considering self as autonomous, developing self-control, and understanding how to fit in
- Daily living skills—becoming more independent with feeding, dressing, sleeping, and toileting activities

Photo 7-1 Opportunities to practice motor skills build confidence.

Photo 7-2 When toddlers are engaged in solitary play, they do not seem to notice the presence of other children.

critical to future development and learning (Marotz & Allen, 2016). However, their acquisition is not achieved in isolation, but depends upon advancements that are occurring simultaneously, and not always at the same rate, across all developmental areas. For example, a toddler's ability to roll a ball back and forth between themself and a parent requires a combination of several advanced skills. They must be able to understand and process the request to roll the ball (causal thinking), pick up and release the ball (motor skills), and perhaps, squeal in delight (communication and socialization skills) when their efforts have been successful.

A discussion of the major developmental tasks follows and includes information about toddlers' capabilities, why certain behaviors may be exhibited, and developmentally-appropriate ways that parents (and teachers) can support their learning progress.

7-2a Learning Through Play

In a sense, toddlers are programmed with the desire to learn and to acquire information through their daily experiences. One of the primary ways that they begin to achieve new skills and discover the world around them is through play. Toys and daily play activities provide opportunities for children to explore, manipulate, experiment, observe, understand, and interact with others (Suggestions for Parents 7-1). For these reasons, it is important that parents understand why play is important and how they can create experiences that continue to promote children's skill development.

In a classic study, Mildred Parten (1932) observed that the nature of children's play involved more social interaction as their developmental skills advanced. According to her taxonomy of play, young toddlers engage in **solitary play** and **onlooker play**, whereas older toddlers begin to exhibit more **parallel play**. Although they may attempt limited interaction with one another, it is not until late in the second year that children begin to include each other in activities. **Make-believe play**, or pretend play, also begins to appear at around 18 months of age and represents a higher order of cognitive development. During this stage, toddlers may act out mental images or ideas about things or events they have observed. Vygotsky (1978) believed that pretend play activities provided toddlers with opportunities for thinking, understanding relationships, rehearsing problem-solving skills, using functional language, and developing self-control. Although questions have been raised about whether children are able to

Developmentally Appropriate Toys for Toddlers

Examples of safe toy choices that are designed to promote toddlers' development include:

- large rubber balls for kicking; riding toys
- large non-toxic markers and crayons and paper
- cloth or cardboard books
- simple wooden puzzles; pegboards
- large plastic or wooden building blocks; nesting cups
- cardboard boxes (in various sizes)
- dress-up clothes
- construction toys, large plastic animals, kitchen utensils (plastic bowls, spoons, kettles)
- puppets, dolls
- plastic buckets, sieves, and shovels

make-believe play children's imaginary reenactment of real-life ideas and occurrences, such as pretending to be a veterinarian or a chef, or taking a train ride to a fictional city.

symbolic play a child's use of play objects as representations of real objects or ideas: a block becomes a motorboat, a broom becomes a hockey stick, a chair becomes a car.

generalize and apply what they learn during make believe play, researchers have shown that some learning does occur (Hopkins, Dore, Lillard, 2015).

Symbolic play, or using an object to represent something else, becomes evident at around age 2 (NAEYC, 2009). For example, a child may pick up a block and pretend that it is a telephone or move it through the air as if it were an airplane. Each stage of play represents an increase in cognitive complexity, and opens the door for parents to provide opportunities that advance children's skills across all developmental areas.

The dynamics and outcomes of children's play are also influenced by the quality of parent-child interactions. Giving toddlers supportive guidance and constructive feedback during play activities helps to increase their persistence with difficult tasks now and in the future (Wang, Morgan, & Biringen, 2014). Parents can also encourage persistence by creating challenging opportunities that are slightly beyond what the child is able to do on his own (i.e., *zone of proximal development*) and helping the child to complete the task as needed (Lillard, 2012). For example, a parent may tell the child "Wow, you did a great job of putting the blocks together. You have the red on the bottom, then a blue, and then the yellow one on top." As the child attempts to add another block, the tower may fall (an opportunity for learning about gravity). The parent can support the child's persistence by encouraging her to try again, and when she gets to the final block, hold the base of the tower and describe how to slowly place the block on the top. Each time the child attempts to add another block, the parent can gradually reduce the amount of verbal and physical support given. By encouraging the child's efforts, describing what the child is doing, playing along with the child, and being enthusiastic during play, parents are developing a positive relationship with their child that provides a basis for continued learning.

Photo 7-3 Toddlers use make-believe play to imitate and practice activities they have observed.

The cognitive, motor, language, and social skills that toddlers are developing and ways that parents can promote these skills during daily interactions and play are described in the following sections.

7-2b Fostering Cognitive Development

Toddlers are rapidly developing the intellectual capacity to think, understand, problem solve, imitate, and remember. They seem to have an insatiable curiosity for learning that can sometimes get them into trouble. As challenging as parents might find this behavior to be, it represents a significant step in the toddler's cognitive development. Every positive or negative experience adds to the toddler's ideas and understanding, and either creates new neural connections or refines and strengthens existing neural networks in the brain. Given a nurturing and stimulating environment, toddlers will develop synapses, or connections between neurons, faster than they will at any other point in their lifetime; and, they will have twice as many synapses than they will as an adult (Urban Child Institute, 2015). Later, these connections will be refined and pruned so that the brain works more efficiently. These continuously-forming network connections provide the critical infrastructure upon which all future learning is based.

Four important developments occur in the brain during the toddler years. First, significant development takes place in the brain's language region as toddlers learn the meaning and expression of words. Second, maturational changes in the hippocampus, the main area of the brain involved in memory, make it possible for toddlers to begin remembering events that happened a few hours ago or the day before (e.g., the animals seen at the zoo). However, Piaget noted that children are not able to grasp the true concept of time for several more years (e.g., a trip to the zoo two weeks ago, taking a trip in three days) (Piaget, 1927/1969). Third, at around age 2, there is an increase in the amount of myelin that covers axons, which enables the brain to send messages more efficiently and clearly, and also allows for the development of higher-order skills such as self-awareness (Urban Child Institute, 2015). Lastly, the child's frontal lobe, which is associated with self-control or the ability to regulate emotions and actions, shows some developmental changes at around ages 2 to 3 years, but will not be fully developed until early adulthood.

Maturational brain changes make it possible for the toddler to develop a variety of new skills and to refine those currently in place. For example, 1-year-olds are perfecting their skills in identifying and naming pictures, placing items in and out of containers, understanding spatial relationships, finding hidden objects, playing with items in functional ways, and following simple directions. Two-year-olds are better able to put together puzzles, use objects for different purposes, recognize items as similar and different, understand cause and effect, and sit and focus on activities for longer periods. Toddlers of all ages enjoy looking at picture books and having stories, especially rhymes, read aloud to them. Most of what toddlers are learning during this stage is acquired through play experiences. While mothers are more likely to talk with children during play, guide, and use activities for teaching purposes, fathers tend to engage in play that is often more spontaneous, physical, and challenging in nature (John, Halliburton, & Humphrey, 2013). Both styles of play are necessary because they help children to develop different skills.

The nature of parent-child interactions during play also affects brain development and the quality of cognitive outcomes for children (Takeuchi, et al., 2015).

Photo 7-4 Improved hand-eye coordination enables toddlers to manipulate objects and puzzle pieces.

Researchers have shown that children's cognitive and vocabulary skills are more advanced when parents participated in their play activities, acknowledged and responded to their behaviors, demonstrated developmentally appropriate expectations, encouraged their efforts, and showed enjoyment (Earhart & Zamora, 2015). Children's language development also improved when parents elaborated on the child's verbalizations, discussed themes and actions, and described concepts, such as cause-effect during play (Conner, et al., 2014).

7-2c Promoting Motor Skill Development

Toddlers enjoy exploring their environment, but coordination often lags behind their desire to effectively complete tasks. Consequently, falls, bumps, and spills are common. At age 1, children are learning to pull themselves up, stand independently, take steps, stack blocks, and scribble in big motions. By age 2 years, children are beginning to run, kick a ball, walk up and down stairs with support (e.g., holding an adult's hand or on to a railing), stand on tiptoes, unzip zippers, and draw lines and circles.

Toddlers typically show intermittent activity patterns, engaging in low to high intensity activity approximately half of the time they are awake (Johansson, 2015). However, without structured opportunities and an appropriate environment, toddler's free play is predominately sedentary (Fees et al., 2015). Given the increase in childhood obesity rates, the Society of Health and Physical Educators (SHAPE) has developed physical activity recommendations for toddlers (see Figure 7-2).

The SHAPE guidelines highlight the need to incorporate physical activity into children's daily routines. Indoor and outdoor activities provide toddlers with opportunities to release excess energy, expand language and social skills, and develop and refine large and fine motor skills through repetition and practice. It is important that parents provide safe environments (e.g., safety gates, locks on cabinets, breakable and small items placed out of reach) that encourage toddlers to explore without the risk of serious injury or exposure to hazardous materials, such as cleaning supplies and medications. Safe environments reduce the need for frequent reprimands and are less stressful for adults to monitor.

Photo 7-5 Stirring, mixing, and pouring strengthen motor and problem-solving skills.

Figure 7-2 SHAPE Guidelines for Toddler Physical Activity

Guideline 1. Toddlers should engage in a total of at least 30 minutes of structured physical activity each day.

Guideline 2. Toddlers should engage in at least 60 minutes—and up to several hours—per day of unstructured physical activity and should not be sedentary for more than 60 minutes at a time, except when sleeping.

Guideline 3. Toddlers should be given ample opportunities to develop movement skills that will serve as the building blocks for future motor skillfulness and physical activity.

Guideline 4. Toddlers should have access to indoor and outdoor areas that meet or exceed recommended safety standards for performing large-muscle activities.

Guideline 5. Adults who are in charge of toddlers' well-being are responsible for understanding the importance of physical activity and promoting movement skills by providing opportunities for structured and unstructured physical activity and movement experiences.

Source: Society of Health and Physical Educators (SHAPE) (2009).

Photo 7-6 Safe, active play promotes healthy growth and development.

In unstructured play, toddlers lead the activities. Having access to toys that encourage toddlers to walk, kick, and throw, such as riding toys, balls, pull toys, or a small wagon helps them to build a variety of motor, cognitive, and language skills. As children's skills progress, they can be given opportunities to help carry items, turn pages in a book, and run and kick a ball. Fine motor skills can be practiced through activities such as coloring, placing shapes in shape sorters, playing with blocks, and imitating actions to common nursery rhymes and songs.

Although unstructured play activities are effective for advancing motor and cognitive skill development, toddlers should also participate in at least 30 minutes of structured physical activity each day (SHAPE, 2009). Structured activities are organized and guided by an adult who then prompts the child to join in. For example, a parent may invite a child to partake in a game of pretending to move about like various animals (e.g., hopping like a rabbit, galloping like a horse, crawling like an inch worm), flying a plastic bag kite, or dancing to music. Parents' involvement in these activities provides opportunities to foster children's enjoyment, as well as to reinforce and advance their developmental skills across all domains. Researchers have demonstrated that children are more likely to maintain a physically active lifestyle when parents model similar behaviors and encourage and support their child's participation (Yao & Rhodes, 2015).

It is important to note that children do not need access to high tech or expensive equipment to build motor skills. Everyday items such as boxes (crawling in and out, pushing the box, putting items into the box), bowls and pans (filling and emptying, banging like a drum), and plastic containers (stacking, pouring) can provide hours of practice and entertainment. Spending time outdoors is also highly recommended as children tend to be more active and spontaneous when they are in open areas. Taking walks together can be an enjoyable activity that encourages exploration, language, and motor skill practice. Adults must be patient during these adventures as toddlers are easily distracted by little things along the way, like picking up leaves or looking at ants, and are not in a hurry to reach a particular destination.

7-2d Language Skill Development and Communication

expressive vocabulary words that a child uses to convey a thought or request.

receptive vocabulary words that a child understands and may respond to, but is not able to produce.

nonverbal communication the use of gestures and facial expressions to convey a feeling.

holophrastic speech uttering a single word to express a complete thought.

telegraphic speech using a two- or three-word phrase to express a complete thought.

Toddlers are rapidly becoming thinkers, talkers, and doers. Their ability to hear and to understand what is being said (**receptive vocabulary**), use language to convey thoughts (**expressive vocabulary**), and communicate emotions through facial expressions and gestures (**nonverbal communications**) progresses at a remarkable rate. Toddlers are quickly learning how to use words, especially for making requests and gaining attention. They can often be overheard talking to themselves as they practice new words and conversation. They enjoy stories and rhymes, and are becoming increasingly able to follow simple directions.

At age 1, children know between 5 to 50 words and their speech is primarily **holophrastic**. For example, a child may say the word "ball," to mean "I see a ball," "I want the ball," or "No ball." It is important that caregivers listen to the toddler's words as well as note the inflection, or tone of voice, and the context in which the word is being used to be sure they understand what the child is attempting to communicate. By age 2, toddlers know approximately 50 to 300 words and their speech pattern typically becomes **telegraphic**.

Toddlers' ability to understand language far exceeds their expressive skills (Beuker, 2013). This discrepancy can be frustrating for the child and parent, especially when the toddler's needs cannot be understood because of limited communication. Although a 1-year-old's speech is only 25–50 percent intelligible to others, it becomes 65–70 percent understandable by 2 years of age (Marotz & Allen, 2016). Parents and familiar caregivers often understand what a toddler is saying, but it may be necessary for them to interpret the child's words for other people (ASHA, 2015).

The first three years of life are vital to early language development. What parents say and how they respond to a toddler's communication efforts can hinder or strengthen future progress. For many years, scientists have observed that young children who grow up in low-income families are at greater risk for having delayed language development, primarily because they were thought to have fewer literacy opportunities (e.g., books, verbal interactions) (Hoff, 2013; Rodriquez & Tamis-LeMonda, 2011; Hart & Risley, 1995). Fernald (2013) and her colleagues noted that many of these children already present significant language deficits by the time they turn 2 which, in turn, affect reading and writing skills when they enter school. However, several researchers have identified parents' (particularly mothers') educational level as responsible for the observed disparities in children's language development (Bridges et al., 2015). Rindermann and Baumeister (2015) noted similar results when they reanalyzed data from the original Hart and Risley (1995) study.

Photo 7-7 Reading to children regularly builds early literacy skills and enjoyment of books.

When toddlers are exposed to a literacy-rich environment and have quality interactions with adults they are more likely to develop stronger language skill trajectories (Nobel et al., 2015; Norris, 2014). Morgan et al. (2015) determined that 2-year-olds who have larger vocabularies tend to achieve better academic success and have fewer behavioral problems later on. Parents can create a literacy-rich environment by having books and related materials available in the home, reading books frequently with the child, playing games with words and sounds, and modeling their own enjoyment of reading when children are around (Hudson et al., 2015) (Suggestions for Parents 7-2). Treiman et al. (2015) noted that children whose parents' emphasized alphabetical letters during conversations and play activities (e. g., "milk starts with the letter m"; "baby begins with a b," "Shala starts with a s") when they were young were better readers and learners in kindergarten.

Suggestions for Parents 7-2

Strategies to Foster Toddlers' Language Development

Parents can encourage toddler's language development in numerous ways:

- Use language frequently. Get down on the floor and look at your toddler when speaking.
- Label and repeat the names of objects, foods, colors, feelings, and actions.
- Play games with rhymes and sounds (e.g., stretch out and emphasize sounds in words); have your child make up words to a familiar song.
- Place toys out of reach and encourage the child to ask for them.
- Describe daily routines and activities during play.
- Listen to your toddler and build on what he/she says: "What color is the ball?" "Yes, it is a ball. It is a big, red ball."
- Read books aloud and together; make print materials accessible; check books out from your local book mobile or library or exchange children's books with friends; take toddlers to library-sponsored story hours.
- Take walks together and play word games: "What do you see that is green (or red, yellow)?"; "What animal flies in the sky (crawls on the sidewalk, hops in the grass)?"
- Acknowledge and reinforce the child's efforts to communicate.

⌄ Professional Resource Download

Childhood speech problems are one of the most common developmental delays, and without treatment, place children at long-term risk for negative outcomes. A child's vocabulary has been identified as one of the most reliable predictors of academic and behavioral success in school (Cooper et al., 2014). Furthermore, toddlers who have language delays show poorer **self-regulation** in kindergarten which, in turn, interferes with their academic performance (Aro et al., 2014). Children who have language delays should be referred to a speech-language pathologist for evaluation and intervention to decrease the risk for potential long-term problems (Roberts & Kaiser, 2015).

7-2e Supporting Social-Emotional Development

Toddlers have many positive qualities that are sometimes overshadowed by their lack of social skills and emotional regulation. Their enthusiastic responses to a novel discovery or the mastery of a new task reflect the tremendous desire and learning potential that each child possesses. However, toddlers are also quite **egocentric** as they attempt to determine who they are (self), how they differ from other people and things around them, and how they ultimately fit in. As a result, they have difficulty playing with other children, sharing, and following directions. They frequently resort to physical means such as hitting or snatching toys away from another child because their language skills limit the ability to express needs and frustration. Immature brain development also contributes to the toddler's impulsive and poor decision-making tendencies.

For these reasons, parents report the toddler years to be one of the most stressful child-rearing periods. They describe the toddler's intense desire to be independent, limited developmental skills, stubborn and defiant behaviors, and lack of self-regulation as particularly troubling (Kwon, et al., 2015). These feelings are often intensified in families that are living in poverty, caring for a child with a disability or medical condition, recently immigrated, or have a parent on deployment in the military (Mortensen & Barnett, 2015; Robinson & Neece, 2015).

Photo 7-8 The egocentric toddler has difficulty understanding why things cannot always go his way.

Scientists have long-studied the role that parents play in children's emotional socialization (Miller, Dunsmore, & Smith, 2015; Waugh, Brownell, & Pollock, 2015; Gottman, Katz, & Hooven, 1996). They have consistently determined that a parent's personal beliefs and emotional expressions have a direct shaping effect on children's ability to understand, regulate, and express emotions. Shewark and Blandon (2015) observed that fathers and mothers often differ in their responses to children's emotions and, thus, make unique contributions to their emotional development. Brown, Craig, and Halberstadt (2015) and others have noted that a child's gender and ethnic differences in parents' gender role expectations may help to explain these differences.

It is important to understand that all toddler behavior has meaning. Facial expressions and gestures provide clues about what a child may be thinking but unable to verbalize. When parents learn to recognize these early signs, they often can intervene and prevent the toddler's frustration from escalating. For example, a parent who observes her toddler getting ready to throw a wooden block after the tower she was building falls down might say: "I know you are upset because your tower fell down. Let's build a bigger one together." Helping toddlers to identify and label their feelings is an important first step in advancing communication skills and developing emotional control.

Although toddler behaviors can be challenging to manage and support at times, they also present unique opportunities for teaching social skills that reflect family and cultural values. For example, turn-taking and cooperation can be modeled during a simple game of rolling a ball back and forth, showing excitement with each turn, and applauding the toddler's efforts when the ball is returned. When parents assume an active role in fostering qualities, such as sharing, empathy, cooperation, and helping, toddlers exhibit better self-control and prosocial behaviors (Miller, Dunsmore, & Smith, 2015). Researchers have also observed that toddlers develop more positive social skills when parents provide consistent routines, involve them in simple tasks (e.g., putting papers away, carrying a bag with a few groceries into the house), establish limits, and set aside quality time each day for reading or playing together (Waugh, Brownell, & Pollock, 2015). Because toddlers seek out and thrive on adult attention, it too can be used strategically to foster appropriate behaviors and discourage misbehavior.

Children's social-emotional development encompasses several critical components, including becoming autonomous, handling uncertainty during separations, developing awareness of gender identity and stereotypes, and beginning to learn self-control.

Autonomy. As toddlers approach their second birthday, they become increasingly independent in their play and interactions with adults. Erikson (1950) referred to this stage as autonomy vs. shame and doubt. Whereas 1-year-olds rely heavily on parents for guidance and reassurance, 2-year-olds are developing an instinctive desire to do things for themselves. The words "no," "mine," and "I do it" are uttered frequently. Although this behavior may easily be mistaken for defiance, it represents the toddler's efforts to make independent choices and establish their own personal identity. Parents in many Western cultures typically place a high value on helping toddlers achieve self-care skills (e.g., feeding, toileting, dressing) so they can learn to function independently. Efforts to control or to interfere with toddlers' autonomous interests can lead to poor self-regulatory behaviors, decreased persistence, and an increase in anxiety disorders (Wang, Morgan, & Biringen, 2014; Green, Caplan, & Baker, 2013).

However, not all cultures value or promote children's autonomy in the same manner. As a result, toddlers may exhibit behaviors in the classroom that are a function of the family's cultural values and practices, and not inappropriate behavior. Although early autonomy and self-control are qualities that are more typically emphasized in urban, middle class Western families, respect, proper demeanor, restraint, and communal cohesiveness are valued in many other cultures (Johnson, Radesky, & Zuckerman, 2013). For example, parents in African, Asian, and Latin American cultures are less likely to teach children to become self-reliant or self-assertive, and more likely to foster interdependence or social relationships within a family or group. Children reared in collectivist cultures such as these are taught to share and to consider the welfare and needs of the group before their own. Parents begin to encourage interdependency values through practices such as co-sleeping (bed-sharing) and prolonged breastfeeding, delayed self-feeding, and carrying children around while performing their daily tasks. As a result, toddlers in these cultures tend not to separate or spend time away from parents until they are considerably older (Mindell et al., 2013).

Several other factors are also known to affect the quality of a child's autonomous development. Of particular significance is the nature of the parent-child relationship—the frequency of interactions, the variety of activities that parents engage in with their child, and the manner in which parents respond to the child's behavior. Toddlers who have established a trusting and secure attachment with parents are typically ready to move beyond the boundaries of safety and to attempt new challenges. Parents can support the toddler's interest in becoming self-sufficient by establishing limits and rules and maintaining environments that are safe for exploration. Stating rules in positive terms teaches the child what to do rather than what not to do: "Roll the ball on the floor like this" as opposed to, "Stop throwing the ball." Toddlers also learn best through modeling of appropriate behavior, repeated experience with constructive feedback, and consistent rule enforcement.

Toddlers' autonomous interests can also be encouraged by offering choices. Allowing children to make decisions builds self-esteem and minimizes conflict because it promotes a sense of control and independence. For example, a child might be given a choice of which shoes or coat to wear when getting ready to leave the house. Parents control the choices that are presented, but the child gains a feeling of confidence, responsibility, and self-importance by making the final selection.

The moment the babysitter arrives, Jackson runs to his mother, clings to her leg, and begins to sob. He thrashes about when the babysitter attempts to pick him up, so she puts him back down on the floor. Jackson's mother tries to calm him, but he immediately starts kicking and screaming. Why is Jackson likely behaving in this manner? How would you advise Jackson's mother to respond to his behavior?

Fears and Uncertainty. Toddlers experience a heightened awareness of the people, objects, sounds, shapes, light, and darkness in their surroundings. Their immature ability to understand and explain what is occurring often gives rise to increased anxiety and fear. The most common fears revolve around being left alone in the dark, loud noises (e.g., wind, thunder, toilet flushing, vacuum cleaner), strangers, and monsters. Toddlers who observe others (especially parents) display anxious behaviors, or are reinforced for showing anxious behaviors tend to experience anxiety that is often more severe and intense (Aktar et al., 2014).

Many 1-year-olds continue to show some anxiety during separations from their parents, although their worries are becoming less frequent and intense. Abrupt changes in a toddler's routine can sometimes cause regression and an increased resistance when parents leave. For example, a child who had been separating easily when left at the child development center may suddenly have difficulty following a move to a different room, the birth of a sibling, or death of a close loved one.

The way that parents handle separations is important. Anxiety behaviors that are reinforced (e.g., parent lingers, parent returns to reassure the child), are more likely to persist and be repeated in the future. Parents can help toddlers overcome some of their anxiety by showing them what to do when afraid, practicing brief separations in familiar places, visiting places that may be anxiety-provoking (e.g., meeting the teacher at school before attendance begins), developing a consistent good-bye routine (do not sneak out or prolong the good-bye), and remaining calm when it is time to leave.

Some parents have difficulty following through consistently with separations because of their own anxiety or trauma. Mothers who have a history of post-traumatic stress disorder show a higher fear response and report greater stress during separations than do mothers who have not experienced trauma (Schechter et al., 2015). These parents may need additional support and information about how to best handle separations in order to prevent the intergenerational transmission of undue anxiety. Teachers and other caregivers can encourage greater consistency by affirming the parent's efforts: "You did a great job with the goodbye routine today. Jordyn started smiling and playing much sooner than he has in the past."

Photo 7-9 Separations are still difficult for many toddlers.

Gender Awareness. Toddlers are becoming increasingly aware of gender differences. Their ability to identify male and female is a function of gender socialization and improved language and cognitive skills. Gender labeling is typically one of the first descriptive characteristics that toddlers use to categorize people. Although they are able to correctly identify a person's gender, their determination is based primarily on physical features, such as hair length and type and color of clothing. As a result, young children's ideas about gender are quite rigid. They believe that gender can be changed simply by altering one's appearance (e.g., changing clothes, cutting off hair, putting on a mask or costume, shaving off a mustache) or by desiring it to happen (Halim et al., 2014).

Researchers have shown that children as young as 1 year understand gender labels and are able to match voices with the appropriate gendered pictures (Pascalis et al., 2014). Between 18 and 24 months, toddlers correctly label themselves and others according to gender, and begin to imitate gender-typed activities during play. Girls tend to develop these skills several months earlier than do boys. However, children who live in more egalitarian households often take longer to label themselves and to develop gender role stereotypes (Halim & Ruble, 2010).

Children's stereotypical beliefs about gender and gender roles are shaped by a variety of sociocultural factors, including child-rearing practices, religion, family structure and values, ethnicity, language, and the media. Toddlers first begin to notice gender differences by observing the way that the adults around them look, act, and speak. These early ideas continue to be refined and reinforced over the years through association with gender-specific toys, colors, clothing, books, activities, and peer interactions (Weisgram, Fulcher, & Dinella, 2014; Zosuls, Ruble, & Tamis-LeMonda, 2014).

Parents can take steps to help toddlers develop healthy gender attitudes and avoid harmful gender biases. Gender-neutral toys (e.g., large Legos, stacking blocks, puzzles, plastic garden tools, art supplies, balls), books, games, and activities should be made available for all children to enjoy. It is important that toddlers have ample opportunities to explore and experiment with a variety of toys and activities that are not limited by preconceived gender expectations. Care should also be taken to avoid labeling or suggesting that certain toys, activities, or behaviors are more appropriate for boys than for girls, or vice versa.

Learning Self-Control and Self-Regulation. Human feelings, including pain, anger, fear, happiness, empathy, and loneliness, are experienced universally. How children are socialized to manage and express these feelings is a reflection of the parenting styles, values, and cultural norms to which they are exposed. Although tantrums, hitting, biting, and defiance are considered typical toddler behaviors, they are observed far less often in non-Western cultures. Researchers have attributed this contrast to sociocultural differences in parenting styles, sensitivity to children's needs, perception of what constitutes negative behavior, and typical response methods (Lansford, 2014).

There are several developmental reasons why parent-child conflict tends to occur more often during the toddler years (see Figure 7-3). One-year-olds are just beginning to learn about parent's expectations and are able to comply on occasion. However, 2-year-olds are better able to understand the difference between appropriate and inappropriate behavior, to internalize adult standards for behavior, and to develop some self-control (Kochanska & Sanghag, 2014). Toddlers who have more positive interactions with caregivers are less likely to engage in problematic behaviors than children who have experienced negativity and minimal parental responsiveness

Figure 7-3 Common Causes of Parent-Toddler Conflict

Developmental characteristics that can lead to parent-toddler conflict include:

- Toddlers have a strong urge to be independent and to assert themselves.
- Toddlers have limited language and ability to express their needs.
- Toddlers may become easily frustrated because they lack some of the skills necessary to complete a task.
- Toddlers have limited self-control and experience intense emotional swings.
- Toddlers tend to be active and not always fully aware of their physical limitations.
- Toddlers are impatient and have difficulty when they must wait to get what they want.
- Toddlers are unable to see things from another person's perspective, and cannot think logically or abstractly.

Photo 7-10 Learning to help with their own personal care is an important step in a toddler's efforts to become independent.

(Boyd & Waanders, 2013). However, sleep disturbances and lack of adequate sleep can interfere with the toddler's ability to develop healthy behavioral responses and self-control (Miller et al., 2015).

Parents can promote toddlers' emotional and social understanding by helping them to begin labeling and talking about their feelings (Brophy-Herb et al., 2015). For example, when a toddler appears to be upset, parents can label the emotion ("You look upset."), respond in a sensitive manner, and help the child to resolve the problem ("It looks like the train keeps coming apart. Let's see if we can fix it together."). As children learn to associate words with different emotions, parents can help children to express their own feelings and describe how other people might feel. Care must be taken to always use language that the child understands and to avoid reasoning and lengthy discussions because they are not effective strategies for changing behavior.

7-2f Daily Living Skills

Growing up involves learning to feed, dress, bathe, brush teeth, and go to the bathroom independently. The age at which a toddler attempts these activities is highly variable and depends upon the child's developmental readiness. Some toddlers demand to feed themselves at an early age, while others are content to be fed for a much longer time. The same toddler may insist on dressing herself, but express little interest in bathing or tooth-brushing tasks. Individual variations in interest and abilities are also influenced by the environmental and cultural opportunities that are available to the child. For example, a toddler who grows up in a culture that does not value early independence may not be encouraged to attempt self-care activities, or a child's desire to achieve daily living skills may be delayed by a medical condition or developmental disability.

The toddler's desire for autonomy can be intense and difficult to manage at times. Although they may be fiercely determined to dress or to feed themselves with minimal adult assistance, toddlers' best intentions can quickly turn into frustration when the advanced motor and cognitive skills needed to complete these tasks have not yet been developed. In addition, toddlers are also becoming aware of the power they possess in these situations, and they do not hesitate to use it to refuse help or to test parental limits. Parents must not interpret these behaviors as signs of rejection, but should understand that they are typical and a necessary part of the learning process.

Patience may be one of the most important virtues that parents can offer to toddlers as they are learning various self-care skills. Although it is often easier and faster for an adult to put on a toddler's shoes or to brush their teeth, children must be given opportunities to practice new skills, to make decisions, and to learn from their mistakes. It is also important that parents acknowledge a toddler's efforts, and not dwell on their failures. Repeated criticism can eventually extinguish any interest or initiative a toddler may have for attempting new challenges. A simple, sincere statement acknowledging the toddler's behavior can be effective in moving them closer to success: "I know you are really trying hard to put on your own shoes." Supporting and encouraging toddlers' efforts also helps to build self-esteem, self-confidence, and socialization skills.

Responsive Parenting

Mee, age 20 months, throws herself on the floor, kicking and squealing, or runs away whenever her mother tries to put on her shoes and stockings. Mee's mother has tried punishing her and bribing her with candy, but neither method has worked. Why does Mee behave in this manner? How would you advise Mee's mother to address this behavior the next time it occurs?

Self-Feeding. Parents report that mealtimes are among the most consistently stressful and challenging toddler behaviors with which they must contend (Yoon, Newkirk, & Perry-Jenkins, 2015; Wiggins, 2014). However, potential power struggles can often be avoided when parents understand why toddlers might resort to these behaviors and how positive management strategies can be used to address undesirable conduct.

Most toddlers begin to show an interest in feeding themselves at around 12 to 15 months of age. Learning to eat independently is a slow process and requires toddlers to develop a whole new set of skills. They must learn to grasp a spoon (fine motor), maneuver it to their mouth (hand-eye coordination), close their lips around the contents (oral-motor skills), and chew with an up/down (bite release) motion before swallowing. Drinking from a cup requires a similar sequence of refined skills: picking up the cup, directing it to their mouth, and tipping the cup to obtain the milk inside.

By 18 months of age, most toddlers are able to pour juice or milk into their own cup, use a spoon with relative accuracy, hold their own cup, and help to clean up spills when they occur. They also enjoy helping with simple food preparation tasks, such as washing fruits and vegetables, stirring cold foods, and placing eating utensils on the table. Their involvement becomes a source of pride and provides opportunities for practicing important motor skills.

In the early stages, toddlers' best intentions and enthusiasm often exceed their motor and cognitive skills. As a result, strong emotional outbursts that may include crying or throwing food about are not uncommon, and should be anticipated. Mealtimes can become messy affairs, with frequent spills and food ending up in places where it doesn't belong. Although toddlers are eager to use utensils, they often end up eating with their hands if food is difficult to manage or they become impatient.

Toddlers are also notorious for resisting meals and refusing to come to the table when called. They are beginning to discover their ability to exert some control over mealtime behaviors, as evidenced by their unrestrained "no" responses. At the same time, they are experiencing a significant decrease in their appetite and caloric needs due to a slower growth rate. What parents may perceive as "picky eating" or "not eating" are toddlers who may consume only a few bites before proclaiming that they are done, or who may eat one meal and refuse the next two. It is not uncommon for toddlers to skip an occasional meal, but it is rare for them to stop eating altogether.

In order to maintain healthy growth and an active lifestyle, toddlers need to consume approximately 1000 calories a day. Convincing toddlers to eat this much food can be challenging given their smaller appetite and inconsistent eating patterns. The American Academy of Pediatrics recommends that toddlers follow a daily pattern that includes three meals and two or three small snacks spaced several hours apart so that children are hungry when it is time to eat (AAP, 2015b).

Foods served to toddlers should be nutritious and include a variety of items selected to meet critical dietary requirements for protein, vitamins, and minerals. Foods of poor nutritive value (i.e., high fat, high sugar content), such as chips, cookies, candy, and fruit drinks must be limited to ensure that the toddler consumes those that are nutrient-rich. Offering food in small portions can improve the toddler's willingness to eat. All foods, especially grapes, raw fruits and vegetables, and hot dogs should be cut into small pieces so they are easier to chew and prevent choking.

There are several steps that parents can take to promote children's healthy eating behaviors (Suggestions for Parents 7-3). A positive feeding relationship is based on a mutual respect for the roles that children and their parents each play. Satter (2000) refers to this partnership as the "division of responsibility." Adults are responsible for providing safe and nutritious food within reasonable limits, and serving it in a pleasant mealtime environment. Toddlers are responsible for determining which foods and how much of the food they are willing to eat. Initially, parents may find it uncomfortable to relinquish their

Photo 7-11 Toddlers are becoming increasingly able to feed themselves.

Promoting Healthy Mealtime Behaviors

Steps taken to create a pleasant mealtime environment can encourage children's healthy eating behaviors and reduce family stress.

- Remove potential distractors (e.g., toys, pets, television) from the immediate area.
- Play quiet, relaxing background music.
- Offer a variety of nutritious food items (don't cater to picky eating).
- Involve children in meal preparation (e.g., place napkins on the table; carry fruit to the sink for washing).
- Let children know several minutes in advance when meals will be served so they can anticipate a change in activities. Have them wash their hands.
- Provide safe and appropriately-sized chairs and eating utensils.
- Place a small, damp cloth under bowls or plates to keep them from moving about while a child is trying to eat.
- Eat meals together with toddlers; use the opportunity to model appropriate eating behaviors.
- Engage toddlers in pleasant mealtime conversation. Reinforce language skills by encouraging toddlers to name and talk about different foods, colors, tastes, and textures.
- Limit negative comments about children's mealtime behaviors to avoid distracting or discouraging them from eating. Remain positive and respect the amount of food that is eaten.

control over the toddler's food choices and consumption. However, children should never be forced to eat or punished for not eating; doing so is likely to increase a child's resistance and result in a power struggle. Parents must anticipate that toddlers are going to experience fluctuations in their appetite from meal to meal and day to day. Knowing that they will eat when hungry should alleviate unnecessary concerns and make it easier for parents to accept children's occasional food rejections. However, frequent or prolonged food refusal may indicate a more serious feeding problem that should be evaluated.

Toddlers are notorious for resisting new or unfamiliar foods and expressing strong reactions to foods they dislike. These behaviors are thought to be primitive responses that are designed to protect a child from ingesting harmful substances. In addition, young children have many more taste buds than do adults, so they experience an enhanced sense of textures and flavors that can lead to food rejection. Refused foods should not be eliminated from the toddler's diet. Research has shown that it may take as many as 10 to 15 exposures to a new or rejected food before a child is receptive to trying it (Wadhera et al., 2015). Sometimes disliked foods can be prepared and served in different ways to make them more appealing. Involving toddlers in meal preparations, such as retrieving items from the refrigerator or washing vegetables in the sink, is also an effective way to increase their interest in tasting a previously refused food item.

Some toddlers experience occasional periods when they refuse all foods to the exclusion of one or two favorites (e.g., macaroni and cheese, hot dogs, peanut butter sandwiches). These phases, commonly referred to as selective eating or **food jags**, can create considerable parent-child tension. Cano et al. (2015) observed that 46 percent of children experience periods of selective eating during early childhood and, thus, considered it typical development. They also noted that prolonged picky eating behaviors are more common among children from socially disadvantaged backgrounds. Although giving

food jag periods when a child will only eat certain preferred foods to the exclusion of all others.

into the toddler's demands may seem the easiest way to avoid conflict, doing so may actually prolong food refusals. Repeated prompts, reprimands, and rewards offered for eating should also be avoided because they too can strengthen the undesirable behavior.

Toddlers should not be expected to eat everything on their plate. Food refusals and other negative mealtime behaviors can be handled in a positive, yet firm and caring manner. A gentle warning that the meal will soon end should be issued if, after five minutes, a toddler has shown little interest in eating. At this point, food should be removed from the table. Uneaten food can be saved and offered at the next meal or snack. If toddlers beg for something to eat soon after leaving the table, parents must resist the temptation to give in until it is again time to eat. Children are likely to be hungry and ready to eat when food is again served. Respecting the toddler's decision not to eat in a positive manner builds self-esteem and teaches important lifelong skills, including healthy eating habits and valuing social expectations.

Toddlers should be monitored closely for food allergies when new foods are introduced into their diet. Rashes and digestive upsets (i.e., diarrhea, vomiting) may be signs of a food allergy, and should be discussed with the child's health care provider. It is also important that parents inform teachers and care providers about any food allergies, **food intolerances**, religious restrictions, or cultural food preferences their child may have.

Toddlers who have disabilities, developmental delays, or certain medical conditions (e.g., gastroesophageal reflux disease, diabetes, failure to thrive) tend to experience a higher rate of feeding problems (e.g., difficulty chewing or swallowing, choking, gagging) that may require special foods or mealtime modifications. Advice can be sought from dietitians and intervention specialists to determine if a toddler is receiving the proper nutrition. Occupational and physical therapists can evaluate the child's eating behaviors and assist the family in making adjustments that will facilitate independence.

food intolerance a sensitivity reaction to food that can cause digestive upsets (e.g., gas, diarrhea, nausea), but is not a true food allergy.

Self-Dressing. Toddlers typically begin showing an interest in dressing and undressing themselves at around 15 to 18 months of age. However, the process to achieve complete independence takes several years and involves extensive trial and error. Toddlers must figure out how things work and in what order each step occurs. Although they find zippers, buttons, and snaps especially intriguing, toddlers still lack the fine motor skills necessary to successfully manipulate them. As a result, these objects often become a source of considerable frustration for children.

Parents can support toddlers' interests in dressing themselves by providing clothing that is soft, loose, and easy to manage (e.g., doesn't have to be pulled over their head, has an elastic waistband). Toddlers' early attempts to dress themselves are generally concentrated on taking things off, especially shoes and socks, because they are the easiest to reach. Young toddlers are usually cooperative when asked to push their arm into a shirt sleeve or to stretch out their legs to put on pants or socks. However, as they approach their second birthday, they become more adamant about dressing themselves without any adult assistance. Shouts of, "No, me do it!" are typical. Even though both feet may end up in the same pant leg or shoes are placed on the wrong feet, it is the toddler's effort, and not the result, that is most important (Erikson's autonomy vs. shame and doubt). However, if a toddler's efforts end in repeated failure, it may be necessary to intervene. Parents can demonstrate the process for the toddler to follow, or they can complete a portion of the process and have the toddler finish; "I'll put the sock on your foot, and then you can pull it up."

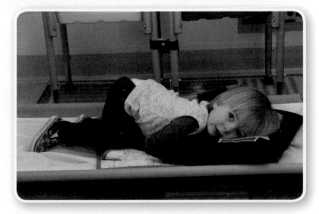

Photo 7-12 Adequate sleep is essential to support toddlers' healthy growth and development.

Older toddlers may begin to insist on selecting their own clothes to wear, and may vehemently refuse to dress in items that a parent has chosen. Power struggles can often be avoided by giving the toddler options, "Do you want to wear the red shirt or the blue shirt?" or, "Do you want to put on your sandals or tennis shoes?" Allowing toddlers to make the final decision reduces the potential for conflict and reinforces their sense of initiative, autonomy, and self-worth.

Bedtimes. Children's sleep routines develop in the context of their family. Cultural, socioeconomic, and structural differences influence family routines and decisions about when children are put to bed, where they will sleep, and how they are expected to behave. For example, although early evening bedtimes (i.e., 7:00 or 8:00 P.M.) are common in many Western cultures, children in some European and Asian countries typically do not go to bed until 9:00 or 10:00 P.M. or even later. **Co-sleeping** is also commonly practiced in many non-Western countries and can take several forms, including children sleeping in their parent's bed (with or without a co-sleeper present), sleeping in a crib or bed adjacent to their parent's bed, or simply sleeping in the same room (El-Sheikh & Sadeh, 2015; Mindell et al., 2015).

Although most toddlers begin sleeping soundly through the night, there are occasions when a child may have difficulty falling asleep or wake up crying after having been asleep. Toddlers' quest for independence may also contribute to occasional bedtime resistance. Approximately 30 percent of parents' express concern about their child's sleep habits (Staples, Bates, & Petersen, 2015). Inadequate sleep has been linked to poor emotional control and cognitive development (Miller et al., 2015; Meltzer et al., 2014). Sleep disturbances and bedtime resistance are especially notable among children who have medical and developmental disorders, such as attention deficit hyperactivity disorder (ADHD), Down syndrome, autism, Prader-Willi syndrome, and gastroesophageal reflux disease (GERD) (Montgomery & Wiggs, 2015; Valicenti-McDermott et al., 2015). Environmental conditions, including television viewing before bedtime, and inconsistent sleep routines have also been identified as factors that contribute to disrupted sleep (McDonald, et al., 2014). Although toddlers' sleep patterns vary, it is recommended that they get 10 to 12 hours of uninterrupted nighttime sleep plus a 1 to 3 hour-long nap each day to maintain their active lifestyle and growth (National Sleep Foundation, 2015).

Sleep specialists agree that it is especially important to establish and maintain consistent bedtimes and bedtime routines for toddlers. However, their approaches to the management of challenging bedtime behaviors differ. Dr. Richard Ferber (1985) suggests that children be put to bed when they are fully awake so that they can learn how to settle themselves for sleep. He discourages parents from cuddling or rocking children to sleep because they will begin to rely on these activities. Furthermore, he advocates waiting progressively longer periods (e.g., 5, 10, 15 minutes) each time the child cries out for a parent to return. When the parent does return, interactions are to be kept brief (1 or 2 minutes) and are only intended to reassure the child that someone is nearby. Ferber believes this method gradually extinguishes problematic behaviors and helps children learn how to self-quiet and fall asleep on their own. However, he also suggests that it may not be appropriate for all children or for all types of sleep problems. Dr. William Sears (2005) offers a contrasting approach and suggests that failing to respond to a child's demands could potentially lead to undue stress, insecure feelings, and future sleep problems. Instead, he advocates that parents assume a more nurturing, attachment-style approach to children's bedtime issues that includes holding, rocking, and soothing a child to sleep, as well as co-sleeping.

The American Academy of Pediatrics (2015a) has issued guidelines that reflect a more moderate approach to children's bedtime routines. They suggest that bedtime preparations be initiated as soon as a toddler begins to appear sleepy. If parents wait too long, children may regain their 'second wind' and have difficulty relaxing and falling asleep. A typical bedtime routine might include a brief period of active play followed by a series of calming activities, such as a warm bath, a favorite story, a light snack, cuddling, and/or dancing quietly to music. When it is time, parents are encouraged to tuck the toddler into bed, say their goodnights, and leave the room. Some children find comfort in taking a soft toy or blanket to bed with them, or having a night light or hall light left on.

Once the toddler has been settled in bed, parents are urged to resist the child's pleas to have them return. Although it may be difficult to do so, responding more than once or twice to their repeated calls increases the probability that the toddler will continue

co-sleeping child sleeping in a parent's bed, in an adjacent bed, or in the same room with parents.

making demands. If parents are confident that the toddler is safe and all immediate needs (e.g., a trip to the bathroom, a drink, a goodnight kiss) have been satisfied, then it is best to allow them time to soothe themselves to sleep. Once asleep, parents may want to quietly check to be sure that the child is okay.

Some toddlers still experience separation anxiety, especially if they awake from a sound sleep and are disoriented. Teething discomfort or a noise or shadow that isn't immediately familiar may also cause a toddler to awaken and call out for a parent. In these situations, it is best to comfort, reassure, and quietly tuck the toddler back under her covers. Prolonged conversation or lingering should be avoided because it may disrupt the toddler's ability to settle herself back to sleep.

It is important that parents carefully evaluate any method they may read about in popular books or on the Internet to determine if it is consistent with their family values and appropriate for the child's developmental stage and personality. Once they settle on a method, it should be implemented consistently. Toddlers find comfort and security in knowing what to expect and are also more likely to cooperate when they have a familiar routine to follow.

Toilet Training. Learning to use a toilet for elimination purposes represents another important step in the toddler's efforts to become independent. However, it is also one of the few opportunities over which a toddler can exercise complete control. As a result, the toilet training process seldom proceeds as smoothly or as quickly as parents anticipate. Some children catch on quickly while others may take many months. Slow progress causes some parents to experience considerable stress, tension, and an increased risk for abusing children (Palusci & Covington, 2014). For these reasons, it is important for parents to understand that frequent accidents and occasional regressions are normal and do not represent a child's willful intention to upset or to disobey parents.

Thoughts about when and how toilet training should be conducted are wide-ranging, and often change from year to year (see, "Trending Now"). Toilet training

Trending Now Toilet Training Infants

An Internet search for the latest in toilet training trends turns up a technique commonly referred to as "elimination communication." The concept touts the idea that infants can be trained to use the toilet for elimination purposes. Infants are allowed to go diaper-free so they become aware of sensations associated with the need to urinate or to defecate. Parents learn to recognize the infant's behavioral signals that suggest elimination is imminent so they can hold the child over a toilet (sink, or other functional container) to "perform." Some parents practice diaper-free training only in their own home. Others adhere to the practice when infants are taken out in public and allow them to urinate in the street or a park.

Many parents have shared their success stories on blogs and websites. Some claim that they have been able to teach 2- and 3-month-old infants to go on demand, and that by 15 months of age, toddlers are able to use the toilet unassisted. Ardent followers of the diaper-free training method cite early cultural practices that did not rely on the use of disposable diapers. They promote the method as being eco-friendly, saving landfills from massive amounts of disposable diapers and valuable resources that would otherwise be used for laundering cloth diapers. Some parents describe a deeper feeling of closeness with their infant. Others are appreciative of the fact that infants are unlikely to experience diaper rash or other skin conditions.

A recent increase in urinary tract infections among young children has caused medical experts to re-examine current toilet training practices. Hodges et al. (2014) determined that initiating toilet training procedures earlier than 24 months and later than 36 months is associated with a higher incidence of urinary tract dysfunction. Wen et al. (2014) reported similar findings, and found that the bladder continues to grow and mature throughout infancy. Voluntary sphincter control develops as a result of physiological maturation and, in turn, contributes to increased bladder capacity and improved bladder-emptying function. These and similar outcomes have led the American Academy of Pediatrics (AAP) (2015c) and the Canadian Paediatric Society (CPS) (2014) to recommend a conservative approach to toilet training. Although they recognize that social and cultural variants influence parents' decisions about when and how to conduct toilet training, they advise waiting until a child is older and, thus, more mature. Why might early toilet training appear to work? How would you respond if a parent asked for your opinion about whether infants could be toilet trained?

methods posted by so-called "experts," and abundant success stories appearing on websites and blogs can add to parents' confusion in their attempt to make an informed decision (Porter & Ispa, 2013). Personal factors, including work schedules, socioeconomic values, culture, religion, ethnicity, and a child's developmental disabilities or medical conditions also affect a family's ideas about what method is most appropriate (Frank & Esbensen, 2015). For example, a two-working parent family may decide to delay toilet training until they have more time to devote to the project. Infants in the Vietnamese culture seldom wear diapers and are often toilet trained by 9 months of age (Duong, Jansson, & Hellström, 2013). In contrast, toilet training is typically not initiated until after a child's second birthday in Scandinavian, Asian, and many Western countries (Duong, et al., 2013). Whatever method parents eventually choose, it should be one that takes into account a toddler's unique personality, developmental readiness, and learning style.

Many toddlers begin to show an interest in using the toilet at around 20 to 24 months of age. Waiting until they are curious and have the requisite skills to begin toilet training can improve a child's chances for success and make the process less stressful for everyone involved. Indicators that suggest a child is physically and emotionally ready to begin toilet training include:

- child is able to initiate and control elimination
- child remains dry for several hours during the daytime
- child has a regular pattern of elimination
- child recognizes when he is urinating or having a bowel movement
- child understands and follows simple directions
- child is able to communicate the need to go
- child has developed the necessary motor skills (e.g., able to walk, pull clothing up and down, sit down and get up off a toilet seat or potty)

It is also prudent to wait to begin toilet training until there are no major changes expected in the toddler's daily routine, such as a move to a new home, the birth of a sibling, an illness, a transition from crib to a 'grown-up' bed, or a long road trip. Such events will distract the toddler's attention from the task at hand and slow progress.

There are several things that parents can do to prepare toddlers for this experience. Words to describe elimination (e.g., pee, tinkle, urine, BM, poop, bowel movement) should be used consistently so that a toddler begins to associate them with the appropriate actions. Disposable diapers (which whisk away moisture) can be replaced with training pants or cloth diapers during daytime hours so that toddlers begin to recognize when their pants are wet or soiled. Clothing should be loose and easy for children to manage, especially when it is necessary to hurry. Parents should decide whether to purchase a child-size potty chair or training seat that fits over a toilet seat (along with a non-slip footstool to support the child's feet). Toddlers can then begin to practice sitting on their potty chair or training seat (with or without training pants) whenever a parent or sibling is using the toilet (modeling) so they learn what it is used for.

A consistent routine is important to establish and follow once the decision has been made to initiate toilet training. This helps toddlers know what to expect and improves their chances for success. For example, a toddler might be placed on the potty whenever he wakes up with a dry diaper (a sign of bladder maturity) or 30 minutes after drinking fluids to help him recognize the sensation of a full bladder. Some parents follow a 2-hour routine whereby a toddler is asked every 2 hours if she needs to use the potty. Parents may also encourage a toddler to try and urinate every night before going to bed. Because children are more likely to have a bowel movement shortly after eating, it may be ideal to have them sit on the toilet for a short time following a meal. Parents should also discuss their toilet training routine with the child's teachers or caregivers so they can follow the same procedures.

Successful toilet training requires that parents exercise considerable patience, support, and encouragement. Children should not be punished for accidents, which are normal and to be expected, because this can cause regression or withholding elimination. Occasional accidents should be handled matter-of-factly, soiled clothing removed and replaced, and children reassured that they will do better the next time. It may be necessary to suspend toilet training for a few days if a child who was toilet trained begins having frequent accidents. Offering praise when children experience success can encourage them to keep on trying. Some parents also opt to reward children with a sticker, a story, or other small reinforcement.

Toilet training toddlers who have special needs requires an individualized approach. Procedures may need to be modified to address a child's unique abilities and limitations. Some children take much longer to achieve toilet training if the developmental disability or delay affects their cognitive and motor skills (especially the muscles involved in urination and defecation). Medical conditions, such as diabetes and urinary tract infections, may cause a child to urinate frequently and have difficulty staying dry. Dietary patterns, physical limitations, and some medications can increase the risk for constipation and cause hard stools that may be difficult for children to pass. Parents should work closely with a health care provider who can assist them in implementing appropriate toilet training procedures, and offer medical treatment for conditions that may interfere with the child's success.

Photo 7-13 Prosocial behaviors are learned through consistent, positive adult guidance.

7-3 Developmentally Appropriate Behavior Guidance

Parents' ideas about what it means to be a 'good child' serve as the standard for expectations, rule- and limit-setting, and disciplinary responses. These beliefs are highly variable and often reflect a combination of family diversity and current trends. However, when parents are familiar with developmentally appropriate expectations, they are better able to respond to children's behavior in a reliable, effective, and positive manner. Because toddlers are likely to present parents with significant behavioral challenges from time to time, this is an especially important consideration. Knowing how to establish and enforce consistent limits and use constructive strategies, such as communication, redirection, active ignoring, and rewards to address undesirable behavior will help toddlers develop the positive social and emotional qualities they will need to succeed (Kwon et al., 2015). It is also important for parents to learn how to manage their own feelings in these situations and to model positive behaviors (Suggestions for Parents 7-4).

For many years, parents were encouraged to use time-out procedures exclusively when young children misbehaved. However, the technique was soon being employed too often and usually incorrectly (e.g., child made to sit in a chair or corner while an adult explained the reason for being disciplined). When implemented correctly, time-out involves having the child sit quietly in-place or move to a designated location without toys or attention from adults or other children. When the child is calm, the child is allowed to return to the original situation.

Time-outs were never meant to be punitive, but rather to allow the child a few quiet moments to settle down and regain composure. However, because toddlers are just beginning to learn about self-control it is unlikely that they will be able to quiet themselves during an emotional outburst. It is also doubtful that they will remember the 'lesson' that a time-out session was intended to teach due to their limited memory and recall abilities. For these reasons, it is recommended that time out only be used sparingly and as a last resort. Positive guidance techniques, such as prevention (avoiding a

Suggestions for Parents 7-4

Positive Steps for Managing Angry Feelings

It is normal for parents to feel angry and frustrated at times. Responding to intense emotions in a positive manner also teaches children to behave in similar ways.

- Recognize when you are upset or angry, and avoid taking any immediate action that you might later regret.
- Take a deep breath, and evaluate the situation. If necessary, walk away until you regain self-control.
- Choose your battles. Not all misbehavior is worth getting upset about.
- Have empathy and try to understand why a child may be upset.
- Listen to what the child says and show understanding, but remain focused on the behavior in question.
- Avoid using physical discipline, such as hitting or spanking, or making threats. These methods teach children to handle anger in a negative manner.
- Remain calm and speak in a normal tone of voice.
- Set aside "me" time each day to do something that you enjoy and that relieves stress.

❯❯ Professional Resource Download

trip to the grocery store when a toddler is tired, giving positive attention), active ignoring, modeling, physical guidance, and redirection often prove to be the most effective behavior management strategies to use with this age group.

7-3a Tantrums

Children's tantrums can cause parents and caregivers considerable distress. Temper tantrums tend to peak between 15 and 20 months of age, and are the most common concern that parents report to pediatricians (Godoy et al., 2014). They occur at an especially high rate among children who have developmental or intellectual disabilities (Ngashangva & Dutt, 2015). Most tantrums last less than 5 minutes and are of relatively low intensity. During a tantrum, children may display behaviors that range from mild whining and pouting to rage, robust kicking, shrieking, tossing of objects, throwing themselves on the floor, and/or breath holding.

Before parents respond to a child's tantrum, it is important to consider why the tantrum is happening (Daniels, Mandleco, & Luthy, 2012). **Temperamental tantrums** occur when children are tired, overly stimulated, hungry, or not feeling well. In this case, caregivers may simply need to hold and comfort the child and talk quietly once the child calms down. **Manipulative tantrums** are frequently triggered by feelings of anger or frustration following noncompliance. They happen because children are testing adult limits, trying to get attention, wanting a toy that another child has, or trying to escape from someone or a situation. If parents give in to demands during a tantrum, children quickly learn that they are likely to get their way whenever they repeat the behavior.

Determining the reason for a child's tantrums provides valuable information about ways to address and prevent the behavior from recurring (Suggestions for Parents 7-5). For example, if a child always tantrums to get attention when the telephone rings (i.e., manipulative tantrum), parents can offer the child something to do while they talk, give periodic attention (e.g., pat on the back, smile, hand a toy,

temperamental tantrum an emotional outburst that may occur because a child is overly tired or hungry.

manipulative tantrum acting out to get attention or what is wanted.

Preventing Temper Tantrums

Several steps can be taken to reduce the potential for children's temper tantrums.

- Establish simple limits and rules, and enforce them consistently.
- Maintain predictable schedules (e.g., mealtimes, bedtimes) so that children know what to expect and do not become overly hungry or tired.
- Give only one instruction at a time. Tell the child what to do, and be sure the direction is something the child understands and is able to follow.
- Model appropriate ways to handle anger or frustration; young children learn best by observing how others act.
- Offer toddlers simple choices. Allowing them to make some decisions improves cooperation and helps them to gain a sense of control.
- Provide an advanced warning when a transition is approaching: "It is almost time to go to the store, so we will need to stop playing soon."
- Avoid negotiating with a noncompliant toddler.
- Note times and situations that typically provoke a tantrum or behaviors that precede a tantrum. This allows you to intervene before the child's behavior escalates into a meltdown, and to model appropriate ways to manage frustration (e.g., asking for help, trying a different way).

⌄ Professional Resource Download

give specific praise), keep the conversation short so that the child can be successful in waiting, and/or provide special play time when the conversation has ended. If the child is most likely to tantrum when it is time to get ready for sleep (i.e., temperamental tantrum), it may be helpful to initiate an earlier bedtime and a consistent routine with calming activities.

Additional techniques that can be used to address tantrums include redirecting the child's attention, active ignoring, and giving attention when the child begins to quiet or relax. If a child's behavior suggests that a tantrum is imminent, the parent can try redirecting the child's attention to another object or person of interest ("Oh look, the puppy wants to play ball with you."). Active ignoring involves the parent looking away, showing interest in something else (e.g., a book, toy, sibling), and not talking to the child for a brief time.

These strategies will not work if time-in is not in place. Time-in involves the parent paying attention and engaging in positive interactions with the child when good behaviors are shown (Nelsen, Erwin, & Duffy, 2015). In other words, the parent is catching the child being good. The overall goal is to be predictable, consistent, and for there to be a difference or contrast in how the adult responds so that the child begins to understand what behaviors are desired and will get attention.

Tantrums in public places are a dreaded, but common experience for parents. In these settings, it is especially tempting to give in to unreasonable demands and try to rationalize with a toddler in order to get the tantrum to stop. However, giving in can lead to more frequent and intense public tantrums in the future. Before going into public settings, the expected behaviors should be briefly explained and practiced with the toddler. It is best to keep outings short, especially in the beginning, so that children can be successful. Timing of outings can also be planned for the child's best time of the day (e.g., not right before nap or meals).

Photo 7-14 Toddlers frequently resort to the use of physical aggression.

During the outing, toddlers can be given a task to keep them engaged, such as placing items into the cart, looking for colors or animals on cereal boxes, or playing with a small toy that they have brought along. Offering specific praise and an opportunity to spend special time with the parent can also be used effectively to reinforce a child's good behavior during the trip. If a tantrum occurs in public, it is important to remain calm and matter-of-fact. A warning can be given, but if the tantrum continues, the child should be removed from the situation until he can regain emotional control. If the tantrum is manipulative, the outing can be continued once the child is briefly reminded of how he is expected to behave and regains his composure. If the tantrum is temperamental, it may be necessary to leave and complete the outing at a better time (e.g., after taking a nap, after getting a snack, when the child is not ill).

7-3b Biting and Hitting

Hitting and biting behaviors are not uncommon during the toddler stage. In most instances, they are spontaneous and occur when a toddler becomes overly frustrated or angry and loses control. Seldom do toddlers plan to cause intentional harm to another person or consider the consequences of their actions. Because the mouth is one of the most well-developed parts of the body, it is not surprising that children use it for immediate defense. Bites are typically directed to an upper extremity, and are most likely to happen when there is a dispute with another child.

Environmental arrangements, including having adequate space for movement, close supervision, and multiple and duplicate toys for children to play with, can help to decrease biting and hitting. These behaviors can also be avoided by noting if certain times or situations tend to provoke a toddler's hitting or biting, and then intervening before problems arise. Children can be taught appropriate words and actions to use when they are upset so they will be less likely to resort to physical aggression. In addition, parents can model effective coping skills and practice them with children to build confidence. Gradually, appropriate or desired behaviors will become a natural part of the child's response repertoire when they are consistently acknowledged and reinforced.

If a bite does occur, attention should first be given to the victim and later to the child who did the biting. It is not recommended that children be bitten or spanked to show them how it feels because this consequence models using inappropriate and aggressive behavior when a person is frustrated.

7-3c Defiance

The majority of toddlers' difficult behaviors are not purposely intended to be defiant. Young toddlers are not capable of planning ahead or of understanding logic, and they have little or no self-control. However, around the age of 2, children may begin to assert themselves more often by not doing what they are told or refusing to stop a behavior when asked (Zero to Three, 2016). This change reflects the toddler's efforts to test adult expectations and to gain independence.

Several positive behavior strategies can be followed to decrease defiant and other problematic behaviors (Suggestions for Parents 7-6). It is important for parents to remain calm, yet firm, and follow through with directions given. Toddlers who present with more intense or repetitive behavior problems, such as self-injury or aggression, should receive early intervention supports to lessen the potential impact these behaviors may have on daily functioning and peer relationships (Schroeder et al., 2014; Baillargeon, Keenan, & Cao, 2012).

Positive Behavior Guidance

Toddler behavior can be challenging, but when parents create a safe and consistent environment and respond patiently to children, significant behavior problems can be prevented.

- Childproof the environment to decrease the number of rules and redirections needed.
- Set a positive example, because children learn to behave by watching others.
- Establish predictable routines and clear rules so that children know what is expected.
- Use warnings to signal when transitions are about to happen: "It is almost time to leave for the store."
- Give brief directions that the child is able to complete one at a time, and state them in a positive way: "It is time to leave for the store. Please put the cars in the bucket."
- Offer choices to help the child feel control over situations: "Do you want to pick up the cars or the books?"
- Catch toddlers when they are behaving appropriately. Give them attention by describing and playing along with them as well as providing descriptive praise: "You did a great job of putting the cars in the bucket quickly when I asked!"
- Follow through with directions in a calm, yet firm manner by showing and guiding the child's actions: "Put the cars in the bucket like this" (take the child's hand to put a car in the bucket).
- Recognize that toddlers may misbehave to get attention. Attention-seeking behaviors can be ignored as long as they do not cause harm to the child or to others, and toddlers are taught more appropriate ways to gain attention.

Summary

- Despite experiencing a slower growth rate, increased height and weight give the toddler a more streamlined and childlike appearance by age 2. Dramatic changes in the toddler's cognitive, motor, language, and social-emotional abilities also occur between 1 and 2 years of age as new neural connections and patterns form in the brain.

- Toddlers focus the majority of their time and energy on developing locomotion and fine motor skills, acquiring and using language, establishing autonomy, learning social-emotional skills, and becoming more independent with daily living skills. Parent's encouragement, involvement, and positive guidance are essential for promoting toddlers' early skill development and self-esteem. Parents play an important role in providing safe environments that encourage toddlers' independence and exploration, showing interest and encouragement in their emerging skills, establishing routines, and setting limits that are developmentally appropriate and consistently enforced.

- Toddlers' social and emotional development depends on adult guidance. Several positive guidance techniques, including communication, active ignoring, and redirection can be used to effectively address a variety of challenging toddler behaviors, including aggression (e.g., hitting, biting, throwing objects), tantrums, and noncompliance.

Key Terms

autonomy (p. 191)

co-sleeping (p. 206)

egocentric (p. 198)

expressive vocabulary (p. 196)

food intolerance (p. 205)

food jag (p. 204)

holophrastic speech (p. 196)

make-believe play (p. 192)

manipulative tantrum (p. 210)

nonverbal communication (p. 196)

onlooker play (p. 192)

parallel play (p. 192)

receptive vocabulary (p. 196)

self-regulation (p. 198)

solitary play (p. 192)

symbolic play (p. 193)

telegraphic speech (p. 196)

temperamental tantrum (p. 210)

Questions for Discussion and Self-Reflection

1. How do growth and development differ? What activities can parents use to support toddlers in achieving important developmental tasks in the areas of: cognition; locomotion and motor skill; language and communication; social-emotional skills; and daily living?

2. What purpose does play serve in toddlers' development? How might a toddler's development be affected if parents do not provide or encourage any play opportunities?

3. Why is it important that toddlers participate in structured and unstructured physical activity every day? Describe two developmentally appropriate structured and unstructured activities for toddlers. How could these activities be modified for a toddler who has limited physical mobility or a visual impairment?

4. What suggestions could you offer to parents who have limited financial resources for promoting and supporting toddler's language development?

5. Describe how the "division of responsibility" in the feeding relationship fosters toddlers' autonomy and self-esteem.

Field Activities

1. Make arrangements to observe a small group of toddlers (e.g., birthday party, family celebration, play group, story hour) for at least 30 minutes. Based on what you have learned in this chapter, prepare a brief narrative (to post online or distributed to parents) that explains what behaviors they should anticipate, and include guidelines for how to organize successful toddler playgroups.

2. Interview the parents of several toddlers. Ask them to describe the challenges they face at bedtime, the methods they have used to address noncompliance, and if the strategy has been effective. Design a plan for one family that could be used to improve their child's bedtime routine.

REFERENCES

Agrati, D., Browne, D., Jonas, W., Meaney, M., Atkinson, L., Steiner, M., & Flemin, A. (2015). Maternal anxiety from pregnancy to 2 years postpartum: Transactional patterns of maternal early adversity and child temperament. *Archives of Women's Mental Health*, 18(5), 693–705.

Aktar, E., Majdandžić, M., de Vente, W., & Bögels, S. (2014). Parental social anxiety disorder prospectively predicts toddlers' fear/avoidance in a social referencing paradigm. *Journal of Child Psychology and Psychiatry*, 55(1), 77–87.

American Academy of Pediatrics (AAP). (2015a). A lullaby for good health. Retrieved on June 4, 2015 from https://www.healthychildren.org/English/ages-stages/toddler/Pages/A-Lullaby -for-Good-Health.aspx.

American Academy of Pediatrics (AAP). (2015b). Toddlers: Food and feeding. Retrieved on March 25, 2015 from https://www.aap.org/en-us/advocacy-and-policy/aap-health-initiatives /HALF-Implementation-Guide/Age-Specific-Content/Pages/Toddler-Food-and-Feeding.aspx.

American Academy of Pediatrics (AAP). (2015c). Toilet training your child: The basics. Retrieved on April, 12, 2015, from http://www2.aap.org/sections/scan/practicingsafety/Toolkit_Resources /Module7/barton_schmitt_protocol_guide_for_parents_1.pdf.

American Speech-Language-Hearing Association (ASHA). (2015). How does your child hear and talk? Retrieved on April 2, 2015 from http://www.asha.org/public.

Aro, T., Laakso, M., Maatta, S., Tolvanen, A., & Poikkeus, A. (2014). Associations between toddler-age communication and kindergarten-age self-regulatory skills. *Journal of Speech, Language, and Hearing Research, 57*(4), 1405–1417.

Baillargeon, R., Keenan, K., & Cao, G. (2012). The development of opposition-defiance during toddlerhood: A population-based cohort study. *Journal of Developmental & Behavioral Pediatrics, 33*(8), 608–617.

Beuker, K., Rommelse, N., Donders, R., & Buitelaar, J. (2013). Development of early communication skills in the first two years of life. *Infant Behavior & Development, 36*(1), 71–83.

Boyd, R., & Waanders, C. (2013). Protective factors for depression among African American children of predominantly low-income mothers with depression. *Journal of Child and Family Studies, 22*(1), 85–95.

Bridges, M., Cohen, S., Scott, L., Fuller, B., Anguiano, R., Figueroa, A., & Livas-Dlott, A. (2015). Home activities of Mexican American children: Structuring early socialization and cognitive engagement. *Cultural Diversity and Ethnic Minority Psychology, 21*(2), 181–190.

Brophy-Herb, H., Bocknek, E., Vallotton, C., Stansbury, K., Senehi, N., Dalimonte-Merckling, D., & Lee, Y. (2015). Toddlers with early behavioral problems at higher family demographic risk benefit most from maternal emotion talk. *Journal of Developmental & Behavioral Pediatrics, 36*(7), 512–520.

Brown, G., Craig, A., & Halberstadt, A. (2015). Differences in emotion socialization behaviors vary by ethnicity and child gender. *Parenting: Science and Practice, 15*(3), 135–157.

Calzada, E., Huang, K., Linares-Torres, H., Singh, S., & Brotman, L. (2014). Maternal *familismo* and early childhood functioning in Mexican and Dominican immigrant families. *Journal of Latina/o Psychology, 2*(3), 156–171.

Canadian Paediatric Society (CPS). (2014). *Toilet learning: Anticipatory guidance with a child-oriented approach.* Retrieved on April 11, 2015, from http://www.cps.ca/en/documents /position/toilet-learning.

Cano, S., Tiemeier, H., Van Hoeken, D., Tharner, A., Jaddoe, V., Hofman, A., Verhulst, F., & Hoek, H. (2015). Trajectories of picky eating during childhood: A general population study. *International Journal of Eating Disorders, 48*(6), 570–579.

Conner, J., Kelly-Vance, L., Ryalls, B., & Friehe, M. (2014). A play and language intervention for two-year-old children: Implications for improving play skills and language. *Journal of Research in Childhood Education, 28*(2), 221–237.

Cooper, B., Moore, J., Powers, C., Cleveland, M., & Greenberg, M. (2014). Patterns of early reading and social skills associated with academic success in elementary school. *Early Education and Development, 25*(8), 1248–1264.

Cuellar, J., Jones, D., & Sterrett, E. (2015). Examining parenting in the neighborhood context: A review. *Journal of Child and Family Studies, 24*(1), 195–219.

Daniels, E., Mandleco, B., & Luthy, K. (2012). Assessment, management, and prevention of childhood temper tantrums. *Journal of the American Academy of Nurse Practitioners, 24*(10), 569–573.

Duong, T., Jansoon, U., Holmdahl, G., Sillén, U., & Hellström, A. (2013). Urinary bladder control during the first 3 years of life in healthy children in Vietnam: A comparison study with Swedish children. *Journal of Pediatric Urology, 9*(6), 700–706.

Duong, T., Jansson, U., & Hellström, A. (2013). Vietnamese mothers' experiences with potty training procedure for children from birth to 2 years of age. *Journal of Pediatric Urology, 9*(6), 808–814.

Earhart, J., & Zamora, I. (2015). Achievement together: The development of an intervention using relationship-based strategies to promote positive learning habits. *Infants and Young Children, 28*(1), 32–45.

El-Sheikh, M., & Sadeh, A. (2015). Sleep and development: Introduction to the monograph. *Monographs of the Society for Research in Child Development, 80*, 1–14.

Erikson, E. (1950). *Childhood and society.* New York: Norton.

Fees, B., Fischer, E., Haar, S., & Crowe, L. (2015). Toddler activity intensity during indoor free-play: Stand and watch. *Journal of Nutrition Education and Behavior, 47*(2), 170–175.

Ferber, R. (1985). *Solve your child's sleep problems.* New York: Fireside.

Fernald, A., Marchman, V., & Weisleder, A. (2013). SES differences in language processing skill and vocabulary are evident at 18 months. *Developmental Science, 16*(2), 234–248.

Frank, K., & Esbensen, A. (2015). Fine motor and self-care milestones for individuals with Down syndrome using a retrospective chart review. *Journal of Intellectual Disability Research, 59*(8), 719–729.

Godoy, L., Carter, A., Silver, R., Dickstein, S., & Seifer, R. (2014). Infants and toddlers left behind: Mental health screening and consultation in primary care. *Journal of Developmental & Behavioral Pediatrics, 35*(5), 334–343.

Gottman, J., Katz, L., & Hooven, C. (1996). Parental meta-emotion philosophy and the emotional life of families: Theoretical models and preliminary data. *Journal of Family Psychology, 10*(3), 243–268.

Green, S., Caplan, B., & Baker, B. (2013). Maternal supportive and interfering control as predictors of adaptive and social development in children with and without developmental delays. *Journal of Intellectual Disability Research, 58*(8), 691–703.

Halim, M., & Ruble, D. (2010). Gender identity and stereotyping in early and middle childhood. In J.C. Chrisler, D.R. McCreary (Eds.), *Handbook of Gender Research in Psychology*, New York: Springer.

Halim, M., Ruble, D., Tamis-LeMonda, C., Zosuls, K., Lurye, L., & Greulich, F. (2014). Pink frilly dresses and the avoidance of all things "girly": Children's appearance rigidity and cognitive theories of gender development. *Developmental Psychology, 50*(4), 1091–1101.

Hart, B., & Risley, T. *(1995). Meaningful differences in the everyday experience of young American children.* Baltimore, MD: *Brookes.*

Ho, J. (2015). Bicultural children: What parents and teachers should know. *Childhood Education, 91*(1), 35–40.

Hoff, E. (2013). Interpreting the early language trajectories of children from low-SES and language minority homes: Implications for closing achievement gaps. *Developmental Psychology, 49*(1), 4–14.

Hodges, S., Richards, K., Gorbachinsky, I., & Krane, L. (2014). The association of age of toilet training and dysfunctional voiding. *Research and Reports in Urology, 6*, 127–130.

Hopkins, E., Dore, R., & Lillard, A. (2015). Do children learn from pretense? *Journal of Experimental Child Psychology, 130*, 1–18.

Hudson, S., Leviciks, P., Down, K., Nicholls, R., & Wake, M. (2015). Maternal responsiveness predicts child language at ages 3 and 4 in a community based sample of slow-to-talk toddlers. *Journal of Language & Communication Disorders, 50*(1), 136–142.

Johansson, E., Hagströmer, M., Svensson, V., Ek, A., Forssén, M., Nero, H., & Marcus, C. (2015). Objectively measured physical activity in two-year-old children—levels, patterns and correlates. *International Journal of Behavioral Nutrition and Physical Activity, 12*(3), 1–7. doi: 10.1186/s12966-015-0161-0.

John, A., Halliburton, A., & Humphrey, J. (2013). Child–mother and child–father play interaction patterns with preschoolers. *Early Child Development and Care, 183*(3–4), 483–497.

Johnson, L., Radesky, J., & Zuckerman, B. (2013). Cross-cultural parenting: Reflections on autonomy and interdependence. *Pediatrics, 131*(4), 631–633.

Kochanska, G., & Sanghag, K. (2014). A complex interplay among the parent–child relationship, effortful control, and internalized, rule-compatible conduct in young children: Evidence from two studies. *Developmental Psychology, 50*(1), 8–21.

Kwon, K., Han, S., Jeon, H., & Bingham, G. (2015). Mothers' and fathers' parenting challenges, strategies, and resources in toddlerhood. *Early Childhood Development and Care, 183*(3–4), 415–429.

Lansford, J. (2014). Parents' aggression toward children and children's own aggression. *Parenting Across Cultures, 7*, 445–458.

Li, X., Zou, H., Liu, Y., & Zhou, Q. (2014). The relationships of family socioeconomic status, parent-adolescent conflict, and filial piety to adolescents' family functioning in Mainland China. *Journal of Child and Family Studies, 23*(1), 29–38.

Lillard, A. (2012). Preschool children's development in classic Montessori, supplemented Montessori, and conventional programs. *Journal of School Psychology, 50*(3), 379–401. doi:10.1016/j.jsp.2012.01.001.

Marotz, L., & Allen, K. (2016). *Developmental profiles: Pre-birth through adolescence.* Boston, MA: Cengage Learning.

McDonald, L., Wardle, J., Llewellyn, C., van Jaarsveld, C., & Fisher, A. (2014). Predictors of shorter sleep in early childhood. *Sleep Medicine, 15*(5), 536–540.

Meltzer, L., Plaufcan, M., Thomas, J., & Mindell, J. (2014). Sleep problems and sleep disorders in pediatric primary care: Treatment recommendations, persistence, and health care utilization. *Journal of Clinical Sleep Medicine, 10*(4), 421–426.

Miller, R., Dunsmore, J., & Smith, C. (2015). Effort control and parents' emotion socialization patterns predict children's positive social behavior: A person-centered approach. *Early Education and Development*, 26(2), 167–188.

Miller, A., Seifer, R., Crossin, R., & Lebourgeois, M. (2015). Toddler's self-regulation strategies in a challenge context are nap-dependent. *Journal of Sleep Research*, 24(3), 279–287.

Mindell, J., Sadeh, A., Kwon, R., & Goh, D. (2015). Relationship between child and maternal sleep: A developmental and cross-cultural comparison. *Journal of Pediatric Psychology*, 40(7), 689–696.

Mindell, J., Sadeh, A., Kwon, R., & Goh, D. (2013). Cross-cultural differences in the sleep of preschool children. *Sleep Medicine*, 14(12), 1283–1289.

Montgomery, P., & Wiggs, L. (2015). Definitions of sleeplessness in children with attention-deficit hyperactivity disorder (ADHD): Implications for mothers' mental state, daytime sleepiness and sleep-related cognitions. *Child: Care, Health and Development*, 41(1), 139–146.

Mortensen, J., & Barnett, M. (2015). Risk and protective factors, parenting stress, and harsh parenting in Mexican origin mothers with toddlers. *Marriage & Family Review*, 51(1), 1–21.

National Association for the Education of Young Children (NAEYC). (2009). Developmentally Appropriate Practice in Early Childhood Programs Serving Children from Birth through Age 8. Position Statement. Retrieved on April, 12, 2016, from http://www.naeyc.org/files/naeyc/file/positions/PSDAP.pdf.

National Sleep Foundation. (2015). Children and sleep. Retrieved on June 4, 2015 from http://sleepfoundation.org/sleep-topics/children-and-sleep.

Nelsen, J., Erwin, C., & Duffy, R. (2015). *Positive discipline: The first three years*. New York: Harmony Books.

Ngashangva, P., & Dutt, S. (2015). Profile of behavioural problems among children with intellectual and developmental disabilities. *Psychological Studies*, 60(1), 101–107.

Noble, K., Engelhardt, L., Brito, N., Mack, L., Nail, E., Angal, J., Barr, R., Fifer, W., & Elliot, A. (2015). Socioeconomic disparities in neurocognitive development in the first two years of life. *Developmental Psychobiology*, 57(5), 535–551.

Norris, D. (2014). Comparing language and literacy environments in two types of infant-toddler child care centers. *Journal of Early Childhood Education*, published online November 2014. doi: 10.1007/s10643-014-0679-9.

Palusci, V., & Covington, T. (2014). Child maltreatment deaths in the U.S. National Child Death Review case reporting system. *Child Abuse & Neglect*, 38(1), 25–36.

Parten, M. (1932). Social participation among preschool children. *Journal of Abnormal and Social Psychology*, 28(3), 136–147.

Pascalis, O., Loevenbruck, H., Quinn, P., Kandel, S., Tanaka, J., & Lee, K. (2014). On the links among face processing, language processing, and narrowing during development. *Child Development Perspectives*, 8(2), 65–70.

Piaget, J. (1927/1969). *The child's conception of time*. New York: Ballantine Books.

Porter, N. & Ispa, J. (2013). Mothers' online message board questions about parenting infants and toddlers. *Journal of Advanced Nursing*, 69(3), 559–568.

Rindermann, H., & Baumeister, A. (2015). Parents' SES vs. parental educational behavior and children's development: A reanalysis of the Hart and Risley study. *Learning and Individual Differences*, 37, 133–138.

Roberts, M., & Kaiser, A. (2015). Early intervention for toddlers with language delays: A randomized controlled trial. *Pediatrics*, 135(4), 686–693.

Robinson, M., & Neece, C. (2015). Marital satisfaction, parental stress, and child behavior problems among parents of young children with developmental delays. *Journal of Mental Health Research in Intellectual Disabilities*, 8(1), 23–46.

Rodriguez, E., & Tamis-LeMonda, C. (2011). Trajectories of the home learning environment across the first 5 years: Associations with children's vocabulary and literacy skills in prekindergarten. *Child Development*, 82(4), 1058–1075.

Satter, E. (2000). *Child of mine: Feeding with love and good sense*. Boulder, CO: Bull Publishing Company.

Schechter, D., Moser, D., Reliford, A., McCaw, J., Coates, S., Turner, J., Serpa, S., & Willheim, E. (2015). Negative and distorted attributions towards child, self, and primary attachment figure among posttraumatically stressed mothers: What changes with clinician assisted videofeedback exposure sessions (CAVES). *Child Psychiatry & Human Development*, 46(1), 10–20.

Schroeder, S., Richman, D., Abby, L., Courtemanche, A., & Oyama-Ganiko, R. (2014). Functional analysis outcomes and comparisons of direct observations and informant rating scales in the assessment of severe problems of infants and toddlers at-risk for developmental delays. *Journal of Developmental and Physical Disabilities, 26*(3), 325–334.

Sears, W., & Sears, M. (2005). *The baby sleep book: The complete guide to a good night's rest for the whole family.* New York, NY: Little, Brown, & Co.

Shewark, E., & Blandon, A. (2015). Mother's and father's emotion socialization and children's emotion regulation: A with-in family model. *Social Development, 24*(2), 266–284.

Society of Health and Physical Educators (SHAPE). (2009). Active Start: A statement of physical activity guidelines for children from birth to age 5. (2nd Ed.). Retrieved on December 15, 2015 from http://www.shapeamerica.org/standards/guidelines/activestart.cfm.

Staples, A., Bates, J., & Petersen, I. (2015). Bedtime routines in early childhood: Prevalence, consistency, and associations with nighttime sleep. *Monographs of the Society for Research in Child Development, 80,* 141–159. doi: 10.1111/mono.12149.

Stephens, N., Markus, H., & Phillips, L. (2014). Social class culture cycles: How three gateway contexts shape selves and fuel inequality. *Annual Review of Psychology, 65,* 611–634.

Takeuchi, H., Taki, Y., Hashizume, H., Asano, K., Asano, M., Sassa, Y., Yokota, S., Kotozaki, Y., Nouchi, R., & Kawashima, R. (2015). The impact of parent-child interaction on brain structures: Cross-sectional and longitudinal analyses. *Journal of Neuroscience, 4*(35), 2233–2245.

Tamis-LeMonda, C., Shannon, J., Cabrera, N., & Lamb, M. (2004). Fathers and mothers at play with their 2- and 3-year-olds: Contributions to language and cognitive development. *Child Development, 75*(6), 1806–1820.

Treiman, R., Schmidt, J., Decker, K., Robins, S., Levine, S., & Demir, O. (2015). Parent's talk about letters with their young children. *Child Development, 86*(5), 1406–1418.

Urban Child Institute. (2015). Baby's brain begins now: Conception to age 3.

Valicenti-McDermott, M., Lawson, K., Hottinger, K., Seijo, R., Schechtman, M., Shulman, L., & Shinnar, S. (2015). Parental stress in families of children with autism and other developmental disabilities. *Journal of Child Neurology, 30*(13), 1728–1735.

Vygotsky, L. (1978). The role of play in development. In, *Mind in society* (pp. 92–104). Cambridge, MA: Harvard University Press.

Wadhera, D., Phillips, E., Wilke, L., & Boggess, M. (2015). Perceived recollection of frequent exposure to foods in childhood is associated with adulthood liking. *Appetite, 89*(1), 22–32.

Walker, C., & Gopnik, A. (2014). Toddlers infer high-order relational principles in causal learning. *Psychological Science, 25*(1), 161–169.

Waugh, W., Brownell, C., & Pollock, B. (2015). Early socialization of prosocial behavior: Patterns in parents' encouragement of toddlers' helping in an everyday household task. *Infant Behavior and Development, 39,* 1–10.

Weisgram, E., Fulcher, M., & Dinella, L. (2014). Pink gives girls permission: Exploring the roles of explicit gender labels and gender-typed colors on preschool children's toy preferences. *Journal of Applied Developmental Psychology, 35*(5), 401–404.

Wen, J., Lu, Y., Cui, L., Bower, W., Rittig, S., & Djurhuus, J. (2014). Bladder function development and its urodynamic evaluation in neonates and infants less than 2 years old. *Neurourology & Urodynamics, 34*(6), 554–560.

Wiggins, S. (2014). Adult and child use of love, like, don't like and hate during family mealtimes. Subjective category assessments as food preference talk. *Appetite, 80,* 7–15.

Yao, C., & Rhodes, R. (2015). Parental correlates in child and adolescent physical activity: A meta-analysis. *International Journal of Behavioral Nutrition and Physical Activity, 12*(10), 2–38.

Yoon, Y., Newkirk, K., & Perry-Jenkins, M. (2015). Parenting stress, dinnertime rituals, and child well-being in working-class families. *Family Relations, 64*(1), 93–107.

Zero to Three. (2016). Coping with defiance. *Zero to Three.* Retrieved on September 12, 2016 from, https://www.zerotothree.org/resources/199-coping-with-defiance-birth-to-three-years.

Zosuls, K., Ruble, D., & Tamis-LeMonda, C. (2014). Self-socialization of gender in African American, Dominican immigrant, and Mexican immigrant toddlers. *Child Development, 85*(6), 2202–2217.

Parenting Preschool-Age Children

8

LEARNING OBJECTIVES

After reading the chapter, you will be able to:

8-1 Briefly discuss how culture influences children's growth and development.

8-2 Describe several activities that parents can use to promote children's cognitive, motor, language, and social-emotional development.

8-3 Explain why parents' positive attention is more effective than punishment for encouraging preschoolers' appropriate behavior.

naeyc Standards Linked to Chapter Content

1a, 1b, and 1c: Promoting child development and learning

2a, 2b, and 2c: Building family and community relationships

4a and 4b: Using developmentally effective approaches to connect with children and families

2 1/2 TO 6 YEARS

Preschoolers are known for their boundless energy, enthusiasm, and curiosity. They seem to be captivated by just about everything in their environment as evidenced by their endless "why," "who," "what," and "how come" questions: "Why is the sky blue?" "What is in that box?" "How come we have to eat now?" "Where are we going?" Their unique personalities begin to

continued on following page

emerge—charming and entertaining at times, obstinate and fiercely independent at others. Although they act with a considerable degree of self-confidence, they still need and often seek out adult reassurance. ■

8-1 Typical Growth and Development Overview

During the preschool years, children become increasingly sophisticated thinkers and doers. As their motor skills continue to advance, preschoolers are able to pursue and act upon their interests, build and manipulate objects, take things apart and put them back together, navigate riding toys, and create fine works of art. They develop a more sophisticated level of understanding that is reflected in their ability to anticipate, problem solve, imagine, communicate, and show empathy toward others. Parents continue to play an influential role in this process by creating learning experiences, guiding and supporting children's efforts, respecting each child's uniqueness, and serving as positive role models for children to emulate.

8-1a Growth

Preschoolers grow at a slow, steady pace. As a result, they require fewer calories (per pound of actual body weight) than they did as a toddler, and are usually interested in eating less food. They typically gain about 2 to 3 inches (5–7.6 cm) in height and approximately 3 to 5 pounds (1.4–2.3 kg) in weight each year, although rates for an individual child may vary due to genetic, health, and nutritional differences. A steady increase in height is a reliable indicator of the child's overall well-being. By the age of 3 years, boys typically reach approximately 53 percent of their adult height; girls reach about 57 percent. A preschooler's body begins to appear more streamlined as arms and legs grow longer and posture becomes more erect. Most 3-year-olds have a full set of baby teeth, which they often begin to lose at around age 5 years. They tend to have better distant than near vision, but overall acuity improves significantly by the time a child turns 5.

8-1b Developmental Tasks

Preschoolers are becoming increasingly aware that the world is a much larger place than they initially realized. Consequently, they have several important tasks to address during this stage in order to determine how they can best fit into a larger group (see Figure 8-1). However, because they are still in the preoperational stage, their thinking remains egocentric (Piaget, 1952). This makes it difficult for preschool-age children to consider other peoples' actions and desires objectively, or to understand that they may have feelings and/or beliefs that are different from their own. Preschoolers must also learn how to balance their desire for assertive control (Erikson's initiative versus guilt) with a willingness to play appropriately and cooperatively with other children. Learning to understand and accept the purpose of rules is an important step in this socialization process.

Although all children develop fundamental skills that are similar, the acquisition rate and pattern may be highly variable as a result of individual cultural, genetic, and environmental factors. Cultural values and beliefs shape parenting values and practices which, in turn, exert a strong influential effect on children's development. For example, American parents tend to encourage children to be independent and assertive;

in contrast, Japanese parents socialize their children to show respect and emotional restraint. Gabrell et al. (2015) noted that Chinese and American children responded differently to the same stressful task. Chinese children exhibited persistence and emotional self-control, whereas American children appeared less focused and were more likely to verbalize their frustration and disappointment. Similar observations have led many researchers to suggest that a child's home environment may be the most significant of those factors that determine what and how children learn (Biedinger, Becker, & Klein, 2015).

8-1c Early Identification and Intervention

It is often during the preschool years that undiagnosed health conditions and developmental delays and disorders become more apparent as children attempt to master increasingly complex tasks (see Figure 8-2). In general, parents are becoming more aware of the early signs of potential developmental problems and often 'just know' when their child's development is not progressing as expected. Teachers and service providers are in a unique position to also monitor children's development and to refer families when they believe there may be a problem. Health care providers typically include developmental screenings in their well-child checkups. The result of these combined efforts has led to significant improvements in the early identification of children who may require in-depth evaluation and support services.

Vision and hearing disorders are among the most common problems that affect preschool-age children. If left untreated, they can have a profound negative effect on learning (ASHA, 2016; NEI, 2016). Speech and language problems, especially those associated with autism spectrum disorder, hearing loss, and difficulty expressing and understanding language also become more apparent during this stage. Any concerns about children's mental health (e.g., anxiety, depression, dramatic mood swings, self-injury), or the persistence of challenging behaviors (e.g., defiance, poor self-regulation, aggression) require professional evaluation. The early identification of developmental disorders and initiation of intervention support services have repeatedly been shown to improve the outcomes for children (Vinh et al., 2016; Spencer, Petersen, & Adams, 2015).

8-2 Supporting the Preschool Child's Development

Healthy development during the preschool years is dependent upon children having access to nutritious food, getting adequate sleep, receiving appropriate medical care, engaging in physical activity, and growing up in safe learning environments. The importance of meeting children's needs in these areas is considered so vital that many countries have identified them as national health priorities and addressed them in large-scale public health initiatives. The World Health Organization (WHO) is also actively engaged in raising international awareness about ways to improve children's health so that they are able to reach their developmental potential.

8-2a Cognitive and Language Development

Brain development during the preschool years is concentrated on "growth, expansion, construction, and blossoming that will later be pruned and tuned with maturation and experience" (Brown & Jernigan, 2012, p. 18). In other words, as preschoolers explore their environment and complete tasks, they use many brain regions (growth). Over time, the brain becomes more efficient and requires fewer regions to be activated in order to complete the same task. Areas of the brain associated with processing visual, touch, and taste sensations begin to decrease in volume; at the same time, regions in the temporal and frontal lobes increase in size (Brown & Jernigan, 2012).

The temporal lobe is associated with hearing and speech comprehension. Continued brain maturation improves the preschool-age child's ability to respond to progressively complex questions (e.g., who, what, where, how many) and reciprocate during social exchanges. Furthermore, children begin to recognize that sentences consist of words and words are formed with letters that have sounds. Vocabulary continues to increase significantly, from 300–1000 words at age 3 years to 1500 words or more by age 5 years. Preschool-age children have speech that becomes more intelligible and complex, they converse in longer sentences, ask many questions, use prepositions correctly, add information to what others say, and begin to use past tense verbs more appropriately.

The frontal lobe is associated with higher order cognitive processes, regulation of thoughts and emotions, planning actions, and goal-directed behavior; development in this region continues into early adulthood. As a result, preschoolers are better able than toddlers to wait their turn, complete two-step directions, and calm down when upset. Children who have neurological disorders, such as fetal alcohol syndrome, are likely to demonstrate poorer skills in these areas because of abnormal brain development (Fuglestad et al., 2015).

According to Piaget (1952), preschoolers' thinking is in the preoperational stage. They understand that they can influence their environment and act intentionally, but their thinking is not always logical. They are able to think in a symbolic manner (e.g., using

Photo 8-1 Parents can encourage children's cognitive development by providing interesting and novel learning activities and experiments.

one item to represent another), grasp simple numerical (e.g., most/fewest, short/longest) and spatial concepts (e.g., over, under, on top of), and begin to correctly distinguish between the past, present, and future. However, preschoolers are unable to focus on more than one task at a time. They also tend to jump to conclusions because they have not yet developed higher order reasoning abilities. As a result, they engage in **magical thinking** to self-explain actions or events that they are not able to comprehend. For example, a child who is lying in bed and hears a crashing sound coming from his closet may believe that there is a monster or ghost making the noise when, in fact, the sound was caused by a box falling off of a shelf.

Preschoolers remain rather egocentric and often have difficulty appreciating or accepting another person's viewpoint. As a result, parents may encounter considerable frustration in their interactions with preschoolers because of the mismatch between children's language skills, their inability to process information in a logical manner, and their desire to complete tasks independently. For example, a parent may recognize a more efficient way to build a structure and present a rationale to the child who rejects the information because he is not able to grasp or accept a perspective that is different from his own. However, as preschoolers continue to mature, they begin to understand that people can have different thoughts, feelings, and beliefs. This ability is referred to as the **theory of mind**. For example, a child may observe a peer fall and scrape her knee, imagine himself in the situation and, as a result, offer to help or ask the girl if she is okay. Imagining oneself in someone else's situation and thinking about their feelings is an important building block for the development of empathy.

Children learn through a variety of methods, including observing others, but their cognitive abilities may restrict what they are able to understand. For example, 4-year-olds, but not 3-year-olds, are able to observe an adult completing a task, such as sorting visually identical objects by weight, and generalize the abstract rules that were observed to a novel task (Wang, Meltzoff, & Williamson, 2015). This ability occurs because 4-year-olds are beginning to understand that objects can have different internal properties even when they look alike.

Cognitive development is influenced by parenting behaviors and opportunities that encourage children to interact with their environment in increasingly complex ways (Suggestions for Parents 8-1). Children are more likely to develop higher level cognitive skills when caregivers respond contingently to their cues, and are warm, accepting, and understanding of their needs (Merz et al., 2015). Caregiver behaviors, such as these, facilitate advanced cognitive skill development by encouraging children's exploratory efforts and allowing them to take the lead.

magical thinking a belief that wishes or desires can cause things to happen.

theory of mind the ability to imagine, understand, explain, or predict the thoughts, beliefs, intentions, and emotions of others.

Responsive Parenting

Four-year-old Janeene was angry with her father because he would not let her watch her favorite television show, and she wished that he would go away. Shortly thereafter, her father left the house following an argument between her parents. Janeene ran to her room and began to cry because she believed that she had caused her parents to argue and her father's departure. Why would Janeene think that she was responsible for these events? How would you advise her parents to respond?

Early Childhood Education. High quality early care and education is associated with better cognitive and achievement scores and social-emotional skills, with the most pronounced improvements occurring among low-income children (Executive Office of the President of the United States, 2014). Comprehensive programs that offer support to preschoolers and their parents have added benefits to families. For example, Benzies and colleagues (2014) evaluated a two-generation preschool program that included preschool education, transportation, nutrition, health and developmental assessments, parenting and life skills education, and family counseling. The authors

Activities to Promote Cognitive and Language Development

- Provide access to more challenging materials, such as puzzles, pegboards, counting, matching, and sorting activities.

- Engage in shared reading. Comment on pictures, encourage the child to talk about the story and pictures, elaborate on what the child says.

- Encourage creativity by using objects for different purposes, such as using a paper towel tube as a guitar or fire hose.

- Involve children in completing simple household responsibilities, such as setting the table, putting water in the dog's bowl, carrying groceries into the house.

- Encourage exploration of the environment. Have children inspect and describe what they see and are doing. Play the "I spy" game ("I spy something red and round.")

- Work on simple science and math activities together, such as determining if a bigger or smaller ice cube melts faster; have children help with measuring and mixing ingredients.

- Provide materials for coloring, painting, writing, and cutting.

- Play games that emphasize word sounds. For example, say a word slowly like a turtle—have the child guess the word or identify the first letter sound.

- Talk about past, current, and future events. Encourage children to ask questions and describe their feelings.

- Build on what children say during conversations, and incorporate more complex vocabulary and relationships (e.g., cause-effect, categories).

Photo 8-2 Preschool programs should reflect a balance between structured preacademic activities and play-based discovery.

found that not only did children show improvements in language and global development, but parents also showed better self-esteem, use of community resources, and stability of the home environment for as long as 7 years after completing the program. The positive effects attributed to early childhood education, especially for low income children, have given impetus to including and expanding early education programs in public schools.

Quality early care and education typically includes some focus on academics, as well as on children's social-emotional, language, and motor skill development. However, there has been controversy regarding the amount of emphasis that should be placed on academic training versus play-based learning (see "Trending Now: Focus on Academics in Early Childhood Education"). A crucial objective during the early years is to help young children develop positive attitudes toward learning and to feel good about themselves in the process. For this reason, it is important that parents consider the goals and philosophy of any early childhood program they are considering to determine if it offers the right approach for their child.

Technology and Electronic Media. Young children are increasingly exposed to various types of electronic media including television, computers, video games, tablets, and smart phones. The effects of media on development are mixed and depend upon the media content, the frequency of use, and amount of parental involvement. Federal regulatory efforts have had mixed results in shaping the industry. For example, the Children's Television Act (1990) was passed in an effort to regulate the design and content of programs that targeted children, but it was never enforced. The National

There continues to be debate over the amount of emphasis that should be placed on teaching academic skills versus learning through play in early childhood education programs. Some parents believe that preschool-age children should develop social-emotional skills that will prepare them for learning in kindergarten, whereas others believe that preschool should be more structured and teach children specific early academic skills to give them an intellectual advantage (Lewis-Brown, 2015). Parents who advocate the teaching of academics may be responding to the rise in high-stakes testing and increased expectations in elementary schools resulting from a "push-down" kindergarten curriculum (Harkins, 2015). For example, although implementation of the Common Core Standards for K-12 clarifies what children should be learning at each grade level, it has placed greater pressure on teachers to meet accountability standards and less emphasis on children's social-emotional skill development. Thus, some preschool parents have expressed concerns about whether or not their child will be ready for the ever-increasing kindergarten expectations. This raises the question as to whether early childhood education programs should increase their focus on teaching academic skills.

Some researchers have noted that although academically-oriented early childhood programs may produce higher initial academic scores, the advantage tends to fade over time and, in some case, even reverse itself. In addition, children who are products of these programs often demonstrate poorer social-emotional skills (Gray, 2015). Researchers have also hypothesized that when children lack play-based interactions with their peers, they are less likely to develop personal responsibility and problem-solving skills. Bell et al. (2016) noted that children in Head Start who engaged in peer interactions and play-based learning achieved the highest academic and social-emotional skills; children who experienced low levels of peer-play interactions had significantly poorer academic and social-emotional skills.

Parents may feel pressured to choose one or the other philosophical approach, but many experts note that this should not be about an either/or decision. They argue that early childhood programs should reflect a balance between structured academic activities and play-based discovery (Harkins, 2015). Preschool-age children need opportunities to be creative and to refine and expand basic developmental skills in addition to acquiring factual information (Snow, 2011). Interactive and hands-on experiences, as opposed to sitting still, memorizing, and completing worksheets, best support this type of learning. Many questions remain about the most effective ways to encourage development through play and direct instruction. For example, what skills should be taught using direct instruction? How much unstructured play time should children be given? How can teachers best scaffold learning during play?

Ready to Learn Act (1993, and amended in 1996) outlined specific criteria (e.g., time program was aired, program length, learning objectives that met children's learning or informational needs) for programs that were designated as educational, and required stations to broadcast at least three additional hours of educational programming per week. Examples of programs that meet the educational programming criteria include *Sesame Street*, *Bill Nye the Science Guy* (now on Netflix), *Super Why!*, *Daniel Tiger's Neighborhood*, *Between the Lions*, and *The Electric Company*. High quality programs such as these are associated with positive outcomes for preschool children. For example, Kearney and Levine (2015) found that children who watched *Sesame Street* were more likely to progress through school at an appropriate rate for their age. This effect was particularly significant for boys, African American children, and those from economically disadvantaged areas.

Technology and media used in moderation can facilitate children's cognitive learning and social abilities. The National Association for the Education of Young Children, in collaboration with the Fred Rogers Center for Early Learning and Children's Media (2012), issued a position statement that outlines principles for the appropriate use of technology with young children. These principles emphasize the need for caregivers to carefully select technology and media to ensure that they are developmentally appropriate for individual children; monitor children's use of the tool; use interactive media to support children's learning, creativity, and exploration; connect use of media to other activities that encourage interaction between children and adults; intentionally integrate use of technology into daily routines to extend learning; and to provide access to assistive technology for children with special needs. Furthermore, children's early exposure to technology can help them begin to develop digital literacy skills which are becoming increasingly important to have in many careers (NAEYC, 2012). For example, a child must learn to navigate using a mouse or touch screen before they can use a software program to trace letters or select the correct answer to a math problem.

Although technology and media can have beneficial outcomes for children, caution is warranted, especially when the media is passive or non-interactive. For example, preschoolers who live in homes where the television is left on, whether or not it is being watched, and view programs in the evening are less likely to get sufficient quality sleep (Natahanson & Fries, 2014). Preschool children are most likely to be misled when viewing programs that use special effects or other ways of altering reality and involve real people (as opposed to cartoons), because they have difficulty determining if what they see on television is real or fantasy (Li, Boguszewski, & Lillard, 2015). Furthermore, children who view physically aggressive models in the media are more likely to exhibit similar aggressive behavior, especially when the behaviors are reinforced (e.g., a superhero punches a villain and is rewarded). They are also more likely to show increases in relational aggression, particularly if the programs that are viewed model and reinforce indirect aggression or require young children to follow a plot—young children are more likely to attend to the aggressive behaviors and not to how the problem was solved (Ostrav, Gentile, & Mullins, 2013). Videogame exposure is also associated with increased hyperactive behavior in preschool children; however, the negative impact is lessened when parents are involved and responsive (Linebarger, 2015). Nathanson and colleagues (2014) outlined three additional reasons why media viewing may be detrimental during early childhood:

1. Many programs aimed at children are fast-paced, leading children to reactively respond to the changes and thereby discouraging any processing that accompanies thoughtful actions.

2. Background television causes children to continuously orient towards the television which interferes with their play. In addition, having the television on may distract caregivers and limit their interactions with children.

3. Television exposure may be most detrimental to young children when certain synaptic connections are forming in the brain.

The Council on Communications and Media (2015) recommends that:

- children have less than 1 or 2 hours of entertainment screen time per day
- parents create "screen free" zones at home (e.g., TVs and other electronic devices are removed from bedrooms, television is turned off during meals)
- parents monitor the media that children use
- parents co-view and discuss media content with their child

Preschool children are more likely to respond to restrictive parental mediation (e.g., setting rules for the amount of television exposure, the type of shows that can be watched) as opposed to active mediation (Coyne et al., 2014). Active mediation, or talking about show content, may be less beneficial when programs include inappropriate behaviors because children's attention is directed to the antisocial messages, which increase the potential to learn about, and develop, undesirable behaviors. In addition, parental controls should be set on all television remotes, handheld devices, and computers to decrease the likelihood that children will access inappropriate content.

In general, it is recommended that parents select media that is developmentally appropriate, portrays appropriate and prosocial behaviors, and emphasizes positive messages. Parents can build on the prosocial messages and learning objectives by introducing a game, modeling appropriate coping and good sportsmanship, and reinforcing the child's use of these skills after watching a segment on being a good sport. Or, a parent may take the child on a scavenger hunt to find bugs and plants that were discussed in a science episode.

8-2b Social-Emotional Development

According to Erikson (1963), preschoolers experience a conflict between initiative and guilt. Through their interactions with peers and adults, children begin to learn about social roles and how to take risks by initiating control and seeing tasks through to completion. They gradually gain a better understanding about how routines, rules, and adult expectations operate, and how they are expected to fit in. Children who successfully resolve these conflicts gain a sense of pride, self-confidence, and purpose. Those who are less successful may experience greater inhibition, self-doubt, and peer rejection.

Although older toddlers began to include peers in their play activities, preschoolers become more interactive and begin to establish close relationships with one another. Some may even begin to have a best friend. Peer acceptance is important to a child's mental health, and is influenced by the way that parents and teachers provide opportunities and support for positive, reciprocal relationships. Brighi et al. (2015) examined reciprocal peer nominations in preschoolers, and found that children who received a greater number of nominations from their peers had higher scores in social orientation, positive emotionality, motor activity, and linguistic skills. The findings also indicated that children tend to select peers who share similar qualities, and that children who exhibited symptoms of social withdrawal were more likely to play alone and be isolated by their peers.

Photo 8-3 Children begin to develop closer friendships during the preschool years.

These observations have important implications for parents and teachers because they suggest that improved social relationships can be achieved through the creation of environments that support children's independence and development of specific skills, such as cooperation, helping others, and resolving conflict (see Figure 8-3). Although preschool-age children resort to less physical aggression, they are more likely to engage in emotional outbursts, name calling, and excluding others from play. Because these reactions can have a negative effect on peer relationships, it is important that parents and caregivers provide children with constructive feedback and guide them in learning self-control and positive emotional expression. Children can be taught specific social-emotional skills through a combination of instruction, modeling of the skill, practicing it in pretend situations, prompting children to use the skills in situations with peers, and providing praise when they use the targeted skill appropriately.

Self-Concept. Self-concept refers to the way people view themselves in comparison to others (self-image) and the value they place on their own self-worth (self-esteem). During the preschool years, children begin to develop a more consistent self-concept, describing themselves in terms of concrete characteristics, such as appearance, habits, and possessions. More recently, researchers have found that preschoolers also have some understanding of their own psychological characteristics. Jia and colleagues (2015) identified three higher-order psychological self-concept qualities that preschool-age children possess:

1. Sociability: a view of the self as happy and approach-oriented in social situations as opposed to negative and withdrawn.

2. Control: a view of the self as behaviorally and emotionally controlled versus out-of-control.

3. Assurance: a view of the self as one who wants to achieve and is open to challenges as opposed to wanting easy, risk-free tasks.

Children's self-perceived assessments of these qualities were linked to how well they adapted in the school setting. For example, children who rated themselves high in sociability were less likely to demonstrate internalizing behavioral problems and to have higher social competence. Boys who perceived themselves as having greater social control

Figure 8-3 Typical Social-Emotional Behaviors and Strategies to Encourage Development

Age	Typical Social-Emotional Behaviors	Strategies to Encourage Development
3 Years	• May understand taking turns, but not always willing to do so • Observes and joins in play with peers for short periods of time • May be aggressive if toys or other possessions are taken away • Eager to please and laughs often • May have nightmares or fears about the dark, monsters, or being left somewhere • Talks to self and engages in make-believe play	• Model and praise appropriate turn-taking • Play games that encourage children to take turns • Provide bursts of high quality attention and praise prosocial behaviors • Elaborate on children's self-talk to reinforce ideas and problem solving • Acknowledge children's efforts • Encourage children's persistence toward achieving small goals • Provide a safe, secure base for exploration
4 Years	• Changes mood quickly and tantrums over minor frustrations • Establishes close relationships with playmates and is more cooperative with others • Bends or exaggerates the truth • Shows desire to do things independently, but becomes frustrated when problems arise • Uses more verbal than physical aggression • Takes pride in accomplishments	• Help children learn and practice positive ways to handle frustration • Provide opportunities to be around the same peers • Teach the importance of telling the truth and praise children when they are honest • Support children in labeling and communicating their feelings • Continue to provide children with a safe, secure base; acknowledge their efforts and persistence
5 Years	• Continues to develop close friendships • Is better able to share, cooperate, and take turns • Follows more complex directions • Has better self-control • Has fewer and less dramatic mood changes • Enjoys telling jokes and making others laugh • Continues to take pride in accomplishments	• Assist children with learning how to problem solve • Praise and provide attention when children follow directions, use prosocial behaviors with peers, and handle frustration or other emotions appropriately • Continue to provide children with a safe, secure base; acknowledge their efforts and persistence

Adapted from: Marotz & Allen (2016).

showed fewer externalizing problems. These findings illustrate how important positive self-concept is for children's mental health and their ability to gain peer acceptance.

Parenting style has also been closely linked to children's self-concept development. For example, LeCuyer and Swanson (2016) noted that African American and European children whose mothers followed an authoritative parenting style exhibited better social competence and had a more positive self-concept than other children. DiBiase and Miller (2015) observed that children in their cross-cultural study were more likely to develop a positive self-concept when their parents permitted an appropriate level of freedom, set clear expectations, used effective communication strategies, and maintained a balance between nurturing and controlling interactions.

self-esteem feelings about one's self-worth.

Self-esteem is a key component of a child's self-concept. Children who have positive self-esteem show more confidence in their abilities, increased self-acceptance, better social skills, and greater optimism than those who have a poor self-image. Although preschool-age children tend to have an overly positive view of themselves, their ideas gradually become more realistic as they develop cognitively, are better able to understand the meaning of experiences and feedback, and begin to make social comparisons (Lecompte et al., 2014).

Healthy attachments with primary caregivers set the stage for children's positive self-esteem development. These feelings influence the quality of children's social skills and, in turn, peer acceptance. Preschool-age children who have disorganized attachments with caregivers are more likely to exhibit poor self-esteem, experience peer rejection, and develop problems with anxiety and depression during adolescence (Groh et al., 2014; Lecompte et al., 2014).

Parents and caregivers can promote children's positive self-esteem through their warmth, acknowledgement of children's efforts, encouragement of children's persistence toward achieving small goals, and provision of sincere praise when children meet expectations. Preschool-age children's self-esteem development is also influenced by their increased awareness of the social world, and the nature of interactions that occur among people. For example, Clements et al. (2014) found that preschoolers who perceive high levels of interparental conflict, especially when the conflict is child-focused, unresolved, and expressed physically, are more likely to report low self-esteem and to experience an increase in behavioral problems. The authors hypothesized that declines in self-esteem may be related to children blaming themselves for the conflict or feeling that they are helpless in resolving it. These misled perceptions are directly related to the preschool-age child's concept of magical thinking. Thus, parents are encouraged to manage conflicts related to children in private, work to resolve their differences, and seek support when needed to improve family relationships.

Sibling Relationships. The birth of another child affects family system dynamics, and often leads to changes in the roles and expectations of its members. Although most children adapt well to the addition of a new brother or sister, there are steps that parents can take to ease children's transition (Suggestions for Parents 8-2). For example, involving older children in preparations for the baby's arrival, emphasizing the importance of their new role as a 'big' brother or sister, and enlisting their help with the infant's care make it

Suggestions for Parents 8-2

Helping Children Cope with the Birth of a Sibling

- Before the baby arrives:
  - Talk with children about the importance of their new role as a sibling.
  - Let children help with preparations. For example, involve them in picking out the color of bedding or making a picture for the baby.
  - Watch age-appropriate videos together and read books about becoming a big brother/sister.
- After the baby arrives:
  - Attend to children's good behaviors; give lots of praise, feedback, and attention.
  - Acknowledge children's feelings.
  - Do not allow hurtful behaviors.
  - Point out children's positive qualities (e.g., being gentle, being a good helper by retrieving a blanket to keep baby warm).
  - Involve children in the infant's care.
  - Set limits and rules (e.g., only adults can pick up the infant).
  - Show and provide specific praise for gentle interactions.
  - Set aside time to spend alone with older children.

⌄ Professional Resource Download

Photo 8-4 Children adjust better to the addition of a sibling when they are involved in the infant's care and continue to receive high-quality attention from parents.

easier for children to accept change. It is also important that parents are sensitive to the older child's needs and continue to share quality time with her. For example, before feeding the infant, a new mother may help her preschooler begin an activity (e.g., art, building, puzzle) and then continue to comment on the child's actions and good behavior during the feeding; then, when the baby falls asleep, the mother and preschooler can play a quiet game together.

Preschool-age children desire parents' undivided attention, and may experience initial feelings of loss and resentment when they are forced to share it with another person. However, the way that parents handle the arrival and introduction of a new baby sister or brother can have positive or negative effects on children's long-term relationships. Children's adjustment is more likely to be positive toward a sibling when parents treat them with warmth and sensitivity, include them in the sibling's care, and spend quality time together.

Sibling conflict is more common among first- and second-born children and between same gender children, especially boys. However, Walton and Ingersoll (2015) noted that siblings of children with developmental disabilities, such as autism spectrum disorder, displayed lower rates of involvement and less aggression toward one another than is often reported among brothers and sisters who do not have a disability. Children who believe that a sibling is being favored or receiving preferential treatment often exhibit increased sibling conflict and persistent jealousy (Jeannin & Leeuwen, 2015). Parental response to sibling rivalry, including praising appropriate interactions, setting clear rules and consequences for hurtful behavior, and helping children to identify peaceful solutions, can improve the quality of relationship that children experience with one another.

Moral Development. Preschoolers begin to develop an understanding of moral behavior through their interactions with others. They follow social and moral norms related to right and wrong because they are told to do so by parents, teachers, and other caregivers. They consider rules to be factual and unchangeable regardless of a person's intentions. Dahl and Kim (2014) outlined four different types of transgressions that preschoolers are able to judge as being wrong:

1. *Pragmatic*: actions that create an inconvenience for others, such as spilling something. These types of transgressions are most prevalent during the preschool years.

2. *Conventional*: behaviors that break a rule or disrupt social order, such as wearing pajamas to preschool because doing so may cause other children to want to do the same. Preschoolers are most likely to reference breaking rules.

3. *Prudential*: actions that create physical or psychological harm to one's self, such as sustaining a burn if a hot stove is touched despite parental warnings.

4. *Moral*: behaviors that create physical or psychological harm to others (e.g., he will get hurt if he jumps off of the swing), are an evaluation of the act (e.g., she is nice or mean), or refer to property ownership (e.g., the ball belongs to John). Preschool-age children are most likely to emphasize harm to others in their evaluation of moral dilemmas.

Younger preschoolers recognize pragmatic transgressions as being less serious than other types of moral behavior because they are not fully able to comprehend how the inconvenience may affect others (Dahl & Kim, 2014). Although preschoolers believe that they have the choice to make a moral or immoral decision, they tend to focus on outcomes that follow the rules and avoid harm to others (Chernyak & Kushnir, 2014). Preschoolers also begin to make decisions based on fairness and whether or not they believe that others are deserving. For example, Hamann and colleagues (2014) found that when 3-year-olds were given a collaborative task to complete—one in which one child was required to complete more work than the other—the children who received a larger reward for doing less work were more likely to share with their partner. However, children were less likely to share if the task was completed in a side-by-side arrangement with their partner. The authors highlighted the importance of peer collaboration for encouraging children to attend to norms of fairness.

Lying is also a common behavior during the preschool years because children do not always understand that it is wrong or how others are affected. Children may intentionally exaggerate the truth or lie to obtain something they want (e.g., a toy that another child has) or to avoid punishment (e.g., blame for an object that was broken). Rather than shaming or reprimanding preschoolers for lying, parents can use these instances to teach children about why it is important to be honest and truthful. They should also set a positive example by telling the truth, and praising children when they do admit to doing something that they know is wrong.

As preschoolers mature, they are better able to manage their emotions, develop a stronger sense of responsibility, and understand rules and other peoples' perspectives. As a result, they are also more likely to report wrongdoing and attempt to correct the problem (Bafuno & Camodeca, 2013). However, children's sense of responsibility and sensitivity to feelings of shame and guilt are highly socialized by cultural beliefs. For example, children are less likely to show signs of regret when adults are not present, which may be related to cultural beliefs that shaming is a way to teach social and moral development (Bafuno & Camodeca, 2013). Parents and caregivers can support children's development of moral reasoning by providing guidance and feedback on specific actions and relationships (e.g., it is not nice to hit friends) as opposed to focusing on global attributions (e.g., you are naughty).

Gender Identity. There are two main theories of gender identity development. First, social learning theory suggests that children learn to be male or female through their observations and imitations of same-gendered individuals. In addition, children are usually reinforced for behaving in a "correct" manner. For example, parents and teachers may be more accepting of boys' roughhousing and acting loudly than if girls were to do the same. Furthermore, boys and girls may be offered different toys or opportunities that further shape their gendered thoughts and behaviors.

Second, cognitive theories suggest that children actively construct ideas about what it means to be a boy or girl. Piaget (1952) believed that preschoolers develop schemas about stereotypical masculine and feminine roles and behavior appropriate for each gender. For example, they may create a schema that labels all firefighters and police officers as being male. If they encounter a female police officer, the new information would not fit into their existing schema. As a result, the schema would need to be modified through assimilation and accommodation processes.

By the age of 3 years, most children are able to correctly identify themselves as being either a boy or a girl. However, their gender determinations of other children are based primarily on physical appearance, such as hair length and clothing type. By the age of 4 and 5 years, children begin to understand that gender is established more on genitalia differences. Preschoolers maintain fairly rigid ideas about gender, and are likely to play only with

Responsive Parenting

Five-year-old Jordan's mother told him to put his dirty clothes in the laundry basket before going downstairs to play. A few minutes later, she saw Jordan playing with his trains and asked if he had put his clothes away. He replied that he did. Later in the morning, she noticed that his clothes were still lying on the floor in his bedroom. Why was Jordan not truthful, and how would you encourage Jordan's mother to respond?

Photo 8-5 Preschoolers become more aware of gender differences, with girls being more prone to gender stereotyping than boys.

same-gender peers and avoid cross-gender play. Researchers have noted that these childhood tendencies are fairly consistent across all cultures (Hamlin et al., 2013).

It is common for preschoolers to begin exploring their body parts and to be interested in looking at, or showing, them to others as they learn about gender differences. Their curiosity is likely to lead to questions about male and female differences, and pregnancy. Although parents and caregivers may find these questions challenging, it is important that they be answered in a calm, honest, and factual manner. In most instances, children are only looking for simple answers. Turning their questions around can be effective for determining exactly what a child knows and is interested in learning. For example, if a child asks, "Where do babies come from?" a parent might respond by saying, "Where do you think they come from?" If the child says she believes they come from the hospital, then a simple statement correcting this assumption may be all that the child wants and needs at this time. Many good books about gender, pregnancy, and appropriate sexual behavior are available that parents can read together with children. These opportunities also invite children to ask questions and, thereby, decrease the likelihood that they will receive inaccurate information from other sources.

Female preschoolers typically engage in more gender stereotyping than do males. Specifically, Baker and colleagues (2015) found that preschool girls are more likely than boys to say that only girls can be teachers or nurses and only boys can be police officers. The authors hypothesized that this finding may be due to the increased opportunities for socialization that girls receive, and that female gender norms are prescriptive (e.g., girls wear dresses) and related to traits (e.g., clothing colors, hair length), whereas male gender norms are proscriptive (e.g., boys *don't* wear dresses) and related to activities (e.g., playing basketball), which enable girls to assimilate information more easily.

The media also influences and reinforces children's gender stereotypical ideas. Boys who view superheroes are more likely to engage in male-stereotyped play (Coyne et al., 2014). These data point to the importance of exposing children to individuals in gender-incongruent positions in order to decrease gender stereotyping. Weisgram, Fulcher, and Dinella (2014) found that girls are more likely to play with masculine toys when the toys were pink. However, they note that even though girls may be more likely to play with these toys, it may increase, rather than decrease, stereotypes—that pink, for example, may signal a feminine way to play with toys and prohibit important masculine building skills. Interestingly, companies such as Lego have begun marketing toys to girls that are typically viewed as masculine by simply changing the toy's colors. Wong and Hines (2015) made similar observations, and suggested that eliminating gender-typical coloring of toys could increase gender-neutral play opportunities.

Researchers have also found that teachers' attitudes about gender roles can influence children's future academic achievements. For example, when preschool teachers held traditional gender role attitudes, boys showed lower motivation to read, which predicted poorer reading skills at the end of first grade (Wolter, Braun, & Hannover, 2015). Similarly, girls performed poorer on science and math tasks when focus was placed on traditional gender role expectations—that boys are better at math and science (Shenouda & Danovitch, 2014). In contrast, Simpson and Linder (2016) observed only minimal differences in teachers' math conversations with preschool boys and girls, and noted that any variations were more likely to be influenced by the classroom context (e.g., block area, dress-up play, science activity) in which they were occurring.

Fears. Fears are influenced by a variety of factors, including global events (e.g., war, terrorism, natural disasters), television and media (e.g., violent shows), and societal changes (e.g., increase in single-parent households) (Burnham, 2009). Young children are most likely to worry about the death of a parent, their own death, being attacked by animals, war, fire, being injected, natural disasters, and having bad dreams (Oghii, 2015).

Preschool-age children fear death more than anything else, in part, because it is a difficult concept for them to understand, and parents often avoid discussing it. From a cognitive perspective, children younger than age 5 years are not able to understand death as inevitable and permanent because these are abstract concepts. From a social perspective, children are often exposed to death differently today than in the past when families cared for ill members at home. As a result, death becomes an abrupt rather than gradual experience for which children can prepare. Some parents also believe that children should be shielded from illness and death in order to spare them from experiencing grief. However, avoiding the topic is not a healthy way to help children understand the reality and finality of death.

Children can be expected to respond in unique ways following a death, with some adjusting more readily than others depending upon their developmental stage. For example, infants may respond to such a loss by crying more often, clinging to caregivers, or having difficulty with sleep and eating. Preschoolers may show an increase in regressive behaviors, fears or fantasies related to guilt concerning the death, and fluctuating moods (e.g., anger, sadness, anxiety, outbursts). In addition, cultural and religious beliefs exert a strong socializing effect on children's ideas about death and how grief is to be expressed. For example, Asian Americans tend to internalize their feelings and appear stoic so that they are not seen as a burden to others and avoid the shame associated with losing control. In contrast, Puerto Ricans and Haitians are more likely to show intense hysterical emotions in public. White clothing is often worn by African-Americans as a sign of mourning in contrast to dark-colored clothing that is more typical at European-American funerals. Lee et al. (2014) also noted that cultural variations, such as naturalistic and supernatural explanations of death, were often depicted in children's books.

Open and honest discussions with children are beneficial for helping them to cope with death and avoid resorting to magical thinking explanations. A lack of information may add to children's fear and confusion about what may have caused a death, and worries about their own mortality. Parents can also help children by sharing their emotions (e.g., crying, feeling sad), providing simple and clear explanations, and answering their questions in a factual manner (Suggestions for Parents 8-3). Many of these same

Helping Children Cope with Death

- Provide simple, straightforward explanations about the death, funeral or memorial service, and what will happen to the body.
- Answer children's questions calmly. Parents can reverse their questions to better understand what the child is thinking and how to provide a developmentally appropriate answer.
- Be a good listener, and let children know that you are there to comfort them.
- Encourage children to express their feelings and ask questions without judgment.
- Share your feelings of grief and loss. It is okay for children to see that their parent is sad because this can be an effective way to teach them how family members can be supportive of one another.
- Be honest.
- Avoid euphemisms or expressions such as "gone to sleep," "watching over you," "went on a long trip," or "we lost Grandma" because children will interpret the information literally.
- Read books about death together.
- Help children find a way to say goodbye, such as drawing a picture, planting a tree, or lighting a candle.

⌄ Professional Resource Download

strategies can be used effectively to help children work through other difficult experiences, such as divorce, natural disasters, fears, and harm to self or others. Maintaining consistent routines and a positive relationship during times of transition also help children to make difficult adjustments.

Teaching children how to cope with fears, including death, at an early age is beneficial for reducing the frequency and intensity of fears, and promoting resilience to future stressors. The use of **inferential language** also supports children's reasoning skill development and ability to express difficult emotions (Merz et al., 2015). For example, parents and caregivers can help children to recognize their feelings, use words to communicate emotions, challenge negative or unrealistic thoughts, and focus on positive behaviors (Leppma, Szente, & Brosch, 2015). Parents can also explain the difference between reality and imagination, define words at an age-appropriate level, discuss cause and effect, and provide honest and concrete information relative to fears; in addition, they can model appropriate ways to stay calm, and teach specific behaviors such as diaphragmatic breathing to help children gain control when they are faced with a frightening situation.

> **inferential language** includes connecting the present to past events, talking about feelings, summarizing, predicting, explaining cause and effect, and defining words.

8-2c Motor Development

Although preschool-age children have mastered most basic gross motor skills, their strength, coordination, and accuracy in performing these actions continues to increase. Stability or balance, locomotion (e.g., jumping and hopping), and object-control (e.g., catching and throwing) pave the way for the development of more complex movements (Foulkes et al., 2015). Furthermore, improved motor skill competence is associated with better physical fitness and lower rates of childhood obesity (Vlahov et al., 2014; Rodrigues et al., 2015). Researchers have noted that preschoolers who have poor motor coordination are at increased risk for emotional-behavioral problems, such as aggression and withdrawal (King-Dowling et al., 2015). These antisocial behaviors may reflect the child's way of handling frustration associated with poor motor abilities.

Preschool-age children are also in the early stages of developing fine motor skills that are used in eating, dressing, drawing, cutting with scissors, building, and manipulating small items. These skills are important precursors of more advanced skills that children will use later on for reading, writing, numeracy, and self-care. Children growing up in higher socio-economic families often have more opportunities to practice fine and gross motor skills. As a result, their skills tend to be more advanced than those of children from lower-SES families (Morley et al., 2015). Kim et al. (2016) noted that children with developmental disabilities experienced better social and cognitive skills that were directly related to improvements in their fine, but not gross, motor skills.

It is important that children have ample developmentally appropriate structured and unstructured opportunities to practice their motor skills, given the significant influence they have on promoting overall development. For example, Piek et al. (2015) found that children's motor and social skills improved when they participated in a structured program that focused on motor skills (gross and fine motor) as well as social-emotional development. The authors hypothesized that organized program activities encouraged children, who may otherwise withdraw from participation in physical activity opportunities, to interact in positive play contexts with their peers. Parents and teachers play a valuable role in facilitating children's motor development by creating safe environments (e.g., equipment, supplies, activities), providing encouragement and instruction, and safeguarding their well-being through quality supervision.

Parents can easily incorporate age- and developmentally-appropriate motor skills into children's daily activities. For example, they can create opportunities for 3-year-olds to climb up stairs, kick large balls, jump in place, build higher towers, carry containers, and practice controlling crayons and other writing utensils. They can encourage 4-year-olds to practice walking a straight line, hopping on one foot, climbing ladders, running and maneuvering around obstacles, copying shapes and letters, holding crayons with correct grasp, and threading beads on a string. They can give

5-year-olds opportunities to practice walking backward, skipping, balancing on one foot, coloring in the lines, fitting puzzle pieces into the correct spaces, and cutting paper with scissors.

Gender differences in preschool children's motor skill competence provide opportunities for targeted instruction. Specifically, boys tend to show better object-control skills, and girls perform better on running, hopping, and galloping tasks. Researchers have also noted that girls typically demonstrate fine motor skills that are more advanced than those exhibited by boys (Morley et al., 2015). In part, these differences may be related more to the types of games and physical activities that boys and girls typically engage in (i.e., cultural and environmental factors) than to any physiological differences (Foulkes et al., 2015). Parents can address this matter by modeling and playing active games (e.g., baseball, soccer, golf) with girls that promote skills typically mastered earlier by boys, and vice versa (e.g., coloring, cooking, making clay figures with boys).

By the end of the preschool years, children usually show a hand preference, with the majority of children being right-handed. It is interesting to note that although left-handed preschool children may reach and use utensils with their left hand, they tend to use their right hand when pointing and making symbolic gestures (Cochet et al., 2015). Once established, hand preference remains stable as children grow into adulthood (Gonzalez, Flindall, & Stone, 2014).

Photo 8-6 Parents can encourage motor skill development by participating in fun play activities with children.

8-2d Physical Activity

Although preschool-age children have a natural propensity for being physically active, researchers are finding that they are becoming increasingly sedentary. Senso et al. (2015) tracked the activity patterns of preschool children who were at-risk for being overweight or obese and found that they engaged in moderately vigorous physical activity (MVPA) only 2–8 minutes per hour, and spent between 27 and 35 minutes per hour in sedentary behavior. These totals are in sharp contrast to the Society of Health and Physical Educators (SHAPE) (2015) recommendations that children 2 years of age and older engage in at least 60 minutes of moderately vigorous physical activity daily (see Figure 8-4). Pate et al. (2014) noted that less than 50 percent of children enrolled in preschool programs achieved the daily physical

---

Figure 8-4 SHAPE's Physical Activity Guidelines for Preschool-Age Children

Guideline 1. Preschoolers should accumulate at least 60 minutes of structured physical activity each day.

Guideline 2. Preschoolers should engage in at least 60 minutes—and up to several hours—of unstructured physical activity each day, and should not be sedentary for more than 60 minutes at a time, except when sleeping.

Guideline 3. Preschoolers should be encouraged to develop competence in fundamental motor skills that will serve as the building blocks for future motor skillfulness and physical activity.

Guideline 4. Preschoolers should have access to indoor and outdoor areas that meet or exceed recommended safety standards for performing large-muscle activities.

Guideline 5. Caregivers and parents in charge of preschoolers' health and well-being are responsible for understanding the importance of physical activity and for promoting movement skills by providing opportunities for structured and unstructured physical activity.

Source: Society of Health and Physical Educators (SHAPE) (2009).

activity recommendations. The results of these and similar studies have important implications for parents and teachers, and the need to incorporate additional physical activity into children's daily schedules.

Children derive many positive benefits from physical activity, including weight control, improved motor coordination and fitness, increased self-confidence, fewer behavioral problems, and increased bone strength and development (Foweather et al., 2015; Jackowski et al., 2015; Copeland et al., 2012). However, not all children have access to safe places to play. For example, although Latino mothers in farmworker families believe that physical activity is important for their children, they are reluctant to let them play outdoors due to concerns about chemical and environmental hazards, unfamiliar neighborhoods, and distance to playgrounds and parks (Grzywacz et al., 2014). Other parents have cited similar concerns, such as activities being located too far away to walk to, strangers and unsafe neighborhoods, and high traffic volume in the recreational areas (Faulkner et al., 2015; Kercood et al., 2015). City planners are taking note of these concerns and attempting to address them as new parks and open green spaces in urban areas are being designed (Wang et al., 2016).

Daily physical activity is equally important for children who have developmental disabilities as it is for those who are developing along a typical path (Klein & Hollingshead, 2015). Ziereis and Jansen (2015) determined that physical activity was an effective intervention for children with ADHD when it was used alone or in conjunction with medication. Other researchers also have found that children with disabilities showed improved focus and cognitive performance, improved motor skills, and a decrease in inappropriate behaviors when they participated in daily physical activity (Gawrilow et al., 2016). Although many children who have disabilities express a desire to participate in physical activities, the opportunities available to them are often limited (Must et al., 2015; Bloemen et al., 2014). Continued efforts are needed to modify activities and provide appropriate equipment so that children of all abilities can participate.

It is important that parents and teachers help children to enjoy and engage in an active lifestyle. Teachers can incorporate physical activity throughout the curriculum and reduce the amount of sedentary time that children spend during the day. Parents can set a positive example by maintaining their own daily physical activity routine and planning activities that are appropriate for, and include, children (Suggestions for Parents 8-4). An active lifestyle is easy for children to maintain when it is fun, safe, and done together with other family members and/or peers.

Suggestions for Parents 8-4

Fun Physical Activities with Children

Preschool-age children enjoy:

- Tossing, catching, and kicking balls of all sizes (a plastic grocery bag stuffed with newspapers with ends tied makes a safe 'ball' alternative for use indoors).
- Dancing, waving scarves, or imitating different animal movements to music.
- Turning a walk into a scavenger hunt, or finding and naming objects along the way that are of the same color (e.g., green grass, green house, green bug, green car).
- Helping with household activities (e.g., raking leaves, carrying groceries into the house, pulling weeds, planting a garden, washing the car, taking the dog for a walk).
- Building an obstacle course with chairs, pillows, ramps, and cardboard boxes.
- Playing tag, hide and seek, hopscotch, and kickball.
- Swimming, playing in the park.

Introducing Children to New Foods

- Offer new foods when children are hungry and more likely to try them.
- Involve children in preparations (e.g., grocery shopping, stirring, washing fruits and vegetables, helping to serve).
- Introduce only one new food at a meal and serve it along with other "favorites."
- Serve a child only a small amount (one bite, one teaspoon).
- Let the child watch you enjoying the food item.
- Talk about the food's properties: its color, shape, texture, where it grows.
- Ask what the child doesn't like about the food.
- Remember, new foods may need to be served multiple times before a child feels comfortable eating them.

8-2e Healthy Eating Behaviors

Optimal growth and development, illness reduction, energy, and long-term well-being are closely related to a nutritious diet. Adequate protein, vitamins, minerals, and approximately 1200 to 1400 calories are required by preschool-age children to support their continued growth and high energy needs. Because children are still in the process of forming lifelong eating patterns and food preferences, this is also an important time to introduce a wide variety of **nutrient-dense foods**, and to model healthy eating behaviors that they can emulate. However, convincing preschoolers to eat foods that are good for them is not always easy. Young children have a heightened sense of taste and texture that can deter their acceptance of unfamiliar foods, particularly fruits and vegetables (Fildes et al., 2016; Mennella, Reiter, & Daniels, 2016). Such items may need to be served ten or more times before children are willing to taste them (Suggestions for Parents 8-5).

Preschool-age children become better able to use eating utensils, pour liquids, and chew and swallow without choking (see Figure 8-5). Their appetite often fluctuates from day to day—they are seemingly ravenous one day and refuse most foods the next. Food preferences also change abruptly—a "favorite" food today may be rejected tomorrow. Preschoolers continue to have difficulty sitting still and remaining at the dinner table for very long, and may proceed to leave their chair as soon as they have finished eating.

nutrient-dense foods foods high in essential nutrients (e.g., protein, vitamins, minerals, fiber) and low in processed ingredients and empty calories.

Figure 8-5 Typical Preschool Eating Behaviors
Three-, four-, and five-year-olds:

- are able to feed themselves independently, especially when hungry
- pour juice and milk into a glass with fewer spills
- have distinct food likes and dislikes, and may adamantly refuse them if offered
- use eating utensils (e.g., use fork to spear food, a table knife to spread peanut butter)
- resort occasionally to eating with their hands, especially if tired or frustrated
- chatter frequently throughout meals and may forget to eat
- are easily distracted by activities in the room
- show interest in helping to prepare and serve meals and snacks

Adapted from: Marotz & Allen (2016).

Although parents may be tempted to stop children from leaving, it is important that they remember their role in the feeding process: adults plan, prepare, and serve nutritious foods, and decide when and where meals and snacks will be served; children decide what and how much they are willing to eat (Satter, 2000). Respecting these boundaries can instill trust and teach children how to regulate their food intake. Pressuring children to eat when they are no longer hungry is likely to increase mealtime conflict and long-term eating disorders (Ellis et al., 2016). Food should never be used as a reward because this approach can lead to similar problems.

Children with Special Needs. Children who have developmental disabilities often present parents with special feeding challenges (e.g., poor appetite due to medication, difficulty chewing or swallowing, increased need for particular nutrients, extreme food rejections). Parents may also need to address weight management issues with children who have some genetic disorders (e.g., Down syndrome, Prader-Willi syndrome, Fragile X syndrome), because they have a tendency to overeat and to gain excess weight (Nordstrøm et al., 2015). Children who have autism spectrum disorder are often willing to eat only a few food items, which makes it difficult for parents to meet their dietary needs. Because a healthy diet is so important during the preschool years, parents who encounter feeding problems with their children should be encouraged to consult a dietitian for help in managing eating behaviors.

Food Insecurity. Many children in the United States grow up in families that are experiencing food insecurity. Approximately 19 percent (17.4 million) of U.S. households were identified as food insecure during 2014; 7.9 million children were living in these food-insecure households (see Figure 8-6) (USDA, 2015). Although poverty is often a problem for many of these families, it is not always the only causative factor. Maternal depression, substance abuse, family structure (e.g., single, immigrant, or incarcerated parent), lack of transportation, and poor nutrition knowledge are known to increase the risk of food insecurity in families (Gundersen & Ziliak, 2014). Preschool-age children are especially vulnerable to the malnourishing effects of a poor-quality diet and, as a result, are more likely than older children to experience life-long growth and neurocognitive deficits. They also experience higher rates of illness and hospitalization, growth failure, poor academic performance, and social and behavioral problems (Fram et al., 2015; Kimbro & Denney, 2015).

Nutritious meals can be planned, even on a limited budget. Dietitians affiliated with local public health departments and county extension offices are often available to consult with parents about nutritional needs and planning healthy meals. Shopping, meal

Figure 8-6 U.S. Household Food Insecurity, 2014

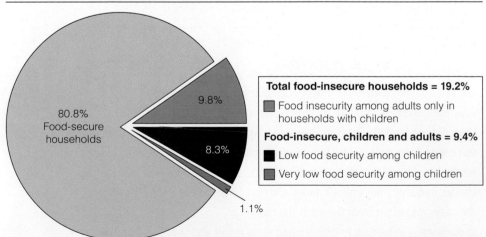

Source: Calculated by ERS using data from the December 2014 Current Population Survey Food Security Supplement.

planning, and budgeting information can also be accessed on several U.S. Department of Agriculture (USDA) websites, including ChooseMyPlate, Nutrition.gov, and SNAP-Ed Connection. Families may also be eligible to receive assistance through local food banks and the Supplemental Food Assistance Program (SNAP).

Childhood Obesity. Childhood obesity continues to be a serious dietary problem in the United States and many countries around the world. Approximately 8.4 percent (2.9 million) of U.S. children between the ages of 2 and 5 years are obese; 27 percent are considered to be overweight or obese (CDC, 2015; Ogden, Carroll, & Flegal, 2012). Obesity rates among preschool-age children declined by almost 40 percent between 2004 and 2012, although the total number of affected children remains undesirably high. However, these figures must also be viewed with caution because they mask the significantly higher incidence of obesity that occurs among certain ethnic groups, particularly Hispanic and non-Hispanic Black children and those living in poverty. The prevalence of childhood obesity is also significantly higher in families headed by parents who have less than a high-school education; a 50 percent lower rate occurs when children's parents have a college education (CDC, 2015). Parents who are concerned about a child's weight should consult their health care provider or a dietitian for guidance. Comprehensive resources are also available on several government websites (e.g., ChooseMyPlate, National Institute of Diabetes and Digestive and Kidney Diseases—*Helping your overweight child*).

Parents and early childhood teachers have many opportunities to influence preschool children's ideas about eating, physical activity, and positive lifestyle behaviors. Researchers have noted that eating family meals together, making nutritious food items available, and parent modeling are factors directly associated with children's development of healthy eating behaviors (de Wit et al., 2015; Montaño et al., 2015). Pleasant mealtime environments that encourage positive social interaction and quality time spent together also help children to develop positive attitudes about food and its role in keeping bodies healthy.

8-2f Sleep Patterns and Problems

Children's sleep patterns often change during the preschool years. Most children will sleep between 11 and 13 hours through the night and begin to forgo a daytime nap. Younger children may still benefit from an hour-long rest period during midafternoon but may have difficulty sleeping at night if they are allowed to sleep too long during the daytime. Positive associations have been established between the duration and quality of children's sleep and improved growth and brain development, emotional control, peer acceptance, memory, receptive language skills, and cognitive functioning (Gómez & Edgin, 2015; Vaughn et al., 2015; Wilson et al., 2015).

Following a consistent bedtime routine is especially beneficial for improving children's sleep quality and reducing the potential for resistance. However, there are significant cross-cultural differences in children's sleep patterns and bedtime practices (Mindell et al., 2015). Ahn et al. (2016) examined the sleep routines of preschool children in multiple cultures and observed, for example, that Korean children went to bed later, slept fewer total hours, and were less likely to take naps than Caucasian or Asian children. They also noted that Australian and New Zealand parents allowed their children to fall asleep without an adult nearby and to self-soothe themselves back to sleep when they awakened during the night; as a result, these children experienced the longest sleep duration and fewest night awakenings. Children in India typically did not go to bed until after 10:00 P.M., whereas children in Australia and New Zealand went to bed early. Wilson et al. (2014) examined the sleep patterns of

Photo 8-7 Preschoolers begin to forgo daytime naps, but some still benefit from having a quiet rest period.

children enrolled in Head Start programs and found that minority children in low-income families slept fewer hours per night than their Caucasian peers, often because their home environments were not conducive to restful sleep.

Sleep problems are relatively common during the preschool years. It is estimated that between 10 and 50 percent of young children experience a form of sleep disturbance from time to time (Carter, Hathaway, & Lettieri, 2014). Some children have difficulty falling asleep, especially when parents fail to maintain consistent bedtimes or routines that help them to relax. Children who did not learn how to settle themselves back to sleep when they were younger may continue to experience prolonged nighttime awakenings and call for a parent to comfort them. Sleep disorders are also common among children who have developmental disorders, such as autism, Down syndrome, cerebral palsy, and Williams syndrome (Blackmer & Feinstein, 2016).

Nightmares and Night Terrors. Bad dreams and occasional nightmares also tend to peak during the preschool years (Suggestions for Parents 8-6). Children of this age have a vivid imagination and are just beginning to develop fears (e.g., ghosts, monsters, thunderstorms, snakes). Although the cause of most nightmares is unknown, they can be triggered by medication (e.g., ADHD drugs), stress and anxiety (e.g., parents' divorce or military deployment, a recent move, scary movie), lack of adequate sleep, or a traumatic event (e.g., car accident, getting lost, grandparent's death) (Sinha, Jhaveri, & Banda, 2015). They are thought to be childrens' ways of working through feelings and experiences that they may have encountered. Nightmares typically occur during the last half of the sleep cycle and usually cause children to wake up.

A small percentage of preschool children will have an occasional night terror, and will wake up crying or screaming and be extremely frightened. The episode usually occurs during the first few hours of the sleep cycle, seldom lasts more than a few minutes, and is not likely to be remembered because children are not awake. Night terrors tend to peak between the ages of 4 and 10 years and then disappear. A review of research

Suggestions for Parents 8-6

Responding to Children's Nightmares and Night Terrors

Nightmares:

- Comfort (hold, cuddle) children, and let them know that you understand their fear is real and that you will keep them safe.
- Empower children by involving them in problem solving a solution: ask them questions like "What can we do to scare the monsters away?" and "What can we do to make you feel safe?"
- Ask if there is something special (e.g., toy, blanket, hall light, quiet music) that would make them feel safer.
- Remain until the child has calmed down and is ready to go back to sleep.
- Monitor the environment for unusual sounds or shadows that could be misinterpreted; be sure the child's bedtime routine is not overstimulating or contributing to his/her fears.

Night terrors:

- Stay with the child and make sure that he is safe, but do not attempt to awaken him.
- Avoid talking about the experience the next day; children won't remember what happened.
- If night terrors occur around the same time each night, it may be possible to interrupt the routine by waking the child up 10 or 15 minutes beforehand, keeping her awake for a few minutes, and then calmly helping her return to sleep.
- Make sure the child is getting enough sleep and has a relaxing bedtime routine.

studies suggested that 50 percent of children who experienced night terrors also had obstructive sleep apnea (Carter, Hathaway, & Lettieri, 2014).

Children's sleep problems can cause parents considerable stress and sleep loss. An effort should be made to assess the child's environment and bedtime routine for conditions that may not be conducive to sleep, such as family conflict, household chaos, or disturbing television shows or video games. Young children may even find some scenes in cartoons and children's movies troubling because they have difficulty understanding that characters are not real. Following a consistent bedtime routine (e.g., warm bath, quiet story, favorite pajamas, dimmed lights, quiet music) may be one of the most important factors in promoting healthful sleep. A cross-cultural study conducted by Mindell et al. (2015) examined the bedtime routines of more than 10,000 children in 14 countries and determined that consistency led to better quality sleep, fewer night awakenings, and longer sleep duration. Children should be put to bed when they are sleepy and at approximately the same time each evening to avoid getting their "second wind." Making sure that they are physically active during the daytime also improves the quality of nighttime sleep. Parents should be encouraged to consult their child's health care provider if sleep disturbances do not respond to these measures or they increase in frequency.

Bedwetting. Occasional nighttime bedwetting is a common occurrence among preschool-age children. Because many children are still in the process of achieving bladder control, nighttime accidents should not be cause for concern. Although most children outgrow this tendency by age 5 or 6 years, an estimated 20 percent experience frequent or persistent nighttime incontinence beyond this point (AAP, 2016). Enuresis (involuntary nighttime urination) is more typical in boys, and has a strong inherited tendency (von Gontard, Heron, & Joinson, 2011). Children who have sleep apnea, which is often associated with obesity, are difficult to arouse from a deep sleep and, thus, more likely to experience enuresis (Carter, Hathaway, & Lettieri, 2014). Other causes include constipation (which puts pressure on the bladder), consuming too much liquid before bedtime, stress, illness, and excess fatigue. Urinary tract infections, diabetes, and other medical conditions can also be a factor and should be evaluated.

Bedwetting incidents are embarrassing for children and frustrating for parents. However, getting angry, blaming, or punishing children for these occurrences has been shown to increase poor self-esteem, depressive symptoms, and lower academic performance (Al-Zaben & Sehlo, 2015). The use of bedding that can easily be laundered and protective coverings on mattresses can make it easier to manage accidents. Encouraging older children to help change the bed may help to ease some of their embarrassment. Limiting children's liquid consumption several hours before bedtime, making sure they go to the bathroom before crawling into bed, and waking them to urinate several hours after they have been asleep can gradually reduce the frequency of accidental nighttime bedwetting.

8-2g Communicable Illness and Immunizations

Preschool-age children are highly susceptible to communicable illnesses and experience an average of six to eight viral infections per year (Douros et al., 2016). There are several reasons why 3-, 4-, and 5-year-olds are more likely than older children to have frequent illnesses. Distances between the ears, nose, and throat are short and allow germs to reach their destinations quickly. In addition, the preschooler's immune system is not yet fully matured and, thus, provides limited protection against many of the common illnesses to which children are exposed. Many preschool-age children spend time in early childhood programs, play groups, or activities where they are in close proximity to other children. Good hygiene is also not well understood (or practiced)—children's hands frequently end up in their mouth, coughs are not always

Photo 8-8 Promoting good hygiene skills is important for preventing illness.

covered, and physical contact is frequent (Toyama, 2016). As a result, communicable illnesses are able to spread rapidly from one child to another.

Continued supervision and guidance of children's hygiene practices (e.g., hand-washing, covering coughs and sneezes) can have a positive impact on the reduction of communicable illness. Keeping children's immunizations current affords protection against diseases that can have serious and sometimes harmful consequences (Hendrix et al., 2016). However, many parents fail to have their children immunized, despite consistent research evidence supporting vaccine safety (Moran et al., 2016). Continued efforts are needed to help parents understand the importance of universal immunization and empower them to make sound decisions that will protect children's well-being.

8-2h Safety Concerns

Unintentional injuries are the leading cause of death among children 1–4 years of age (Xu et al., 2016). The majority of these deaths are the result of drowning, motor vehicle accidents, suffocation, and burns. Curious and exuberant preschool-age children lack the foresight and motor abilities that are often necessary to avoid serious injury and/or death. For this reason, adults have a moral responsibility to protect young children by creating safe environments and supervising their activities. Knowledge of children's developmental abilities enables parents to anticipate children's actions and take steps to reduce the risk of injury by planning ahead, providing developmentally appropriate toys and play equipment, eliminating environmental hazards, and establishing protective safety rules (Ablewhite et al., 2015; Marotz, 2015). For example, knowing that 4-year-olds are extremely curious, quick, and able to climb means that poisonous items (e.g., cleaning supplies, medications, cosmetics, pesticides) are not safe on a high shelf, but must be locked in a cabinet. Rules should set clear limits, be explained in simple terms, and enforced consistently. Stating them in positive terms teaches children about behaviors that are considered safe and acceptable. For example, telling children "Hold onto the railing and go down the stairs one foot at a time" informs them of a safe way to use the stairs versus, "I told you not to jump down off the stairs."

8-3 Developmentally Appropriate Behavior Guidance

Disruptive behavior is the single most common cause for mental health referrals involving preschool-age children. Although preschoolers will occasionally lose their temper, engage in low-intensity lying or stealing, and low level destruction of property, those who exhibit more intense problems including aggression, deceitfulness, and peer problems should be referred for treatment to prevent more significant behavioral problems from developing (Hong, Tillman, & Luby, 2015).

Positive behavior strategies can be used to encourage appropriate behavior and decrease problematic behaviors (Suggestions for Parents 8-7). Maintaining a positive relationship with the child provides a basis for setting and enforcing limits. Preschool-age children generally continue to seek adult attention and are more likely to follow directions when they have a high-quality relationship with their parent. In addition, children demonstrate lower levels of aggression when their parents have high social support and use parenting strategies that are characterized by warmth and reasoning (Arsenio & Ramos-Marcuse, 2014). Parent-child relationships are enhanced when parents provide preschoolers with positive time and attention, set clear expectations, and provide structure. Caregivers can spend quality time playing with preschoolers describing what they are doing, providing praise, reflecting and elaborating on what they say, and limiting directions given. Responding consistently to behavior and establishing routines are also essential because children are able to predict what will happen next.

Positive Behavior Guidance

- Provide extra time for children to complete tasks independently. Remain calm and patient.

- Give preschoolers something to do while waiting: "We need to wait in line for our turn, let's see if we can find something shaped like a circle" or "Sing 'Baa baa Black Sheep' quietly while I finish talking to your teacher."

- Reassess the environment to make sure that it remains childproofed, checking especially that dangerous materials and items are out of reach, because preschoolers are able to reach higher and are more inventive at getting into household items (e.g., pulling a chair over to reach food from the cabinet).

- Set a positive example, because children learn to behave from watching others.

- Establish predictable routines and clear rules so that children know what is expected.

- Set limits and give a simple explanation for why it is necessary: "We hold hands when crossing the street so that we are safe." "We put our toys in gently like this so that they don't break."

- Use warnings to signal when transitions are about to happen: "We will need to clean up in 5 minutes to go to preschool."

- Give clear, positively stated directions. If children are following one-step directions well, begin giving simple two-step directions: "We have two things to do. First, put your pants on, then put your pajamas in the laundry."

- Offer choices to help the child feel control over situations: "Do you want to brush your teeth or put on your clothes first?"

- Catch preschoolers when they are behaving appropriately. Give them attention by describing and playing along with them as well as providing descriptive praise: "You did an awesome job putting the puzzle together. You kept trying until you figured it out."

- Notice tasks that the child wants to complete on his own and provide scaffolding to help him learn to do the task independently.

- Allow preschoolers time to calm down when angry or frustrated so that they learn how to control their strong emotions.

- Involve older children in problem solving: "If you want to play with the red car that Jason has, what could we do? We could try asking him if he wants to trade or play with a different car until he is done."

- Provide a quiet place where children can settle down if inappropriate behavior continues to occur. Remain calm and limit attention given to the inappropriate behaviors.

Summary

- Preschool-age children grow at a rate that is slower than when they were younger. Parents play a vital role in identifying hearing and vision problems and developmental concerns that may warrant early intervention.

- Parents and other caregivers can support preschoolers' efforts to achieve a variety of developmental tasks, including refining cognitive, language, social-emotional, and motor skills. Parents can also facilitate physical activity, healthy eating, and sleeping habits that will carry over into adulthood.

- During the preschool years, children are better able to engage in higher-order cognitive processes, regulate their thoughts and emotions, plan their actions, and engage in goal-directed behavior. They are also actively refining their motor skills, and learning about how to fit in with social roles, norms, and expectations. It is important that parents be patient and understanding of children's desire to experience independence and success.

- Preschoolers continue to benefit from having warm and responsive parenting that encourages exploration and assistance with problem solving. Parents' use of positive behavioral strategies, including establishing safe environments, developing consistent routines, providing opportunities for children to complete tasks independently, and modeling and encouraging adaptive coping skills help to promote appropriate behavior.

Key Words

inferential language (p. 234)

magical thinking (p. 223)

nutrient-dense foods (p. 237)

self-esteem (p. 228)

theory of mind (p. 223)

Questions for Discussion and Self-Reflection

1. What information is important to know and understand when evaluating a child's developmental progress?

2. Why are preschoolers especially prone to misinterpret information presented in the media? How can parents use media appropriately to encourage cognitive and social-emotional development?

3. What can parents and teachers do to encourage children's cognitive development?

4. Why might a 3-year-old have nightmares after watching a children's movie in which a baby bear's mother is killed by a hunter?

5. What is food insecurity, and how does it affect a child's development?

Field Activities

1. Contact local preschools to obtain information about how the preschool day is structured. What are the similarities and differences? Would you change the amount of time spent on different activities or learning methods? Develop a list of questions that parents should consider when selecting a preschool based on the information you gather.

2. Identify and prepare a list of organizations (governmental and non-profit) in your community that offer food and other forms of assistance to families in need. Contact each group to determine what services they offer and how families qualify.

3. Explore the following websites that offer information to help parents promote children's development: Office of Head Start, National Association for the Education of Young Children, InfoAboutKids.org, KidsHealth.org, National Institute of Child Health and Human Development, and the U.S. Department of Health and Human Services. How could these resources be used in your work with families?

4. Conduct an Internet search to learn more about various interventions that have been suggested to address bedwetting issues. Briefly describe one empirically-based method and explain what makes it effective; describe a second method and discuss why you think it may be questionable. How would you share the information you learned with a concerned parent?

REFERENCES

Ablewhite, J., McDaid, L., Hawkins, A., Peel, I., Goodenough, T., Deave, T., . . . & Kendrick, D. (2015). Approaches used by parents to keep their children safe at home: A qualitative study to explore the perspectives of parents with children aged under five years. *BMC Public Health*, *15*(983). Retrieved on February 25, 2016 from http://bmcpublichealth.biomedcentral.com/articles/10.1186/s12889-015-2252-x.

Al-Zaben, R., & Sehlo, M. (2015). Punishment for bedwetting is associated with child depression and reduced quality of life. *Child Abuse & Neglect, 43*, 22–29.

American Academy of Pediatrics (AAP). (2016). Bedwetting. Retrieved on February 22, 2016 from http://www.healthychildren.org/English/ages-stages/toddler/toilet-training/Pages /Bedwetting.aspx.

American Speech-Language-Hearing Association (ASHA). (2016). Causes of hearing loss in children. Retrieved February 19, 2016 from http://www.asha.org/public/hearing/Causes -of-Hearing-Loss-in-Children/.

Arsenio, W., & Ramos-Marcuse, F. (2014). Children's moral emotions, narratives, and aggression: Relations with maternal discipline and support. *Journal of Genetic Psychology: Research and Theory on Human Development, 175*(6), 528–546.

Baker, E., Tisak, M., & Tisak, J. (2015). What can boys and girls do? Preschoolers' perspectives regarding gender roles across domains of behavior. *Social Psychology of Education*. Advance online publication. doi: 10.1007/s11218-015-9320-z.

Bell, E., Greenfield, D., Bulotsky-Shearer, R., & Carter, T. (2016). Peer play as a context for identifying profiles of children and examining rates of growth in academic readiness for children enrolled in Head Start. *Journal of Educational Psychology.* doi.org/10.1037 /edu0000084.

Benzies, K., Mychasiuk, R., Kurilova, J., Tough, S., Edwards, N., & Donnelly, C. (2014). Two-generation preschool programme: Immediate and 7-year-old outcomes for low income children and their parents. *Child & Family Social Work, 19*, 203–214.

Biedinger, N., Becker, B., & Klein, O. (2015). Turkish-language ability of children of immigrants in Germany: Which contexts of exposure influence preschool children's acquisition of their heritage language? *Ethnic and Racial Studies, 38*(9), 1520–1538.

Blackmer, A., & Feinstein, J. (2016). Management of sleep disorders in children with neurodevelopmental disorders: A review. *Pharmacotherapy: The Journal of Human Pharmacology and Drug Therapy, 36*(1), 84–98.

Bloemen, M., Backx, F., Takken, T., Wittink, H., Benner, J., Mollema, J., & De Groot, J. (2014). Factors associated with physical activity in children and adolescents with a physical disability: A systematic review. *Developmental Medicine & Child Neurology, 57*(2), 137–148.

Brighi, A., Mazzanti, C., Guarini, A., & Sansavini, A. (2015). Young children's cliques: A study on processes of peer acceptance and cliques aggregation. *The International Journal of Emotional Education, 7*(1), 69–83.

Brown, T., & Jernigan, T. (2012). Brain development during the preschool years. *Neuropsychology Review, 22*(4), 313–333.

Carter, K., Hathaway, N., & Lettieri, C. (2014). Common sleep disorders in children. *American Family Physician, 89*(5), 368–377.

CDC. (2015). Prevalence of childhood obesity in the United States, 2011-2012. Retrieved February 20, 2016 from http://www.cdc.gov/obesity/data/childhood.html.

Chernyak, N., & Kushnir, T. (2014). The self as a moral agent: Preschoolers behave morally but believe in the freedom to do otherwise. *Journal of Cognition and Development, 15*(3), 453–464.

Clements, M., Martin, S., Randall, D., & Kane, K. (2014). Child and parent perceptions of interparental relationship conflict predict preschool children's adjustment. *Couple and Family Psychology: Research and Practice, 3*(2), 110–125.

Cochet, H., Centelles, L., Jover, M., Plachta, S., & Vauclair, J. (2015). Hand preferences in preschool children: Reaching, pointing and symbolic gestures. *Laterality: Asymmetries of Body, Brain and Cognition, 20*(4), 501–516.

Council on Communications and Media. (2015). Media and children. American Academy of Pediatrics. Retrieved on February 27, 2016 from http://www.aap.org/en-us/advocacy-and -policy/aap-health-initiatives/pages/media-and-children.aspx.

Copeland, K., Kendeigh, C., Saelens, B., Kalkwarf, H., & Sherman, S. (2012). Physical activity in child-care centers: Do teachers hold the key to the playground? *Health Education Research, 27*, 81–100.

Coyne, M., Linder, J., Rasmussen, E., Nelson, D., & Collier, K. (2014). It's a bird! It's a plane! It's a gender stereotype!: Longitudinal associations between superhero viewing and gender stereotyped play. *Sex Roles, 70*(9-10), 416–430.

Dahl, A., & Kim, L. (2014). Why is it bad to make a mess? Preschoolers' conceptions of pragmatic norms. *Cognitive Development, 32*, 12–22.

de Wit, J., Stok, F., Smolenski, D., de Ridder, D., de Vet, E., Gaspar, T., . . . & Luszczynska, A. (2015). Food culture in the home environment: Family meal practices and values can support health eating and self-regulation in young people in four European countries. *Applied Psychology: Health and Well-Being, 7*, 22–40.

DiBiase, R., & Miller, P. (2015). Self-perceived peer acceptance in preschoolers of differing economic and cultural backgrounds. *The Journal of Genetic Psychology: Research and Theory on Human Development, 176*(3), 139–155.

Douros, K., Kotzia, D., Kottaridi, C., Giotas, A., Boutopoulou, B., Karakitsos, P., & Priftis, K. (2016). Many children aged two to five have a persistent presence of respiratory viruses in their nasopharynx. *Acta Paediatrica, 105*(2), e89–e92.

Ellis, J., Galloway, A., Webb, R., Martz, D., & Farrow, C. (2016). Recollections of pressure to eat during childhood, but not picky eating, predict young adult eating behavior. *Appetite, 97*(1), 58–63.

Erikson, E. (1963). *Childhood and society (2nd Ed)*. New York: W. W. Norton.

Executive Office of the President of the United States. (2014). The economics of early childhood investments. Retrieved January 17, 2016 from http://www.whitehouse.gov/sites/default/files /docs/early_childhood_report1.pdf.

Faulkner, G., Mitra, R., Buliung, R., Fusco, C., & Stone, M. (2015). Children's outdoor playtime, physical activity, and parental perceptions of the neighbourhood environment. *International Journal of Play, 4*(1), 84–97.

Fildes, A., van Jaarsveld, C., Cooke, L., Wardle, J., & Lewellyn, C. (2016). Common genetic architecture underlying young children's food fussiness and liking for vegetables and fruit. *American Journal of Clinical Nutrition, 103*(4), 1099–1104.

Foulkes, J., Knowles, Z., Fairclogh, S., Stratton, G., O'Dwyer, M., Ridges, N., & Foweather, L. (2015). Fundamental movement skills of preschool children in northwest England. *Perceptual & Motor Skills: Physical Development & Measurement, 121*(1), 260–283.

Foweather, L., Knowles, Z., Ridgers, N., O'Dwyer, M., Foulkes, J., & Stratton, G. (2015). Fundamental movement skills in relation to weekday and weekend physical activity in preschool children. *Journal of Science and Medicine in Sport, 18*(6), 691–696.

Fram, M., Ritchie, L., Rosen, N., & Frongillo, E. (2015). Child experience of food insecurity is associated with child diet and physical activity. *The Journal of Nutrition, 145*(3), 499–504.

Fuglestad, A., Whitley, M., Carlson, S., Boys, C., Eckerle, J., Fink, B., & Wozniak, J. (2015). Executive functioning deficits in preschool children with fetal alcohol spectrum disorders. *Child Neuropsychology, 21*(6), 716–731.

Gawrilow, C., Stadler, G., Langguth, N., Naumann, A., & Boeck, A. (2016). Physical activity, affect, and cognition in children with symptoms of ADHD. *Journal of Attention Disorders, 20*(2), 151–162.

Gómez, R., & Edgin, J. (2015). Sleep as a window into early neural development: Shifts in sleep-dependent learning effects across early childhood. *Child Development Perspectives, 9*(3), 183–189.

Gonzalez, C., Flindall, J., & Stone, K. (2014). Hand preference across the lifespan: Effects of end-goal, task nature, and object location. *Frontiers in Psychology, 5*, 1579.

Grabell, A., Olson, S., Miller, A., Kessler, D., Felt, B., Kaciroti, N., . . . & Tardif, T. (2015). The impact of culture on physiological processes of emotion regulation: A comparison of US and Chinese preschoolers. *Developmental Science, 18*(3), 420–435.

Gray, P. (2015). Early academic training produces long-term harm. *Psychology Today*. Retrieved February 25, 2016 from https://www.psychologytoday.com/blog/freedom-learn/201505/early -academic-training-produces-long-term-harm.

Groh, A., Fearon, R., Bakermans-Kranenburg, M., IJzendoorn, M., Steele, R., & Roisman, G. (2014). The significance of attachment security for children's social competence with peers: A meta-analytic study. *Attachment & Human Development 16*(2), 103–136.

Grzywacz, J., Arcury, T., Trejo, G., & Quandt, S. (2014). Latino mothers in farmworker families' beliefs about preschool children's physical activity and play. *Journal of Immigrant and Minority Health, 18*(1), 234–242.

Gundersen, C., & Ziliak, J. (2014). Childhood food insecurity in the U.S.: Trends, causes, and policy issues. *The Future of Children, 24*(2), 1–19.

Halim, M., Ruble, D., Tamis-LeMonda, C., & Shrout, P. (2013). Rigidity in gender-typed behaviors in early childhood: A longitudinal study of ethnic minority children. *Child Development, 84*(4), 1269–1284.

Hamann, K., & Bender, J. (2014). Meritocratic sharing is based on collaboration in 3-year-olds. *Developmental Psychology, 50*(1), 121–128.

Harkins, J. (2015). Academic vs. play-based preschool debate fading in favor of intellectual discovery. *Pittsburgh Post-Gazette*. Retrieved February 25, 2016 from http://www.post-gazette.com/news/education/2015/04/01/Academic-vs-play-based-preschool-debate-fading-in-favor-of-intellectual-discovery/stories/201503310025.

Hendrix, K., Sturm, L., Zimet, G., & Meslin, E. (2016). Ethics and childhood vaccination policy in the United States. *American Journal of Public Health*, 106(2), 273–278.

Hong, J., Tillman, R., & Luby, J. (2015). Disruptive behavior in preschool children: Distinguishing normal misbehavior from markers of current and later childhood conduct disorder. *Journal of Pediatrics*, 166(3), 723–730.

Jackowski, S., Baxter-Jones, A., Gruodyte-Raciene, R., Kontulainen, S., & Erlandson, M. (2015). A longitudinal study of bone area, content, density, and strength development at the radius and tibia in children 4-12 years of age exposed to recreational gymnastics. *Osteoporosis International*, 26(6), 1677–1690.

Jia, R., Lang, S., & Schoppe-Sullivan, S. (2015, June 22). A developmental examination of the psychometric properties and predictive utility of a revised psychological self-concept measure for preschool-age children. *Psychological Assessment*, 28(2), 226–238.

Kearney, M., & Levine, P. (2015). Early childhood education by MOOC: Learning from Sesame Street. *NBER* working paper no. 21229. Cambridge, MA: National Bureau of Economics Research.

Kercood, S., Conway, T., Saelens, B., Frank, L., Cain, K., & Sallis, J. (2015). Parent rules, barriers, and places for youth physical activity vary by neighborhood walkability and income. *Children, Youth, and Environments*, 25(1), 100–118.

Kim, H., Carlson, A., Curby, T., & Winsler, A. (2016). Relations among motor, social, and cognitive skills in pre-kindergarten children with developmental disabilities. *Research in Developmental Disabilities*, 53, 43–60.

Kimbro, R., & Denney, J. (2015). Transitions into food insecurity associated with behavioral problems and worse overall health among children. *Health Affairs*, 34(11), 1945–1955.

King-Dowling, S., Missiuna, C., Rodriguez, C., Greenway, M., & Cairney, J. (2015). Co-occurring motor, language and emotional-behavioral problems in children 2-6 years of age. *Human Movement Science*, 39, 101–108.

Klein, E., & Hollingshead, A. (2015). Collaboration between special and physical education. The benefits of a healthy lifestyle for all students. *Teaching Exceptional Children*, 47(3), 163–171.

Landry, S., Zucker, T., Taylor, H., Swank, P., Williams, J., Assel, M., . . . & Klein, A. (2014). Enhancing early child care quality and learning for toddlers at risk: The responsive early childhood program. *Developmental Psychology*, 50(2), 526–541.

Lecompte, V., Moss, E., Cyr, C., & Pascuzzo, K. (2014). Preschool attachment, self-esteem and the development of preadolescent anxiety and depressive symptoms. *Attachment & Human Development*, 16(3), 242–260.

LeCuyer, E., & Phillips Swanson, D. (2013, December 12). African American and European American mothers' limit setting and their 36-month-old children's responses to limits, self-concept, and social competence. *Journal of Family Issues*, 37(2), 270–296.

Lee, J., Kim, E., Choi, Y., & Koo, J. (2014). Cultural variances in composition of biological and supernatural concepts of death: A content analysis of children's literature. *Death Studies*, 38(8), 538–545.

Leppma, M., Szente, J., & Brosch, M. (2015). Advancement in addressing children's fears: A review and recommendations. *The Professional Counselor*, 5(2), 261–272.

Lewis Brown, L. (2015). Comparing preschool philosophies: Play-based vs. academic. Retrieved February 25, 2016 from http://www.pbs.org/parents/education/going-to-school/choosing/comparing-preschool-philosophies/.

Li, H., Boguszewski, K., & Lillard, A. (2015). Can that really happen? Children's knowledge about the reality status of fantastical events in television. *Journal of Experimental Child Psychology*, 139, 99–114.

Linebarger, D. (2015). Contextualizing video game play: The moderating effects of cumulative risk and parenting styles on the relations among video game exposure and problem behaviors. *Psychology of Popular Media*, 4(4), 375–396.

Marotz, L. (2015). *Health, safety, and nutrition for the young child*. Stamford, CT: Cengage Learning.

Marotz, L., & Allen, K. (2016). *Developmental profiles: Pre-Birth through adolescence*. Boston, MA: Cengage Learning.

Mennella, J., Reiter, A., & Daniels, A. (2016). Vegetable and fruit acceptance during infancy: Impact of ontogeny, genetics, and early experiences. *Advances in Nutrition, 7*(1), 211S–219S.

Merz, E., Zucker, T., Landry, S., Williams, J., Assel, M., Taylor, H., . . . & de Villiers, J. (2015). Parenting predictors of cognitive skills and emotion knowledge in socioeconomically disadvantaged preschoolers. *Journal of Experimental Child Psychology, 132*, 14–31.

Mindell, J., Li, A., Sadeh, A., Kwon, R., & Goh, D. (2015). Bedtime routines for young children: A dose-dependent association with sleep outcomes. *Sleep, 38*(5), 717–722.

Mindell, J., Sadeh, A., Kwon, R., & Goh, D. (2013). Cross-cultural differences in the sleep of preschool children. *Sleep Medicine, 15*(12), 1595–1596.

Montaño, Z., Smith, J., Dishion, T., & Shaw, D. (2015). Longitudinal relations between observed parenting behaviors and dietary quality of meals from ages 2 to 5. *Appetite, 87*, 324–329.

Moran, M., Frank, L., Chatterjee, J., Murphy, S., & Baezconde-Garbanati, L. (2016). Information scanning and vaccine safety concerns among African American, Mexican American, and non-Hispanic White women. *Patient Education and Counseling, 99*(1), 147–153.

Morley, D., Till, K., Ogilvie, P., & Turner, G. (2015). Influences of gender and socioeconomic status on the motor proficiency of children in the UK. *Human Movement Science, 44*, 150–156.

Must, A., Phillips, S., Curtin, C., & Bandini, L. (2015). Barriers to physical activity in children with autism spectrum disorders: Relationship to physical activity and screen time. *Journal of Physical Activity & Health, 12*(4), 529–534.

Nathanson, A., Aladé, F., Sharp, M., Rasmussen, E., & Christy, K. (2014). The relation between television exposure and executive function among preschoolers. *Developmental Psychology, 50*(5), 1497–1506.

Nathanson, A., & Fries, P. (2014). Television exposure, sleep time, and neuropsychological function among preschoolers. *Media Psychology, 17*(3), 237–261.

National Association for the Education of Young Children and the Fred Rogers Center for Early Learning and Children's Media. (2012). Technology and interactive media as tools in early childhood programs serving children from birth through age 8. Retrieved April 14, 2016 from http://www.naeyc.org/files/naeyc/PS_technology_WEB.pdf.

National Eye Institute (NEI). (2016). Uncorrected farsightedness linked to literacy deficits in preschoolers. Retrieved February 19, 2016 from http://nei.nih.gov/news/pressrelease/farsightedness_linked_literacy_deficits.

Nordstrøm, M., Paus, B., Andersen, L., & Kolset, S. (2015). Dietary aspects related to health and obesity in Williams syndrome, Down syndrome, and Prader-Willi syndrome. *Food and Nutrition Research, 59*. Retrieved February 20, 2016 from http://www.ncbi.nlm.nih.gov/pmc/articles/PMC4317472/.

Ogden, C., Carroll, K., & Flegal, K. (2012). Prevalence of obesity and trends in body mass among US children and adolescents, 1999–2010. *JAMA, 307*(5), 483–490.

Oghii, O. (2015). Fears of preschool and primary school children with regard to gender, age, and cultural identity: Cross-cultural study. Unpublished master's thesis. Middle East Technical University. Retrieved from http://etd.lib.metu.edu.tr/upload/12618795/index.pdf.

O'Farrelly, C., & Hennessy, E. (2014.) Watching transitions unfold: A mixed-method study of transitions within early childhood care and education settings, *Early Years, 34*(4), 329–347.

Ostrav, J., Gentile, D., & Mullins, A. (2013). Evaluating the effect of educational media exposure on aggression in early childhood. *Journal of Applied Developmental Psychology, 34*(1), 38–44.

Pate, R., O'Neill, J., Brown, W., Pfeiffer, K., Dowda, M., & Addy, C. (2014). Prevalence of compliance with a new physical activity guideline for preschool-age children. *Childhood Obesity, 11*(4), 415–420.

Piaget, J. (1952). *The origins of intelligence in children.* New York: International University Press.

Piek, J., Kane, R., Rigoli, D., McLaren, S., Roberts, C., Rooney, R., et al. (2015). Does the Animal Fun program improve social-emotional and behavioural outcomes in children aged 4–6 years? *Human Movement Science, 43*, 155–163.

Rodrigues, L., Stodden, D., & Lopes, V. (2016). Developmental pathways of change in fitness and motor competence are related to overweight and obesity status at the end of primary school. *Journal of Science and Medicine in Sport, 19*(1), 87–92.

Satter, E. (2000). *Child of mine: Feeding with love and good sense.* Boulder, CO: Bull Publishing Company.

Senso, M., Trost, S., Crain, A. Seburg, E., Anderson, J., & Sherwood, N. (2015). Activity patterns of preschool-aged children at risk for obesity. *Journal of Physical Activity and Health, 12*(6), 861–868.

Shenouda, C., & Danovitch, J. (2014). Effects of gender stereotypes and stereotype threat on children's performance on a spatial task. *Revue Internationale de Psychologie Sociale, 27* (3-4), 53–77.

Simpson, A., & Linder, S. (2016). The indirect effect of children's gender on early childhood educators' mathematical talk. *Teaching and Teacher Education, 54,* 44–53.

Sinha, S., Jhaveri, R., & Banga, A. (2015). Sleep disturbances and behavioral disturbances in children and adolescents. *Psychiatric Clinics of North America, 38*(4), 705–721.

Snow, K. (2011). Research news you can use: Debunking the play vs. learning dichotomy. Retrieved February 25, 2016 from http://www.naeyc.org/content/research-news-you-can-use-play-vs-learning.

Society of Health and Physical Educators (SHAPE). (2015). SHAPE America. Retrieved on February 20, 2016 from http://www.shapeamerica.org/standards/guidelines/activestart.cfm.

Spencer, T., Petersen, D., & Adams, J. (2015). Tier 2 language intervention for diverse preschoolers: An early-stage randomized control group study following an analysis of response to intervention. *American Journal of Speech-Language Pathology, 24,* 619–636.

Toyama, N. (2016). Preschool teachers' explanations for hygiene habits and young children's biological awareness of contamination. *Early Education and Development, 27*(1), 38–53.

U.S. Department of Agriculture (USDA). (2015). Household food security in the United States in 2014. Retrieved February 20, 2016 from http://www.ers.usda.gov/topics/food-nutrition-assistance/food-security-in-the-us/key-statistics-graphics.aspx.

Vaughn, B., Elmore-Staton, L., Shin, N., & El-Sheikh, M. (2015). Sleep as a support for social competence, peer relations, and cognitive functioning in preschool children. *Behavioral Sleep Medicine, 13*(2), 92–106.

Vinh, M., Strain, P., Davidon, S., & Smith, B. (2016). One state's systems change efforts to reduce child care expulsion. Taking the pyramid model to scale. *Topics in Early Childhood Special Education.* doi: 10.1177/0271121415626130.

Vlahov, E., Baghurst, T., & Mwavita, M. (2014). Preschool motor development predicting high school health-related physical fitness: A prospective study. *Perceptual & Motor Skills, 119*(1), 279–291.

von Gontard, A., Heron, J., & Joinson, C. (2011). Family history of nocturnal enuresis and urinary incontinence: Results from a large epidemiological study. *Journal of Urology, 185*(6), 2303–2306.

Walton, K., & Ingersoll, B. (2015). Psychosocial adjustment and sibling relationships in siblings of children with autism spectrum disorder: Risk and protective factors. *Journal of Autism and Developmental Disorders, 45*(9), 2764–2778.

Wang, Y., Chau, C., Ng, W., & Leung, T. (2016). A review on the effects of physical built environment attributes on enhancing walking and cycling activity levels within residential neighborhoods, *Cities, 50,* 1–15.

Wang, Z., Meltzoff, A., & Williamson, R. (2015). Social learning promotes understanding of the physical world: Preschool children's imitation of weight sorting. *Journal of Experimental Child Psychology, 136,* 82–91.

Weisgram, E., Fulcher, M., & Dinella, L. (2014). Pink gives girls permission: Exploring the roles of explicit gender labels and gender-typed colors on preschool children's toy preferences. *Journal of Applied Developmental Psychology, 35*(5), 401–409.

Wilson, K., Lumeng, J., Kaciroti, N., Chen, S., LeBourgeois, M., Chervin, R., & Miller, A. (2015). Sleep hygiene practices and bedtime resistance in low-income preschoolers: Does temperament matter? *Behavioral Sleep Medicine, 13*(5), 412–423.

Wilson, K., Miller, A., Lumeng, J., & Chervin, R. (2014). Sleep environments and sleep durations in a sample of low-income preschool children. *Journal of Clinical Sleep Medicine, 10*(3), 299–305.

Wolter, I., Braun, E., & Hannover, B. (2015). Reading is for girls!? The negative impact of preschool teachers' traditional gender role attitudes on boys' reading related motivation and skills. *Frontiers in Psychology, 6,* Article 1267.

Wong, W., & Hines, M. (2015). Effects of gender color-coding on toddlers' gender-typical toy play. *Archives of Sexual Behavior, 44*(5), 1233–1242.

Xu, J., Murphy, S., Kochanek, K., & Bastian, B. (2016). National Vital Statistics Report *64*(2). Deaths: Final data for 2013. Centers for Disease Control and Protection. Retrieved February 25, 2016 from http://www.cdc.gov/nchs/data/nvsr/nvsr64/nvsr64_02.pdf.

Ziereis, S., & Jansen, P. (2015). Effects of physical activity on executive function and motor performance in children with ADHD. *Research in Developmental Disabilities, 38,* 181–191.

Parenting School-Age Children

9

LEARNING OBJECTIVES

After reading the chapter, you will be able to:

9-1 Describe typical growth and development during the school-age years, and common impairments that require intervention.

9-2 Discuss how parents can support cognitive and social development during the school-age years, and how this influences children's readiness for, transition to, and success in, school.

9-3 Briefly describe the role of co-regulation in the parent-child relationship.

naeyc Standards Linked to Chapter Content

1a, 1b, and 1c: Promoting child development and learning

2a, 2b, and 2c: Building family and community relationships

4a and 4b: Using developmentally effective approaches to connect with children and families

6 TO 12 YEARS

Children become increasingly sophisticated in many ways between the ages of 6 and 12 years. Their unbridled enthusiasm, curiosity, and zest for life are only tempered by limited reasoning, social skills and, occasionally, motor skills which will continue to develop through complex processes during the coming years. They learn quickly that the world is a much bigger

continued on following page

place than they have so-far experienced, and that it offers adventures and opportunities that they could not have imagined. Although they are becoming more dependable and able to make independent decisions, they continue to need adult-established limits, guidance, and nurturing which are provided in safe and secure environments. ■

9-1 Typical Growth and Development Overview

For children in most cultures, this period coincides with the beginning of formal, structured education. School serves as a place to meet and make friends, engage in new activities, develop advanced cognitive, language, and social skills, and gain increasing independence. Successful adaptation requires that children learn to follow directions, focus on tasks at hand, problem solve, and accept failure and criticism—skills that also become increasingly important and useful in their daily lives.

Parents may find this transitional phase confusing and hurtful at times, unless they understand that children's behaviors reflect typical developmental changes that occur during this age. For example, school-age children often begin to question parental authority, refuse parents' efforts to show affection in public, and prefer spending more time with their friends than at home. Parents should avoid misinterpreting these behaviors as signs of disrespect or rejection, and to appreciate children's needs for achieving greater independence by modifying their parenting style and behavior guidance efforts.

9-1a Growth

Children continue to grow taller and heavier, but at a slower rate than during their earlier years. Six- to nine-year-olds tend to gain about 5–6 pounds (2.3–2.7 kg) per year, and add 2–2.5 inches (5–6.25 cm) in height, although genetics, diet, and illness will influence these rates. Arms and legs grow longer, giving children a more adult-like appearance. They begin to lose their 'baby' teeth, which are replaced with teeth much larger in size. Vision is almost equivalent to that of an adult's (20/20) although some children may still be farsighted. This is an important time for parents to provide children with information about healthy eating habits, physical activity behaviors, and about physical and mental changes that are taking place.

Children's growth rate and developmental pattern begin to change between the ages of 10 and 12 years. Girls experience irregular and dramatic growth spurts which may temporarily cause them to appear physically awkward, whereas boys grow more slowly and usually remain smaller than girls at equivalent ages. However, boys are adding considerable muscle mass and becoming stronger during this period; girls will almost reach their maximum muscle strength by age 12. Girls begin to experience early hormonal changes associated with puberty (e.g., enlarged breasts, pubic and underarm hair, rounded hips, menses); boys may also notice some prepuberty changes (e.g., spontaneous erections, pubic and underarm hair, penis enlargement).

9-1b Developmental Tasks

Most basic motor, language, and thinking skills are in place at the beginning of this stage. Children are able to use them intentionally to execute and achieve desired outcomes. They also continue to develop other advanced abilities which will enable them to function more competently and independently (see Figure 9-1). School-age children are gaining a

Figure 9–1   School-Age Children's Developmental Tasks

School-age children invest considerable time and energy toward the achievement of several important developmental tasks:

- Improving cognitive, motor, and language skills—grasping more advanced concepts; approaching and mastering activities with increased understanding and purpose

- Developing socialization skills—learning about social expectations and behavioral consequences; respecting and internalizing limits and rules; coping with frustration

- Becoming more responsible and independent

- Establishing healthy lifestyles—nutrition, physical activity, and sleep

sense of self-identity, self-efficacy, and are learning how they fit into a larger social order throughout this developmental process. They are usually eager to learn and often attempt a host of novel activities (e.g., organized games, sports, crafts, building projects, cooking, club participation, skating) that serve to test newly-acquired skills. Learning to read may present one of the most complex perceptual tasks that children will encounter during this stage, and it may take them several years to master the skill successfully.

Cultural differences play an important role in the way children are socialized to learn, including the developmental tasks that they are expected to acquire. For example, Frewen et al. (2015) found that Chinese parents placed a higher value on children's conforming behaviors than on their development of creative and practical skills—more so than parents from other Asian backgrounds. Rodic et al. (2015) attributed variations in children's mathematical abilities to cross-cultural differences in the emphasis that parents from the United Kingdom, China, and Russia placed on early number training prior to school attendance. In contrast, Crosnoe et al. (2016) noted that foreign-born Latina mothers who had lower educational attainment were less likely than White, African American, and Latina U.S.-born mothers to encourage children's learning, provide enrichment materials and activities, or become involved in their children's schools. As a result, these children were less likely to be successful academically. Researchers have shown repeatedly that parents who value and support education are more likely to have children who are actively engaged in learning and experience greater academic success (Hoglund et al., 2015; Jeynes, 2015).

9-1c Early Identification and Intervention

It is often during the early elementary school years that certain physical problems (e.g., vision and hearing deficits), speech and language impairments, and developmental disorders (e.g., attention deficit disorder, Tourette syndrome, learning disabilities) become more apparent as the result of increased academic and social demands. Teachers may be the first to notice that children are having difficulty following instructions, comprehending language or number concepts, or grasping early reading skills. Children who are struggling in school are likely to develop significant anxiety, poor self-esteem, and related psychological disorders as a result of physical and mental limitations (Charman et al., 2015; Reardon, Gray, & Melvin, 2015). Failure to recognize these problems in their early stages may lead children to lose self-confidence and to eventually stop their efforts to perform in the classroom.

Many children, especially those with physical or developmental disabilities, have undetected vision and hearing impairments. Because most learning is dependent upon a child's ability to hear and see, it is critical that parents and teachers refer children who may exhibit signs of vision or hearing problems for professional evaluation (see Figure 9-2). **Amblyopia** is one of the most common vision impairments identified in school-age children, and can cause a child to gradually lose sight in the affected eye

> **amblyopia** blurry or reduced vision in one or both eyes related to a muscle imbalance; sometimes referred to as "lazy eye."

Photo 9-1 Vision, hearing, and speech problems are often detected in school-age children because of increased academic and social demands.

Figure 9-2 Signs of Vision and Hearing Impairment

Observe children carefully for the following signs of a vision impairment:

- Becomes irritable or tired when engaged in close-up work (e.g., reading, writing)
- Is inattentive or loses interest after a short time
- Turns head to one side in order to see better
- Rubs eyes frequently; complains of headache or tired eyes
- Trips over objects; is clumsy
- Has poor hand-eye coordination

Observe children carefully for the following signs of a hearing impairment:

- Has delayed or irregular speech development
- Talks loudly or responds inappropriately to requests
- Is successful at tasks that do not depend upon hearing ability
- Asks to have statements repeated; turns up the volume (e.g., music player, television)
- Uses gestures often in place of words
- Is reluctant to join other children in groups

⌄ Professional Resource Download

unless it is detected and treated (ideally before the age of 5 or 6 years). Xiao et al. (2015) noted that the condition was most prevalent among Hispanic children and lowest among African American children. Amblyopia can be especially problematic for school-age children because it reduces their reading speed and efficiency (Kelly et al., 2015). The earlier this condition is identified and treated, the more likely it is that some lost vision can be restored, further loss is prevented, and children's academic performance will improve.

Hearing impairments also occur frequently among school-age children, particularly those who have certain medical conditions (e.g., allergies, frequent ear infections, prematurity) and developmental disabilities, such as Down syndrome and fetal alcohol syndrome. A child's ability to hear well is essential for learning and speech development. However, noisy classrooms can make it difficult for children who have even minimal to mild hearing loss to succeed (Lewis, Valente, & Spalding, 2015). Children are seldom aware that they are not hearing well. As a result, they are dependent upon parents and teachers to recognize when they may have a hearing problem and to refer them for a professional evaluation.

It is also imperative that parents and teachers are aware of potential mental health disorders that children may be experiencing. Although behavioral signs may have been present for some time, it is often not until children find themselves in structured situations where they are expected to perform, that an unusual pattern becomes more apparent. The early identification and treatment of mental health problems is essential to prevent them from interfering with children's academic success and ability to make and keep friends.

Children's dental health also warrants early identification and intervention. Approximately 18 percent of school-age children have untreated dental decay; 17 percent had not seen a dentist in the previous year (CDC, 2014a). Chronic dental problems can cause children to experience pain, difficulty eating and speaking, embarrassment, and may interfere with their ability to concentrate and learn. Poverty and lack of dental insurance create significant disparities in children's access to essential dental care (Capurro et al., 2015). Efforts to help parents locate affordable dental care and to understand the importance of teaching children good dental hygiene practices are critical to improving children's learning potential (Heima et al., 2015).

9-2 Supporting the School-Age Child's Development

For parents, the span between a child's sixth and twelfth birthdays is often one of the most enjoyable. Children are able to manage most of their own personal needs without adult assistance. They listen, follow directions (for the most part), enjoy spending time with their family, are energetic, and usually eager to help. However, some children will begin the process of separating themselves from family by asserting their independence at times, talking back, and searching for a more adult-like identity as they approach their eleventh and twelfth years. They often vacillate between the desire for adult-status recognition and the desire and need for parental support, reassurance, and love. The school-age years also remain an important time for parents to monitor and guide children's health and well-being.

9-2a Promoting Cognitive Development

By age 5 years, a child's brain has completed approximately 85 percent of its overall physical growth. Language and sensory pathways are well-established, but important cognitive developments continue to occur throughout the school-age years. More energy within the brain is utilized in areas involved with interpreting social and emotional cues (Angier, 2011). Connections between neurons—cells that process information—improve children's ability to absorb information that they are exposed to during daily activities (Donaldson, 2013). Piaget (1952) described 7- to 11-year-olds' thinking as "concrete operational," which involves the ability to think more logically in order to understand cause and effect, **conservation** (e.g., liquid, mass, and number), and **classification** (e.g., shape, use, and color) concepts.

Children are able to understand objects and their relationships, but they are not able to comprehend abstract thoughts until the end of this period. This developmental path allows children to learn basic mathematical skills (e.g., addition, subtraction, time) and more complex concepts, such as death and gender (see Figure 9-3). Continued brain maturation enables children to remain attentive for longer periods, follow multi-step directions, understand causal relations, recall events or information more precisely, and differentiate between reality and fantasy. Parents begin to notice that children are much more reasonable and better able to regulate their own behavior and emotions than when they were younger.

> **conservation**
> understanding that something (e.g., liquid, solid) is the same even when the appearance changes.
>
> **classification** ability to organize or group objects based on different features of items including form, use, and color.

Figure 9-3 Developmental Stages in Understanding Death

Concept	Age Developed	Children's Thinking Before the Concept of Death is Developed	Children's Thinking After the Concept of Death Forms
Permanence (finality)	5–6 years	Believes that death is reversible. Uses magical thinking to explain death. For example, if a child said "I wish Uncle Bill would go away," she may believe that her words caused her uncle's death.	Understands that death is permanent and not reversible
Universality (inevitability)	6–7 years	Believes that death is avoidable and will only happen to other people	Understands that everything alive will at some point die
Non-functionality (cessation)	7–8 years	Believes that a person continues to function normally even after death. For example, even though the person's heart is no longer beating, he can still feel, think, or eat	Understands that body functions (e.g., thought, feelings, movements) cease at death

Parents play a key role in creating positive, secure, and nurturing learning environments which foster optimal brain development (neural connections) and learning. Safe and predictable environments encourage higher rates of self-control and prosocial behaviors; dangerous and unpredictable environments often lead to earlier maturation, relationship instability, impulsivity, risk taking, and aggression (Del Guidice, 2015). Parents, teachers, and other professionals can coordinate their efforts to encourage discovery, creativity, and development of academic skills within safe, nurturing environments (Suggestions for Parents 9-1).

Children become increasingly adept at using their advanced language skills for a variety of purposes, including engaging in social interactions with peers. In addition, they are able to consider others' perspectives, anticipate outcomes, and are becoming increasingly less egocentric. Children also show a greater understanding of social language rules, or **pragmatics**. Pragmatics involve language usage for different purposes (e.g., greeting, requesting, informing), language alteration to fit the needs of the listener (e.g., talking differently to a peer than to a teacher or parent), and the following of rules for social conversations (e.g., taking turns in conversation, staying on topic, using nonverbal communication) (American Speech-Language-Hearing Association, 2016).

pragmatics using language in different ways and for different purposes.

Suggestions for Parents 9-1

Facilitating Children's Cognitive Development

- Allow children to select books that appeal to their interests, are appropriate for their level of understanding, and encourage independent reading as they develop reading skills.

- Read and discuss books, articles, and magazines together. Help children relate material to their existing knowledge, make predictions, organize information, and summarize what they have read.

- Match learning opportunities to children's skill level and interests.

- Encourage discovery and creativity in everyday activities. Ask and answer questions about the way things work ("What would happen if…?"). Allow children to make, and learn from, mistakes.

- Gather everyday materials (e.g., boxes, cardboard, and straws), and challenge children to construct buildings, bridges, space stations, etc.

- Conduct experiments together. Help children make predictions and estimations of what might happen, and then evaluate the outcomes.

- Include children in baking and other food preparations. Discuss mathematical information such as counting, measurements, fractions, and science information such as the purpose of recipe ingredients (e.g., baking powder makes corn bread rise).

- Provide various art supplies and allow children freedom to determine what to make; discuss the process for turning their ideas into reality.

- Play games that require a moderate level of strategy (e.g., checkers, chess, dominoes, cards).

- Attend educational opportunities in the community. Include children in outings to the library, zoo, park, and stores (e.g., building supply, gardening, grocery). Introduce and use vocabulary words relevant to the outing.

- Give children specific tasks to complete at home (e.g., putting clothes away, feeding pets, setting the table). Gradually give children more complex, multistep directions.

- Provide learning opportunities at home which reinforce and expand upon topics that children are learning in school.

School-age children are able to develop more complex narratives, tell detailed stories, demonstrate a better grasp of conversational elements, understand figurative language, and use persuasion.

Transition to School and Readiness. The transition to kindergarten poses new challenges and opportunities for children and their families. Although schools often focus on child-level social-emotional, physical, and cognitive competencies when assessing school readiness, readiness itself is a very complex, inclusive construct that encompasses the child, family, school, and community at various levels (Quirk et al., 2015). These levels all interact and influence children's academic and social-emotional outcomes. If a child is considered to be ready for school, they are expected to attend to and show persistence with tasks, cooperate with peers, express excitement and interest in school, recognize their written name, shapes, colors, and upper case letters, and demonstrate an understanding that numbers represent quantities (Bates & Furlong, 2014). Readiness behaviors are associated with academic achievement, classroom adjustment, and mental health concerns.

Photo 9-2 Parents can provide valuable learning opportunities that promote creativity and exploration.

Quirk et al. (2015) found that Latino children who started school with higher levels of cognitive readiness showed better literacy achievement patterns. English language learners who demonstrate greater initiative, self-control, attachment, and fewer behavior problems prior to school entry tend to be more successful in attaining English language proficiency and to adapt more readily to the educational environment (Winsler, Kyong Kim, & Richard, 2014). Conversely, children with limited adaptive behavior skills and/or those who exhibit problem behaviors during preschool are more likely to have difficulty adjusting to the classroom and learning because they lack necessary "survival" skills (e.g., compliance, turn-taking, sharing, independent task completion, frustration tolerance, duration of attention, learning engagement) that are essential in a new, more structured kindergarten setting (McDermott, Rikoon, & Fantuzzo, 2016; Welchons, & McIntyre, 2015). The most common problematic behaviors reported by kindergarten teachers are an inability to, or difficulty with, following directions and working independently (Robinson & Diamond, 2014). Poor social-emotional skills exhibited in a kindergarten setting have also been associated with future problems in multiple domains including employment, criminal activity, substance use, and mental health problems (Jones, Greenberg, & Crowley, 2015).

Children who have experienced stress due to maltreatment often show poor language and limited social stimulation which leads to lower cognitive development. During the transition to school, maltreated children are more likely to internalize problems if family conflict continues; those with higher cognitive abilities show less internalization, externalization, and emotional dysregulation (Appleyard et al., 2015). Temperamentally shy children may also experience greater adjustment problems during the transition to kindergarten. Often there is a poor fit between the child's temperament and expectations (e.g., participating in activities, socializing with peers) which leads to decreased behavioral engagement and poorer academic performance (O'Connor et al., 2014). Parents and teachers can support these children by recognizing and monitoring their reactions, rehearsing events and expectations, assisting with problem solving, structuring graduated practice opportunities, and providing affirmation for efforts (O'Connor et al., 2014).

Most children have a positive attitude toward school, but a few (1–6 percent) express negative feelings; some children report a change from positive to negative feelings about particular school events (Harrison &Murray, 2015). Harrison and Murray (2015) noted that children form an initial concept about school and what it means to be a student. They rely upon school rules, routines, and structure to cope with new school challenges. Familiarity gradually leads to more active problem solving and less reliance on classroom structural expectations. Daily conversations with children about school can help parents identify any negative feelings, provide support with coping and problem solving skills, and collaborate with teachers to increase positive outcomes.

Parental readiness for their child to begin formal schooling can also affect the transitional phase that both are about to encounter. Parent's memories about their own experiences (e.g., school transitions, negative social experiences, receipt of special education services) influence how they prepare children for school, their self-efficacy for helping children to make the transition, and their ongoing collaboration with teachers (Miller, 2015a). Parents with higher incomes and mothers with more education often provide stimulating learning activities and experiences at home that help to prepare their children for school (Iruka et al., 2014). However, Puccioni (2015) found that regardless of socioeconomic status, parents who placed greater importance on school readiness also engaged in more pre-kindergarten transition practices (parent-child interactions to prepare children for school), and their children showed higher achievement at the beginning of kindergarten.

Cultural factors can influence whether parents become involved and how they prepare children for the transition to school. Parents whose ethnic group is not well represented in the classroom are less likely to participate in learning activities because they may feel less empowered or that their ethnic group is not respected (Benner & Yan, 2015). They may also be reluctant to become involved if teachers contact parents only when they encounter problems with a child. Lau (2014) interviewed Chinese parents during the school transition phase. Parents reported that they shifted to more academic home-based involvement to support knowledge acquisition which was consistent with cultural expectations for high achievement. Lau pointed out that parents should try to understand the multifaceted nature of school readiness, including social adjustment, and to avoid focusing solely on academic achievements.

Miller (2015b) identified four themes that were related to school transition among parents from low-income backgrounds:

1. The transition is ongoing: refers to children's and parents' continuous adjustment to the kindergarten setting and experiences, and the development of a sense of belonging.

2. Logistics were the toughest part: describes challenges associated with the enrollment process, transportation, and school policies and procedures for starting school.

3. I told you this would happen: summarizes parents' initial concerns or aspirations for children that were confirmed during the transitional phase (e.g., poor treatment because a sibling had problems in the same school, teacher's acknowledgement of a child's exceptional performance).

Photo 9-3 School transitions are more likely to be successful when parents have information about the knowledge and skills that children will need.

4. The first time is the hardest: refers to parents' feelings that they were initially naïve about what the transition process entailed, and frustrated in their first attempts to navigate the system; however, parents also felt that they had gained important knowledge and felt more comfortable transitioning subsequent children.

Parents of children with disabilities often experience concerns associated with the transition to school and may turn to the Internet for information. Curle (2015) evaluated school transitioning information that agencies had posted online for parents of children who are deaf and hard of hearing, and found that it was of limited use, particularly for families who were located in rural areas and those with limited English skills. The information provided also placed little emphasis on parent involvement and collaborative decision-making with regard to available services and placement. Curle concluded that schools should provide better information for parents on their websites, and that school personnel must work collaboratively with families to help them navigate and understand these systems.

Such results highlight the importance of providing families with information and support to increase their understanding about the skills and attributes that contribute to school readiness (Puccioni, 2015) (Suggestions for Parents 9-2). Better parental awareness and preparedness is likely to lead to more successful transitional outcomes for children as they enter school. Family-school partnerships are also important for children's academic achievement and social-emotional well-being, especially for children who struggle with ready-to-learn behaviors, and for parental confidence in helping their child to succeed (McDremott et al., 2016) (see Chapter 3). Teachers and other professionals should reach out to parents in an effort to identify families' individual strengths, needs, and effective methods for collaboration.

Many parents may also benefit from participation in structured transition programs. Bierman et al. (2015) found that children's literacy skills, academic performance, self-directed learning, and social competence improved when parents were engaged in teacher-initiated home visitations. Teachers were able to focus on targeted interactive learning games, stories, and pretend play activities that parents could use with their children before and after the kindergarten transition period. The study authors also noted that parents continued to use more advanced reading strategies and were more involved in conversations with their children following the transition. Furthermore, Dawson-McClure et al. (2015) found that a family-centered intervention increased parent's

Suggestions for Parents 9-2

Facilitating Children's Transition to School

Parents can provide opportunities at home to prepare children for school.

- Cognitive:
  - Read and talk about stories together
  - Engage in activities that encourage children to practice counting, recognizing shapes, colors, and letters
  - Ask open-ended questions and engage in conversations (e.g., daily activities, how things work)
- Physical:
  - Play games and do activities that involve large (e.g., running, skipping, jumping) and fine motor skills (e.g., drawing, painting, placing beads on string)
  - Provide a healthy, balanced diet
  - Attend routine well-child medical checkups
- Social-emotional skills:
  - Encourage children to concentrate on tasks for increasingly longer periods of time and to persist with difficult tasks
  - Model and help children learn to problem solve, label their emotions, and cope with frustration and disappointment
  - Encourage participation in cooperative play
  - Teach children to play independently, and to seek help when needed
  - Continue to provide a nurturing, supportive learning environment
- School knowledge:
  - Help children become familiar with the school facilities (e.g., visit the school, playground, cafeteria)
  - Help children to learn the routines, rules, and expectations
  - Support children in making friends
  - Talk daily about school and children's feelings
  - Collaborate and maintain open communication with teachers

involvement and use of positive behavior techniques, which also resulted in decreased rates of problem behaviors for at-risk male students.

Schools' efforts to screen incoming students' readiness, and provide appropriate, targeted interventions can help to decrease the risk of future negative outcomes, such as retention, academic and behavioral difficulties, and peer rejection (Stormont et al., 2015). There is also increasing evidence that long-term cost savings are associated with programs that facilitate school transition. Peters et al. (2016) found that for every dollar the government invested in programs that focused on healthy development, prevention of social, behavioral, and cognitive problems, and enhancements in family and community environments for children ages 4 to 8 years, there was a savings of $2.50 per family because fewer costly interventions were needed in subsequent years.

Learning and Attention Problems. Specific learning disabilities and attention problems are often first recognized during the school-age years as the demands of school increase and discrepancies between expectations and academic and attention skills become more apparent. Several factors may contribute to these problems, including genetic/heritability, prenatal exposure to malnutrition, oxygen deprivation, drugs and alcohol, and premature or prolonged labor; and postnatal factors, such as traumatic brain injuries, nutritional deprivation, homelessness, or exposure to poisonous substances, such as lead (Cortiella & Horowitz, 2014). Thompson et al. (2015) found that children were at increased risk for specific reading disabilities when there was a family history of dyslexia, for example, and when the child showed poor language skills (e.g., letter knowledge, phonological awareness) at school entry.

Attention Deficit Hyperactivity Disorder (ADHD) is often diagnosed as school expectations increase and students are required to attend to tasks for longer periods, control their impulses, and plan and organize their materials more independently. ADHD is a neurogenetic condition (i.e., differences in the brain, particularly the frontal lobe) that tends to run in families and is associated with poor persistence toward goals or tasks, greater reactivity to distractions, and impaired working memory (remembering how to perform a task). It is also associated with impaired verbal and motor inhibition, impulsive decision making, difficulty delaying gratification, excessive movement or restlessness, and emotional impulsivity (e.g., impatience, low frustration to tolerance, quick to anger, easily excitable). More than half of all children with ADHD have another mental health concern (e.g., oppositional defiant disorder), and are more likely than those without ADHD to perform below an average academic level, have a tendency to get in trouble at school or with the law, and to have difficulty making and keeping friends (Cuffe et al., 2015). Similarly, one in every two students with a learning disability will be suspended or expelled from school (Cortiella & Horowitz, 2014). Furthermore, maladaptive behavior and academic difficulties often occur together. Some children show an increase in problem behaviors in order to avoid work tasks that are too difficult; others may exhibit problematic behavior that subsequently interferes with work completion.

Parents of children with learning and attention impairments respond to the challenges in different ways. Approximately 35 percent struggle with their attitudes and ability to accept the child's problems, 31 percent have conflicting feelings, and 34 percent are optimistic about the child's future (Cortiella & Horowitz, 2014). Those who struggle may find the challenges daunting, experience increased financial pressures, feel isolated, have difficulty maintaining positive relationships, and have trouble coping with feelings of stress and guilt. Parents and caregivers of children with ADHD may become frustrated with the child's behavior because he or she typically understands instructions or has the skills to complete tasks, but does not do so in a timely manner. Children with ADHD often respond well to medication in combination with behavior therapy.

Parents can also structure the home environment in ways that will produce positive and corrective consequences which may help to decrease the negative impact of ADHD on daily functioning. Cortiella & Horowitz (2014) noted that optimistic parents were able to advocate for their child, manage stress, teach their child to cope with situational difficulties, and develop confidence in handling everyday issues.

However, they also found that most parents of children with learning disabilities (75 percent) believe they could do more to help their child with these skills (Cortiella & Horowitz, 2014).

Parents who suspect that their child may have a learning disability or attention problems can request an evaluation through their local school district and/or meet with a physician or psychologist to determine if children meet criteria for a disability and would benefit from treatment. If a child qualifies for special education services, an Individualized Education Program (IEP) that outlines specific goals, intervention services needed, and appropriate classroom accommodations will be developed (see Chapter 14). If ADHD does not appear to have a detrimental effect on a child's academic skills or ability to function in the classroom, a 504 Plan may be developed to protect the student's rights (as having a disability) and provide access to basic and necessary accommodations. For all students, but particularly those with disabilities and attention difficulties, collaboration between home and school is essential to their academic success and to healthy family functioning.

Photo 9-4 When learning and attention problems are identified early, appropriate services can be delivered to improve achievement.

The use of early identification screening tools in schools has become increasingly common. Such tools encourage teachers and schools to take a Response to Intervention (RIT) approach to identifying children with disabilities. This approach uses a data-based decision-making process, tiered levels of support to prevent and ameliorate learning and behavioral problems, and quality instruction matched to students' needs. Children are better able to overcome barriers to learning when they are given an appropriate type and amount of instruction, support, and accommodation. Multi-tiered intervention support systems also appear to be more effective than retention for meeting students' needs. Retention is controversial and associated with mixed results with regard to student achievement and social-emotional functioning. Vandecandelaere et al. (2016) found that retention is less harmful overall if it is implemented in kindergarten versus first grade. They hypothesized that early grade repeaters would score higher in mathematics over time if they were promoted each year. The conjecture was based upon the idea that children who are promoted may be more likely to receive instruction appropriate to their developmental stage (zone of proximal development), which may lead to better achievement. Children who are retained may experience poor self-esteem and a self-fulfilling prophesy of low expectations and performance. However, if children do not receive instruction appropriate for their level after being promoted, they too may experience lower self-esteem, problematic behaviors, and poor academic performance. Thus, retention or promotion without an appropriate instructional match to children's unique needs may prove equally consequential for learning outcomes.

9-2b Supporting Social-Emotional Development

School-age children begin to exhibit a need for greater independence. This desire coincides with an improved ability to control and regulate their own behavior, and to understand the consequences of their actions. They make friends easily, and often prefer spending more time with them than with their family.

Socialization. While preschoolers were likely to view themselves in an overly positive light, school-age children's views are more realistic (Lecompte et al., 2014). In fact, children's self-esteem tends to decrease at around age 7 years and remain in question throughout adolescence (Del Giudice, 2015). This change in perspective is described by Erikson (1963) as a conflict between industry and inferiority. Children develop a sense of industry through successful interactions and experiences with others which, in turn, contributes to feelings of confidence, accomplishment, competence, and positive self-esteem. Parents and caregivers can support a child's sense of industry by providing developmentally appropriate tasks, and scaffolding more advanced tasks that are within their zone of proximal development. Acknowledgement of children's efforts and

David Elkind, author of *The hurried child* (1981), was among the first scholars to express concern about the detrimental effects that parental pressure and extracurricular activity overscheduling could have on children's development. Concerns are re-emerging again about the same subjects, and the negative effects that such a pattern can have on children's well-being and academic performance (Moran, 2016; Stracciolini et al., 2015; Brown et al., 2011).

Parental involvement in children's education has been encouraged for many years. Research results have shown that it makes a significant difference in children's adjustment to school and in academic achievements (Jeynes, 2016; Hoglund, 2015). However, some well-intentioned parents have misinterpreted professional advice and have overscheduled children in multiple after-school extracurricular activities—from music lessons and 4-H to enrichment classes and competitive youth sport teams. In some families, overscheduling also extends to weekends when school doesn't interfere with all-day competitions or tournaments.

The rationale for following this path is based on the belief that such experiences will give children a competitive advantage (e.g., cognitive, motor, social)—especially in sport-related endeavors—over their peers who do not participate in such activities. As a result, children may find themselves being transported from one activity to another (often on the same evening) which leaves them limited time to complete homework, to eat, and to sleep. Children have reported feeling pressured, anxious, and stressed as a result of maintaining such nonstop schedules (Dent, 2013).

Do multiple activities and a complex schedule have a positive effect on children's academic performance and socialization? Schiffrin et al. (2015) did not find any direct associations between young children's involvement in extracurricular activities and improvement in their developmental skills

(e.g., cognitive, social, motor). However, the authors noted that children who felt pressured by their parents experienced more stress and anxiety. High absenteeism and injury rates have also been observed among children who are highly involved in extracurricular activities on a regular basis (Hansen et al., 2016).

However, not all researchers would agree that children's participation in structured extracurricular activities is associated with negative consequences. Some children do thrive on activity and involvement in after-school activities. Researchers have also concluded that children learn important self-regulation skills when they participate in supervised activities outside of the classroom (Piché, Fitzpatrick, & Pagani, 2015). Schuepbach (2015) noted that first- through third-grade Swiss children showed improved academic achievement when they participated in extracurricular activities. Similarly, Schwartz, Capella, and Seidman (2015) found that children who participated in several community or athletic activities during the school year had higher GPAs. However, they also noted that participation in more than two such activities had negative effects on academic performance.

Parents desire health and happiness for their children, and want them to explore opportunities that may help them to succeed. However, pressuring children to pursue too many activities or activities in which they have limited interest or required skills can lead to psychological problems, particularly if they decide to drop out or terminate the experience (Vella et al., 2015). Parents must work together with their children to create a healthy balance between scheduled activity involvement and unstructured time. Activities should be fun for children and not something that parents believe they should do, especially if they feel anxious or academic performance is affected. Too much pressure can lead to anxiety and burnout. How can a parent determine if an activity is right for their child? What behavioral indications might suggest that a child is overscheduled?

persistence toward achieving goals, and provision of honest feedback are also important strategies for reinforcing children's feelings of self-worth.

School-age children begin to form an expanded network of friendships with peers who exert a considerable influence on their thoughts and actions. However, peers are not just friends; they also become competitors for social status and rewards, which can lead to conflict (Del Giudice, 2015). Although acceptance within a peer group is important, it is not necessary for children to have multiple friends or to be a popular student. Indeed, research supports the conclusion that children benefit most from having one close friendship.

Bullying problems often arise as children begin comparing themselves to others and competing for peer attention. Bullying is defined as repeated aggressive behavior that involves a real or perceived power imbalance. Aggressive behaviors may be verbal (e.g., name calling, taunting, teasing), social or relational (e.g., hurting someone's reputation by spreading rumors, excluding others on purpose), or physical (e.g., hitting, spitting, breaking another's possessions) (U.S. Department of Health and Human Services, 2015). Research results are beginning to show that bullying may lead to long-term negative effects on brain development. Bullying can cause stress, which increases cortisol levels in the brain, weakens the immune system, and destroys nerve cells in the area associated with memory (Bates, 2015). Such changes are associated with poor self-esteem, increased drug use, aggression directed toward others, and disorders such as depression and anxiety (Bates, 2015).

School personnel have a professional and ethical responsibility to create safe environments for all students and to implement policies that protect children who are at increased risk of being victimized, such as lesbian, gay, bisexual, and transgender students (Russell et al., 2016). Gower et al. (2014) examined the impact of physical and **relational aggression** in kindergarten children. They noted that children who are physically aggressive upon school entry are less likely to be accepted by their peers, and more likely to have conflict with teachers. Children who exhibit relational aggression are more likely to be accepted by, and have a closer relationship with, teachers than with their peers. Children who bully or intimidate others often have better social skills and an ability to establish their standing in a group, manipulate interactions, and hide aggressive behaviors.

Despite the fact that relationally-aggressive children experience fewer social problems, the impact they have on victims can be significant (Gower et al., 2014). Therefore, interventions to increase the use of prosocial skills by school-age children who show physically and relationally-aggressive behavior are important to the development of a positive environment in which all children are able to flourish. Parents can also take several steps to prevent and intervene when children are being bullied (Suggestions for Parents 9-3).

Photo 9-5 Supportive relationships with parents and teachers enhance children's resilience.

relational aggression hurtful behavior, such as bullying, used to manipulate or disrupt peer relationships to gain personal recognition.

Suggestions for Parents 9-3

Preventing and Intervening with Bullying

Parents' role in preventing bullying:

- Help children understand what bullying is, how to respond appropriately to bullies, and how to get help from adults who are responsible for maintaining safety.

- Keep the lines of communication open. Talk with children daily about school (e.g., friends, concerns, accomplishments). Mention bullying directly to determine if they have concerns or are affected. Remain calm, do not overreact, listen attentively, and acknowledge the child's feelings.

- Stay up to date with school and extracurricular activities. Be aware of school policies that relate to bullying.

- Encourage children to do what they enjoy. Children gain self-confidence when they are engaged in pleasurable activities and are able to meet and develop friendships with peers who have shared interests. Enjoyable activities that children can successfully participate in also promote positive mood and thinking.

- Model how to treat others with kindness and respect. Children learn from observing adults, noting how they interact with others and work to solve conflicts.

Parents' role in intervening when children are being bullied:

- Listen and focus on the child. Assure the child that the bullying is not their fault.

- Encourage children to talk about it or seek mental health support.

- Help the child learn how to respond:
  - Suggest that the child look directly at the person initiating the bullying activity and tell them to stop in a calm, confident voice. Use humor, but do not insult the bully.

continued on following page

- If the bullied child does not feel safe or verbally able to respond, he/she should walk away, find an adult, and ask for help so that the bullying behavior is stopped right away.
- Do not encourage the child to be aggressive in return.
- Advise the child to stay away from places where bullying is likely to occur, or to stay near a trusted adult.
- Work with others (e.g., teachers, coaches) to resolve the situation, and to keep children safe.
- Understand that it may take time to fully address bullying problems. Remain supportive and persistent.
- Avoid the following common mistakes:
  - Never tell children that the bullying is their fault or blame children for being bullied.
  - Do not tell children to ignore the bullying or to fight back.
  - Do not contact the other parent(s) involved because this may escalate the problem.

Adapted from: U.S. Department of Health and Human Services (2015). *How to talk about bullying and support the kids involved.*

❯❯ Professional Resource Download

resilience the ability to adapt to and overcome adversity.

Parents can also work with children to enhance their social-emotional skills and build **resilience** to adversity. Increasing children's positive experiences and adaptive coping skills can help to counterbalance the negative effects of exposure to significant or repeated adversity. The Center on the Developing Child (2016) has identified several factors that promote resilience:

1. Facilitating supportive relationships
2. Increasing self-efficacy and control
3. Providing opportunities to improve adaptive skills and self-regulation
4. Mobilizing sources of faith, hope, and cultural traditions

Forming a stable relationship with at least one caring adult, such as a teacher or coach, is the most important protective factor for increasing a child's resilience (Gower et al., 2014). Parents can also promote children's self-efficacy by acknowledging their efforts and successes, encouraging persistence, increasing their involvement in activities in which they are successful and enjoy, and continuing to provide a friendly, nurturing environment. In addition, parents can help children to learn behaviors that are appropriate for different settings, become aware of their feelings and positive ways to express them, and to use effective coping and problem-solving strategies.

Mental Health Disorders. Children's mental health is attracting increased attention worldwide as more is learned about the early signs and importance of securing prompt treatment. Teachers, health care providers, and other professionals are assuming a more active role in identifying children who exhibit negative behaviors that prevent them from being successful. Parents also play a critical role in recognizing changes in children's behavior and seeking early evaluation and treatment (see Figure 9-4).

Mental health problems can cause children to experience low self-esteem and self-worth, academic failure and school expulsion, substance abuse, criminality, and suicide unless they receive treatment. Some circumstances place children at higher risk for developing mental health problems, including living in poverty, foster care, abusive homes, military or incarcerated families, or being homeless (Alfano et al., 2016; Bitsko et al., 2016; Waters et al., 2015). Some disorders have a genetic predisposition (e.g., schizophrenia, depression), whereas others may develop in response to environmental conditions, such as experiencing severe emotional trauma or stress (e.g., illness

Figure 9-4 Signs of Children's Mental Health Problems

All children will show some of these behaviors from time to time. If they occur frequently or persist, the child's health care provider should be consulted. Serious signs (e.g., talk of suicide, hurting themselves) require immediate professional attention.

- Develops sudden behavior changes (e.g., declining grades, aggression, withdrawn)
- Has difficulty sleeping, frequent nightmares, or loss of interest in eating
- Experiences sudden, excessive, or prolonged sadness, worry, fear, irritability, anger, anxiety, hopelessness, or tearfulness
- Has difficulty focusing or staying on task
- Withdraws and prefers to spend time alone; avoids friends and family
- Destroys property; hurts self, animals, or other people
- Hears voices, is overly suspicious, or talks about suicide

Adapted from Mental Health America (2016).

or death of a parent or close family member, divorce, maltreatment, witnessing a violent crime).

Mood and anxiety disorders are among the most common causes of mental health problems experienced by school-age children. Approximately 3.7 percent of children age 8 to 15 years experience mood disorders which include serious depression, persistent, low-grade depression, and bipolar conditions (NIMH, 2016a). These disorders are typically characterized by a sudden or prolonged change in children's emotional and daily living behaviors (e.g., sleeping, eating, social interactions). Anxiety disorders include a variety of conditions, such as generalized anxiety disorders, panic disorder, obsessive-compulsive disorder (OCD), separation disorders, social and specific phobias, and posttraumatic stress disorder (PTSD). Cognitive behavioral therapy, alone or in combination with medication is often used successfully to treat children's mood and anxiety disorders (NIMH, 2016b; Gordon-Hollingsworth et al., 2015; Weinstein et al., 2015).

Oppositional defiant disorder (ODD) also becomes more apparent during the school-age years. It is characterized by a pattern of disruptive, disobedient behavior that includes anger and irritable mood, argumentative and defiant behavior, and vindictiveness directed toward family members and/or peers (APA, 2013). Because it is not uncommon for children to occasionally exhibit some of these behaviors, a diagnosis of ODD requires that the symptoms be observed at least once a week over a 6-month period. Children should also be evaluated for the presence of other disorders that may be contributing to these behaviors, such as learning disabilities, mood and anxiety disorders, and ADHD (Mayes et al., 2016). Effective treatment strategies include parent management training and cognitive behavioral therapy (Sukhodolsky et al., 2016).

Parents often find it difficult to accept that their child may have a mental health disorder. Some parents rationalize the child's challenging behaviors as 'just a phase' that will eventually be outgrown or even deny that a problem exists. Parents may feel guilty and fear that the child's disorder reflects poorly on their parenting abilities. Cultural differences and perceived stigma associated with mental health disorders also create barriers that can keep families from obtaining treatment for children (Ohan et al., 2015; Polaha et al., 2015). Turner et al. (2015) reported that African-American parents felt more stigmatized than European-American or Hispanic-American parents and, thus, were less likely to acknowledge or seek professional mental health care for their children. However, Hispanic American parents also felt stigmatized and, thus,

Photo 9-6 School age children are better able to consider a peer's perspective and empathize.

were reluctant to seek treatment for mental health problems. These findings may help to explain, in part, the disparity that exists in the utilization of mental health services among minority populations.

Moral Reasoning. Moral behavior encompasses children's sense of justice, fairness, responsibility, caring, and helping. As children develop and gain a better understanding of right and wrong, parents may become frustrated when children appear to overlook or ignore moral standards. Research, however, supports the idea that moral reasoning is sensitive to changes in maturity and social demands (Lapsley & Carlo, 2014). For example, young children may engage in moral behavior (e.g., sharing, helping others, taking turns) and are able to recognize whether their behaviors are right or wrong based upon rules and expectations. Such moral understanding becomes more sophisticated during the school-age years (Lapsley & Carlo, 2014). New cognitive skills enable children to consider the personal and situational features of moral events, and to appreciate that people can have different thoughts, feelings, and beliefs. Thus, they begin to understand that rules and moral situations are more complex, and less rigid than simply being right or wrong. For example, older school-age children are better able to understand the reasons for why inequality may be acceptable in some situations, and to differentiate between legitimate (e.g., based on merit, need, or rules) and idiosyncratic (e.g., desire to have more without justification) inequality (Schmidt et al., 2016).

The development of moral reasoning is shaped by a combination of cultural practices, customs, and beliefs and ongoing social interactions. For example, moral behavior is predicted by *familism* in Latino youth (i.e., value and importance of family ties) and by parental chore assignments in Kenyan youth (Lapsley & Carlo, 2014). Parents and teachers can teach children moral reasoning by encouraging them to consider other people's viewpoints and actions, and how they might be related (Brownlee et al., 2015). Parents can also play games with children to highlight the importance of rules, provide brief rationales for consequences associated with correct and incorrect behavior, assist children with problem solving, and involve children in complex situations, such as the seemingly unequal division of materials among group members (e.g., mom and dad get more food because their bodies are bigger and need more energy to function). Positive parent-child relationships are also associated with higher moral behavior and lower levels of aggression (Sengsvang & Krettenauer, 2015). Over time, children learn by observing behaviors that are valued and modeled by significant adults in their lives, such as respecting others' views, being generous, admitting errors, showing loyalty, helping others, being honest, and demonstrating commitment to justice.

Children's behavior and reasoning are sensitive to factors, such as emotions, potential punishments or rewards, and a desire to impress or protect others. Given a scenario, school-age children are able to determine the appropriate moral behavior, but they also begin to realize that they may behave differently in the same situation. For example, if asked by a parent what grade was received on a test, a child may understand that she should tell the truth, but may not because she wants the parent to view her in a positive light. If she lies, she gains approval and can continue to play; if she tells the truth she may have to stop playing and study (a consequence of poor performance).

It is important that parents pay attention to feelings of shame, guilt, and empathy that may underlie children's moral reasoning. Parents should refrain from negative shaming when giving children feedback and, instead, focus on problem solving and persistence toward completing challenging tasks. Stuewig et al. (2015) found that school-age children who were more prone to feelings of **shame** versus feelings of **guilt** were more likely to show deviant behaviors in late adolescence, including illicit and

shame a feeling of embarrassment or remorse for behavior that a person knows is wrong.

guilt feelings associated with regret and motivation to repair a misdeed.

unprotected sex, drug use, and activities that led to involvement with the criminal justice system. These undesirable outcomes may be related to children's peer relationship problems, negative evaluations of self-worth, and adverse behaviors (e.g., withdrawal, depression, defensive or irrational anger). In general, guilt appears to be more adaptive and associated with fewer negative feelings.

Empathy refers to a person's ability to understand, be sensitive to, and share another's feelings. Parents are important for fostering empathy development in children. In fact, children with responsive, playful, and nurturing parents show higher empathy levels (Narvaez et al., 2013). Empathy facilitates positive social interactions because it enables prosocial behaviors, inhibits aggression, increases helping behavior, and supports moral behavior (Decety, 2015). Parents can reflect upon their child's thoughts, feelings, and actions and provide support during everyday interactions. For example, given the previous scenario, a parent might say "I understand that you were afraid to tell me the truth about your test score because you thought that I would disapprove and you would get in trouble. But, it is important for us to be honest with each other. Let's make a plan so that you feel more confident about taking your next test." Parents can also point out examples, encourage, and reinforce caring behaviors (e.g., listening, showing concern) that are related to empathy development.

Sexuality. Six-year-old children begin to understand that gender is based on genitalia differences, and that gender is constant and cannot be changed (Halim & Ruble, 2010). They understand that a girl will grow up to be a woman and a boy will become a man. They also understand that gender is consistent even when superficial changes are made in appearance. For example, they know that a girl remains a girl even if she dresses like a boy and plays football. Although a 5-year-old's ideas about what people can and cannot do (e.g., occupations, sports, parental roles) are quite rigid, they will gradually become more flexible at around age 7 years (Halim & Ruble, 2010). Boys and girls tend to go their separate ways, and show more interest in spending time and engaging in activities with same-sex peers (Marotz & Allen, 2016). To support healthy development of gender identity and to decrease gender stereotypes, parents and caregivers should allow children freedom to select activities of interest, even if those interests diverge from typical activities for their gender. School-age children continue to be influenced by their parents' and teachers' attitudes about gender roles, and the way that genders are portrayed in the media.

It is important that parents continue to educate children about sexuality as their bodies begin to mature and their knowledge of gender identity, roles, and expressions improve. Children should be taught about appropriate and inappropriate touches and what to do if someone were to touch, ask them to touch, or look at their private parts. Children also need information about bodily changes that occur during puberty. Initiating these conversations early, being honest, and remaining nonjudgmental during these conversations can help to keep open the lines of communication and encourage children to continue asking questions in the future.

Some children may begin to express gender non-conformity. They may feel that they do not fit into either gender category, but are somewhere in between. Other children may express an identification with the opposite gender (transgender) or be attracted to the same or both genders (e.g., gay, lesbian, bisexual). Some young children, particularly those between the ages of 9 and 10 years may identify with the opposite gender and then, later, change to identify with their birth gender. It is unknown whether these children decided to hide their true feelings or if their feelings were simply a passing phase (American Academy of Pediatrics, 2015). Unfortunately, some of these children experience rejection in their school, the community, or home and are at increased risk for entering the foster care or juvenile justice system. Thus, it is important for children to have a connection with a supportive physician or mental health provider who has expertise in this area and can work with them to achieve positive gender outcomes (Sherer et al., 2015). Parents can also take important steps to support children who have non-conforming gender identities (Suggestions for Parents 9-4).

empathy ability to understand, be sensitive to, and share another's feelings and motivation to care for others.

Parental Support for Gender Non-Conforming Children

- Respond to children's disclosure in an affirming, supportive way.
- Recognize that gender identity cannot be changed through intervention and is not a result of inadequate parenting.
- Accept and love children as they are; support is beneficial for their healthy development.
- Stand up for children when they are mistreated or subjected to jokes and slurs.
- Watch for signs of anxiety, insecurity, depression, and low self-esteem, especially when children have limited social support.
- Connect children with gender non-conforming organizations, resources, and events so they understand that they are not alone.
- Support children's self-expression through choices of clothing, jewelry, hairstyle, friends, and room decoration.
- Help school personnel create a welcoming environment for children.
- Strengthen your own understanding of gender non-conforming youth experiences.

Adapted from: American Academy of Pediatrics (2015). Gender non-conforming & transgender children.

Responsive Parenting

Seven-year-old Jayden's favorite colors are pink and lavender, and he will only wear shirts to school that are these colors. His mother, a single parent, continuously criticizes his clothing choices and tells him that "only girls wear pink and lavender." Yesterday, Jayden came home from school in tears and told his mother that the kids were making fun of his clothes. She laughed and responded, "I told you so. If you would only listen and dress like a real boy that would not have happened." What assumptions is Jayden's mother making? How are her comments likely to make Jayden feel? How would you advise her to respond in a way that is more supportive?

9-2c Promoting Healthy Eating Behaviors

School-age children typically have a good appetite, are willing to try new foods, and often enjoy assisting with food shopping and meal preparation. It is important that they continue to consume a nutritious diet during this period to maintain growth, supply energy, improve resistance to illness, and perform well in school (Marotz, 2015). However, many U.S. children are failing to meet the recommendations established in the 2010 Dietary Guidelines for Americans (Banfield et al., 2016). Poor dietary intake of essential nutrients (e.g., proteins, carbohydrates, fats, vitamins, minerals, water) is associated with adverse health effects in childhood as well as in the future (Marotz, 2011). Conversely, Cheng et al. (2016) observed that the nutrient quality of Chinese school-age children's diet, particularly that of girls, was closely aligned with the Chinese Children Dietary Index, and that children were less likely to be overweight and inactive.

Why are U.S. children not receiving the nutrients they require? Parents often cite busy lifestyles, children's picky-eating, food costs, and distance to grocery stores as barriers that interfere with healthy eating behaviors (Robson, Crosby, & Stark, 2016; Ranjit et al., 2015; Cano et al., 2015). Children who are picky eaters, for example, often consume a diet that lacks variety, fruits and vegetables and, thus, critical vitamins, minerals, and fiber. Food refusal and high food selectively are often characteristic behaviors in children with autism spectrum disorder, and are associated with poor nutrient intake (Curtin et al., 2015; Zimmer et al., 2012). Cultural patterns also influence children's food preferences. Jahns et al. (2015) surveyed fifth-grade Northern Plains American-Indian children and evaluated the types of foods they typically ate and those they rejected. Children who participated in the study reported personal preferences and environmental issues (e.g., food costs, transportation, distance to grocery stores) as factors that limited their consumption of foods from all food groups, especially whole grains, fruits, and vegetables. These findings are especially alarming given the high incidence of obesity and diabetes that occurs among this population.

Parents play an unquestionably influential role in the formation of children's eating habits and attitudes toward certain foods and food groups. For example, Fraught et al. (2016) examined the relationship between parental practices and their fifth-grade children's weight and fruit and vegetable consumption. Children who reported that their parents showed concern about what they ate, encouraged them to eat nutritious foods, and made such foods available in the home had better overall dietary quality and were less likely to be overweight. Researchers have also noted that children are more likely to indulge in unhealthy snacking in homes where less parental concern and control are exercised. For example, Taillie et al. (2015) found that Mexican children who ate more than the average three meals and one or two snacks per day were more likely to be overweight and to consume foods that were poor in nutrient quality (e.g., candy, cookies, salty snacks, soda). These findings reinforce the significant positive or negative effect that parents have on children's eating behaviors, particularly during the school-age years (Boots et al., 2015).

Photo 9-7 Parents can encourage healthy habits and decrease the risk of obesity by serving regular meals, making sleep a priority, and participating in physical activity with children.

Childhood Obesity and At-Risk Populations. Although the rates of childhood obesity in the U.S. appear to have reached a plateau, the number of children who are overweight or obese remains high, especially among minority groups (e.g., Black, Hispanic, Native American), those living in poverty, and those who have disabilities (e.g., intellectual, physical, developmental). Childhood obesity can lead to significant health complications (e.g., diabetes, cardiovascular heart disease, sleep apnea) and have a negative effect on children's self-esteem, academic performance, and peer relationships (Carey et al., 2015; Gurnani, Birken, & Hamilton, 2015).

A child's risk for becoming overweight is highly influenced by a combination of interacting factors, including maternal education and food-related practices, neighborhood environment, and family resources. Researchers have found that ethnic minority parents, particularly African American and Hispanic parents, were more likely to underestimate their child's weight and not to perceive being overweight as problematic (Natale et al., 2016; Alexander et al., 2015). Parents in these studies believed that children's health and happiness were more important than concerns about their weight. Ford et al. (2016) also noted that African American, Hispanic, and Asian children who were overweight or obese engaged in fewer hours of physical activity, slept less, spent more time with electronic devices, skipped breakfasts and meals, and had high consumption of sweetened beverages and/or juice. Skipped meals, reduced sleep, and insufficient physical activity rates were highest among school-age and adolescent girls. These are areas where parents can take positive steps to help children improve habits that are conductive to better health.

Children with physical, intellectual, and developmental disorders are also more likely than their typically developing peers to be overweight or obese (Gillette et al., 2015; Slevin et al., 2014). Several factors that contribute to this pattern have been identified, including lower rates of physical activity, increased time spent in sedentary activities (e.g., watching television, playing video games, reading), and a preference for consuming fatty, sugary foods (Cermak et al., 2015; Cook, Li, & Heinrich, 2015). Boddy et al. (2015) noted that children with intellectual disabilities (particularly those

Examples of Fitness Activities for Children with Autism

Physical activity improves children's balance, coordination, strength, flexibility, and cardiovascular fitness. Activities should appeal to children's interests, be safe, and be consistent with their abilities.

- Walking around the neighborhood or to a nearby park or playground, jogging around a local track
- Assisting with household tasks—putting away laundry, vacuuming, washing the car, walking the dog, watering the garden
- Tossing beanbags, playing catch or kicking balls of different sizes
- Swimming, skating, shooting basketballs, playing golf, jumping rope, riding a bike, swinging, playing hopscotch, flying a kite
- Dancing to music, doing jumping jacks
- Walking on a treadmill, riding a stationary bike, participating in a martial arts or yoga class
- Pulling a wagon, moving gardening supplies in a wheelbarrow

with autism spectrum disorder) did not participate in group games or sport-related activities during recess. Instead, they spent the majority of their time playing alone, behavior that is consistent for children who have impaired communication and social skills. These findings have important implications for parents and caregivers, and the need to identify fitness opportunities that will appeal to, and address, a child's unique interests and individual needs (Suggestions for Parents 9-5).

Food Insecurity. Many families are struggling to feed their school-age children, especially minority families and those headed by a single female. Over 60 percent of the 3500 California children participating in a recent study reported that they had experienced food insecurity during the previous 24 hours (Fram et al. (2015). Food insecure diets are typically high in calories, fat, and sugar and low in protein, fruit, vegetables, and fiber. They are also associated with higher obesity rates, low physical activity, learning and behavior disorders, and negative health and economic outcomes in adulthood (Kaur, Lamb, & Ogden, 2015; Ke & Ford-Jones, 2015).

For many children, the meals and snacks they receive at school are their primary food source for the day. The National School Lunch Program (NSLP) and School Breakfast Program (SBP) served approximately 21 million children during the 2014–2015 school year; the Summer Food Service Programs (SFSP) served approximately 200 million meals to hungry children in 2015 (see Figure 9-5) (USDA, 2016). Recent cost increases for full- and reduced-price meals have resulted in decreased participation and caused many families to begin packing children's lunches. However, researchers have noted that the packed lunches children are bringing to school fail to meet nutrient recommendations. Farris et al. (2015) reported that an estimated 40 percent of elementary school children bring a packed lunch to school each day. These lunches typically included a sugary beverage and dessert (high sugar, fat, calories), and were low in vitamins and minerals (typically found in fruits and vegetables), and protein. Efforts to improve parents' nutrition knowledge and understanding about the important role that a healthy diet plays in children's growth and development would help to alleviate some school lunch issues.

9-2d Promoting Physical Activity

Although time constraints and conflicting schedules become more challenging as children age, it is important that they engage in at least 60 minutes of vigorous physical activity each day, and muscle- and bone-building activities every other day. School-age children

Figure 9-5 National School Lunch Program Participation Rates By Eligibility Category, Fiscal 2007–2014

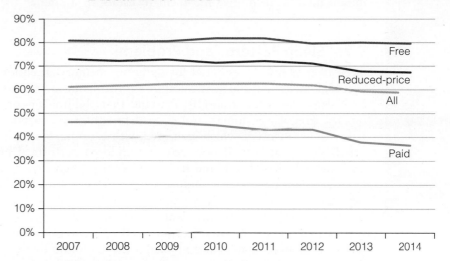

Note: Participation rates are calculated as average daily participation divided by the number of students in each category.

Source: USDA Economic Research Service using data from USDA, Food and Nutrition Service.

should be discouraged from remaining inactive for longer than 2 hours at a time (SHAPE America, 2016). Moderate daily activity has been shown to reduce school absenteeism, improve cognitive function, increase academic motivation, and foster positive social skills and self-esteem as well as promote fitness and health (Hansen et al., 2015; Eime et al., 2013).

It becomes imperative that children have opportunities to be active because many schools have decreased or eliminated recess periods, and school-age children spend long hours in sedentary school activities. Encouraging children to walk or ride their bike to school is one way to increase their daily activity. Duncan, Strycker, and Nigel (2015) noted that African American, Latino, and White girls who enjoyed physical education classes were more likely to walk or ride their bikes to school than were girls who disliked these classes. This finding should provide schools with an incentive to make physical education classes more interesting and fun for students. Echeverría, Ohri-Vachaspati, and Yedidia (2015) examined the type and quantity of physical activity among a sample of Latino children living in a poor New Jersey neighborhood. They noted that Latino children whose parents had lived in the United States for less than 10 years were almost twice as likely to walk, ride their bike, or use a skateboard to travel to school than children whose parents were born here. Ideally, parents can walk to and from school with their children and enjoy the benefits of spending time together and creating a healthier lifestyle. Researchers have also observed that children from higher income families are often driven to school by their parents and, thus, tend to engage in less than the recommended amount of daily activity.

Study results show that children are more likely to value and participate in organized physical activities when they perceive parental encouragement and support (Sterdt, Liersch, & Walter, 2014). Parents convey their interest through verbal encouragement, attending events, initiating and completing the enrollment process, and transporting children to and from activities. The availability of equipment, such as a basketball goal or skateboard, increased the likelihood that boys would engage in physical activity when they arrived home after school; parental encouragement was more strongly correlated with girls' participation in physical activities (Lau et al., 2015).

The school-age years are an opportune time for children to experiment with a variety of different sports and physical activities, and to discover those that they find

Photo 9-8 Sleep problems can have a significant negative impact on learning.

most enjoyable. Researchers have shown that children who find pleasure in being physically active are likely to maintain this pattern into adulthood (Smith et al., 2015). Parents who are physically active and engage in activities together with their children play an important role in motivating them to establish a similar lifelong pattern.

9-2e Sleep Patterns and Problems

Sleep is known to be essential for optimum memory, attention, decision-making, math fluency, emotional control, and decreased daytime sleepiness. Cho et al. (2015) found that children's poor sleep quality, irregular bedtimes, and sleep deprivation led to poor verbal working memory, which interfered with learning. Similarly, van Schalkwijk et al. (2015) observed that children performed poorly on a memory-based task and had more errors when they received less sleep. During sleep, the brain reorganizes verbal memories and experiences so that children are able to learn new skills faster and more efficiently when they are awake. Inadequate sleep has also been shown to have a negative effect on children's emotions and emotional regulation. Kouros and El-Sheikh (2015) found that children who took longer to fall asleep exhibited a more negative mood and had difficulty regulating their emotions the next day. These behaviors are likely to also have a negative effect on a child's social interactions and peer relationships.

Quality sleep is essential for children's health, academic performance, mood and emotional stability, and unintentional injury prevention (Erath et al., 2015; Tan et al., 2015). Researchers have established a strong link between inadequate sleep and weight gain, including obesity (Chaput, 2016). Insufficient sleep appears to contribute to increased food consumption (frequency, quantity) and a preference for high-calorie foods. Franckle et al. (2015) reported that children who slept less than 10 hours a day consumed soda more often, ate fewer vegetables, but showed no difference in their fruit consumption. These findings have important implications given current child obesity rates, and should alert parents to the urgency of ensuring that children receive adequate sleep (Suggestions for Parents 9-6). Parents are advised to avoid giving children sleep medications, and to consult with their health care provider if children's sleep disturbances persist.

Suggestions for Parents 9-6

Tips for Improving Children's Sleep Habits

Adequate sleep is critical for children's growth, development, and short- and long-term health. Consider:

- Creating an environment that is conducive to restful sleep (e.g., remove clutter, turn off cell phones and computers, provide quiet, turn down room temperature)

- Maintaining a regular bedtime routine, even on weekends and holidays (e.g., similar bedtime and wake schedule, warm shower or bath, a light snack, a few minutes of 'winding down' time engaged in reading or listening to quiet music).

- Talking with children about the importance of sleep.

- Encouraging children to be physically active during the daytime.

- Avoiding products that contain caffeine (e.g., regular and decaffeinated coffees, brewed and instant teas, cocoa, sodas, coffee-flavored ice cream).

Children between the ages of 6 and 12 years require 9 to 11 hours of uninterrupted nighttime sleep. According to a National Sleep Foundation (2014) poll, parents reported that their school-age children slept an average of 8.2 to 8.6 hours per night. However, when parents were asked how many hours of sleep 6- to 12-year-olds should be getting, 26 percent of the parents estimated one hour less than is currently recommended. Most children sleep well during this stage and experience fewer disturbances once they fall asleep than when they were younger. However, homework, extracurricular activities, social media, and video games begin to keep school-age children up later at night and distract them from getting as much sleep as is needed.

School-age children typically experience few sleep problems, although a small percentage may continue to have occasional nightmares. Periodic insomnia accounts for the most common sleep-related complaints reported to health care providers. However, sleep disturbances are especially common among children with neurodevelopmental disorders (e.g., autism, attention deficit hyperactivity disorder (ADHD), Down syndrome, Fragile X syndrome); an estimated 80 percent of these children experience significant difficulty falling and staying asleep (Blackmer & Feinstein, 2016; Lambert et al., 2016). Children who have other health conditions, such as allergies, asthma, arthritis, and cerebral palsy also experience a higher rate of sleep disturbances (Koinis-Mitchell et al., 2016; Félis, Cardosa, & Hall, 2016).

Exposure to light-emitting electronic devices (e.g., computer screens, eReaders, cell phones) shortly before bedtime has been shown to increase alertness and suppress melatonin production which regulates the sleep-wake cycle. Researchers observed that individuals who use such devices within an hour of bedtime had difficulty falling asleep, less sleepiness, lower melanin production, and increased difficulty waking up in the morning (Chang et al., 2015). Ogunleye, Voss, and Sandercock (2015) also found that boys (42 percent) were more likely than girls (37 percent) to go to bed late, that late bedtimes were highly correlated with increased computer use, and that both factors resulted in sleep deprivation. Parents should share such information with children to help them understand why electronic devices should be turned off or removed from bedroom areas in order to promote better sleep quality.

9-2f Communicable Illness and Prevention

Schools are ideal settings for the rapid spread of common communicable illnesses. Close contact among children in groups allows illnesses to travel quickly from one child to another. Frequent respiratory, gastrointestinal illnesses, and ear infections are common during children's first years in school. However, children become increasingly more resilient and are sick less often as they grow older. This change is due, in part, to their maturing biological defense mechanisms, coupled with an improved understanding of how illnesses are transmitted and the ability to practice precautionary measures (e.g., handwashing, covering coughs and sneezes properly) without an adult reminder (Marotz, 2015).

Parents and school personnel play an important, collaborative role in limiting children's exposure to communicable illnesses, which reduces absenteeism. Teachers and other school personnel have a responsibility to maintain healthy environmental conditions (e.g., surface cleaning, sanitary bathrooms and kitchen areas, proper ventilation) and promote frequent handwashing among children and staff (Ban et al., 2015; Bonnesen et al., 2015; Lee et al., 2015). Their daily observations of children's health and communication with parents also provide effective opportunities for limiting unnecessary exposure. Parents are more likely to keep ill children home from school when they are informed about exclusion policies and the early signs of communicable illnesses that may be present in classrooms. Their efforts to provide children with a nutritious diet, encourage physical activity, ensure adequate sleep, obtain essential immunizations, and to teach them healthy habits are most essential for improving children's resilience to, and recovery from, communicable illness.

Photo 9-9 Children's close contact enables communicable illnesses to spread rapidly.

Photo 9-10 The parent-child relationship changes as school-age children become more independent.

9-2g Safety

Unintentional injuries are the primary cause of death among children 6 to 12 years of age (CDC, 2014b). More than half of all childhood deaths and injuries are vehicle-related (e.g., as passengers, as pedestrians, on bicycles) (NHTSA, 2015). An estimated 172,000 children were injured in traffic accidents in 2012; an average of three children die every day in the United States (NHTSA, 2015). Of all child traffic fatalities, 55 percent involved boys.

School-age children's increased independence and involvement in a variety of new activities (e.g., attending school, participating in sports, spending time alone with friends) may require them to make decisions that they previously have not had to make. They arc also easily distracted, and still limited by immature cognitive abilities that make it difficult for them to always anticipate the consequences of their actions or to make safe choices (Morrongiello et al., 2015). Children who have behavior or developmental disorders are at particularly high risk in these situations and, as a result, experience a significantly higher rate of unintentional injuries (Zhang et al., 2016; Shilon et al., 2012).

Although it is important for parents to gradually relinquish some control over children's decision-making endeavors, it is equally necessary that they continue to set reasonable limits for school-age children (e.g., places they may go, people they may see, things they are allowed to do) and know where they are at all times. Parents must also continue to talk with children about how to act responsibly, and teach them safety precautions to take in unpredictable or uncomfortable situations. Several areas warrant parent's special attention because of the potentially harmful consequences that can occur if school-age children make poor choices (Suggestions for Parents 9-7).

Suggestions for Parents 9-7

Guidelines for Children's Safety

Safety issues that are particularly important for parents to address with school-age children include:

- *Firearms*
  - Always check with the families of your child's friends to be sure firearms in their homes are locked up and not accessible to children.
  - Teach children about the dangers of firearms, and instruct them to report a found gun to an adult.
- *Water*
  - Teach children to swim, and to do so only when an adult is present.
  - Teach children about water safety rules (e.g., no rough-housing in the water, always wear a fitted flotation vest when in a boat or involved in water sports, and to avoid inflatable "floaties").
  - Always wear sun protection.
  - Stay out of water in the event of a storm.
  - Always wash hands after playing in beach sand.

- *Animals*
  - Avoid approaching an unfamiliar animal, or running away from one quickly.
  - Leave wild animals and snakes undisturbed.
  - Always wash hands thoroughly after touching any animal.
- *Traffic*
  - Teach children where and when it is safe to ride bicycles, skateboards, and scooters.
  - Teach children about stop lights, and the necessity to look both ways at street corners for oncoming traffic before crossing.
  - Instruct younger children to dismount and walk their bike across a street.
  - Make sure that children have and wear appropriate safety equipment (e.g., helmet, protective gear) that is in good condition when they ride bikes, a skateboard, or are on rollerblades.
  - Insist that children always have an appropriate safety seat or that they buckle up when riding in a car with family or friends.
- *Internet*
  - Set security controls on televisions and computers, talk with children about accessing inappropriate sites, and monitor their online activities.
  - Teach children not to give out personal information or respond to marketing requests.
  - Talk with children about cyberbullying and sexting, and let them know that these are inappropriate (and illegal in some states) behaviors to engage in.
  - Limit children's media time (e.g., cell phones, television, video games) and encourage their interests in other activities (including physical activity).

9-3 Developmentally Appropriate Behavior Guidance

The relationship between parents and children undergoes significant change during the school-age years because of an increase in peer influence and decrease in children's reliance on others to meet their physical needs. Although the bonds that parents share with their children become less exclusive as children develop close peer relationships, they continue to need—and will often seek—parental approval and nurturance (Del Giudice, 2015). Parents serve as an invaluable resource and foundation for children's development of autonomy and self-regulation. During the school-age years, parents should begin to establish a **co-regulation** relationship with their children. By gradually relinquishing some control over children's behavior, parents help children become more confident in their ability to make logical and goal-directed decisions.

Co-regulation involves a bi-directional process between a parent and child that leads to emotional and behavioral stability. Parents continue to provide rules and structure, set limits, and respond consistently, but begin to give children some control so that they gain confidence in making decisions, managing responsibilities, regulating their emotions, and solving problems. For example, a parent may set expectations for homework or reading that is to be done every day after school, but children are given the opportunity to decide the order in which the work will be completed and how much homework must be finished before taking a short break.

As children's ability to think about and process their own behavior continues to develop, they often need reassurance and direction from parents to help regulate their emotions. For example, a 6-year-old child who shows anxious behaviors (e.g., shaking,

co-regulation
bi-directional process between a parent and child that leads to emotional and behavioral stability.

sweating, desires to leave an uncomfortable situation) may not be able to effectively identify triggers and bodily changes that signal the need to use coping skills. In these situations, a parent can provide support to help the child regulate such behavior, remain in the situation, and experience success. Over time, parents can decrease the level of support they provide and, thereby, enhance the child's responsibility and control of their own behavior.

Positive Behavior Guidance

- Provide unconditional love. When problems or mistakes arise, focus on the behavior, rather than on individual characteristics.

- Establish limits and rules and state directions clearly and in positive terms to teach children what to do rather than focusing on negative behaviors. Allow children to make decisions, and provide opportunities for increasing their freedom within safe limits.

- Involve children in setting expectations and limits, and enforce expectations consistently.

- Acknowledge children's accomplishments, feelings, and frustrations.

- Show enjoyment in interactions with children. Give children positive attention and feedback, especially when they seek it out.

- Continue to provide specific praise for good behaviors.

- Consider children's perspective, and help children learn to compromise when appropriate.

- Keep lines of communication open and positive by using active listening, acknowledging thoughts and feelings even if you have a difference of opinion, and providing brief rationales for your actions. Be open to talking about important topics such as sexuality, peer relations, and common fears and worries.

- Refrain from engaging in arguments with children. Continue to model appropriate ways to handle frustration and stress. Model and help children to express their feelings in appropriate ways. Support effective problem solving and conflict resolution.

- Ignore minor, non-harmful behaviors (e.g., whining) and provide praise for desirable behavior.

- Use natural (receiving no points on a homework assignment because the child forgot to put the assignment in her bag) and logical (not being able to play outside without an adult because the child rode her bike down the street further than she was supposed to the day before) consequences for behaviors to encourage compliance.

Responsive Parenting

When 11-year-old George came home from school, his father gave him a list of four chores to complete. George asked his father if he could complete the chores after having a snack and playing outside for a little while. George's father said "no" and told him to get to work on the chores. George yelled, "That's not fair, you get to choose when you do chores at home." His father responded, "I can do what I want because I'm an adult." George ran to his room and slammed the door. How would you recommend that George's father use this situation as an opportunity to encourage his son's autonomy, decision making skills, and appropriate coping responses? What advice would you give to George's father for changing the nature of his statements to make the communication more positive?

Summary

- Children experience fewer dramatic physical changes during the school-age years. Girls will begin to undergo hormonal and body changes associated with puberty during the last half of this stage; boys often do not experience puberty for several more years. Children's vision and hearing, mental health, and dental health should be monitored closely to ensure that undetected problems do not interfere with learning efforts.

- Cognitive advancements make it possible for school-age children to process and recall increasingly complex information and to think in abstract terms. Children are developing a better understanding of grammatical rules, and becoming more adept at using language for different purposes (e.g., conversation, writing stories). Parents continue to play an important role in supporting children's development in these areas.

- The transition to formal school represents a significant change for children and their families. Children are exposed to new learning experiences and socialization opportunities. Parents can take steps to prepare children for this transition, support their adjustment, and work collaboratively with teachers to maximize learning.

- Healthy dietary, physical activity, and sleep patterns are essential if children are to benefit from learning and socialization opportunities and experience fewer communicable illnesses. Habits established during the school-age years are often carried over into adulthood.

- Ideally, parents should gradually relinquish some of their authority and control, and begin to engage children in a co-regulation relationship that involves some joint decision-making and behavior regulation.

Key Terms

amblyopia (p. 253)

classification (p. 255)

co-regulation (p. 275)

conservation (p. 255)

empathy (p. 267)

guilt (p. 266)

pragmatics (p. 256)

relational aggression (p. 263)

resilience (p. 264)

shame (p. 266)

Questions for Discussion and Self-Reflection

1. Why is it important to evaluate school-age children's hearing and vision? In what ways is learning affected if these sensory systems are not functioning at optimum levels?

2. What is a learning disability, and what signs would suggest that a child needs to be evaluated?

3. Why do some children engage in bullying or intimidating behaviors toward their peers?

4. In what ways does the school-age child's concept of sexuality differ from the ideas they held during the preschool years?

5. How does the parent-child relationship change during the school-age period? Describe three strategies that parents can use to encourage children's self-regulation development.

Field Activities

1. Attend a kindergarten roundup session and note how children's readiness for school is assessed. What learning skills were evaluated? Were children's cultural differences taken into consideration? What information or feedback did parents receive following the assessment? In general, how well do you think the children in attendance were prepared to enter kindergarten? What developmental skills did they seem to be lacking?

2. Arrange to sit in on an IEP (Individualized Education Plan) parent-team conference for a child with a physical or developmental disorder. Summarize your experience, and describe the type of information that was exchanged. If you were the child's parents, would you be satisfied with the experience? If not, what would have made it better? Alternatively, conduct an Internet search to learn more about IEPs and the process that schools are required to follow.

3. Interview five elementary school-age children and ask them to recall their first days in school. How would they describe their feelings on that day? What would have made the transition easier? What could teachers have done to make the experience less intimidating? How could parents have prepared them beforehand?

REFERENCES

Alfano, C., Lau, S., Balderas, J., Bunnell, B., & Beidel, D. (2016). The impact of military deployment on children: Placing developmental risk in context. *Clinical Psychology Review*, *43*, 17–29.

Alexander, D., Alfonso, M., & Hansen, A. (2015). Childhood obesity perceptions among African American caregivers in a rural Georgia community: A mixed methods approach. *Journal of Community Health*, *40*(2), 367–378.

American Psychiatric Association (APA). (2013). *Diagnostic and statistical manual of mental disorders* (5th Ed.). Washington, DC: Author.

American Speech-Language-Hearing Association. (2016). Social language use (pragmatics). Retrieved April 17, 2016 from http://www.asha.org/public/speech/development/Pragmatics/.

Appleyard, K., Haskett, M., Loehman, J., & Rose, R. (2015). Physically abused children's adjustment at the transition to school: Child, parent, and family factors. *Journal of Child and Family Studies*, *24*(4), 957–969.

Ban, Q., Li, T., Shen, J., Li, J., Peng, P., Ye, H., & Zhang, L. (2015). Effects of multiple cleaning and disinfection interventions on infectious diseases in children: A group randomized trial in China. *Biomedical and Environmental Science*, *28*(11), 779–787.

Banfield, E., Liu, Y., Davis, J., Chang, S., & Frazier-Wood, A. (2016). Poor adherence to US Dietary Guidelines for children and adolescents in the National Health and Nutrition Examination survey population. *Journal of the Academy of Nutrition and Dietetics*, *116*(1), 21–27.

Bates, M. (2015). Bullying and the brain. Retrieved April 17, 2016 from http://www.brainfacts.org/in-society/in-society/articles/2015/bullying-and-the-brain/.

Bates, M., & Furlong, M. (2014, July). *Kindergarten students entrance profile*. Paper presented at the Quality Rating and Improvement Systems National Meeting, Denver, CO. Retrieved April 21, 2016 from http://qrisnetwork.org/sites/all/files/session/presentations/Kindergarten%20Student%20Entrance%20Profile%20(Featured%20Sponsor%20Presentation%20by%20Mosaic%20Network,%20Inc.)%20PART%20ONE%20PPT%20as%20PDF.pdf.

Benner, A., & Yan, N. (2015). Classroom race/ethnic composition, family-school connections, and the transition to school. *Applied Developmental Science*, *19*(3), 127–138.

Bierman, K., Welsh, J., Heinrichs, B., Nix, R., & Mathis, E. (2015). Helping Head Start parents promote their children's kindergarten adjustment: The research-based developmentally informed parent program. *Child Development*, *86*(6), 1877–1891.

Bitsko, R., Holbrook, J., Robinson, L., Kaminski, J., Ghandour, R., Smith, C., & Peacock, G. (2016). Health, family, and community factors associated with mental, behavioral, and developmental disorders in early childhood – United States, 2011-2012. *Morbidity and Mortality Weekly Report (MMWR)*, *65*: 221–226. http://dx.doi.org/10.15585/mmwr.mm6509a1.

Blackmer, A., & Feinstein, J. (2016). Management of sleep disorders in children with neurodevelopmental disorders: A review. *Pharmacotherapy*, *36*(1), 84–98.

Boddy, L., Downs, S., Knowles, Z., & Fairclough, S. (2015). Physical activity and play behaviours in children and young people with intellectual disabilities: A cross-sectional observational study. *School Psychology International*, *36*(2), 154–171.

Bonnesen, C., Plauborg, R., Denbaek, A., Due, P., & Johansen, A. (2015). Process evaluation of a multi-component intervention to reduce infectious diseases and improve hygiene and well-being among school children: The Hi Five study. *Health Education Research*, *30*(3), 497–512.

Boots, S., Tiggemann, M., Corsini, N., & Mattiske, J. (2015). Managing young children's snack food intake. The role of parenting style and feeding strategies. *Appetite, 92*(1), 94–101.

Brown, S., Nobiling, B., Teufel, J., & Birch, D. (2011). Are kids too busy? Early adolescents' perceptions of discretionary activities, overscheduling, and stress. *Journal of School Health*, *81*(9), 574–580.

Brownlee, J., Johansson, E., Cobb-Moore, C., Boulton-Lewis, G., Walker, S., & Ailwood, J. (2015). Epistemic beliefs and beliefs about teaching practices for moral learning in the early years of school: Relationships and complexities. *Education*, *43*(2), 164–183.

Brugman, D., Keller, M., & Sokol, B. (2013). Introduction: Meaning, measurement, and correlates of moral development. *European Journal of Developmental Psychology, 10*(2), 99–105.

Cano, S., Tiemeier, H., Van Hoeken, D., Tharner, A., Jaddoe, V., Hofman, A., Verhulst, F., & Hoek, H. (2015). Trajectories of picky eating during childhood: A general population study. *International Journal of Eating Disorders*, *48*(6), 570–579.

Capurro, D., Iafolla, T., Kingman, A., Chattopadhyay, A., & Garcia, I. (2015). Trends in income-related inequality in untreated caries among children in the United States: Findings from NHANES I, NHANES III, and NHANES 1999–2004. *Community Dentistry and Oral Epidemiology*, *43*(6), 500–510.

Carey, F., Singh, G., Brown, H., & Wilkinson, A. (2015). The science of childhood obesity: An individual to societal framework. *International Journal of Behavioral Nutrition and Physical Activity*, *12*(Suppl 1): S3. doi:10.1186/1479-5868-12-S1-S3.

Centers for Disease Control and Prevention (CDC). (2014a). Oral and dental health. Retrieved April 22, 2016 from http://www.cdc.gov/nchs/fastats/dental.htm.

CDC. (2014b). 10 Leading causes of death by age group. Retrieved April 22, 2016 from http://www.cdc.gov/injury/wisqars/pdf/leading_causes_of_death_by_age_group_2014-a.pdf.

Center on the Developing Child. (2016). Key Concepts: Resilience. Retrieved April 22, 2016 from http://developingchild.harvard.edu/science/key-concepts/resilience/.

Cermak, S., Katz, N., Weintraub, N., Steinhart, S., Raz-Silbiger, S., Munoz, M., & Lifshitz, N. (2015). Participation in physical activity, fitness, and risk for obesity in children with developmental coordination disorder: A cross-cultural study. *Occupational Therapy International*, *22*(4), 163–173.

Chang, A., Aeschbach, D., Duffy, J., & Czeisler, C. (2015). Evening use of light-emitting eReaders negatively affects sleep, circadian timing, and next-morning alertness. *Proceedings of the National Academy of Sciences of the United States of America*, *112*(4), 1232–1237.

Charman, T., Ricketts, J., Dockrell, J., Lindsay, G., & Palikara, O. (2015). Emotional and behavioural problems in children with language impairments and children with autism spectrum disorders. *International Journal of Language & Communication Disorders*, *50*(1), 84–93.

Chaput, J., (2016). Is sleep deprivation a contributor to obesity in children? *Eating and Weight Disorders*, *21*(1), 5–11.

Cheng, G., Duan, R., Kranz, S., Libuda, L., & Zhang, L. (2016). Development of a dietary index to assess overall diet quality for Chinese school-age children: The Chinese children dietary index. *Journal of the Academy of Nutrition and Dietetics*, *116*(4), 608–617.

Cho, M., Quach, J., Anderson, P., Mensah, F., Wake, M., & Roberts, G. (2015). Poor sleep and lower working memory in grade children: Cross-sectional, population-based study. *Academic Pediatrics*, *15*(1), 111–116.

Cook, B., Li, D., & Heinrich, K. (2015). Obesity, physical activity, and sedentary behavior of youth with learning disabilities and ADHD. *Journal of Learning Disabilities*, *48*(6), 563–576.

Cortiella, C., & Horowitz, S. (2014). *The State of Learning Disabilities: Facts, Trends and Emerging Issues*. New York: National Center for Learning Disabilities.

Crosnoe, R., Ansari, A., Purtell, K., & Wu, N. (2016). Latin American immigration, maternal education, and approaches to managing children's schooling in the United States. *Journal of Marriage and Family*, *78*(1), 60–74.

Cuffe, S., Visser, S., Holbrook, J., Danielson, M., Greryk, L., Wolraich, M., & McKeown, R. (2015). ADHD and psychiatric comorbidity: Functional outcomes in a school-based sample of children. *Journal of Attention Disorders*. Online before print, November 25, 2015. doi:10.1177/1087054715613437.

Curle, D. (2015). An examination of web-based information on the transition to school for children who are deaf or hard of hearing. *Deafness & Education International, 17*(2), 63–75.

Curtin, C., Hubbard, K., Anderson, S., Mick, E., Must, A., & Bandini, L. (2015). Food selectivity, mealtime behavior problems, spousal stress, and family food choices in children with and without autism spectrum disorder. *Journal of Autism and Developmental Disorders, 45*(10), 3308–3315.

Dawson-McClure, S., Calzada, E., Huang, K., Kamboukos, D., Rhule, D., Kolawole, B., . . . & Brotman, L. (2015). A population-level approach to promoting healthy child development and school success in low-income, urban neighborhoods: Impact on parenting and child conduct problems. *Prevention Science, 16*(2), 279–290.

Decety, J. (2015). The neural pathways, development and functions of empathy. *Current Opinion in Behavioral Sciences, 3*, 1–6.

Del Giudice, M. (2015). Attachment in middle childhood: An evolutionary–developmental perspective. In G. Bosmans & K. A. Kerns (Eds.), *Attachment in middle childhood: Theoretical advances and new directions in an emerging field. New Directions for Child and Adolescent Development, 148*, 15–30.

Dent, M. (2013). Calming our students' lives. *Educating Young Children: Learning and Teaching in the Early Childhood Years, 19*(3), 23–25.

Donaldson, R. (2013). Elementary age brain development.

Duncan, S., Strycker, L., & Nigel, R. (2015). School influences on the physical activity of African American, Latino, and White girls. *Journal of School Health, 85*(1), 43–52.

Echeverría, S., Ohri-Vachaspati, P., & Yedidia, M. (2015). The influence of parental nativity, neighborhood disadvantage and the built environment on physical activity behaviors in Latino youth. *Journal of Immigrant and Minority Health, 17*(2), 519–526.

Eime, R., Young, J., Harvey, J., Charity, M., & Payne, W. (2013). A systematic review of the psychological and social benefits of participation in sport for children and adolescents: Informing development of a conceptual model of health through sport. *International Journal of Behavioral Nutrition and Physical Activity*, 10:98, 1–21. http://www.ijbnpa.org /content/10/1/98.

Elkind, D. (1981). *The hurried child*. Boston, MA: Addison-Wesley.

Erath, S., Tu, K., Buckhalt, J., & El-Sheikh, M. (2015). Associations between children's intelligence and academic achievement: The role of sleep. *Journal of Sleep Research, 24*(5), 510–513.

Erikson, E. (1963). *Childhood and society*. (2nd Ed). NY: W.W. Norton.

Farris, A., Misyak, S., Duffey, K., Mann, G., Davis, G., Hosig, K., . . . & Serrano, E. (2015). A comparison of fruits, vegetables, sugar-sweetened beverages, and desserts in the packed lunches of elementary school children. *Childhood Obesity, 11*(3), 275–280.

Ford, M., Gordon, N., Howell, A., Green, C., Greenspan, L., Chandra, M., Mellor, G., & Lo, J. (2016). Obesity severity, dietary behaviors, and lifestyle risks vary by race/ethnicity and age in a Northern California cohort of children with obesity. *Journal of Obesity*, 2016, 1–10. http://dx.doi.org/10.1155/2016/4287976.

Fram, M., Ritchie, L., Rosen, N., & Frongillo, E. (2015). Child experience of food insecurity is associated with child diet and physical activity. *Journal of Nutrition, 145*(3), 499–504.

Franckle, R., Falbe, J., Gortmaker, S., Ganter, C., Taveras, E., Land, T., & Davison, K. (2015). Insufficient sleep among elementary and middle school students is linked with elevated soda consumption and other unhealthy dietary behaviors. *Preventive Medicine, 74*, 36–41.

Fraught, E., Ploeg, K., Chu, Y., Storey, K., & Veugelers, P. (2016). The influence of parental encouragement and caring about healthy eating on children's diet quality and body weights. *Public Health Nutrition, 19*(5), 822–829.

Frewen, A., Chew, E., Carter, M., Chunn, J., & Jotanovic, D. (2015). A cross-cultural exploration of parental involvement and child-rearing beliefs in Asian cultures. *Early Years: An International Research Journal, 35*(1), 36–49.

Gillette, M., Borner, K., Nadler, C., Poppert, K., Odar, C., Swinburne, R., & Davis, A. (2015). Prevalence and health correlates of overweight and obesity in children with autism spectrum disorder. *Journal of Developmental & Behavioral Pediatrics, 36*(7), 489–496.

Gordon-Hollingsworth, A., Becker, E., Ginsburg, G., Keeton, C., Compton, S., Birmaher, B., . . . & March, J. (2015). Anxiety disorders in Caucasian and African American children: A comparison of clinical characteristics, treatment process variables, and treatment outcomes. *Child Psychiatry & Human Development, 46*(5), 643–655.

Gower, A., Lingras, K., Mathieson, L., Kawabata, Y., & Crick, N. (2014). The role of preschool relational and physical aggression in the transition to kindergarten: Links with social-psychological adjustment. *Early Education and Development, 25*(5), 619–640.

Gurnani, M., Birken, C., & Hamilton, J. (2015). Childhood obesity: Causes, consequences, and management. *Pediatric Clinics of North America, 62*(4), 821–840.

Halim, M., & Ruble, D. (2010). Gender identity and stereotyping in early and middle childhood. In J.C. Chrisler, D.R. McCreary (Eds.), *Handbook of Gender Research in Psychology,* 494–525. doi:10.1007/978-1-4419-1465-1_24.

Hansen, A., Pritchard, T., Melnic, I., & Zhang, J. (2016). Physical activity, screen time, and school absenteeism: Self-reports from NHANES 2005–2008. *Current Medical Research Opinion, 32*(4), 651–659.

Harrison, L., & Murray, E. (2015). Stress, coping, and wellbeing in kindergarten: Children's perspective on personal, interpersonal, and institutional challenges of school. *International Journal of Early Childhood, 47*(1), 79–103.

Heima, M., Lee, W., Milgrom, P., & Nelson, S. (2015). Caregiver's education level and child's dental caries in African Americans: A path analytic study. *Caries Research, 49*(2), 177–183.

Hoglund, W., Jones, S., Brown, J., & Aber, J. (2015). The evocative influence of child academic and social-emotional adjustment on parent involvement in inner-city schools. *Journal of Educational Psychology, 107*(2), 517–532.

Iruka, I., Gardner-Neblett, N., Matthews, J., & Winn, D. (2014). Preschool to kindergarten transition patterns for African American boys. *Early Childhood Research Quarterly, 29*(2), 106–117.

Jahns, L., McDonald, L., Wadsworth, A., Morin, C., Liu, Y., & Nicklas, T. (2015). Barriers and facilitators to following the Dietary Guidelines for Americans reported by rural, Northern Plains American-Indian children. *Public Health Nutrition, 18*(3), 482–489.

Jeynes, W. (2016). A meta-analysis: The relationship between parental involvement and African American school outcomes. *Journal of Black Studies, 47*(3), 195–216.

Jeynes, W. (2015). A meta-analysis: The relationship between father involvement and student academic achievement. *Urban Education, 50*(4), 387–423.

Jones, D., Greenberg, M., & Crowley, M. (2015). Early social-emotional functioning and public health: The relationship between kindergarten social competence and future wellness. *American Journal of Public Health, 105*(11), 2283–2290.

Kaur, J., Lamb, M., & Ogden, C. (2015). The association between food insecurity and obesity in children—The National Health and Nutrition Examination survey. *Journal of the Academy of Nutrition and Dietetics, 115*(5), 751–758.

Ke, J., & Ford-Jones, E. (2015). Food insecurity and hunger: A review of the effects on children's health and behaviour. *Paediatrics & Child Health, 20*(2), 89–91.

Kelly, K., Jost, R., De La Cruz, A., & Birch, E. (2015). Amblyopic children read more slowly than controls under natural, binocular reading conditions. *JAAPOS, 19*(6), 515–520.

Koinis-Mitchell, D., Kopel, S., Boergers, J., Ramos, K., LeBourgeois, M., McQuaid, E., . . . & Klein, R. (2016). Asthma, allergic rhinitis, and sleep problems in urban children. *Journal of Clinical Sleep Medicine, 11*(2), 101–110.

Kouros, C., & El-Sheikh, M. (2015). Daily mood and sleep: Reciprocal relations and links with adjustment problems. *Journal of Sleep Research, 24*(1), 24–31.

Kuzawa, C., Chugani, H., Grossman, L., Lipovich, L., Muzik, O., Hof, P., . . . & Lange, N. (2014). Metabolic costs and evolutionary implications of human brain development. *Proceedings of the National Academy of Sciences, 111,* 13010–13015.

Lambert, A., Tessier, S., Rochette, A., Scherzer, P., Mottron, L., & Godbout, R. (2016). Poor sleep affects daytime functioning in typically developing and autistic children not complaining of sleep problems: A questionnaire-based and polysomnographic study. *Research in Autism Spectrum Disorders, 23,* 94–106.

Lapsey, D., & Carlo, G. (2014). Moral development at the crossroads: New trends and possible futures. *Developmental Psychology, 50*(1), 1–7.

Lau, E., Barr-Anderson, D., Dowda, M., Forthofer, M., Saunders, R., & Pate, R. (2015). Associations between home environment and after-school physical activity and sedentary time among 6th grade children. *Pediatric Exercise Science, 17*(2), 226–233.

Lau, E. (2014). Chinese parents' perceptions and practices of parental involvement during school transition. *Early Child Development and Care, 184*(3), 403–415.

Lee, R., Leung, C., Tong, W., Chen, H., & Lee, P. (2015). Comparative efficacy of a simplified handwashing program for improvement in hand hygiene and reduction of school absenteeism among children with intellectual disability. *American Journal of Infection Control, 43*(9), 907–912.

Lélis, A., Cardosa, M., & Hall, W. (2016). Sleep disorders in children with cerebral palsy: An integrative review. *Sleep Medicine Reviews, 30*, 63–71.

Lewis, D., Valente, D., & Spalding, J. (2015). Effect of minimal/mild hearing loss on children's speech understanding in a simulated classroom. *Ear & Hearing, 36*(1), 136–144.

Marotz, L. (2015). *Health, safety, and nutrition for the young child*. Stamford, CT: Cengage Learning.

Marotz, L. (2011). Children's dietary needs: Nutrients, interactions, and their role in health. In D. Kilcast & F. Angus (Eds.), *Developing children's food products*. Cambridge, UK: Woodhead Publishers.

Marotz, L., & Allen, K. (2016). *Developmental profiles: Pre-birth through adolescence*. (8th Ed). Boston, MA: Cengage Learning.

McDermott, P., Rokoon, S., & Fantuzzo, J. (2016). Transition and protective agency of early childhood learning behaviors as portents of later school attendance and adjustment. *Journal of School Psychology, 54*, 59–75.

Mayes, S., Waxmonsky, J., Calhoun, S., & Bixler, E. (2016). Disruptive mood dysregulation disorder symptoms and association with oppositional defiant and other disorders in the general population child sample. *Journal of Child and Adolescent Psychopharmacology, 26*(2), 101–106.

Mental Health America. (2016). Children's mental health. Retrieved from http://www.mentalhealthamerica.net/conditions/childrens-mental-health.

Miller, K. (2015a). From past to present: How memories of school shape parental views of children's schooling. *International Journal of Early Years Education, 23*(2), 153–171.

Miller, K. (2015b). The transition to kindergarten: How families from lower-income backgrounds experienced the first year. *Early Childhood Education, 43*(3), 213–221.

Moran, K. (2016). Anxiety in the classroom: Implications for middle school teachers. *Middle School Journal, 47*(1), 27–32.

Morrongiello, B., Stewart, J., Pope, K., Pogrebtsova, E., & Boulay, K. (2015). Exploring relations between positive mood state and school-age children's risk taking. *Journal of Pediatric Psychology, 40*(4), 406–418.

Narvaez, D., Wang, L., Gleason, T., Cheng, Y., Lefever, J., & Deng, L. (2013). The evolved developmental niche and child sociomoral outcomes in Chinese 3-year-olds. *European Journal of Developmental Psychology, 10*(2), 106–127.

Natale, R., Uhlhorn, S., Lopez-Mitnik, G., Camejo, S., Englebert, N., Delamater, A., & Messiah, S. (2016). Caregiver's country of birth is a significant determinant of accurate perception of preschool-age children's weight. *Health Education & Behavior, 43*(2), 191–200.

National Institute of Mental Health (NIMH). (2016a). Any disorder among children. Retrieved April 22, 2016 from http://www.nimh.nih.gov/health/statistics/prevalence/any-disorder-among-children.shtml.

National Institute of Mental Health (NIH). (2016b). Treatment of children with mental illness. Retrieved April 22, 2016 from http://www.nimh.nih.gov/health/publications/treatment-of-children-with-mental-illness-fact-sheet/index.shtml.

National Sleep Foundation. (2014). Sleep in America poll finds children sleep better when parents establish rules, limit technology, and set a good example. Retrieved April 21, 2016 from https://sleepfoundation.org/media-center/press-release/national-sleep-foundation-2014-sleep-america-poll-finds-children-sleep.

National Highway Traffic Safety Administration (NTHSA). (2015). Traffic safety facts: 2013 data. Retrieved April 22, 2016 from http://www-nrd.nhtsa.dot.gov/Pubs/812154.pdf.

O'Conner, E., Cappella, E., McCormick, M., & McClowry, S. (2014). Enhancing the academic development of shy children: A test of the efficacy of INSIGHTS. *School Psychology Review, 43*(3), 239–259.

Ogunleye, A., Voss, C., & Sandercock, G. (2015). Delayed bedtime due to screen time in schoolchildren: Importance of area deprivation. *Pediatrics International, 57*(1), 137–142.

Ohan, J., Seward, R., Stallman, H., Bayliss, D., & Sanders, M. (2015). Parents' barriers to using school psychology services for their child's mental health problems. *School Mental Health, 7*(4), 287–297.

Peters, R., Petrunka, K., Khan, S., Howell-Moneta, A., Nelson, G., Pancer, M., & Loomis, C. (2016). Cost-savings analysis of the Better Beginnings, Better Futures community-based project for young children and their families: A 10-year follow-up. *Prevention Science, 17*(2), 237–247.

Piaget, J. (1952). *The origins of intelligence in children.* New York: International University Press.

Piché, G., Fitzpatrick, C., & Pagani, L. (2015). Associations between extracurricular activity and self-regulation: A longitudinal study from 5 to 10 years of age. *American Journal of Health Promotion, 30*(1), e32–e40.

Polaha, J., Williams, S., Heflinger, C., & Studts, C. (2015). The perceived stigma of mental health services among rural parents of children with psychosocial concerns. *Journal of Pediatric Psychology, 40*(10), 1095–1104.

Puccioni, J. (2015). Parents' conceptions of school readiness, transition practices, and children's academic achievement trajectories. *Journal of Educational Research, 108*(2), 130–147.

Quirk, M., Grimm, R., Nylund Gibson, K., & Furlong, M. (2015). The association of Latino children's kindergarten school readiness profiles with grade 2-5 literacy achievement trajectories. *Journal of Educational Psychology.* Published online. doi:10.1037/edu0000087.

Ranjit, N., Wilkinson, A., Lytle, L., Evans, A., Saxton, D., & Hoelscher, D. (2015). Socioeconomic inequalities in children's diet: The role of the home food environment. *International Journal of Behavioral Nutrition and Physical Activity, 12*(Suppl 1): S4. doi:10.1186/1479-5868-12-S1-S4.

Reardon, T., Gray, K., & Melvin, G. (2015). Anxiety disorders in children and adolescents with intellectual disability: Prevalence and assessment. *Research in Developmental Disabilities, 36*, 175–190.

Robinson, C., & Diamond, K. (2014). A quantitative study of Head Start children's strengths, families' perspectives, and teachers' ratings in the transition to kindergarten. *Early Childhood Education, 42*(2), 77–84.

Robson, S., Crosby, L., & Stark, L. (2016). Eating dinner away from home: Perspectives of middle- to high-income parents. *Appetite, 96*(1), 147–153.

Rodic, M., Zhou, X., Tikhomirova, T., Wei, W., Malykh, S., Ismatulina, V., . . . & Kovas, Y. (2015). Cross-cultural investigation into cognitive underpinnings of individual differences in early arithmetic. *Developmental Science, 18*(1), 165–174.

Russell, S., Day, J., Ioverno, S., & Toomey, R. (2016). Are school policies focused on sexual orientation and gender identity associated with less bullying? Teachers' perspectives. *Journal of School Psychology, 54*, 29–38.

Schmidt, M., Svetloya, M., Johe, J., & Tomasello, M. (2016). Children's developing understanding of legitimate reasons for allocating resources unequally. *Cognitive Development, 37*, 42–52.

Schuepbach, M. (2015). Effects of extracurricular activities and their quality on primary school-age students' achievement in mathematics in Switzerland. *School Effectiveness and School Improvement: An International Journal of Research, Policy, and Practice, 26*(2), 279–295.

Schwartz, K., Cappella, E., & Seidman, E. (2015). Extracurricular participation and course performance in the middle grades: A study of low-income, urban youth. *American Journal of Community Psychology, 56*(3-4), 307–320.

Schiffrin, H., Godfrey, H., Liss, M., & Erchull, M. (2015). Intensive parenting: Does it have the desired impact on child outcomes? *Journal of Child and Family Studies, 24*(8), 2322–2331.

Sengsvang, S., & Krettenauer, T. (2015). Children's moral self-concept: The role of aggression and parent-child relationships. *Merrill-Palmer Quarterly, 16*(2), 213–235.

SHAPE America. (2016). Physical activity guidelines. Retrieved April 18, 2016 from http://www.shapeamerica.org/standards/guidelines/pa-children-5-12.cfm.

Sherer, I., Baum, J., Ehrensaft, D., & Rosenthal, S. (2015). Affirming gender: Caring for gender-atypical children and adolescents. *Contemporary Pediatrics*, Published online, http://contemporarypediatrics.modernmedicine.com/contemporary-pediatrics/news/affirming-gender-caring-gender-atypical-children-and-adolescents?page=full.

Slevin, E., Truesdale-Kennedy, M., McConkey, R., Livingstone, B., & Fleming, P. (2014). Obesity and overweight in intellectual and non-intellectually disabled children. *Journal of Intellectual Disability Research, 58*(3), 211–220.

Shilon, Y., Pollak, Y., Aran, A., Shaked, S., & Gross-Tsur, V. (2012). Accidental injuries are more common in children with attention deficit hyperactivity disorder compared with their non-affected siblings. *Child: Care, Health, and Development, 38*(3), 366–370.

Smith, L., Gardner, B., Aggio, D., & Hamer, M. (2015). Association between participation in outdoor play and sport at 10 years old with physical activity in adulthood. *Preventive Medicine, 74,* 31–35.

Sterdt, E., Liersch, S., & Walter, U. (2014). Correlates of physical activity of children and adolescents: A systematic review of reviews. *Health Education Journal, 73*(1), 72–89.

Stormont, M., Herman, K., Reinke, W., King, K., & Owens, S. (2015). The kindergarten academic and behavior readiness screener: The utility of single-item teacher ratings of kindergarten readiness. *School Psychology Quarterly, 30*(2), 212–228.

Stracciolini, A., Casciano, R., Friedman, H., Meehan, W., & Micheli, L. (2015). A closer look at overuse injuries in the pediatric athlete. *Clinical Journal of Sport Medicine, 25*(1), 30–35.

Stuewig, J., Tangney, J., Kendall, S., Folk, J., Reinsmith Meyer, C., & Dearing, R. (2015). Children's proneness to shame and guilt predict risky and illegal behaviors in young adulthood. *Child Psychiatry and Human Development, 46*(2), 217–227.

Sukhodolsky, D., Smith, S., McCauley, S., Ibrahim, K., & Piasecka, J. (2016). Behavioral interventions for anger, irritability, and aggression in children and adolescents. *Journal of Child and Adolescent Psychopharmacology, 26*(1), 58–64.

Taillie, L., Afeiche, M., Eldridge, A., & Popkin, B. (2015). Increased snacking and eating occasions are associated with higher energy intake among Mexican children aged 2-13 years. *Journal of Nutrition, 145*(11), 2570–2577.

Tan, Y., Ma, D., Chen, Y., Cheng, F., Liu, X., & Li, L. (2015). Relationships between sleep behaviors and unintentional injury in Southern Chinese school-aged children: A population-based study. *International Journal of Environmental Research and Public Health, 12*(10), 12999–13015.

Thompson, P., Hulme, C., Nash, H., Gooch, D., Hauiou-Thomas, E., & Snowling, M. (2015). Developmental dyslexia: Predicting individual risk. *Journal of Child Psychology and Psychiatry, 56*(9), 976–987.

Turner, E., Jensen-Doss, A., & Heffer, R. (2015). Ethnicity as a moderator of how parents' attitudes and perceived stigma influence intentions to seek child mental health services. *Cultural Diversity and Ethnic Minority Psychology, 21*(4), 613–618.

U.S. Department of Agriculture (USDA). (2016). Child nutrition tables. Retrieved April 19, 2016 from http://www.fns.usda.gov/pd/child-nutrition-tables.

U.S. Department of Health and Human Services. (2015). Bullying definition. Retrieved April 16, 2016 from http://www.stopbullying.gov/what-is-bullying/definition/.

Vandecandelaere, M., Vansteelandt, S., De Fraine, B., & Van Damme, J. (2016). The effects of early grade retention: Effect modification by prior achievement and age. *Journal of School Psychology, 54,* 77–93.

van Schwalkwijk, F., Benjamins, J., Migliorati, F., de Nooijer, J., van Someren, E., van Gog, T., & van der Werf, Y. (2015). The role of sleep timing in children's observational learning. *Neurobiology of Learning and Memory, 125,* 98–105.

Vella, S., Cliff, D., Magee, C., & Ok, A. (2015). Associations between sports participation and psychological difficulties during childhood: A two-year follow up. *Journal of Science and Medicine in Sport, 18*(3), 304–309.

Waters, S., Boyce, W., Eskenazi, B., & Alkon, A. (2015). The impact of maternal depression and overcrowded housing on associations between autonomic nervous system reactivity and externalizing behavior problems in vulnerable Latino children. *Psychophysiology, 53*(1), 97–104.

Weinstein, S., Henry, D., Katz, A., Peters, A., & West, A. (2015). Treatment moderators of child- and family-focused cognitive-behavioral therapy for pediatric bipolar disorder. *Journal of the American Academy of Child & Adolescent Psychiatry, 54*(2), 116–125.

Welchons, L., & McIntyre, L. (2015). The transition to kindergarten: Predicting socio-behavioral outcomes for children with and without disabilities. *Early Childhood Education Journal.* Published online. doi:10.1007/s10643-015-0757-7.

Winsler, A., Kyong Kim, Y., & Richard, E. (2014). Socio-emotional skills, behavior problems, and Spanish competence predict the acquisition of English among English language learners in poverty. *Developmental Psychology, 50*(9), 2242–2254.

Xiao, O., Morgan, I., Ellwein, L., & He, M. (2015). Prevalence of amblyopia in school-aged children and variations by age, gender, and ethnicity in a multi-country refractive error study. *Ophthalmology, 122*(9), 1924–1931.

Zhang, H., Li, Y., Cui, Y., Song, H., Zu, Y., & Lee, S. (2016). Unintentional childhood injury: A controlled comparison of behavioral characteristics. *BMC Pediatrics, 16*:21. doi:10.1186/s12887-016-0558-1.

Zimmer, M., Hart, L., Manning-Courtney, P., Murray, D., Bing, N., & Summer, S. (2012). Food variety as a predictor of nutritional status among children with autism. *Journal of Autism and Developmental Disorders, 42*(4), 549–556.

Parenting Early Adolescent Children

10

LEARNING OBJECTIVES

After reading the chapter, you will be able to:

10-1 Explain gender differences in adolescent growth, and conditions that require early intervention.

10-2 Discuss how parents can support adolescents' cognitive, social-emotional, and healthy lifestyle development.

10-3 Identify positive behavioral guidance strategies that parents can use to encourage adolescents' independence, confidence, and self-esteem.

naeyc Standards Linked to Chapter Content

1a, 1b, and 1c: Promoting child development and learning

2a, 2b, and 2c: Building family and community relationships

4a and 4b: Using developmentally effective approaches to connect with children and families

13 TO 14 YEARS

Ready or not, parents are about to embark on a new chapter in their children's endeavors. In a matter of months, children seemingly transform from kind, caring, and willing-to-listen individuals into fiercely independent, self-determined adolescents who question authority and, at times, are even surprised by their own rebellious behaviors. Parents often find this transformation

continued on following page

just as confusing as do their children, and they struggle to figure out what adjustments are necessary to maintain an effective and supportive parent-child relationship. ∎

10-1 Typical Growth and Development Overview

Although it is easy for parents to focus on behavioral matters during this stage, it is equally important that they notice and appreciate the potential and endearing personal qualities that early adolescent children possess. They are intellectually curious, capable, industrious, and basically "good" kids. They ask many questions, develop an interest in worldly affairs, and begin to form their own opinions. At the same time, they struggle with ambivalent feelings about bodily changes, relationships, morals, and social adjustments. As a result, parents and their children each face different challenges during this stage, and they must find ways to respect and relate to one another in new and healthy ways.

10-1a Growth

There are significant individual and gender differences in growth patterns among 13- and 14-year-olds. Ethnicity plays an important role in determining height/weight parameters, facial features, and puberty onset. Environmental conditions can either optimize children's growth or restrict it (e.g., early neglect, poor dietary quality, prenatal drug exposure, traumatic experiences) (Miller et al., 2015; Richardson et al., 2015; Pervanidou & Chrousos, 2012). Some genetic and developmental disorders, such as Turner and Down syndrome, fetal alcohol syndrome, and autism spectrum disorder can also impair growth (Lee, Chien, & Hwu, 2016; Green, Dissanayake, & Loesch, 2015).

Gender also affects growth differently during early adolescence. Boys tend to gain height in spurts, while girls generally grow taller at a slower and steadier rate. Girls have almost achieved their adult height by this age, whereas boys tend to continue growing taller well into their early twenties. Children's weight also varies widely and is dependent upon genetic makeup and dietary and physical activity habits.

The most striking alterations in children's physical appearance result from sexual developments that are caused by hormonal changes. Acne may form, sexual organs (e.g., breasts, penis) enlarge, underarm and public hair develop, body odor becomes more noticeable, and girls begin (if they haven't already) to have monthly periods. Boys develop facial hair, a deeper voice, and have nocturnal emissions. Hormones also trigger additional developments in the brain.

Puberty may be occurring several years earlier among children in industrialized, high-income countries according to some reports (Zhai et al., 2015; Herman-Giddens et al., 2012). Girls as young as 8 and 9 years are reaching menarche; the average age is normally between 12 and 13 years. Researchers have attributed early puberty onset in girls to overweight and obesity (Fu et al., 2015). Lundeen and colleagues (2016) noted similar results, and also found that greater height-for-age and height-to-weight (BMI) measurements at age 5 and 8 years were directly associated with early puberty in boys. The later results are especially important given that few studies have examined this connection among early adolescent boys.

Children who experience early-onset puberty report being subjected to increased and unwanted peer attention, sexual harassment, rumors, and bullying (Skoog, Özdemir, & Stattin, 2016; Reynolds & Juvonen, 2011). As a result, they experience high rates of anxiety and depression. This circumstance is particularly common among Caucasian girls and African American boys, due to an apparent disconnect between physical maturity, psychosocial immaturity, and social expectations based upon physical appearances (Winer et al., 2016; Zhai et al., 2015; Hamlat, Stange, & Abramson, 2014). Parents should continue to treat children who experience early puberty according to their chronological age and not based on their more mature physical appearance. Children also need continued parental reassurance, understanding, and help in developing self-confidence and a positive body image. Professional counseling may be warranted for adolescents who experience significant difficulty accepting these changes and/or coping with peer reactions.

Photo 10-1 Adolescents are adjusting to the physical changes that accompany puberty as well as trying to figure out who they are and how they fit in.

10-1b Developmental Tasks

Thirteen- and fourteen-year-olds often find themselves overwhelmed by the many physical changes, new experiences, and unexplained feelings that confront them on any given day. One moment they are 'kids' playing games with their friends and seemingly the next day parents and teachers expect them to think and act like adults. Is it any wonder that they seem confused or make poor decisions at times?

A child's transition from childhood to adolescence is celebrated in many countries worldwide, and is usually associated with the onset of puberty (Ginsberg, Kariuki, & Kimamo, 2014; Gentina, Palan, & Fosse-Gomez, 2012). For example, a ritual circumcision has long been practiced in many African tribes to signify children's adolescence and entry into adulthood; however, such practices are beginning to change (Kang'ethe, 2013). Navajo girls may participate in a pubertal coming-of-age ceremony called Kinaaldá to recognize their adolescence (Markstrom & Iborra, 2003). Similar recognitions do not occur until several years later for boys. These transitions are also accompanied by the assumption of new adult roles and responsibilities.

Although there are no similar initiation rituals or celebrations typically held in this country when children become adolescents, there are developmental tasks and implicit social expectations that are associated with this change, such as the expectation that they will act more responsibly and autonomously (see Figure 10-1). Children need considerable parental support and guidance to help them make a successful adjustment during this transitional stage. They need parents who will listen to their concerns without being critical or judgmental, allow them to learn from simple mistakes, and discuss the consequences of their actions together. They need parents who continue to provide safety and structure by establishing reasonable limits and routine. And, perhaps most importantly, they need parents who acknowledge healthy decisions and provide unconditional love regardless of their occasional mistakes.

10-1c Early Identification and Intervention

Efforts to support 13- and 14-year-olds through their adjustment to adolescence requires that parents, teachers, and other significant adults (e.g., clergy, coaches, club leaders) continue to observe closely for signs of any potential physical or mental health problems. For example, mild learning disabilities that children have been able to manage

---

Figure 10-1 Developmental Tasks during Early Adolescence

- Achieving independence
- Developing advanced cognitive and social skills
- Adjusting to sexual changes and feelings
- Establishing a sense of personal and sexual identity
- Forming mutual peer and intimate relationships

or hide until this stage may become more problematic as a result of hormonal changes and increased stress. Unidentified learning problems can cause academic and social struggles and increased feelings of low self-worth, anxiety, and depression unless they are recognized and addressed (Panicker & Chelliah, 2016). Vision and hearing acuity should also be monitored to ensure that early adolescents are able to benefit fully from learning activities in school.

Early adolescents report high levels of anxiety and stress as they attempt to work through many uncertainties related to their sexuality, social relationships, and peer pressures. Schwartz and Maric (2015) found that young teens have a tendency to overestimate and overgeneralize the negative aspects of situations and to underestimate their ability to cope; both increase anxiety, stress, and depressive symptoms. Minority and female adolescents report especially high stress and anxiety levels (Wyatt et al., 2015). However, researchers have also noted that early adolescent youth who maintained strong ethnic affiliations tend to experience academic, psychosocial, and health outcomes that are significantly more positive than young teens who do not have such associations. Results from some studies suggest that ethnic identity offers protective qualities which enable youth to cope with adverse situations and, thus, they experience lower levels of stress and depression when they find themselves faced with difficult circumstances (Rivas-Drake et al., 2014).

Thirteen- and fourteen-year-olds have important developmental tasks to address, and many are unprepared and vulnerable to low self-esteem during this adjustment process. Parents and teachers who are alert to early signs that a child may be having personal or academic difficulties can provide supportive guidance to help them overcome occasional obstacles. Children who grow up in a positive family environment and have parents who encourage open communication are more likely to move through this stage successfully. Professional referral may be necessary if children exhibit negative behaviors that include talk of suicide, substance use, or depression.

10-2 Supporting the Early Adolescent's Development

Thirteen- and fourteen-year-olds are in the process of forming a new personality and self-identity in response to a host of biological, physical, and social-emotional changes that are occurring simultaneously. As a result, 13-year-olds are often unsure of themselves. They vacillate between considering themselves to be "grown up" and yet quickly retreat to the secure feelings of childhood when demands become too difficult. However, they begin to regain their self-confidence during the following year as they become more comfortable with school, peer relationships, and their own advanced cognitive and social-emotional skills. Parental patience, support, encouragement, and guidance are especially important during this time if children are to be successful in coping with so many developmental changes as they strive for autonomy.

10-2a Promoting Cognitive Development

Adolescents have almost reached physical maturity and they are able to think both logically and abstractly, yet they have difficulty meeting expectations, handling multiple tasks, planning ahead, organizing, and delaying gratification. In addition, they periodically make poor decisions and engage in behaviors that they know are wrong. Although parents may find these behaviors distressing at the times, they may be more accepting when they understand that changes in the adolescent's brain may be a contributing factor.

The brain undergoes significant changes during the adolescent years. Unused neural connections continue to be eliminated (pruned) while myelination and white matter increase in volume and complexity. These developments enable the brain to take in new information, operate more efficiently, and send messages between regions faster (Vijayakumar et al., 2016). In addition, hormonal changes that accompany puberty onset are associated with reorganization of the prefrontal cortex and the way in which the brain processes information (Juraska & Willing, 2016). This area of the brain is associated with planning, organization, emotional regulation, and the ability to anticipate consequences. Given that females tend to enter puberty earlier than do males, the associated changes may help to explain why female brains show accelerated maturation (Vijayakumar et al., 2016). For example, girls tend to perform better on tasks that involve attention and episodic memory, which may be related to increased hippocampal volume (Satterthwaite et al., 2014). However, prefrontal cortex maturation will not be complete until individuals reach their early twenties.

Thus, although adolescents' physical appearance may be more adult-like, they do not necessarily think, respond to information, or make decisions in the same way as do adults. For example, adolescents can typically consider different perspectives and solutions when they are given a scenario or reflect back on an incident, but in the moment, they are more likely to act impulsively and less likely to think before they act. In other words, the brain is still undergoing construction, with the majority of systems in place, but the brakes and mental GPS are not fully functional.

Adolescent brains are also more sensitive to emotional input (i.e., increased reactivity in the amygdala), which often leads to immediate and intense emotional responses (Stephanou et al., 2016; National Institute of Mental Health, 2011). As a result, adolescents tend to react to emotional situations without taking time to consider the consequences of their decisions. Over time, the prefrontal cortex will begin to modulate activity in the amygdala and ventral striatum to suppress impulsive emotional responses and enable more thoughtful actions to occur (Casey et al., 2016).

Furthermore, adolescents favor immediate gratification and are less likely to show sensitivity to long-term gains and/or consequences; those who have been exposed to adverse childhood events show more problems in these particular areas (Mackey et al., 2016). In other words, teens show an increased sensitivity for novelty and rewards, which biases their decision-making and increases their desire for larger, more intense rewards (e.g., risk-taking, and thrill seeking behaviors). Their response to smaller rewards (e.g., pat on the back, thank you) is much more muted. They are also more sensitive to peer-initiated rewards because of the shift in socialization focus away from parents. Increased interest and motivation in social interactions, as well as the development of new neural circuits, may also facilitate improved recognition of more complex facial expressions that signal states of mind and intention (e.g., surprise, fear, and disgust); girls show a slight advantage in this ability (Lawrence et al., 2015).

Despite these challenges, the adolescent brain also makes it possible for youth to explore and learn new information, oftentimes with greater speed than adults. Piaget (1952) described advances in adolescents' cognition as they enter into the formal operational stage of cognitive development. He suggested that this stage is characterized by more advanced abstract thinking, which allows adolescents to solve problems through visualization, think hypothetically, and understand the use of metaphors and analogies. More complex thinking patterns, in turn, spur adolescents to explore their own personal values, beliefs, and philosophies.

As youth progress through adolescence, they show improvements in social cognition, concept formation, task-switching, and working memory related to prefrontal cortex maturation (Juraska & Willing, 2016). However, adolescents continue to need parental structure and guidance to help them make good choices and progress toward their goals. In addition, adolescents need parents to be patient and understanding, while also helping them to learn from their mistakes.

Family Engagement and Effect on Learning Outcomes. During early adolescence, youth show declines in engagement and self-efficacy in academic subjects (Martin et al., 2015).

Photo 10-2 Adolescents show higher levels of school success and fewer risky behaviors when their parents are engaged in their education.

Gender and cultural factors also influence teen's educational attainment during this period. Girls are more likely to report higher levels of academic motivation, view education as more valuable, focus more on learning, and manage tasks more effectively, but they also report uncertainties and anxieties related to school (Bugler et al., 2015). Jethwani (2015) described that within the Black Bermudian culture, boys are viewed as troublemakers and less educationally focused than females. They are also less likely to seek social-emotional support from teachers which interferes with their educational attainment. American, but not Chinese, children report a perceived decline in the value of education and school engagement during early adolescence. Qu and Pomerantz (2015) found that such divergent trajectories are related to Chinese youths' sense of responsibility or obligation to parents.

Despite the typical developmental declines that occur in engagement and achievement during this period, parents continue to have a significant impact on a youth's success. Indeed, parental engagement in school is one of the most prominent factors that serve to improve healthy behavior, school success, and decrease risky behaviors such as drug use and early sexual activity (Centers for Disease Control [CDC], 2015). Involvement of both parents appears to be important for school engagement, particularly for boys (Raufelder et al., 2015). Engagement means that parents and teachers collaborate in a bi-directional manner with a focus on mutual decision-making and support for common goals that facilitate adolescent development. Parents and schools have a shared goal to help adolescents develop positive identities that will allow them to contribute to society in constructive ways as adults. Interventions designed to reach and engage high-risk families within the school system have been associated with decreased substance use through early adulthood (Véronneau et al., 2016). Schools can encourage parents to participate and support learning in numerous different ways (Suggestions for Parents 10-1).

Quality parent-child relationships also influence and predict academic outcomes. Authoritative parenting (high in acceptance, supervision, and autonomy support) is associated with a decreased risk of school dropout (Blondal & Adalbjarnardottir, 2014). In general,

---

Suggestions for Parents 10-1

Supporting Adolescents' Academic Engagement and Learning

- *Parenting:* Provide monitoring/supervision, unconditional acceptance, autonomy support, set limits that encourage academic engagement and participation in an appropriate amount of after-school activities, remain calm in the face of conflicts, and involve youth in problem-solving.

- *Communicating:* Remain informed about school policies and activities; establish open, positive communication with teachers; talk daily with students about school; communicate the value of education; and provide encouragement and confidence in adolescents' skills.

- *Volunteering:* Participate in after-school activities, attend school meetings, respect boundaries and adolescents' desire for independence.

- *Learning at home:* Provide a space for homework with few distractions, provide access to learning resources (e.g., computer in home or library), discuss academic content, and help adolescents relate information to their own lives.

- *Decision-making:* Provide educators with feedback about the school atmosphere and policies that support all students to succeed.

when parents provide structure and support autonomy in academic task completion, youth show higher levels of competence, motivation, engagement, and academic achievement (Grolnick et al., 2015). Parental warmth involves unconditional acceptance and feedback that is focused on reassurance of worth, approval, and praise. Adolescents who feel that their parents accept them regardless of their actions show more positive academic adjustment, whereas those who receive more conditional feedback perceive added pressure and show lower academic adjustment (Makri-Botsari, 2015). Rather than providing critical or negative feedback, parents should try to communicate a desire to help the young adolescent focus on behaviors and beliefs that will improve their performance. Hill and Wang (2015) found that parental warmth supported African American and European American students' aspirations, engagement, and achievement. However, differences between the ethnicities were also found; African American students' achievement and engagement was associated with higher levels of parental monitoring; autonomy support contributed more to achievement among European American students.

Parent-adolescent conflicts regarding school issues (e.g., doing homework, learning schedule, grades, future academic plans) tend to increase steadily from late elementary through the middle school years. They are typically most problematic for males who also experience a larger decline in academic achievement (Brković et al., 2014). However, conflicts and declines in academic achievement are also likely bidirectional; conflicts increase when youth perform poorly, and poor performance increases when conflict is present. Higher than average conflict levels are associated with declining grades, lower levels of school self-esteem (e.g., feeling proud of work) and bonding (e.g., feeling close to others at school). High levels of parental warmth and support can promote adolescents' sense of competence and autonomy at home and in school settings and, thereby, increase self-esteem (Dotterer et al., 2013).

Parents can also have a positive influence on adolescents' academic values by reinforcing what is learned in school, and communicating the value of an education for future success. Often, these messages increase an adolescent's likelihood of selecting peers who have similar academic interests and values (Hayes et al., 2015). Young adolescents who have involved parents and strong affiliations with peers who are engaged in school show higher academic achievement (Im et al., 2016).

The way that adolescents spend their time outside of school also influences their adjustment to school. Students who dedicate more time to academic activities are more likely to have a positive outlook and adjustment. For instance, students, particularly low-income, lower-achieving, and immigrant youth who participate in extracurricular school activities tend to be more engaged and to perform better academically (Camacho & Fuligni, 2015). Poor academic performance and increased problematic behaviors are associated with more time spent in social activities outside of school; a majority of this time is often devoted to electronic activities and, in turn, is associated with even lower levels of intrinsic motivation (Wolf et al., 2015). Parents can promote adolescents' successful adjustment to school by helping them to find a healthy balance between their social and academic activities.

10-2b Supporting Social-Emotional Development

Adolescence is a time of much personal and emotional development. Youth begin to question who they are in relation to others, what they would like to become, and what they believe in. Questions about sexuality, attractions, and relationships begin to arise as well. Although teens begin spending more time with peers—and peers become more influential—parents must remember that they have laid a foundation that will guide the child's decision-making when they are not present. In addition, although teens express an increased desire for autonomy, children need their parents' continued guidance and emotional support.

Social-emotional learning is associated with improved academic outcomes, more positive attitudes and motivation to learn, fewer disruptive behaviors, and reduced emotional distress (e.g., depression, withdrawal) (Collaborative for Academic, Social, and

Photo 10-3 Adolescents strive to fit in with their peers—they are often self-conscious and tend to believe that others are always evaluating them.

Emotional Learning [CASEL], 2015; Oberle et al., 2014). Therefore, it is not surprising that the use of structured social-emotional programs has increased in schools. Many of these programs encourage a focus on improving competencies in five areas of social-emotional learning: self-awareness, self-management, social awareness, relationships, and decision-making (CASEL, 2015). Parents can also take steps to promote these same skills by showing, in various ways, that they care about adolescents' well-being, and by creating an environment in which youth feel safe to express themselves (Tennant et al., 2015) (Suggestions for Parents 10-2).

Suggestions for Parents 10-2

Supporting Adolescents' Development of Core Social-Emotional Competencies

Competency	Support Strategies
Self-awareness: ability to recognize one's emotions, thoughts, and influence on behavior	• Model labeling of emotions and discuss how your thoughts and emotions affect your behavior • Help youth to reflect on their emotions, thoughts, and behaviors in different situations • Encourage participation in valued activities
Self-management: ability to regulate emotions, thoughts, behavior	• Model adaptive ways to cope with strong emotions • Teach adaptive coping skills • Reinforce use of adaptive coping skills
Social awareness: ability to take another's perspective and empathize with others	• During problem solving, discuss how others will be affected by different solutions • Show empathy during daily interactions with youth • Provide opportunities to give back to the community or support meaningful causes
Relationship skills: ability to establish and maintain healthy relationships	• Demonstrate healthy relationships within the family system that are characterized by love, respect, and trust • Discuss the roles of friends and the characteristics of good friends • Encourage youth to be kind and respectful of others • Encourage a sense of commitment and belonging (e.g., family, church, sports teams)
Responsible decision-making: ability to make constructive and respectful choices independently and in social interactions	• Provide brief rationales for the decisions made to give youth an example of how to consider different perspectives and outcomes • Involve youth in setting limits and rules • Give opportunities for daily decision-making • Teach time management and organizational skills • Discuss and help youth plan ahead for difficult decisions they are likely to face (e.g., alcohol, bullying, sexual relationships)

A recent Pew Foundation study (Lenhart et al., 2015) found that 92 percent of adolescents use the Internet daily, with 24 percent reporting that they were online continuously using their mobile devices. Eighty-eight percent of teens have access to a cellphone and, of those, 90 percent use them to exchange text messages. A typical teen sends and receives more than 30 text messages per day. Furthermore, the majority of teens use more than one social media site, the most popular of these being Facebook (71 percent), Instagram (52 percent), Snapchat (41 percent), and Twitter (33 percent). Many concerns arise given that so many young adolescents are communicating online. Are youth developmentally ready to use social media? What effects does social media have on their mental health and relationships? Are youth safe communicating with others in this manner?

Underwood and Faris (2015) examined the social media communications of 13-year-olds, and concluded that "there is no firm line between their real and online worlds. Social media is an extension of their social lives ..." This continuous real-time feedback can have beneficial or detrimental consequences on adolescents as they are actively trying to figure out who they are and how they fit in, and have an intense desire to be popular and accepted. Social media makes it easy for adolescents to extend their friendships, find emotional support that might be lacking in traditional relationships (especially for those with disabilities or non-conforming gender), deal with daily stressors, gain information, and learn about new interests (Frison & Eggermont, 2015; Caroll & Kirkpatrick, 2011). Adolescents who have poor social skills often find social media non-threatening and useful for developing friendships and/or romantic relationships (Korchmaros, 2015).

Social media also brings identity development to the forefront. Adolescents are able to develop online profiles, display photographs, and add comments that create a composite identity for others to see. However, they may also post information impulsively without considering its immediate and long-term consequences. For example, a student may post inappropriate pictures or make emotional and hurtful comments to get back at a peer. Unfortunately, it is virtually impossible to erase these errors in judgment.

Adolescents often view social media use and postings as a reflection of their social standing. This can have positive and reinforcing effects for those who are considered to be popular. However, it can also be a painful and even demoralizing experience for adolescents who may be left out. For example, a student who was not invited to a party may be able to access online pictures of the event as it is occurring, whereas they may not have known about the omission until days later prior to the advent of the Internet (Wallace, 2015). Students can also see immediately how quickly others respond or fail to respond to their postings, and whether 'friends' are supportive or rejecting. This information can place young adolescents, particularly females, at increased risk for depression, especially when feedback is negative or they compare themselves to peers who are viewed as being more 'popular' by their online friends (Nesi & Prinstein, 2015). Similarly, adolescents may experience a decline in mood when they do not receive the emotional support they anticipated from others online (Frison & Eggermont, 2015). Psychological distress tends to be greater for teens who use social media to direct attention to themselves, constantly comment on others' postings, receive inappropriate pictures, follow more people than others follow them, and check others' statuses and profiles frequently without posting (i.e., "lurking") (Underwood & Faris, 2015).

Social media is often addicting, even for adults. There is a thrill in seeing what others are posting, how many "likes" are received, and who is making comments about things that others have commented on. The desire for a high number of "likes" and social media connections has been taken to another level by recent apps that allow users to fake texts, conversations, comments, posts, and "likes" (Elgersma, 2015). For example, some apps allow users to receive points by liking others' posts. In turn, these points can then be spent on likes to add to their own posts, which makes them appear even more popular.

Parental monitoring is essential to buffer the potential negative effects that social media use may have for young adolescents. Adolescents whose parents monitor their social media involvement tend to experience less distress and online conflict (Underwood & Faris, 2015). However, this requires that parents be familiar with the way sites operate in order to effectively monitor the intricacies of adolescents' communication. Parents can access information about how to facilitate conversations with teens about appropriate online behavior and safety from several websites (CommonSenseMedia.org, Enough.org, StopCyberbullying.org, and SafetyNet.aap.org).

Parents must also be cognizant about how social media communications may be affecting their child's mood and/or behavior. Sixty percent of parents underestimate how lonely, worried, and depressed their children are, and 94 percent underestimate the amount of online fighting that occurs (Underwood & Faris, 2015). Parents must also keep in mind that adolescents respond to situations differently than do adults. They are more likely to react in an emotionally urgent and intense manner—they jump to conclusions and are very sensitive to peer feedback. How can parents help adolescents put the use of social media and online responses into a healthy perspective? Should parents set limits for the amount of time adolescents can spend online each day?

Peer Relationships. The focus of adolescent social behavior shifts from peer-focused play with parents as a base to full integration and acceptance with large peer groups; adolescents experience distress if this social target is impeded (Nelson et al., 2016). Popularity becomes increasingly important. Youth begin to adopt or adjust their behavior to fit the norms of specific groups that they wish to join, and are more likely to attend to social cues involving acceptance, integration, and evaluation (Nelson et al., 2016). Peer relationships are further complicated by adolescents' increased capacity to view themselves in ways that they believe others see them. This perspective change contributes to **egocentrism**, a focus more on themselves, which leads to increasing self-consciousness and sensitivity to criticism. The sense of an **imaginary audience** also develops; youth believe that others are continuously thinking about them and evaluating their appearance and behavior. Furthermore, adolescents are more likely to believe that they are invincible; thinking that even though bad things can happen to others (e.g., falling when doing a risky skateboard trick, getting caught drinking at a party), they can engage in the same behavior without experiencing negative repercussions.

egocentrism a tendency to focus on one's own thoughts and opinions, and to disregard those of other individuals.

imaginary audience an adolescent's belief that he or she is the center of everyone's concern and attention.

Characteristics of peer relationships differ by gender and are influenced by culture. Early adolescent female relationships are characterized more by validation, trust, disclosure, nurturance, enhancement of worth, and closeness, which promote more positive, supportive responses during self-disclosures (Altermatt & Painter, 2016). Male adolescent relationships tend to be organized more around shared activities (Kornienko & Santos, 2014). Gender differences in disclosure and responses may be related to the way that parents discuss emotions with their children.

Parents can help children learn to balance their desire to appear competent with an ability to maintain positive relationships (Altermatt & Painter, 2016). Kang noted that adolescents' belief in their ability to control life events (locus of control) is associated with more initiative in peer relations, higher social status, and greater peer acceptance for Caucasian youth. African American, Hispanic, and Asian ethnicities' internal locus of control may be associated with behaviors that are in conflict with their collective culture and that pose a threat to their peer groups (Kang et al., 2015).

Adolescents show a heightened need for belongingness and conformity which also increases the likelihood of social exclusion. Girls who experienced pressure for gender conformity showed increased academic self-efficacy, but boys exhibited a decrease and more antisocial attitudes (Vanteighem & Van Houtte, 2015). A heightened sense of group conformity also begins to exert a powerful influence on how youth respond to moral transgressions. Mulvey and Killen (2016) found that although youth understood actions that constituted incorrect behavior and had a positive view of students who stood up for others, they themselves would not intervene because of concerns about social standing repercussions within their peer group. Young adolescents often make exclusionary decisions based upon individual characteristics, the nature of their group's goals, and whether or not they believe an individual would interfere with the group's functioning (Richardson et al., 2014). Younger adolescents are more likely to base their decisions on reference group stereotypes, whereas older adolescents are more likely to use gender stereotypes—an indication that the individual is not likely to enjoy group membership due to certain personal characteristics (Richardson et al., 2014).

Parents should be patient and understanding of the need and challenges involved in adolescent peer relationships. Such associations can provide safe gathering spaces for youth (e.g., movie night at the home, meeting at a game center), model healthy relationship behaviors, and help adolescents consider multiple perspectives and the "evidence" for irrational or unhelpful thoughts. Parents should be sensitive to the need for autonomy and respect boundaries and desire for privacy (e.g., knock before entering room, not interject during conversations). Parents should also remain calm and not overreact when adolescents make inappropriate decisions or commit mistakes, given their strong motivation to fit

Photo 10-4 Adolescents begin to show an interest in forming romantic relationships, and some are in a relationship before entering high school.

Shandra posted an unflattering photo of one of her teammates on Instagram. She was tired of the girl's constant criticisms about her performance in games and why she was even on the team. Shandra thought that her other teammates were on her side, and that she would gain increased acceptance (and likeability) by posting the photo. When Shandra's mother found out about the photo and message from a teammate's parent, she promptly took away Shandra's cell phone and grounded her for a month. What does this punishment teach Shandra? How might Shandra's mother have handled this experience differently in order to help her learn more constructive ways to manage her feelings?

in and heightened levels of emotionality and impulsivity. Rather, parents should focus their attention on helping adolescents explore their own identity, how their actions affect others, and how to formulate constructive solutions for challenging situations.

Personal Identity and Self-Esteem. Early adolescents often feel confident one moment and insecure and in need of reassurance from others the next (Marotz & Allen, 2016). This fluctuation describes what Erikson (1963) defined as conflict between a sense of personal identity and role confusion. Adolescents who successfully resolve this conflict develop a positive sense of self and commitment to their beliefs and future. Youth today face numerous challenges to their development of a personal identity. For example, increased globalization (e.g., exposure to different cultures, ease of travel) has exposed this generation of adolescents to more options as they struggle to form an identity and determine what social groups they want to be a part of, what they believe in, and what they eventually want to become (Fuligini & Tsai, 2015). Indeed, immigrant youth often develop a "hybridized" personal identity to negotiate this crisis, which combines ethnic categories and cultural switching based on the particular setting or context (Fuligini & Tsai, 2015).

As youth begin to define who they are, they begin to separate themselves more from parents in order to gain autonomy, or emotional independence. This renewed drive for autonomy can be a difficult transition for parents because their child no longer wants shows of affection in public and often questions their beliefs and decisions. Although adolescents begin to rely more on their own internal monitoring processes when making decisions, they continue to respond to external feedback related to behavioral control (Ferdinand et al., 2016). However, the drive and focus on autonomy differs by culture, and is typically more prevalent in European and North American countries. In contrast, there is a greater emphasis on interdependence, family cohesion, and solidarity in Asian, Latin American, and African cultures. There, adolescents are encouraged to consider their identity in relation to the family rather than as separate individuals (Fuligini & Tsai, 2015).

Parents can encourage youth to explore and reflect on their sense of identity within reasonable limits. Some parents may show a tendency to shelter children from potentially difficult or questionable activities; however, these decisions may have a negative impact on adolescents' self-concept development and interactions with peers. For example, Ekinci et al. (2016) noted that parents of teens with epilepsy often restrict their child's daily activities due to a fear that the child may have a seizure in a public place. Such protective attitudes and restrictive behaviors are associated with adolescents' forming a more negative self-concept and perception about their popularity with peers. Parents should promote respect and trust within the family relationship and remember that adolescents' protests and challenges are a natural part of the developmental process.

Adolescents continue to show a decline in self-esteem throughout adolescence as they continue to evaluate themselves against others (Del Guidice, 2015). Fear of negative evaluation by others is related to social status and depressive symptoms in both genders (Kornienko & Santos, 2014). Insufficient sleep is also associated with lower levels of self-confidence and use of ineffective coping strategies, which can lead to peer problems such as bullying (Kubiszewski et al., 2014). DesRoches and Willoughby (2014) recommend that parents support and encourage teens to participate in social activities. Increased engagement in meaningful activities is often associated with higher levels of optimism, greater feelings of purpose, and more positive mood and self-esteem. Parents can also encourage positive feelings of self-worth by acknowledging and supporting their adolescent's positive attributes and achievements.

Sexuality. Adolescents often experience a heightened awareness of, and interest in, what it means to be male or female, the extent to which they "fit" their gender, and how important it is to belong to their gender (Rogers et al., 2015). They worry about their physical attractiveness and whether they are normal. Youth today are more likely to view gender identity and sexual orientation as more fluid and changeable, with beliefs and emotions falling on a continuum, rather than a simple dichotomy (either male or female) (Eagly, 2013; Galinsky et al., 2012). Offering support during the tumultuous adolescent years as gender identity develops is beneficial to positive adjustment, especially for gender non-conforming youth who are more likely to have problems with depression, anxiety, self-harm, and suicidal thoughts (Reisner, 2015).

Romance and sex are dominant preoccupations during early adolescence; they influence youth's motivations, interactions with others, emotional responses, social learning, decision-making, and identity formation (Suleiman & Harden, 2016). Before entering high school, almost 85 percent of adolescents reported being interested in romantic relationships (Suleiman & Deardorff, 2015). Thirteen-year-olds often begin to explore and talk about sexual relationships with their peers, but they tend to have mixed feelings about such relationships; 14-year-olds begin to develop an interest in forming romantic relationships that are more serious (Marotz & Allen, 2016). Teens are most likely to have an initial sexual experience with a steady partner. The average age of first intercourse in the United States is 17 years; however, 2 percent of adolescents are sexually active by age 12 years (Guttmacher Institute, 2014). Early adolescent relationships are briefer than those of adults and less emotionally intimate, but these new relationships help adolescents to explore their gender identity, sexual orientation, relationship values (e.g., characteristics of a desired partner, what it means to be in a relationship), and competence in future relationships (Marotz & Allen, 2016; Suleiman & Harden, 2016).

Peers exert an influence on the development of romantic relationships. Suleiman and Deardorff (2015) found that friends who pressured others into relationships did so, in part, to gain popularity and social status. Although adolescents typically meet romantic partners at school or through friends and acquaintances, the normality and acceptance of using the Internet to form relationships increases as they grow older (Korchmaros et al., 2015). Consequently, parents should discuss online safety measures and monitor adolescents' use of social media. Adolescents who form online relationships are at increased risk for substance abuse, delinquency, and teen dating violence because the relationships do not have the same level of supervision or family and peer support (Korchmaros et al., 2015).

Many teens receive formal sexual education at school; the most successful programs are comprehensive and include encouragement to delay sex (as opposed to advocating abstinence only) and to have responsible, healthy relationships (Guttmacher Institute, 2016). Although the majority of adolescents talk to their parents about some sexual education topics (70 percent of males and 78 percent of females), their knowledge about contraception and related topics is often inaccurate or incomplete. Adolescents often consult the Internet without knowledge that many websites provide misinformation (up to 46 percent of those addressing contraception and 35 percent of those addressing abortion) (Guttmacher Institute, 2016). Establishing open communication about sensitive topics, such as sexual behaviors, is important for healthy development and to ensure that adolescents have appropriate and correct information.

Quality parent-adolescent relationships are associated with lower rates of risky sexual behaviors. This may be related to adolescents' feelings of closeness, trust, security, open communication, and perceived parental disapproval (i.e., communicated values regarding sex). Although parental monitoring is needed, parents' efforts to control or coerce youth from engaging in risky sexual behaviors are not associated with a decrease in these behaviors (Kerpelman et al., 2015).

10-2c Maintaining Healthy Eating Habits

Dramatic growth, emotional changes, and active lifestyles during the early adolescent years demand a diet that includes adequate calories, protein, vitamins, and minerals. Unfortunately, researchers have found that young adolescents often fail to consume a diet that adequately meets U.S. Dietary Guidelines (Banfield et al., 2016). Their intake of fruits, vegetables, and grains, met less than half of the daily required amounts, with the exception of dairy products and protein which were considered to be adequate. An interesting trend also emerged from this data. Young adolescents consumed fewer fruits, vegetables, and grains than younger children (4–8 years) but more than older adolescents (14–18 years). Their diet also included more sodium, empty calories (junk foods), and processed grains than younger children. In other words, the nutrient quality of children's diets appears to decline with age.

Photo 10-5 Eating disorders are not uncommon as young adolescents struggle with their body image.

Competing interests, increased autonomy, and busy schedules often begin to interfere with the quality of young adolescents' diet. Peers begin to exert a stronger influence on adolescents' eating behaviors, especially as more time is spent away from home and involvement in after-school activities increases. de la Haye et al. (2014) found that peer influence had a significant socializing effect on adolescents' eating behaviors, and that their consumption of poor nutrient quality foods (junk foods) typically increased as the eating habits of their closest friends were adopted. Research results also showed that eating meals together as a family had positive and protective outcomes for adolescents, including improved academic performance and lower rates of depression, substance abuse rates, and school problems (de Wit et al., 2015; Goldfarb et al., 2015; Meier & Musick, 2014).

Eating disorders often become more apparent during the early adolescent years as girls and boys struggle to accept their body image, experience lower self-esteem, and are more susceptible to the persuasive messages about weight and appearance presented in the media. Messages about overweight health issues and obesity also bombard teens on a daily basis and at a time when they are predisposed to height and weight gains associated with normal growth. Contradictory messages can add to the body image confusion that many 13- and 14-year-olds experience. Mothers' perceived comments about their daughters' weight and appearance further increase the risk of eating disorders among adolescent girls (Thøgersen-Ntoumani et al., 2016).

anorexia nervosa an eating disorder in which a person severely limits food intake due to an obsessive fear of becoming fat.

bulimia nervosa an eating disorder in which a person overeats or binges and then compensates by self-induced vomiting or use of laxatives or diuretics to prevent weight gain.

binge eating disorder repeated episodes of excessive, uncontrolled eating, usually occurring at least once a week, followed by feelings of guilt, remorse, or embarrassment.

The American Psychiatric Association recognizes three major categories of eating disorders in its *Diagnostic and Statistical Manual of Mental Disorders (DSM-V)*: **anorexia nervosa**, **bulimia nervosa**, and **binge eating disorder** (APA, 2013). These conditions represent serious eating and emotional disorders that range along a continuum from starvation (anorexia) to excessive overeating (binge eating). Although eating disorders tend to occur more often in girls, researchers have estimated that 1.2 percent of 14-year-old boys experience eating disorders; this percentage more than doubles by age 17 (Allen, 2013). Bucchianeri et al. (2016) noted a strong correlation between boys' high body dissatisfaction and unhealthy weight control behaviors. However, they also determined that African American boys who were dissatisfied with their body were almost 50 percent less likely than White, Asian, or mixed/other race boys to engage in unhealthy weight control behaviors. Eating disorders are also more common among female athletes who participate in aesthetic events (e.g., gymnastics, dance, cheerleading) and male athletes who participate in weight-class sports or events where lighter weights are advantageous (e.g., wrestling, boxing, cycling) (Bratland-Sanda & Sundgot-Borgen, 2013).

Parents, peers, and other significant people in an adolescent's life must recognize the early signs of an eating disorder and ensure that the teen receives professional help (Suggestions for Parents 10-3). Untreated eating disorders are associated with long-term negative outcomes, including intentional self-harm, substance abuse, and significant psychiatric disorders (Micali et al., 2015). Nutrition education is also an important component of any treatment program. Castillo et al. (2015) surveyed adolescents, with and without an eating disorder, and their parents to assess their basic nutrition knowledge. The results showed that no group correctly answered more than 50 percent of the questions, and fewer than 20 percent of the participants were able to identify the recommended daily intake for calories, fats, protein, and carbohydrates. These findings highlight the lack of accurate nutrition knowledge that exists among the general population and the negative effects that it can have on adolescents' dietary quality.

10-2d Staying Physically Active

Voluminous research evidence supports the positive effects that physical activity has on health and weight control. Although children tend to be quite active when they are young, they become less so as they approach adolescence. Organizations such as the Centers for Disease Control and Prevention (CDC) and World Health Organization (WHO) recommend that adolescents engage in a minimum of 60 minutes of moderate to vigorous physical activity daily and muscle- and bone-strengthening activity three times per week (WHO, 2016; CDC, 2015). Most studies show that young adolescents worldwide are not achieving this level. Cooper et al. (2015) used data from several international studies to analyze the physical activity levels of over 10,000 children between the ages of 9 and 12 years from eight different countries. They observed that boys in this sample consistently achieved more physical activity than girls, but it was not sufficient to meet recommended guidelines. They also noted that the United States had the lowest proportion of 13- to 14-year-old girls and boys who achieved at least 60 minutes of moderate to vigorous activity on a given day; children in Spain, Australia, and Norway were among those achieving the highest proportion. Overweight and obese children were found to engage in less physical activity than their normal-weight peers.

Suggestions for Parents 10-3

Signs of an Eating Disorder

Not all adolescents will exhibit the same behaviors, but the most common signs of an eating disorder include:

- displaying a strong preoccupation with food, dieting, or compulsive exercising
- monitoring food intake closely; keeping track of calories and fat in food
- denying feelings of hunger or finding excuses to avoid meals
- having a distorted body image (e.g., shape, weight, clothing size); experiencing significant weight loss but still considering self too heavy
- complaining about feeling cold, dizzy, or tired
- ceasing to have periods or having irregular periods
- withdrawing socially
- developing dry skin and hair loss
- experiencing unusually slow heartbeat and blood pressure
- developing a fine layer of downy hair on skin surfaces

Source: National Eating Disorders Association.

The researchers also noted that physical activity levels declined by approximately 4.2 percent each year after age 5 years, and that sedentary or light activity replaced vigorous physical activity.

Children's opportunities to participate in daily physical activity often diminish when they transition from grade to middle school. Recess is no longer an option, and participation in many sport-related activities is often determined by a child's skills. Researchers have also identified several additional perceived barriers that adolescents cite as interfering with their engagement in physical activity, including a lack of energy, other competing leisure activities, BMI, number of children in the household, and self-evaluation of athletic competence (Eime et al., 2015; McClanahan et al., 2015). Neighborhood and park safety and increased travel distances to recreational facilities have also been identified as limiting adolescents' participation in physical activity (Babey, et al., 2015). As a result, sedentary activities begin to occupy an increased amount of adolescents' time.

Thirteen- and fourteen-year olds benefit from daily participation in moderate to vigorous physical activity. This is an important time when weight-bearing (impact) activity promotes calcium deposition, which builds bone mass and density. Physical activity also reduces the risk of adolescent obesity, fosters neural connections that lead to improved cognitive functioning, and produces brain chemicals that decrease stress and improve mood (Basterfield et al., 2015; Piepmeier et al., 2015). For these reasons, efforts must be made to encourage young adolescents, particularly girls and children with disabilities, to maintain an active lifestyle. Neighborhood parks and recreational facilities are needed in locations that are safe and accessible for children. Recreational areas should include surfaces and adaptive equipment that allow young adolescents with physical limitations to participate in physical activity. However, parents' own activity habits may be the most motivating and influential factor in terms of instilling a long-term enjoyment of an active lifestyle in children (Wing, Bélanger, & Brunet, 2016).

Photo 10-6 Adolescents are more likely to engage in physical activity when their parents model good activity habits, encourage participation, and provide safe opportunities.

10-2e The Need for Adequate Sleep

Growth and developmental changes occurring during early adolescence increase the need for adequate sleep. Unfortunately, many students get less than the recommended 8 to 10 hours per night, despite the fact that sleep is considered vital to their health and academic performance (Kronholm et al., 2015; National Sleep Foundation, 2015). Paksarian et al. (2015) conducted a large national, cross-sectional survey that involved over 7000 adolescents and found that they averaged 7.71 hours of sleep per weeknight; girls slept approximately 7.6 hours per night, boys slept an average of 7.81 hours. Shorter sleep was typically associated with children's transition from grade to middle school. Students began staying up later at night but still got up at the same time in the morning.

These findings are consistent with other research studies that describe significant changes in adolescents' sleep patterns. Scientists have discovered that brain structure modifications, brain wave alterations, and shifts in circadian rhythm begin to occur during early puberty, and are associated with adolescents' later bedtimes and reduced sleep needs (Skeldon, Derks, & Dijk, 2016; Crowley et al., 2015). Sleep disturbances and insomnia are also more common among young adolescents than in older adolescents. Racial/ethnic differences in sleep duration have also been noted. Caucasian and Asian adolescents report sleeping more hours than do African American and Hispanic students (Organek et al., 2015).

The culmination of numerous research findings has prompted experts to recommend that schools consider later start times in order to improve adolescent sleep duration. Parents should help young adolescents to understand the positive effects that adequate sleep has on health, grades, injury prevention, and athletic performance. Treatment should be sought for emotional disturbances (e.g., stress, anxiety, depression) that adolescents may be experiencing. Parents should also take steps to minimize parent-child conflict, provide nutritious meals, and encourage children to engage in physical activity daily—measures that may be conducive to restful sleep for all family members.

10-2f Mental Health

Adolescents are notorious for their unpredictable emotional mood swings. One moment they are laughing and enjoying life, and within seconds they are angry or sulking because of something that was said. Parents are often puzzled by this behavior and unsure of how to respond for fear that they may trigger yet another emotional outburst. Adolescents also find their reactions confusing at times, especially when they reconsider the event. They also have difficulty figuring out why other people do not understand their viewpoint. Thirteen- and fourteen-year-olds face a major developmental task that involves learning how to regulate their own feelings and behavior. Although most are able to navigate successfully through this process, a small percentage will find the experience stressful and overwhelming. They may exhibit persistent symptoms associated with chronic anxiety and depression that require professional treatment.

Depression and Suicide. Depression is a chronic mental illness that is characterized by prolonged sadness, low energy, lack of interest in daily activities, difficulty sleeping, loss of appetite, and thoughts of self-harm (APA, 2016). The onset in adolescents usually occurs between ages 14 and 15 years, and girls present symptoms earlier than do boys (Siu, 2016). Several explanations have been offered for why young adolescents appear to be more vulnerable to early depression. Hankin et al. (2015) found that girls typically developed depression around the time of puberty (12.5 years) and that peer pressure, combined with physical and hormonal changes, was a major causative factor. They noted that adolescents were 2.5 times more likely to develop symptoms of depression shortly after experiencing puberty. Researchers have also suggested that depression may have an inherited tendency, but study results to date have been inconsistent. A recent study based on MRI brain scans, found that girls whose mothers had been diagnosed with depression (and, thus, may have been at higher risk for developing it themselves) had thinner gray matter compared to girls whose risk was low (Foland-Ross et al., 2015). This finding may help to explain the hereditary predisposition that has long been associated with depression in families.

Fortunately, depression can be treated successfully with therapy and medication, especially if it is identified and treated early. Parents are in a position to notice changes in children's behavior that may indicate undue stress or signs of depression. Parents must also be aware of children's exposure to bullying or excessive peer pressure, provide support if they are being victimized, and take action if necessary (Claes et al., 2015). Exercise has also been found to improve depression in adolescents, and is something that parents can encourage and participate in with their children.

Suicide ranks sixth as a leading cause of death among children 5 to 14 years of age (AACAP, 2013). Boys are more likely to attempt and to die from suicide, whereas girls are more likely to engage in non-fatal suicide efforts. Chronic interpersonal stress, mood disorders, low self-efficacy, low perceived social support, and depression increase adolescents' risk of committing suicide (Buitron et al., 2016; Giletta et al., 2015). Sexual minority adolescents (e.g., gay, lesbian, bisexual, transsexual) may experience family rejection in addition to many of these feelings and, thus, are at higher risk for committing suicide (Mueller et al., 2015). Suicide rates are also reported to be significantly higher among multiracial, American Indian/Alaskan Native, and Native Hawaiian/Pacific Islander youth than for Asian, African American, Hispanic, and Caucasian adolescents (Wong et al., 2012).

Peers, parents, and adults with whom children have frequent contact should be cognizant of changes in young adolescents' behavior and conversations that may indicate despondency or suicidal thoughts (Suggestions for Parents 10-4). Recognition, referral, and prompt professional treatment are necessary to prevent adolescents from harming

Suicide Warning Signs

Although suicide among adolescents is rare, early warning signs may include:

- Exhibiting a personality change—becoming lethargic, apprehensive, withdrawn, irritable, sad
- Experiencing a loss of appetite, weight loss
- Having difficulty sleeping, or sleeping for extended periods
- Complaining frequently of physical ailments (e.g., headache, stomachache, pain)
- Expressing feelings of worthlessness, being a burden to others, lacking hope; running away
- Talking about dying or 'not being around much longer'; giving away personal possessions
- Becoming careless about appearance; failing to do homework
- Using drugs and/or alcohol

themselves. Treatment usually includes a combination of individual and family therapy and medication for depression. Adolescents can also call the National Suicide Prevention Lifeline (800-273-8255) or the National Suicide Hotline (800-784-2433) 24 hours a day, 365 days a year to speak with a counselor, or they can visit their websites for further information. Parents can support adolescents in maintaining a healthy lifestyle (e.g., eating, exercising, sleeping), encouraging open communication with a significant adult, and getting involved in activities that are meaningful, enjoyable, and build self-confidence as important steps in the healing process.

Photo 10-7 Parents must adjust their communication strategies to maintain a positive relationship with their early adolescents.

10-2g Promoting Personal Safety

Young adolescents sometimes find themselves experimenting with high-risk, health-compromising behaviors, including drinking and drugs, crime, body art (tattoos, piercings), or engaging in unprotected sex. Their involvement in these activities may, in part, reflect an increased interest in exploring new activities and asserting their independence. However, parents may question why their children begin to make such poor decisions when they have always acted responsibly and rationally in the past. Seldom is there a simple answer to this question, or even one that adolescents are able to fully articulate. Some teens have identified stress at home and harsh parenting as factors that contributed to their decision to experiment with drugs, sex, or other risky behaviors (Hinnant, Erath, & El-Sheikh, 2015). Others say they do these things simply to gain attention, express their individuality, or for no particular reason (Armstrong et al., 2014). Adolescents who have developmental disorders, such as ADHD and autism spectrum disorder, are especially vulnerable to participating in risky behaviors due to their limited decision-making abilities (Pollack et al., 2016).

Researchers have linked chemical and structural changes in the adolescent's brain to an inability to accurately assess risk, control impulsivity, and make sound decisions (see, *Promoting Cognitive Development*) (Khundrakpam et al., 2016). They have also identified the adolescents' intense desire for peer acceptance as one of the most influential motivators underlying their involvement in risk-taking behaviors (Telzer et al., 2015). Peer acceptance stimulates pleasurable reward centers in the brain and reduces the adolescent's likelihood of engaging in risky behaviors, whereas low peer support increases their chances of doing so.

Thirteen-year-old Jenny asked her mother if she could attend a party at Ben's house. Her mother quickly responded "no," and left the room. Jenny made a disrespectful comment and slammed her door. Jenny then texted her best friend to share the bad news, but rather than receiving sympathy, her friend informed her that she "will not be included in their group any longer if she does not show up at the party." Jenny replied to the message, but did not hear back from her friend. Why would Jenny's friends treat her this way? How might the lack of access to social media and her friends affect her mood? How would you suggest that Jenny's mother involve her in a more productive and respectful conversation about the party next time?

These explanations do not excuse children's thrill-seeking or risk-taking behaviors, but they can help parents understand why 13- and 14-year-olds may be acting in this manner and how best to respond. This is important because many risky behaviors have serious long-term consequences, including pregnancy, sexually transmitted diseases, and addiction. The adolescent's immature physiological development makes them particularly susceptible to infections and addiction, and increases the probability that they will continue to engage in multiple risk behaviors (e.g., drinking and sex, drugs and sex) (Ritchwood et al., 2015). However, parents should not discourage all risk-taking behavior. Adolescents need to be given freedom to make low-consequence decisions so they can learn from their mistakes, gain confidence in their abilities, and build resilience to destructive risky activities.

10-3 Developmentally Appropriate Behavior Guidance

The transition to adolescence can be made smoother when parents provide a stable, safe, and loving environment, and create an atmosphere of honesty, mutual trust, respect, and open communication (American Academy of Child and Adolescent Psychiatry, 2015). Parents must adjust their parenting style to create a healthy balance between protecting children's well-being and supporting their individuality and autonomy (Suggestions for Parents 10-5).

Young adolescents have an increased desire for independence and experimentation that often leads to conflict with parents. Although they may protest rules and limits that parents have set, adolescents continue to need parental nurturance, guidance, consistency, patience, and understanding. Limits and rules should allow adolescents room to explore, experiment, and express themselves while helping them to avoid destructive and serious consequences. Conflict and rebellious behaviors are likely to decrease when a good balance between control and freedom is achieved. Parents must also remember that adolescents are likely to act impulsively, have some difficulty making spontaneous decisions, and experience emotional ups and downs until their brain is fully matured.

Although it may be challenging to communicate with adolescents at times, doing so is important to their continued development. Parents must make themselves available to talk, exercise patience, and be nonjudgmental when addressing difficult topics. Adolescents are more likely to discuss their concerns with a parent who remains calm, listens actively, and allows the adolescent to take the lead in deciding how to address a problem, as opposed to a parent who overreacts and offers an immediate solution. Adolescents benefit from positive communication opportunities that allow them to express themselves, have their questions answered, process information, and problem solve. Parents must also be sensitive to what adolescents desire from conversations. They may simply want someone to listen at times, or they may be looking for advice or help in considering solution alternatives on other occasions.

Positive Behavior Guidance

- Spend quality time together, and encourage adolescents to take the lead; play catch, watch a movie, play board games, ride bikes, go for a hike.

- Make time for family dinners and time away from electronics to encourage meaningful conversation.

- Take time to let adolescents teach you a new skill that they have developed; show interest in things that are of interest to them.

- Show support and appreciation for efforts and accomplishments.

- Continue to involve adolescents in setting limits; enforce them consistently and expect compliance. Use short-term consequences (e.g., no cell phone access for a day, as opposed to a month).

- Be available to talk. Use open-ended questions and nonjudgmental listening. Guide adolescents to identify their own solutions rather than providing immediate answers.

- Model appropriate ways to manage conflict; remain calm, patient, and refrain from arguing. Focus on the behavior in question and help the child to problem solve ("I noticed that you haven't been finishing your assigned chores. Let's figure out a plan."), rather than threatening to punish the adolescent's failures (e.g., "You're always so lazy! You're not going to play in your baseball game if you don't get your chores done.").

- Think before saying "no"; when it is necessary to do so, acknowledge the adolescents' feelings and briefly explain your reasoning for the decision (even if they don't agree).

- Continue to use natural consequences (going without lunch because the adolescent forgot to put it in his backpack before leaving for school) and logical consequences (not being allowed to go to a movie with friends because she did not tell you where she was going the last time) to encourage compliance.

- Reinforce family values and expectations; provide opportunities to teach the importance of responsibility.

- Find someone your adolescent can talk to about drugs and sex if these are uncomfortable subjects for you to discuss.

Summary

- Growth is characterized by changes associated with puberty. Girls typically experience puberty several years earlier than do boys and, as a result, begin to appear more adult-like. Young adolescents may experience increased stress and anxiety as they adjust to new feelings and body image.

- Significant developments are occurring in the brain which enable adolescents to learn faster, understand concepts that are more abstract, and think in complex patterns. However, restructuring of the brain also disrupts their emotional and decision-making processes.

- Peer acceptance and group belonging are vital to adolescents' feelings about social order, self-identity, and self-esteem. Strong interests in romantic relationships become apparent.

- Young adolescents need encouragement to maintain healthy lifestyle habits (e.g., eating, physical activity, sleeping). Eating disorders and sleep deficits become more common during this stage.
- Parents can facilitate adolescents' development by continuing to provide a stable, supportive home environment and setting limits that are developmentally appropriate, supportive of their individuality, and protective of their well-being.

Key Words

anorexia nervosa (p. 297) **binge eating disorder** (p. 297) **imaginary audience** (p. 294)

bulimia nervosa (p. 297) **egocentrism** (p. 294)

Questions for Discussion and Self-Reflection

1. In what ways do girls and boys experience growth differently during early adolescence? How are these differences manifested in their cognitive and social-emotional development?

2. Why do advanced cognitive abilities often fail to protect young adolescents from making unwise decisions and engaging in risk-taking behaviors?

3. Why do young adolescents typically experience a decline in their self-esteem? How might this development contribute to depression and other mental health disorders?

4. Why are eating disorders more likely to develop during early adolescence?

5. What suggestions would you offer to parents for protecting children's personal safety and improving their resilience during this vulnerable period?

Field Activities

1. Conduct an Internet search, and locate the PBS video, *Inside the Teenage Brain*. How is the young adolescent's ability to regulate emotion, plan, and problem-solve explained by changes that are occurring in the brain? Why is there often an increase in miscommunication between parents and adolescents during this stage? What effect does sleep have on brain development and functioning?

2. Think back to the time when you were in middle school or junior high, and identify one event/experience that was particularly stressful. Why did you find it stressful? How might the stress you perceived have been related to your developmental stage? What advice would you now give to yourself about how to handle these feelings based on what you have learned in this chapter?

3. Explore several websites that offer advice to parents about protecting children's safety when online or using social media. Prepare a list of topics that parents should address with children regarding their use of common apps (e.g., Instagram, Yik Yak, Snapchat).

REFERENCES

Allen, K., Byme, S., Oddy, W., & Crosby, R. (2013). DSM-IV-TR and DSM5 eating disorders in adolescents: Prevalence, stability, and psychosocial correlates in a population-based sample of male and female adolescents. *Journal of Abnormal Psychology, 122,* 720–732.

Altermatt, E., & Painter, J. (2016). I did well. Should I tell? Gender differences in children's academic success disclosures. *Sex Roles, 74,* 46–61.

American Academy of Child and Adolescent Psychiatry (AACAP). (2015). Parenting: Preparing for adolescence. Retrieved April 28, 2016 from https://www.aacap.org/AACAP/Families_and _Youth/Facts_for_Families/FFF-Guide/Parenting-Preparing-For-Adolescence-056.aspx.

American Academy of Child and Adolescent Psychiatry (AACAP). (2013). Teen suicide. Retrieved April 29, 2016 from http://www.aacap.org/AACAP/Families_and_Youth/Facts _for_Families/FFF-Guide/Teen-Suicide-010.aspx.

American Psychiatric Association (APA). (2013). Feeding and eating disorders. Retrieved April 28, 2016 from http://www.dsm5.org/documents/eating%20disorders%20fact%20sheet.pdf.

American Psychological Association (APA). (2016). Depression. Retrieved April 29, 2016 from http://www.apa.org/topics/depression/.

Armstrong, M., Tustin, J., Owen, D., Koch, J., & Roberts, A. (2014). Body art education: The earlier, the better. *Journal of School Nursing, 30*(1), 12–18.

Babey, S., Tan, D., Wolstein, J., & Diamant, A. (2015). Neighborhood, family and individual characteristics related to adolescent park-based physical activity. *Preventive Medicine, 76,* 31–36.

Banfield, E., Liu, Y., Davis, J., Chang, S., & Frazier-Wood, A. (2016). Poor adherence to US Dietary Guidelines for children and adolescents in the National Health and Nutrition Examination survey population. *Journal of the Academy of Nutrition and Dietetics, 116*(1), 21–27.

Basterfield, L., Reilly, J., Pearce, M., Parkinson, K., Adamson, A., Reilly, J., & Vella, S. (2015). Longitudinal associations between sports participation, body composition and physical activity from childhood to adolescence. *Journal of Science and Medicine in Sports, 18*(2), 178–182.

Blondal, K., & Adalbjarnardottir, S. (2014). Parenting in relation to school dropout through student engagement: A longitudinal study. *Journal of Marriage and Family, 76*(4), 778–795.

Bratland-Sanda, S., & Sundgot-Borgen, J. (2013). Eating disorders in athletes: Overview of prevalence, risk factors, and recommendations for prevention and treatment. *European Journal of Sport Science, 13*(5), 499–508.

Brković, I., Keresteš, G., & Puklek Levpušček, M. (2014). Trajectories of change and relationship between parent-adolescent school-related academic conflict and academic achievement in early adolescence. *Journal of Early Adolescence, 34*(6), 792–815.

Bucchianeri, M., Fernandes, N., Loth, K., Hannan, P., Eisenberg, M., & Neumark-Sztainer, D. (2016). Body dissatisfaction: Do associations with disordered eating and psychological well-being differ across race/ethnicity in adolescent girls and boys? *Cultural Diversity and Ethnic Minority Psychology, 22*(1), 137–146.

Bugler, M., McGeown, S., & St Clair-Thompson, H. (2015). Gender differences in adolescents' academic motivation and classroom behaviour. *Educational Psychology, 35*(5), 541–556.

Buitron, V., Hill, R., Pettit, J., Green, K., Hatkevich, C., & Sharp, C. (2016). Interpersonal stress and suicidal ideation in adolescence: An indirect association through perceived burdensomeness toward others. *Journal of Affective Disorders, 190,* 143–149.

Camacho, D., & Fuligni, A. (2015). Extracurricular participation among adolescents from immigrant families. *Journal of Youth and Adolescence, 44*(6), 1251–1262.

Carroll, J., & Kirkpatrick, R. (2011). *Impact of social media on adolescent behavioral health.* Oakland, CA: California Adolescent Health Collaborative. Retrieved May 3, 2016 from http://www.phi.org/uploads/application/files /g9g6xbfghdxoe3yytmc1rfvvm8lt1ly9sr3j369pstkojdly15.pdf.

Casey, B., Galván, A., & Somerville, L. (2016). Beyond simple models of adolescence to an integrated circuit-based account: A commentary. *Developmental Cognitive Neuroscience, 17,* 128–130.

Castillo, M., Feinstein, R., Tsang, J., & Fisher, M. (2015). An assessment of basic nutrition knowledge of adolescents with eating disorders and their parents. *International Journal of Adolescent Medicine and Health, 27*(1), 11–17.

Centers for Disease Control and Prevention (CDC). (2015). How much physical activity do children need? Retrieved April 28, 2016 from http://www.cdc.gov/physicalactivity/basics /children/index.htm.

Claes, L., Luyckx, K., Baetens, I., Van de Ven, M., & Whitteman, C. (2015). Bullying and victimization, depressive mood, and non-suicidal self-injury in adolescents: The moderating role of parental support. *Journal of Child and Family Studies, 24*(11), 3363–3371.

Collaborative for Academic, Social, and Emotional Learning (CASEL). (2015). Effective social and emotional learning programs. Retrieved April 29, 2016 from http://secondaryguide .casel.org/casel-secondary-guide.pdf.

Cooper, A., Goodman, A., Page, A., Sherar, L., Esliger, D., van Sluijs, E., . . . & Ekelund, U. (2015). Objectively measured physical activity and sedentary time in youth: The international children's accelerometry database (ICAD). *International Journal of Behavioral*

Nutrition and Physical Activity, 12:113. doi:10.1186/s12966-015-0274-5. Retrieved April 28, 2016 from http://ijbnpa.biomedcentral.com/articles/10.1186/s12966-015-0274-5.

Crowley, S., Cain, S., Burns, A., Acebo, C., & Carskadon, M. (2015). Increased sensitivity of the circadian system to light in early/mid-puberty. *Journal of Clinical Endocrinology and Metabolism, 100*(11), 4067–4073.

de la Haye, K., Robins, G., Mohr, P., & Wilson, C. (2013). Adolescents' intake of junk food: Processes and mechanisms driving consumption similarities among friends. *Journal of Research on Adolescence, 23*(2), 524–536.

de Wit, J., Stok, F., Smolenski, D., de Ridder, D., de Vet, E., Gasper, T., . . . & Luszczynska, A. (2015). Food culture in the home environment: Family meal practices and values can support healthy eating and self-regulation in young people in four European countries. *Applied Psychology: Health and Well-Being, 7*(1), 22–40.

DesRoches, A., & Willoughby, T. (2014). Bidirectional associations between valued activities and adolescent positive adjustment in a longitudinal study: Positive mood as a mediator. *Journal of Youth and Adolescence, 43*(2), 208–220.

Dotterer, A., Lowe, K., & McHale, S. (2013). Academic growth trajectories and family relationships among African American youth. *Journal of Research on Adolescence, 24*(4), 734–747.

Eagly, A. (2013). *Sex differences in social behavior: A social-role interpretation.* New York: Psychology Press.

Eime, R., Casey, M., Harvey, J., Swyer, N., Symons, C., & Payne, W. (2015). Socioecological factors potentially associated with participation in physical activity and sport: A longitudinal study of adolescent girls. *Journal of Science and Medicine in Sport, 18*(6), 684–690.

Ekinci, O., Isik, U., Gunes, S., Yildirim, C., Killi, Y., & Guler, G. (2016). Self-concept in children and adolescents with epilepsy: The role of family functioning, mothers' emotional symptoms and ADHD. *Brain and Development.* Epub ahead of print. doi:10.1016/j .braindev.2016.02.015.

Elgersma, C. (2015). Catfishing apps let kids fake everything from texts to tweets. Retrieved May 3, 2016 from https://www.commonsensemedia.org/blog/catfishing-apps-let-kids-fake -everything-from-texts-to-tweets.

Erikson, E. (1963). *Childhood and society* (2nd Ed). New York: W.W. Norton.

Ferdinand, N., Becker, A., Kray, J., & Gehring, W. (2016). Feedback processing in children and adolescents: Is there a sensitivity for processing rewarding feedback? *Neuropsychologia, 82,* 31–38.

Foland-Ross, L., Gilbert, B., Joormann, J., & Gotlib, I. (2015). Neural markers of familial risk for depression: An investigation of cortical thickness abnormalities in healthy adolescent daughters of mothers with recurrent depression. *Journal of Abnormal Psychology, 124*(3), 476–485.

Frison, E., & Eggermont, S. (2015). The impact of daily stress on adolescents' depressed mood: The role of social support seeking through Facebook. *Computers in Human Behavior, 44,* 315–325.

Fu, J., Liang, J., Zhou, X., Prasad, H., Jin, J., Dong, G., & Rose, S. (2015). Impact of BMI on gonadorelin-stimulated LH peak in premenarcheal girls with idiopathic central precocious puberty. *Obesity, 23*(3), 637–643.

Fuligini, A., & Tsai, K. (2015). Developmental flexibility in the age of globalization: Autonomy and identity development among immigrant adolescents. *Annual Review of Psychology, 66,* 411–431.

Galinsky, E., Aumann, K., & Bond, J. (2012). Times are changing: Gender and generation at work and at home in the USA. In M. A. Shaffer, J. R. Joplin, & Y. S. Hsu (Eds.), *Expanding the boundaries of work–family research: A vision for the future* (pp. 279–296). New York: Macmillan.

Gentina, E., Palan, K., & Fosse-Gomez, M. (2012). The practice of using makeup: A consumption ritual of adolescent girls. *Journal of Consumer Behaviour, 11*(2), 115–123.

Giletta, M., Calhoun, C., Hastings, P., Rudolph, K., Nock, M., & Prinstein, M. (2015). Multi-level risk factors for suicidal ideation among at-risk adolescent females: The role of hypothalamic-pituitary-adrenal axis responses to stress. *Journal of Abnormal Child Psychology, 43*(5), 807–820.

Ginsberg, P., Kariuki, P., & Kimamo, C. (2014). The changing concept of adolescence in Kenya. *Psychological Thought, 7*(1). doi:10.5964/psyct.v7i1.97.

Goldfarb, S., Tarver, W., Locher, J., Preskitt, J., & Sen, B. (2015). A systematic review of the association between family meals and adolescent risk outcomes. *Journal of Adolescence, 44*, 134–149.

Green, C., Dissanayake, C., & Loesch, D. (2015). A review of physical growth in children and adolescents with Autism Spectrum Disorder. *Developmental Review, 36*, 156–178.

Grolnick, W., Raftery-Helmer, J., Flamm, E., Marbell, K., & Cardemil, E. (2015). Parental provision of academic structure and the transition to middle school. *Journal of Research on Adolescence, 25*(4), 668–684.

Guttmacher Institute. (2016). Fact Sheet: American teens' sources of sexual health education. Guttmacher Institute, Washington, DC. Retrieved May 1, 2016 from https://www.guttmacher.org/fact-sheet/facts-american-teens-sources-information-about-sex.

Guttmacher Institute. (2014). Fact Sheet: American teens' sexual and reproductive health. Guttmacher Institute, Washington, DC. Retrieved May 1, 2016 from https://www.guttmacher.org/fact sheet/american-teens-sexual-and-reproductive-health.

Hamlat, E., Stange, J., Abramson, L., & Alloy, L. (2014). Early pubertal timing as a vulnerability to depression symptoms: Differential effects of race and sex. *Journal of Abnormal Child Psychology, 42*(4), 527–538.

Hankin, B., Young, J., Abela, J., Smolen, A., Jenness, J., Gulley, L., . . . & Oppenheimer, C. (2015). Depression from childhood into late adolescence: Influence of gender, development, genetic susceptibility, and peer stress. *Journal of Abnormal Psychology, 124*(4), 803–816.

Hayes, D., Bloake, J., Darensbourg, A., & Castillo, L. (2015). Examining the academic achievement of Latino adolescents: The role of parent and peer. *Journal of Early Adolescence, 35*(2), 141–161.

Herman-Giddens, M., Steffes, J., Harris, D., Slora, E., Hussey, M., Dowshen, S., . . . & Reiter, E. (2012). Secondary sexual characteristics in boys: Data from the pediatric research in office settings network. *Pediatrics, 130*, e1058–1068.

Hill, N., & Wang, M. (2015). From middle school to college: Developing aspirations, promoting engagement and indirect pathways from parenting to post high school enrollment. *Developmental Psychology, 51*(2), 224–235.

Hinnant, J., Erath, S., & El-Sheikh, M. (2015). Harsh parenting, parasympathetic activity, and development of delinquency and substance use. *Journal of Abnormal Psychology, 124*(1), 137–151.

Im, M., Hughes, J., & West, S. (2016). Effect of trajectories of friends' and parents' school involvement on adolescents' engagement and achievement. *Journal of Research on Adolescence*. Advance online publication. doi:10.1111/jora.12247.

Jethwani, M. (2015). "Girls have more of an educational brain": A qualitative exploration of the gender gap in educational achievement among Black Bermudian adolescents. *Journal of Adolescent Research, 30*(3), 335–364.

Juraska, J., & Willing, J. (2016). Pubertal onset as a critical transition for neural development and cognition. *Brain Research*. Published online. doi:10.1016/j.brainres.2016.04.012i.

Kahn, R., Holmes, C., Farley, J., & Kim-Spoon, J. (2015). Delay discounting mediates parent-adolescent relationship quality and risky sexual behavior for low self-control adolescents. *Journal of Youth and Adolescence, 44*(9), 1674–1687.

Kang, H., Chang, K., Chen, C., & Greenberger, E. (2015). Locus of control and peer relations among Caucasian, Hispanic, Asian, and African American adolescents. *Journal of Youth and Adolescence, 44*(1), 184–194.

Kang'ethe, S. (2013). The panacea and perfidy of cultural rites of circumcision in African countries: Examples from Kenya, Botswana, and South Africa. *Eastern Africa Social Science Research Review, 29*(1), 107–123.

Kerpelman, J., McElain, A., Pittman, J., & Adler-Baeder, F. (2015). Engagement in risky sexual behavior. Adolescents' perceptions of self and the parent-child relationship matter. *Youth & Society, 48*(1), 101–125.

Khundrakpam, B., Lewis, J., Zhao, L., Chouinard-Decorte, F., & Evans, A. (2016). Brain connectivity in normally developing children and adolescents. *NeuroImage, 134*(1), 192–203.

Korchmaros, J., Ybarra, M., & Mitchell, K. (2015). Adolescent online romantic relationship initiation: Differences by sexual and gender identification. *Journal of Adolescence, 40*, 54–64.

Kornienko, O., & Santos, C. (2014). The effects of friendship network popularity on depressive symptoms during early adolescence: Moderation by fear of negative evaluation and gender. *Journal of Youth and Adolescence, 43*, 541–553.

Kronholm, E., Puusniekka, R., Jokela, J., Villberg, J., Urrila, A., Paunio, T., . . . & Tynjälä, J. (2015). Trends in self-reported sleep problems, tiredness, and related school performance among Finnish adolescents from 1984 to 2011. *Journal of Sleep Research, 24*(1), 3–10.

Kubiszewski, V., Fonatine, R., Porard, C., & Gimenes, G. (2014). Bullying, sleep/wake patterns and subjective sleep disorders: Findings from a cross-sectional survey. *Chronobiology International, 31*(4), 542–553.

Lawrence, K., Campbell, R., & Skuse, D. (2015). Age, gender, and puberty influence the development of facial emotion recognition. *Frontiers in Psychology*. Published online. doi:10.3389/fpsyg.2015.00761.

Lee, N., Chien, Y., & Hwu, W. (2016). Integrated care for Down syndrome. *Congenital Anomalies, 56*(3), 104–106.

Lenhart, A., Duggan, M., Perrin, A., Stepler, R., Rainie, L., & Parker, K. (2015). Teens, social media & technology overview 2015: Smartphones facilitate shifts in communication landscape for teens. Washington, DC: Pew Research Center.

Lundeen, E., Norris, S., Martorell, R., Suchdev, P., Mehta, N., Rishter, L., & Stein, A. (2016). Early life growth predicts pubertal development in South African adolescents. *Journal of Nutrition, 146*(3), 622–629.

Mackey, S., Chaarani, B., Kan, K., Spechler, P., Orr, C., Banaschewski, T., . . . & Garavan, H. (2016). Brain regions related to impulsivity mediate the effects of early adversity on antisocial behavior. *Biological Psychiatry*. Advance online publication. doi:10.1016/j.biopsych.2015.12.027.

Maki-Botsari, E. (2015). Adolescents' unconditional acceptance by parents and teachers and educational outcomes: A structural model of gender differences. *Journal of Adolescence, 43*, 50–62.

Markstrom, C., & Iborra, A. (2003). Adolescent identity formation and rites of passage: The Navajo Kinaaldá ceremony for girls. *Journal of Research on Adolescence, 13*(4), 399–425.

Marotz, L., & Allen, K. (2016). *Developmental profiles: Pre-birth through adolescence.* (8th Ed). Boston, MA: Cengage Learning.

Martin, A., Way, J., Bobis, J., & Anderson, J. (2015). Exploring the ups and downs of mathematics engagement in the middle years of school. *Journal of Early Adolescence, 35*(2), 199–244.

McClanahan, B., Stockton, M., Klesges, R., Slawson, D., Lanctot, J., & Klesges, L. (2015). Psychosocial correlates of physical activity in African-American girls. *Health Behavior and Policy Review, 2*(2), 100–109(10).

Meier, A., & Musick, K. (2014). Variation in associations between family dinners and adolescent well-being. *Journal of Marriage and Family, 76*(1), 13–23.

Micali, N., Solmi, F., Horton, N., Crosby, R., Eddy, K., Calzo, J., . . . & Field, A. (2015). Adolescent eating disorders predict psychiatric, high-risk behaviors and weigh outcomes in young adulthood. *Journal of the American Academy of Child & Adolescent Psychiatry, 54*(8), 652–659.e.

Miller, B., Spratt, E., Himes, J., Condon, D., Summer, A., Papa, C., & Brady, K. (2015). Growth failure associated with early neglect: Pilot comparison of neglected US children and international adoptees. *Journal of Pediatric Endocrinology and Metabolism, 28*(1-2), 111–115.

Mueller, A., Wesley, J., Abrutyn, S., & Levin, M. (2015). Suicide ideation and bullying among US adolescents: Examining the intersections of sexual orientation, gender, and race/ethnicity. *American Journal of Public Health, 105*(5), 980–985.

Mulvey, K., & Killen, M. (2016). Keeping quiet just wouldn't be right: Children's and adolescents' evaluations of challenges to peer relational aggression and physical aggression. *Journal of Youth and Adolescence*. Epub ahead of print. doi:10.1007/s10964-016-0437-y.

National Institute of Mental Health. (2011). The teen brain: Still under construction. Retrieved on April 28, 2016 from http://www.nimh.nih.gov/health/publications/the-teen-brain-still-under-construction/index.shtml#pub3.

Nelson, E., Jarcho, J., & Guyer, A. (2016). Social re-orientation and brain development: An expanded and updated view. *Developmental Cognitive Neuroscience, 17*, 118–127.

Nesi, J., & Prinstein, M. (2015). Using social media for social comparison and feedback-seeking: Gender and popularity moderate associations with depressive symptoms. *Journal of Abnormal Child Psychology, 43*(8), 1427–1438.

Organek, K., Taylor, D., Petrie, T., Martin, S., Greenleaf, C., Dietch, J., & Ruiz, J. (2015). Adolescent sleep disparities: Sex and racial/ethnic differences. *Sleep Health, 1*(1), 36–39.

Oberle, E., Schonert-Reichl, K., Hertzman, C., & Zumbo, B. (2014). Social–emotional competencies make the grade: Predicting academic success in early adolescence. *Journal of Applied Developmental Psychology, 35*(3), 138–147.

Paksarian, D., Rudolph, K., He, J., & Merikangas, K. (2015). School start time and adolescent sleep patterns: Results from the US National Comorbidity Survey–Adolescent Supplement. *American Journal of Public Health, 195*(7), 1351–1357.

Pervanidou, P., & Chrousos, G. (2012). Metabolic consequences of stress during childhood and adolescence. *Metabolism, 61*(5), 611–619.

Piaget, J. (1952). *The origins of intelligence in children.* New York: International University Press.

Piepmeier, A., Shih, C., Whedon, M., Williams, L., Davis, M., Henning, D., . . . & Etnie, J. (2015). The effect of acute exercise on cognitive performance in children with and without ADHD. *Journal of Sport and Health Science, 4*(1), 97–104.

Pollak, Y., Oz, A., Nevenstal, O., Rabi, O., Kitrossky, L., & Maeir, A. (2016). Do adolescents with attention deficit/hyperactivity disorder show risk seeking? Disentangling probabilistic decision making by equalizing the favorability of alternatives. *Journal of Abnormal Psychology, 125*(3), 387–398.

Qu, Y., & Pomerantz, E. (2015). Divergent school trajectories in early adolescence in the United States and China: An examination of underlying mechanisms. *Journal of Youth and Adolescence, 44*(11), 2095–2109.

Raufelder, D., Hoferichter, F., Ringeisen, T., Regner, N., & Jacke, C. (2015). The perceived role of parental support and pressure in the interplay of test anxiety and school engagement among adolescents: Evidence for gender-specific relations. *Journal of Child and Family Studies, 24*, 3742–3756.

Reisner, S., Vetters, R., Leclarc, M., Zaslow, M., Wolfrum, S., Shumer, D., & Mimiaga, M. (2015). Mental health of transgender youth in care at an adolescent urban community health center: A matched retrospective cohort study. *Journal of Adolescent Health, 56*(3), 274–279.

Reynolds, B., & Juvonen, J. (2011). The role of early maturation, perceived popularity, and rumors in the emergence of internalizing symptoms among adolescent girls. *Journal of Youth and Adolescence, 40*(11), 1407–1422.

Richardson, C., Hitti, A., Mulvey, K., & Killen, M. (2014). Social exclusion: The interplay of group goals and individual characteristics. *Journal of Youth and Adolescence, 43*(8), 1281–1294.

Richardson, G., Goldschmidt, L., Larkby, C., & Day, N. (2015). Effects of prenatal cocaine exposure on adolescent development. *Neurotoxicology and Teratology, 49*, 41–48.

Ritchwood, T., Ford, H., DeCoster, J., Sutton, M., & Lochman, J. (2015). Risky sexual behavior and substance use among adolescents: A meta-analysis. *Children and Youth Services Review, 52*, 74–88.

Rivas-Drake, D., Seaton, E., Markstrom, C., Quintana, S., Syed, M., Lee, R., . . . & Yip, T. (2014). Ethnic and racial identity in adolescence: Implications for psychosocial, academic, and health outcomes. *Child Development, 85*(1), 40–57.

Rogers, L., Scott, M., & Way, N. (2015). Racial and gender identity among black adolescent males: An interdisciplinary perspective. *Child Development, 86*(2), 407–424.

Satterthwaite, T., Vandekar, S., Wolf, D., Ruparel, K., Roalf, D., Jackson, C., . . . & Gur, R. (2014). Sex differences in the effect of puberty on hippocampal morphology. *Journal of the American Academy of Child & Adolescent Psychiatry, 53*(3), 341–350.

Schwartz, J., & Maric, M. (2015). Negative cognitive errors in youth: Specificity to anxious and depressive symptoms and age differences. *Behavioural and Cognitive Psychotherapy, 43*(5), 526–537.

Skeldon, A., Derks, G., & Dijk, D. (2016). Modelling changes in sleep timing and duration across the lifespan: Changes in circadian rhythmicity or sleep homeostasis? *Sleep Medicine Reviews, 28*, 92–103.

Skoog, T., Özdemir, S., & Stattin, H. (2016). Understanding the link between pubertal timing in girls and the development of depressive symptoms: The role of sexual harassment. *Journal of Youth and Adolescence, 45*(2), 316–327.

Siu, A. (2016). Screening for depression in children and adolescents: U.S. Preventive Services Task Force recommendation statement. *Annals of Internal Medicine, 164*(1), 360–366.

Stephanou, K., Davey, C., Kerestes, R., Whittle, S., Pujol, J., Yücel, M., . . . & Harrison, B. (2016). Brain functional correlates of emotion regulation across adolescence and young adulthood. *Human Brain Mapping, 37*(1), 7–19.

Suleiman, A., & Deardorff, J. (2015). Multiple dimensions of peer influence in adolescent romantic and sexual relationships: A descriptive, qualitative perspective. *Archives of Sexual Behavior, 44*(3), 765–775.

Suleiman, A., & Harden, P. (2016). The importance of sexual and romantic development in understanding the developmental neuroscience of adolescence. *Developmental Cognitive Neuroscience, 17*, 145–147.

Tennant, J., Demaray, M., Malecki, C., Terry, M., Clary, M., & Elzinga, N. (2015). Students' ratings of teacher support and academic and social-emotional well-being. *School Psychology Quarterly, 30*(4), 494–512.

Telzer, E., Fuligni, A., Lieberman, M., Miernicki, M., & Galván, A. (2015). The quality of adolescents' peer relationships modulates neural sensitivity to risk taking. *Social, Cognitive, and Affective Neuroscience, 10*(3), 389–398.

Thøgersen-Ntoumani, C., Ng, J., Ntoumanis, N., Chatzisarantis, N., Vlachopoulos, S., Katartzi, E., & Nikitaras, N. (2016). "Mum's the word': Predictors and outcomes of weight concerns in pre-adolescent and early adolescent girls. *Body Image, 16*, 107–112.

Underwood, M., & Faris, R. (2015). #Being thirteen: Social media and the hidden world of young adolescents' peer culture. Retrieved May 3, 2016 from https://www.documentcloud.org/documents/2448422-being-13-report.html.

Vantieghem, W., & Van Houtte, M. (2015). Are girls more resilient to gender-conformity pressure? The associate between gender-conformity pressure and academic self-efficacy. *Sex Roles, 73*(1), 1–15.

Véronneau, M., Dishion, T., Connell, A., & Kavanagh, K. (2016). A randomized, controlled trial of the Family Check-Up model in public secondary schools: Examining links between parent engagement and substance use progressions from early adolescence to adulthood. *Journal of Consulting and Clinical Psychology, 84*(6), 526–543.

Vijayakumar, N., Allen, N., Youssef, G., Dennison, M., Yücel, M., Simmons, J., & Whittle, S. (2016). Brain development during adolescence: A mixed-longitudinal investigation of the cortical thickness, surface area, and volume. *Human Brain Mapping, 37*(6), 2027–2038.

Wallace, K. (2015). Parents: Here's how to stop the worst of social media. CNN. Retrieved May 3, 2016 from http://www.cnn.com/2015/10/04/health/being13-social-media-teens-parents-stress/index.html.

World Health Organization (WHO). (2016). Physical activity and young people. Retrieved April 28. 2016 from http://www.who.int/dietphysicalactivity/factsheet_young_people/en/.

Winer, J., Parent, J., Forehand, R., & Breslend, N. (2016). Interactive effects of psychological stress and early pubertal timing on youth depression and anxiety: Contextual amplification in family and peer environments. *Journal of Child and Family Studies, 25*(5), 1375–1384.

Wing, E., Bélanger, M., & Brunet, J. (2016). Linking parental influences and youth participation in physical activity in- and out-of-school: The mediating role of self-efficacy and enjoyment. *American Journal of Health Behavior, 40*(1), 31–37.

Wolf, S., Aber, L., & Morris, P. (2015). Patterns of time use among low-income urban minority adolescents and association with academic outcomes and problem behavior. *Journal of Youth and Adolescence, 44*(6), 1208–1225.

Wong, S., Sugimoto-Matsuda, J., Chang, J., & Hishinuma, E. (2012). Ethnic differences in risk factors for suicide among American high school students 2009: The vulnerability of multiracial and Pacific Islander adolescents. *Archives of Suicide Research, 16*(2), 159–173.

Wyatt, L., Ung, T., Park, R., Kwon, S., & Trinh-Shevrin, C. (2015). Risk factors of suicide and depression among Asian American, Native Hawaiian, and Pacific Islander youth: A systematic literature review. *Journal of Health Care for the Poor and Underserved, 26*(2), 191–237.

Zhai, L., Liu, J., Zhao, J., Liu, J., Bai, Y., Jai, L., & Yao, X. (2015). Association of obesity with onset of puberty and sex hormones in Chinese girls: A 4-year longitudinal study. PLoS ONE, *10*(8), e0134656. doi:10.1371/journal.pone.0134656.

Parenting Middle and Late Adolescent Children

11

LEARNING OBJECTIVES

After reading the chapter, you will be able to:

11-1 Describe typical growth and developmental changes that occur during middle and late adolescence, and the emotional and/or behavioral conditions that may require intervention.

11-2 Discuss how parents can foster adolescents' cognitive and social-emotional development in preparation for adulthood.

11-3 Briefly describe why parental supervision continues to be important, and how parents can create positive relationships that will support their older adolescent's development.

naeyc Standards Linked to Chapter Content

1a, 1b, and 1c: Promoting child development and learning

2a, 2b, and 2c: Building family and community relationships

4a and 4b: Using developmentally effective approaches to connect with children and families

15 TO 19 YEARS

Pressmaster/Shutterstock.com

Children are about to embark upon the last years of the adolescent voyage, and to refine the many positive qualities that they have been developing in the process. They begin to devote more attention to friends than to their parents, but this trend will reverse itself within a few years. As adolescents struggle to gain acceptance into new peer groups, their choices may sometimes

continued on following page

cause parental concern, but their decision-making skills will gradually improve as they mature and gain experience. ∎

11-1 Typical Growth and Development Overview

Children enjoy a period of relative stability and exhibit fewer dramatic developmental changes in the years before they exit late adolescence and enter early adulthood. Children aged 15 and 16 years are still likely to experience occasional periods when they believe that they deserve greater respect, independence, and lessening of parental limits and control. They can be moody, introspective and rebellious at times when their efforts are thwarted. Navigating the social scene, spending more time with friends, and gaining peer acceptance consume a considerable amount of their time and emotional energy. Friends are of utmost importance because they serve as a trusted information source and can provide answers to tough questions that parents "just don't get." Parents must be able to look past these occasional transgressions, and appreciate the fact that 15- and 16-year-olds are developing and testing skills that they will need as adults.

When children reach the ages of 17 and 18 years, they attain a sense of calm and purpose. They are less dependent upon friends to meet their social and emotional needs, and develop a renewed respect for their parents in the process. They begin to think rationally, act more responsibly, and make plans for the future. They regain and build self-confidence, express interest in many worldly topics, and are able to carry on intellectual conversations. However, 17- and 18-year-olds still consider themselves invincible and continue to experiment with risky behaviors—often just for the thrill that seems to occur when they try something novel and outside of mainstream behavioral norms.

11-1a Growth

Growth changes are relatively uneventful for girls. Most will have reached their adult height by the middle of this period. Boys, however, will continue to experience growth spurts which usually stop around the end of late adolescence. They develop wider shoulders and their arms and legs grow longer than girls'. Boys add considerable muscle mass which gives them an adult-like appearance; girls who are athletic also add muscle mass. Bodily changes associated with puberty become less noticeable as hormone levels stabilize. Weight fluctuations are influenced by a combination of diet, activity, and genetics. Most adolescents enjoy relatively good health and experience fewer illnesses, although they may continue to tire easily with physical exertion.

11-1b Developmental Tasks

Adolescents have several remaining developmental tasks to accomplish before they are ready to transition to adulthood (see Figure 11-1). However, there is considerable personal and cultural variability in the timing, expression, and value assigned to these developmental behaviors. For example, adolescents in some cultures are often discouraged to strive for autonomy until much later than is typical in many Western countries. This delay is particularly notable among collectivist cultures (e.g., Asian, Latino, Native American, African American), and especially with respect to girls (Lui, 2015). Boys are customarily expected to be assertive, independent, and to exhibit a leadership role while girls are encouraged to maintain strong emotional connections to their family.

Researchers have also noted that intergenerational conflict tends to occur more often when adolescents of immigrant parents feel trapped between two contrasting cultural expectations (Jensen & Dost-Gözkan, 2015). For example, Indian adolescents

Figure 11-1 Developmental Tasks during Middle to Late Adolescence

- Forming a clear sense of personal and sexual identity
- Achieving stable and meaningful relationships with peers of both sexes
- Identifying future educational and career goals and plans
- Establishing a gradual emotional and economic independence from family
- Achieving improved self-regulation and impulse control

living in the United States may not be allowed to date or engage in mixed-sex relationships because parents traditionally still arrange their children's marriages. Roblyer et al. (2015) observed similar discrepancies among Latino adolescents living in the United States whose immigrant parents disapproved of their Western clothing choices, sexual behavioral displays, and materialistic desires as non conforming to cultural standards.

Fifteen- and sixteen-year-olds lose some of the self-confidence that they had developed during early adolescence. Girls may fret about their appearance, social acceptance, and sexual attractiveness and spend considerable time selecting "just the right outfit," fixing their hair, applying makeup, and worrying about blemishes. Boys also have concerns about their body image, appearance, and muscle and genital development (Alexander, Storm, & Cooper, 2015; Sutter, Nishina, & Adam, 2015). Friends often take precedence over family and tend to serve as confidants in whom adolescents can relate their innermost concerns and fears.

Photo 11-1 Anxiety and depression rates increase during middle adolescence.
Fresnel/Shutterstock.com

Seventeen- and eighteen-year-olds regain their self-esteem, are more self-assured, and begin to focus their attention on planning for the future. Their need for peer acceptance diminishes, and is often replaced by individual friendships and romantic relationships. Older adolescents begin to separate themselves emotionally from their parents, but still seek out, listen to, and respect their advice. They are also in the final stages of formulating their own personal belief system (e.g., morals, values) by integrating parental teachings with their social experiences.

11-1c Early Identification and Intervention

The primary focus of early intervention efforts during this stage is to identify individuals who are experiencing significant behavioral and emotional problems. It is not uncommon for adolescents to experience brief periods of sadness, lack of motivation, or low self-esteem from time-to-time. However, treatment interventions may be needed when these feelings are prolonged or they interfere with daily life-functioning.

Depression rates tend to escalate during the middle-to-late adolescent years. An estimated 2.8 million (11.4 percent) U.S. teens, particularly girls, between the ages of 12 and 17 years experience significant depression (see Figure 11-2) (National Institute of Mental Health, 2014). Major or clinical depression is characterized by feelings of extreme sadness, distress, or hopelessness that disrupt the adolescent's daily functioning (e.g., sleeping, eating, concentration, self-esteem, interest, social interaction) and last longer than two weeks (see Suggestions for Parents 11-1) (American Psychiatric Association, 2013). Various causes have been identified, including hormonal imbalance, brain chemicals, genetics, trauma (e.g., death, illness, environmental disaster, maltreatment, exposure to family violence, homelessness, substance use, peer victimization), and learned patterns of negative thinking (Kerig et al., 2016; Edlund et al., 2015; Hankin et al., 2015; Schwartz et al., 2015). Early identification and treatment are essential to minimize the negative effects on an adolescent's daily life.

Figure 11-2 Prevalence of Major Depressive Episode
among U.S. Adolescents (2014)

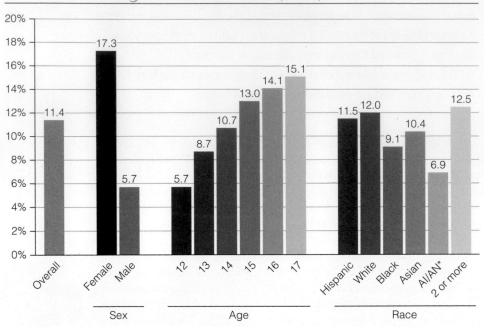

*AI/AN = American Indian/Alaska Native

Source: National Institute of Mental Health (2014).

Suggestions for Parents 11-1

Signs of Major Depression

Professional treatment should be sought if an adolescent exhibits signs of significant depression for longer than two weeks.

- social withdrawal
- irritability and uncharacteristic anger
- tearfulness, sadness, feeling hopeless
- overreaction to criticism
- loss of interest in normal activities
- increased physical complaints (e.g., body aches, headaches, stomach pain)
- increase or decrease in hours of sleep or food eaten
- difficulty making decisions
- engagement in risky behaviors (e.g., skipping school, stealing, drinking or using drugs)
- ignoring homework; academic performance and grades decline

≫ Professional Resource Download

---

oppositional defiant disorder (ODD) a behavioral disorder characterized by a pattern of persistent defiance, negativity, disrespect, and hostility.

conduct disorder (CD) a cluster of persistent antisocial behaviors characterized by difficulty in following rules, showing aggression toward others, destroying property, and engaging in deceitfulness.

Early recognition of other serious behavioral and emotional conditions, including **oppositional defiant disorder (ODD)** and **conduct disorder (CD),** is also crucial for arranging treatment and protecting the adolescent and others from serious harm (see Figure 11-3). Oppositional defiant disorder affects approximately 3.5 percent of children, especially boys, and may initially appear during the preschool and early school-age years. It often

Figure 11-3 Signs of Oppositional Defiant and Conduct Disorders

Oppositional defiant disorder

- argues and blames others for own mistakes
- defies rules and requests
- is often irritable and easily upset
- loses temper and lashes out in anger
- has few friends or friends of "the wrong kind"
- is repeatedly in trouble at school

Conduct disorder

- initiates fights; may use an object (e.g., stick, stone, gun, knife) to cause physical harm to others
- bullies or intimidates others
- forces another person to engage in sexual activity
- sets fire to structures; breaks windows; forces entry into a building or someone's house
- harms animals
- lies, steals, or shoplifts to obtain what is wanted
- runs away from home; is truant from school
- defies parental rules

precedes the development of a conduct disorder (SAMHSA, 2015b). Conduct disorder occurs in approximately 8.5 percent of youth, particularly boys; the incidence increases with age (SAMHSA, 2015b). Both conditions are thought to be due to a combination of genetics and environmental factors, such as harsh parenting, growing up in a dysfunctional family, and association with delinquent peers. Adolescents who have ADHD, depression, or a learning disability are at increased risk for developing a conduct disorder. Researchers have also identified a strong correlation between child sexual abuse and the subsequent development of a conduct disorder (Maniglio, 2015). Noordermeer, Luman, & Oosterlaan (2016) identified brain abnormalities (in the amygdala) that are thought to be directly associated with conduct and oppositional defiant disorders.

Adolescents who have conduct problems typically have a poor relationship with their parents (Simons et al., 2016; Cummings, Koss, & Davi, 2015). They are also likely to engage in antisocial behaviors that pose a risk to themselves and to others (Frick, 2016). A combination of medication and long-term family and behavioral therapy is required to help the adolescent learn behaviors that are more socially acceptable.

11-2 Supporting the Middle- and Late Adolescent's Development

Many new experiences in and outside of school await adolescents during this stage. Their ability to think abstractly, logically, and scientifically enables them to tackle academic demands that are more complex and challenging. Their efforts to establish friendships and gain peer acceptance consume considerable attention outside of the classroom. They mistakenly believe that everyone is watching and evaluating them and, as a result, they lose some of the self-confidence and self-esteem they had developed earlier. Some adolescents may become anxious, lonely, or depressed during this phase and engage in risky behaviors (e.g., alcohol, drugs, unprotected sex). However, most teens will begin to regain their self-confidence by the time they reach their 16th

Photo 11-2 Adolescents are capable of learning complex material and testing hypotheses. racorn/Shutterstock.com

higher-order thinking complex learning that requires the application of multiple skills to solve problems, draw conclusions, or make inferences.

and 17th birthdays. Even though adolescents may outwardly reject parental caring and concern at this stage, they need their parent's guidance, support, and protection now more than ever.

11-2a Promoting Cognitive Development

As children progress through adolescence, the brain continues to develop, which promotes gradual improvements in planning, organization, impulse control (for behavior and emotions), and ability to delay gratification. Neural connections associated with **higher-order thinking** processes are refined and show stronger connectivity (Vendetti et al., 2015). Higher-order thinking enables adolescents to learn more complex information that goes beyond simple memorization. They are better able to use multiple skills to solve problems, draw conclusions, and make inferences; attend to more than one element or dimension at a time; apply information in new ways; connect to other knowledge; and, use mental representations. Adolescents also learn to inhibit responses (i.e., not respond until they have used higher-order thinking), so that they can apply more adaptive behaviors required for future learning and life success (Greiff et al., 2016).

Adolescents show improvements in deductive reasoning, complex problem solving, and analogical reasoning. In deductive reasoning, adolescents are able to test hypotheses and make inferences by considering hypothetical alternatives based upon a general principle or premise. Complex problem solving (CPS) involves the analysis, synthesis, evaluation, information generation, creation of mental representations, reactions to changes and feedback, and application of solutions (Greiff et al., 2016). Analogical reasoning involves attention to relevant information, relationship extraction within and across items, connection with other knowledge to figure out the common principles underlying the relationship, and inferential constructions (Vendetti et al., 2015). Higher-order skills are related to earlier working memory and fluid reasoning performance (Greiff et al., 2016). However, adolescents who receive specific instruction in planning, monitoring, and personal learning evaluation (metacognitive skills) show increased motivation (e.g., beliefs, goals, and dispositions) and better task performance (Zepeda et al., 2015). Parents can reinforce higher-order thinking by encouraging adolescents to apply it in everyday situations (Suggestions for Parents 11-2).

Parental involvement and interest in adolescents' education and the communication of high expectations continue to have positive outcomes for students' achievement and self-control (Núñez et al., 2015; Shute et al., 2011). Parents can help adolescents

Suggestions for Parents 11-2

Encouraging Higher-Order Thinking

- Encourage adolescents to ask questions, and respond to their questions in a way that requires them to consider and evaluate alternative explanations or solutions.
- Help adolescents connect learned information to previous knowledge or experiences.
- Involve adolescents in identifying problems, considering the pros and cons of various solutions, and developing rationales for chosen solutions.
- Discuss thoughts and ideas related to current events and policies. Ask 'why' questions.
- Provide rationales for limits, rules, and decisions.
- Help adolescents to make connections and point out similarities and differences among concepts.
- Encourage reflection on learning (e.g., "How did you come to that conclusion?").
- Encourage planning and thinking about the future and hypothetical situations.
- Provide opportunities for creativity (e.g., designing a garden, decorating bedroom).

during the transitional process following high school by encouraging them to explore their interests, values, and the opportunities available for postsecondary education and/or career training. Adolescents who examine and understand the values that are personally important tend to experience a more positive well-being during the post–high school years (Williams, Ciarrochi, & Heaven, 2014). This transitional period is also accompanied by many parental tasks and potential stressors, such as college visits, arranging for financial assistance to continue an education, networking to identify work opportunities, supporting adolescents in assuming responsibility for their own affairs, and preparing for adolescents to move out of the home. For some families, the transition is a smooth process, but others may encounter barriers that interfere with adolescents' and parents' values and future plans. For example, despite many parents' belief in the importance of postsecondary education, they often have difficulty providing adequate financial assistance; this is particularly true for middle class families who may not qualify for governmental support (Napolitano, Pacholok, & Furstenberg, 2014).

For students who are receiving special education services, the transition process requires more direct planning. The Individuals with Disabilities Education Improvement Act (IDEA) requires schools to initiate a transitional plan when students turn 16 to help them understand options that are available after high school, and to develop specific skills to achieve future success. Parent and adolescent involvement in the process is invaluable for identifying goals and the steps needed to accomplish them. For example, the transition team might conclude that a student needs to learn how to manage money, how to advocate for his own needs, and how to use public transportation in order to live independently.

Students are no longer eligible to receive special education services under IDEA after graduating from high school. However, they can provide documentation of a disability to their college, vocational training program, or workplace in order to receive special accommodations and support through a 504 Plan or through the Americans with Disabilities Act (U.S. Department of Education and Office for Civil Rights, 2011).

Unfortunately, parents often feel that adolescents with special needs do not receive the academic and social support services they need upon entering postsecondary schooling. Parents may try to provide substantial support and facilitate the transitional process in the absence of guidance from other sources (Suggestions for Parents 11-3) (Cai & Richdale, 2016).

Suggestions for Parents 11-3

Keys to Successful Transition to Postsecondary Education

Parents, educators, and other professionals can encourage adolescents to:

- Have a positive outlook.
- Advocate for their needs.
- Understand their disabilities.
- Accept responsibility for their own success.
- Take an appropriate preparatory curriculum.
- Learn time management skills.
- Acquire computer skills.
- Research postsecondary education or vocational training program requirements and accommodations to identify the 'best fit'.
- Get involved in campus and/or community activities.

Source: U.S. Department of Education and Office for Civil Rights (2011).

Photo 11-3 Transition plans must be initiated when students who have an Individualized Education Program (IEP) turn 16 years of age. IMAGE LAGOON/Shutterstock.com

Parents of adolescents who have more significant developmental disabilities often face unique stressors which include long-term decisions about caregiving, the most appropriate living arrangements, overcoming disappointments related to the disability, and negotiating new health provider systems (Glidden & Natcher, 2009). However, parents who focus on personal growth, create positive meaning, and use an analytical approach to solve problems show improved adjustment and better well-being compared to those who distance themselves or avoid problems (Glidden & Natcher, 2009).

11-2b Supporting Social-Emotional Development

As children progress through adolescence, they continue to explore and to develop a sense of self-identity and how they fit into society. It can be a perplexing time—adolescents are trying to establish themselves as separate from their families, yet they have a desire to be liked and to be accepted by their peer groups. They may question parental beliefs, explore different ideas about sexuality and religion, and speak out on issues about which they are passionate. At the same time, they may change the way they dress or act to become part of groups that they determine to be popular. Throughout the adolescent period, parents can support their children in safe exploration and facilitate their healthy social-emotional adjustment into adulthood.

Self-Identity. As adolescents seek to define themselves, most go through a period of exploration that is followed by commitment. Marcia (1966) outlined four identity formation stages, noting that they are not linear, but rather change in response to a crisis or event (e.g., change in education/work, exposure to another religion):

- *Identity diffusion*: has no identity commitment; a crisis leads to a change in status; adolescents often sample from several different outlooks or may not have any concerns about their personal identity.
- *Identity foreclosure*: commitment to aspects of identity without exploring options; adolescents may follow parental goals and values, feel threatened by negative feedback, endorse authoritarian values, and have unrealistic goals.
- *Identity moratorium*: active exploration with low commitment; parental wishes are important, but adolescents try to compromise those with societal demands and personal capabilities; they show variability in responding to different situations.
- *Identity achievement*: commitment to aspects of identity following exploration; adolescents make decisions based on personal terms, which may be a variation of parental wishes; they show greater perseverance, develop realistic goals, and exhibit less vulnerability to negative feedback.

Exploration allows adolescents to learn more about gender, race, values, religion, sexual orientation, disability status, professional opportunities, educational alternatives, and political views, and to determine what meaning they have to their sense of self. When adolescents explore and then reach identity achievement as opposed to identity foreclosure, they show higher self-esteem, greater life satisfaction, and fewer symptoms of depression and anxiety (Sumner, 2016). This exploration period is perhaps the most challenging for parents because adolescents are likely to question parental beliefs and values. However, when parents understand that such exploration is normal and beneficial, they may find the adolescent's behavior less stressful.

Although many youth struggle to determine who they are, identity development is often more complex for those with unique situations (e.g., different beliefs, ethnic origin, sexual orientation, family structure). Some adolescents must negotiate their ethnic-racial identity, which can be particularly difficult given the strong influence of peer feedback and common racial/ethnic teasing that occurs among teens. Many adolescents view racial/ethnic teasing as harmless. However ethnic minority adolescents who experience teasing, find the process of negotiating their identity to be complex and are more prone to developing mental health problems (Douglass et al., 2016). Race and ethnicity exert a strong influence on the development of self-identity in youth of minority cultures (ACT for Youth Center of Excellence, 2016). These adolescents are more likely to experience feelings of dissonance when their cultural beliefs and practices are marginalized (Atkinson, Morten, & Sue, 1993).

Atkinson, Morten, and Sue (1979) and Sue and Sue (2008) proposed a model of minority identity development:

- *Conformity*: identifies with the white majority culture, shows little interest in learning about own ethnic heritage and perceives own racial/cultural group negatively which is consistent with the way it is viewed by the majority culture

- *Dissonance*: questions the majority culture, shows interest in own ethnic group, shows awareness that racism exists and questions stereotypes

- *Resistance and immersion*: withdraws from the majority culture (viewed as an oppressor), explores own heritage as a means to define their identity, shows strong sense of commitment to their minority group

- *Introspection*: attempts to incorporate aspects of their ethnic identity with that of the majority culture without compromising aspects of ethnic identity

- *Integrative awareness*: develops a positive self-image and sense of self-worth and confidence; views self as more autonomous, has a sense of pride in their ethnic group, is more open to constructive elements of the dominant culture, and appreciates aspects of own and dominant culture

Many adolescents are able to embrace cultural differences through a process of identification, connection, and involvement in their traditional culture (Kulis et al., 2016). Adolescents from minority groups often have greater ability to shift their perspectives, identify with the views of the dominant culture and their own group, and understand characteristics associated with race (Gaither et al., 2014). Interventions and support for marginalized populations should take a strengths-based approach in order to encourage healthy development. The approach should include: development of sound coping skills, means of self-expression, self-efficacy, and a sense of belonging; consistency with cultural values and beliefs; and, delivery within the community (Antonio & Chung-Do, 2015).

Parents can help adolescents explore their identity by discussing their values, beliefs, and goals; providing opportunities for youth to see role models who have interests associated with their own future goals; talking about their own explorations and reasons for committing to aspects of identity; and, providing reasonable rules and limits that protect adolescents' safety during exploration (Sumner, 2016). In later adolescence, most youth gain self-confidence as they begin to see themselves as part of a larger world, and to refine their values and identity based on increasingly realistic goals and cultural norms (Marotz & Allen, 2016).

Friends and Relationships. Although adolescents are strongly influenced by peers, parents continue to serve an important role: they affect youth's friend selection, and their support buffers the potential negative influences of delinquent peers (Wang et al., 2016). Strong, positive friendships provide adolescents with a source of social support for discussions about topics (e.g., depressed mood, sex, alcohol) that can be difficult to have with parents (Olsson et al., 2016). When a peer describes a potential problem, girls are more likely to provide support and ask questions while boys tend to use humor during such discussions (Rose et al., 2016). Talking about problems leads to an increase in emotional closeness with peers. Adolescents who have established quality friendships tend to use more constructive coping skills and show greater resilience (Graber, Turner, &

Photo 11-4 Although friends are important, older adolescents also enjoy spending time by themselves.
© Lynn Marotz

Madill, 2016). Lack of social connections and limited friendship competence, on the other hand, are related to potential future problems with depression and social withdrawal (Chango et al., 2015).

Popularity and being liked or socially preferred are important concerns for adolescents. Both are associated with prosocial skills and the presence of mutual friendships. Socially-preferred youth are more likely to show positive academic achievement; those who are popular are more likely to demonstrate aggressive behaviors and to use alcohol and nicotine (French, Niu, & Purwono, 2016). Popular adolescents may use their prosocial skills in combination with relational aggression to maintain their status. These findings are consistent across some cultures (e.g., Western, Indonesian), but research in other cultures (e.g., Chinese) shows inconsistent results, likely due to the way that popularity is defined (French, Niu, & Purwono, 2016). Therefore, interventions to address the problematic behaviors of popular adolescents have the potential to improve prosocial and appropriate behavior of peers, but must be done with sensitivity to cultural differences.

Adolescents may engage in behaviors that do not always follow their beliefs or morals due to strong desires to gain popularity or peer acceptance. For example, adolescents may change their drinking and smoking behavior to match their peers. However, parental caring, support, and monitoring have been shown to help decrease negative behaviors (Wang et al., 2016). It is important for parents to remember that, given adolescent brain development (e.g., impulsivity, difficulty planning and considering consequences, emotional urgency), lapses in judgment are likely and may not be

Trending Now Adolescents and Cosmetic Surgery

Concerns about body image and peer acceptance punctuate much of the adolescent's thought processes. "Does this dress make me look fat?" "Everybody is going to laugh at this pimple on my chin!" "My nose is too big." Although adults tend to find this behavior trivial and inconsequential, it represents an important developmental step in the adolescent's adjustment to bodily changes associated with puberty. Most adolescents will gradually accept and become comfortable with their body image. However, a small percent will continue to fixate on specific parts that cause them to feel uncomfortable, embarrassed, or to have low self-esteem. Their body dissatisfaction only increases when they make comparisons with digitally-enhanced photos in magazines or posted online. As a result, some adolescents will go so far as to convince their parents that they need cosmetic surgery to correct perceived imperfections.

Cosmetic surgery was originally developed to correct congenital deformities and injuries, but gained popularity when surgeons realized that adults would pay for procedures just to improve their appearance. Soon adolescents were exploring and demanding similar options. Each year, plastic surgeons report an increase in the number of adolescents under age 18 years who request surgical and nonsurgical (e.g., laser, chemical peels, soft tissue fillers) cosmetic procedures (see Figure 11-4) (American Society of Plastic Surgeons, 2016). Adolescents represent only a small percentage of the patients who are treated annually, but the upward trend certainly raises questions about why teens of all races and ethnicities are so dissatisfied with their body and

body image that they feel pressured to have their lips plumped, nose re-contoured, or thighs reduced in size.

Researchers have noted that girls are more likely than boys to undergo cosmetic surgery, and they attribute this to an increased sensitivity to socially accepted standards of attractiveness (Dakanalis et al., 2015; Furnham & Levitas, 2012). Many are driven to achieve an idealized appearance such as that of their favorite movie stars or celebrities who appear in the media or online. For example, Lunde and Gyberg (2016) noted that women are more likely than men to respond to parental pressures to seek cosmetic surgery in order to achieve certain appearance-related physical forms. However, increased gender equality has begun to make it more socially acceptable for males to also express interest in their appearance which, in turn, has led to an increase in cosmetic procedures among young boys (Lunde, 2013).

Some plastic surgeons are refusing to perform procedures on adolescents that are requested strictly for cosmetic improvement. Others encourage adolescents to wait until they are considerably older and their bodies have reached a more mature state. However, they are unlikely to hesitate if an adolescent has a specific deformity that is affecting their self-esteem and quality of life. The American Society of Plastic Surgeons (ASPS) encourages parents to consider their adolescent's emotional and physical maturity before they decide if cosmetic surgery is appropriate. They also advise parents to consider how actively and for how long the adolescent has requested a procedure. This recommendation helps to assess if the request is impulsive, or a

(continued)

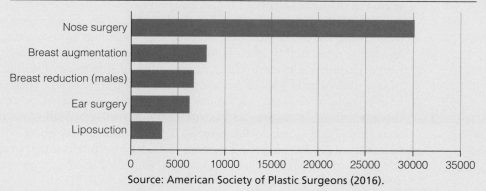

Figure 11-4 Top Five Cosmetic Surgical Procedures in Adolescents 18 and Under

Source: American Society of Plastic Surgeons (2016).

carefully considered need. Parents should also determine if the adolescent understands the risks involved, is realistic about the benefits, and if they are emotionally mature enough to tolerate the discomfort and temporary disfigurement that accompanies a particular procedure (ASPS, 2016). Should parents support and facilitate cosmetic surgery procedures for adolescents? In what other ways can parents help adolescents develop a positive and realistic body image? What other factors beside acceptance of one's body image contribute to the formation of a healthy self-esteem?

an indication of negative peer influence. As adolescents continue to develop and learn from their experiences, they become less reliant upon peer approval, are better able to accept responsibility for their actions, and respond to adult feedback and advice with greater ease (Marotz & Allen, 2016).

Sexuality. Adolescents establish friendships with peers of both genders. Romantic relationships also become more commonplace during adolescence, which help youth refine their self-identity, determine their sexual orientation, learn about characteristics they want in a partner, and establish values about intimacy—all of which can set the stage for successful adult relationships. Toward the end of adolescence, youth begin to develop intimate relationships based upon shared interests and not simply on a romantic attraction or desire (Marotz & Allen, 2016). Researchers are beginning to reframe their studies from a focus on sexual risk during adolescence to issues of sexual well-being and the role of sexuality in healthy development (Fortenberry, 2016). Sexual well-being includes concepts such as sexual self-esteem (perceptions of worth and attractiveness), sexual self-efficacy (perceived control of sexual situations, such as the right to consent or refuse), arousal, desire, and pleasure, as well as the absence of pain, anxiety, and negative affect (Fortenberry, 2016). Adolescent relationships and sexual activity can facilitate healthy development if the experiences are positive.

One of the first steps toward achieving sexual well-being involves understanding one's own sexual identity and orientation. Adolescents begin to define their sexual identity, including their understanding and feelings about sexual attractions, desires, behaviors, values, and relationships. However, identity may change over time given differences in awareness, understanding, and experience (Morgan, 2013). Morgan (2013) noted that heterosexual sexual identity development is relatively unmarked or happens without much consideration, but lesbian, gay, bisexual, and transgender (LGBT) identity development is often more evident because it diverges from the norm. Sexual minority adolescents usually go through three progressive steps in "coming out": (1) awareness of being different, (2) recognition and exploration of same-sex and other-sex attraction

Photo 11-5 Adolescents begin to form a sexual identity and feelings about their self-worth and attractiveness to others.
Stock Rocket/Shutterstock.com

and behavior, and (3) coming out to self and others, including acceptance and integration of their identity. In the past, it was believed that solidification of LGBT identity did not occur until early adulthood, but researchers have noted that more adolescents are solidifying their sexual identity due to an increase in normalization of same-sex sexuality (Morgan, 2013).

Many LGBT youth face unique challenges as a result of being part of a marginalized group, including increased violence (e.g., bullying, harassment, physical assault), and being ostracized by their families or community, which may result in limited social support and homelessness (CDC, 2014; Office of Adolescent Health, 2016; Substance Abuse and Mental Health Services Administration, 2015a). These challenges place LGBT youth at elevated risk for emotional problems: some 31 percent report suicidal thoughts; those identifying as bisexual show particularly high levels of emotional distress (Eisenberg, Gower, & McMorris, 2016; Whitaker, Shapiro, & Shields, 2016). One national survey found that 61 percent of LGBT youth felt unsafe or uncomfortable in school because of their sexual orientation, which led some to experience excessive absenteeism and resulting academic difficulties (CDC, 2014).

Parents who discover that their child is LGBT may have a variety of reactions, from feelings of guilt, devastation, and worry to feelings of acceptance. Questions may arise: "Did I cause this?" "Should we have done something differently?" and "This does not fit with my beliefs, so how is it possible?" It is important for parents to understand that individuals do not choose to be LGBT; reflection and discussion provide time for parents to gradually accept their child unconditionally (American Academy of Pediatrics, 2015). Parental rejection or attempts to change the youth's gender identity are associated with negative well-being (CDC, 2014). A report by the Substance Abuse and Mental Health Services Administration (SAMHSA) (2015a) specified three key findings after reviewing the literature related to LGBT youth and treatment:

1. Same-gender sexual orientation (including identity, behavior, and attraction) and variations in gender identity and gender expression are a part of the normal spectrum of human diversity, and do not constitute a mental health disorder.

2. There is limited research on conversion therapy efforts among children and adolescents; however, none of the existing research supports the premise that mental or behavioral health interventions can alter gender identity or sexual orientation.

3. Interventions aimed at a fixed outcome, such as gender conformity or heterosexual orientation, including those aimed at changing gender identity, gender expression, and sexual orientation are coercive, can be harmful, and should not be part of behavioral health treatment.

Parents are integral to the healthy development of LGBT teens. When parents create a positive family environment and provide high levels of support with low conflict, teens are more likely to feel valued and less likely to experience depression, attempt suicide, use drugs and alcohol, or engage in sexual risk behaviors (CDC, 2014). Even if parents struggle to accept their child's sexual orientation due to personal beliefs and values, they can support the adolescent's well-being by talking and trying to understand the child's experiences, requiring family members to be respectful, and standing up for their child when others mistreat or discriminate against the child (SAMHSA, 2015a).

Adolescents who are LGBT exhibit lower levels of suicidal ideation when they are connected to school (Whitaker, Shapiro, & Shields, 2016). A positive and accepting school environment allows them to behave in a manner consistent with their gender identity. The U.S. Departments of Justice and Education (2016) released a letter stating that transgender students should be permitted to use the public facilities (e.g., restrooms and locker rooms) that match their gender identity (i.e., one's internal sense of gender, which may be different from their biological gender). Schools may be at-risk for litigation due to discriminatory practices (i.e., violating Title IX) if the recommendations are not followed. Youth should not be discriminated against based upon their sexual orientation; adolescents benefit when their orientation is respected, even if others disagree.

Dating Violence and Safe Sex. The increase in romantic relationships during adolescence gives rise to parental concerns about pregnancy and dating violence. Teen pregnancy rates have been declining in recent years, but remain problematic. In some cases, pregnancy could have been prevented if youth were better informed. The majority of adolescents' report the receipt of formal instruction about sexually transmitted diseases and how to say no to sex, but only 55 percent of males and 60 percent of females report that they received information about birth control; even fewer received information about where to get or how to use birth control measures (Guttmacher Institute, 2016). The average age of first intercourse is 17 years, which suggests that parents should start conversations about dating, relationships, and sex when children are young (Guttmacher Institute, 2016). Adolescents who perceive their parents as competent and effective in communicating with them are less likely to engage in sexual risk-taking behaviors (Holman & Kellas, 2015). There are several steps that parents can take to reduce the potential for teen pregnancy (Suggestions for Parents 11-4).

Unfortunately, dating violence is a significant concern. If not addressed, it can lead to similar patterns in adulthood. Dating violence is defined as violence (e.g., physical, emotional, sexual, or stalking) that occurs between two people in a close relationship. More recently, violence activity has entered into social media. Drouin et al. (2015) found that 20 percent of young adults who engaged in sexting felt pressured or forced

Photo 11-6 Pressured dating or sexual coercion should never be tolerated.
marylooo/Shutterstock.com

Suggestions for Parents 11-4

Talking to Adolescents about Relationships and Pregnancy Prevention

- Start conversations early about dating expectations, contraception and condoms, avoiding pregnancy and sexually transmitted diseases, and having healthy relationships.

- Be clear and specific about family values and rules for dating and sexual behavior. Provide rationales for your values and rules.

- Recognize that you have the power to affect change. Adolescents may appear as if they are not listening, but they often report that parents have a stronger influence on their decisions regarding sex than do friends.

- Monitor, supervise, and follow through with rules, curfews, and expectations. Get to know your child's friends and be aware of what they are watching in the media.

- Discourage early dating because it is related to earlier sexual activity and risky behaviors.

- Take your child to regular visits with a medical provider and allow them to have private time to ask any questions they might have.

- Talk about the future and encourage your child's aspirations and achievements because youth who feel they have a bright future are less likely to engage in risky behaviors.

Source: Office of Adolescent Health (2016).

⌄⌄ Professional Resource Download

to participate. Such coercion is also likely to lead to physical sexual coercion, intimate partner violence, greater anxiety symptoms, depression, and trauma. About 21 percent of females and 10 percent of males are victims of dating violence during high school (CDC, 2016). Another study found that 37 percent of adolescents reported relationship abuse in the last year and 69 percent during their lifetime; rates increased with age (Taylor & Mumford, 2016). Psychological abuse was the most commonly reported form of abuse (Taylor & Mumford, 2016). Oftentimes, the violence starts out with behaviors that may seem to be normal teasing, but then escalates into significant violence. The perpetrator may be male or female; perpetrators may also be victims and vice versa. Recent studies have indicated higher perpetration rates among females (Taylor & Mumford, 2016).

The Centers for Disease Control and Prevention (CDC, 2016) have identified several risk factors that increase the likelihood of an individual harming a dating partner:

- belief that dating violence is acceptable
- depression, anxiety, and other trauma symptoms
- aggression toward peers and other antisocial behavior
- substance use
- early sexual activity and having multiple sexual partners
- having a friend involved in dating violence
- conflict with partner
- witnessing or experiencing violence in the home

Dating violence is associated with negative outcomes for victims and perpetrators. Victims may be injured (sometimes fatally) and are at risk for depression, suicide, anxiety, poor academic performance, and delinquent behaviors. Perpetrators are more likely to have lower educational aspirations, more family conflict, greater likelihood of marijuana use, and an increased risk for suicide (Foshee et al., 2016). Parents are key players in decreasing the risk of dating violence. They can facilitate healthy teen relationships by maintaining quality parent-child relationships, having open communications about dating and sex, providing monitoring that indicates trust and communication, setting dating rules, and modeling healthy relationships and appropriate ways of managing conflict in relationships (Mumford, Lui, & Taylor, 2016). Parenting styles that are characterized by disengagement/harshness and strictness/harshness increase the likelihood of dating violence (Mumford, Lui, & Taylor, 2016). Interventions that seek to prevent or eliminate dating violence must consider not only the adolescent but also parents so that they can learn more effective ways to manage youth's behavior, solve problems, and handle their own anger or relationship problems.

Parents should discuss (not lecture) several topics with adolescents: what it means to be in a relationship, characteristics of healthy relationships, how to set boundaries, effective ways to handle conflict, considerations for using social media (e.g., sexting, posting personal information), and considerations for entering into a sexual relationship. Parents should also be aware of dating violence warning signs (Suggestions for Parents 11-5). The CDC has developed an online training program, *Dating Matters*, to help educators and others working with youth to identify dating violence, risk and protective factors, and how to provide effective support. Parents should address concerns early in a nonjudgmental way that expresses caring and unconditional love for their child (Suggestions for Parents 11-5). Despite parents' efforts to maintain open communication, it can be difficult for youth to talk with their parents about violence they may experience in a relationship. In these situations, parents can provide adolescents with alternative information resources (e.g., loveisrespect.org) and access to professional support if needed.

Potential Warning Signs of Dating Violence and How Parents Can Help

Potential warning signs of dating violence:

- makes changes in daily routines
- withdraws from family and friends
- gives up activities they once enjoyed
- receives frequent messages or checks in often with their partner
- has unexplained marks or bruises
- has a partner who is jealous, controlling, loses temper easily, or makes insulting comments and threats
- has a partner who abuses other people or animals

How parents can help:

- Communicate concern for the adolescent's safety.
- Provide access to a counselor or attorney, as well as information about support organizations.
- Be supportive, understanding, and nonjudgmental. Remind adolescents that you are on their side.
- Let them know that it is not their fault, and that no one deserves to be abused.
- Take your adolescent seriously, and validate their feelings when they voice concerns.
- Help adolescents develop a safety plan; connect them with support groups and professionals who can help them to leave the relationship.
- Recognize that there are many reasons why an adolescent may not leave a relationship. Continued support may help them to accept that the relationship is unhealthy, and take steps to end it.

Source: National Domestic Violence Hotline & Break the Cycle (2013).

Responsive Parenting

Jared's father tells him to put his cell phone away during dinner. The 15-year-old places it on the kitchen counter and heads into the dining room to eat. During the meal, Jared seems withdrawn and on-edge as he hears his phone vibrating whenever a text message comes in. His father asks how soccer is going, and Jared informs him that he has decided to quit because his girlfriend is upset that he is always at practice and not able to spend the afternoons with her. As his father heads into the kitchen to retrieve an item from the refrigerator, he sees part of a text message on Jared's phone: "I told you never to talk to her again!!! You're mine. I'll tell Matt what you said about him if it happens again. You're such an **** sometimes!" What warning signs may suggest that dating violence is occurring? How would you advise Jared's father to approach his son about his concerns?

11-2c Maintaining Healthy Eating Habits

Adolescents are in the final stages of establishing a lifelong eating-behavior pattern. Increased time spent away from home and erratic daily schedules often mean that adolescents are making many more independent decisions about their food choices. On any given day they may be eating meals at home, school, and/or from fast food establishments. Researchers have noted that dietary quality tends to decline (e.g., fewer fruits, vegetables, and grains; increased fats, sugar, and calories) as more food is eaten away from home (Altman et al., 2015; Jones et al., 2015). Adolescents who consumed breakfast, ate more family meals together, and brought their lunches from home, were more likely to follow a healthier diet (Zewditu et al., 2015).

Although adolescents may understand the importance of healthy dietary habits, they often succumb to peer pressure and the perceived need to conform. Guidetti, Cavazza, and Conner (2016) found that adolescents who grew up with an authoritative parenting style were more likely to emulate their parents', and not peers', food choices. This correlation actually became stronger as the adolescent aged. The researchers hypothesized that adolescents were less likely to submit to peer influence and more likely to make positive food choices because they had learned how to regulate their own decisions and behavior.

Body image sensitivity also continues to play an influential role in the adolescent's eating patterns and dietary intake quality. Researchers have found that adolescents often modify their own eating behaviors (e.g., diet, consume more fattening foods, show no concern) based upon perceived weight comparisons with their peers. Perkins, Perkins, and Craig, (2015) noted that adolescent boys who overestimated their peers' weight were more likely to be overweight themselves; boys who were underweight were more likely to have underestimated the weight of their peers. Girls' assessments followed a similar pattern, although they were less likely to over- or underestimate their peers' weight than did boys. Adolescents, particularly boys, who were of a normal weight but perceived themselves to be overweight were more likely to engage in unhealthy dieting practices (e.g., vomiting, fasting, taking laxatives) (Sutin & Terracciano, 2015). They were also at an increased risk for becoming obese during adulthood. These findings illustrate the strength that peer influence has on adolescents' emotional self-efficacy and, in turn, on their eating behaviors and health.

Although adolescents' eating habits are susceptible to peer influence, parents also continue to have an effect. For example, Chng and Fassnacht (2016) found that parental comments about their adolescents' weight contributed to greater body dissatisfaction and disordered eating among boys and girls. Yamazaki and Omori (2016) also found that mothers' transferred their social value for thinness to their children who, in turn, engaged in weight-loss behaviors to comply with perceived body preferences. In contrast, Zamora-Kapoor, Nelson, and Buchwald (2016) found that maternal obesity was strongly correlated with obesity in adolescents (sons and daughters) across all racial/ethnic groups, and was only moderated by higher maternal educational attainment. Mothers who have more education may understand what constitutes a healthy diet and which nutritious foods are lower in calories.

11-2d Getting Adequate Sleep

School and social demands continue to compete with adolescent sleep duration and quality. According to the American Psychological Association, adolescents report sleeping approximately 7.4 hours on school nights and 8.1 hours on non-school nights, and almost 25 percent indicate that their quality of sleep is fair or poor (APA, 2013). Numerous research studies have shown that sleep is positively associated with improved learning, academic performance, behavior, and health outcomes (Wheaton, Chapman, & Croft, 2016; Schmidt & Van der Linden, 2015; Tonetti et al., 2015). Researchers have noted that sleep quality and duration increases the body's stress-responsive systems and

Photo 11-7 Busy school days and involvement in extracurricular activities can result in more meals being eaten away from home.
Lynn Marotz

enhances an individual's alertness and ability to function during the daytime (Lenten & Doane, 2016).

Adolescents have identified stress, particularly emotions associated with negative peer relationships (e.g., rejection, humiliation, disgrace, sadness, loneliness), as having a detrimental effect on their ability to sleep; positive emotions (e.g., happiness, excitement) were associated with favorable sleep outcomes (Tavernier et al., 2016). Umlauf et al. (2015) examined the sleep patterns of African American adolescents who lived in impoverished and violent neighborhoods, and found that they experienced increased levels of stress and hopelessness which contributed to poorer sleep quality. They also noted that sleep problems (e.g., sleep apnea, nightmares, insomnia) and daytime sleepiness were most apparent when adolescents were exposed to both poverty and violence, and that females were most severely affected by these conditions. Researchers have noted that adolescents who report sleeping even one hour less on weekdays experienced greater feelings of hopelessness, depression, anxiety, suicidal tendencies, impulsiveness, and substance use; adequate sleep was associated with a positive mood and outlook (Tavernier et al., 2016; Winsler et al., 2015; Hasler, Soehner, & Clark, 2015; van Zundert et al., 2015).

Adolescents may occasionally need gentle reminders about managing their time wisely so that they are able to get adequate sleep. Although it may seem counterintuitive to adolescents, learning and retention are improved by sleep versus staying up late at night to study (Horváth et al., 2015; Tononi & Cirelli, 2014). Parents can also encourage adolescents to consume nutritious foods and build time into their day for physical activity to improve sleep quality. Turning off electronic devices, taking a warm shower, and relaxing for a short while before bedtime can also contribute to a good night's sleep.

11-2e Protecting Adolescents from Risky Behaviors

Researchers have found that adolescents' propensity for engaging in risky behaviors peaks between the ages of 15 and 16 years and gradually declines by late adolescence (Defoe et al., 2015). These findings parallel neurodevelopmental changes associated with puberty that affects decision-making abilities, impulsivity, and desire for immediate gratification (Littlefield et al., 2016; Qu et al., 2015). Statistics show a significant increase in the three major causes of death during this particular adolescent stage: unintentional injuries (e.g., driver of motor vehicle, passenger in motor vehicle, poisoning/drug overdose, firearms), suicide, and homicide.

Photo 11-8 Poor judgment and reckless abandon increase adolescents' risk-taking behaviors. Hero Images/Getty Images

Parents play a critical role in protecting adolescents' welfare and safeguarding them from harm. This is not always an easy role to fulfill, especially as adolescents begin to disregard parental concern and advice. Researchers have identified early parental warmth, caring, and involvement, family cohesion, and positive behavior guidance practices as qualities that improve adolescents' resilience to participation in risky behaviors (Hayakawa et al., 2016; Sánchez-Queija, Oliva, & Parra, 2016; Reeb et al., 2015).

Motor Vehicles and Unlicensed Motorized Transportation. Adolescents' poor judgment and belief that they are invincible make them especially prone to taking risks that may threaten their well-being and that of others. This is apparent in terms of motor vehicles and other motorized transportation forms (e.g., motorcycles, all-terrain vehicles, boats) which are the number-one cause of adolescent injury and death. According to the CDC, approximately 2000 adolescents die each year (6 per day) (CDC, 2015). A majority of these accidents are due to a combination of driver inexperience and distracted driving. Ten percent of all drivers 15 to 19 years old involved in fatal crashes were found to have been distracted (e.g., using a cell phone, texting, eating, talking to passengers, adjusting the radio) at the time of a crash, which is the largest proportion of distracted drivers of all ages that are involved in such incidents (NHTSA, 2016). Researchers have also found a similar pattern in their studies. For example, Barr et al. (2015) surveyed more than 700 high school adolescent drivers and found that males were 20 percent less likely than females to wear their seat belt when driving. They were also 12 percent more likely than females to use their cell phone and 80 percent more likely to text while driving. Kahn et al. (2016) also found that almost 60 percent of teens reported talking on their cell phones (many also texted while driving) even though they knew that it was dangerous.

The increasing popularity and use of unlicensed recreational motorized transportation modes (e.g., motocross, all-terrain vehicles [ATVs], boats, jet skis) among adolescents has resulted in a significant rise in the number of deaths and serious injuries associated with these devices. According to a report issued by the U.S. Consumer Product Safety Commission (CPSC) approximately 23 percent (3098) of ATV fatalities and 26 percent (24,362) of ATV injuries treated in emergency departments involved adolescents under the age of 16 years (CPSC, 2015). Jinnah and Stoneman (2016) found that the ATV injury rate was four times higher among adolescents than adults. A lack of safety rule knowledge and engagement in risk-taking behaviors (e.g., allowing passengers to ride, not wearing a helmet, driving too fast, driving on public roads), especially among boys, creates a volatile situation that many adolescents are unprepared to manage. Similar injury rates have been observed among adolescents who participate in motocross or operate various watercraft forms (e.g., jet skis, boats, windsurfing) and fail to use proper flotation devices or follow safety rules (Daniels et al., 2015; Quistberg et al., 2014).

Substance Use and Abuse. Tobacco use is a major cause of preventable illness and death worldwide; it kills almost half of its users (WHO, 2015). Approximately 6,000,000 people die each year from tobacco product usage; approximately 600,000 of these deaths are attributable to secondhand smoke exposure (WHO, 2015). More than 4000 chemicals have been identified in tobacco smoke, with more than 250 known to be harmful and 50 known to cause cancer.

Despite these frightening statistics, adolescents continue to use various tobacco products (e.g., cigarettes, cigars, smokeless tobacco, electronic cigarettes, hookahs [water pipes used to smoke tobacco], pipe tobacco, and bidis [small imported cigarettes wrapped in a tendu leaf]) at an alarming rate. Singh et al. (2016) found that approximately 4.7 million U.S. middle and high school students were currently using or had used tobacco products in the previous 30 days. E-cigarette use among adolescents tripled between 2013 and 2014, and has now become the most commonly used and preferred tobacco product (CDC, 2015). These numbers are particularly disconcerting given the known risk for dependency and a significantly increased likelihood that a student who smokes at an early age will go on to use marijuana, cocaine, and other addictive substances (Keyes, Hamilton, & Kandel, 2016).

Numerous studies have been undertaken in an effort to understand what entices adolescents to engage in substance use (e.g., drinking, smoking, illicit drugs). One of the most substantiated explanations involves brain change developments which increase an adolescent's impulsive behavior, poor judgment, and pleasure derived from alcohol and drugs. Researchers have also identified strong associations among adolescent substance use and family conflict, stress, anxiety and depression, low self-esteem, and peer (for males) and romantic relationships (for females) (Cerdá et al., 2016; Holliday & Gould, 2016; Kuhn, 2015). Trucco et al. (2016) suggest that the adolescent's tendency to engage in substance use may actually develop during early childhood. Children who have a difficult temperament often exhibit problematic behaviors and poor coping skills which, in turn, elicit negative adult and peer responses. Their history of alienation increases the likelihood that, as adolescents, they will experiment with various substances and associate with deviant peers who also engage in impulsive behaviors and substance use.

Crime and Delinquency, Group Affiliation, and Gangs. Adolescents' involvement in crime and delinquency represents another form of risky behavior that has been attributed to a combination of immature brain development and environmental factors. Antisocial behaviors tend to peak between the ages of 15 and 19 years and then slowly decline (National Institute of Justice, 2014). Some adolescents who engage in delinquent or criminal activity begin to exhibit a pattern of aggressive, deceptive, or destructive behaviors during childhood. Others develop antisocial behaviors shortly after the onset of puberty when neurocognitive changes reduce the adolescent's ability to resist impulsive responses (Zhou et al., 2016).

According to National Gang Center statistics, approximately 50 percent of the gang members in small towns and 60 percent in rural areas are under the age of 18 years; 32 percent of the gang members in large cities and 37 percent in suburban areas are younger than 18 years (National Gang Center, 2014). Over 90 percent of gang members are male and of Hispanic/Latino (46 percent), African American (35 percent), or White (11 percent) ethnicities. They are also more likely to live in poverty and single-parent households (Pyrooz & Sweeten, 2015).

Researchers have also identified a number of social factors that increase the likelihood of adolescents engaging in delinquent behavior, including racial discrimination, maltreatment, dysfunctional parenting (e.g., substance use, acceptance of, and engagement in, antisocial behavior), and exposure to community violence (Evans, Simons, & Simons, 2016; Maguire & Fishbein, 2016; Baglivio et al., 2015; Fix & Burkhart, 2015). Repeated exposure to violent video games has also been acknowledged as a contributory risk factor for delinquent behavior (Exelmans, Custers, & Van den Bulck, 2015).

Adolescents experience a significant developmental need for peer acceptance and belonging, especially as they begin to separate themselves from parents and establish greater independence. This desire makes them eager to join with friends who are supportive and share similar deviant or non-deviant interests. Adolescents who engaged in delinquent behaviors and experienced frequent peer rejection during childhood are more likely to affiliate with other deviant peers (Chen, Drabick, & Burgers, 2015). Membership in these peer groups often socializes adolescents to engage in increased antisocial behaviors which, in turn, strengthen affiliation bonds. Dong and Krohn (2016) noted that adolescents typically join these groups because they experienced comfort and security in having friends who would look out for them. The researchers also found that the majority of adolescents who joined gangs when they were young did so in large numbers before the age of 14 years; the number of adolescents who joined gangs when they were older did so around the age of 17 years. The "late joiners" were more likely to use drugs and to commit violent crimes.

Photo 11-9 Truant adolescents often also engage in risky sexual, substance, and/or crime-related behaviors. Axente Vlad/Shutterstock.com

Truancy and School Drop Out. Frequent unexcused absences from school are associated with poor educational outcomes, and have also been linked to engagement in risky behaviors, including substance use, delinquency, and sexual activity (Holtes, 2015; Dembo et al., 2015b).

Truancy tends to peak at around age 15 years, and involves almost an equal number of boys and girls (Truancy Prevention, 2016). Truant females are more often Caucasian and likely to report being depressed; males tend to be African American and cite poor academic performance as the reason for their truancy (Dembo et al, 2015b). Adolescents who identify themselves as LGBT experience high truancy rates due to reported bullying and victimization (Birkett, Russell, & Corlis, 2014). Poor peer relationships and the failure of teachers to address bullying behaviors are also reasons often cited by truant adolescents (Havik, Bru, & Ertesvåg, 2015). Parental behavior is also known to contribute to truancy, especially if parents show low involvement with their adolescent or they condone the use of physical punishment (Dembo et al., 2015a).

Truancy creates significant challenges for adolescents and society in general. Many participate in risky sexual behaviors, drug use, and crime during times when they are away from school (Dembo et al., 2016). Adolescents who are frequently truant also tend to drop out of school at significantly high rates. Those from low-income families are six times more likely than their peers to drop out of high school (U.S. Department of Education, 2011). Years of low self-esteem, peer rejection, and poor academic performance cause adolescents to lose hope in ever achieving academic success. However, failure to complete a high school education increases their risk of health problems and results in significant financial loss over a lifetime. It is estimated that adults who do not complete a high school degree earn approximately $650,000 less during their working years, and cost the economy approximately $250,000 in lost tax revenue and increased medical care coverage, welfare support, and law enforcement costs (Stark, Noel, & McFarland, 2015).

11-3 Developmentally Appropriate Behavior Guidance

Attachment continues to be an important predictor for positive youth outcomes. Attachment with a caregiver during the adolescent years is characterized by being 'in tune' with one another and using effective communication and conflict negotiation (Mumford, Liu, & Taylor, 2016). Parents who maintain trusting and respectful relationships with their adolescents are more likely to have children who reciprocate such behaviors and meet parental expectations. Modeling prosocial behavior and showing warmth and responsiveness during interactions also reinforces adolescents to develop similar qualities (Padilla-Walker, Nielson, & Day, 2016; Missotten et al., 2016). Hostile or psychologically-controlling parental behaviors (e.g., anger, frustration, disappointment, sarcasm, emotional abuse) should be avoided because they are associated with lower prosocial behavior and more destructive resolution (Padilla-Walker, Nielson, & Day, 2016; Missotten et al., 2016).

Family cohesion and supportive relationships with parents are related to lower levels of risky behavior, especially for girls (Sasson & Mesch, 2016). Adolescents whose parents are caring, supportive, and aware of their child's behaviors are less likely to be in situations where drinking and smoking are occurring (Wang et al., 2016). Behavioral monitoring should imply support, trust, and caring versus behavioral restrictions that are imposed without a rationale and/or discussion. Adolescents whose parents use restrictive parental mediation, or focus on controlling behavior exclusively, may find ways to circumvent parents' efforts (Sasson & Mesch, 2016). Furthermore, when parents use more intrusive behaviors that attempt to control or inhibit adolescents' thoughts, feelings, and emotional expression (e.g., manipulation, guilt, love withdrawal), relationship hostility tends to increase and, in turn, fosters emotional and behavioral problems (Weymouth & Buehler, 2016).

Although adolescents are likely to turn to their peers for social support, they continue to need and want parental guidance (Olsson et al., 2016). Open, respectful communication enables parents to better understand their child's perspectives and behaviors. Parents tend to underreport (e.g., unaware of issues) or overreport (e.g., observes hostile behaviors and assumes that there is a disagreement) the amount of conflict in their relationship with adolescents when communication is lacking. Discrepancies in acknowledging conflict can have detrimental outcomes for adolescents, including increased anxiety and depression (Ehrlich et al., 2016).

Parents should continue to set high expectations and maintain their authority, communicate trust and respect, and encourage and support emotional independence during adolescence (Suggestions for Parents 11-6). They may find it difficult to relinquish control at times, but adolescent involvement in decision-making and goal-setting plans builds skills (e.g., banking, completing applications, making purchases) that they will need in adulthood (Marotz & Allen, 2016).

Suggestions for Parents 11-6

Positive Behavior Guidance

- Communicate unconditional love and a sense of trust and respect.
- Spend quality time together; let adolescents guide activities to be done during this time. Have family dinners together, volunteer for a meaningful cause, watch a movie, play board games, and/or ride bikes.
- Notice and reinforce appropriate, responsible behavior; celebrate progress toward goals.
- Involve adolescents in decision-making and problem solving processes.
- Be available for discussion. Use open-ended questions and active listening to engage adolescents in conversations about risky behaviors (e.g., "What have you heard about sexting?" "What do you think you would do if you were in that situation?").
- Remain patient and calm when conflict arises, and model appropriate ways to manage anger and use effective coping skills.
- Model and encourage healthy diet, exercise, sleep, and time management.
- Set limits and respond consistently to risky/harmful behaviors. Communicate your beliefs, values, and perspectives regarding such behaviors.
- Get to know your adolescent's friends, and monitor your adolescent's behavior in a supportive and caring manner.
- Recognize that adolescents make mistakes. Remain patient, calm, and understanding. Help adolescents to learn from their mistakes, but refrain from lecturing or giving too much advice.
- Continue to use natural (forgoing breakfast because the adolescent took too long to get ready for school) and logical (earlier curfew because teen came home late the previous night) consequences for behaviors to encourage compliance.
- Provide guidance in assuming responsibility for their own affairs; support planning for the future by listening to the adolescents' ideas and arranging opportunities so that they can explore their interests.

Responsive Parenting

Romona had invited several girl and boy friends to come over to her house after school. Romona's mother detected the odor of cigarette and marijuana smoke on the clothing of her daughter's friends when she walked into the room. Later that evening, she confronted Romona and threatened a severe punishment if she found out that her daughter was smoking or using drugs. Romona denied that she had ever participated in these activities, yelled, "You never trust me!," ran to her bedroom, and slammed the door. What potential effects may her mother's accusations have had on future communications and guidance? Why was it important that Romona's mother raise questions about her daughter's behavior? How would you advise Romona's mother to handle this situation differently, and in a more positive manner, in the future?

Summary

- Growth is less dramatic during adolescence, with females reaching their adult height around the age of 16 years, and males continuing to experience growth spurts until the end of this developmental stage.

- Parents should be aware of the warning signs associated with depression, oppositional defiant disorder, and conduct disorder, and help adolescents access services to improve daily functioning.

- By the end of adolescence, children show improvements in planning, organization, impulse control, and ability to delay gratification; they are also able to use higher-order thinking processes to address complex problems.

- A major developmental task during adolescence is the formation of a personal identity. Parents can support adolescents' identity development by encouraging safe exploration, discussing rationales for personal values and beliefs, and showing an interest in their future goals.

- Peer relationships become increasingly important as adolescents prepare for adulthood. Parents play a critical role in the adolescent's development of positive friendships and healthy dating relationships.

- Adolescents often struggle to maintain a healthy diet, body image, and sleep routines. Parents can support adolescents' healthy behaviors by providing access to healthy snacks, prioritizing family dinners, modeling and communicating a positive body image, encouraging appropriate physical activity, and creating an environment conducive to quality sleep.

- Children in middle and late adolescence may engage in risky behaviors from time to time. Parental warmth, caring, involvement, and positive behavior guidance practices are associated with improved resilience and reduced involvement in such activities.

- Parents need to continue relinquishing some control as adolescent children approach adulthood. Positive parent-adolescent relationships help children to make sound choices, and are characterized by being in tune with one another, showing trust and respect, maintaining open communication, and using appropriate conflict resolution strategies.

Key Terms

conduct disorder (CD) (p. 314)

higher-order thinking (p. 316)

oppositional defiant disorder (ODD) (p. 314)

Questions for Discussion and Self-Reflection

1. What are some typical signs of adolescent emotional and behavioral problems? How might depression, oppositional defiant disorder, and conduct disorder affect the parent-adolescent relationship?

2. How does belonging to a minority or marginalized group influence identity development? What can parents do to help adolescents develop a positive self-identity?

3. In what ways do dietary and sleep quality change during middle and late adolescence, why do these changes often occur, and what can parents do to promote a healthier lifestyle?

4. Why are adolescents prone to engage in risky behaviors?

5. How does the parent-child relationship change during middle and late adolescence? How can parents effectively monitor and promote a sense of trust and respect while also supporting increased autonomy?

Field Activities

1. Interview several parents of adolescents to identify the three biggest behavioral challenges they have encountered and how they dealt with them. Write a brief statement about how you would respond to each of the challenges based upon the chapter content.

2. Compile a list of quality websites for parents and teens focused on education and prevention of risky behaviors.

3. Discuss your own adolescence with a peer. Develop a list of topics that you would have liked to receive more information about. Brainstorm how parents can effectively communicate this information to an adolescent.

REFERENCES

ACT for Youth Center of Excellence. (2016). Ethnic and racial identity development. Retrieved May 12, 2016 from http://www.actforyouth.net/adolescence/identity/ethnic_racial.cfm.

American Academy of Pediatrics. (2015). Gay, lesbian, and bisexual teens: Facts for teens and their parents. Retrieved May 12, 2016 from https://www.healthychildren.org.

Alexander, S., Storm, D., & Cooper, C. (2015). Teasing in school locker rooms regarding penile appearance. *Journal of Urology*, *193*(3), 983–988.

Altman, M., Holland, J., Lundeen, D., Kolko, R., Stein, R., Saelens, B., …. & Wilfley, D. (2015). Reduction in food away from home is associated with improved child relative weight and body composition outcomes and this relation is mediated by changes in diet quality. *Journal of the Academy of Nutrition and Dietetics*, *115*(9), 1400–1407.

American Psychiatric Association. (2013). *Diagnostic and statistical manual of mental disorders*. (5th Ed., DSM-5). Arlington, VA: American Psychiatric Publishing.

American Psychological Association (APA). (2013). Stress and sleep. Retrieved May 11, 2016 from http://www.apa.org/news/press/releases/stress/2013/sleep.aspx.

American Society of Plastic Surgeons (ASPS). (2016). Plastic surgery for teenagers briefing paper.

Antonio, M., & Chung-Do, J. (2015). Systematic review of intervention focusing on indigenous adolescent mental health and substance use. American Indian and Alaska Native Mental Health Research: Centers for American Indian and Alaska Native Health. Retrieved May 12, 2016 from http://www.ucdenver.edu/academics/colleges/PublicHealth/research/centers/CAIANH/journal/Documents/Volume%2022/22(3)_Antonio_Adolescent_interventions_36-56.pdf.

Atkinson, D., Morten, G., & Sue, D. (1979). *Counseling American minorities: A cross-cultural perspective*. Dubuque, IA: Brown Company.

Atkinson, D., Morten, G., & Sue, D. (1993). *Counseling American minorities: A cross-cultural perspective*. (4th Ed). Dubuque, IA: Brown Company.

Baglivio, M., Wolff, K., Piquero, A., & Epps, N. (2015). The relationship between adverse childhood experiences (ACE) and juvenile offending trajectories in a juvenile offender sample. *Journal of Criminal Justice*, *43*(3), 229–241.

Barr, G., Kane, K., Barraco, R., Rayburg, T., Demers, L., Kraus, C., …. & Kane, B. (2015). Gender differences in perceptions and self-reported driving behaviors among teenagers. *The Journal of Emergency Medicine*, *48*(3), 366–370.e3.

Birkett, M., Russell, S., & Corliss, H. (2014). Sexual-orientation disparities in school: The mediational role of indicators of victimization in achievement and truancy because of feeling unsafe. *American Journal of Public Health*, *104*(6), 1124–1128.

Cai, R., & Richdale, A. (2016). Educational experiences and needs of higher education students with autism spectrum disorder. *Journal of Autism and Developmental Disorders*, *46*(1), 33–41.

Centers for Disease Control and Prevention. (2016). Understanding teen dating violence: Fact sheet. Retrieved May 6, 2016 from http://www.cdc.gov/violenceprevention/pdf/teen-dating-violence-factsheet-a.pdf.

Centers for Disease Control and Prevention (CDC). (2015). E-cigarette use triples among middle and high school students in just one year. Retrieved May 13, 2016 from http://www.cdc.gov/media/releases/2015/p0416-e-cigarette-use.html.

Centers for Disease Control and Prevention. (2014). Lesbian, gay, bisexual, and transgender health. Retrieved May 12, 2016 from http://www.cdc.gov/lgbthealth/youth.htm.

Cerdá, M., Prins, S., Galea, S., Howe, C., & Pardini, D. (2016). When psychopathology matters most: Identifying sensitive periods when with-in person changes in conduct, affective and anxiety problems are associated with male adolescent substance use. *Addiction, 111*(5), 924–935.

Chango, J., Allen, J., Szwedo, D., & Schad, M. (2015). Early adolescent peer foundations of late adolescent and young adult psychological adjustment. *Journal of Research on Adolescence, 25*(4), 685–699.

Chen, D., Drabick, D., & Burgers, D. (2015). A developmental perspective on peer rejection, deviant peer affiliation, and conduct problems among youth. *Child Psychiatry & Human Development, 46*(6), 823–838.

Chng, S., & Fassnacht, D. (2016). Parental comments: Relationship with gender, body dissatisfaction, and disordered eating in Asian young adults. *Body Image, 16*, 93–99.

Cummings, E., Koss, K., & Davi, P. (2015). Prospective relations between family conflict and adolescent maladjustment: Security in the family system as a mediating process. *Journal of Abnormal Child Psychology, 43*(3), 503–515.

Dakanalis, A., Timko, A., Madeddu, F., Volpato, C., Clerici, M., Riva, G., & Zanetti, A. (2015). Are the Male Body Dissatisfaction and Drive for Muscularity Scales reliable and valid instruments? *Journal of Healthy Psychology, 20*, 48–59.

Daniels, D., Clarke, M., Puffer, R., Luo, T., McIntosh, A., & Wetjen, N. (2015). High occurrence of head and spine injuries in the pediatric population following motocross accidents. *Journal of Neurosurgery: Pediatrics, 15*(3), 261–265.

Defoe, I., Dubas, J., Figner, B., & van Aken, M. (2015). A meta-analysis on age differences in risky decision making: Adolescents versus children and adults. *Psychological Bulletin, 141*(1), 48–84.

Dembo, R., Briones-Robinson, R., Schmeidler, J., Wareham, J., Ungaro, R., Winters, K., ... & Belenko, S. (2016). Brief intervention impact on truant youth's marijuana use: Eighteen-month follow-up. *Journal of Child & Adolescent Substance Abuse, 25*(1), 18–32.

Dembo, R., Briones-Robinson, R., Barrett, K., Winters, K., Ungaro, R., Karas, L., & Belenko, S. (2015a). Parenting practices among biological mothers of drug-involved truant youths: A latent profile analysis. *Journal of Child & Adolescent Substance Abuse, 24*(5), 282–294.

Dembo, R., Wareham, J., Krupa, J., & Winters, K. (2015b). Sexual risk behavior among male and female truant youths: Exploratory, multi-group latent class analysis. *Journal of Alcoholism & Drug Dependency, 3*, 226. doi:10.4172/2329-6488.1000226.

Dong, B., & Krohn, M. (2016). Dual trajectories of gang affiliation and delinquent peer association during adolescence: An examination of long-term offending outcomes. *Journal of Youth and Adolescence, 45*(4), 746–762.

Douglass, S., Mirpuri, S., English, D., & Yip, T. (2016). "They were just making jokes": Ethnic/racial teasing and discrimination among adolescents. *Cultural Diversity and Ethnic Minority Psychology, 22*(1), 69–82.

Drouin, M., Ross, J., & Tobin, E. (2015). Sexting: A new, digital vehicle for intimate partner aggression? *Computers in Human Behavior, 50*, 197–204.

Edlund, M., Forman-Hoffman, V., Winder, C., Heller, D., Kroutil, L., Lipari, R., & Colpe, L. (2015). Opioid abuse and depression in adolescents: Results from the National Survey on Drug Use and Health. *Drug and Alcohol Dependence, 152*, 131–138.

Ehrlich, K., Richards, J., Lejuez, C., & Cassidy, J. (2016). When parents and adolescents disagree about disagreeing: Observed parent-adolescent communication predicts informant discrepancies about conflict. *Journal of Research on Adolescence*. Epub ahead of print. doi: 10.1111/jora.12197.

Eisenberg, M., Gower, A., & McMorris, B. (2016). Emotional health of lesbian, gay, bisexual and questioning bullies: Does it differ from straight bullies? *Journal of Youth and Adolescence, 45*(1), 105–116.

Evans, S., Simons, L., & Simons, R. (2016). Factors that influence trajectories of delinquency throughout adolescence. *Journal of Youth and Adolescence, 45*(1), 156–171.

Exelmans, L., Custers, K., & Van den Bulck, J. (2015). Violent video games and delinquent behavior in adolescents: A risk factor perspective. *Aggressive Behavior, 41*(3), 267–279.

Fix, R., & Burkhart, B. (2015). Relationships between family and community factors on delinquency and violence among African American adolescents. *Race and Justice, 5*(4), 378–404.

Fortenberry, D. (2016). Adolescent sexual well-being in the 21st century. *Journal of Adolescent Health, 58*(1), 1–2.

Foshee, V., Gottfredson, N., Reyees, H., Chen, M., David-Ferdon, C., Latzman, N., . . . & Ennett, S. (2016). Developmental outcomes of using physical violence against dates and peers. *Journal of Adolescent Health, 58*(6), 665–671.

French, D., Niu, L., & Purwono, U. (2016). Popularity of Indonesian adolescents: Do the findings from the USA generalize to a Muslim majority developing country? *Social Development, 25*(2), 405–421.

Frick, P. (2016). Current research on conduct disorder in children and adolescents. *South African Journal of Psychology, 46*(2), 160–174.

Furnham, A., & Levitas, J. (2012). Factors that motivate people to undergo cosmetic surgery. *Canadian Journal of Plastic Surgery, 20*(4), e47–e50.

Gaither, S., Chen, E., Corriveau, K., Harris, P., Ambady, N., & Sommers, S. (2014). Monoracial and biracial children: Effects of racial identity saliency on social learning and social preferences. *Child Development, 85*(6), 2299–2316.

Glidden, L., & Natcher, A. (2009). Coping strategy use, personality, and adjustment of parents rearing children with developmental disabilities. *Journal of Intellectual Disability, 53*(12), 998–1013.

Graber, R., Turner, R., & Madill, A. (2016). Best friends and better coping: Facilitating psychological resilience through boys' and girls' closest friendships. *British Journal of Psychology, 107*(2), 338–358.

Greiff, S., Wüstenberg, S., Goetz, T., Vainikainen, M., Hautamäki, J., & Bornstein, M. (2016). A longitudinal study of higher-order thinking skills: Working memory and fluid reasoning in childhood enhance complex problem solving in adolescence. *Frontiers in Psychology, 6,* Article 1-60, 1–9.

Guidetti, M., Cavazza, N., & Conner, M. (2016). Social influence processes on adolescents' food likes and consumption: The role of parental authoritativeness and individual self-monitoring. *Journal of Applied Social Psychology, 46*(2), 114–128.

Guttmacher Institute. (2016). Fact Sheet: American teens' sources of sexual health education. Guttmacher Institute, Washington, DC. Retrieved May 1, 2016 from https://www.guttmacher.org/fact-sheet/facts-american-teens-sources-information-about-sex.

Hankin, B., Young, J., Abela, J., Smolen, A., Jenness, J., Gulley, L., . . . & Oppenheimer, C. (2015). Depression from childhood into late adolescence: Influence of gender, development, genetic susceptibility, and peer stress. *Journal of Abnormal Psychology, 124*(4), 803–816.

Hasler, B., Soehner, A., & Clark, D. (2015). Sleep and circadian contributors to adolescent alcohol use disorder. *Alcohol, 49*(4), 377–387.

Havik, T., Bru, E., & Ertesvåg, S. (2015). School factors associated with school-refusal and truancy-related reasons for school non-attendance. *Social Psychology of Education, 18*(2), 221–240.

Hayakawa, M., Giovanelli, A., Englund, M., & Reynolds, A. (2016). Not just academics: Paths of longitudinal effects from parent involvement to substance abuse in emerging adulthood. *Journal of Adolescent Health, 58*(4), 433–439.

Holliday, E., & Gould, T. (2016). Nicotine, adolescence, and stress: A review of how stress can modulate the negative consequences of adolescent nicotine abuse. *Neuroscience & Biobehavioral Reviews, 65,* 173–184.

Holman, A., & Kellas, J. (2015). High school adolescents' perceptions of the parent-child sex talk: How communication, relational, and family factors relate to sexual health. *Southern Communication Journal, 80*(5), 388–403.

Holtes, M., Bannink, R., Joosten, E., van As, E., Raat, H., & Broeren, S. (2015). Associations of truancy, perceived school performance, and mental health with alcohol consumption among adolescents. *Journal of School Health, 85*(12), 852–860.

Horváth, K., Myers, K., Foster, R., & Plunkett, K. (2015). Napping facilitates word learning in early lexical development. *Journal of Sleep Research, 24*(5), 503–509.

Jensen, L., & Dost-Gözkan, A. (2015). Adolescent-parent relations in Asian Indian and Salvadoran immigrant families: A cultural-developmental analysis of autonomy, authority, conflict, and cohesion. *Journal of Research on Adolescence, 25*(2), 340–351.

Jinnah, H., & Stoneman, Z. (2016). Age- and gender-based patterns in youth all-terrain vehicle (ATV) riding behaviors. *Journal of Agromedicine, 21*(2), 163–170.

Jones, A., Hammond, D., Reid, J., & Leatherdale, S. (2015). Where should we eat? Lunch source and dietary measures among youth during the school week. *Canadian Journal of Dietetic Practice and Research, 76*(4), 157–165.

Kahn, D., Fofie, F., Buchanan, G., Qazi, Z., Wilson-Byrne, T., LeGrow, T., & Shuler, F. (2016). Teen perception of texting and driving in rural West Virginia. *Marshall Journal of Medicine*, *2*(2), 45–53.

Kerig, P., Bennett, D., Chaplo, S., Modrowski, C., & McGeen, A. (2016). Numbing of positive, negative, and general emotions: Associations with trauma, exposure, posttraumatic stress, depressive symptoms among justice-involved youth. *Journal of Traumatic Stress*, *29*(2), 111–119.

Keyes, K., Hamilton, A., & Kandel, D. (2016). Birth cohorts analysis of adolescent cigarette smoking and subsequent marijuana and cocaine use. *American Journal of Public Health*, *106*(6), 1143–1149.

Kuhn, C. (2015). Emergence of sex differences in the development of substance use and abuse during adolescence. *Pharmacology & Therapeutics*, *153*, 55–78.

Kulis, S., Robbins, D., Baker, T., Denetsosie, S., Parkhurst, N. (2016). A latent class analysis of urban American youth identities. *Cultural Diversity and Ethnic Minority Psychology*, *22*(2), 215–228.

Lenten, S., & Doan, L. (2016). Examining multiple sleep behaviors and diurnal salivary cortisol and alpha-amylase: Within- and between-person associations. *Psychoneuroendocrinology*, *68*, 100–110.

Littlefield, A., Stevens, A., Ellingson, J., King, K., & Jackson, K. (2016). Changes in negative urgency, positive urgency, and sensation seeking across adolescence. *Personality and Individual Differences*, *90*, 332–337.

Lui, P. (2015). Intergenerational cultural conflict, mental health, and educational outcomes among Asian and Latino/a Americans: Qualitative and meta-analytic review. *Psychological Bulletin*, *141*(2), 404–446.

Lunde, C. (2013). Acceptance of cosmetic surgery, body appreciation, body ideal internalization, and fashion blog reading among late adolescents in Sweden. *Body Image*, *19*(4), 632–635.

Lunde, C., & Gyberg, F. (2016). Maternal and paternal influences on young Swedish women's and men's cosmetic surgery acceptance. *Sex Roles*, *74*(5), 242–253.

Maguire, E., & Fishbein, D. (2016). The influence of family characteristics on problem behaviors in a sample of high-risk Caribbean adolescents. *Family Relations*, *65*(1), 120–133.

Maniglio, R. (2015). Significance, nature, and direction of the association between child sexual abuse and conduct disorder. *Trauma, Violence, & Abuse*, *16*(3), 241–257.

Marcia, J. E. (1966). Development and validation of ego identity status. *Journal of Personality and Social Psychology 3*(5), 551–558.

Marotz, L., & Allen, K. (2016). *Developmental profiles: Pre-birth through adolescence*. (8th Ed). Boston, MA: Cengage Learning.

Missotten, L., Luyckx, K., Van Leeuwen, K., Klimstra, T., & Branje, S. (2016). Adolescents' conflict resolution style toward mothers: The role of parenting and personality. *Journal of Child and Family Studies*. Advance online publication. doi:10.1007/s10826-016-0421-x.

Morgan, E. (2013). Contemporary issues in sexual orientation and identity development in emerging adulthood. *Emerging Adulthood*, *1*(1), 52–66.

Mumford, E., Liu, W., & Taylor, B. (2016). Parenting profiles and adolescent dating relationship abuse: Attitudes and experiences. *Journal of Youth and Adolescence*, *45*(5), 959–972.

Napolitano, L., Pacholok, S., & Furstenberg, F. (2014). Educational aspirations, expectations, and realities for middle-income families. *Journal of Family Issues*, *35*(9), 1200–1226.

National Domestic Violence Hotline & Break the Cycle. (2013). Help your child. Retrieved May 6, 2016 from http://www.loveisrespect.org/resources/download-materials/.

National Gang Center. (2014). *National Youth Gang Survey Analysis*. U.S. Department of Justice. Retrieved May 13, 2016 from http://www.nationalgangcenter.gov/Survey-Analysis.

National Highway Traffic Safety Administration (NHTSA). (2016). Distracted driving 2014. Retrieved May 13, 2016 from http://www-nrd.nhtsa.dot.gov/Pubs/812260.pdf.

National Institute of Justice. (2014). From juvenile delinquency to young adult offending. Retrieved May 13, 2016 from http://www.nij.gov/topics/crime/Pages/delinquency-to-adult-offending.aspx.

National Institute of Mental Health. (2014). Major depression among adolescents. Retrieved May 10, 2016 from http://www.nimh.nih.gov/health/statistics/prevalence/major-depression-among-adolescents.shtml.

Noordermeer, S., Luman, M., & Oosterlaan, J. (2016). A systematic review and meta-analysis of neuroimaging in oppositional defiant disorder (ODD) and conduct disorder (CD) taking attention-deficit hyperactivity disorder (ADHD) into account. *Neuropsychology Review*, *26*(1), 44–72.

Núñez, J., Suárez, N., Rosário, P., Vallejo, G., Valle, A., & Epstein, J. (2015). Relationships between perceived parental involvement in homework, student homework behaviors, and academic achievement: Differences among elementary, junior high, and high school students. *Metacognition and Learning, 10*(3), 375–406.

Office of Adolescent Health. (2016). Teen pregnancy & childbearing: Tips for parents. Retrieved May 6, 2016 from http://www.hhs.gov/ash/oah/adolescent-health-topics /reproductive-health/teen-pregnancy/tips-for-parents.html.

Olsson, I., Hagekull, B., Giannotta, F., & Ahlander, C. (2016). Adolescents and social support situations. *Scandinavian Journal of Psychology, 57*(3), 223–232.

Padilla-Walker, L., Nielson, M., & Day, R. (2016). The role of parental warmth and hostility on adolescents' prosocial behavior toward multiple targets. *Journal of Family Psychology, 30*(3), 331–340.

Perkins, J., Perkins, H., & Craig, D. (2015). Misperception of peer weight norms and its association with overweight and underweight status among adolescents. *Prevention Science, 16*(1), 70–79.

Pyrooz, D., & Sweeten, G. (2015). Gang membership between ages 5 and 17 years in the United States. *Journal of Adolescent Health, 56*(4), 414–419.

Qu, Y., Galvan, A., Fuligni, A., Lieberman, M., & Telzer, E. (2015). Longitudinal changes in prefrontal cortex activation underlie declines in adolescent risk taking. *The Journal of Neuroscience, 35*(32), 11308–11314.

Quistberg, D., Bennett, E., Quan, L., & Ebel, B. (2014). Low life jacket use among adult recreational boaters: A qualitative study of risk perception and behavior factors. *Accident Analysis & Prevention, 62*, 276–284.

Reeb, B., Chan, S., Conger, K., Martin, M., Hollis, N., Serido, J., & Russell, S. (2015). Prospective effects of family cohesion on alcohol-related problems in adolescence: Similarities and differences by race/ethnicity. *Journal of Youth and Adolescence, 44*(10), 1941–1953.

Roblyer, M., Bámaca-Colbert, M., Rojas, S., & Cervantes, R. (2015). "Our child is not like us:" Child conflict among U.S. Latino families. *Family Science Review, 20*(2), 3–22.

Rose, A., Smith, R., Glick, G., & Schwartz-Mette, R. (2016). Girls' and boys' problem talk: Implications for emotional closeness in friendships. *Developmental Psychology, 52*(4), 629–639.

Sánchez-Queija, I., Oliva, A., Parra, A., & Camacho, C. (2016). Longitudinal analysis of the role of family functioning in substance use. *Journal of Child and Family Studies, 25*(1), 232–240.

Sasson, H., & Mesch, G. (2016). Gender differences in the factors explaining risky behavior online. *Journal of Youth and Adolescence, 45*, 973–985.

Schmidt, R., & Van der Linden, M. (2015). The relations between sleep, personality, behavioral problems, and school performance in adolescents. *Sleep Medicine Clinics, 10*(2), 117–123.

Schwartz, D., Lansford, J., Dodge, K., Pettit, G., & Bates, J. (2015). Peer victimization during middle childhood as a lead indicator of internalizing problems and diagnostic outcomes in late adolescence. *Journal of Clinical Child & Adolescent, 44*(3), 393–404.

Shute, C., Hansen, E., Underwood, J., & Razzouk, R. (2011). A review of the relationship between parental involvement and secondary school students' academic achievement. *Education Research International, 2011*, 1–10.

Simons, L., Wickrama, K., Lee, T., Landers-Potts, M., Cutrona, C., & Conger, R. (2016). Testing family stress and family investment explanations for conduct problems among African American adolescents. *Journal of Marriage and Family, 78*(2), 498–515.

Singh, T., Arrazola, R., Corey, C., Husten, C., Neff, L., Homa, D., & King, B. (2016). Tobacco use among middle and high school students–United States, 2011-2015. *Morbidity and Mortality Weekly (MMWR), 65*(14), 361–367.

Stark, P., Noel, A., & McFarland, J. (2015). Trends in high school dropout and completion rates in the United States: 1972-2012. U.S. Department of Education. Retrieved May 13, 2016 from http://nces.ed.gov/pubs2015/2015015.pdf.

Substance Abuse and Mental Health Services Administration (SAMHSA). (2015a). Ending conversion therapy: Supporting and affirming LGBTQ youth. HHS Publication No. (SMA) 15-4928. Rockville, MD: Substance Abuse and Mental Health Services Administration.

Substance Abuse and Mental Health Services Administration (SAMHSA). (2015b). Mental disorders. Retrieved May 10, 2016 from http://www.samhsa.gov/disorders/mental.

Sue, D., & Sue, D. (2008). *Counseling the culturally diverse: Theory and practice* (5th Ed). Hoboken, NJ: John Wiley & Sons.

Sumner, R. (2016). "Who am I"—Identity formation in adolescence. Retrieved May 12, 2016 from http://www.actforyouth.net/adolescence/identity/.

Sutin, A., & Terracciano, A. (2015). Body weight misperception in adolescence and incident obesity in young adulthood. *Psychological Science, 26*(4), 507–511.

Sutter, C., Nishina, A., & Adam, R. (2015). How you look versus how you feel: Associations between BMI z-score, body dissatisfaction, peer victimization, and self-worth for African American and white adolescents. *Journal of Adolescence, 43*, 20–28.

Tavernier, R., Choo, S., Grant, K., & Adam, E. (2016). Daily affective experiences predict objective sleep outcomes among adolescents. *Journal of Sleep Research, 25*(1), 62–69.

Taylor, B., & Mumford, E. (2016). A national descriptive portrait of adolescent relationship abuse: Results from the National Survey on Teen Relationships and Intimate Violence. *Journal of Interpersonal Violence, 31*(6), 963–988.

Tononi, G., & Cirelli, C. (2014). Sleep and the price of plasticity: From synaptic and cellular homeostasis to memory consolidation and integration. *Neuron, 81*(1), 12–34.

Tonetti, L., Fabbri, M., Filardi, M., Martoni, M., & Vincenzo, N. (2015). Effects of sleep timing, sleep quality and sleep duration on school achievement in adolescents. *Sleep Medicine, 16*(8), 936–940.

Truancy Prevention. (2016). Truancy definition, facts and laws. Retrieved on May 14, 2016 from http://www.truancyprevention.org/.

Trucco, E., Hicks, B., Villafuerte, S., Nigg, J., Burmeister, M., Zucker, R. (2016). Temperament and externalizing behavior as mediators of genetic risk on adolescent substance use. *Journal of Abnormal Psychology, 125*(4), 565–575.

Umlauf, M., Bolland, A., Bolland, K., Tomek, S., & Bolland, J. (2015). The effects of age, gender, hopelessness, and exposure to violence on sleep disorder symptoms and daytime sleepiness among adolescents in impoverished neighborhoods. *Journal of Youth and Adolescence, 44*(2), 518–542.

U.S. Consumer Product Safety Commission (CPSC). (2015). 2014 Annual report of ATV-related deaths and injuries. Retrieved May 15, 2016 from http://www.cpsc.gov//Global/Research-and-Statistics/Injury-Statistics/Sports-and-Recreation/ATVs/2014atvannualreport.pdf.

U.S. Department of Education. (2011). National Center for Education Statistics. The Digest of Education Statistics 2010 (NCES 2011-015) (Washington, DC: U.S. Government Printing Office, 2011), Table 116, p. 181.

U.S. Department of Education and Office for Civil Rights. (2011). Transition of students with disabilities to postsecondary education: A guide for high school educators. Retrieved May 15, 2016 from http://www2.ed.gov/about/offices/list/ocr/transitionguide.html.

U.S. Department of Justice & U.S. Department of Education. (2016). Dear colleague letter on transgender students. Retrieved on May 13, 2016 from http://www2.ed.gov/about/offices/list/ocr/letters/colleague-201605-title-ix-transgender.pdf.

van Zundert, R., van Roekel, E., Engels, R., & Scholte, R. (2015). Reciprocal associations between adolescents' night-time sleep and daytime affect and the role of gender and depressive symptoms. *Journal of Youth and Adolescence, 44*(2), 556–569.

Vendetti, M., Matlen, B., Richland, L., & Bunge, S. (2015). Analogical reasoning in the classroom: Insights from cognitive science. *Mind, Brain, and Education, 9*(2), 100–106.

Wang, C., Hipp, J., Butts, C., Jose, R., & Lakon, C. (2016). Coevolution of adolescent friendship networks and smoking and drinking behaviors with consideration of parental influence. *Psychology of Addictive Behaviors, 30*(3), 312–324.

Wehman, P., Sima, A., Ketchum. J., West, M., Chan, F., & Luecking, R. (2015). Predictors of successful transition from school to employment for youth with disabilities. *Journal of Occupational Rehabilitation, 25*(2), 323–334.

Weymouth, B., & Buehler, C. (2016). Adolescent and parental contributions to parent-adolescent hostility across early adolescence. *Journal of Youth and Adolescence, 45*(4), 713–729.

Wheaton, A., Chapman, D., & Croft, J. (2016). School start times, sleep, behavioral, health, and academic outcomes: A review of the literature. *Journal of School Health, 86*(5), 363–381.

Whitaker, K., Shapiro, V., & Shields, J. (2016). School-based protective factors related to suicide for lesbian, gay, and bisexual adolescents. *Journal of Adolescent Health, 58*(1), 63–68.

Williams, K., Ciarrochi, J., & Heaven, P. (2014). Relationships between valued action and well-being across the transition from high school to early adulthood. *Journal of Positive Psychology, 10*(2), 127–140.

Winsler, A., Deutsch, A., Vorona, R., Payne, P., & Szklo-Coxe, M. (2015). Sleepless in Fairfax: The difference one more hour of sleep can make for teen hopelessness, suicidal ideation, and substance use. *Journal of Youth and Adolescence, 44*(2), 362 378.

World Health Organization (WHO). (2015). Tobacco. Retrieved May 13, 2016 from http://www.who.int/mediacentre/factsheets/fs339/en/.

Yamazaki, Y., & Omori, M. (2016). The relationship between mothers' thin-ideal and children's drive for thinness: A survey of Japanese early adolescents and their mothers. *Journal of Health Psychology, 21*(1), 100–111.

Zamora-Kapoor, A., Nelson, L., & Buchwald, D. (2016). Maternal correlates of body mass index in American Indian/Alaska Native and White adolescents: Differences between mother/son and mother/daughter pairs. *Eating Behaviors, 20*(1), 43–47.

Zepeda, C., Richey, J., Ronevich, P., & Nokes-Malach, T. (2015). Direct instruction of metacognition benefits adolescent science learning, transfer, and motivation: An in vivo study. *Journal of Educational Psychology, 107*(4), 954–970.

Zewditu, D., Eaton, D., Lowry, R., Kim, S., Park, S., Grimm, K., ... & Harris, D. (2015). The association of meal practices and other dietary correlates with dietary intake among high school students in the United States, 2010. *American Journal of Health Promotion, 29*(6), e.203–e213.

Zhou, X., Zhu, D., King, S., Lees, C., Bennett, A., Salinas, E., . . . & Constantinidis, C. (2016). Behavioral response inhibition and maturation of goal representation in prefrontal cortex after puberty. *Proceedings of the National Academy of Sciences of the United States of America, 113*(2), 3353–3358.

Parenting Young Adult Children

12

LEARNING OBJECTIVES

After reading the chapter, you will be able to:

12-1 Understand the developmental characteristics that are unique during the early adulthood years, and what meaning they have for the individual's future.

12-2 Discuss how parents can support young adults' social-emotional development, and promote healthy independence.

naeyc Standards Linked to Chapter Content

2a, and 2b: Building family and community relationships

4a: Using developmentally effective approaches to connect with children and families

mangostock/Shutterstock.com

The journey from adolescence to adulthood is analogous to arrival in a foreign country: new adventures await, there are expectations to fulfill, and many navigational uncertainties exist in unfamiliar territory. Metaphorically, all children start out in essentially the same country, but on different roads. They meet at intersections like school, but choose different means

continued on following page

and routes to arrive at a chosen destination, which they hope will be the one that leads to their dreams and meets their expectations.

Preparations for this lifetime trip have been underway since birth. Parents guide, encourage, and protect children while they develop the cognitive, language, and social-emotional skills that are needed to complete the journey. Some children and adolescents will encounter more obstacles (e.g., poverty, health, disability, family) along the way and, as a result, be more or less successful than others in following a particular path. Cultural and environmental influences also determine when and how the trip will unfold. Nevertheless, all children will eventually become adults and, thus, begin a series of new and unanticipated adventures. ■

12-1 Developmental Overview

At what point does a child become an adult? During the Middle Ages, children as young as 7 years of age were considered adults who were expected to enter the workforce (Aries, 1962). G. Stanley Hall (1904) defined adulthood as beginning at age 24 years. Erik Erikson (1963) described young adulthood as occurring between the ages of 18 and 40 years. Dictionary definitions usually include phrases such as, "an adult is a fully mature, sensible, grown, and not childish person." In the United States, adult status is often equated with legal status. For example, the legal age one can marry without parental consent is 18 years; a person must be 18 years to serve in the military (or 17 years with parental consent); the legal voting age is 18 years; a person must be 21 years to drink alcoholic beverages legally; and, an unrestricted driver's license can be obtained in most states at 16 years (although the legal age varies from state to state). It is clear that the term "adult" is a fluid concept that depends upon its usage context.

In many Western cultures, adulthood has long been synonymous with expectations that children would complete secondary education, move out of their parent's home, find a job to support themselves, get married, and have children. However, this pattern has become far less typical in recent years as young adults delay marriage, pursue advanced degrees or vocational training, focus more attention on their career development, choose to travel and experience different cultures, or have difficulty finding jobs and supporting themselves financially. J. Arnett (2000, 2006), an American psychologist, introduced the term *emerging adult* to distinguish the developmental processes that tend to occur between the ages of 18 and 28 years with respect to contemporary demographic societal changes:

- *time of instability*: experiencing flux and uncertainty; young adults may be heading off to school, moving to another city for employment, or spending time in various relationships. Challenges and conflicts encountered along the way must be resolved and revised.

- *time of possibilities*: creating a vision of future goals; exploring and making decisions about options that one wants to pursue, including continued education, employment, finances, relationships, living arrangements, and other personal aspirations.

- *time of self-focus*: making independent decisions and focusing primary attention on satisfying one's own personal needs and interests.

Figure 12-1 Developmental Tasks During Early Adulthood

- Learning adult roles; accepting adult responsibilities
- Establishing and building a career
- Forming a mature personal and sexual identity
- Developing mature and meaningful relationships
- Becoming emotionally and financially independent

Photo 12-1 Parental guidance and support are important during an adolescent's transition to adulthood. © Lynn Marotz

- *time of uncertainty*: feeling sandwiched between two developmental stages: no longer being treated like an adolescent, but not yet considering themselves full-fledged adults. During this time, emerging adults must learn how to balance personal freedom and independence with adult responsibility and cultural obligations to family.
- *time of identity exploration*: forming and reforming one's self-concept as a result of new possibilities and experiences.

The emerging adult phase is most evident in industrialized cultures, such as the United States, Canada, Europe, Japan, New Zealand, and Australia, but it does not exist in many collectivist societies, such as American Indian, African, Chinese, Latin American, and South Korean groups (Adams et al., 2016; Zeng & Greenfield, 2015; Arnett, 2000).

Young adults have few physical and social-emotional tasks left to achieve, but they provide a developmental framework for the attainment of meaning and purpose. All have a formidable effect on an individual's life course (see Figure 12-1). Many factors, including race/ethnicity, culture, gender, health, educational achievement, and family resources affect the timing and manner in which individuals address and achieve these tasks (Keijer, Nagel, & Liefbroer, 2016; Fingerman et al., 2015; Gordon & Cui, 2015). Researchers have also noted that parental guidance, interaction, advice, and support may be the most protective and influential factors in helping adolescents' transition successfully to adulthood (Lee, & Goldstein, 2016; Inguglia et al., 2015). In many ways, their experience is analogous to that of toddlers' who are able to experiment and explore their environment only when they feel safe and have a secure relationship with their parents.

12-2 Supporting Social-Emotional Development

The traditional adulthood benchmarks (e.g., marriage, children, job) that once denoted adulthood appear to be far less relevant today. As a result, young adults' social and emotional development is occurring later and at a slower pace (Furstenberg, 2015). They tend to feel less social and parental pressure to achieve adult-associated developmental milestones by a particular age. They are more likely to proceed slowly and assume a less-serious and categorical attitude toward life (Eliason, Mortimer, & Vuolo, 2015; South & Lei, 2015). Many young adults appear to be in no hurry to rush the process because they assume that they will eventually arrive at some stage that will be financially rewarding as well as lifestyle appropriate given their goals.

This attitudinal behavior may have, at least in part, a biological explanation. Scientists once thought that brain development was complete around mid-adolescence. A National Institute of Mental Health longitudinal study, initiated in 1991 to learn more about brain development progression, was intended to validate these assumptions.

Researchers planned to follow approximately 5000 children until middle adolescence. However, what they and other neuroscientists soon discovered was that the adolescent brain continues to undergo structural changes (pruning and strengthening of neural connections) which peak at around age 25 years and then gradually continue to occur, but at a slower pace, until the late twenties (Lebel & Beaulieu, 2011; Johnson, Blum, & Giedd, 2009; Giedd, 2004).

The structural changes noted in these studies affect areas of the brain that are involved in cognition and social-emotional behaviors, including identity formation, anticipation and evaluation of alternatives, planning, relationship formation, and goal orientation (Barrasso-Catanzaro & Eslinger, 2016). These skills are integral to the decisions that young adults' must make, many of which have significant long-term ramifications. So, how do these findings account for the apparent maturity differences in the way young adults transition into adulthood today as compared to years past? The answer is most likely due to an increase in lifestyle options and choices that young adults have today (e.g., jobs, travel, relationships), and to a greater societal and parental acceptance of their delayed assumption of adult roles and responsibilities.

Researchers have noted that young adults also undergo personality changes during these transitional years. They begin to experience fewer negative emotions (e.g., stress, unfriendliness, aggression, neuroticism) and an increase in positive traits (e.g., self-control, perceptiveness, thoughtfulness, sociability) (Durbin et al., 2016; Silvers et al., 2015; Landsford et al., 2014). In addition, young adults have a tendency to migrate toward individuals and environments that reflect and reinforce personality traits which are similar to their own (Penke & Jokela, 2016). As a result, these traits become more consistent with time and experience, and usually stabilize at around age 30 years (Biley & Tucker-Drob, 2014; Raznahan et al., 2014). The culmination of developmental processes, thus, cause young adults to behave in ways that are more likely to conform to the social expectations associated with adulthood in their particular culture (Bleidorn, 2015; Bleidorn et al., 2013).

12-2a Family Relationships

Families play a significant role in the way that parents help or hinder children's transition to adulthood. Although adolescents begin to distance themselves from parents and are eager to assume their independence, they tend to form a new respect and relationship with them during the early adulthood period (Guan & Fuligni, 2015). Parents and children typically become less antagonistic and more compassionate and mutually understanding of one another. This seems to be particularly true if parents maintain nonjudgmental communication and limit their control and intervention in young adults' affairs. Although children may experience a temporary increase in stress during this transitional process, they gradually regain confidence with repeated experience. Parra, Oliva, and Reina (2015) noted that the amount of parent-child communication tends to decrease during young adulthood, but that discussions and interactions often focused on more important matters and much less time was spent on criticism and attempts to resolve conflict.

However, the dynamics in some families are not always conducive to children's healthy transition to adulthood. For example, negative parental reactions to a son's or daughter's disclosure of same-sex preference may disrupt parent-child relations, contribute to a child's psychological problems, and compromise an otherwise successful transition (D'amico et al., 2015). Children who grow up in economically disadvantaged families often encounter significant challenges, including violence, conflict, and dependency that make this transition difficult to attain. In some cases, adolescents may be forced to assume adult roles despite a lack of preparation for these responsibilities (Roy et al., 2014).

Photo 12-2 Culture defines what it means to be an adult.
antoniodiaz/Shutterstock.com

Oman et al. (2015) found that such experiences had long-lasting and negative effects on young adults' self-perception and later adjustment to adulthood, even though they had previously been fulfilling many of these same responsibilities.

Cultural Differences and Expectations. All cultures define what it means to be an adult, what responsibilities are associated with an adult role, and when this transition is typically expected to occur. Some cultures encourage behaviors that lead to an early transition to adulthood, particularly in developing countries where citizens have less access to education and must attempt to enter the workforce at a young age. This pattern is in contrast to what occurs in many industrialized nations where an increasing number of young adults have extended their postsecondary education for 5 or more years longer than in the past (Furstenberg, 2013). As a result, young adults delay marriage and the start of a family, rely on their families for greater financial support, and live with their parents for an extended time period (see Figure 12-2).

Some young adults do not transition to adulthood in a traditional way (e.g., move out of their parent's home, get married, have children) because they feel a strong sense of duty or responsibility to their families. This is particularly true among Asian and Latino groups, which tend to be collectivist cultures. Upholding these beliefs can become a source of considerable intergenerational conflict, and can cause young adults who emigrate to individualistic societies, such as the United States or Germany, to experience psychological distress and depression (Lee, Dik, & Barbara, 2015; Lui, 2015). However, some tensions may gradually dissolve as their home countries experience a greater Western influence. For example, researchers have noted that an increasing number of young adults in China and Japan are experimenting with behaviors (e.g., premarital sex, cohabitation) that are considered contradictory to their traditional cultural values (Yeung & Hu, 2013). Emigration subsequent to cultural changes in their own countries lessens these adaptive requirements.

Photo 12-3 High living costs and low wages challenge young adults' ability to live independently.
bikeriderlondon/Shutterstock.com

Figure 12-2 Young Adults Living in Their Parental Home, 1960–Present

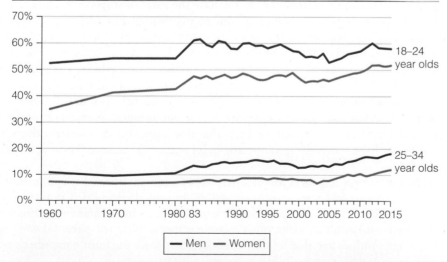

Note: Unmarried college students living in dormitories are counted as living in group quarters in decennial data but as living in their parental home in CPS data.

Source: U.S. Census Bureau, Decennial Censuses, 1960 to 1980, and Current Population Survey, Annual Social and Economic Supplements, 1983 to 2015.

Socioeconomic developments in recent years have also caused changes in some of the cultural traditions associated with youths' transition to adulthood. High unemployment, expensive housing, and low wages in countries such as Spain, Greece, Africa, China, and Japan have resulted in fewer young adults who live independently (Hu & Chou, 2016; Parra, Oliva, & Reina, 2015). Lei and South (2016) noted a similar pattern among Black and Mexican youth who were significantly more likely than Caucasians to remain in their parents' household because of economic constraints (e.g., no job, low wages, high rent). Hispanic youth were also less likely to leave home because they felt a strong tie to siblings and a need to help support their family. Cultural differences in attitudes among Black and Hispanic youth also resulted in lower marriage rates and a lesser likelihood that they would leave their parental home (Britton, 2013).

12-2b Prolonged Parenting

Researchers have identified three general pathways into adulthood: some young adults (without children) enter higher education or employment; some assume traditional family roles (e.g., women have children, often early in their relationship, and fathers work to provide support); and, some are "slow starters" who live with their parents for a longer period of time while or until they establish a clearer path to adulthood (Birkeland et al., 2014). A fourth pathway is becoming increasingly more common; adult children return home after living independently for a period. Slow starters, or those who "fail to launch," as well as those who return home, or "boomerang," influence the entire family system and outcomes for individual family members.

Encouraging Dependence. Physical, emotional, and financial dependence can occur for a variety of reasons, including parenting style and mental health needs. Overinvolved (with low warmth) or overly protective parents, for example, are more likely to encourage children's prolonged dependence. Adult children in these families often exhibit lower levels of self-worth and greater maladjustment problems (Nelson, Padilla-Walker, & Nielson, 2015). Further, young adults whose parents do not support their autonomy and are psychologically controlling tend to have more maladaptive outcomes (e.g., depression, anxiety) and lower life satisfaction, especially if they feel that their psychological needs are unmet (Mageau et al., 2015; Costa et al., 2015).

Overparenting may lead to inadequate, blurred, or inflexible boundaries within the family that foster interpersonal dependency and depression in adulthood (Rousseau & Scharf, 2015). For example, children may give up their own needs in order to fulfill parental needs; they may be drawn in to mediate the relationship between parents; or, they may engage in dependent behaviors due to psychological control (e.g., high nurturance-seeking, low emotional independence, low functional independence). These actions and reactions are associated with lower levels of adult adjustment (Rousseau & Scharf, 2015; Mayseless & Scharf, 2009). In addition, adult children are likely to remain fused with the family system (i.e., they do not differentiate their circumstances as apart from the family) and experience role confusion (i.e., have not developed a strong sense of identity) because their autonomy is not encouraged. In turn, they are less likely to commit to an occupation or they abandon opportunities when others arise, which promotes little motivation to become independent (Sandberg-Thoma, Snyder, & Jang, 2015).

Children who have a mental illness often have an increased need for support which may cause parents to feel a sense of inescapable duty to their child (Lindgren, Söderberg, & Skär, 2016). The reverse can also be true if parents have their own unmet mental health needs and adult children must assume responsibility for parental well-being. However, when families are able to access services that meet the family member's needs, the burden of caregiver responsibility becomes more manageable.

Socioeconomic status also influences the type of support that parents are able to provide to young adults. Parents who have higher income and more education are typically able to offer increased emotional and financial support. Goodsell et al. (2015)

noted that parents often provided financial assistance to help adult children continue their education, establish a family, and make large purchases (e.g., house, car, furniture). They also found that parents were more likely to assist children financially if they lived nearby and had a close relationship with their mother. Girls were more likely than boys to receive financial help from their parents, but the more sisters (not brothers) an adult child had, the less financial assistance (but not advice or in-kind assistance, such as babysitting) they received. Researchers have also found that parents are more likely to provide resources to their biological children, as opposed to adopted or stepchildren (Kalmijn, 2013).

Photo 12-4 Parents often provide some financial assistance during the early adult years. Luna Vandoorne/Shutterstock.com

Parents who have less education and income are more likely to provide children with intangible support (e.g., live together with their child or provide advice and companionship), which can be taxing on their time and personal health (Fingerman et al., 2015). As a result, young adults and their parents may become reliant upon one another to meet intermingled emotional and financial needs. For example, parents who experience poverty, have limited education, and few work opportunities are more likely to live with their children and grandchildren which, in many cases, makes it easier for them to provide necessary intangible supports (Ellis & Simmons, 2014). Adult children whose parents have higher incomes may become dependent upon them to help meet their financial needs.

Parents face a significant financial burden when children move back home. Many young adults have acquired substantial debt (e.g., credit card, school loans, car payments) that they are unable to address (Dettling & Hsu, 2014). As a result, parents may find that they must help children make their debt payments while also meeting their own mortgage and daily living expenses. This arrangement seldom leaves parents with much ability to save for their retirement and, in some cases, may require that they sacrifice the savings they have managed to accumulate. The average U.S. married couple has less than $50,000 in a retirement savings account; single- and minority parents are likely to have significantly less (see Figure 12-3). According to Morrissey (2016), fewer than half of all Black and Hispanic families have any retirement savings; those who do have saved an average of $22,000 compared to White non-Hispanic families who have saved approximately $73,000. Thus, it is important that parents establish clear financial arrangements with children who intend to move back home so that their own quality of life isn't jeopardized.

Figure 12-3 Family Retirement Savings, 1989–2013

Note: Retirement account savings include 401(k)s, IRAs, and Keogh plans.
Source: Morrissey (2016).

Situations Which May Necessitate Continued Dependence. Having a child with special medical or developmental needs and/or caring for an aging or ill parent often necessitates continued involvement and dependence within the parent-child relationship. Young adults who have mild developmental disabilities may be able to live independently, but are likely to require some routine support to ensure that their needs are being met. Those who have moderate to severe disabilities typically need more intensive caregiving, including housing and financial support and help with daily living skills. As parents age, they become increasingly aware of their caregiving limitations and own mortality, which can raise anxiety about their children's future, safety, and vulnerability for abuse (Thackeray & Eatough, 2015).

Parents may require assistance in planning how to meet children's special needs as they transition into adulthood; initiating the planning process at an early age is important and often beneficial. Once a child is diagnosed with a disability that has a significant impact on their ability to function independently, parents can usually gain access to various public assistance forms (e.g., Medicaid, Medicare, and Social Security). Continuation of financial support for young adults with exceptionalities can be accomplished through careful estate planning, which may include the establishment of a trust that specifies how funds or other assets should be dispersed over time (Wright, 2013). It is also important that parents make arrangements for guardianship protection in the event that they are no longer able to care for the child.

Although prolonged parenting of young adults has become increasingly common in American families, the opposite phenomenon (role reversal) is also becoming equally significant. People are living much longer, which means that aging parents may require significantly more assistance from their adult children, especially if they are unable to afford the high costs associated with the type of care they need. The National Alliance for Caregiving (NAC) and the AARP Public Policy Institute (2015) have produced a comprehensive report on caregiving in the United States. Several key findings include:

- Of the estimated 39.8 million American adults who provide care for another adult, 49 percent are caring for a parent or parent-in-law.
- Most caregivers are female and live with the person they are caring for.
- Caregivers spend an average of 24 hours per week providing care.
- Caregivers provide assistance with a variety of daily living activities (e.g., getting in and out of bed, bathing, preparing meals), instrumental support (e.g., transportation, shopping), and nursing tasks. Those who assist with multiple daily living activities report greater difficulty in fulfilling these responsibilities. Demands rise, but available time does not.
- Half of all caregivers feel that they had no choice but to assume the caregiver role. These individuals are more likely to report experiencing negative consequences related to the care they were providing.
- Caring for a parent is emotionally stressful.

Some caregivers face significant financial strain and personal work-related challenges (e.g., task completion difficulties, reduced work hours, transportation costs). Roach, Drummond, and Keady (2016) found that a parental illness diagnosis, such as early onset dementia, requires familial adjustment to the diagnosis, presents financial implications, and produces changes in the parent-adult child relationship. These challenges, in turn, influenced adult coping and involvement in meaningful activities. Adult children expressed worries about parental safety, observations of parental behavioral changes, and planning for parental wishes (e.g., residing in the family home as long as possible). Parent and family caregivers who engaged in non-caregiving activities (e.g., work, volunteering) were better able to cope with transitions that were related to a parent's illness.

Photo 12-5 Many adult children live with their parents while completing an education. Dragon Images/Shutterstock.com

In general, caregivers are more likely than non-caregivers to be diagnosed with depression, to report higher levels of worries, and to have health problems, such as high blood pressure and pain (Witters, 2011a, 2011b). Families that receive structured palliative care often have reduced physical and emotional stress associated with a parent's illness (Dionne-Odom et al., 2014). Adult children who are caring for parents should be encouraged to set aside time to care for themselves and to engage in pleasurable activities. They may also be eligible to receive financial support for the care they are providing (this varies by state; see www.Benefits.gov) or to access support services through their local area Agency on Aging (e.g., Meals-on-Wheels, transportation, respite care) to help reduce stress.

Renested Families. A recent Gallup poll found that it is quite common for children ages 18 to 23 years (51 percent; many of whom are still completing their education) to live with their parents. Perhaps a more surprising outcome of the poll is the response that 14 percent of children ages 24 to 34 years also reside in their parental home (Jones, 2014). Older children are more likely to live at home if they are not married, do not work full time, or have not graduated from college. Marriage is the strongest predictor of whether they will/will not live with their parents, likely because (a) it is less feasible to live at home with a spouse, and (b) because a spouse's second income provides additional financial resources that make it feasible to live independently. Adult children may also find it necessary to live at home due to high housing costs and a weak job market. Although living with family can provide support and be beneficial for some young adults and their parents, for others, it may interfere with their sense of autonomy and self-identity (Burn & Szoeke, 2015).

Reasons for remaining in the family home, or for returning to it at a later time, affect children's adjustment differently. For example, those who "boomerang" due to practical motivations (e.g., employment problems) are more likely to experience depressive symptoms compared to those with intrinsic motivations (e.g., enjoy living with parents) (Copp et al., 2015). A report from the Pew Research Foundation found that young adults (25- to 34-year-olds) are more likely to report that continuing to live with their parents or moving back into the family home has worked against the parent-child relationship (25 percent) (Parker, 2012). The return of children ages 18 to 24 years produced slightly less than half of the same response (12 percent). Younger adults report experiencing fewer negative feelings, perhaps because so many are currently living with their family today: 61 percent of adults surveyed knew someone who lives with their family; those who were living at home knew of other individuals in their same situation. Younger adults also tend to be more optimistic about their future. Educational level does not predict a return home for younger adults, but those without a college education are more likely to return in later years.

Photo 12-6 An advanced degree increases the likelihood that adult children will be able to establish their independence. g-stockstudio/Shutterstock.com

Children ages 18 to 23 years who are living at home experience slightly better physical health and access to basic necessities than those who are struggling financially and not living at home (Newport, 2014). However, young adults between the ages of 24 and 34 years who live at home are less likely to report that they are thriving, which is an indication of lower levels of well-being across several domains, including life evaluation, physical health, emotional health, healthy behaviors, and access to basic things that promote healthy living (Newport, 2014).

The effects associated with living in a renested family vary for parents as well as for adult children. Some find that living with an adult child can be mutually beneficial and positive if rules, roles, and responsibilities within the family are negotiated in advance. Other parents experience negative effects when adult children return home, including financial, social, and emotional stress (Burn & Szoeke, 2015). Living with grandchildren can also have a negative impact on health, stress level, and income stability (Ellis & Simmons, 2014). The number of multigenerational family configurations has increased significantly in recent decades: some 67 percent of coresident households are maintained by a grandparent (see Figure 12-4) (Ellis & Simmons, 2014). Native Hawaiian, American Indian/Alaska Native, Asian, and African American parents are more likely to live with grandchildren, but their level of responsibility varies: younger parents (under 60) and African American, Alaska Native, and White parents are more likely to be responsible for their grandchild's care than those

Figure 12-4 Households with Coresident Grandparents and Grandchildren

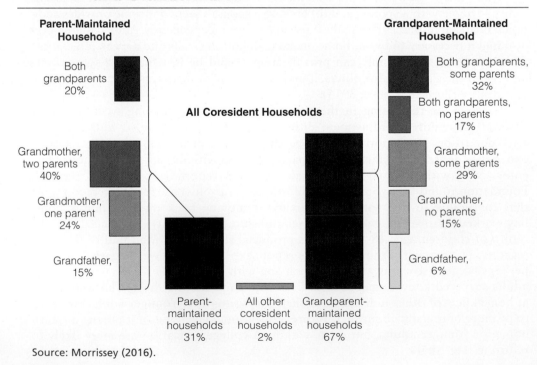

Source: Morrissey (2016).

Anese was the first person in her family to earn a college degree. Her parents had worked two jobs each to help pay for her tuition and living expenses so that she wouldn't have a large student loan to repay. Anese was grateful for the opportunity that they had made possible for her, and wanted to show her appreciation by "giving back" to society. She accepted a job in a large, nearby city as a middle school teacher in a primarily Hispanic school. However, she didn't find teaching or the salary particularly rewarding, so she resigned from her position at the end of the school year and decided to move back home. Anese plans to remain with her parents until she can decide what to do next.

According to U.S. Census data, an estimated 36 percent (21.6 million) of young adults between the ages of 18 and 31 years were living with their parents; more than half were between 18 and 24 years of age (2012). Men were more likely than women to return to their parent's home, and those who had some college education (43 percent) or only a high school degree (40 percent) comprised the majority (Fry, 2013). More often than not, these young adults were in between jobs or in jobs that they didn't find satisfying or intend to keep. Parents found these attitudes especially puzzling because they were counter to beliefs that they had held at the same age.

Krahn and Galambos (2014) compared the work values of Generation X (graduated from high school in 1985) and Generation Y (graduated from high school in 1996) young adults, and found distinct intrinsic and extrinsic differences. Generation Y young adults placed a high value on job entitlement and extrinsic rewards (e.g., salary, opportunity for promotion, job security), particularly during their early years of employment (18 to 25 years). These feelings were similarly expressed by individuals in both generational groups. However, they tended to be replaced by an increased interest in intrinsic rewards (e.g., independent decision-making, interesting work, feeling of accomplishment) among older (late twenties) Generation X individuals. Young adults who place a high value on extrinsic rewards are more likely to remain in their jobs than to move from one job to another. Krahn, Howard, & Galambos (2015) noted that a pattern of fluctuating employment is associated with lesser career development and much lower lifetime earnings.

Are the work-related expectations of Generation Y poor and/or incorrect, or might there be some positive aspects to consider? Why might Anese's parents view her job resignation as a failure on their part? What approach might her parents employ to help Anese analyze her situation and develop a new career plan?

who are Asian or Hispanic; as a result, they are more likely to experience stress associated with the living situation (Ellis & Simmons, 2014).

Management Strategies. An adult child's move back into their parental home often disrupts the family system, and causes imbalance or instability based upon family systems theory. Families that operate from implied rules and roles and have closed outside boundaries are more likely to experience problems with this transition. Families that successfully adjust, set explicit rules, roles, and routines are more likely to return to a state of homeostasis. Parenting practices that were once used with adolescent children are not likely to be effective with adult children because both parties have grown and developed different behavior patterns, routines, and expectations. Thus, it is imperative that the roles and expectations for parents and adult children be carefully redefined (Burn & Szoeke, 2015).

Photo 12-7 Ground rules and expectations must be worked out before adult children return to live with their parents. Iakov Filimonov/Shutterstock.com

Parents should discuss, negotiate, and agree upon familial arrangements and practices with adult children before they move in and begin living together (Suggestions for Parents 12-1). Families may also consider the development of a more formal agreement (contract) that outlines the expectations and conditions under which the living arrangement would be terminated.

Strategies to Increase Success of Parents Living with Their Adult Children

- Discuss and establish explicit roles and responsibilities (e.g., chores, food preparation, cleaning, child care).
- Develop an agreement related to household financial obligations (e.g., rent, food, supplies).
- Set clear expectations for respectful behavior (e.g., quiet times, language use).
- Negotiate limits and rules, use mutual problem solving when concerns arise.
- Use effective communication strategies.
- Allow for privacy within the home.
- Let adult children be responsible for their own behavior.
- Establish clear reasons to end the living arrangement (e.g., drugs, alcohol abuse, lack of assistance, or failure to make financial contributions.).

Responsive Parenting

Ms. Beacon's daughter, Hannah, and 3-year-old grandson, Ben, recently moved in with her following a divorce. She agreed to this arrangement because she knew that her daughter needed time to adjust, and she enjoyed spending time with her daughter and grandson. However, in recent weeks, Hannah has become more dependent upon her mother for Ben's daily care (e.g., taking him to and from daycare, preparing dinner, watching him on weekends when she goes out with her friends, putting him to bed), leaving little time to spend with her own activities and friends. In addition, Hannah has stopped paying her share of the rent that she had agreed to at the onset. How would you recommend that Ms. Beacon address this situation with her daughter?

Summary

- The term adult has different cultural meanings and, in Western societies, is often associated with the idea that children will move out of their parent's home, become financially independent, and establish a family of their own. Socioeconomic conditions have delayed and made this transition difficult for many young adults.
- The brain continues to undergo developmental changes until a person's late twenties. A young adult also experiences personality changes that tend to stabilize by the mid-twenties.
- Family dynamics and culture influence expectations about an adolescent's transition to adulthood. Parents who are overinvolved or psychologically controlling may prolong their adult child's dependence. Circumstances, such as having a child with special medical or developmental needs or a mental health problem may necessitate prolonged reliance on their parents.

- Renested families are becoming increasingly common, especially for younger adults who often move back home after finishing college. The effects of living with one's parents vary depending upon the motivation for moving back (i.e., practical or intrinsic) and parent's age; older adults often have greater difficulty making this adjustment.

- Living with an adult child requires that families formally renegotiate rules, roles, and expectations.

Questions for Discussion and Self-Reflection

1. What factors may be contributing to delayed adulthood in the United States and other Western countries?

2. What are some ways that parents can help their children transition successfully to adulthood that don't entail moving back home?

3. What roles and expectations should families establish before an adult child moves back home, and why is this step important?

4. What positive and negative consequences are associated with renesting in families?

Field Activities

1. Imagine that you are the parent of an 18-year-old daughter who has moderate cerebral palsy and uses a wheelchair. Develop a list of service agencies and resources in your area that may provide beneficial support to you and your family. Prepare a similar list of services that would assist with long-term care for an older family member.

2. A 22-year-old is planning to return home to live with his/her parents because he/she has recently graduated from college, but is unable to find work. Develop a sample written contract agreement for the family.

3. Survey your classmates to learn about their current living arrangements. What do they consider to be the positives and negatives associated with this arrangement? For those who are living with their parents, how would they describe their current relationship?

REFERENCES

Adams, B., Abubakar, A., Van de Vijver, F., De Bruin, G., Arasa, J., Fomba, E., . . . & Murugami, M. (2016). Ethnic identity in emerging adults in Sub-Saharan Africa and the USA, and its associations with psychological well-being. *Journal of Community & Applied Social Psychology, 26*(3), 236–252.

Aries, P. (1962). *Centuries of childhood: A social history of family life.* New York: Vintage Books.

Arnett, J. (2006). *Emerging adulthood: The winding road from the late teens through the twenties.* New York: Oxford University Press.

Barrasso-Catanzaro, C., & Eslinger, P. (2016). Neurobiological bases of executive function and social-emotional development: Typical and atypical brain changes. *Family Relations, 65*(1), 108–119.

Birkeland, M., Leversen, I., Torsheim, T., & Wold, B. (2014). Pathways to adulthood and their precursors and outcomes. *Scandinavian Journal of Psychology, 55*(1), 26–32.

Bleidorn, W. (2015). What accounts for personality maturation in early adulthood? *Current Directions in Psychological Science, 24*(3), 245–252.

Bleidorn, W., Klimstra, T., Denissen, J., Rentfrow, P., Potter, J., & Gosling, S. (2013). Personality maturation around the world: A cross-cultural examination of social-investment theory. *Psychological Science, 24*(12), 2530–2540.

Britton, M. (2013). Race/ethnicity, attitudes, and living with parents during young adulthood. *Journal of Marriage and Family, 75*(4), 995–1013.

Burn, K., & Szoeke, C. (2015). Boomerang families and failure-to-launch: Commentary on adult children living at home. *Maturitas, 83*, 9–12.

Copp, J., Giordano, P., Longmore, M., & Manning, W. (2015). Living with parents and emerging adults' depressive symptoms. *Journal of Family Issues*. Advance online publication. doi: 10.1177/0192513X15617797.

Costa, S., Soenens, B., Gugliandolo, M., Cuzzocrea, F., & Larcan, R. (2015). The mediating role of experiences of need satisfaction in associations between parental psychological control and internalizing problems: A study among Italian college students. *Journal of Child and Family Studies, 24*(4), 1106–1116.

D'amico, E., Julien, D., Tremblay, N., & Chartrand, E. (2015). Gay, lesbian, and bisexual youths coming out to their parents: Parental reactions and youths' outcomes. *Journal of GLBT Family Studies, 11*(5), 411–437.

Dettling, L., & Hsu, J. (2014). Returning to the nest: Debt and parental co-residence among young adults. Federal Reserve Board. Retrieved May 22, 2016 from http://www.federalreserve .gov/econresdata/feds/2014/files/201480pap.pdf.

Dionne-Odom, J., Kono, A., Frost, J., Jackson, L., Ellis, D., Ahmed, A., . . . & Bakitas, M. (2014). Translating and testing the ENABLE: CHF-PC concurrent palliative care model for older adults with heart failure and their family caregivers. *Journal of Palliative Medicine, 17*(9), 995–1004.

Eliason, S., Mortimer, J., & Vuolo, M. (2015). The transition to adulthood: Life course structures and subjective perceptions. *Social Psychology Quarterly, 78*(3), 205–227.

Ellis, R., & Simmons, T. (2014). Coresident grandparents and their grandchildren: 2012. *Current Population Reports*, P20-576. Washington, DC: U.S. Census Bureau.

Erikson, E. (1963). *Childhood and society* (2nd Ed). New York: W.W. Norton.

Fingerman, K., Kyungmin, K., Eden, D., Furstenberg, F., Birditt, K., & Zarit, S. (2015). 'I'll give you the world': Socioeconomic differences in parental support of adult children. *Journal of Marriage and Family, 77*(4), 844–865.

Fry, R. (2013). A rising share of young adults live in their parents' home. Pew Research Center. Retrieved May 22, 2016 from http://www.pewsocialtrends.org/2013/08/01/a-rising-share-of -young-adults-live-in-their-parents-home/.

Giedd, J. (2004). Structural magnetic resonance imaging of the adolescent brain. *Annals of the New York Academy of Sciences, 1021*, 77–85.

Goodsell, T., James, S., Yorgason, J., & Vaughn, R. (2015). Intergenerational assistance to adult children: Gender and number of sisters and brothers. *Journal of Family Issues, 36*(8), 979–1000.

Gordon, M., & Cui, M. (2015). Positive parenting during adolescence and career success in young adulthood. *Journal of Child and Family Studies, 24*(3), 762–771.

Hu, F., & Chou, K. (2016). Understanding the transition to independent living among urban youth: A decomposition analysis for Hong Kong. *Habitat International, 51*, 141–148.

Inguglia, C., Ingoglia, S., Liga, F., Lo Coco, A., & Lo Cricchio, M. (2015). Autonomy and relatedness in adolescence and emerging adulthood: Relationships with parental support and psychological distress. *Journal of Adult Development, 22*(1), 1–13.

Johnson, S., Blum, R., & Giedd, J. (2009). Adolescent maturity and the brain: The promise and pitfalls of neuroscience research in adolescent health policy. *Journal of Adolescent Health, 45*(3), 216–221.

Jones, J. (2014). In U.S., 14% of those aged 24 to 34 are living with parents. Gallup. Retrieved May 16, 2016 from http://www.gallup.com/poll/167426/aged-living-parents.aspx.

Kalmijn, M. (2013). Adult children's relationships with married parents, divorced parents, and stepparents: Biology, marriage, or residence? *Journal of Marriage and Family, 75*(5), 1181–1193.

Keijer, M., Nagel, I., & Liefbroer, A. (2016). Effects of parental cultural and economic status on adolescents' life course preferences. *European Sociological Review*. First published online. doi:10.1093/esr/jcw007.

Krahn, H., & Galambos, N. (2014). Work values and beliefs of "Generation X" and "Generation Y." *Journal of Youth Studies, 17*(1), 92–112.

Krahn, H., Howard, A., & Galambos, N. (2015). Exploring or floundering? The meaning of employment and educational fluctuations in emerging adulthood. *Youth Society, 47(2),* 245–266.

Lebel, C., & Beaulieu, C. (2011). Longitudinal development of human brain wiring continues from childhood into adulthood. *Journal of Neuroscience, 31*(30), 10937–10947.

Lee, C., & Goldstein, S. (2016). Loneliness, stress, and social support in young adulthood: Does the source of support matter? *Journal of Youth and Adolescence, 45*(3), 568–580.

Lei, L., & South, S. (2016). Racial and ethnic differences in leaving and returning to the parental home: The role of life course transitions, socioeconomic resources, and family connectivity. *Demographic Research, 34*(4), 109–142.

Lindgren, E., Söderberg, S., & Skär, L. (2016). Being a parent to a young adult with mental illness in transition to adulthood. *Issues in Mental Health Nursing, 37*(2), 98–105.

Lui, P. (2015). Intergenerational conflict, mental health, and educational outcomes among Asian and Latino/a Americans: Qualitative and meta-analytic review. *Psychological Bulletin, 141*(2), 404–446.

Mageau, G., Ranger, F., Koestner, R., Moreau, E., & Forest, J. (2015). Validation of the Perceived Parental Autonomy Support Scale (P-PASS). *Canadian Journal of Behavioural Science, 47*(3), 251–262.

Mayseless, O., & Scharf, M. (2009). Too close for comfort: Inadequate boundaries with parents and individuation in late adolescent girls. *American Journal of Orthopsychiatry, 79*(2), 191–202.

Morrissey, M. (2016). The state of American retirement: How 401(k)s have failed most American workers. Economic Policy Institute. Retrieved May 22, 2016 from http://www.epi.org/publication/retirement-in-america/.

National Alliance for Caregiving (NAC) and the AARP Public Policy Institute. (2015). *Caregiving in the U.S. 2015.* Retrieved May 17, 2016 from http://www.caregiving.org/wp-content/uploads/2015/05/2015_CaregivingintheUS_Final-Report-June-4_WEB.pdf.

Nelson, L., Padilla-Walker, L., & Nielson, M. (2015). Is hovering smothering or loving? An examination of parental warmth as a moderator of relations between helicopter parenting and emerging adults' indices of adjustment. *Emerging Adulthood, 3*(4), 282–285.

Newport, F. (2014). Young adults living at home less likely to be "thriving." Gallup. Retrieved May 16, 2016 from http://www.gallup.com/poll/167429/young-adults-living-home-less-likely-thriving.aspx?g_source=living with parents&g_medium=search&g_campaign=tiles.

Oman, R., Vesely, S., Aspy, C., & Tolma, E. (2015). Prospective associations among assets and successful transition to early adulthood. *American Journal of Public Health, 105*(1), e51–e56.

Parker, K. (2012). The boomerang generation: Feeling ok about living with mom and dad. Pew Research Center. Retrieved May 15, 2016 from http://www.pewsocialtrends.org/2012/03/15/the-boomerang-generation/.

Parra, A., Oliva, A., & Reina, M. (2015). Family relationships from adolescence to emerging adulthood: A longitudinal study. *Journal of Family Issues, 36*(14), 2002–2020.

Penke, L., & Jokela, M. (2016). The evolutionary genetics of personality revisited. *Current Opinion, in Psychology, 7*, 104–109.

Raznahan, A., Shaw, P., Lerch, J., Clasen, L., Greenstein, D., Berman, R., . . . & Giedd, J. (2014). Longitudinal four-dimensional mapping of subcortical anatomy in human development. *Proceedings of the National Academy of Sciences of the United States of America, 111*(4), 1592–1597.

Roach, P., Drummond, N., & Keady, J. (2016). 'Nobody would say that it is Alzheimer's or dementia at this age': Family adjustment following a diagnosis of early-onset dementia. *Journal of Aging Studies, 36*, 26–32.

Rousseau, S., & Scharf, M. (2015). "I will guide you" The indirect link between overparenting and young adults' adjustment. *Psychiatry Research, 228*(3), 826–834.

Roy, K., Messina, L., Smith, J., & Waters, D. (2014). Growing up as "Man of the house": Adultification and transition into adulthood for young men in economically disadvantaged families. *New Directions for Child and Adolescent Development, 2014*(143), 55–72.

Sandberg-Thoma, S., Snyder, A., & Jang, B. (2015). Exiting and returning to the parental home for boomerang kids. *Journal of Marriage and Family, 77*(3), 806–818.

Silvers, J., Shu, J., Hubbard, A., Weber, J., & Ochsner, K. (2015). Concurrent and lasting effects of emotion regulation on amygdala response in adolescence and young adulthood. *Developmental Science, 18*(5), 771–784.

South, S., & Lei, L. (2015). Failures-to-launch and boomerang kids: Contemporary determinants of leaving and returning to the parental home. *Social Forces, 94*(2), 863–890.

Thackeray, L., & Eatough, V. (2015). 'Well the future, that is difficult': A hermeneutic phenomenological analysis exploring the maternal experience of parenting a young adult with a developmental disability. *Journal of Applied Research in Intellectual Disabilities, 28*(4), 265–275.

Witters, D. (2011a). In U.S., caregivers' emotional health often suffers. Gallup. Retrieved May 17, 2016 from http://www.gallup.com/poll/147815/Caregivers-Emotional-Health-Often -Suffers.aspx.

Witters, D. (2011b). In U.S., caregivers suffer from poorer physical health. Gallup. Retrieved May 17, 2016 from http://www.gallup.com/poll/145940/Caregivers-Suffer-Poorer-Physical -Health.aspx.

Wright, P. (2013). Special needs: Planning for the future. Retrieved May 18, 2016 from http://www.wrightslaw.com/info/future.plan.index.htm.

Yeung, W., & Hu, S. (2013). Coming of age in times of change: The transition to adulthood in China. *The Annals of the American Academy of Political and Social Science*, 646(1), 149–171.

Zeng, R., & Greenfield, P. (2015). Cultural evolution over the last 40 years in China: Using the Google Ngram Viewer to study implications of social and political change for cultural values. *International Journal of Psychology, 50*, 47–55.

Family Violence and Child Maltreatment

13

LEARNING OBJECTIVES

After reading the chapter, you will be able to:

13-1 Identify the family violence theories.

13-2 Describe the adult, child, environmental, and cultural factors that increase the likelihood of household violence.

13-3 Understand how victims and their children are affected by intimate partner violence.

13-4 Discuss the different child maltreatment forms and their indicators.

13-5 Explain legal and professional obligations associated with the identification and reporting of child maltreatment.

13-6 Provide examples of how parents and the community can support and strengthen children's resilience to maltreatment.

naeyc Standards Linked to Chapter Content

1a, 1b, and 1c: Promoting child development and learning

2a, and 2b: Building family and community relationships

6b: Growing as a professional

Family violence and **child** maltreatment are significant concerns in the United States. Hundreds of thousands of children are victims of violence every year, and over half of all children will be exposed to violence at home or in their community (U.S. DHHS, 2016; Finkelhor, 2015).

continued on following page

Family violence can be defined as "any act or omission by persons who are cohabitating that results in serious injury to other members of the family." Serious injury can be physical, emotional, or the restriction or violation of another's rights (Wallace & Roberson, 2014, p. 3). Child maltreatment may occur within or outside of the family, and involve abuse or neglect that is committed by any adult the child encounters. Professionals play an important role in observing children's well-being and taking steps to protect them from intentional harm. ∎

child a minor under the age of eighteen years.

13-1 Theoretical Models

Several models have been proposed to explain why child abuse and neglect are more likely to occur, and what steps can be taken to prevent their repetition.

13-1a Psychiatric: Psychopathology and Substance Abuse

The *psychiatric model* assumes that individuals who are abusive towards family members are deviant, mentally ill, or substance abusers. In other words, the illness (psychopathology) causes them to engage in violent or neglectful behavior. Although psychiatric disorders are associated with increased risk of child maltreatment, not all individuals who have a mental illness become abusive or neglectful, or vice versa. Researchers have not been able to identify specific psychological characteristics or personality traits that are consistent and can be used in practice to prevent abuse (Wallace & Roberson, 2014).

It is also commonly assumed that substance abuse (e.g., excessive alcohol consumption, drug use) causes maltreatment. Although substance use may impair a parent's judgment and increase the likelihood of maltreatment, researchers have not found a direct path or causal relationship between the two (Wallace & Roberson, 2014). In other words, there may be factors in addition to substance use that contribute to the incidence of maltreatment. For example, the context in which alcohol consumption occurs may be more influential than the amount of alcohol consumed. Freisthler, Wolf, and Johnson-Motoyama (2015) found that parents who drink with friends are more likely to leave their child alone at home, a potentially neglectful behavior; those who drink with family were less likely to leave children unattended, but they often did not provide proper monitoring by an adult or similarly responsible person.

13-1b Sociocultural: The Culture of Violence and Patriarchy

The *culture of violence theory* presumes that there are societal subcultures within which individuals learn violent behaviors and are socialized to view these behaviors as acceptable (Wallace & Roberson, 2014). Violence is prevalent throughout the general U.S. population, although it is more likely to occur in urban minority neighborhoods. Many children's television shows model and reinforce aggression, which is subsequently associated with increases in aggressive behaviors (Ostrav, Gentile, & Mullins, 2013). Video games (e.g., points for killing characters), sports (e.g., hitting others in hockey or football), and toys (e.g., guns, light sabers) also depict and reinforce violent behaviors.

The *patriarchy model* emphasizes the acceptance of male dominance as a major cause of family violence. A power differential between men and women continues to exist, and is pervasive in some cultures where women are viewed as possessions. In this model, violence is believed to be one way to establish control and maintain power over people who are viewed as being in subordinate positions. Bartolomei (2015) interviewed abused women who confirmed that one of the most difficult problems related to violence towards women is that patriarchal and sexist attitudes result in legitimization of violence, which may lead to stigmatizing or blaming the victim. The patriarchy model does not address or account for the violence towards men.

13-1c Social-Psychological: Social Learning and Ecological Theory

Social learning theory stresses the concept that violent behavior is learned and, therefore, often leads to generational patterns of violence. Adults within the child's environment serve as models that children emulate. Children observe adult behaviors (e.g., aggression, name calling, threats) and consequences (e.g., makes the person stop doing something, causes the person to do what they wanted). The more often children view such behaviors, the more likely they are to consider them acceptable and appropriate ways to deal with frustration and stress (Kimber et al., 2015). Parents may also unknowingly reinforce inappropriate behaviors that children observe, thus strengthening the likelihood that they will demonstrate the same behavior in the future. For example, if a parent laughs when one child attacks another child in order to retrieve a toy, the child is more likely to repeat the behavior, because it was: a) reinforced by the parent's attention, and b) successful in gaining access to the desired toy.

The *exchange* or *social control theory* suggests that violence occurs when the rewards (e.g., personal gratification) for committing violent behavior are greater than the penalties. In other words, individuals carefully weigh the benefits and costs for engaging in abusive behaviors. Violence, therefore, is often more prevalent in private or closed family systems because there are fewer social costs or controls associated with the abusive behaviors (Wallace & Roberson, 2014). Critics have raised concern that social-psychological theories do not have an explanation for spontaneous forms of aggression. For example, a parent who has never before engaged in violent behavior spontaneously hits a crying child (Wallace & Roberson, 2014).

Ecological theory examines maltreatment from a systems perspective and attempts to explain violence as a consequence of interacting level variables (e.g., individual, community, society). Huang et al. (2015) explained that children are affected not only by their direct relationships (microsystem) but also by the interactions that occur among caregivers (mesosystem) even if there is no direct contact with a perpetrator. For example, a child may not witness violence or unresolved disagreements between parents but their interactions with the child are likely to be different than if parents had a positive relationship and resolved their disagreements amicably.

School policies and accessible support organizations can influence the extent to which basic needs are met within a family (exosystem features). For example, stress increases as socioeconomic disadvantage, housing instability, single parenting, and limited access to resources and social support increase. The result of unmet needs may, in turn, contribute to increased maltreatment (Mohammad et al., 2015). Cultural beliefs and values also serve as exosytemic features that may influence the acceptability, prevalence, and rate of violence and aggression within families. Lastly, factors of time, such as divorce or exposure to war or terrorism, influence how violence is viewed and used (chronosystem features).

Garbarino (1977) outlined two specific conditions that must be in place for maltreatment to occur from an ecological systems perspective: a) a culture that supports the use of physical force against children and b) an inadequate availability and use of support systems. He noted that maltreatment arises when there is a mismatch between the parent, child, and family to the neighborhood and community.

Photo 13-1 Child maltreatment is a complex problem that is influenced by individual, relationship, community, and societal factors.

13-2 Characteristics of Violent and Neglectful Households

Researchers have identified a combination of factors which increase the likelihood that family violence and/or child maltreatment will occur.

13-2a Adult Factors

Adults from all walks of life (e.g., socioeconomic, religious, education, urban and rural settings) may become abusive or neglectful. Specific adult characteristics that are commonly associated with child maltreatment include history of child abuse, substance misuse, criminality, and violence towards others outside of the family (González et al., 2016). Parents who have significant mental health concerns, such as schizophrenia, bipolar disorder, or depression are also more likely to engage in abuse or neglect. Berthelot et al. (2015) found that child maltreatment occurred in 46 percent of such families, compared to 30 percent of families in the general population.

Adults who were abused during childhood, particularly women, are at increased risk for developing psychiatric disorders and abusing children in their care (Widom, Czaja, & DuMont, 2015; Medley & Sachs-Ericsson, 2009). Leach et al. (2016) did not find a similarly strong relationship between childhood male sexual abuse and subsequent abuse of children. Specifically, the authors found that only a small proportion (3 percent) became adult sex offenders. However, **polyvictimization** significantly increased the risk of becoming an adult offender (Leach, Stewart & Smallbone, 2016).

The likelihood of maltreatment may also be influenced by parental understanding of child development, tolerance levels, and acceptable reactivity to typical childhood misbehaviors. Parents who approve of harsher disciplinary practices, and those who interpret child misbehavior negatively, or do not show empathy with the child's perspective are at increased risk of using harsh parenting practices which may turn into child maltreatment at some time in the future (Rodriguez, Smith, & Silvia, 2016). Parental stress levels and relationship satisfaction may also affect the way children are treated within a family. In fact, rates of **emotional abuse** and sibling victimization are higher in families in which there is frequent parental conflict (Turner et al., 2012).

Alcohol usage, coupled with specific personality traits and exosystem factors such as unemployment, is associated with increased intimate partner violence and child maltreatment (Choenni, Hammink, & van de Mheen, 2015). Substance abuse combined with psychiatric problems decreases parental nurturance, compromises child safety, and increases the risk for abuse and safety concerns (Turner et al., 2012).

13-2b Child Characteristics

Children, particularly males, under the age of 1 year are at the highest risk for **physical abuse** (see Figure 13-1) (Afifi et al., 2015; King et al., 2015). Girls between the ages

---

polyvictimization
exposure to multiple maltreatment forms (e.g., physical, sexual, neglect).

emotional abuse
a pattern of verbal assaults, such as threats and intimidation, that have a negative effect on a child's emotional well-being and sense of self-worth.

physical abuse
non-accidental injuries inflicted upon a child by an adult.

Responsive Parenting

Two-year-old Jake was playing with his cars at the table. He reached across to grab his favorite blue car and knocked an expensive vase off of the table. Water spilled across the floor and the vase broke into pieces. His mother came running into the room and yelled, "You made another mess, I told you to be careful! What's wrong with you?!" She grabbed him, spanked his bottom and threw him on the sofa in the living room. How did Jake's mother interpret his behavior? What adult characteristics and theory or theories of violence might explain his mother's reaction? What information about toddler development would be useful for her to know? What would be a more positive way for Jake's mother to prevent and handle the behavior?

Figure 13-1 Victimization Rates by Gender and Age from 2010–2014

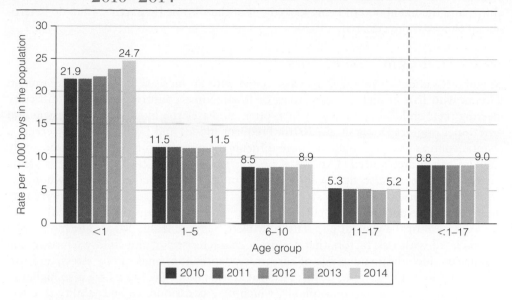

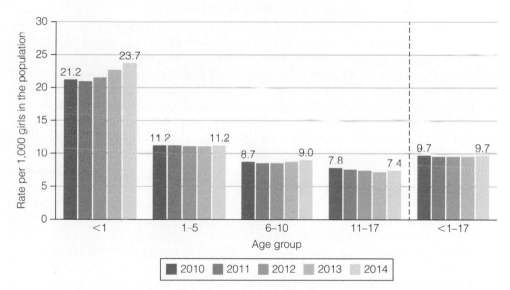

Source: U.S. Department of Health & Human Services (2016).

of 2 and 17 years are more likely to be victims of sexual abuse. More than 60 percent of the children who experienced sexual abuse were also subjected to physical abuse (polyvictimization) (Afifi et al., 2015). Rates of abusive and neglectful treatment are also notably high among infants who are born prematurely or with low birth weight (Risch et al., 2014). These infants are often more irritable and difficult to manage during the 1st year than are full-term infants, due to their immature development.

Children who have a difficult temperament and those with functional impairments (e.g., physical, intellectual, behavioral) are also at increased risk for maltreatment (Palusci, Datner, & Wilkins, 2015). For example, children who demonstrate hostile and oppositional behavior and have frequent temper outbursts often have caregivers who tend to user harsher forms of punishment to control the child's behavior (Lin et al., 2016). In turn, the harsh punishment may escalate the child's negative behavior and create a coercive cycle of control.

Statistical maltreatment data suggest that minority children are at significantly greater risk for maltreatment than are Caucasian children. However, researchers have found that this difference is strongly correlated with poverty and living in a single-parent household, and not minority status (Afifi et al., 2015; Lanier et al., 2014). Lesbian, gay, bisexual, and transgender children also report more physical, emotional, and sexual abuse, and the likelihood of being kicked out of their home by parents, than do heterosexual children (Snyder et al., 2016).

13-2c Environmental Factors

Neighborhood disadvantage is also associated with an increase in child maltreatment. Parents who live in high poverty areas or low-income countries may have difficulty meeting their child's basic needs, which often increases the likelihood of physical and **emotional neglect** (Viola et al., 2016). Frequent moves and family adversity create a chaotic context that also make it more difficult for parents to monitor and effectively respond to children's needs (Afifi et al., 2015; Turner et al., 2012). Rates of intimate partner violence are also significantly higher among these families, many of whom are involved with the child welfare system. Estimates are that approximately 36 percent of these partners experience personal violence during their lifetime, compared with about 1 to 6 percent of the general population (Millett, Seay, & Kohl, 2015). The higher rate is associated with risk factors that are often characteristic of the child welfare system population, including young age of caregivers, depression, high family stress, and low social support (Millett et al., 2015). Physical abuse and neglect rates are also higher in families when services are unavailable, which may contribute to an inability to effectively cope with stress (Maguire-Jack & Negash, 2016).

Nearly 60 percent of children and adolescents are exposed to violence in their home, school, or community every year (Finkelhor et al., 2015). Rates of exposure are even higher (80 to 90 percent) in poor urban areas, single-parent households, and for African American youth who experience more violence across all socioeconomic classes (Mohammad et al., 2015; Mrug, Madan, & Windle, 2015). There is increasing evidence that individuals who are exposed to repeated violence become desensitized to its effects, especially when the violence happens across different settings. Observing a person being beaten on the street typically brings about strong, often empathetic emotions. However, if a person is repeatedly exposed to such violence, their emotional response lessens, which can decrease empathetic feelings and desire to help others; repeated exposure may also increase the likelihood that the observer would become violent with others (Mrug, Madan, & Windle, 2015). Similarly, exposure to media violence may lead to desensitization, which is associated with lower behavioral inhibition, increased aggression, and decreased prosocial behavior (Stockdale et al., 2015). Overall, exposure to violence in multiple settings may lead to more family violence, because the violent behaviors are modeled more frequently, the responses become more acceptable, and the emotional reaction that would typically keep a person from harming others is no longer experienced.

13-2d Cultural Context and Differences

Cultural context also has an impact on how family violence is viewed and when violence is most likely to occur. Native American, Alaska Native, and African American children are at higher risk for maltreatment, which may be related to a lack of appropriate services to meet families' needs, to intra-system discrimination, and to problems with jurisdictional responsibility for addressing child maltreatment (Commission to Eliminate Child Abuse and Neglect Fatalities [CECANF], 2016). The lack of services to meet basic needs often leads to increased stress within the family system, which is associated with higher rates of violence. In addition, individuals may be more prone to report or prosecute violence towards children from these ethnic groups due to underlying prejudice. Furthermore, confusion and difficulty navigating legal systems are common on tribal reservations because responsibility for protection and prosecution of perpetrators varies by state and reservation (i.e., sometimes the responsibility lies with the tribe, sometimes with the state, and sometimes with the federal government or a

---

emotional neglect an adult's failure to attend and be responsive to a child's social and emotional needs.

combination of the three), which can result in a longer time period before action is taken and services are provided. The acceptability of fathers' use of harsher discipline practices within a culture may also lead to different effects on children. For example, fathers are viewed as strict disciplinarians in the Chinese culture; children exposed to harsh physical punishment by Chinese fathers were less likely to develop anxiety symptoms than those whose mothers also used physical forms of punishment (Wang et al., 2016).

Chrombach and Bambonyé (2016) explored factors that increase risk for child maltreatment in an African country. They found that men were more likely to act violently towards their children when they perceived their partner as an intimidating person. This may be related to an assumption that aggression is the way to reassert their manhood in a culture where violence is trivialized when women are the perpetrators. New immigrants are also at risk for perpetrating intimate partner violence or child maltreatment due to the many stressors that are involved in the transition to a new country. Stressors may include loss of family ties in the country of origin, financial difficulties, language challenges, and differences in gender role expectations and parenting practices between the country of origin and the new dominant culture (Kimber et al., 2015).

Photo 13-2 Stress and the acceptability of harsh disciplinary practices place children in immigrant families at increased risk for maltreatment.

13-3 Intimate Partner Violence

Intimate partner violence is a significant issue in the United States. Approximately 19 percent of women and about 2 percent of men are raped; severe physical violence affects about 22 percent of women and 14 percent of men during their lifetimes (Breiding et al., 2014). Men are more likely to be victims of physical abuse; women are more likely to be victims of multiple forms of violence including rape, physical abuse, and stalking (Breiding et al., 2014).

Why do victims stay in such dangerous relationships? Reasons that are often cited include the cycle of abuse, poor self-esteem, feelings of helplessness, fear of retaliation, economic and/or religious reasons, or a desire to maintain the family system whatever the costs. Victims often experience significant effects, including job absenteeism, job loss due to illness or physical harm, social isolation, and safety concerns (Bartolomei, 2016) (see Figure 13-2). Victimization can also lead to increased stress that, in turn, has a negative impact on the parent's ability to provide good parenting practices for children (Telman et al., 2016). In addition, there is a strong relationship between intimate partner violence and child maltreatment; children who try to intervene in a parental dispute or try to prevent harm to a sibling are at the highest risk for harm to themselves (Smith & Eklund, 2016).

Intimate partner violence can affect children even if they are not the direct recipient of the abusive behavior. Boys who witness violence between their parents are more likely to display clinically significant externalizing and internalizing problems. In particular, they show higher rates of aggression and hostility and are more likely to become violent in future intimate partner relationships (Blair et al., 2015; González et al., 2016). Girls are more likely to show internalizing problems such as depression and anxiety, and often try to behave 'perfectly' in the hopes of diffusing parental fighting (Blair et al., 2015). Exposure to violence also increases the risk of early delinquency, which has profound negative effects on academic achievement (Huang et al., 2015).

Not all children who are exposed to intimate partner violence show problematic symptoms. However, children are more likely to meet criteria for post-traumatic stress

Figure 13-2 Lifetime Prevalence of Contact Sexual Violence, Physical Violence, or Stalking by an Intimate Partner with Intimate Partner Violence (IPV)-Related Impact, by Sex

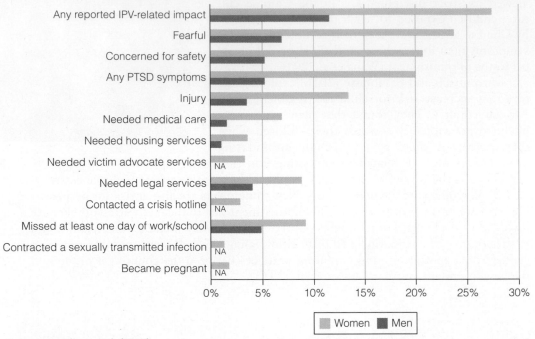

Source: Breiding et al. (2014).

disorder (PTSD) when the violence is chronic, and/or severe, there are high levels of parental stress, and when additional stressful life events, such as divorce, parent incarceration, or residence relocation are present (Telman et al., 2016). In addition, the process that underlies partner violence appears important for predicting the effect violence will have on children. Jouriles and McDonald (2014) found that beyond the frequency of violence, children showed poorer adjustment when the violence was coercive (i.e., hostile, threatening, controlling, intended to make someone do what the person wants) versus violence committed for other reasons.

13-4 Child Maltreatment

Data collected by the U.S. Department of Health and Human Services (U.S. DHHS, 2016) show that in 2014, 702,000 children were victims of maltreatment. Of those, 75 percent were victims of neglect, 17 percent suffered physical abuse, and about 8 percent experienced sexual abuse (see Figure 13-3). Approximately 1,580 children died in 2014 as a result of neglect or abuse; the majority of those were under the age of 3 years. In most cases (78 percent), the perpetrator was the victim's parent; most perpetrators were female (54 percent). In 3.4 percent of maltreatment cases, the perpetrator was unknown to the child or the child's family (i.e., not related, not a caretaker, and not a family friend). Many children were exposed to multiple forms of victimization (i.e., polyvictimization) including physical, emotional or sexual abuse, neglect, and/or witnessing family violence (Turner et al., 2012).

13-4a Physical Neglect

Physical neglect involves a family's failure to provide for a child's basic physical needs and care, such as food, clean and safe housing, and appropriate clothing. In recent years, medical neglect, which is defined as the failure to obtain necessary medical care,

physical neglect an adult's failure to provide for the child's basic physical and medical needs and care, including access to food, clean and safe housing, and appropriate clothing.

Figure 13-3 Reported Abuse and Neglect among Children under Age 18 years, by Type of Maltreatment (2012)

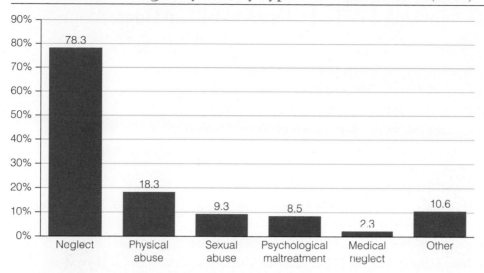

Notes: Estimates do not total 100 percent, as children may experience more than one type of maltreatment. "Other" includes types of maltreatment not mentioned above such as threats of abuse or congenital drug addiction.

Source: U.S. Department of Health & Human Services (2012).

thereby placing the child at risk for disability or death, also has been considered a form of physical neglect (see "Trending Now: Medical Neglect and Religious Beliefs"). Physical neglect can have significant implications for children's health and well-being, with most fatalities due to malnourishment or lack of appropriate supervision (e.g., toddler drowns in a pool or bathtub) (CECANF, 2016).

Failure to protect children from endangerment is another form of physical neglect. For example, provision of alcohol, nicotine, or illegal substances to underage children places them in potentially dangerous situations; adults can be prosecuted for allowing children access to these substances. Adults also can be held liable for leaving children unattended (e.g., locked in a car, left home alone to care for a younger sibling). Some states have laws that establish minimum age requirements for when a child can be at home without an adult present (e.g., age 14 years in Illinois, 8 years in Maryland, and 10 years in Oregon). However, most states consider one or more of the following factors to determine if a child may be at risk (Child Welfare Information Gateway, 2013):

- child's age
- mental ability
- physical condition
- length of the parent's absence
- home environment

Caregivers should always consult state recommendations to determine if and when it is appropriate to leave children home alone, as well as the child's readiness to be left alone (Suggestions for Parents 13-1). If parents do not feel that their child is ready to

Photo 13-3 Parents must be aware of state laws and consider their children's maturity before leaving them home alone.

Determining if a Child is Ready to Be Left Home Alone

Questions to determine if a child is ready to be left home alone:

- What are the state laws or recommendations?
- Is the child able to care for him- or herself?
- Is the child able to follow rules and demonstrate maturity?
- Does the child know how to respond to stressful or unsafe situations that may arise?
- Does the child know how to contact the parent or another trusted adult in case of an emergency?
- Does the child feel comfortable being left alone?
- How long will the child be alone? Does the child have the skills to stay alone for the length of time required, or to manage preparations that may be needed (e.g., dinner, snack)?
- If other children will also be left home, is the older child prepared to care for them?
- Is the home environment safe (e.g., are dangerous items such as firearms, medications, cleaning materials locked up)?

Preparing your child for being left home alone:

- Review what to do in case of emergencies.
- Set clear rules for behavior and activities that are allowed when home alone.
- Practice how to handle different situations that may arise (e.g., someone coming to the door, answering the telephone).
- Practice leaving your child home alone for brief periods, gradually increasing the amount of time until a child demonstrates that he/she is comfortable.
- Set times to check in with the child during the period when he/she is alone.

Adapted from: Child Welfare Information Gateway (2013).

⌄⌄ Professional Resource Download

manage this responsibility, they should arrange for care with a family member, vetted babysitter, youth organization, or respite services.

13-4b Emotional Neglect

Parents who are emotionally neglectful may not be responsive to a child's distress or social needs, or they may require children to complete tasks that are unsafe or beyond their ability (Teicher & Samson, 2016). For example, a parent may not show affection (e.g., hugging, kissing, touching) or provide a sufficient amount of attention (e.g., talking and conversing, proximity) needed to establish a strong attachment or support children's development. Infants who are exposed to emotional neglect may show slower physical growth and development due to the lack of nurturing interactions or mental stimulation (Marotz, 2015).

Children who do not establish a secure attachment are also at risk for future problems, such as disruptive and emotional disorders (Allely et al., 2013). In addition, they are more likely to have problems with interpersonal relationships within and outside of the family unit (Lin et al., 2016). Geoffroy et al. (2016) found that child neglect was

Medical neglect may occur for several reasons, including economic hardship, lack of access to care, lack of information about available treatments, limited trust in medical providers, cognitive impairment in caregivers, and perhaps (a controversial reason), religious beliefs (Jenny, 2007). The Child Abuse Prevention and Treatment Act (CAPTA) specifies that there is no federal requirement for a parent to provide medical treatment that is against their religious beliefs. However, medical neglect definitions and repercussions for parents who do not provide potentially lifesaving medical care for their children vary from state to state. For example, two families living in different states each have a child with type I diabetes. The parents in both families decide to forgo medical treatment for their child because the procedures violate their religious convictions. The children develop complications and become progressively more ill. The parents and community members in both cases pray and provide care in accord with their beliefs. Both children die as a result of their untreated illnesses. The parents of one family are prosecuted for criminal negligence, while the other parents are protected by their state's law and no legal charges are filed.

Significant conflicts arise in such cases if persons outside of the religious group are notified that children are not receiving care that could potentially save their lives. In the United States, 31 states provide an exemption to maltreatment laws for parents who do not seek medical care based on religious beliefs. However, the courts in 16 of those states can order medical treatments deemed essential to the child's well-being (Child Welfare Information Gateway, 2014). Inconsistent definitions can further complicate efforts to provide children with necessary medical care: Seven states define medical neglect as "failing to provide needed medical/mental health care"; four states define it as "withholding medical treatment/nutrition from disabled infants with life-threatening conditions"; and forty states, including the District of Columbia, do not specifically address medical neglect (Child Trends, 2011).

Advocates of such exemptions consider the right to refuse medical treatment as a religious freedom. They do not view refusal as neglect, or agree that their care and love for children should be called into question (Brown, 2016). Thus, these families believe that they are providing for their child's needs in accordance with their beliefs, and that this decision is within their parental rights.

The American Medical Association (AMA, 2016) and other professional groups continue to advocate for the repeal of religious exemptions in child abuse laws. The AMA acknowledges that efforts to change laws must overcome significant barriers, but it urges medical associations to continue to find solutions that address medical neglect. The determination of whether or not a child would benefit from health care is of primary importance. Medical providers may seek feedback from ethical boards if the benefits are probable and, in some cases, a determination may lead to court proceedings to permit medical treatment for the child.

Other organizations, such as the Children's Healthcare Is a Legal Duty, Inc. (CHILD, 2016) seek to protect children from religion-based medical neglect and are advocates for the elimination of exemptions in child maltreatment laws and regulations. CHILD notes that the rate of infant fatalities is higher in certain religious communities and that too many children die from treatable illnesses. Lawmakers in some states have been asked to repeal legislation that protects certain religious groups from prosecution. For example, the Tennessee senate recently voted to repeal the "spiritual treatment" medical exemption (Locker, 2016). In Idaho, a recent report recommended that the state be allowed to intervene if a child's death or disability is imminent and if the child's condition could be treated effectively with medical care (Brown, 2016).

The religious exemption conflict is unlikely to be resolved within the near future, given many existing questions. Is it fair for parents to be treated differently across the United States? Should all parents be treated in the same manner if they refuse, or do not seek, medical treatment? How significant must the medical problem be before a negligent declaration occurs? What data are needed to show that a child would benefit from treatment? What ethical concerns would arise for health care professionals if medical neglect is ignored?

associated with a 15 percent lower cognitive ability at age 16 years and had long term negative effects into adulthood, including poor educational attainment. Furthermore, children raised in neglectful situations had an increase in amygdala volume that is related to processing emotions and survival instincts (Teicher & Samson, 2016). Emotional neglect is much more difficult to identify; not all states include this as a separate category in their reporting laws (Marotz, 2015).

13-4c Educational Neglect

Parents in many states are now being prosecuted for educational neglect (Gleich-Bope, 2014). Educational neglect can occur for a variety of reasons, including lack of information about mandatory education laws, limited or no transportation, significant child behavioral or social problems, and parental work or mental health problems. Failure to enroll children in school, or to ensure that a child receives appropriate educational services (e.g., homeschooling, special education) deprives them of opportunities to learn, and is detrimental to their health and development. Chronic absenteeism reduces academic achievement, school engagement (e.g., approaches to learning, eagerness to learn), and social interaction (e.g., increased internalizing behaviors) (Gottfried, 2014). Parents who allow children to be truant, drop out of school prematurely, or miss excessive school days may face educational neglect charges. High rates of unexcused absences may be an indication of other abusive or neglectful occurrences in the home, and should be investigated (Viezel & Davis, 2015).

13-4d Physical Abuse

Physical abuse occurs when children experience non-accidental injuries that are inflicted by a caregiver. These may include hitting, kicking, beating with an object, burning, throwing, shaking, and pushing that lead to injuries, such as bruises, fractures, scratches, and burns. Physical abuse often begins as punishment for a child's misbehavior (Centers for Disease Control and Prevention [CDC], 2014a), but may continue to be used because it usually has an immediate impact on the child's behavior. Thus, if a parent forcefully hits a child for throwing his cup on the floor for the second time, the child is likely to stop throwing the cup in that instance. Thus, the parent may conclude that hitting has been effective. However, physical punishment does not lead to long-term positive behavioral change and is often associated with increased child aggression over time (CDC, 2014a). Parents may also inadvertently intensify their use of harsh discipline (Rodriguez, Smith, & Silvia, 2016). For example, the use of spanking as a means of disciplining children at age 1 year increases the likelihood that the child and parents will become involved with child protective services in the future (Lee, Grogan-Kaylor, & Berger, 2014).

In adulthood, children who have been abused show reduced hippocampal volume, which is associated with problems in the formation and retrieval of memories and the development of psychiatric disorders including depression, bipolar disorder, and borderline personality disorder (Teicher & Samson, 2016). Repeated exposure to physical abuse is also related to the development of post-traumatic stress disorders and increased aggression (Mohammad et al., 2015). Wang et al. (2016) found that Chinese children who were exposed to parental psychological aggression and maternal corporal punishment (i.e., use of physical force to cause pain and control misbehavior), but not paternal corporal punishment were more likely to develop anxiety symptoms. The outcome differences associated with maternal and paternal use of corporal punishment may be related to traditional Chinese cultural norms, which emphasize fathers as being strict and stern, whereas mothers are supposed to be loving and nurturing. Thus, Wang et al. (2016) hypothesized that the differences in effects on children may be related to whether or not the parental behavior is perceived as rejection. Researchers who studied American children found that both mothers' and fathers' use of corporal punishment was related to internalizing problems (McKee et al., 2007). Although maltreated boys and girls were likely to experience some internalizing problems, reported problems continued to increase with age among girls, but not among boys (Lewis et al., 2016). This finding may be related to normal development during the adolescent years or to re-victimization.

sexual abuse sexual behaviors, including rape, fondling, and pornography that are initiated by an adult and involve a child.

Photo 13-4 Victims of physical abuse are more likely to develop post-traumatic stress disorder and anger control problems. Jeges-Varga Ferenc/Shutterstock.com

13-4e Sexual Abuse and Exploitation

Sexual abuse is committed if an adult engages in sexual behaviors, such as rape, fondling, or pornography, with a child. Perpetrators are often known to the child—a family member, friend, or neighbor. Girls are at increased risk for sexual abuse (U.S. DHHS, 2016). Children who are sexually abused are likely to also experience another form of maltreatment (polyvictimization). Vachon et al. (2015) found that 89 percent of sexual abuse cases were accompanied by another type of nonsexual child maltreatment. Victims of child sexual abuse are at increased risk for psychological and interpersonal problems. Those suffering from intrafamilial abuse, ongoing abuse, and non-disclosure of abuse experience significantly greater psychological and relational impairments and poorer mental adjustment following the abuse (Cantón-Cortés, Cantón, & Cortés, 2016). Children who have been sexually abused are at increased risk for more serious and prolonged mental health concerns, including attempted suicide and committing suicide at a younger age (Lewis et al., 2016; Hoertel, et al., 2015).

Every year, between 100,000 and 300,000 youth in the United States are "at risk" for commercial sexual exploitation by a family member or someone outside of the family (National Center for Missing & Exploited Children and National Council of Juvenile and Family Court Judges, 2015). Traffickers are most likely to target vulnerable youth, including those who have run away from home, are homeless or live in shelters, or have unmet emotional or physical needs. The manipulation or grooming process (e.g., build trust, show caring behaviors, make threats, and/or cause harm) that occurs in the relationship with a pimp or trafficker is significant and often leads to feelings of powerlessness and post-traumatic stress disorder (National Center for Missing and Exploited Youth, 2010). Children in these situations are also at increased risk for academic failure (attending school inconsistently or not at all), unwanted pregnancy, sexually transmitted infections, untreated medical and mental health issues, illegal activity, physical violence, and drug and alcohol use (National Center for Missing & Exploited Children and National Council of Juvenile and Family Court Judges, 2015).

13-4f Emotional Abuse

Emotional abuse harms children's emotional well-being and sense of self-worth (CDC, 2014a). It often involves a caregiver's repeated verbal assaults, including belittling, manipulating, isolating, ignoring, rejecting, shaming, bullying, or destroying a child's objects. This differs from emotional neglect in that the parent is engaging in an active pattern of aversive behaviors, rather than failing to respond to the child's emotional needs. For example, children may be called names ("You're so stupid, you never do anything right"), threatened ("If you don't put your clothes away, you'll go to your room for the rest of the day after a beating"), or rejected ("You don't fit in with our family, you can't even throw a ball five feet"). Emotional abuse is very common; 8 percent of children reported emotional abuse during the past year, and approximately 26 percent of 14- to 17-year-olds reported emotional abuse at some point in their lifetime (Finkelhor et al., 2015). Although emotional abuse occurs frequently and is just as harmful to children as physical abuse, it is less punishable because the evidence is difficult for authorities to document (Vachon et al., 2015). Thus, prevention and intervention efforts are needed to better address and prevent emotional abuse.

Infurna et al. (2016) reviewed multiple studies and concluded that "silent" types of maltreatment (i.e., neglect and emotional abuse) were strongly associated with future depression. High depression rates linked to emotional abuse are known to cause neurological changes that affect how the brain processes rewards (Hanson, Hariri, & Willamson, 2015). For example, Shin et al. (2015) found that children who are emotionally abused experience psychological distress and are more likely to develop problematic drinking behaviors in young adulthood. They hypothesized that children who grow up in hostile environments often fail to learn self-control. As a result, alcohol use may provide an impulsive way to cope with, or temporarily relieve, negative emotions. Relatedly, these children also tend to have difficulty with interpersonal relationships (Lin et al., 2016).

13-4g General Effects on Children's Development

Overall, child maltreatment can have significant long-lasting implications for children's cognitive and social-emotional development. Children who are maltreated often show specific cognitive impairments in executive functioning, attention, learning, memory, working memory, visuospatial perception, and processing speed. These behaviors are directly related to changes in the brain that are the result of maltreatment and related stress (Vasilevski & Tucker, 2016). Children who are removed from their home because of abuse or neglect show lower reading and math achievement, and are more likely to drop out of school, receive special education services, and be retained or suspended (Leonard, Stiles, & Gudino, 2016).

Abuse and neglect are also associated with poor self-esteem, poor response to adversity, and long-lasting mental health concerns (Arslan, 2016; Geoffroy et al., 2016). The neurological impairments attributed to abuse and neglect may help to explain the association between maltreatment and the development of adult psychiatric disorders, including anxiety and depression (Berthelot et al., 2015). In fact, by early adulthood, most maltreated children will meet criteria for at least one such disorder (van der Kolk, 2016). Some estimates suggest that 50 percent of these cases worldwide are attributable to maltreatment (Li, Arcy, & Meng, 2016). Furthermore, if there was a 10 to 25 percent reduction in the number of maltreatment cases, 31 to 80 million cases of depression and anxiety worldwide could be prevented (Li et al., 2016).

Child temperament has also been found to account, in part, for the relationship between child abuse and adult depression; the severity of depression is greater for children who show a depressive, cyclothymic (emotional ups and downs), irritable, or anxious temperament (Nakai et al., 2015). Maladjustment rates (both externalizing and internalizing problems) also increase when children are exposed to more than one type of maltreatment, and the maltreatment occurs with greater frequency and severity (Lin et al., 2016; Vachon et al., 2015).

Because children who experience trauma live in a constant state of fear, they are more likely to act impulsively, and have problems regulating their emotions and engaging in higher-order thinking (Statman-Weil, 2016). Even when these children are in safe environments, they are more likely to interpret events or actions as threats, and to respond as if they are in danger (Statman-Weil, 2016). In sum, maltreatment and chronic stress can have a neurotoxic effect on children's brain development. However, these neurological changes may facilitate survival for children who find themselves in adverse situations, even though the associated behaviors seem maladaptive when they are exhibited in appropriate environments (Teicher & Samson, 2016).

13-5 Early Identification

The economic costs associated with child maltreatment pose a significant public health problem. The CDC (2014b) estimated that the annual cost of maltreatment (e.g., health care, lost productivity, child welfare services, legal expenses, special education) in the United States is approximately $124 billion. Furthermore, if a child dies from maltreatment, the estimated economic loss is approximately $1.3 million (e.g., lost productivity and wages). The lifetime cost for a victim who survives is approximately $210,012, which is similar to the amount associated with health conditions, such as stroke and type II diabetes.

13-5a Legal and Ethical/Professional Obligations

There are legal obligations at the federal and state level for protecting children. The Child Abuse Prevention and Treatment Act (CAPTA; Public Law 93-247) was first authorized in 1974 and most recently amended in 2010. The law requires states to establish definitions, policies, and laws to address child maltreatment, and to designate an agency to oversee the investigation and prosecution of cases. Federal funds are made available to states for prevention, assessment, prosecution, treatment, and grant projects aimed at developing demonstration programs to decrease child maltreatment incidence (Child Welfare Information Gateway, 2011). In addition, CAPTA established the Office on Child Abuse and Neglect and the Child Welfare Information Gateway, which strives to provide comprehensive resources to professionals for protecting, strengthening, and preserving family systems (Child Welfare Information Gateway, 2011). State laws developed through this process provide guidance to professionals in determining what is considered child maltreatment and who has a mandatory responsibility to report instances of suspected abuse or neglect.

Photo 13-5 Most professionals are required to report suspected child maltreatment.

Reporting Requirements. Anyone can report suspected child maltreatment to child protective services. However, state laws typically require people in certain professional occupations to contact authorities:

- School staff—teachers, child care providers, principals, paraeducators, coaches, administrative assistants

- Health care providers—physicians, nurses, dentists, psychologists, mental health counselors

- Law enforcement—police, firemen, emergency responders

- Social service and religious professionals—social workers, clergy

Law enforcement personnel file the majority of reports made to child protective services (18.1 percent), followed by educational personnel (17.7 percent), and social services personnel (11.0 percent) (U.S. DHHS, 2016). State laws often require schools and organizations that serve children to have written procedures that must be followed in the event that there is suspected child maltreatment. Authorities must be notified of any reasonable suspicion of abuse or neglect so they can conduct an investigation if warranted. Service providers should know the contact information and agency to whom a report is to be made. Local social welfare or law enforcement offices or the Childhelp® (1-800-422-4453) hotline can also be contacted for assistance in making an anonymous report.

Teachers and service providers should be knowledgeable about standard screening procedures, how to make appropriate determinations, and when action needs to be taken. An individual who suspects that a child may have been maltreated should always follow up to ensure that a report has been filed with the proper authorities. When making a report, the following information may be requested:

- Reporter's relationship to the child suspected of being maltreated, and the reporter's name (optional)

- Information about the child and other children in the home (e.g., child's name, age, gender, address, others living in the home)

- Name of the person suspected of the abuse or neglect, and parents' names if different

- The nature and extent of injury (e.g., physical markers, behavior changes) or neglect

- Approximate date the maltreatment occurred, and any prior abuse or neglect concerns

- Circumstances or situations in which maltreatment may have taken place as described by the child or caregiver

- Child's location and current safety

Professional personnel must be aware of their own attitudes and cultural biases about child maltreatment and how these feelings may influence judgments about making or substantiating a report and subsequent intervention decisions (Benbenishty et al., 2015). For example, Israeli and Spanish practitioners would not make similar decisions if presented with the same scenario: Israeli practitioners were not, and Spanish practitioners were, likely to recommend a child's removal from the home. When offered the same scenario, personnel in the Netherlands were adamantly against the removal of children, and emphasized family-centered intervention programs as a means for resolving the issue (Benbenishty et al., 2015).

Smith and Eklund (2016) outlined ways that professionals can support families during the difficult transition period that follows a required child maltreatment report:

1. Ensure safety: provide physical safety until the next steps are identified following contact with child protective services and help to identify follow-up care.

2. Mental health: provide information and easy access to affordable mental health services.

3. Community shelter, food, clothing resources: provide information about local resources that are available, especially if the family needs to relocate away from the abuser.

4. Transportation: help families arrange for transportation to school if they have to be relocated in order to increase the child's sense of stability and consistency. (The McKinney-Vento Homeless Assistance Act provides free transportation for children who have been relocated.)

5. School-based mental health support: provide children with counseling support to help them learn anger management, coping, or other related skills.

Ethical and Professional Obligations. Individuals who serve children also have an ethical obligation to protect children against harm. Most ethical codes for professional organizations provide guidance for responsible practice within a given field. For example, the NAEYC Code of Ethics (2011) states:

- P-1.1—Above all, we shall not harm children. We shall not participate in practices that are emotionally damaging, physically harmful, disrespectful, degrading, dangerous, exploitative, or intimidating to children. *This principle has precedence over all others in this Code.*

- P-1.11—When we become aware of a practice or situation that endangers the health, safety, or well-being of children, we have an ethical responsibility to protect children or inform parents and/or others who can.

Professionals who work in a variety of settings are also expected to help protect children's safety and well-being by recognizing the early signs of maltreatment, screening for evidence of maltreatment, and directing families to supportive services. Many professional organizations (e.g., Society for Pediatric Nurses, American Counseling Association, and the American Association of Social Workers) have developed recommendations for the identification, evaluation, and treatment of children who are exposed to violence. For example, personnel who work in hospitals and birthing facilities are obligated under CAPTA to ensure that infants do not leave the hospital without appropriate supports in place. Emergency room personnel have implemented procedures to identify and report children with unexplained or repeated admissions for injuries. Medical providers have an ethical obligation to detect early risk factors, such as parental mental health disorders, domestic violence, substance use, and physical signs of neglect at routine well-child visits. Mental health providers are expected to screen parents for mental illness and assist them in accessing treatment. Domestic violence professionals should assess children's safety when they respond to reports as there is often a link between intimate partner violence and child maltreatment. It is also important that they be aware of the spousal tendency to avoid reporting domestic violence for fear of potential repercussions.

13-6 Breaking the Cycle of Family Violence and Building Resilience

The prevention and treatment of intergenerational family violence and child maltreatment is most effective and beneficial when an ecological approach is taken. This strategy involves a three-pronged approach: increasing public maltreatment awareness and developing community programs to more effectively address broader parenting factors, such as socioeconomic stress and neighborhood violence; collaborating with families to reduce parental distress and improve parenting skills; and, working with children to increase their **resilience** (Chamberland et al., 2015).

13-6a Community Focus

The Commission to Eliminate Child Abuse and Neglect Fatalities (CECANF, 2016) identified core components of the child welfare system that are needed to protect children from harm and to effectively intervene when child maltreatment occurs (see Figure 13-4). The framework highlights the need for a) leadership and accountability across organizations and systems; b) better systems for data collection, data sharing, and analysis to inform practice; and c) cooperation and collaboration among multiple agencies and systems to address families' needs.

The CDC (2014a) encourages communities to assume an active role in reducing the potential for maltreatment by developing resources that strengthen families' ability to create safe, stable, and nurturing environments for children. Information collected locally can assist communities in implementing programs that will address the population's unique needs. For example, a community may respond to a recent influx of new immigrant families by developing programs to support their healthy adjustment to a different cultural context and, in turn, reduce the risk for intimate partner violence and child maltreatment caused by excessive stress (Kimber et al., 2015).

Efforts to improve neighborhood environments also play an important role in maltreatment prevention. Molnar et al. (2016) noted that maltreatment rates were significantly higher in neighborhoods where the rates of robberies and homicides were

resilience the ability to adapt to and overcome adversity.

Figure 13-4 Core Components of the 21st Century Child Welfare System

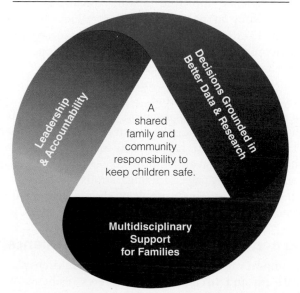

Source: Commission to Eliminate Child Abuse and Neglect Fatalities (2016).

Photo 13-6 Intervention programs to decrease child maltreatment must address parenting skills and help connect families to necessary services.

greater, and lower in neighborhoods where residents had more opportunities for positive social interaction. Community and school violence prevention programs that target prosocial behaviors and decrease emotional desensitization can also be effective for reducing the frequency, intensity, and number of settings in which children are exposed to violence (Mrug, Madan, & Windle, 2015).

13-6b Emphasis on Parenting Improvement

It is important to understand that child maltreatment is often a symptom of a much larger and more complex problem, such as relational conflict, a mental health disorder, substance abuse, inadequate parenting knowledge and skills, or challenging daily living conditions. Thus, in order to disrupt the intergenerational effect of child maltreatment, it is first necessary to identify and address any contributing factors. Simply encouraging an at-risk parent to attend parenting classes is unlikely to prevent future maltreatment incidences if the family is struggling to purchase food or pay the next month's rent. Linking families to essential community services (e.g., health care, housing assistance, job training, child care) can help to alleviate some of their immediate concerns and enable them to begin focusing on other ways to improve parent-child interactions (Maguire-Jack & Negash, 2016).

Intervention efforts that strive to improve parenting skills are numerous, and range from evidence-based parent education and home-visitation programs, to support groups and respite care. An extensive list of current programs, resources, and support information is available on the Child Welfare Information Gateway website supported by the Children's Bureau, Administration for Children and Families, U.S. Department of Health and Human Services. The primary objective of most parent education programs is to strengthen parent-child relationships by creating a positive environment. Such a situation promotes consistent routines, developmentally-appropriate behavior guidance, positive communication, and improved understanding of children's development (Chen & Chan, 2016).

Programs that include home visits show promise for reducing child maltreatment, especially for vulnerable families that may include young parents and parents who have spent time in the foster care system (CECANF, 2016; Oxford et al., 2016). For example, the Nurse Family Partnership program provides in-home support to first-time mothers throughout pregnancy and until her child turns 2 years. Mothers in these programs experience improved health, educational attainment, economic self-sufficiency, self-efficacy in parenting, and a reduction in maltreatment incidences (Olds et al., 2013). Researchers have also substantiated positive parent and child behavioral outcomes associated with many other home-visiting intervention programs (Chen & Chan, 2016; Oxford et al., 2016).

Interventions to reduce stress also contribute to improved parenting skills and lower child maltreatment rates (Steele et al., 2016). Parents who experience less stress are not as likely to engage in hostile, demeaning, and rejecting behaviors that are often associated with physically and emotionally abusive treatment directed toward children (Turner et al., 2012). Suggestions to help parents manage their own anger can have a beneficial effect on stress reduction and improved relationships with children and other family members (see Chapter 7, page 213, Suggestions for Parents 7–5). Parents who have mental health or substance abuse problems should also be linked to community resources for treatment (Choenni, Hammink, & van der Mheen, 2015).

13-6c Building and Supporting Children's Resilience

Parents and other important adults who work with children play a critical role in preventing maltreatment and strengthening children's resilience when violence does occur. Resilience refers to an individual's ability to adapt to, and overcome, adversity. It reduces the potential for maltreatment and impact that negative life events can have

Figure 13-5 Protective and Risk Factors That Influence Outcomes of Exposure to Violence

Protective Factors	Risk Factors
• Easy child temperament	• Repeated and severe violence
• Communication, problem-solving, and decision-making skills	• Maternal mental health problems
• Positive self-esteem and self-image	• Stressful life events
• Positive parenting	• Minority status in addition to low income
• Positive relationship with at least one caring, non-abusive adult	• Socioeconomic factors including poverty, neighborhood disadvantage, and community violence
• Parents or peers who disapprove of antisocial behavior	
• Involvement in a religious community	

Adapted from: Huang, Vikes, & Yi, (2015).

on children's development. Several protective and risk factors that influence the outcome of children's exposure to violence and aversive acts have been identified in the literature (see Figure 13-5).

Social support is an essential ingredient in the comprehensive prevention and treatment of child maltreatment (van der Kolk, 2016). Early targeted interventions that focus on increasing personal skills and minimizing the negative impact of adverse experiences are key to building resiliency among maltreated children (Vasilevski & Tucker, 2016). For example, children who have poor self-esteem are at increased risk for developing long-term emotional and behavioral disorders subsequent to maltreatment (Arslan, 2016). Strategies implemented to increase their communication skills and self-esteem, such as creating caring relationships with children, acknowledging their efforts, encouraging their persistence, and providing positive feedback for accomplishments, may help to buffer the negative effects of abusive treatment. School engagement or connections to other meaningful adults or social networks (e.g., religious affiliations, sports and other organized activities) in the community have also been shown to improve children's resilience to adverse situations. In fact, children who were removed from their home due to maltreatment showed higher achievement and fewer mental health concerns when they were engaged in school (Leonard, Stiles, & Gudino, 2016).

Several programs have demonstrated success in supporting children who may be at-risk for or have experienced maltreatment (see Figure 13-6) (Leonard et al., 2016). For example, the Check and Connect program focuses on building quality relationships, providing encouragement and monitoring, and increasing children's problem-solving skills (What Works Clearinghouse, 2015). The Safe Child Program (grades K-3) empowers children by engaging them in "what if" scenarios to help them gain confidence in knowing how to respond in uncomfortable situations (Brassard & Fiorvanti, 2015).

Teaching children coping, communication, problem solving, and self-regulation strategies can also bolster their resilience, confidence, and buffer the detrimental effects of exposure to violence (Mohammad et al., 2015). The Communities That Care (CTC) program has been used to prevent child abuse and neglect and increase the resilience

Photo 13-7 Communication, problem solving, and self-regulation skills increase children's resilience to potential maltreatment.

Figure 13-6 Strategies to Support Children Who Are Exposed to Trauma

Strategy	How It Helps	Example
Maintain consistent routines	Helps children to learn that the world is predictable and safe.	Each morning, the teacher uses a visual schedule to review the day's activities.
Inform children of changes in typical routines	Prepares children for unexpected events and reduces stress due to uncertainty or an association with prior trauma.	A foster parent discusses upcoming changes in routines and addresses any concerns children may have. She prepares the children for an event by role-playing or describing what will happen (e.g., showing pictures of a visitor who will be coming later to talk).
Offer developmentally appropriate choices	Builds self-esteem by providing children some control over their environment.	Children are allowed to select which center they want to participate in, or where they want to sit during story-time.
Anticipate and provide support during difficult periods	Creates a feeling of safety and security during periods that may remind children of trauma; helps them to feel more at ease.	Hearing a teacher call out in a loud voice for students to line up following recess may remind a child of shouting that occurred during physical abuse; to prevent this reaction, the teacher can quietly explain to the child what to expect before she raises her voice to tell the students that it is time to go indoors (alternatively, she might use a whistle).
Support self-regulation	Helps children learn how to manage their emotions and respond appropriately to stress.	A counselor teaches children deep, belly breathing (diaphragmatic breathing) and other relaxation strategies, such as guided imagery and mindfulness. The teacher models the use of these skills and reminds children to use them when they begin to feel anxious or stressed.
Understand that children make sense of their experiences through interactions with others	Helps children to recognize, problem solve, and learn how to manage their feelings.	The teacher calmly encourages the children to develop a positive solution when they become upset about being asked to complete a task that they don't want to do, or are having difficulty with a peer.
Be nurturing, but also sensitive to children's triggers	Provides reassurance in a comfortable and nurturing way.	A service provider asks children if they would like to be hugged before providing affection.
Use positive guidance	Provides opportunities for students to observe and learn appropriate ways to interact with others.	A teacher helps a child to understand how his actions affect a peer's feelings, and sets up opportunities for the child to practice desired behaviors with support.

Adapted from: Statman-Wei (2015).

of children (birth to age 10 years) who have experienced maltreatment (Salazar et al., 2016). Providing access to quality therapy is also important for disrupting the cycle of violence. In fact, Maxwell et al. (2015) found that participation in therapy may decrease the likelihood of children becoming perpetrators as adults. Thus, intervention can successfully change children's trajectory towards more positive, long-term outcomes.

Responsive Parenting

Whenever the principal, Mr. Beckel, or other males come into the room, 7-year-old Nichole begins to cower and will not respond to their questions. After talking to her mother, you learn that Nichole has witnessed her father hitting her mother in the past. Although Nichole has not had contact with her father for the last year, her mother has noticed similar problems during interactions with males at their church, in restaurants, and stores. What could be done to support Nichole at school, home, and in the community?

Summary

- Many theories of child maltreatment have been proposed, but none fully explain why some adults abuse or neglect children. However, many factors that increase the risk of child maltreatment have been identified, including:

  - Adult factors—mental health problems, history of maltreatment, and substance abuse

  - Child factors—under the age of 1 year, difficult temperament, special needs, and non-gender conforming

  - Environmental factors—poverty, limited access to services, frequent moves, single parenting, exposure to violence in the community and media

  - Cultural factors—disproportionate representation of Native Americans, Alaska Natives, and African American children, discrimination within systems, cultural acceptance of violent behavior.

- The majority of child maltreatment incidents involve neglect; however, some children are victims of multiple abuse and/or neglect forms. Child maltreatment occurs across all socioeconomic, religious, educational, ethnic, and cultural groups.

- Child maltreatment can have significant effects on children's cognitive and social-emotional development. Alterations in brain functioning influence children's emotional regulation, ability to engage in higher order thinking, and interpretation of events as threats; however, these differences may be adaptive for violent settings. Children are also more likely to have short- and long-term mental health disorders and substance use problems.

- Professionals must be knowledgeable about their legal and ethical responsibilities for reporting suspected child maltreatment.

- Breaking the cycle of child maltreatment will involve systems and organizations working together to deliver preventative programs and to screen children and families, make appropriate judgments to ensure child safety, and provide access to needed services. Teachers and other service providers can create positive nurturing environments that support and enhance childrens' resilience.

Key Terms

child (p. 357)

emotional abuse (p. 360)

emotional neglect (p. 362)

physical abuse (p. 360)

physical neglect (p. 364)

polyvictimization (p. 360)

resilience (p. 373)

sexual abuse (p. 368)

Questions for Discussion and Self-Reflection

1. What risk factors are associated with child maltreatment? What physical and behavioral indicators are commonly associated with various forms of child maltreatment?

2. What legal and ethical responsibilities apply in your role? What should be done if child maltreatment is suspected?

3. What effects does child maltreatment have on children's growth, development, relationships, and functioning in threatening and non-threatening environments (e.g., at school, therapy)?

4. What strategies and supports can be provided to help children and families who have experienced violence to build resilience?

Field Activities

1. Obtain a copy of reporting laws for three states, including your own. Compare and contrast the regulations. How is child maltreatment defined? Who is a mandated reporter? What are the repercussions if a report is not made?

2. Develop a list of resources in your area that are available to families who have experienced violence. Resources might include shelters, affordable mental health services, and assistance for housing, food, transportation, and clothing.

REFERENCES

Afifi, T., Taillieu, T., Cheung, K., Katz, L., Tonmyr, L., & Sareen, J. (2015). Substantiated reports of child maltreatment from the Canadian Incidence Study of Reported Child Abuse and Neglect 2008: Examining child and household characteristics and child functional impairment. *Canadian Journal of Psychiatry, 60*(7), 315–323.

Allely, C., Purves, D., McConnachie, A., Marwick, H., Johnson, P., Doolin, O., & Wilson, P. (2013). Parent-infant vocalisations at 12 months predict psychopathology at 7 years. *Research in Developmental Disabilities, 34*(3), 985–993.

American Medical Association. (2016). H-515.988 Repeal of religious exemptions in child abuse and medical practice statutes. Retrieved April 3, 2016 from https://www.ama-assn.org/ssl3/ecomm/PolicyFinderForm.pl?site=www.ama-assn.org&uri=/resources/html/PolicyFinder/policyfiles/HnE/H-515.988.HTM.

Arslan, G. (2016). Psychological maltreatment, emotional and behavioral problems in adolescents: The mediating role of resilience and self-esteem. *Child Abuse & Neglect, 52*, 200–209.

Bartolomei, M. (2015). Domestic violence and human rights. An anthropological view. *Ex æquo, 31*, 91–104.

Benbenishty, R., Davidson-Arad, B., López, M., Devaney, J., Spratt, T., Koopmans, C., . . . & Hayes, D. (2015). Decision making in child protection: An international comparative study on maltreatment substantiation, risk assessment and interventions recommendations, and the role of professionals' child welfare attitudes. *Child Abuse & Neglect, 49*, 63–75.

Berthelot, N., Paccalet, T., Gilbert, E., Moreau, I., Mérette, C., Gingras, N., . . . & Maziade, M. (2015). Childhood abuse and neglect may induce deficits in cognitive precursors of psychosis in high-risk children. *Journal of Psychiatry & Neuroscience, 40*(5), 336–343.

Blair, F., McFarlane, J., Nava, A., Gilroy, H., & Maddoux, J. (2015). Child witness to domestic abuse: Baseline data analysis for a seven-year prospective study. *Pediatric Nursing, 41*(1), 23–29.

Brassard, M., & Fiorvanti, C. (2015). School-based child abuse prevention programs. *Psychology in Schools, 52*(1), 40–60.

Breiding, M., Smith, S., Basile, K., Walters, M., Chen, J., & Merrick, M. (2014). Prevalence and characteristics of sexual violence, stalking, and intimate partner violence victimization—National Intimate Partner and Sexual Violence Survey, United States, 2011. *Surveillance Summaries, 63*(8), 1–18. Division of Violence Prevention, National Center for Injury Prevention and Control, CDC. Retrieved on March 31, 2016 from http://www.cdc.gov/mmwr/preview/mmwrhtml/ss6308a1.htm?s_cid=ss6308a1_e.

Brown, N. (2016). Child deaths bring urgency to debate over faith healers. *Times-News Magic Valley*. Retrieved April 3, 2016 from http://magicvalley.com/news/local/govt-and-politics/child-deaths-bring-urgen/cy-to-debate-over-faith-healers/article_c9b98e8d-69df-5dec-99c6-fae3e5e2fbd0.html#utm_source=magicvalley.com&utm_campaign=%2Femail-updates%2Fdaily-headlines%2F&utm_medium=email&utm_content=headline.

Cantón-Cortés, D., Cantón, J., & Cortés, M. (2016). Emotional security in the family system and psychological distress in female survivors of child sexual abuse. *Child Abuse & Neglect, 51*, 54–63.

Centers for Disease Control and Prevention (CDC). (2014a). Essential for childhood: Steps to create safe, stable, nurturing relationships and environments. Retrieved on March 17, 2016 from http://www.cdc.gov/violenceprevention/pdf/essentials_for_childhood_framework.pdf.

Centers for Disease Control and Prevention (CDC). (2014b). Cost of child abuse and neglect rival other major public health problems. Retrieved March 17, 2016 from http://www.cdc.gov/violenceprevention/childmaltreatment/economiccost.html.

Chamberland, C., Lacharité, C., Clément, M., & Lessard, D. (2015). Predictors of development of vulnerable children receiving child welfare services. *Journal of Child and Family Studies, 24*(10), 2975–2988.

Chen, M., & Chan, K. (2016). Effects of parenting programs on child maltreatment prevention: A meta-analysis. *Trauma, Violence, & Abuse, 17*(1), 88–104.

Child Trends. (2011). Medical neglect specifically defined in statute. Retrieved April 2, 2016 from http://www.childwelfarepolicy.org/maps/single?id=144.

Child Welfare Information Gateway. (2011). About CAPTA: A legislative history. Retrieved March 25, 2016 from https://www.childwelfare.gov/pubPDFs/about.pdf#page=2&view =Summary of Legislative History.

Child Welfare Information Gateway. (2013). Leaving your child home alone. Retrieved March 11, 2016 from https://www.childwelfare.gov/pubs/factsheets/homealone.cfm.

Child Welfare Information Gateway. (2014). *Definitions of child abuse and neglect*. Washington, DC: U.S. Department of Health and Human Services, Children's Bureau.

Children's Healthcare Is a Legal Duty, Inc. (2016). Victims of religion-based medical neglect. Retrieved on April 3, 2016 from http://childrenshealthcare.org/?page_id=132.

Choenni, V., Hammink, A., & van de Mheen, D. (2015). Association between substance use and the perpetration of family violence in industrialized countries: A systematic review. *Trauma, Violence, & Abuse*. Published online. doi: 10.1177/1524838015589253.

Chrombach, A., & Bambonyé, M. (2016). Intergenerational violence in Burundi: Experienced childhood maltreatment increases the risk of abusive child rearing and intimate partner violence. *European Journal of Psychotraumatology, 6*, 1–7.

Commission to Eliminate Child Abuse and Neglect Fatalities. (2016). *Within our reach: A national strategy to eliminate child abuse and neglect fatalities*. Washington, DC: Government Printing Office. Retrieved March 31, 2016 from http://www.acf.hhs.gov/programs/cb/resource/cecanf -final-report.

Finkelhor, D., Turner, H., Shattuck, A., Hamby, S., & Kracke, K. (2015). Children's exposure to violence, crime, and abuse: An update. Juvenile Justice Bulletin, Laurel, MD: U.S. Department of Justice. Retrieved March 27, 2016 from http://www.ojjdp.gov/pubs/248547.pdf.

Freisthler, B., Wolf, J., & Johnson-Motoyama, M. (2015). Understanding the role of context-specific drinking in neglectful parenting behaviors. *Alcohol and Alcoholism, 50*(5), 542–550.

Garbarino, J. (1977). The human ecology of child maltreatment: A conceptual model for research. *Journal of Marriage and Family, 39*(4), 721–735.

Geoffroy, M., Pereira, S., Li, T., & Power, C. (2016). Child neglect and maltreatment and childhood-to-adulthood cognition and mental health in a prospective birth cohort. *Journal of the American Academy of Child and Adolescent Psychiatry, 55*(1), 33–40.

Gleich-Bope, D. (2014). Truancy laws: How are they affecting our legal systems, our schools, and the students involved? *The Clearing House: A Journal of Educational Strategies, Issues and Ideas, 87*(3), 110–114.

González, R., Kallis, C., Ullrich, S., Barnicota, K., Keersd, R., & Coidc, J. (2016). Childhood maltreatment and violence: Mediation through psychiatric morbidity. *Child Abuse & Neglect, 52*, 70–84.

Gottfried, M. (2014). Chronic absenteeism and its effects on students' academic and socioemotional outcomes. *Journal of Education for Students Placed at Risk, 19*(2), 53–75.

Hanson, J., Hariri, A., & Willamson, D. (2015). Blunted ventral striatum development in adolescence reflects emotional neglect and predicts depressive symptoms. *Biological Psychiatry, 78*(9), 598–605.

Hoertel, N., Franco, S., Wall, M., Oquendo, M., Wang, S., Limosin, F., & Blanco, C. (2015). Childhood maltreatment and risk of suicide attempt: A nationally representative study. *Journal of Clinical Psychiatry, 76*(7), 916–923.

Huang, C., Vikes, J., Lu, S., & Yi, S. (2015). Children's exposure to intimate partner violence and early delinquency. *Journal of Family Violence, 30*(8), 953–965.

Infurna, M., Reichl, C., Parzer, P., Schimmenti, A., Bifulco, A., & Kaess, M. (2016). Associations between depression and specific childhood experiences of abuse and neglect: A meta-analysis. *Journal of Affective Disorders, 190*, 47–55.

Jenny, C. (2007). Recognizing and responding to medical neglect. *Pediatrics, 120*(6), 1385–1389.

Jouriles, E., & McDonald, R. (2014). Intimate partner violence, coercive control, and child adjustment problems. *Journal of Interpersonal Violence, 30*(3), 459–474.

Kimber, M., Henriksen, C., Davidov, D., Goldstein, A., Pitre, N., Tonmyr, L., & Afifi, T. (2015). The association between immigrant generational status, child maltreatment history and intimate partner violence (IPV): Evidence from a nationally representative survey. *Social Psychiatry and Psychiatric Epidemiology, 50*(7), 1135–1144.

King, A., Farst, K., Jaeger, M., Onukwube, J., & Robbins, J. (2015). Maltreatment-related emergency department visits among children 0 to 3 years old in the United States. *Child Maltreatment, 20*(3), 151–161.

Lanier, P., Maguire-Jack, K., Walsh, T., Drake, B., & Hubel, G. (2014). Race and ethnic differences in early childhood maltreatment in the United States. *Journal of Developmental & Behavioral Pediatrics, 35*(7), 419–426.

Leach, C., Stewart, A., & Smallbone, S. (2016). Testing the sexually abused-sexual abuser hypothesis: A prospective longitudinal birth cohort study. *Child Abuse & Neglect, 51*, 144–153.

Lee, S., Grogan-Kaylor, A., & Berger, L. (2014). Parental spanking of 1-year-old children and subsequent child protective services involvement. *Child Abuse & Neglect, 38*, 875–883.

Leonard, S., Stiles, A., & Gudino, O. (2016). School engagement of youth investigated by child welfare services: Associations with academic achievement and mental health. *School Mental Health*. Published online. doi: 10.1007/s12310-016-9186-z.

Lewis, T., McElroy, E., Harlaar, N., & Runyan, D. (2016). Does the impact of child sexual abuse differ from maltreated but non-sexually abused children? A prospective examination of the impact of child sexual abuse on internalizing and externalizing behavior problems. *Child Abuse & Neglect, 51*, 31–40.

Li, M., Arcy, D., & Meng, X. (2016). Maltreatment in childhood substantially increases the risk of adult depression and anxiety in prospective cohort studies: Systematic review, meta-analysis, and proportional attributable fractions. *Psychological Medicine, 46*(4), 717–730.

Lin, X., Li, L., Chi, P., Wang, Z., Heath, M., Du, H., & Fang, X. (2016). Child maltreatment and interpersonal relationship among Chinese children with oppositional defiant disorder. *Child Abuse & Neglect, 51*, 192–202.

Locker, R. (2016). State may remove 'spiritual treatment' shield to child abuse law. *The Commercial Appeal*. Retrieved April 3, 2016 from http://www.commercialappeal.com/news/government/state/state-may-remove-spiritual-treatment-shield-to-child-abuse-law-2dcd0e88-33f4-749f-e053-0100007f5a90-371844621.html.

Maguire-Jack, K., & Negash, T. (2016). Parenting stress and child maltreatment: The buffering effect of neighborhood social service availability and accessibility. *Children and Youth Services Review, 60*, 27–33.

Marotz, L. (2015). *Health, safety, and nutrition for the young child.* (9th Ed). Stamford, CT: Cengage Learning.

Maxwell, K., Callahan, J., Ruggero, C., & Janis, B. (2016). Breaking the cycle: Association of attending therapy following childhood abuse and subsequent perpetration of violence. *Journal of Family Violence, 31*(2), 251–258.

McKee, L., Roland, E., Coffelt, N., Olson, A., Forehand, R., Massari, C., & Zens, M. (2007). Harsh discipline and child problem behaviors: The roles of positive parenting and gender. *Journal of Family Violence, 22*(4), 187–196.

Medley, A., & Sachs-Ericsson, N. (2009). Predictors of parental physical abuse: The contribution of internalizing and externalizing disorders and childhood experiences of abuse. *Journal of Affective Disorders, 113*(3), 244–254.

Millett, L., Seay, K., & Kohl, P. (2015). A national study of intimate partner violence risk among female caregivers involved in the child welfare system: The role of nativity, acculturation, and legal status. *Child and Youth Services Review, 48*, 60–69.

Mohammad, E., Shapiro, E., Wainwright, L., & Carter, A. (2015). Impacts of family and community violence exposure on child coping and mental health. *Journal of Abnormal Child Psychology, 43*(2), 203–215.

Molnar, B., Goerge, R., Gilsanz, P., Hill, A., Subramanian, S., Holton, J., . . . & Beardslee, W. (2016). Neighborhood-level social processes and substantiated cases of child maltreatment. *Child Abuse & Neglect, 51*, 41–53.

Mrug, S., Madan, A., & Windle, M. (2015). Emotional desensitization to violence contributes to adolescents' violent behavior. *Journal of Abnormal Child Psychology, 44*(1), 75–86.

Nakai, Y., Inoue, T., Chen, C., Toda, H., Toyomaki, A., Nakato, Y., . . . & Kusumi, I. (2015). The moderator effects of affective temperaments, childhood abuse and adult stressful life events on depressive symptoms in the nonclinical general adult population. *Journal of Affective Disorders, 187*, 203–210.

National Association for the Education of Young Children. (2011). Code of Ethical Conduct and Statement of Commitment. Retrieved March 31, 2016 from https://www.naeyc.org/files/naeyc/image/public_policy/Ethics%20Position%20Statement2011_09202013update.pdf.

National Center for Missing & Exploited Children and National Council of Juvenile and Family Court Judges. (2015). *Missing children, state care, and child sex trafficking: Engaging the judiciary in building a collaborative response. Technical assistance brief*. Retrieved May 20, 2016 from http://www.missingkids.org/en_US/publications/missingchildrenstatecare.pdf.

National Center for Missing and Exploited Children. (2010). Commercial sexual exploitation. Retrieved on May 20, 2016 from http://www.missingkids.org/en_US/documents/CCSE_Fact_Sheet.pdf.

Olds, D., Holmberg, J., Donelan-McCall, N., Luckey, D., Knudtson, M., & Robinson, J. (2013). Effects of home visits by paraprofessional and by nurses on children: Follow-up of a randomized trial at ages 6 and 9 years. *JAMA Pediatrics, 168*(2), 114–121.

Ostrav, J., Gentile, D., & Mullins, A. (2013). Evaluating the effect of educational media exposure on aggression in early childhood. *Journal of Applied Developmental Psychology, 34*(1), 38–44.

Oxford, M., Marcenko, M., Fleming, C., Lohr, M., & Spieker, S. (2016). Promoting birth parents' relationships with their toddlers upon reunification: Results from Promoting First Relationships® home visiting program. *Children and Youth Services Review, 61*,109–116.

Palusci, V., Datner, E., & Wilkins, C. (2015). Developmental disabilities: Abuse and neglect in children and adults. *International Journal of Child Health and Human Development, 8*(4), 407–428.

Risch, E., Owora, A., Nandyal, R., Chaffin, M., & Bonner, B. (2014). Risk for child maltreatment among infants discharged from a neonatal intensive care unit. *Child Maltreatment, 19*(2), 92–100.

Rodriguez, C., Smith, T., & Silvia, P. (2016). Multimethod prediction of physical parent–child aggression risk in expectant mothers and fathers with Social Information Processing theory. *Child Abuse & Neglect, 51*, 106–119.

Salazar, A., Haggerty, K., de Haan, B., Catalano, R., Vann, T., Vinson, J., & Lansing, M. (2016). Using communities that care for community child maltreatment prevention. *American Journal of Orthopsychiatry, 86*(2), 144–155.

Shin, S., Hassamal, S., & Groves, L. (2015). Examining the role of psychological distress in linking childhood maltreatment and alcohol use in young adulthood. *The American Journal on Addictions, 24*(7), 628–636.

Smith, R., & Eklund, K. (2016). Children's exposure to domestic violence: How school psychologists can help. *National Association of School Psychologists Communiqué, 43*(6). Retrieved March 18, 2016 from http://www.nasponline.org/publications/periodicals/communique/issues/volume-43-issue-6/childrenandaposs-exposure-to-domestic-violence-how-school-psychologists-can-help.

Snyder, S., Hartinger-Saunders, R., Brezina, T., Beck, E., Wright, E., Forge, N., & Bride, B. (2016). Homeless youth, strain, and justice system involvement: An application of general strain theory. *Children and Youth Services Review, 62*, 90–96.

Statman-Weil, K. (2015). Creating trauma sensitive classrooms. *Young Children*, 70(2), 72–79.

Steele, H., Bate, J., Steele, M., Dube, S., Danskin, K., Knafo, H., . . . & Murphy, A. (2016). Adverse childhood experiences, poverty, and parenting stress. *Canadian Journal of Behavioural Science, 48*(1), 32–38.

Stockdale, L., Morrison, R., Kmiecik, M., Garbarino, J., & Silton, R. (2015). Emotionally anesthetized: Media violence induces neural changes during emotional face processing. *Social Cognitive and Affective Neuroscience*. Published online. doi: 10.1093/scan/nsv025.

Teicher, M., & Samson, J. (2016). Annual research review: Enduring neurobiological effects of childhood abuse and neglect. *Journal of Child Psychology and Psychiatry, 57*(3), 241–266.

Telman, M., Overbeek, M., Schipper, C., Lamers-Winkelman, F., Finkenauer, C., & Schuengel, C. (2016). Family functioning and children's post-traumatic stress symptoms in a referred sample exposed to interparental violence. *Journal of Family Violence, 31*, 127–136.

Turner, H., Finkelhor, D., Ormrod, R., Hamby, S., Leeb, R., Mercy, J., & Holt, M. (2012). Family context, victimization, and child trauma symptoms: Variations in safe, stable, and nurturing relationships during early and middle childhood. *American Journal of Orthopsychiatry, 82*(2), 209–219.

U.S. Department of Health & Human Services, Administration of Children, Youth, and Families, Children's Bureau. Child maltreatment 2012. Available at http://www.acf.hhs.gov/cb/resource/child-maltreatment-2012.

U.S. Department of Health & Human Services, Administration for Children and Families, Administration on Children, Youth and Families, Children's Bureau. (2016). *Child maltreatment 2014*. Available from http://www.acf.hhs.gov/programs/cb/research-data-technology/statistics-research/child-maltreatment.

Vachon, D., Krueger, R., Rogosch, F., & Cicchetti, D. (2015). Assessment of the harmful psychiatric and behavioral effects of different forms of child maltreatment. *Journal of the American Medical Association Psychiatry, 72*(11), 1135–1142.

van der Kolk, B. (2016). Commentary: The devastating effects of ignoring child maltreatment in psychiatry—a commentary on Teicher and Samson 2016. *Journal of Child Psychology and Psychiatry, 57(3)*, 267–270.

Vasilevski, V., & Tucker, A. (2016). Wide-ranging cognitive deficits in adolescents following early life maltreatment. *Neuropsychology, 30*(2), 239–246.

Viezel, K., & Davis, A. (2015). Child maltreatment and the school psychologist. *Psychology in the Schools, 52*(1), 1–8.

Viola, T., Salum, G., Kluwe-Schiavon, B., Sanvicente-Vieira, B., Levandowski, M., & Grassi-Oliveira, R. (2016). The influence of geographical and economic factors in estimates of childhood abuse and neglect using the Childhood Trauma Questionnaire: A worldwide meta-regression analysis. *Child Abuse & Neglect, 51*, 1–11.

Wallace, H., & Roberson, C. (2014). *Family violence: Legal, medical, and social perspectives* (7th Ed). Abingdon, Oxford, UK: Taylor and Francis.

Wang, M., Wang, X., & Liu, L. (2016). Paternal and maternal psychological and physical aggression and children's anxiety in China. *Child Abuse & Neglect, 51*, 12–20.

What Works Clearinghouse. (2015). WWC Intervention Report: Check & Connect. Retrieved March 24, 2016 from http://ies.ed.gov/ncee/wwc/pdf/intervention_reports/wwc_checkconnect_050515.pdf.

Widom, C., Czaja, S., & DuMont, K. (2015). Intergenerational transmission of child abuse and neglect: Real or detection bias? *Science, 347*(6229), 1480–1485.

Parenting Children with Exceptionalities

14

LEARNING OBJECTIVES

After reading the chapter, you will be able to:

14-1 Discuss how philosophical and legislative developments have changed educational opportunities for children with disabilities.

14-2 Describe how having a child with a disability affects parents and parenting.

14-3 Identify some of the challenges that parents typically experience as children with exceptionalities age.

14-4 Explain the family-centered approach.

naeyc Standards Linked to Chapter Content

1a, 1b, 1c: Promoting child development and learning

2a, 2b: Building family and community relationships

4a, 4b: Using developmentally effective approaches to connect with children and families

Every child is unique in some way from all other children. Those who excel at mathematics or music, or have behavioral issues or a developmental disability, may pose challenges which parents may be unprepared to handle. A child's deviation from an idealized image may also cause parents to experience a range of unanticipated events and emotions. Although it is easy to focus

continued on following page

Denis Kuvaev/Shutterstock.com

on children's potential limitations, it is important to remember that all children have the same fundamental needs and are more alike than they are different. The purpose of this chapter is not to elaborate on specific medical conditions or developmental disabilities, but to focus on some of the more common parenting challenges that parents of children with exceptionalities are likely to encounter. ■

14-1 Philosophical and Legislative Developments

An improved understanding of developmental disorders, brain development, and interventions to promote optimal learning has contributed to significant changes in the way that children with unique needs are treated and educated. For example, prior to 1960, parents were encouraged to place children with disabilities in residential institutions, because they were considered an uneducable burden on society (Pfieffer, 1993). However, study results showed that children who were living in these institutions experienced declining health and cognitive development regression (Nelson et al., 2007; Zigler, Balla, & Watson, 1972). Parents who refused to exercise this option had few alternative choices: they could care for and educate their children at home or they could pay for expensive private instruction, if any was available.

Public attention was increasingly drawn to the rights and humane treatment of individuals with disabilities during the mid-1960s to early 1970s. Some public schools offered separate programs for children who were considered "trainable," but they often were not accessible to thousands of other children who had disabilities (Meisels & Shokoff, 2000). Legislation that authorized the founding of Head Start programs (1965) and experimental university-affiliated special education preschool classrooms (1968) helped to establish approaches that would create major changes in the way that children with disabilities were treated and educated.

Studies conducted in these settings yielded conclusive evidence that the early identification and an interdisciplinary approach for educating children who had, or were at-risk for, developmental disorders significantly improved their lives and long-term achievements. Professional attention and advocacy also led to the passage of legislation that would expand educational opportunities and protect the rights of individuals with disabilities (see Figure 14-1) (Cicirelli, 1969; Lazar et al., 1982; Hubbell, 1983; Lee et al., 1990). Research findings also fostered increased interest in preventive measures (e.g., prenatal health care, prenatal and infant nutrition, infant immunization, health insurance) which could reduce the incidence of many developmental disabilities. As a result, professionals and parents continue to lobby policymakers in an effort to improve upon, and expand, existing programs and services to further reduce the incidence of developmental disabilities and to maximize every child's learning potential. They have also drawn attention to the importance of using people-first language to communicate respectfully about individuals with disabilities. This type of language focuses on the person, and not the disability (see Figure 14-2).

Photo 14-1 Head Start embodies the concept of early identification and intervention.

Figure 14-1 Major Legislative Acts Affecting Educational Opportunities for Children with Disabilities

Legislation	Provisions
Mental Retardation Facilities Construction Act (1963) PL 88-164	• Provided funds to establish university-affiliated centers staffed by interdisciplinary professionals. • Provided educational services to people with disabilities, staff training, and research support.
Head Start Act (1965) PL 89-10	• Established part-day Head Start programs for low-income at-risk children ages 3–5 years. • Provided developmental screenings, health services, nutrition, and parent training. • 1972 and 1974 amendments required programs to serve children with disabilities. • 1994 reauthorization created Early Head Start programs to serve infants, toddlers, and their parents.
Handicapped Children's Early Education and Assistance Act (1968) PL 90-538	• Provided funds to establish model preschool classrooms for children diagnosed with developmental disabilities.
Section 504 of the Rehabilitation Act (1973; 2008)	• Prohibits discrimination and protects the rights of individuals with disabilities in schools and programs that receive Federal funding from the U. S. Department of Education. • Provides for accommodations that allow children to learn in educational and extracurricular environments.
Education for All Handicapped Children Act (1975) PL 99-142	• Landmark law that required states to provide "free and appropriate" comprehensive education for all children 3–21 years, who had, or were at-risk for, developmental disabilities. • Included provisions for nondiscriminatory evaluation, due process, and zero rejection.
Education of the Handicapped Act Amendments (1986) PL 99-457	• Extended mandated service provisions of PL 99-142 to include infants, toddlers, and their families. • Stipulated multidisciplinary assessment, a family-centered approach, and service coordination.
Americans with Disabilities Act (ADA) (1990) PL 101-336	• Protects individuals with disabilities from discrimination in schools, public, and the workplace. • Requires child care facilities and schools to make facilities accessible to all persons with disabilities.
Individuals with Disabilities Education Act (IDEA) (1990) PL 101-476	• Amends and reframes PL 94-142 to reflect person-first language ("person with disabilities" vs "handicapped person"). • Mandates school districts to maintain Child Find screening programs. • Established Part B services for children 3–21 years, and Part C services for children birth to age 3 years and their families. • 1997 amendment (PL 105-17) emphasized students' and families' role in the educational process; it also required schools to begin transition planning at age 16 years for employment and adult living beyond high school.
Individuals with Disabilities Education Improvement Act (2004, 2011) PL 108-446	• Increased state accountability for children's educational outcomes, stipulated "highly qualified teachers," addressed better identification methods, and reduced some required planning paperwork
No Child Left Behind (2002) PL 107-110	• Established to improve children's math and reading proficiency; requires schools to demonstrate yearly score improvement or lose federal Title 1 funding. • Holds schools and teachers accountable for children's progress or lack of progress. • Emphasizes parent involvement and parent-school partnerships.

(Continued)

Figure 14-1 Major Legislative Acts Affecting Educational Opportunities for Children with Disabilities (*Continued*)

Legislation	Provisions
Every Student Succeeds Act (ESSA) (2015) PL 114-95	• Reauthorized the Elementary and Secondary Education Act (1965) and reformed No Child Left Behind. • Requires schools to reduce testing while maintaining high academic standards to help students succeed in careers and college. • Provides additional funding to schools for innovative instructional approaches. • Expands children's access to high-quality preschool.

Figure 14-2 Language for Communicating with and About People with Disabilities

People First Language	Languages to Avoid
Person with a disability	The disabled, handicapped
Person without a disability	Normal person, healthy person
Person with an intellectual disability	Retarded, slow, special person
Person with a mental health disability	Crazy, psycho, nuts
Person who is deaf or blind/visually impaired	Deaf, mute, the blind
Person who uses a wheelchair	Crippled, lame, deformed
Person with epilepsy, cerebral palsy, multiple sclerosis	Epileptic, cerebral palsy victim, afflicted by multiple sclerosis
Accessible services or locations	Handicapped parking, handicapped bathroom
Person who is successful, productive	Has overcome a disability

Source: Centers for Disease Control and Prevention (n.d.).

14-1a Early Identification and Intervention

Legislative and financial support for the early identification of children with disabilities and intervention programs developed slowly, despite evidence linking these strategies to many positive outcomes. Advocates for this approach referred to Marie Montessori's (2002) work with intellectually disabled children, as well as other studies which demonstrated the ability of children in orphanages to learn after they were adopted and living in stimulating environments (Meisels & Shonkoff, 2000; Pfeiffer, 1993; Zigler, Balla, & Watson, 1972). They also espoused the importance of learning during children's earliest years, as suggested by Piaget (1954) and Vygotsky (1986), and the critical role that environment plays in shaping children's development (Bronfenbrenner, 1979). The idea that intelligence was malleable and not genetically fixed also lent additional credibility to their push for early identification and intervention services.

The establishment of Head Start programs (1965) was an acknowledgement of such research endeavors. The idea that environmental factors—particularly poverty—played a major role in shaping children's development, placed them at high risk for learning disabilities and academic failure, and that such factors could be addressed successfully convinced policymakers to invest in a compensatory program. Children would benefit and society would also realize substantial savings in health care and remedial education costs (Choi et al., 2016; Hindman & Wasik, 2015). Head Start visionaries also understood that a comprehensive approach (e.g., preventive health, nutrition, parent education) was vital to children's well-being and ability to learn. As a result, many children with developmental disabilities and health conditions that may otherwise have gone unnoticed, interfered with learning, or increased their need for special education placements, remediation, or retention have been identified and have received early intervention services (Teutsch, Herman, & Teusch, 2016; Lumeng et al., 2015).

For example, Harden et al. (2012) found that African American children who participated in Early Head Start programs experienced significant improvements in their language, attention, social, and communication skills. They also observed that parent interventions included in the program led to improved behavioral management and increased parental support. Other researchers also have noted that children enrolled in Head Start programs exhibited improved social-emotional competence and experienced an easier transition to kindergarten (Bierman et al., 2015; Eggum-Wilkens et al., 2014).

Several long-term effects are also attributed to children's participation in early intervention programs, including increased educational attainment, greater lifetime earning potential, lower depression rates, and decreased criminal activity (Heckman & Raut, 2016; Duncan & Magnuson, 2013). Researchers have estimated that every dollar invested in early intervention programs returns approximately $7 to $8.50 in savings (Executive Office of the President of the United States, 2014; Karoly, Kilburn, & Cannon, 2005).

Mandated **Child Find** programs represent another major effort to identify children with potential disabilities. The program was established in 1960 and included in the Individuals with Disabilities Education Act (IDEA) 1990 amendments. It requires all states to establish Child Find screening programs for the purpose of identifying, locating, and evaluating children with, or at risk for, developmental disabilities. These programs are typically administered through local school districts, and apply to all children, including those who attend public and private schools, are children of migrants, are homeless, or are in state custody. The 1997 IDEA amendments eliminated the provision of special education services to children in private schools, but Child Find screening programs remain accessible (Lane & Jones, 2015). The IDEA Act also identified 14 disability categories that qualify children for intervention services (see Figures 14-3 and 14-4).

Successful early intervention efforts have led to other strategies for the identification of children with exceptionalities. For example, hospitals now screen newborns for a variety of disorders (e.g., blood, heart, genetic, neurological, hearing) prior to their discharge. Health care providers are encouraged to include developmental and behavioral screenings in all of their well-child check-ups (AAP, 2016). Parents can arrange for comprehensive developmental screenings through their local school district or public health department, and they can also access developmental milestone information

Child Find a national screening program, mandated by IDEA (1990), that is responsible for identifying, locating, and evaluating children with potential disabilities and increasing public awareness about these services.

Photo 14-2 Many children with exceptionalities have not been identified.

Figure 14-3 Disability Categories Eligible for Special Education Services (IDEA)

- ✔ Autism
- ✔ Deaf-blindness
- ✔ Deafness
- ✔ Developmental delay
- ✔ Emotional disturbance
- ✔ Hearing impairment
- ✔ Intellectual disability

- ✔ Multiple disabilities
- ✔ Orthopedic impairment
- ✔ Other health impairment (e.g., ADD/ADHD, diabetes, sickle cell, epilepsy, Tourette syndrome)
- ✔ Specific learning disability
- ✔ Speech or language impairment
- ✔ Traumatic brain injury
- ✔ Visual impairment, including blindness

Figure 14-4 Percentage Distribution of Children Ages 3–21 years Served under the Individuals with Disabilities Education Act (IDEA), Part B, by Disability Type: School Year 2012–2013

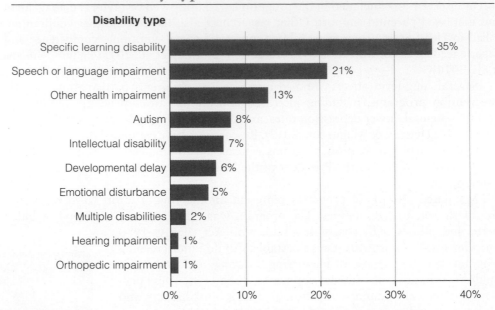

Note: Deaf-blindness, traumatic brain injury, and visual impairments are not shown because they each account for less than 0.5 percent of children served under IDEA. Some categories are not shown, so detail does not sum to total.

Source: U.S. Department of Education, National Center for Statistics (2016).

on reliable websites (e.g., AAP-Ages & Stages; CDC-Learn the Signs/Act Early; Zero to Three). Teachers are also assuming a pivotal role in the monitoring of children's development and referring those who may require additional evaluation to professionals.

Despite these multifaceted efforts, however, there are still many children who fail to be identified. Reasons commonly noted for this failure include an absence of screening programs in some communities, lack of language-appropriate screening instruments, limited parental and professional awareness, and poor service coordination (Leon, Holliker, & Pepe, 2015; Macy, Marks & Towle, 2014; Zuckerman et al., 2013). New experimental approaches, such as telemedicine, are being tested to determine if alternative identification and service delivery methods can improve access to developmental information, especially for high-risk, low-income populations (Ciccia et al., 2015).

14-2 Understanding How Having a Child with Exceptionalities Affects Parenting

The parent of a child with special health or developmental needs often faces unique challenges, such as operating specialized equipment, administering therapeutic procedures, and/or addressing behavioral issues, that typically are added to an already demanding parental role. The resulting workload and responsibility this creates can be highly stressful. Parents of children with significant medical or developmental disabilities consistently report experiencing added financial concerns, emotional stress and strain, additional care-taking responsibilities, and social stigma (Walker et al., 2016; Woodman, Mawdsley, & Hauser-Cram, 2015).

Interestingly, the severity of a child's disability is not a primary predictor of parental well-being; rather, factors such as access to services, resources, and supports, parent problem solving ability, child age, number of children living in the home, and household income better account for variations in well-being (Resch, Benz, & Elliott, 2012). All of these characteristics create a better person-environmental match. For example, parents become more knowledgeable, aware, and involved in services to support their child and family as their child ages. As a result, children often show improvements in self-care tasks, which increase the time that parents can devote to other tasks. Furthermore, parents who have high hopefulness and low despair in relation to thoughts about their child's future, regardless of the child's symptom severity, show lower levels of stress and higher life satisfaction (Faso, Neal-Beevers, & Carlson, 2013). Parents of children with severe functional impairments also report more perceived growth and self-efficacy in response to daily challenges (Resch et al., 2012).

14-2a Relationship Conflict

Researchers have noted that parental stress levels are significantly higher if their child has autism which, in turn, can lead to an increased risk for marital conflict and divorce (Namkung et al., 2015). Results from some studies run counter to the conclusion that elevated stress levels are solely responsible for the negative effect on couples' relationships (Brenner et al., 2016; Baeza-Velasco et al., 2013). Brenner et al. (2016) noted that differences in marital separation rates were not specifically linked to having a child with special medical needs or disabilities, but were positively associated with lower parental education and higher poverty levels. Thus, a child's disability may add to a parent's financial hardship which may push them beyond and exceed their coping abilities. Researchers also have observed that separation rates were higher among couples when the child with a disability was not their firstborn, a situation that produced an increased workload to their already demanding caregiving responsibilities. Parkes et al. (2015) noted that mothers who had more education were able to take advantage of alternative and respite child care arrangements, which contributed to lower stress levels.

14-2b Health Effects

Research results show that parents of children with developmental disabilities, particularly autism, experience a high rate of mental health disorders, physical ailments (e.g., headaches, backaches, exhaustion), sleep deficits, and poorer overall quality of life (Mcbean & Scholsnagle, 2016; Giallo et al.; 2013; Smith, Seltzer, & Greenberg, 2012). Sleep disturbances are consistently reported and are often associated with memory impairments and poor physical and mental health (Miodrag et al., 2015). Depression also is more common and is usually related to the child's behavior or concerns about their future.

Parents' perceptions of what they consider to be stressful are highly variable and influenced by their personal characteristics (e.g., self-efficacy, resilience, coping skills, temperament), culture, and social support. Mothers typically report feeling greater stress and anxiety than do fathers. They often feel resentful because they have had to forego their careers, assume a disproportionate responsibility for providing children's daily care, and sacrifice time to socialize with friends (Jones et al., 2013). Although fathers admit that they too feel stressed, they seem less willing than mothers to talk about their feelings. Lee and colleagues (2015) noted that mothers who were gradually able to accept their child's disability and reframe their negative attitude from a focus on the child's limitations to an acknowledgement of their strengths reported feeling less stress (Lee, Par, & Recchia, 2015). Although this transitional process required time to achieve, parents felt empowered and believed that it also strengthened their relationship (Minnes, Perry, & Weiss, 2015). In contrast, parents who lacked self-esteem and confidence in their caregiving skills and ability to manage children's behavior experienced significantly higher stress and depression levels than parents of children whose development was typical (Cantwell, Muldoon, & Gallagher, 2015; Miranda et al., 2015). Parents who have access to information about their child's disability are less likely to experience depression and excessive stress.

Photo 14-3 Parents who are informed and supported are empowered to be their child's best advocate.

The Center for Parent Information and Resources maintains an interactive website where parents can find extensive information about exceptionalities and supportive services in their area.

14-2c Social Support

The social support that mothers and fathers receive has an important influence on their parenting and quality of life. Couples report that having a supportive partner improves marital satisfaction and family cohesion. Cohen et al. (2105) noted that Latino and White parents enjoyed greater life satisfaction when they felt emotionally supported by their partners. Latino mothers, in particular, experienced the strongest positive effect in their self-efficacy as a result of partner support. Mothers have also reported feeling significantly less stressed when fathers participated in children's care and play activities (Hsiao, 2016; Laxman et al., 2015). Although fewer studies have examined the effects of social support on alternative parenting arrangements (e.g., single parenting, same gender parenting), those that have been conducted report similar findings. For example, Whitley et al. (2016) reported that custodial African American grandmothers who were rearing their grandchildren experienced increased stress and potential for depression because of little social interaction. After participating in a 12-month-long social support intervention, the grandparents showed significant improvement in their mental health state.

Parents with strong social support systems outside of family (e.g., friends, support groups) generally report lower stress and improved coping skill. Gallagher et al. (2016) observed that parents of children with disabilities often turned to their spiritual beliefs when social support was limited. They also noted that—to their surprise—parents who had stronger spiritual feelings also experienced higher depression rates which, they hypothesized, may be related to feelings of desperation and despair. These findings reveal an important void in the lives of parents with children who have disabilities, and suggest that the creation of opportunities for social interaction and social support (e.g., online, video-conferencing, smart technology, peer groups, community activities) could potentially mediate the rates of isolation, stress, and depression that are commonly reported.

14-2d Cultural Influence

Cultural beliefs exert a strong influence on parents' attitudes regarding their child's disability, parenting practices, and their willingness to utilize supportive services. For example, there is no equivalent for the term 'disability' in some cultures. In some societies, children who have disabilities are typically kept out of sight, supposedly to protect them from harm (Ripat & Woodgate, 2011). Similarly, Ahmed et al. (2013) noted that Pakistani children with Down syndrome are considered unusual and to be pitied; families that include a child with disabilities are stigmatized and isolated from the rest of the community.

Some cultures blame mothers for a child's disability, or they believe that the family is being punished for some misdeed. For example, disabilities are often viewed as a sign of failure and shame in some traditional Asian cultures; families are not expected to share their circumstances with outsiders. As a result, many traditional Asian American families refuse treatment and services because they consider a child's disability the family's responsibility (Yan et al., 2014). Delayed identification and treatment of autism spectrum disorders is also fairly common among African American groups in which members are encouraged to protect and care for one another (Burkett et al., 2015). Ratto et al. (2015) noted that Latino children with autism spectrum disorder (ASD) were diagnosed at an older age. They attributed this delay to the mother's lack of knowledge about autism spectrum disorder and typical developmental milestone achievements.

Parents of children with disabilities who immigrate to the United States often face additional challenges that are related to language barriers, conflicting cultural beliefs (e.g., traditional versus alternative medical treatments, self-reliance versus public programs), attempts to navigate unfamiliar service and educational systems, and lack of social support (Zechella & Raval, 2016). Immigrant status increases the vulnerability of many parents, especially single parents, to stress and low social support (Radey, 2015). Long et al. (2015) noted that Latina mothers of children with intellectual disabilities experienced higher rates of depression and health problems than their non-Latina White counterparts. However, mothers who were more acculturated and spoke English were less likely to feel socially isolated and depressed. Maternal depression rates were also lowest in families where family relationships and functioning were positive. Because a strong sense of family (*familism*) is highly valued in many Latino cultures, any family dysfunction added to the stress that mothers who were caring for a child with disabilities were already experiencing. Latina mothers also found children's maladaptive behaviors extremely stressful because they believed it reflected poorly on their ability to be a good parent.

14-2e Financial Impact

Children's disabilities can also affect parents' financial well-being. Variations in disability types and family situations make it difficult to obtain an accurate estimate of the annual out-of-pocket expenses that parents are forced to pay. This effort is further complicated by the fact that studies often include different expense variables (e.g., child-only medical and dental expenses, lost parental wages, estimated loss of child's lifetime earning potential, cost of lifetime support programs for aging children) in their calculations. Stabile and Allin (2012) estimated that the direct and indirect costs to a family of a child with disabilities were approximately $30,500. Canadian researchers determined that the annual costs associated with parental caregiving and lost wages were approximately $44,570 Canadian and approximately $53,484 U.S. (Genereaux, van Karenbeek, & Birch, 2015). Boulet et al. (2008) estimated that the medical costs alone for a child with Down syndrome were 12 to 13 times higher than for a child without a disability, and even higher if the child also had any other medical conditions.

Parents of children with an autism spectrum disorder often incur direct costs that are significantly higher than those associated with many other disabilities because of the intensive therapies and special care attendants that children typically require. Parish et al. (2015) noted that parents of children with autism spent approximately 1 percent of their annual income on child care costs. They also found that families with private health insurance were five times more likely than publically-insured families to have additional expenses. They attributed this to the fact that many private insurance companies do not adequately meet the financial needs of families of children with autism. An increasing number of parents also are turning to alternative and complementary medicines and treatments for children's disabilities that insurance does not cover. Bourke-Taylor et al. (2015) reported that many of these parents eliminate purchases for items, such as clothing, entertainment, hobbies, holidays, and their own health care in order to afford services for their children.

Photo 14-4 Families of children with exceptionalities are most effective when they support one another. Jaren Jai Wicklund/Shutterstock.com

14-2f The Positive Effects

Most published study results support the conclusion that having a child with a disability has negative and distressing effects on parents and parenting, but some researchers have found that the opposite is also true. King et al. (2012) identified several positive themes that emerged during interviews with parents including: an appreciation of children for who they are and what they are able to accomplish; parental exposure to new experiences; and, opportunities to interact with parents who face similar circumstances. Scallan, Senior, and Reilly (2011) also noted that parents of children with disabilities expressed an increased sense of family closeness, observations of positive effects on siblings (e.g., respect, tolerance, understanding), and redefinition of what they believed to be important in life.

In a comparison study, Latina mothers were significantly more likely than Caucasian mothers to report that having a child with a disability had a positive impact on them and on their family (Blacher et al., 2013). Latina mothers were also less likely to blame children or themselves for negative behaviors and were more positive about a child's potential. These findings do not suggest that parents who maintain a positive outlook fail to experience negative feelings (e.g., stress, anxiety, depression). Rather, researchers have noted that these parents are able to redirect more attention to the positive aspects of parenting a child with a disability, which then moderates the relationship between stress and family adjustment (Thompson, Hiebert-Murphy, & Trute, 2012).

Trending Now Genetic Testing

Denise, age 37 years, and her husband are expecting their first child. She is 8 weeks pregnant and concerned about the possibility that their child could have a chromosomal birth disorder, such as Down syndrome, given her age and history. During her first routine prenatal exam, the physician assistant learned that Denise has a cousin who was born with Down syndrome. She explained the maternal risks to Denise, and the various screening options (e.g., sonogram, amniocentesis, Chorionic Villus Screening [CVS]) that are available to rule out or confirm a potential birth defect, and encouraged Denise to discuss the information with her husband.

Many couples face a decision situation similar to that of Denise and her husband. Should they proceed with the testing? What are the procedural risks to the fetus? What will the couple do if the screening results are positive and suggest that the fetus may have a genetic disorder? What effect will the results have on their plans for having another child in the future?

Genetic testing performed prior to conception may be used for counseling purposes. Couples can be advised about their potential chances for giving birth to an infant with a particular disorder. The information may help them to make an informed decision about whether to prevent pregnancy, proceed with a pregnancy, or use assisted reproductive technology. Participants in two studies reported that such information proved valuable to them for this purpose (Archibald et al., 2016; Ulph et al., 2014). They expressed gratitude for the discussion about the genetic risks that they might face, and stated that they would use the information in making future plans.

Genetic testing performed in the early months of pregnancy presents couples with a different set of emotional and ethical dilemmas once they receive the information. Guon et al. (2014) reported that more than 60 percent of parents whose fetus tested positive for a genetic disorder felt pressured to terminate the pregnancy after being informed that their infant would likely die. However, 94 percent of these parents choose to continue their pregnancy for reasons that included moral, child-centered beliefs, and religious beliefs, as well as for parent-centered and practical reasons. Guon and her colleagues also noted that parents who made a decision to continue a pregnancy began making preparatory arrangements to address their infant's anticipated special needs. Suzumori et al. (2015) reported that 93 percent of Japanese parents whose fetus tested positive for a chromosomal abnormality with a severe prognosis choose to terminate the pregnancy. Maternal age, length of pregnancy, number of pregnancies, and number of living children did not significantly influence their decision.

A newer, non-invasive prenatal test (prenatal cell-free DNA testing) has been introduced as a safer and more reliable alternative for identifying several genetic disorders, including Down syndrome, sickle cell, and cystic fibrosis. The test is performed from a sample of the mother's blood and, thus, poses no threat to fetal safety (unlike amniocentesis and CVS screening, which carry a miscarriage risk). However, the relative ease and simplicity of this test has also given rise to new ethical questions about paternity consent and whether the test should be administered strictly for curiosity or informational purposes (Deans, Clarke, & Newson, 2015; Skirton, Goldsmith, & Chitty, 2014).

Genetic testing provides an invaluable diagnostic tool for health care providers. However, it can also present couples with wrenching decisions about what to do if they learn that their fetus has a genetic disorder. Ethical concerns have also been raised about who should have access to the testing results. How might insurance companies respond if they know that a child is a carrier of a particular genetic disorder? What potential effect could this information have on a child's future relationships?

14-3 Parenting Children with Exceptionalities Across the Lifespan

The transition to parenthood requires adults to make considerable lifestyle adjustments. These changes may be even greater when parents have a child with special medical or developmental needs. For example, a new parent who anticipates returning to their teaching position after 8 weeks of maternity/paternity leave may be forced to work fewer hours, or to leave their job in order to care for a child's special needs. Unexpected situations such as these may also lead to significant emotional stress, financial strain, and partner conflict unless parents are flexible and able to make necessary adjustments.

Parents often face a lifetime of unpredictable and unforeseen challenges which are related to their child's special health or developmental needs. For example, an unexpected diagnosis received at the time of a child's birth, or at some later life stage, presents an abrupt situation that parents may initially find overwhelming. As a result, it may take them longer to cope, accept, and make the necessary emotional and physical adjustments. In contrast, parents who are planning for a child's transition to public school or implementing a new therapy have time to adapt more gradually to an anticipated change. How well parents in either scenario adjust will continue to influence children's development, as well as family dynamics.

14-3a Parenting Infants and Toddlers with Exceptionalities

For most parents, an infant's birth brings an anticipated sense of joy. On occasion, these expectations are not realized when parents are told that their infant has a serious medical condition or developmental disability. Birth defects (e.g., microcephaly, cleft lip, Down syndrome, muscular dystrophy) occur in approximately 3 percent of infants born in the United States each year, and between 3 and 6 percent of births worldwide (CDC, 2016; March of Dimes, 2016). Some infants will be hospitalized in a neonatal intensive care unit (NICU) for a period of time, some will be discharged to be cared for at home, and a small number may die at, or shortly following, birth. As a result, parents are faced with an unexpected situation and many unknowns.

Some birth defects are immediately apparent at the time of birth, whereas other disabilities (e.g., autism spectrum disorders, neuromuscular disorders, low vision, learning disorders) may not be noted until a toddler or older child fails to make appropriate developmental progress. When parents learn that their child has a birth defect or diagnosed disability, their initial reactions may range from one of shock to extreme disappointment and sense of loss for the idealized, healthy child they had envisioned. Their ability to process, cope with, and accept this information requires time and compassionate understanding, and is often described as being analogous to the stages of mourning that Elisabeth Kübler-Ross (1969) proposed in her book, *On Death and Dying*:

Photo 14-5 Parents may learn about their child's disability at, or shortly after, birth. noBorders-Brayden Howie/Shutterstock.com

- Stage 1: *Denial* — An intense refusal to accept the reality of the situation (e.g., a medical condition, birth defect, or diagnosis) in hopes that it is not true or will go away. Strong emotions often accompany this reaction.

- Stage 2: *Anger* — Denial turns into frustration and blame; intense emotions are redirected toward another person (including the child) or an object ("the teacher should have noticed this sooner," "why didn't the doctor tell me not to run in that marathon while I was pregnant").

- Stage 3: *Bargaining* — Vulnerable feelings of guilt and helplessness are turned into 'if only's," or appeals to a higher power, in an attempt to undo the reality ("if only we would have sought treatment sooner," "if only the doctor had told me this medication could be harmful to take during pregnancy," "I will never ask for anything again if only you will make my child well").

- Stage 4: *Depression* — Feelings of utter sadness, hopelessness, and regret begin to set in as a parent realizes that the situation is not going to change; they may retreat from blaming others to blaming themselves for what has occurred.

- Stage 5: *Acceptance* — Accepting the inevitable fact that a child's birth defect or disability is real and unlikely to change.

Not all parents will experience these feelings in the same way, pass through these stages at the same rate, or ever reach a point of full acceptance. Their ability to adjust to a different set of expectations requires time, accurate information, support and understanding, and individual coping skills (e.g., problem solving, positive reframing, self-confidence). Parents' cultural values, spiritual beliefs, perceived support, and the nature of the child's birth defect or disability also influence this process (Salkas et al., 2016; Fonseca, Nazaré, & Canavarro, 2015). Wei et al. (2016) also noted that parents experience significantly greater stress when a child's condition is perceived to be life-threatening or causes pain, or when they feel overwhelmed or incompetent to meet the child's complex caregiving needs.

Birth defects and disabilities that are discovered during early infancy may disrupt the attachment process. Yaman and Altay (2015) observed that a high percentage of parents whose newborns were hospitalized in a neonatal intensive care unit (NICU) developed post-traumatic stress disorders (PTSD) after being informed of their child's condition. High stress levels and depression are known to lessen the quality of parental attachment and caregiving (e.g., disrupted sensitivity to infant signals, inappropriate behavioral response), including the care of other children at home (Conradt et al., 2016; Leerkes et al., 2015). In addition, the NICU environment and high-tech equipment that an infant may be attached to can be intimidating for parents, and thus requires that staff are sensitive to parental reactions and implement measures which will help parents to establish an emotional bond with their infant.

The birth of a child with a disability also affects the lives of siblings. Most children adjust well to their new sibling role. When they realize the experience as life-changing, they quarrel less with their sibling and become more empathetic, loving, responsible, and appreciative (Ward et al., 2016). Other studies have found increased behavioral problems, social impairments, and externalizing and internalizing problems among the children who have a sibling with a disability. However, these effects appear to be related to complex family dynamics (e.g., higher parental stress and depressive symptoms, lower levels of attention, greater financial strain) rather than simply to having a sibling with a disability (Tudor & Lerner, 2015). Therefore, some but not all, siblings may need and benefit from interventions that support their adjustment and understanding.

It is important that families of infants and toddlers with developmental delays or disabilities be informed of the intervention programs available to them and that they are assisted in making an initial contact. State administered early identification (Child Find) and intervention services are provided through Part C of IDEA to eligible children from birth to age 3 years and their families. A family service coordinator works closely with a family to identify the child's specific needs and family resources, arranges for appropriate services (e.g., assistive technology, physical therapy, mental health services), monitors progress, and amends services to meet the child's needs and support continued progress. An Individualized Family Service Plan (IFSP) provides a procedural outline for achieving identified goals and objectives and is developed for each child eligible to receive services (see Figure 14-4). Whenever feasible, early intervention services are delivered in the child's natural environment (e.g., child's home, care provider's home, early education center). Parents are valued and involved in each step of this interdisciplinary approach, and also are eligible to receive essential services (e.g., mental health, nutrition, financial) that will help to support the child's development.

Parents are an integral member of the IFSP team because they have a thorough and unique understanding of their child. Parents can prepare for IFSP meetings and be an active team member by reviewing the IFSP document (a draft should be given to the parent prior to the meeting), developing a list of their child's and family's strengths and needs to share, learning how service providers work with the child, and requesting information about ways to support their child's development in everyday activities. During the meetings, progress toward achieving the IFSP goals is reviewed, any new information (e.g., assessments completed, changes in family) is discussed, changes are made to the original plan, and team members sign a document to approve the revised plan.

Children who remain eligible after age 3 years are transitioned into the public school system, where they will continue to receive services. Transition planning is required by law to begin at least 6 months prior to the child's third birthday in order to assure a smooth transition and ease parental concerns. Change may be difficult for parents and children who have grown comfortable working with the same staff and service providers. Language barriers, differences in cultural expectations, and lack of familiarity with available services may further hinder the process (Khanlou et al., 2015).

Photo 14-6 Some exceptionalities are not discovered until the preschool years.

14-3b Parenting Preschool-Age Children with Exceptionalities

Delayed or impaired fine/gross motor, speech/language, intellectual, or social/emotional skill development may not be discovered until children reach their preschool years. In some instances, parents may deny or not recognize that their child was not developing as expected, or they may have been unsure of where to go for help (Jacobs, Woolfson, & Hunter, 2016). In other situations, a child's limitations (e.g., dyslexia, autism spectrum disorders, hearing loss) may not become apparent until they are older, or they begin to participate in an organized early education program with teachers who have a sound understanding of children's development. Although parents may have suspected all along that something "wasn't quite right," confirmation is likely to trigger emotional responses similar to those described in the previous section. However, some parents, particularly mothers, are relieved when their suspicions are finally confirmed and they are able to get appropriate help for the child (Lingen et al., 2016).

Developmental screening of preschool-age children (3 to 6 years) has been mandated through Part B of the Individuals with Disabilities Education Act (IDEA) (see Figure 14-5). Children with developmental delays or disabilities who meet state-determined disability criteria are eligible to receive special education services provided through their local public school system. Intervention teams work closely with parents to identify and develop an Individualized Educational Program (IEP), and provide services in children's homes or affiliated early intervention programs (see Figure 14-6). Some children who do not meet the criteria for special education services may qualify for a 504 Accommodations Plan that protects their rights as a student with a disability and provides access to accommodations that enable them to learn in the classroom.

Responsive Parenting

When Jordyn, a second-grader who has Down syndrome, got off the school bus, her mother could see that she had been crying. Jordyn told her mother that several boys on the bus were making fun of her "because she looked funny." How would you advise Jordyn's mother to respond to her daughter's hurt feelings? Would you encourage her to talk with Jordyn's teacher? What steps can the teacher take to help the class develop a better understanding of, and respect for, people with disabilities?

Figure 14-5 Guiding Principles of IDEA

Principle	Requirement
Free and appropriate public education (FAPE)	Guarantees children ages 3–21 years the right to a free public education. Requires schools to actively locate, evaluate and develop an IEP identifying appropriate educational services for any child with a disability.
Zero rejection	Prohibits schools from discriminating against a child with a disability, regardless of the disability severity.
Non-discriminatory evaluation	Evaluations must be conducted in the child's native language, include multiple non-discriminatory (e.g., race, culture, language) assessment methods, and have parental consent.
Least restrictive environment	Special educational services are provided to children in regular classrooms, to the extent possible. IEPs must include justifications for times when it is not appropriate for a child with disabilities to be included in an activity (e.g., lunch, recess, physical education classes).
Due process safeguards	Requires parental permission for their child to be evaluated and to receive services. Parents have the right to access children's records, request an independent evaluation at public expense, and request a hearing if they disagree with any step of the educational process.
Parent- and student-shared collaboration	Establishes a collaborative, team approach that includes decision-making parent and child (if appropriate) input throughout the process.

Figure 14-6 IDEA Part C and Part B Model Comparison

Part C	Part B
Serves children birth to age 3 years.	Serves children 3–21 years.
Provides services for children and their family.	Addresses needs specific to an individual child.
Services are organized by a family service coordinator who works closely with local community-based agencies.	Services are provided and coordinated through the local school district.
Requires an IFSP; is typically reviewed and updated every 6 months.	Requires an annual IEP; a multidisciplinary evaluation must be conducted/reviewed every 3 years to determine if services are still needed.
Delivers services in the child's natural environment (e.g., home, day care provider's home, early childhood center).	Delivers educational services in inclusive classrooms or affiliated early education programs.

14-3c Parenting School-Age Children and Adolescents with Exceptionalities

Parents and children with physical and developmental disabilities face several major school transitions over the course of 12 years: from early childhood to kindergarten, from grade school to middle school, and from middle school to high school. Each transition requires parents to invest additional time in attending planning meetings, making new arrangements with service providers, and supporting children through periods of uncertainty (Mandy et al., 2016; Welchons & McIntyre, 2015). Transitions also increase parental concerns about how children will adjust to new facilities, teachers, classmates, and routines.

As children with disabilities transition into formal inclusive educational settings, parents begin to worry about their child's social competence and ability to establish close friendships (Petrina, Carter, & Stephenson, 2016). Piazza et al. (2016) found that mothers, but not fathers, of children with cerebral palsy rated their child's social interactions and ability to form friendships as significant concerns. Approximately 40 percent

Suggestions for Parents 14-1

Teaching Children Social Skills

Puppets, role-play, matching games (especially for recognizing emotions), and modeling can be used effectively to help children who have developmental disabilities develop and practice social skills that are important for making and keeping friends, including:

- Using appropriate ways to seek attention or join a group
- Respecting other children's personal space
- Taking turns, sharing, and playing cooperatively
- Understanding other people's feelings, showing empathy, and responding appropriately
- Controlling impulses (e.g., anger, frustration) and touches
- Handling conflict in positive ways (e.g., compromise, bargaining)
- Initiating conversation, expressing desires, making requests, and apologizing; then, learning to carry on more complex interactions

of children with disabilities who are entering kindergarten, especially those with autism spectrum disorder, lack the basic social skills (e.g., language, understanding feelings, problem solving, self-regulation) necessary for friendship formation (Meyer & Ostrosky, 2016) (Suggestions for Parents 14-1). Azad et al. (2016) examined the effects of race, disability, and grade level on children's friendships and social network formation. They found that older (grades 3–5) African American and Latino children with autism spectrum disorder usually had fewer friends than their younger (K–2) White peers who did not have a disability. They also noted that older Latino children with autism spectrum disorder were the most likely to experience social isolation.

Some studies have reported an increase in bully victimization related to poor social skills among children with developmental disabilities or significant medical conditions, whereas others have found no difference between children with and without disabilities (see Figure 14-7) (Maïano et al., 2016; Faith et al., 2015; Son et al., 2014). Fink et al. (2015) noted that children with disabilities reported being bullied more often than did children without disabilities. However, researchers in this and other studies have not identified any significant difference in the rate of bullying among children with

Figure 14-7 Talking with Children about Disabilities

Take advantage of opportunities to help children understand, and learn respect for, people with different abilities.

- Ask children questions to determine what they are interested in knowing, and what they know about a disability.
- Provide explanations that are simple and direct (e.g., "she gets around in a wheelchair because her legs don't work"; "he hears with the special device attached to his head").
- Use "child-first" language and name the child's disorder ("she has Down syndrome," "he is blind").
- Teach children appropriate words to use when referring to a person with exceptionalities.
- Help children to understand how much all children are alike, rather than focusing on individual differences.
- Never permit children to bully or to make fun of another person, for any reason.

Photo 14-7 Children with exceptionalities are often subjected to peer teasing and bullying.

and without disabilities. Bear et al. (2015) suggested that discrepancies in reported study findings are likely due to differences in the way that researchers define bullying (e.g., verbal, physical, social-relational) and the frequency with which these behaviors are actually exhibited. Despite perception differences, researchers cite poor emotional control (e.g., angry outbursts, crying, frustration) and poor social skill development as factors that increase the risk of a child with disabilities being subjected to bullying (Hebron, Humphrey, & Oldfield, 2015).

Parents of school-age children also have concerns about the effect that a child's disability may have on sibling relationships and on the ability of their typically developing brothers and/or sisters to make friends. Although it has long been assumed that typically developing children were more likely to experience negative social and emotional problems if they had a sibling with a disability, the results of recent studies have been mixed (Petalas et al., 2015; Goudie et al., 2013). For example, children often express positive feelings and a sense of pride toward a sibling with Down syndrome in contrast to the anger, fear, and resentment experienced by children whose siblings have neurodevelopmental disorders (Gettings, Franco, & Santosh, 2015). Mothers of children with and without disabilities reported no significant difference in the frequency of sibling conflicts (Allison & Campbell, 2015). However, they described siblings as having a relationship that is less warm and close than one that is typically formed between siblings without disabilities. Walton and Ingersoll (2015) noted that, in general, there are no significant differences in the quality of sibling relationships among children with and without disabilities. However, they did find that older (mean of 11.2 years) male children experienced an increased risk for developing emotional and behavioral problems, and were less likely to share common interests, or to interact with a sibling who had an autism spectrum disorder.

Sexuality issues present another challenge that parents of older school-age children and adolescents with disabilities are often uncertain about how to manage and, thus, they may simply avoid the subject (McDaniels & Fleming, 2016). Although adolescents with intellectual and developmental disabilities may learn differently or at a slower rate, their bodies develop and mature at about the same age as do their typically developing peers. Researchers have noted that mothers of adolescent children with disabilities typically discussed fewer sexual topics and initiated conversations about sexuality at a later age than they did with children who were developing typically (Pownall, Jahoda, & Hastings, 2012). Many parents also expressed a lack of knowledge about children's sexual development, what sexual information children with disabilities needed to know, and how to present it in a way that they would understand (Miller et al., 2016).

Photo 14-8 Sex education is equally important for children with and without disabilities.

The disconnect between an adolescent's physical and intellectual development may lead parents to believe that children do not experience the same sexual interests and, thus, that sex education is unimportant. However, children without appropriate information are especially vulnerable to sexual exploitation, rape, sexual abuse, and sex trafficking (Mace, 2016; Miller et al., 2016; Reid, 2016). Linton and Rueda (2015) reported that Native American, African American, and Hispanic adolescents with disabilities experienced significantly higher rates of victimization and pregnancy than White girls. Limited contraception use, cultural beliefs (e.g., acceptance of abusive relationships, value placed on parenthood), and family values that do not discourage early dating and sexual behavior increase the likelihood of pregnancy among minority girls with disabilities (Rutman et al., 2012). Findings such as these point out the continued importance of providing sound sex education to children, with (and without) disabilities, about their sexual development and appropriate expression of sexual desires.

As children with developmental disabilities approach their final secondary school years, parents face another challenge in terms of planning for the future. Transition planning is mandated to begin at age 16 years (and younger in many states and U.S. territories) for students who have an Individualized Education Program (IEP, Part B, Indicator 13) (U.S. Department of Education, 2004). Together, the student and members of his/her IEP team identify desired postsecondary goals that pertain to education, training, employment, independent living skills, as well as the services that the child may need to achieve these objectives until he reaches age 21 years. A transition assessment, included in the planning process, aids students and their families in determining how likely it is that children will be able to achieve the future personal and vocational goals they desire. Parents also play an important role in this process by encouraging children to identify their strengths, limitations, and long-term interests, and to guide them in ways that will help to establish a successful adult life. Parents may find information posted on the National Secondary Transition Technical Assistance Center website helpful in working through this process with school personnel (also see page 317, Suggestions for Parents 11-3).

14-3d Parenting Adult Children with Exceptionalities

Medical advancements have contributed to increased life expectancy for many children with complex medical conditions and developmental disabilities. An estimated 71 percent of individuals with intellectual and developmental disabilities continue to live at home with their parents, and 25 percent of the primary caregivers in these settings are over the age of 60 years (Heller, Gibbons, & Fisher, 2015; Braddock et al., 2013). Researchers have noted that caregivers of children with disabilities experience a higher incidence of chronic stress, depression, health problems, and cognitive decline (Miodrag et al., 2015; Song, 2015).

For these reasons, it is important that parents make long-term plans and arrangements that address their children's needs and begin to move from a system of entitlement (IDEA) to a complex and fragmented service system. This process often raises significant anxiety and may prove to be overwhelming at times, especially if parents are unfamiliar with the available resources and supports that a child may need to live independently. Consequently, many parents fail to discuss, initiate, or establish clear advanced plans (DeJong, 2016; Davys, Mitchell, & Haigh, 2015; Joly, 2015). Davys (2015) and her colleagues found that parents of children with disabilities often simply assume that siblings will step in and accept greater responsibility for a child's care if and when they are no longer able. Although siblings understood that they would likely become more involved as their parents aged, they were also unclear about the specifics (e.g., services, finances, living arrangements).

Parents express many uncertainties as their children with disabilities transition to adulthood. They consistently worry that children are vulnerable to abuse and need to be protected from individuals who may take advantage of their limitations (Pryce et al., 2015; Thackeray & Eatough, 2015). They are concerned about long-term financial support for their child as well as who will continue to provide care when they die or are no longer physically able to do so. Because these questions force parents to consider their own mortality, many find it easier to simply avoid broaching the subject.

Photo 14-9 Early planning is essential to maintaining support services that adolescents need for independent living. karelnoppe/Shutterstock.com

Researchers have also detected a common distrust for service providers among the parents and siblings of children with disabilities. They are often dismayed by a seemingly lack of compassion, coordination, and communication demonstrated by these individuals and organizations (Thackeray & Eatough, 2015; Cook et al., 2013). Siblings have also expressed concerns about the lack of information (e.g., about disorders, how to navigate the service system, available resources), ongoing education (e.g., conferences, workshops), and sibling support groups (Arnold, Heller, & Kramer, 2013). They want to be included earlier in the planning stages so that they are familiar with their sibling's disability needs and service providers before it is necessary for them to assume caregiving responsibilities.

There are several important steps that parents must address as their children with disabilities transition from secondary school to adulthood. Although some preliminary planning for this transition is included in the student's final IEP, it will be necessary for parents to assume responsibility for making service arrangements (e.g., financial, education/training, employment, living accommodations) once the student has left school.

Social security programs (Social Security Disability Insurance [SSDI] and Supplemental Security Income [SSI]) serve as major income sources for many adults with disabilities. In most states, a person who is eligible for SSI also automatically qualifies for Medicaid coverage to help cover their health care expenses. Parents can contact state-operated vocational rehabilitation service programs to learn about employment opportunities, skill training, and assistance in locating jobs available to adults with disabilities. Job training and placement resources are also provided through local Workforce Centers. These programs are established in each state as a result of the Workforce Investment Act (WIA) 1998, and funded through the U.S. Department of Labor. Students who are interested in pursuing a postsecondary education can work with student disability service offices (available at most institutions) for assistance in securing accommodations, financial support, and services to help them succeed in school. Adult children with disabilities may continue to live at home with their parents, or parents may decide to make alternative housing arrangements (e.g., adult residential facilities, foster home placements, independent living housing, in-home care). The Disability.gov website offers an excellent, one-stop information source about everything from benefits, law, and housing options to employment, health, emergency preparedness, and transportation.

Parents of children with disabilities may also want to consider addressing several legal matters in their long-term planning process: will preparation, appointment of a guardian to assist with decision-making, and establishment of a trust for added financial support (Wrightslaw, 2016). It is important that these decisions be made carefully because the options can affect a child's rights and financial benefits (Jameson et al., 2015; Brunetti, 2013). For example, Jameson et al. (2015) describes different types of guardianships, and points out that, although full ("plenary") guardianships are most common, they also remove all individual decision-making rights after a guardian is appointed. In contrast, an individual who has disabilities retains certain declared rights (e.g., financial, personal care) under a "partial or limited" guardianship. Unless an individual's decision-making abilities are in question, removing all rights and responsibilities can be damaging to the person's self-esteem and leave them feeling inadequate to manage any of their own affairs. Trusts and wills must also be set up properly to prevent the child from losing Social Security benefits.

14-3e Parenting Children who are Exceptionally Gifted

By definition, gifted children exhibit exceptional potential or aptitude (e.g., intellectual, leadership, creativity, performance and visual arts, sports). Although there is no official tally, the National Association of Gifted Children (NAGC) estimates that there are approximately 3 to 5 million (6 to 7 percent of the student population) academically gifted U.S. children in the elementary and secondary grades (NAGC, 2016). However, it is likely that many more children, especially minorities, with exceptional talents remain unidentified, because of limited opportunities (e.g., poverty, availability) or lack of encouragement (e.g., cultural values, parental support, discrimination) to express their talents. Ford (2015) noted that 50 percent of Black students and 40 percent of Hispanic students remain unidentified or uninvolved in gifted education programs. Barnard-Brak et al. (2015) also reported that approximately 3 percent of the 13,000 children with disabilities who participated in the Special Education Elementary Longitudinal Study were identified as being gifted; however, only 11 percent of those children were actually involved in programs for gifted and talented students. Particularly underrepresented in these programs were female, African American, and Hispanic children.

The absence of Federal funding or mandates requiring schools to identify and serve exceptionally talented students has typically left these decisions up to individual states and local school districts. However, a lack of funds has forced many districts to eliminate or significantly reduce their enrichment services (Kettler, Russell, & Puryear, 2015). Some schools have responded by adding more advanced placement courses at the secondary level, or exploring online delivery methods (Swan et al., 2015). Additionally, some parents are choosing to homeschool their children or to send them to private schools or specialized magnet schools.

Parents play an important role in recognizing children's unique interests and talents, and serving as advocates on their behalf. They can work closely with teachers to discover enrichment opportunities, resources, and methods to foster children's advanced learning. Researchers have also found that gifted children tend to thrive in family environments where parents are respectful, nurturing, flexible, and responsive (Olszewski-Kublilius, Lee, & Thomson, 2014).

Reports of increased rates of emotional and behavioral problems (e.g., tantrums, lack of friends, poor social skills) among children identified as gifted have been attributed to parents' differential treatment (e.g., setting higher expectations, pressuring children to achieve) (Freeman, 2013). This situation has led some parents to object to having their child labeled "gifted" for fear that they would be teased, judged, or treated differently (Matthews, Ritchotte, & Jolly, 2014). However, recent studies have not found any correlation between giftedness and children's increased risk of developing emotional or social problems (Peyre et al., 2016; Eklund et al., 2015).

14-4 Family-Centered Approach

All parents have hopes and dreams for their children; the journey for some parents may take a different course than they had initially envisioned. As a result, they may follow an alternative path and stop frequently along the way for guidance and direction. Some parts of their journey will be pleasurable and rewarding, while others may present occasional obstacles and hardship. In the process, parents will always remember the person who took time to listen, answer their questions, and provide information in ways that would help them provide the guidance they hoped they could provide for their children.

Working collaboratively with families creates a partnership that has benefits for everyone involved (e.g., children, parents, siblings, extended family members). A **family-centered approach** is based upon principles of trust, effective two-way communication, parent involvement, unbiased support, and on-going education (see Figure 14-8) (see Chapter 3). It acknowledges the important stabilizing role that parents play in children's lives and empowers their efforts in advocating, planning, decision-making, implementing, and evaluating intervention services designed to meet children's needs.

Although most families are satisfied with the family-centered intervention approach, special efforts may be needed to reach out to certain groups. Fox et al. (2015)

family-centered approach a philosophy that supports parental strengths and acknowledges the important role that parents play in a child's life.

Figure 14-8 Fundamental Elements of a Family-Centered Approach

- Establish a trusting and honest relationship with families.

- Work closely with families to identify and strengthen their abilities.

- Engage and involve families in advocating, goal setting, decision-making, and evaluating services to maximize a child's development.

- Facilitate and maintain open and frequent communication between parents and service providers.

- Address children's and parent's needs in a manner that is respectful of cultural, socioeconomic, language, religious, and individual differences.

- Identify appropriate community-based resources and services, and assist families in negotiating arrangements.

Adapted from: Child Welfare Information Gateway. U.S. Department of Health & Human Services. Administration for Children & Families (n.d.)

Photo 14-10 Family involvement and family-centered practices improve service quality and delivery.
wallybird/Shutterstock.com

noted that fathers often faced more obstacles (e.g., work conflicts, stress, financial concerns) that limit their involvement in the intervention process. Those who were engaged experienced improved self-efficacy and were more likely to participate in their child's care. Swafford et al. (2015) reported that single mothers of children who received services often felt stigmatized by their single parent status. Several parents thought that living in a rural community or having a child with more severe disabilities limited the services they were able to receive. Azuine et al. (2015) also noted significant geographical, racial/ethnic, and sociode-mographic disparities in the quality of family-centered services that were provided for families. Particularly noteworthy was their finding that children living in low-income, low-education, minority, and non–English-speaking families in the southern and western United States were less likely to receive family-centered interventions than other children.

Clearly, many opportunities remain for improving family-centered practices, service delivery, and relationships with and among service providers. Because parents are one of a child's most valuable teachers, it is important that they have access to the best information and resources available to support positive outcomes for children and themselves.

Summary

- Significant philosophical and legislative developments occurred between 1965 and 1990 that would forever change the way that children with disabilities would be treated and educated.

- Parents of children with exceptionalities experience additional parenting issues, including relational, health, social, financial, and cultural challenges. Some parents consider the experience of rearing a child with exceptionalities as having a positive effect on their lives.

- Parental challenges and responsibilities change with each developmental stage. Parents of infants and toddlers who have a disability may be singularly focused on adjusting to a recent diagnosis and learning how to meet a child's special caregiving needs, whereas parents of adolescents are beginning to make plans for a child's future and independent living arrangements.

- A family-centered approach acknowledges parents' continuous role in their child's life. It honors a family's unique culture and needs, and builds on their strengths to promote and support children's development.

Key Terms

Child Find (p. 387) **family-centered approach** (p. 401)

Questions for Discussion and Self-Reflection

1. How has the Head Start concept influenced contemporary ideas about early identification and intervention?

2. In what ways are IFSPs and IEPs similar to, and different from, each other?

3. Why is cultural context important to consider when working with a family of a child who has an exceptionality?

4. What long-range plans should the parents of adolescent and adult children make, and why is it important that they begin the process early?

5. What characteristics distinguish a family-centered approach from a traditional service-delivery model?

Field Activities

1. Contact several public and private schools (e.g., primary, secondary) in your area to determine what services they provide for children who are gifted. If few or no special services are offered, identify enrichment resources in the community that parents might consider for a child who is a gifted writer or has a special interest in science.

2. Locate and interview two parents of a child with exceptionalities: one who has an IFSP and another who has an IEP. Compare and contrast their experiences with the intervention process.

3. Spend an hour with a child who has a disability. Note and compile a list of the child's positive qualities (e.g., personality, skills, learning potential) that you observed during this experience. Describe how you think these qualities could be used to encourage and support learning.

REFERENCES

Ahmed, S., Bryant, L., Ahmed, M., Jafri, H., & Raashid, Y. (2013). Experiences of parents with a child with Down syndrome in Pakistan and their views on termination of pregnancy. *Journal of Community Genetics, 4*(1), 107–114.

Allison, M., & Campbell, M. (2015). Mothers' perceptions of the quality of childhood sibling relationships affected by disability. *The Australian Educational and Developmental Psychologist, 32*(1), 56–70.

American Academy of Pediatrics (AAP). (2016). Recommendations for preventive pediatric health care. Retrieved June 15, 2016 from https://www.aap.org/en-us/Documents/periodicity _schedule.pdf.

Archibald, A., Hickerton, C., Wake, S., Jaques, A., Cohen, J., & Metcalfe, S. (2016). "It gives them more options": Preferences for preconception genetic carrier screening for fragile X syndrome in primary healthcare. *Journal of Community Genetics, 27*(2), 159–171.

Arnold, C., Heller, T., & Kramer, J. (2012). Support needs of siblings of people with developmental disabilities. *Intellectual and Developmental Disabilities, 50*(5), 373–382.

Azad, G., Locke, J., Kasari, C., & Mandell, D. (2016). Race, disability, and grade: Social relationships in children with autism spectrum disorders. *Autism*. Advance online publication. doi: 10.1177/1362361315627792.

Azuine, R., Singh, G., Ghandour, R., & Kogan, M. (2015). Geographic, racial/ethnic, and sociodemographic disparities in parent-reported receipt of family-centered care among U.S. children. *International Journal of Family Medicine*. doi:10.1155/2015/168521.

Baeza-Velasco, C., Michelon, C., Rattaz, C., Pernon, E., & Baghdad, A. (2013). Separation of parents raising children with autism spectrum disorders. *Journal of Developmental and Physical Disabilities, 25*(6), 613–624.

Barnard-Brak, L., Johnsen, S., Hannig, A., & Wei, T. (2015). The incidence of potentially gifted students within a special education population. *Roeper Review: A Journal of Gifted Education, 37*(2), 74–83.

Bear, G., Mantz, L., Glutting, J., Yang, C., & Boyer, D. (2015). Differences in bullying victimization between students with and without disabilities. *School Psychology Review, 44*(1), 98–116.

Bierman, K., Welsh, J., Heinrichs, B., Nix, R., & Mathis, E. (2015). Helping Head Start parents promote their children's kindergarten adjustment: The research-based developmentally informed parent program. *Child Development, 86*(6), 1877–1891.

Blacher, J., Begum, G., Marcoulides, G., & Baker, B. (2013). Longitudinal perspectives of child positive impact on families: Relationship to disability and culture. *American Journal on Intellectual and Developmental Disabilities, 118*(2), 141–155.

Boulet, S., & Molinari, N. (2008). Health care expenditures for infants and young children with Down syndrome in a privately insured population. *Journal of Pediatrics, 153*(2), 241–246.

Bourke-Taylor, H., Cotter, C., & Stephan, R. (2015). Complementary, alternative, and mainstream service use among families with young children with multiple disabilities: Family costs to access care. *Physical and Occupational Therapy in Pediatrics, 35*(3), 311–325.

Braddock, D., Hemp, R., Rizzolo, M., Tanis, E., Haffer, L., Lulinski-Norris, A., & Wu, J. (2013). *The state of the states in developmental disabilities: 2013. The Great Recession and its aftermath*. Washington, DC: American Association on Intellectual and Developmental Disabilities (AAIDD).

Brenner, M., Cote, S., Boivin, M., & Tremblay, R. (2016). Severe congenital malformations, family functioning and parents' separation/divorce: A longitudinal study. *Child: Care, Health and Development, 42*(1), 16–24.

Bronfenbrenner, U. (1979). *The ecology of human development experiments by nature and design*. Cambridge, MA: Harvard University Press.

Brunetti, F. (2013). Estate planning: Getting started. Retrieved March 30, 2016 from http://www.wrightslaw.com/info/brunetti.getting.started.pdf.

Burkett, K., Morris, E., Manning-Courtney, P., Anthony, J., & Shambley-Ebron, D. (2015). African American families on autism diagnosis and treatment: The influence of culture. *Journal of Autism and Developmental Disorders, 45*(10). 3244–3254.

Cantwell, J., Muldoon, O., & Gallagher, S. (2015). The influence of self-esteem and social support on the relationship between stigma and depressive symptomology in parents caring for children with intellectual disabilities. *Journal of Intellectual Disability Research, 59*(10), 948–957.

Cantwell, J., Muldoon, O., & Gallagher, S. (2014). Social support and mastery influence the association between stress and poor physical health in parents caring for children with developmental disabilities. *Research in Developmental Disabilities, 35*(9), 2215–2223.

Centers for Disease Control and Prevention (CDC). (n.d.). Communicating with and about people with disabilities. Retrieved from http://www.cdc.gov/ncbddd/disabilityandhealth/pdf/disabilityposter_photos.pdf

Centers for Disease Control and Prevention (CDC). (2016). Birth defects. Retrieved on March 22, from http://www.cdc.gov/ncbddd/birthdefects/data.html.

Child Welfare Information Gateway. U.S. Department of Health & Human Services. Administration for Children & Families (n.d.). Philosophy and key elements of family-centered practice. Retrieved September 1, 2016 from https://www.childwelfare.gov/topics/famcentered/philosophy/.

Choi, J., Elicker, J., Christ, S., & Dobbs-Oate, J. (2016). Predicting growth trajectories in early academic learning: Evidence from growth curve modeling with Head Start children. *Early Childhood Research Quarterly, 36*(3), 244–258.

Ciccia, A., Roizen, N., Garvey, M., Bielefeld, R., & Short, E. (2015). Identification of neurodevelopmental disabilities in underserved children using telehealth (INvesT): Clinical trial study design. *Contemporary Clinical Trials, 45*(Part B), 226–232.

Cicirelli, V. (1969). *The impact of Head Start: An evaluation of the effects of Head Start on children's cognitive and affective development.* Athens, OH: Westinghouse Learning Corporation.

Cohen, S., Holloway, S., Domínguez-Pareto, I., & Kuppermann, M. (2015). Support and self-efficacy among Latino and White parents of children with ID. *American Journal on Intellectual and Developmental Disabilities, 120*(1), 16–31.

Conradt, E., Hawes, K., Guerin, D., Armstrong, D., Marsit, C., Tronick, E., & Lester, B. (2016). The contributions of maternal sensitivity and maternal depressive symptoms to epigenetic processes and neuroendocrine functioning. *Child Development, 87*(1), 73–85.

Cook, K., Siden, H., Jack, S., Thabane, L., & Browne, G. (2013). Up against the system: A case study of young adult perspectives transitioning from pediatric palliative care. *Nursing Research and Practice.* Retrieved on March 30, 2016 from http://dx.doi.org/10.1155/2013/286751.

Davys, D., Mitchell, D., & Haigh, C. (2015). Futures planning–adult sibling perspectives. *British Journal of Learning Disabilities, 43*(3), 219–226.

Deans, Z., Clarke, A., & Newson, A. (2015). For your interest? The ethical acceptability of using non-invasive prenatal testing to test 'purely for information.' *Bioethics, 29*(1), 19–25.

DeJong, N., Wood, C., Morreale, M., Ellis, C., Davis, D., Fernandez, J., & Steiner, M. (2016). Identifying social determinants of health and legal needs for children with special health care needs. *Clinical Pediatrics, 55*(3), 272–277.

Duncan, G., & Magnuson, K. (2013). Investing in preschool programs? *Journal of Economic Perspectives, 27*(2), 109–132.

Eggum-Wilkens, N., Fabes, R., Castle, S., Zhang, L., Hanish, L., & Martin, C. (2014). Playing with others: Head Start children's peer play and relations with kindergarten school competence. *Early Childhood Research Quarterly, 29*(3), 345–356.

Eklund, K., Tanner, N., Stoll, K., & Anway, L. (2015). Identifying emotional and behavioral risk among gifted and nongifted children: A multi-gate, multi-informant approach. *School Psychology Quarterly, 30*(2), 197–211.

Executive Office of the President of the United States. (2014). *The economics of early childhood investments.* Retrieved April 10, 2016 from https://www.whitehouse.gov/sites/default/files/docs/early_childhood_report1.pdf.

Faith, M., Reed, G., Heppner, C., Hamill, L., Tarkenton, T., & Donewar, C. (2015). Fragile youth: A review of risks, protective factors, and recommendations for medical providers. *Journal of Developmental & Behavioral Pediatrics, 36*(4), 285–301.

Faso, D., Neal-Beevers, A., & Carlson, C. (2013). Vicarious futurity, hope, and well-being in parents of children with autism spectrum disorder. *Research in Autism Spectrum Disorders, 7*(2), 288–297.

Fink, E., Deighton, J., Humphrey, N., & Wolpert, M. (2015). Assessing the bullying and victimisation experiences of children with special educational needs in mainstream schools: Development and validation of the Bullying Behaviour and Experience Scale. *Research in Developmental Disabilities, 36*, 611–619.

Fonseca, A., Nazaré, B., & Canavarro, M. (2015). Parenting an infant with a congenital anomaly: How are perceived burden and perceived personal benefits related to parenting stress? *Journal of Clinical Psychology in Medical Settings, 22*(1), 64–76.

Ford, D. (2015). Culturally responsive gifted classrooms for culturally different students. *Gifted Child Today, 38*(1), 67–69.

Fox, G., Nordquist, V., Billen, R., & Savoca, E. (2015). Father involvement and early intervention: Effects of empowerment and father role identity. *Family Relations, 64*(4), 461–475.

Freeman, J. (2013). The long-term effects of families and educational provision on gifted children. *Educational Child Psychology, 30*(2), 7–17.

Gallagher, S., Phillips, A., Lee, H., & Carroll, D. (2015). The association between spirituality and depression in parents caring for children with developmental disabilities: Social support and/or last resort. *Religion and Health, 54*(1), 358–370.

Genereaux, D., van Karnebeek, C., & Birch, P. (2015). Costs of caring for children with an intellectual developmental disorder. *Disability and Health Journal, 8*(4), 646–651.

Gettings, S., Franco, F., & Santosh, P. (2015). Facilitating support groups for siblings of children with neurodevelopmental disorders using audio-conferencing: A longitudinal feasibility study. *Child and Adolescent Psychiatry and Mental Health, 9*(8). doi 10.1186/s13034-015-0041-z.

Giallo, R., Wood, C., Jellett, R., & Porter, R. (2013). Fatigue, wellbeing and parental self-efficacy in mothers of children with an autism spectrum disorder. *Autism, 17*(4), 465–480.

Goudie, A., Havercamp, S., Jamieson, B., & Sahr, T. (2013). Assessing functional impairment in siblings living with children with disability. *Pediatrics, 132*(2), e476–e483.

Guon, J., Wilfond, B., Farlow, B., Brazg, T., & Janvier, A. (2014). Our children are not a diagnosis: The experience of parents who continue their pregnancy after a prenatal diagnosis of trisomy 13 or 18. *American Journal of Medical Genetics, 164A*(2), 308–318.

Harden, B., Sandstrom, H., & Chazan-Cohen, R. (2012). Early Head Start and African American families: Impacts and mechanisms of child outcomes. *Early Childhood Research Quarterly, 27*(4), 572–581.

Hebron, J., Humphrey, N., & Oldfield, J. (2015). Vulnerability to bullying of children with autism spectrum conditions in mainstream education: A multi-informant qualitative exploration. *Journal of Research in Special Educational Needs, 15*(3), 185–193.

Heckman, J., & Raut, L. (2016). Intergenerational long-term effects of preschool-structural estimates from a discrete dynamic programming model. *Journal of Econometrics, 191*(1), 164–175.

Heller, T., Gibbons, H., & Fisher, D. (2015). Caregiving and family support interventions: Crossing networks of aging and developmental disabilities. *Intellectual and Developmental Disabilities, 53*(5), 329–345.

Hindman, A., & Wasik, B. (2015). Building vocabulary in two languages: An examination of Spanish-speaking dual language learners in Head Start. *Early Childhood Research Quarterly, 31*(2), 19–33.

Hsiao, Y. (2016). Pathways to mental health-related quality of life for parents of children with autism spectrum disorder: Roles of parental stress, children's performance, medical support, and neighbor support. *Research in Autism Spectrum Disorders, 23*, 122–130.

Hubbell, R. (1983). A review of Head Start research since 1970. Washington, DC: U.S. Department of Health and Human Services.

Jacobs, M., Woolfson, L., & Hunter, S. (2016). Attributions of stability, control and responsibility: How parents of children with intellectual disabilities view their child's problematic behaviour and its causes. *Journal of Applied Research in Intellectual Disabilities, 29*(1), 58–70.

Jameson, J., Riesen, T., Polychronis, S., Trader, B., Mizner, S., Martinis, J., & Hoyle, D. (2015). Guardianship and the potential of supported decision making with individuals with disabilities. *Research and Practice for Persons with Severe Disabilities, 40*(1), 36–51.

Joly, E. (2015). Transition to adulthood for young people with medical complexity: An integrative literature review. *Journal of Pediatric Nursing, 30*(5), e91–e103.

Jones, L., Totsika, V., Hastings, R., & Petalas, M. (2013*)*. Gender differences when parenting children with autism spectrum disorders: A multilevel modeling approach. *Journal of Autism and Developmental Disorders, 43*(9), 2090–2098.

Karoly, L., Kilburn, R., & Cannon, J. (2005). Proven results, future promise. Retrieved on March 13, 2016 from http://www.rand.org/content/dam/rand/pubs/monographs/2005 /RAND_MG341.pdf.

Kerr, B., & Multon, K. (2015). The development of gender identity, gender roles, and gender relations in gifted students. *Journal of Counseling and Development, 93*(2), 183–191.

Kettler, T., Russell, J., & Puryear, J. (2015). Inequitable access to gifted education: Variance in funding and staffing based on locale and contextual school variables. *Journal for the Education of the Gifted, 38*(2), 99–117.

Khanlou, N., Haque, N., Sheehan, S., & Jones, G. (2015). "It is an issue of not knowing where to go": Service providers' perspectives on challenges in accessing social support services by immigrant mothers of children with disabilities. *Journal of Immigrant and Minority Health, 17*(6), 1840–1847.

King, G., Zwaigenbaum, L., Bates, A., Baxter, D., & Rosenbaum, P. (2012). Parent views of the positive contributions of elementary and high school-aged children with autism spectrum disorders and Down syndrome. *Child: Care, Health, and Development 38*(6), 817–828.

Kubler-Ross, E. (1969). *On death and dying.* New York: Macmillan.

Lane, J., & Jones, D. (2015). Child Find practices in Christian schools. *Journal of Research on Christian Education, 24*(3), 212–223.

Laxman, D., McBride, B., Jeans, L., Dyer, W., Santos, R., Kern, J., . . . & Weglarz-Ward, J. (2015). Father involvement and maternal depressive symptoms in families of children with disabilities or delays. *Maternal and Child Health Journal, 19*(5), 1078–1086.

Lazar, I., Darlington, R., Murray, H., Royce, J., Snipper, A., & Ramey, C. (1982). Lasting effects of early education: A report from the Consortium for Longitudinal Studies. *Monographs of the Society for Research in Child Development, 47*(2/3), 1–151.

Lee, V., Brooks-Gunn, J., Schnur, E., Liaw, F. (1990). "Are Head Start effects sustained? A longitudinal follow-up comparison of disadvantaged children attending Head Start, no preschool, and other preschool programs". *Child Development, 61*(2), 495–507.

Lee, Y., Park, H., & Recchia, S. (2015). Embracing each other and growing together: Redefining the meaning of caregiving a child with disabilities. *Journal of Child and Family Studies*, 24(12), 3662–3675.

Leerkes, E., Supple, A., O'Brien, M., Calkins, S., Haltigan, J., Wong, M., & Fortuna, K. (2015). Antecedents of maternal sensitivity during distressing tasks: Integrating attachment, social information processing, and psychobiological perspectives. *Child Development*, 86(1), 94–111.

Leon, A., Holliker, S., & Pepe, J. (2015). The importance of the first 5 years: Pediatrician identification of developmental delays and other related concerns. *Journal of Social Service Research*, 41(4), 425–444.

Lingen, M., Albers, L., Borchers, M., Haass, S., Gärtner, J., Schröder, S., . . . & Zirn, B. (2016). Obtaining a genetic diagnosis in a child with disability: Impact on parental quality of life. *Clinical Genetics*, 89(2), 258–266.

Linton, K. & Rueda, H. (2015). Dating and sexuality among minority adolescents with disabilities: An application of sociocultural theory. *Journal of Human Behavior in the Social Environment*, 25(2), 77–89.

Long, K., Kao, B., Plante, W., Seifer, R., & Lobato, D. (2015). Cultural and child-related predictors of distress among Latina caregivers of children with intellectual disabilities. *American Journal of Intellectual and Developmental Disabilities*, 120(2), 145–165.

Lumeng, J., Kaciroti, N., Sturza, J., Krusky, A., Miller, A., Peterson, K., . . . & Reischl, T. (2015). Changes in body mass index associated with Head Start participation. *Pediatrics 135*, e449–456.

Mace, S. (2016). Global threats to child safety. *Pediatric Clinics of North America*, 63(1), 19–35.

Macy, M., Marks, K., & Towle, A. (2014). Missed, misused, or mismanaged: Improving early detection systems to optimize child outcomes. *Topics in Early Childhood Special Education*, 34(2), 94–105.

Maïano, C., Aimé, A., Salvas, M., Morin, A., & Normand, C. (2016). Prevalence and correlates of bullying perpetration and victimization among school-aged youth with intellectual disabilities: A systematic review. *Research in Developmental Disabilities*, 49-50, 181–195.

Mandy, W., Murin, M., Baykaner, O., Staunton, S., Hellriegel, J., Anderson, S., & Skuse, D. (2016). The transition from primary to secondary school in mainstream education for children with autism spectrum disorder. *Autism, 20*(1), 5–13.

March of Dimes. (2016). Global report on birth defects. Retrieved March 22, 2016 from http://www.marchofdimes.org/mission/march-of-dimes-global-report-on-birth-defects.aspx#.

Matthews, M., Ritchotte, J., & Jolly, J. (2014). What's wrong with giftedness? Parents perceptions of the gifted label. *International Studies in Sociology of Education*, 24(4), 372–393.

Mcbean, A., & Scholsnagle, L. (2016). Sleep, health and memory: Comparing parents of typically developing children and parents of children with special health-care needs. *Journal of Sleep Research*, 25(1), 78–87.

McDaniels, B., & Fleming, A. (2016). Sexuality education and intellectual disability: Time to address the challenge. *Sexuality and Disability, 34*(2), 215–225.

Meisels, S., & Shonkoff, J. (2000). Early childhood intervention: A continuing evolution. In, J. Shonkoff and S. Meisels, (Eds.), *Handbook of early childhood intervention* (2nd Ed.). New York, NY: Cambridge University Press.

Meyer, L., & Ostrosky, M. (2016). Impact of an affective intervention on the friendships of kindergarteners with disabilities. *Topics in Early Childhood Special Education*, 35(4), 200–210.

Miller, H., Pavlik, K., Kim, M., & Rogers, K. (2016). An exploratory study of the knowledge of personal safety skills among children with developmental disabilities and their parents. *Journal of Applied Research in Intellectual Disabilities*. Advanced online publication. doi: 10.1111/jar.12239.

Minnes, P., Perry, A., & Weiss, J. (2015). Predictors of distress and well-being in parents of young children with developmental delays and disabilities: The importance of parent perceptions. *Journal of Intellectual Disability Research*, 59(6), 551–560.

Miodrag, N., Burke, M., Tanner-Smith, E., & Hodapp, R. (2015). Adverse health in parents of children with disabilities and chronic health conditions: A meta-analysis using the Parenting Stress Index's Health Sub-domain. *Journal of Intellectual Disability Research*, 59(3), 257–271.

Miranda, A., Tarraga, R., Fernandez, M., & Colomer, C. (2105). Parenting stress in families of children with autism spectrum disorder and ADHD. *Exceptional Children*, 82(1), 81–95.

Montessori, M. (2002). *The Montessori method* (1912). Mineola, NY: Dover.

Namkung, E., Song, J., Greenberg, J., Mailick, M., & Floyd, F. (2015). The relative risk of divorce in parents of children with developmental disabilities: Impacts of lifelong parenting. *American Journal of Intellectual and Developmental Disabilities, 120*(6), 514–526.

National Association of Gifted Children (NAGC). (2016). Retrieved March 30, 2016 from http://www.nagc.org/.

Nelson, C., Zeahah, C., Fox, N., Marshall, P., Smyke, A., & Guthrie, D. (2007). Cognitive recovery in socially deprived young children: The Bucharest early intervention project. *Science, 318*(5858), 1937–1940.

Olszewski-Kubilius, P., Lee, S., & Thomson, D. (2014). Family environment and social development of gifted students. *Gifted Child Quarterly, 58*(3), 199–216.

Pfeiffer, D. (1993). Overview of the disability movement: History, legislative record, and political implications. *Policy Studies Journal, 21*(4), 724–734.

Parish, S., Thomas, K., Williams, C., & Crossman, M. (2015). Autism and families' financial burden: The association with health insurance coverage. *American Journal of Intellectual and Developmental Disabilities, 120*(2), 166–175.

Parkes, A., Sweeting, H., & Wight, D. (2015). Parenting stress and parent support among mothers with high and low education. *Journal of Family Psychology, 29*(6), 907–918.

Petalas, M., Hastings, R., Nash, S., & Duff, S. (2015). Typicality and subtle difference in sibling relationships: Experiences of adolescents with autism. *Journal of Child and Family Studies, 24*(1), 38–49.

Petrina, N., Carter, M., & Stephenson, J. (2016). Parental perception of the importance of friendship and other outcome priorities in children with autism spectrum disorder. *European Journal of Special Needs Education, 30*(1), 61–74.

Peyre, H., Ramus, F., Melchoir, M., Forhan, A., Heude, B., & Gauvrit, N. (2016). Emotional, behavioral and social difficulties among high-IQ children during the preschool period: Results of the EDEN mother–child cohort. *Personality and Individual Differences, 94*, 366–371.

Piaget, J. (1954). *The construction of reality in the child*. New York: Basic Books.

Piazza, B., Hennrikus, W., Schell, R., Armstrong, D., & Fortuna, K. (2016). The factors most important for quality of life in children and adolescents with cerebral palsy. *Journal of Pediatric Neurology & Medicine, 1*:102. doi:10.4172/jpnm.1000102.

Pownall, J., Jahoda, A., & Hastings, R. (2012). Sexuality and sex education of adolescents with intellectual disabilities: Mother's attitudes, experiences, and support needs. *Intellectual and Developmental Disabilities, 50*(2), 140–154.

Pryce, L., Tweed, A., Hilton, A., & Priest, H. (2015). Tolerating uncertainty: Perceptions of the future for ageing parent careers and their adult children with intellectual disabilities. *Journal of Applied Research in Intellectual Disabilities*. doi: 10.1111/jar.12221.

Radey, M. (2015). The role of race/ethnicity and acculturation in the functioning of disadvantaged mothers' social support networks and disadvantaged mothers. *Journal of Family Relations, 65*(5), 592–605.

Ratto, A., Reznuck, J., & Turner-Brown, L. (2015). Cultural effects on the diagnosis of autism spectrum disorder among Latinos. *Focus on Autism and Other Developmental Disabilities*. Advance online publication. doi: 1088357615587501.

Reid, J. (2016). Sex trafficking of girls with intellectual disabilities. An exploratory mixed methods study. *Sex Abuse*. Advance online publication. doi: 10.1177/1079063216630981.

Resch, J., Benz, M., & Elliott, T. (2012). Evaluating a dynamic process model of wellbeing for parents of children with disabilities: A multi-method analysis. *Rehabilitation Psychology, 57*(1), 61–72.

Ripat, J., & Woodgate, R. (2011). The intersection of culture, disability, and assistive technology. *Disability and Rehabilitation. Assistive Technology, 6*, 87–96.

Rutman, S., Taualii, M., Ned, D., & Tetrick, C. (2012). Reproductive health and sexual violence among urban American Indian and Alaska Native young women: Select findings from the national survey of family growth (2002). *Maternal and Child Health Journal, 16*, S347–352.

Salkas, K., Magana, S., Marques, I., & Mirza, M. (2016). Spirituality in Latino families of children with autism spectrum disorder. *Journal of Family Social Work, 19*(1), 38–55.

Scallan, S., Senior, J., & Reilly, C. (2011). William syndrome: Daily challenges and positive impact on the family. *Journal of Applied Research in Intellectual Disabilities, 24*, 181–188.

Skirton, H., Goldsmith, L., & Chitty, L. (2014). An easy test but a hard decision: Ethical issues concerning non-invasive prenatal testing for autosomal recessive disorders. *European Journal of Human Genetics, 23*, 1004–1009.

Smith, L., Seltzer, M., & Greenberg, J. (2012). Daily health symptoms of mothers of adolescents and adults with fragile X syndrome and mothers and adults with autism spectrum disorders. *Journal of Autism and Developmental Disabilities*, 42, 36–46.

Son, E., Peterson, N., Pottick, K., Zippay, A., Parish, S., & Lohrmann, S. (2014). Peer victimization among young children with disabilities. *Exceptional Children*, 80(3), 368–384.

Song, J., Mailick, M., Greenberg, J., Ryff, C., & Lachman, M. (2015). Cognitive aging in parents of children with disabilities. *Journals of Gerontology, Series B: Psychological Sciences and Social Sciences*. doi:10.1093/geronb/gbv015.

Stabile, M., & Allin, S. (2012). The economic costs of childhood disability. *The Future of Children*, 22(1), 65–96.

Suzumori, N., Kumagai, K., Goto, S., Nakamura, A., & Sugiura-Ogasawara, M. (2015). Parental decisions following prenatal diagnosis of chromosomal abnormalities: Implications for genetic counseling practice in Japan. *Journal of Genetic Counseling*, 24(1), 117–121.

Swafford, M., Wingate, K., Zagumny, L., & Richey, D. (2015). Families living in poverty: Perceptions of family-centered practices. *Journal of Early Intervention*, 37(2), 138–154.

Swan, B., Coulombe-Quach, X., Huang, A., Godek, J., Becker, D., & Zhou, Y. (2015). Meeting the needs of gifted and talented students. *Journal of Advanced Academics*, 26(4), 294–319.

Teutsch, S., Herman, A., & Teutsch, C. (2016). How a population health approach improves health and reduces disparities: The case of Head Start. *Preventing Chronic Disease*, 13:150565. http://dx.doi.org/10.5888/pcd13.150565.

Thackeray, L., & Eatough, V. (2015). "Well the future, that is difficult": A hermeneutic phenomenological analysis exploring the maternal experience of parenting a young adult with a developmental disability. *Journal of Applied Research in Intellectual Disabilities*, 28(4), 265–275.

Thompson, S., Hiebert-Murphy, D., & Trute, B. (2012). Parental perceptions of family adjustment in childhood developmental disabilities. *Journal of Intellectual Disabilities*, 17(1), 24–37.

Tudor, M., & Lerner, M. (2015). Intervention and support for siblings of youth with developmental disabilities: A systematic review. *Clinical Child and Family Psychology Review*, 18(1), 1–23.

Ulph, F., Cullinan, T., Qureshi, N., & Kai, J. (2015). Parents' responses to receiving sickle cell or cystic fibrosis carrier results for their child following newborn screening. *European Journal of Human Genetics*, 23, 459–465.

U.S. Department of Education. (2004). IDEA Regulations: Secondary transition. Retrieved on March 30, 2016 from http://idea.ed.gov/explore/view/p/,root,dynamic,TopicalBrief,17.

U.S. Department of Education, National Center for Statistics. (2016). Children and youth with disabilities. Retrieved from http://nces.ed.gov/programs/coe/indicator_cgg.asp

Vygotsky, L. (1986). *Thought and language*. (2nd Ed.). Cambridge, MA: MIT Press.

Walker, A., Alfonso, M., Colquitt, G., Weeks, K., & Telfair, J. (2016). "When everything changes": Parent perspectives on the challenges of accessing care for a child with a disability. *Disability and Health Journal*, 9(1), 157–161.

Walton, K., & Ingersoll, B. (2015). Psychological adjustment and sibling relationships in siblings of children with autism spectrum disorder: Risk and protective factors. *Journal of Autism and Developmental Disorders*, 45(9), 2764–2778.

Ward, B., Tanner, B., Mandleco, B., Dyches, T., & Freeborn, D. (2016). Sibling experiences: Living with young persons with autism spectrum disorders. *Pediatric Nursing*, 42(2), 69–76.

Wei, H., Roscigno, C., Swanson, K., Black, B., Hudson-Barr, D., & Hanson, C. (2016). Parents' experiences of having a child undergoing congenital heart surgery: An emotional rollercoaster from shocking to blessing. *Heart & Lung*, 45(2), 154–160.

Weiss-Croft, L., & Baldeweg, T. (2015). Maturation of language networks in children: A systematic review of 22 years of functional MRI. *NeuroImage*, 123, 269–281.

Welchons, L., & McIntyre, L. (2015). The transition to kindergarten for children with and without disabilities: An investigation of parent and teacher concerns and involvement. *Topics in Early Childhood Special Education*, 35(1), 52–62.

Whitley, D., Kelley, S., & Lamis, D. (2016). A longitudinal mediation analysis in African American custodial grandmothers. *International Journal of Aging and Human Development*, 82(2–3), 166–187.

Woodman, A., Mawdsley, H., & Hauser-Cram, P. (2015). Parenting stress and child behavior problems within families of children with developmental disabilities: Transactional relations across 15 years. *Research in Developmental Disabilities*, 36, 264–276.

Wrightslaw. (2016). Special needs: Planning for the future. Retrieved March 30, 2016 from http://www.wrightslaw.com/info/future.plan.index.htm.

Yaman, S., & Altay, N. (2015). Posttraumatic stress and experiences of parents with a newborn in the neonatal intensive care unit. *Journal of Reproductive and Infant Psychology, 33*(2), 140–152.

Yan, K., Accordino, M., Boutin, D., & Wilson, K. (2014). Disability and the Asian culture. *Journal of Rehabilitation Counseling, 45*(2), 4–8.

Zechella, A., & Raval, V. (2016). Parenting children with intellectual and developmental disabilities in Asian Indian families in the United States. *Journal of Child and Family Studies, 25*(4), 1295–1309.

Zigler, E., Balla, D., & Watson, N. (1972). Developmental and experiential determinants of self-image disparity in institutionalized and noninstitutionalized retarded and normal children. *Journal of Personality and Social Psychology, 23*(1), 81–87.

Zuckerman, K., Mattox, K., Donelan, K., Batbayar, O., Baghaee, A., & Bethell, C. (2013). Pediatrician identification of Latino children at risk for autism spectrum disorder. *Pediatrics, 132*(3), 445–453.

Glossary

accommodation process of modifying or creating new schemas based upon additional information.

acculturation the process of adopting the language and customs of another culture.

active listening a communication technique whereby a judgement is deferred until there is mutual understanding; involves attentive listening, paraphrasing for mutual understanding, and noting nonverbal behavior.

amblyopia blurry or reduced vision in one or both eyes related to a muscle imbalance; sometimes referred to as "lazy eye."

anencephaly a malformation of the skull and brain; some areas may be missing.

anorexia nervosa an eating disorder in which a person severely limits food intake due to an obsessive fear of becoming fat.

antibodies substances (proteins) produced by the immune system that protect an individual against specific infectious diseases.

assimilation the process of trying to make new information or experiences fit into existing schemas.

assisted reproduction use of technology (e.g., fertility medications, *in vitro* fertilization, intracytoplasmic sperm insertion, egg and gamete donation, and surrogacy) to conceive a child.

attachment an emotional bond that endures over time.

authoritarian parenting style high in demandingness and rigidity and low in warmth; children raised by authoritarian parents often develop poor impulse control and self-regulation.

authoritative parenting style provides a balance between demandingness and responsiveness and is sometimes referred to as a democratic style; associated with the most positive child outcomes.

autonomy a sense of self and/or being independent.

behaviorism a philosophy of human behavior based upon observable changes that occur in a person's development as the result of environmental experiences.

binge eating disorder repeated episodes of excessive, uncontrolled eating, usually occurring at least once a week, followed by feelings of guilt, remorse, or embarrassment.

bio-behavioral synchrony when biological markers (e.g., heart rate, behaviors such as eye gaze and facial expressions) of an infant and caregiver synchronize or occur at the same time.

boundaries limits that are established within families and between the family and others.

breech birth when a fetus is positioned in the birth canal feet or bottom first versus headfirst.

bulimia nervosa an eating disorder in which a person overeats or binges and then compensates by self-induced vomiting or the use of laxatives or diuretics to prevent weight gain.

child a minor under the age of 18 years.

Child Find a national screening program, mandated by IDEA (1990), that is responsible for identifying, locating, and evaluating children with potential disabilities, and increasing public awareness about these services.

chromosomes thread-like structures (DNA) present in every cell that determine all human characteristics (e.g., eye color, height, vision).

chronosystem factors of time that influence development.

classification ability to organize or group objects based upon different characteristics (e.g., form, use, color).

cleft lip, cleft palate a deformity caused by an incomplete closure of the lip, palate (roof of the mouth), or both.

cohabitation living together without legal or religious sanction (e.g., an unmarried couple).

communication an exchange of information that is mutually understood by both the sender and receiver.

conduct disorder (CD) a cluster of persistent antisocial behaviors characterized by difficulty in following rules, showing aggression toward others, destroying property, and engaging in deceitfulness.

conservation understanding that something (e.g., liquid, solid) is the same even when its appearance changes.

constructivist theory of development in which individuals actively interact with the world to construct meaning.

co-regulation bi-directional process between a parent and child that leads to emotional and behavioral stability.

co-sleeping child sleeping in a parent's bed, in an adjacent bed, or in the same room with parents.

differentiation of the self the degree to which an individual distinguishes him- or herself from, and relies upon, family.

egocentric self-centered.

egocentrism a tendency to focus on one's own thoughts and opinions, and to disregard those of other individuals.

emotional abuse a pattern of verbal assaults, such as threats and intimidation, that have a negative effect on a child's emotional well-being and sense of self-worth.

emotional neglect an adult's failure to attend and be responsive to a child's social and emotional needs.

empathy an ability to understand, be sensitive to, and share another's feelings, including a motivation to care for others.

establishing operations distant antecedents that increase or decrease the value of a consequence.

ethology objective study of animal behavior in the natural environment with a focus on behavior as a result of evolution.

exosystem environments that have an indirect effect on the individual.

expressive vocabulary words that a child uses to convey a thought or request.

family-centered approach a philosophy that supports parental strengths and acknowledges the important role that parents play in a child's life.

fontanels small openings in an infant's bony skull that are covered by a soft tissue membrane.

food intolerance a sensitivity reaction to food that can cause digestive upsets (e.g., gas, diarrhea, nausea), but is not a true food allergy.

food jag periods when a child will only eat certain preferred foods to the exclusion of all others.

free-range parenting giving children freedom to engage in experiences without close parental monitoring; parents believe this builds self-confidence and an independent spirit.

gamete donation sperm donated by a known or anonymous person.

gestational diabetes a form of diabetes that only occurs during pregnancy and is often associated with excessive weight gain, certain ethnicities (e.g., Latina, Native American, African American, Asian, Pacific Islander), or a family history of diabetes.

"goodness of fit" compatibility between caregiver and child temperaments; the caregiver adjusts responses to fit the child's individual temperament style.

guan a dimension of Asian parenting styles characterized by caring, monitoring, and teaching appropriate behaviors such as self-discipline and hard work.

guilt feelings associated with regret and motivation to repair a misdeed.

helicopter parenting overly involved, overly protective parenting that interferes with children's autonomy, lowers self-esteem, and increases anxiety.

heterosexual romantic attraction to a person of the opposite sex.

higher-order thinking complex learning that requires the application of multiple skills to solve problems, draw conclusions, or make inferences.

holophrastic speech uttering a single word to express a complete thought.

homeostasis maintaining equilibrium or balance; remaining the same.

homeschool parent-led, home-based education.

imaginary audience an adolescent's belief that he or she is the center of everyone's concern and attention.

I-messages a communication technique that states how a person feels and avoids placing blame.

implied rules expectations that guide behavior and are usually learned through a process of repetition and experience.

inferential language includes connecting the present to past events, talking about feelings, summarizing, predicting, explaining cause and effect, and defining words.

low birth weight an infant who weighs less than 5.5 pounds (2.5 kg) at birth.

macrosystem the culture of a society, including its beliefs, values, and customs.

magical thinking a belief that wishes or desires can cause things to happen.

make-believe play children's imaginary reenactment of real-life ideas and occurrences, such as pretending to be a veterinarian or a chef, or taking a train ride to a fictional city.

manipulative tantrum acting out to get attention or something that is wanted.

matriarchal family unit in which authority and resources are controlled by the wife.

mesosystem the interactions and relationships that occur between microsystems.

microaggressions everyday, subtle, unintentional forms of bias that convey negative messages about a particular group.

microsystem the direct interactions that occur between an individual and their immediate environments.

mongolian spots bluish-grey patches of normal pigment (melanin) that may be present on the lower back of dark-skinned children.

monogamous being married to, or having a sexual relationship with, one partner at a time.

'motherese' a pattern of speech (e.g., simple words, rhythmic, exaggerated sounds, variable pitch) that adults often use when speaking to infants.

neglectful parenting style low in demandingness and warmth; associated with poor academic achievement and an increase in risky behaviors.

neural plasticity the brain's ability to reorganize and form new connections between cells.

nonverbal communication the use of gestures and facial expressions to convey a feeling.

nuclear family a family consisting of a mother, a father, and their biological children.

nutrient-dense foods foods high in essential nutrients (e.g., protein, vitamins, minerals, fiber) and low in processed ingredients and empty calories.

object permanence an infant's ability to comprehend that an object exists even when out of sight; occurs during the sensorimotor stage (Piaget).

onlooker play watching other children play.

operant conditioning learning through consequences that either increase (reinforcement) or decrease (punishment) the likelihood of the behavior being repeated in the future.

oppositional defiant disorder (ODD) a behavioral disorder characterized by a pattern of persistent defiance, negativity, disrespect, and hostility.

parallel play playing alongside other children and imitating their actions, but not interacting with them in any way.

patriarchal family unit in which authority and resources are controlled by the husband.

permissive parenting style high in nurturing and warmth, but low in demandingness; is associated with poor decision making and long term reliance on parents for guidance.

physical abuse non-accidental injuries inflicted upon a child by an adult.

physical neglect an adult's failure to provide for the child's basic physical and medical needs and care, including access to food, clean and safe housing, and appropriate clothing.

polyandry the practice of having more than one male spouse at the same time.

polygamy the practice of being married to more than one spouse simultaneously.

polygyny the practice of having more than one female spouse at the same time.

polyvictimization exposure to multiple maltreatment forms (e.g., physical, sexual, neglect).

postpartum the months following childbirth.

pragmatics using language in different ways and for different purposes.

preeclampsia a pregnancy complication that can develop after the 20th week; signs include high blood pressure that can damage the kidneys and be fatal to mother and infant unless promptly treated.

premature birth delivery prior to the 37th week following conception.

receptive vocabulary words that a child understands and may respond to, but is not able to produce.

relational aggression hurtful behavior, such as bullying, used to manipulate or disrupt peer relationships to gain personal recognition.

resilience the ability to adapt to and overcome adversity.

respondent conditioning learning through repeated pairings of an unconditioned stimulus (e.g., food) and neutral stimulus (e.g., bell) until the neutral stimulus becomes conditioned to evoke the same response (e.g., salivation).

schemas mental patterns or categories that are used for organizing and storing information.

self-efficacy an individual's confidence in their ability to succeed.

self-esteem feelings about one's self-worth.

self-regulation the ability to control and adjust thoughts, behavior, and emotions.

sensitive periods window of time for optimal development of specific abilities or skills. Although it may be more challenging, development can also occur outside of this window timeframe.

sexual abuse sexual behaviors, including rape, fondling, and pornography that are initiated by an adult and involve a child.

shame a feeling of embarrassment or remorse for behavior that a person knows is wrong.

social learning theory theory of learning in which individuals learn through their experiences and cognitive processes; learning through observation and modeling.

solitary play playing alone.

spina bifida a malformation of the infant's spinal column.

symbolic play a child's use of play objects as representations of real objects or ideas: a block becomes a motorboat, a broom becomes a hockey stick, a chair becomes a car.

telegraphic speech using a two- or three-word phrase to express a complete thought.

teratogens harmful substances that may cause birth defects.

temperamental tantrum an emotional outburst that may occur because a child is overly tired or hungry.

theory of mind the ability to imagine, understand, explain, or predict the thoughts, beliefs, intentions, and emotions of others.

zone of proximal development Vygotsky's term for tasks that are too difficult for children to complete alone, but that they are able to complete with adult assistance or guidance.

Index

Ecological theory, 359
Educate America Act (1994), 71
Education. *See also* Family-school part-
    nerships; School(s)
    of children of same-sex parents, 39–40
    compulsory, 5
    cultural differences in learning
        socialization, 253
    early childhood, 223–224, 225
    ethnic minority families and, 10–11
    family education programs, 142–144
    maternal, prenatal care and, 110f
    parental involvement in, 9, 70–71,
        75–76, 262, 316–317
    of parent, parenting style and, 140
    sex education, 296, 298–299
    transition to postsecondary, 315–317
Educational neglect, 367–368
Education for All Handicapped Children
    Act (1975), 8, 78, 385f
Education of the Handicapped Amend-
    ments (1986), 385f
Educators. *See* Teachers
Egg donation, 102
Eggs (ovum), 96
Egocentrism, 198, 294
    in preschoolers, 220, 223
    in toddlers, 198
Electronic devices, sleep problems and, 273
Electronic media. *See* Media
Electronic tools, for teacher-parent com-
    munication, 85–86
Elementary and Secondary Education Act
    (ESEA), 71f, 78
Elkind, David, 262
Embryo, 98
Embryonic stage of pregnancy, 97–98
Embryos, 103
Emerging adult, 342–343
Emotional abuse, 360, 369
Emotional attachment, 128
Emotional development. *See* Social and
    emotional development
Emotional neglect, 362, 366–367
Empathy, 267
Employment, Industrial Revolution and,
    4–5
Enlightenment, 4
Environmental factors
    child maltreatment and, 362
    ecological systems theory and, 12–13
    family roles/responsibilities and, 29–30
    family-school partnerships and, 81–82
    sleep routines and, 206
Environmental Protection Agency (EPA),
    111
Environmental safety, for infants,
    176–177
Epstein's six keys to successful family
    involvement, 80
Erikson, Erik, 7, 17
Erikson's stages of psychosocial develop-
    ment, 17–18, 18f, 227, 261

Establishing operations, 19
Ethical obligations to protect child's
    safety, 372
Ethnic-racial identity, 318–319
Ethology, 15
Eugenics, 103
Every Student Succeeds Act (ESSA)
    (2015), 71f, 386f
Exceptionalities. *See* Disabilities, children
    with
Exchange theory, 359
Exosystem, 13
Expressive vocabulary, 196
Extended families, 33–34
Extracurricular activities
    academic achievement and, 291
    of overscheduled children, 262
Eye contact, 86, 221f

F

Facebook, 293
Factory work, by children, 4
Families Overcoming Under Stress (FO-
    CUS), 55
Familism, 117, 266
Familismo, 191
Family(ies). *See also* Parents
    adolescent parent, 50–52
    adoptive, 42–44
    child care and household responsibili-
        ties and, 8
    cultural, racial, and ethnic diversity of,
        44–50
    dysfunctional, 30–31, 30f
    ethnic influences on, 1–2
    extended or multigenerational, 33–34
    family-school partnerships benefiting,
        73–74
    foster, 40–42
    functional, 30–31, 30f
    grandparent, 52–54
    historical importance of, 3
    immigrant, 48–49
    with incarcerated parents, 56–57
    meaning of, 2–3, 27–28
    military, 54–55
    multiracial and interethnic, 45–48
    nuclear, 31–33
    parents with disabilities and their,
        55–56
    religious affiliation and, 57–58
    roles and responsibilities of, 29–30
    same-sex partnered, 38–40
    single-parent, 34–36
    socioeconomic status (SES) and, 58–59
    stepfamilies, 36–37
Family and provider/teacher relationship
    quality (FPTRQ), 84
Family-centered approach, 401–402
Family education programs, 142–144,
    143f, 144f

Family Resilience Training, 55
Family school capacity-building frame-
    work, 79
Family-school partnerships, 69–88
    approach for, 80–81
    atmosphere for, 81–82
    attitudes for, 81
    benefits of, 72–74, 72f
    Epsteins' six keys for successful, 80
    fostering open communication for,
        84–88
    four components of, 80–84
    historical developments, 71f
    laws and regulations on, 78–79
    measures that schools can take to
        promote, 82
    NAEYC family engagement principles,
        83f
    organizational policies impacting,
        77–78
    strategies for, 82–84
    tools for measuring, 84
    variables influencing, 74–79
Family size, 2
    in the 1930s, 1940s, 1960s and
        1970s, 7
    influencing parenting style, 139–140
    Middle Ages, 4
Family systems theory, 14–15
Family violence, 357–358. *See also* Child
    maltreatment
    breaking cycle of, 373–376
    culture of violence theory on, 358–359
    defined, 358
    factors increasing likelihood of,
        360–363
    household characteristics, 360–364
    intimate partner violence, 363–364
    male dominance as major cause of,
        358–359
    physical abuse, 368
    protective and risk factors influencing
        outcomes of exposure to, 375f
    psychiatric model on, 358
    social-psychological theories on, 359
    theoretical models, 358–359
Fathers
    depression among, 116
    experiences during pregnancy, 98–99
    factors influencing decision for a
        planned pregnancy, 94
    marital satisfaction and involvement
        by, 117
    stereotypical parental role of, 140
    work commitment and, 119
Fears
    in preschool-age children,
        232–233
    of toddlers, 200
Ferber, Richard, 206
Fertilization (conception), 96, 97
Fetal alcohol spectrum disorders (FASD),
    113, 286

2010 NAEYC Standards
For Initial and Advanced Early Childhood Professional Preparation Programs
Correlations with Chapter Content

These NAEYC Standards provide the foundation for accreditation of early childhood programs in higher education.

NAEYC Standards		Chapters where Addressed
Standard 1:	**Promoting Child Development and Learning**	
1a:	Knowing and understanding young children's characteristics and needs.	1, 5, 6, 7, 8, 9, 10, 11, 13
1b:	Knowing and understanding the multiple influences on early development and learning.	1, 2, 4, 5, 6, 7, 8, 9, 10, 11, 13, 14
1c:	Using developmental knowledge to create healthy, respectful, supportive, and challenging learning environments for young children.	5, 6, 7, 8, 9, 10, 11, 13
Standard 2:	**Building Family and Community Relationships**	
2a:	Knowing about and understanding diverse family and community relationships.	All chapters
2b:	Supporting and engaging families and communities through respectful, reciprocal relationships.	3, 5, 6, 7, 8, 9, 10, 11, 12, 13
2c:	Involving families and communities in young children's development and learning.	3, 5, 6, 7, 8, 9, 10, 11, 13
Standard 3:	**Observing, Documenting, and Assessing to Support Young Children and Families**	
3d:	Knowing about assessment partnerships with families and with professional colleagues to build effective learning environments.	3
Standard 4:	**Using Developmentally Effective Approaches**	
4a:	Understanding positive relationships and supportive interactions as the foundation of their work with young children.	3, 5, 6, 7, 8, 9, 10, 11, 12
4b:	Knowing and understanding effective strategies and tools for early education.	6, 7, 8, 9, 10, 11
4d:	Reflecting on own practice to promote positive outcomes for each child.	3
Standard 6:	**Becoming a Professional**	
6b:	Knowing about and upholding ethical standards and other early childhood professional guidelines.	13